The Waite Group's

Using PC DOS™

RELATED TITLES

The Waite Group's MS-DOS® Bible, Third Edition *(forthcoming)*
Steven Simrin

The Waite Group's MS-DOS® Developer's Guide, Second Edition
John Angermeyer, Kevin Jaeger, et al.

The Waite Group's Understanding MS-DOS®
Kate O'Day and John Angermeyer

The Waite Group's Tricks of the MS-DOS® Masters
John Angermeyer, Rich Fahringer, Kevin Jaeger, and Dan Shafer

The Waite Group's Discovering MS-DOS®
Kate O'Day

The Waite Group's MS-DOS® Papers
The Waite Group

The Waite Group's Desktop Publishing Bible
James Stockford, Editor

The Waite Group's Advanced C Primer ++
Stephen Prata

The Waite Group's C Primer Plus, Revised Edition
Mitchell Waite, Stephen Prata, and Donald Martin

The Waite Group's Microsoft® C Bible
Naba Barkakati

The Waite Group's Microsoft® C Programming for the PC, Revised Edition
Robert Lafore

The Waite Group's QuickC™ Bible
Naba Barkakati

The Waite Group's Turbo C® Bible
Naba Barkakati

The Waite Group's Turbo C® Programming for the PC, Revised Edition
Robert Lafore

The Waite Group's

Using PC DOS™

A Hands-On User-Friendly Reference

Peter Abell
David Blossom
David Chatfield
Raj Dhesikan
Tess Goodrich
Harry Henderson
David Moy
Kay Nelson

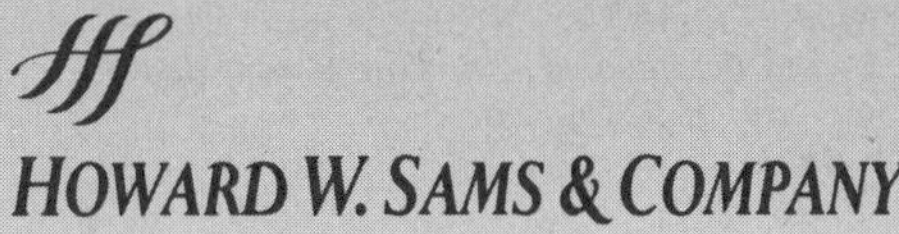

HOWARD W. SAMS & COMPANY
A Division of Macmillan, Inc.
4300 West 62nd Street
Indianapolis, Indiana 46268 USA

FIRST EDITION
FIRST PRINTING—1989

International Standard Book Number: 0-672-22679-0
Library of Congress Catalog Card Number: 89-61053

From The Waite Group

Development Editor: *James Stockford*
Development Advisor: *Mitchell Waite*
Content Editors: *Harry Henderson, Kay Nelson, James Stockford*
Technical Reviewers: *David Blossom, Alexis Benioff, Rhonda Nelson, Sherrell Mack, Evelyn Lopez, Vee Rivera*

From Howard W. Sams & Company

Acquisitions Editor: *Richard K. Swadley*
Development Editor: *James Rounds*
Manuscript Editors: *Diana Francoeur, Katherine Stuart Ewing*
Illustrator: *Wm. D. Basham, T. R. Emrick*
Cover Art: *Dicken or Dicken*
Indexer: *Ted Laux*
Compositor: *Shepard Poorman Communications Corporation*

Printed in the United States of America

Overview

To our families

Contents

List of Tables

Preface

Bookstore shelves are crammed with books about the PC DOS operating system. There are more than 100 in print: some general-purpose tutorials, some detailed references, and some covering special subtopics. Despite this abundance, no single book has really answered all the needs of the PC DOS user.

In *The Waite Group's Using PC DOS*, we address those needs with a combination tutorial and reference that

- trains the new user quickly and inexpensively, whether at home, in school, or on the job
- provides useful information that the reader can find fast when it is needed
- teaches practical, efficient techniques for recognizing and solving common PC DOS problems
- provides a wealth of detail not generally available in PC DOS references
- covers all versions of PC DOS from 2.0 through 4

For students and home or office learners, the Quick Primer provides a progression of user-friendly hands-on examples that get to the heart of what you must understand to become fluent with PC DOS. Most existing PC DOS books present procedures without explaining the underlying concepts. They teach the mechanics of using PC DOS but dismiss the reasons behind them as "too technical." This is like teaching someone to operate a car without giving them a map of the city or telling them that a red light means stop. So this book emphasizes fundamentals like how to use commands, how the PC DOS command line works, how to use "options," "parameters," and simple features to enhance your control, along with explanations of "error messages." Then, to let you practice, the book provides examples based on achievement, letting you build practical skills. Armed with a basic understanding of how the system works and what you can accomplish with commands, you won't get lost as easily, and as you develop advanced skills you will ultimately profit more from the systematic and comprehensive coverage.

Acknowledgments

This book is the result of cooperation, inspiration, guidance, and many midnight phone calls and weekend work sessions among a lot of people. Our true acknowledgments are silent—memories of details and care, struggles and successes. Here we acknowledge the cast of characters.

The Waite Group first expresses its gratitude to the authors for their contributions to this book. Thanks to Harry Henderson for the entire Command Reference as well as chapters on DOS Shell, Installation, Customization, and International Language Support; to Kay Nelson for the Floppy Disk chapter; to David Chatfield for the Quick Primer; to Raj Dhesikan for the chapter on Hard Disks; to Tess Goodrich for her chapters on Advanced Use of the Command Line and Creating a Text File; to Peter Abell for his chapter on PC DOS Files; to David Blossom for his chapter on Batch Files; and to David Moy for his contributions to the Quick Primer as well as the chapters on Hard Disks and Installation.

The Waite Group owes further gratitude to Harry Henderson and Kay Nelson, the content editors for the book, for the hard work and valuable insights and suggestions that guided the development of the manuscript. Thanks also to David Blossom for his technical reviews of the chapters on Installation and Customization and to Alexis Benioff for his review of material used in those chapters. Thanks to Rhonda Nelson, Sherrell Mack, Evelyn Lopez, and Vee Rivera for their review of the Quick Primer, and to Jeff Kessler and Leonard Meuller at the Control Data Institute for their support during the development phase of the Quick Primer. Sincere thanks to the people at Howard W. Sams & Company—Acquisitions Editors James S. Hill and Richard Swadley, Development Editor James Rounds, Cover Coordinator Glenn Santner, Editorial Manager Wendy Ford, Copy Editors Diana Francoeur and Kathy Ewing, and Indexer Ted Laux—for their help in the book production phase. Thanks to Scott Calamar for management support and to Mitchell Waite for development support.

James Stockford

Trademarks

All terms mentioned in this book that are known to be trademarks or service marks are listed below. In addition, terms suspected of being trademarks or service marks have been appropriately capitalized. Howard W. Sams & Company or The Waite Group, Inc., cannot attest to the accuracy of this information. Use of a term in this book should not be regarded as affecting the validity of any trademark or service mark.

COMPAQ is a registered trademark of COMPAQ Computer Corporation.

COPY II PC is a trademark and PC Tools is a registered trademark of Central Point Software.

dBASE IV is a registered trademark of Ashton-Tate Corp.

Fastback is a trademark of Fifth Generation Systems.

IBM, AT, PC, PS/2, and XT are registered trademarks, and PC*jr*, PC DOS, and OS/2, are trademarks of the International Business Machines Corporation.

Intel is a registered trademark of Intel Corporation.

Lotus and Lotus 1-2-3 are registered trademarks of Lotus Development Corporation.

Microsoft, Microsoft Windows, Microsoft Word, MS-DOS, and XENIX are registered trademarks of Microsoft Corporation.

Norton Utilities is a registered trademark of Peter Norton Computing, Inc.

SideKick and SuperKey are registered trademarks of Borland International, Inc.

UNIX is a trademark of American Telephone and Telegraph Corp.

WordPerfect is a registered trademark of WordPerfect Corporation.

WordStar is a registered trademark of MicroPro International Corporation.

XTREE is a trademark of Executive Systems.

To the Reader

Welcome to PC DOS. There's no doubt that the PC DOS operating system is complex, but most of that complexity comes from the large number of commands and their options, not from any intrinsic difficulty in the way things work. In fact, PC DOS responds to you in a few predictable and fairly simple ways. If you really understand how to use the command line, the differences among the different kinds of files, how to organize a directory tree, and a few other basics—such as text strings—learning to use PC DOS skillfully becomes just a matter of looking up the details.

This book is specially designed to teach you the basics you need and to make looking up the details easy. This section orients you to the content of the book, describes its organization, shows you where to find information fast, and tells you about important typographic conventions that will help you understand what you're reading.

Overview of the Book

The Waite Group's Using PC DOS is made up of three parts:

- the Quick Primer
- the Tutorials, and
- the Command Reference

The Quick Primer teaches beginners the fundamental skills and concepts of using a PC DOS computer. It's a complete tutorial with step-by-step instructions, "quick questions" with answers, and plenty of examples and illustrations.

The intermediate Tutorials go beyond the basics to discuss specific PC

DOS topics. These ten chapters also present material step-by-step with examples and illustrations, but they focus on more advanced subjects and treat each one in depth.

The Command Reference is an encyclopedia of all PC DOS commands and features. This is probably the most comprehensive user-level reference you'll find anywhere. It contains the basics, of course, but also special in-depth "detailed reference" sections for intermediate and advanced readers. Commands and other features are arranged alphabetically, with descriptions, syntax, options, examples, tips on how to use them, and cross-references to related commands. In each case, you'll be able to see at a glance whether the specific command is compatible with your version of PC DOS.

The introductions to each of these three parts will tell you more about how to use them. Before you begin reading, here are a few hints for using this book.

If You've Never Used PC DOS . . .

Learning to use a computer system can be like an unpleasant dream. You get the feeling that to learn anything, you must already understand everything. So you memorize steps without knowing why. And if you lose your place, you're stuck until someone comes to help or until you turn off the computer and start over.

Take heart. Nearly everyone who is good with computers has experienced these hopeless feelings. You'll find that there's only a limited amount you have to learn before everything starts to make sense, and then you'll learn a lot, fast. After you've mastered the basic PC DOS principles, you will look back and you won't believe it was so simple.

As a beginner, you'll want to start with the Quick Primer. Each chapter in the Quick Primer can be completed in one sitting. The best way to learn is to practice the examples as you read. They show everything you need to know to use PC DOS commands. So turn on your computer when you sit down to read.

As you go along, answer the "quick questions" to check your understanding, and verify your answers with those at the back of the Quick Primer. Develop the habit of looking things up. Throughout the text, you'll notice references to related material in other chapters. Look up these references in the Tutorials and read further explanations of commands in the Command Reference. Remember that PC DOS is easy to master if you know where to look up the details.

If You've Used PC DOS or Other Operating Systems Before . . .

You may consider yourself an intermediate or advanced user, in search of a detailed understanding of PC DOS commands and special topics. In this case, the Tutorials and the Command Reference will be of particular interest.

You probably already grasp the basic PC DOS principles. A good way to check is to thumb through the Quick Primer to be sure you can answer the "quick questions."

In approaching the Tutorials in Part 2, you may find it helpful to scan the first few pages of each chapter to get a feeling for the PC DOS terrain. Earlier chapters in the section are relevant to building day-to-day skills, like understanding files, using floppy disks, and maintaining order on your hard disk. Later chapters pertain to activities associated with power users and people who set up and install PC DOS systems frequently, for example, setting up batch files to automate routine tasks, adding memory or hardware, and customizing or fine-tuning computer systems. If you browse through the chapters, you'll note that headings often express problems to be solved, with the text going on to show examples and explanations of how to solve them.

As an intermediate or advanced user, you'll benefit especially from the extensive cross-indexing throughout the book and from the "detailed reference" portions of the Command Reference.

Anatomy of a Chapter

Parts 1 and 2 of this book are especially designed to make learning PC DOS skills fast and enjoyable, with special features to help you learn and retain new concepts and skills.

Each chapter begins with an overview statement and a short list of the main topics in the chapter. The text starts out gently, reviewing or defining key concepts and terms. It then presents examples that accomplish practical results, with plenty of illustrations and special information set off in boxes. The text progresses to more advanced material of interest to power users and system experts.

Every chapter ends with a "What's Next" section that identifies relevant chapters and indicates jumping off points to related topics you might like to pursue. Finally, you'll find a complete list of the main concepts and words covered in the chapter, which you can scan to check your understanding.

How to Find It

Special indexing features throughout the book help you find information when you need it.

If you're looking for coverage of a specific topic, check the overview of the chapter titles on page *v* or consult the detailed table of contents showing the main topics and subtopics in each chapter. For a finer level of detail, look through the comprehensive, thoughtfully prepared index at the back of the book.

Much of the general information you'll refer to often is presented in tabular format for easy lookup. A list of all the tables in the book appears right after the table of contents, on page *xix*.

When you're in the middle of a project and need a reminder of how to do a routine task, turn to the "Find It Fast" listing on the inside front and back covers. This "jump table" presents the most common PC DOS problems and routines, with relevant commands and page numbers.

When you need to know about a specific command, its syntax, DOS version compatibility information, or examples of its use, the Command Reference in Part 3 lists all the commands as well as device drivers, settings, and PC DOS resources alphabetically. Dictionary-style headers at the top of each page make it easy to find the command you want.

Equipment You Should Have

To practice the examples in the tutorial sections, you should have an IBM or compatible computer system in working order with the PC DOS operating system installed. A minimum computer system would include a keyboard, a video display, the computer itself, and a floppy disk drive. A larger system might include a hard disk drive, a second floppy disk drive, and a printer.

PC DOS exists in many versions. From version 1, released in 1981, to version 4, released in 1988, each new version offers variations on and improvements over the preceding one. Because IBM has declared versions earlier than 2 obsolete, this book covers versions 2 through 4. As long as you have version 2 or higher, you can learn from the examples in these pages. For easy lookup, the Command Reference shows whether each command is available in your PC DOS version, and material relevant to the latest version 4 is highlighted throughout the book.

Be sure you have several expendable floppy disks to use in trying the examples. No other important information should be stored on these disks, for as you practice, you may accidentally destroy the information (but not the disks themselves). If your system includes a printer, be sure it is connected properly and has paper.

If you've never used a PC DOS computer before, have someone in the office or classroom check that your machine operates correctly and that you have everything you need.

Conventions Used in This Book

This section is very important, because it describes ways we have designed this book to help you learn.

Typography As you read, you'll notice that several typefaces are used and that some terms are in italics, others in boldface, some in all uppercase (all caps), others in upper- and lowercase. These typographic conventions are to help you keep track of different types of terms and their functions.

- PC DOS commands are spelled in uppercase, for example, the FORMAT command or the CHKDSK command.
- Names of files are also in uppercase, for example, the CONFIG.SYS file or the README.TXT file.
- Text that you are to type is shown in a special typeface, for example, "at the system prompt, you type `dir` to get a listing of files."
- Messages that PC DOS prints to the video display are also shown in the special typeface, for example, "you may see the message `File not found`."
- A new term mentioned for the first time is shown in italics, for example, "you will uncover much of the mystery of PC DOS when you understand the structure of the *command line.*"

Use of Second Color

In the Quick Primer, a second color of type is used to show the difference between what PC DOS prints on the video display and what you are to type in response. What you type is shown in blue ink; everything else is in black ink, for example,

```
C:\>dir command.com
Volume in drive C is MyHardDisk
Directory of C:\
COMMAND  COM     425279  7-24-90  12:00:00
          1 File(s)      54239739 bytes free
```

The first element on the first line shows the system prompt (C:\>) that lets you know PC DOS is ready to accept a command. You are supposed to type the text shown in blue, `dir command.com`, exactly as it appears and then press the Enter or Return key. In this example, PC DOS responds to your command by printing further information to the video display as shown in black ink. For now, just remember that the blue ink shows what you are to type in the Quick Primer examples.

System Prompts

The system prompt is a set of characters that tells you the operating system is ready to accept a command. That is, PC DOS expects you to type something on the keyboard to tell the system what to do.

If you're like most PC DOS users, your system includes a hard disk drive, so when the operating system starts, you'll see the system prompt C:\> on the video display, indicating that PC DOS is ready to accept a command from you. If you don't have a hard disk, you'll see A:\> or B:\> on the display, depending on which floppy disk drive is active.

In most of the examples in this book, we use C:\> as the system prompt. If your system has one or two floppy disk drives, simply read the C:\> as A:\> or B:\>.

About the Icons

Throughout the book, small graphic elements or *icons* flag special information.

Points out a clever way that you can use a command or a handy technique to add to your bag of tricks.

Warns you of common pitfalls and problems.

Highlights a way in which the DOS Shell utility offers an alternative to the subject under discussion.

Marks the explanation of a feature found only in PC DOS version 4.

Passages flagged with these icons contain information that's important to know but not essential to the flow of the text presentation. If you prefer to concentrate on the main text, you can skip these passages and come back later to catch what you missed. Also, if you return to a chapter months from now, the icons will help you find information quickly as you browse through the pages.

Part 1
Quick Primer

This Quick Primer is designed to make you comfortable with using the PC DOS operating system. It shows you how PC DOS works and how to control it. You'll learn about the command line and the system prompt, internal and external commands, files, directories and subdirectories, and all the other basics you need. By the end of this section, you will understand how PC DOS stores information and how to use programs to manage your information.

Bookmark

HOWARD W. SAMS & COMPANY

DEAR VALUED CUSTOMER:

Howard W. Sams & Company is dedicated to bringing you timely and authoritative books for your personal and professional library. Our goal is to provide you with excellent technical books written by the most qualified authors. You can assist us in this endeavor by checking the box next to your particular areas of interest.

We appreciate your comments and will use the information to provide you with a more comprehensive selection of titles.

Thank you,

Vice President, Book Publishing
Howard W. Sams & Company

COMPUTER TITLES:

Hardware
☐ Apple 140 ☐ Macintosh 101
☐ Commodore 110
☐ IBM & Compatibles 114

Business Applications
☐ Word Processing J01
☐ Data Base J04
☐ Spreadsheets J02

Operating Systems
☐ MS-DOS K05 ☐ OS/2 K10
☐ CP/M K01 ☐ UNIX K03

Programming Languages
☐ C L03 ☐ Pascal L05
☐ Prolog L12 ☐ Assembly L01
☐ BASIC L02 ☐ HyperTalk L14

Troubleshooting & Repair
☐ Computers S05
☐ Peripherals S10

Other
☐ Communications/Networking M03
☐ AI/Expert Systems T18

ELECTRONICS TITLES:

☐ Amateur Radio T01
☐ Audio T03
☐ Basic Electronics T20
☐ Basic Electricity T21
☐ Electronics Design T12
☐ Electronics Projects T04
☐ Satellites T09
☐ Instrumentation T05
☐ Digital Electronics T11

Troubleshooting & Repair
☐ Audio S11 ☐ Television S04
☐ VCR S01 ☐ Compact Disc S02
☐ Automotive S06
☐ Microwave Oven S03

Other interests or comments: ______________________________

____

____

Name ______________________________
Title ______________________________
Company ______________________________
Address ______________________________
City ______________________________
State/Zip ______________________________
Daytime Telephone No. ______________________________

A Division of Macmillan, Inc.
4300 West 62nd Street Indianapolis, Indiana 46268

22679

Bookmark

NO POSTAGE
NECESSARY
IF MAILED
IN THE
UNITED STATES

BUSINESS REPLY CARD

FIRST CLASS PERMIT NO. 1076 INDIANAPOLIS, IND.

POSTAGE WILL BE PAID BY ADDRESSEE

HOWARD W. SAMS & CO.
ATTN: Public Relations Department
P.O. BOX 7092
Indianapolis, IN 46209-9921

Chapter 1

This chapter is the place to start if you've never used a computer or PC DOS. It guides you gently through the basics of your computer's hardware and its relationship to the PC DOS operating system software. This chapter teaches

- *What PC DOS does*
- *What the various parts of your computer do*
- *How to start your computer and PC DOS*

Before you begin: Be sure you've read To the Reader *at the front of this book, particularly the sections on "If You've Never Used PC DOS" and "Conventions Used in This Book."*

Chapter 1
Hardware and Software

Learning how to use your computer is an adventure! Most people have personal stories to tell about their first experiences. Some people had an easy time, attracted by sheer curiosity about the machine itself and what it can do. Others took their first steps with a great deal of caution—fearing for the worst at every turn—until they became comfortable with their new electronic surroundings.

You are about to join the ranks of millions of PC users, and the job of this Quick Primer section is to get you started right. This chapter presents a basic introduction to the various hardware components of a PC DOS system. If you consider yourself a novice in the PC world, pay careful attention to the examples, try to answer the questions, and follow the discussion at your own pace.

Before going any further, however, take a moment and flip through the pages of this book. Most of the terms and phrases you see in the other chapters may sound unfamiliar and strange now. You may understand very little of what you see, but much of it may draw your curiosity. Note how these pages look to you at this point in time. When you finish this Quick Primer, you will be able to look back at this moment and realize how much you have learned.

The Adventure Begins

What exactly is the PC DOS operating system? What kind of role does it play in the way you use your PC? At a very simple level, PC DOS is a piece of *software*. In general, software consists of a set of commands, or a program, that serves some kind of useful purpose when executed on a computer. PC DOS falls into a special category of software: It is an *operating system*. The IBM software product called *PC DOS* consists of some manuals and some disks. The manuals explain what is on the disks. The disks contain the PC

DOS operating system program and some other programs called *external commands*.

The PC DOS oeprating system program is always used when the computer is turned on. The other programs, the external commands, each perform helpful utility functions.

To use a command, you type its name, and PC DOS responds by loading the proper program. Learning to use PC DOS, in large measure, is learning what the PC DOS commands do and how to use them. The last part of this book contains a Command Reference section, which is a small encyclopedia that explains each PC DOS command in alphabetical order. You will learn how to use PC DOS commands in Chapter 2, "Internal Commands and Files," and Chapter 3, "External Commands and the DOS Shell."

Every computer must have an operating system, which is the program that supplies an *interface* (or bridge) between you and the physical equipment that makes up your PC.

The actual letters *PC DOS* stand for *Personal Computer Disk Operating System*. Without PC DOS, you could not possibly hope to direct all the electronic traffic that flows inside your machine. PC DOS handles many important jobs that you may take for granted. Without it, a simple task, like asking the printer to print HELLO, would be all but impossible for even an experienced PC user. The following sections look at the pieces of hardware that are part of your PC. Figure 1.1 may be helpful in showing how this relationship works.

As you read on, you should keep in mind that PC DOS plays a critical role in managing all these valuable resources when your programs are running.

Your Computer's Hardware

As a new user, you may have been lucky enough to obtain the services of a skilled PC expert to help assemble your hardware and install your new machine. If so, you may be sitting in front of your PC with the power turned on and a strange-looking set of characters called a *prompt* (probably either `C>` or `C:\>`) staring you in the face—and you're wondering what to do next.

Otherwise, you may be stuck with the job of setting it up yourself and making sure the various parts are properly connected. Most PCs these days come with an easy-to-follow illustrated setup guide. If you run into trouble, however, you may want to seek skilled help instead of trying to finish the whole job by yourself. (You might even try borrowing your precocious niece or nephew for the afternoon. Any chance to let them show you up is an opportunity you should use to your best advantage!) You also may want to consult Chapter 12, "Installing a PC DOS System," in this book, which gives some tips on installing the various pieces of hardware and software for your PC DOS system.

Clones and the "Real Thing"

By the way, the discussion here applies equally to IBM machines and the ubiquitous clones from other manufacturers. The one major difference comes with the "laptop" computer, which has everything, including the video display, in a single case and is not intended to be taken apart by the average user.

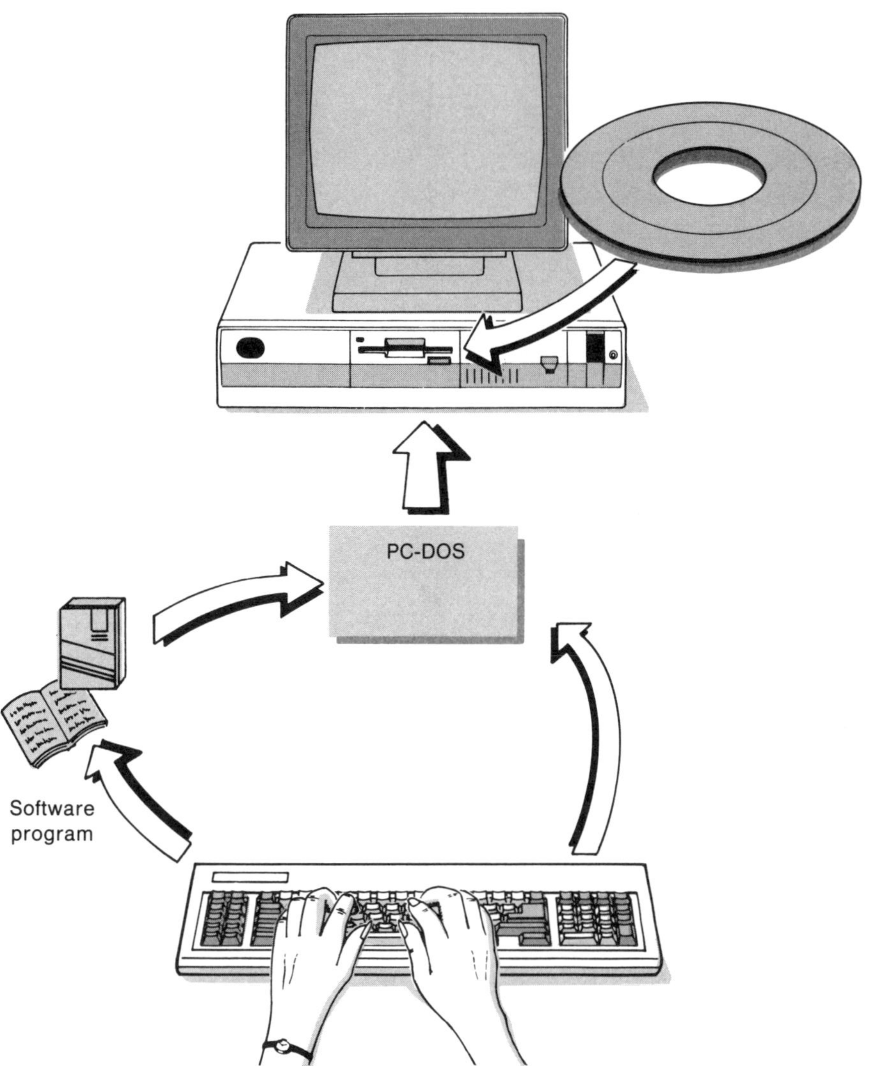

Figure 1.1. ***The relationships among the user, PC DOS, and the PC.***

The Components of Your Computer System

To examine the components of a PC DOS system, look at Figure 1.2A through D. This figure shows the important devices you see in front of you when your PC is assembled. Each item serves you in some way as you use your computer. You will use some of the components more than others, but they are all designed to help you interact with the PC.

The key component of any PC is the large rectangular box, which is often called the *base unit*. The base unit contains the *central processing unit* (CPU), which performs most of the actual computing within your PC. It also contains the *read-only memory* (ROM), which permanently stores a number of internal computer instructions—including those that are executed when your PC is first powered up—and a certain amount of *random access memory* (RAM), which the CPU uses to store results of various computations, program instructions awaiting execution, and other data read from disk.

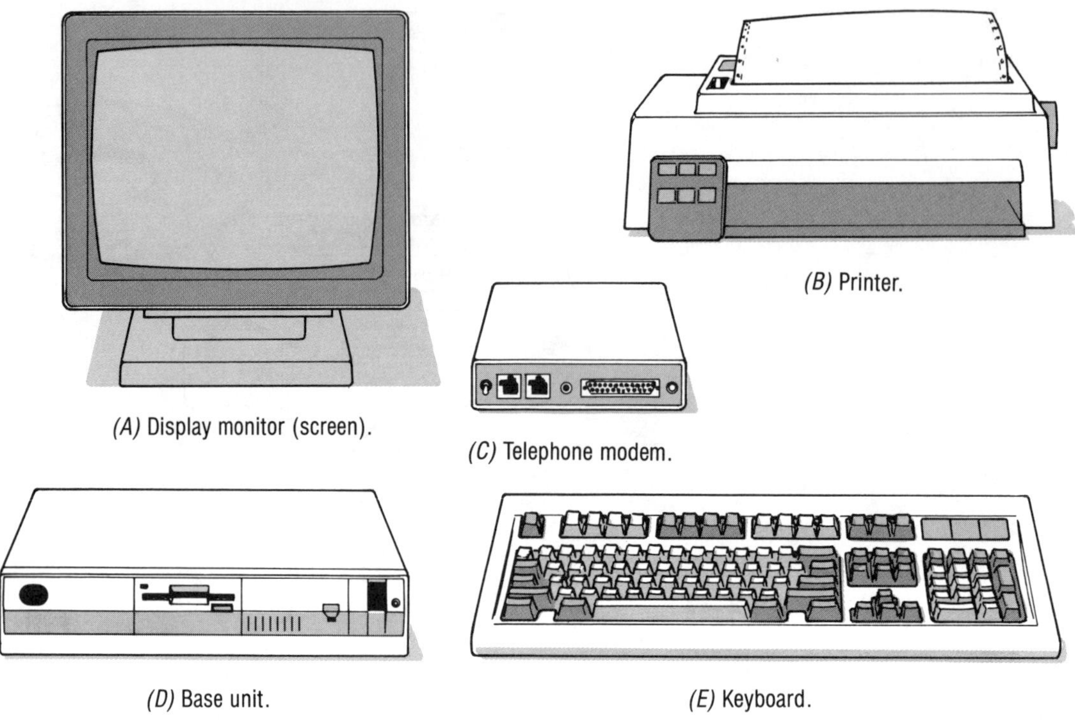

(A) Display monitor (screen).

(B) Printer.

(C) Telephone modem.

(D) Base unit.

(E) Keyboard.

Figure 1.2. *The external components of a PC.*

In addition, the base unit normally contains your floppy disk and your hard disk drives (although you may in some cases be using an external hard disk drive).

Note that the IBM documentation refers to the hard disk drive as a *fixed disk*, meaning that unlike floppy disks, the recording surface is not removable. In everyday use, however, the more common terms, *hard disk* or *hard drive* are used, referring to the fact that the recording surface is rigid, not flexible as in the case of floppy disks. You should know that both hard disk and fixed disk mean exactly the same thing. This book always uses hard disk and hard disk drive to mean your fixed disk.

The only distinguishing features about the base unit from the outside include one or more floppy disk drives (slots where you insert floppy disks) on the front and a number of curious-looking sockets to connect cables that are on the back of the unit.

Each of the rest of the hardware components connects to the base unit by some sort of cable. The *display monitor* (sometimes called *video monitor*, or simply *the screen*), serves as your visual connection, a window into the PC. The keyboard, usually attached to the base unit by a coiled cable, accepts and sends your typed commands to the base unit for processing. You probably also have a printer, which stands ready to print documents.

Another optional device that is increasingly useful these days is the *modem* (short for *mod*ulator/*dem*odulator), which you use to transmit information over phone lines.

The Keyboard

The keyboard is your most important way of communicating with your PC. For this reason, take a few moments to examine the different keys that are available on the standard PS/2 and older PC- and AT-type keyboards, which are displayed in Figure 1.3A and B.

(A) PC keyboard.

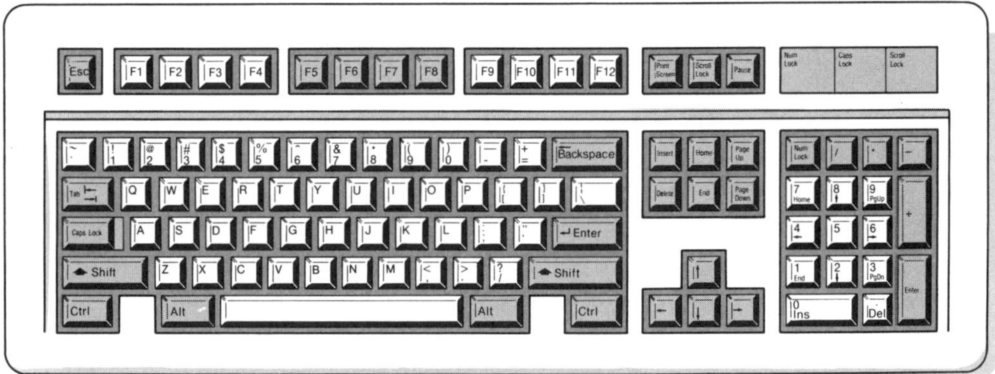

(B) AT and PS/2 keyboard.

Figure 1.3. ***The standard PS/2, AT, and PC keyboards.***

The Typewriter Keys The largest part of the keyboard consists of the traditional typewriter keyboard. This intentional design was used to encourage an easier transition from the typewriter to a personal computer. The standard typewriter keys are highlighted in Figure 1.4.

The Numeric Keypad The numeric keypad was added to the PC in its earliest years. Many people enjoy having the ability to use it for "rapid-fire" entry of calculations—an especially useful feature for those people who use accounting or spreadsheet

Figure 1.4. ***The typewriter keys on the keyboard.***

programs such as Lotus 1-2-3. The numeric keypad also serves double-duty for those who want to use it as a directional arrow keypad. The choice between directional or numeric keypad use is determined by pressing the Num Lock key. When the Num Lock key is pressed, it sets the keypad into numeric mode, and the other keys on the pad are interpreted as numerals. In other words, when the Num Lock key is pressed, the keys on the numeric keypad function like the keys on a pocket calculator. If you press the Num Lock key again, the same keys function as ways to control where the cursor is displayed on the video monitor (more on this shortly).

Thus, the Num Lock key is a *toggle*. Each time you press it, the keyboard goes into the alternate mode, changing from cursor controller to numeric keypad and back. (The PS/2 and AT keyboards have a little light on the keyboard that comes on when the keypad is in numeric mode and turns off when it is in directional mode.) Figure 1.5 shows the location of the numeric keypad and the Num Lock key.

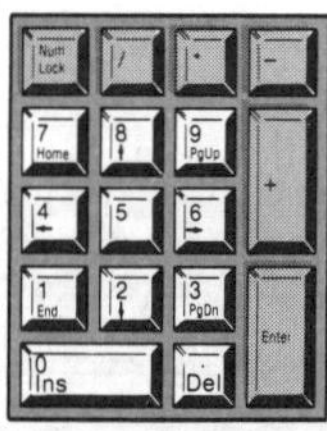

Figure 1.5. ***The numeric keypad and the Num Lock key.***

Control and Function Keys

The function keys, which are labeled F1 through F12, sit across the top of the keyboard. On older PC keyboards, you may find that there are only ten function keys (F1 through F10). Also, older keyboards have the function keys down the left side of the keyboard rather than across the top.

These keys serve many important purposes. When you are looking at the PC DOS prompt, some of these keys have predefined functions that help you manipulate PC DOS commands in some way. When you are running a program, however, you may be surprised to find that the program effectively "takes over" the function keys to represent commands that exist only within that program.

The cursor keys, also known as directional keys, are the four keys that look like an upside-down letter T between the typewriter and keypad portions of the keyboard. On older PC keyboards, these keys do not exist by themselves. Instead, users must use the directional arrow keys on the numeric keypad. This means that you cannot use the keypad for numeric entry and directional movement at the same time.

For the PS/2 machines, IBM thought better of this inconvenience and supplied duplicate directional cursor keys as a separate group. A group of six keys that lie directly above the directional arrow keys are also direct carry-overs from the numeric/directional keypad. Some companies offer replacement keyboards that provide modern features for older machines. Figure 1.6 illustrates the position of some of these important keys.

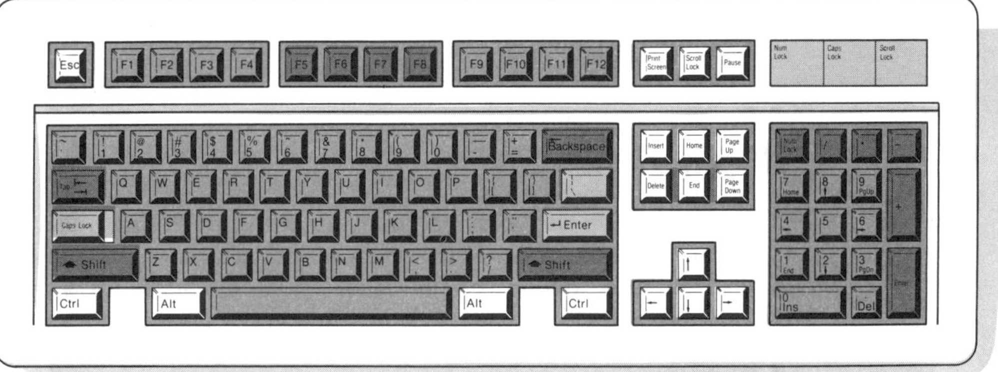

Figure 1.6. ***The remaining keys on the PS/2 keyboard.***

As you do the exercises in the Quick Primer, you will be told which keys to use. After you finish this Quick Primer, you can find out more about the special keys on your keyboard by reading Chapter 9, "Creating Text Files."

Memory and Storage

Before you do much work with your computer, you should understand the distinction between memory and storage. Both are measured in *bytes*, which is a unit of memory. You can think of a byte as representing a single character—a letter of the alphabet, a numeral, a punctuation mark such as a period or comma, or one of a number of other special characters. Quantities of bytes are usually represented as either *kilobytes* (1 kilobyte equals 1,024 bytes) or as *megabytes* (1 megabyte equals 1,024 kilobytes equals 1,048,576 bytes). (These measurements are not round numbers, like 1,000 or 1,000,000, because they are ultimately based on the binary numbering that is actually used by computers.) You also will find that kilobyte and megabyte are usually abbreviated by a capital K and M, respectively (or sometimes KB and MB).

Most PC DOS computers have 640K bytes of random-access memory (RAM), although others have 512K or less. This type of memory, RAM, is what the computer uses to hold various parts of the operating system, as well as the program you are working with and the data you are working on. When you turn off your computer, all the information in RAM is erased.

You use disks to store information permanently. When you first turn on your computer, its RAM is empty. The machine is designed to load automatically PC DOS from a disk into RAM. Then, it is your job to load other programs and information from your disks into RAM so that you can use the programs to change the information. When you're ready to turn off the machine, you must remember to store the information you changed on the disks. If you forget this important step, the changes you made will be erased and you will have to redo them. All your information is stored on the disk as a "file" or as a group of files. PC DOS provides simple commands that you can use to find your files, make PC DOS load them into RAM, save changes on the disk, and do other tasks you will learn soon. For now, what is important is that your disks store all of your programs and your information, usually referred to as *data*.

Floppy Disks

Disk capacities are also measured in bytes. Soft-shell floppy disks (the 5.25-inch kind) can hold either 360K or 1.2MB of data, but hard-shell (3.5-inch) floppy disks have larger capacities: either 720K or 1.44MB. If your 5.25-inch disks are labeled DSDD (double-sided double-density), they have 360K capacity. The newer 1.2MB disks are usually labeled *quad density* or *high density* (see Chapter 7, "All About Floppy Disks," for details).

When you want to use a floppy disk to access your programs or data, you put the disk in its drive. You then use PC DOS commands to tell the operating system to copy the information from the floppy disk into the memory of your computer. (Once the data is in the computer's memory, you can read it and change it, and if you want a permanent record of your changes, remember to write a copy of it (*save it*) onto the disk.

Get out a floppy disk now so that you can use it in the exercises in the Quick Primer. The disks you use must match the size of your disk drive. Figure 1.7A and B shows a comparison of 5.25-inch and 3.5-inch disk drives.

The 5.25-inch floppy drives are equipped with a spring-loaded door that you have to lower and close after inserting the disk. The 3.5-inch drives do not have a drive door. Instead, you have to insert a 3.5-inch disk until you hear and feel a distinctive "snap" that tells you the disk is in place. To release the disk, you push the ejector button sitting underneath the slot opening until the disk is pushed out of the drive.

Soft-Shell Floppy Disks, 360K and 1.2M

Soft-shell floppy disks have been with us for well over a decade in the personal computer environment. Floppy disks are what most PC users think of when they refer to a disk. Figure 1.8 shows a traditional soft-shell floppy disk.

A soft-shell floppy disk can be damaged much more easily than a hard-shell floppy disk, so be sure to handle it with care.

Caution

Minimizing Risks in Using Soft-Shell Disks

- Always keep the disk in its paper envelope when not in use.
- Always hold the disk by the corner or edge, not the exposed film surface.

- Don't keep disks near sources of magnetism, such as audio speakers, telephones, motors, the display monitor, or other metal objects that may be magnetic. Magnetism can erase or garble the stored information.
- Don't keep disks near hot surfaces or in direct sunlight.
- If you send a disk through the mail, use one of the disk mailers available in office supply stores.

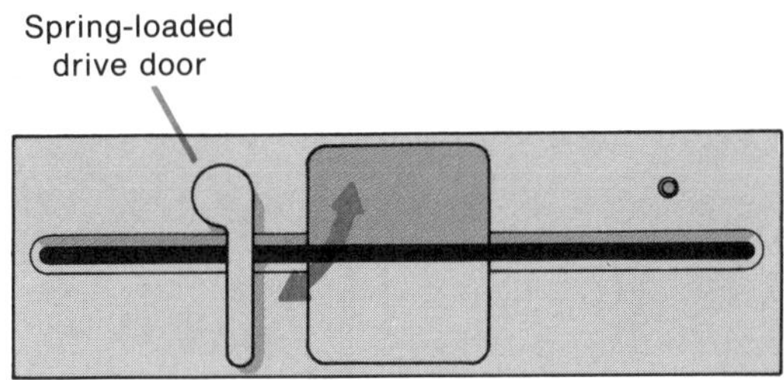

(A) PC/XT/AT floppy disk drive.

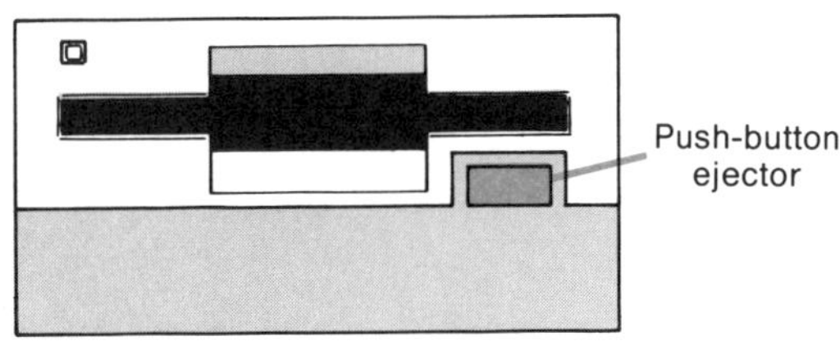

(B) PS/2 floppy disk drive.

Figure 1.7. ***A 5.25-inch floppy disk drive versus a 3.5-inch floppy disk drive.***

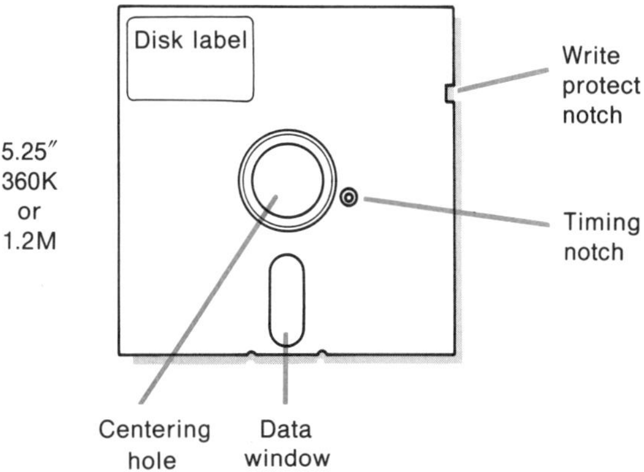

Figure 1.8. ***A soft-shell floppy disk.***

If you are using 5.25-inch floppy disks for the exercises in the Quick Primer, check to see that their write-protect notch is not covered. Covering this notch prevents anyone from changing information on or adding information to a particular disk, so if the notch is covered, you (or someone else) probably wanted to protect the data on that disk—don't use it. Use another disk if this is the case. In Chapter 7, "All About Floppy Disks," you will see that having a write-protected disk is useful when the data stored on the disk should never be changed.

Hard-Shell Floppy Disks, 720K and 1.44M

The other, newer type of floppy disk that is used on PS/2 machines is illustrated in Figure 1.9. It is protected by a rigid plastic case as well as by a metal shutter that slides open when the disk is inserted in the disk drive.

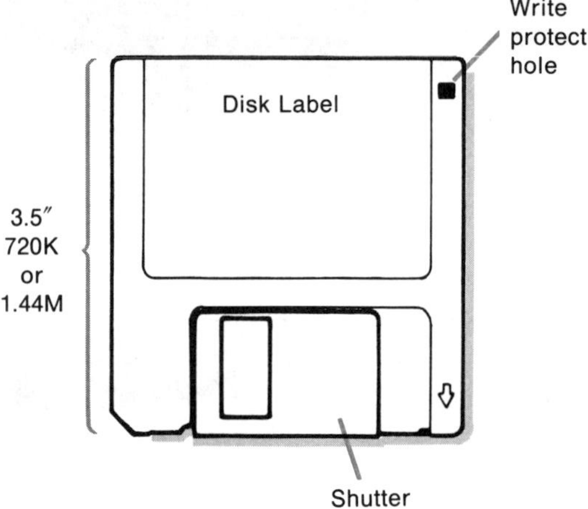

Figure 1.9. ***A hard-shell floppy disk.***

Caution

Don't Confuse *Hard-Shell Floppy Disk* with *Hard Disk*
The hard disk is your fixed (nonremovable) disk.

If you are using this type of disk for the exercises in the Quick Primer, check to see that the small square hole (labeled the *write protect hole* in Figure 1.9) is closed. If it is open, you (or someone else) probably wanted to protect the data on that disk. Use a new disk if this is the case.

Caution

Magnetism and Heat Are Still Factors
Remember that even hard-shelled floppies are vulnerable to magnetism or extreme heat despite the added protection provided by the hard shell.

The PC DOS Operating System

IBM does not automatically supply a copy of PC DOS as a part of a PC machine. Although PC DOS must be purchased separately, it is not an optional purchase! PC DOS must always be the first program loaded into your computer after you turn the power on. Without it, your programs are not able to use the printer, disk drives, screen, or anything else. In fact, without PC DOS, most programs cannot run at all.

Installing PC DOS

To get the most out of this Quick Primer, you should be ready to experiment with the commands and other features of PC DOS as they are presented. To do so, you must have PC DOS installed on your system so that the programs that make up the operating system are stored on your hard disk (or on a floppy disk), ready for action. If you turn on the computer and the system does not start as described in the next section, you need to install PC DOS on your system. Turn to Chapter 12, "Installing a PC DOS System," for instructions; then, return here.

Quick Questions

These questions appear throughout the Quick Primer to help you determine how well you have understood the lessons. Answers are found at the end of the Quick Primer.

1. Identify the location of the Central Processor Unit (CPU) on your system.
   a. on the rear panel of your display monitor
   b. mounted inside the base unit
   c. underneath the keypad on your keyboard
   d. inside your printer
2. *Double-sided, double-density* refers to the capacity of a
   a. 3.25-inch high-density disk
   b. hard-shell floppy disk
   c. hard disk
   d. 360K 5.25-inch floppy disk
3. What do the letters PC DOS stand for?
4. The purpose of the PC DOS operating system is to
   a. control the operation of the hardware components of your system
   b. control the interaction between you and your computer
   c. control the operation of the software programs you purchase
   d. all of the above

Life Before PC DOS Enters Your PC

When you turn on the power to your computer, it is transformed from a quiet collection of idle machinery into a whirring wonder of the electronic age with a life of its own. You will see many things happen, beginning with the first step.

How to Turn It On

As with any electrical device, you must first turn on the power to your computer and its various components. On the newer IBM PS/2 machines, the power switch is located on the far right side of the front of the base unit. On all the PC/XT/AT machines, you can find the power switch at the back of the right side of the base unit, just around the corner from the back panel. Figure 1.10 shows these positions.

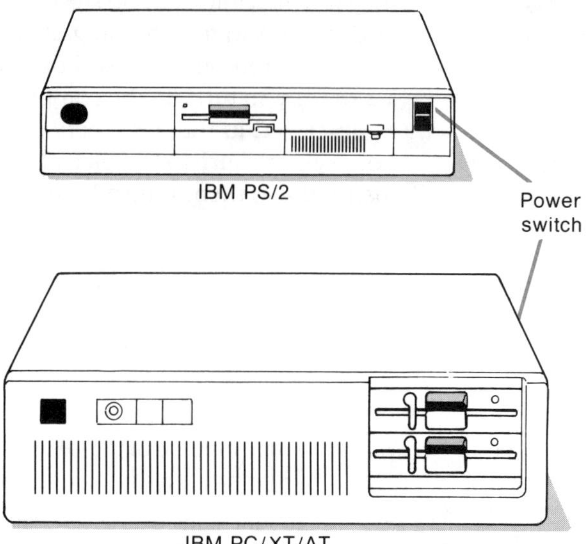

Figure 1.10 ***Power switches on the PS/2 and PC/XT/AT models.***

You may also have to turn on your display monitor. The monitors for the older monochrome and color monitors for the PC/XT/AT systems have their power switches located on the front, along with the contrast and brightness knobs. On the newer PS/2 equipment, the power switch is located on the right side of the display monitor, and the brightness and contrast knobs are located on the left side.

You should note that these descriptions refer to the various IBM models of the base unit and display monitors. Switch types and locations vary on some IBM-compatible systems from other manufacturers. Many people use non-IBM monitors, especially with the older IBM PC/XT/AT machines, and the switch types and locations vary on such monitors, too.

If your computer is not on, turn it on now and see what happens. (If you do not have a hard disk, see the section "Loading PC DOS from a Floppy Disk" later in this chapter, because you need to take a couple of additional steps.)

How to Start Your PC

Many new users are surprised to see what happens when they turn on their machine for the first time. Instead of seeing PC DOS come up immediately, many other things occur. You should take note of what is happening. You may see the screen blink or display strange characters. The small lights that are mounted on the floppy and hard drives may flicker, as do the "lock" key lights on your keyboard. Listen to the whirring sound of the hard drive or the abrupt sounds coming from floppy drive.

These actions are not happening at random. They are part of what is called the PC's *startup program*, which automatically executes each time you start your PC. All PC systems are equipped with a startup program that is executed every time you flip on the power switch.

The process of starting the PC ends when you see the C:\> prompt. That is a sign that PC DOS is fully loaded into your system.

When the power is turned on, the startup program inside every PC has to accomplish two tasks. First, it has to test the hardware (especially the memory chips) to make sure everything is working correctly. If something is not working correctly, you want to know immediately, instead of finding out the hard way later, perhaps after several hours of work.

Second, it has to load the PC DOS operating system program into RAM. Only after PC DOS is properly loaded is the system ready for use.

The startup program runs a routine called the *Power On Self Test*, (POST) which performs several important tests before permitting PC DOS to be loaded into memory. First, it must ensure that all of the memory in the system is working properly and without error. If the POST finds an error, it reports that information to the display screen, in the form of code numbers that refer to the location of the bad chip(s), and then stops. The code numbers enable a trained technician to find the bad memory chip and replace it. In addition to checking memory, the POST examines all the other electronic components. The POST must also check to see whether the connections between the PC and its keyboard and display monitor are solid. Obviously, if these tests fail, the PC will not be of much use. Finally, the POST also checks to see that the floppy and/or hard drives are *on-line*—available to the system for retrieving information. This is a critical step, because the PC startup program loads PC DOS from either a floppy disk or the hard disk.

The POST performs several other tests, although the only one that shows on your screen is the test for random-access memory (RAM). This is the area of memory where PC DOS (and later, your application programs) is loaded.

In the upper-left corner of the screen, the amount of RAM being checked is displayed as the startup program progresses.

Once the POST has checked the hardware, the startup program must load PC DOS into memory and then configure PC DOS so that it can properly control the internal connections to the screen, disk drives, printer, and other devices. The process by which the startup program loads PC DOS into memory is called *booting* your PC. This term comes from the expression "to pull yourself up by your own bootstraps." Before your PC can operate at all, it needs a program that tells it how to do the most basic tasks—including how to fetch programs from the disk! Obviously, the program that tells the computer how to load programs from the disk can't itself be on disk. These most basic instructions for the boot process are stored as part of the startup program in read-only memory (ROM), which makes them instantly available as soon as there is power in the PC's circuits.

When the startup program is ready to load the PC DOS operating system itself from the disk, it always first tries to load PC DOS from a floppy drive. If it does not find a disk containing a copy of PC DOS on the floppy drive, it tries to locate the PC DOS operating system on the hard drive (if you have one). If the startup program cannot locate a working copy of PC DOS anywhere in the system, it returns an error message (`Non-system disk or disk error`) to the display monitor and asks you to insert a PC DOS system disk. (Older IBM PC machines may not display an error message but instead display the opening screen information that lets programmers use a built-in BASIC programming language—ignore this, get a PC DOS system disk, and reboot.)

Quick Questions

5. Which of the following does the startup program perform?
   a. checks to see that your printer is functioning correctly
   b. checks for any errors in your modem
   c. checks for a specific version of PC DOS
   d. checks to see that RAM memory is working properly
6. What is the indication that PC DOS is loaded and ready to use?
   a. the disk drive light comes on
   b. the message `Non-system disk or disk error` appears
   c. the C:\> prompt appears
   d. you see the amount of RAM being checked

PC DOS and Your System

The process of loading PC DOS into your PC is important to understand. PC DOS can be loaded from either a hard disk or floppy disk, and you will see how both of these processes work. As you read through this section, however, you will notice that the examples usually assume that you are using a hard disk drive. This is because most newer PCs are equipped with hard disks as standard equipment, and most serious application programs used today do not work well without a hard disk. If you do not have a hard disk and are using only floppy disks, you should still try these examples. In general, floppy disk users should substitute the drive letter A: for C: when typing the examples. If you have a hard disk, you will find many useful tips for its most efficient use in Chapter 6, "Managing Your Hard Disk."

Loading PC DOS from the Hard Drive

If PC DOS has been stored on a hard disk, the startup program still first tries to boot PC DOS from the floppy drive and then loads PC DOS from the hard drive. If you have a hard disk, by all means store PC DOS on it. (Chapter 12, "Installing a PC DOS System," tells you how.) Using a hard disk rather than a floppy disk for this purpose allows system startup to proceed much faster, and because you don't have to worry about swapping floppy disks, there is less work for you to do.

Assuming that PC DOS is on your hard disk, turn on your computer, if you have not done so already. Notice that the light for the floppy drive comes on as the floppy drive makes an attempt to activate itself. Very quickly, however, the startup program discovers that no disk is present and activates the hard disk drive.

Loading PC DOS from a Floppy Disk

If you are booting your system from a floppy disk, you should have a disk marked *startup disk, boot disk, PC DOS system disk*, or something similar; use one of these disks to start the system. If you are using PC DOS 4 with 5.25-inch disks, you have disks marked *startup* and *shell*. Use the disk marked *startup* to boot the system.

Whichever version of PC DOS you have, insert the system disk in your floppy drive and close the drive door. If you have two floppy drives, insert the PC DOS system disk in the first floppy drive. (The first floppy drive is either to the left of—or directly above—the second floppy drive. If you accidentally insert your PC DOS disk in the wrong drive, you won't cause any damage, but your PC may not function!)

Then, turn on the power. When PC DOS is fully loaded, you will see some information on the screen. (If you do not see anything on the screen, but your disk drive has stopped whirring, you may have forgotten to turn on the power to your monitor. If you get a `Non-System disk` or `disk error` message (or if BASIC is loaded instead), you probably do not have a disk containing PC DOS in your first floppy drive. If you see this message, remove the disk that is in the drive, insert the PC DOS system disk correctly, and press the keys marked Ctrl, Alt, and Del—all three of them—simultaneously. This restarts your computer.)

Quick Questions

7. What does the term *system disk* or *bootable disk* mean?
8. If you have two floppy drives, which one do you use?
    a. the first one, the one above or to the left of the second one
    b. the second one, the one above or to the left of the first one
    c. the first one, which is always below the second one
    d. the second one, which is always above the first one

What's Next

What happens when PC DOS is loaded into memory? How can you tell that it has been loaded successfully? What can you do with your machine once PC DOS has been loaded? These important questions are answered in Chapter 2, "Internal Commands and Files," which introduces you to PC DOS commands, the PC DOS prompts, and the PC DOS command line.

Key Concepts and Words

Before you read further, use the following list to test your understanding of the concepts and words in this chapter.

Disk Operating System	Hard (fixed) disks and drives
Computer system components	Floppy disks and drives
Central processing unit	Memory
Display monitor	Storage
Keyboard	Booting
Printer	Starting PC DOS

Chapter 2

You control PC DOS by using its commands. This chapter presents the fundamental concepts of using the PC DOS operating system, and in the process teaches a dozen easy-to-remember, built-in commands that you'll use every day. You'll learn

- *How to recognize the PC DOS prompt and command line*
- *How to use the internal commands of PC DOS*
- *How to manage and organize your files*
- *How to specify any files by using "wildcards"*
- *How to create your own subdirectories*
- *How to create and read text files*

Before you begin: You should read Chapter 1, which explains the components of a PC DOS computer system, including the keyboard, display monitor, CPU and memory, disk drives, and other fundamentals. You should also know the material in the To the Reader *section in the Introduction, especially, "Conventions Used in This Book."*

Chapter 2
Internal Commands and Files

The fun of PC DOS is in using the commands, making the system respond to what you want. There are lots of different commands, and each does a special task. Using a command is easy—you type its name and then watch it run.

You probably want to start using commands right away, so the following short section presents just what you need to understand in order to start using commands fast.

Getting the PC DOS Prompt: The Fundamentals

When you turn on the power for your PC DOS machine, you begin a sequence of actions called the "boot" process. A built-in startup program initiates some hardware checks to be sure the machine is in proper working order and then begins to load the PC DOS operating system program from a disk drive. When PC DOS is finally loaded, it displays a "prompt" to let you know it is ready to accept your commands and a "cursor" to indicate where you can enter commands.

This section explains what you may have to do as PC DOS is being loaded, as well as the concepts of the prompt, the cursor, and other fundamentals. The next sections present your introduction to using commands as well as understanding and organizing files, with lots of examples you can try.

Setting the Current Date: Some Basic Concepts

If your system has been in use for a while, the chances are that someone customized it to set the date and time automatically at startup. If not, PC DOS asks you for this information before accepting any other commands. Having the correct date and time is important because they combine to form a "date-time stamp" that PC DOS uses whenever it references any of the programs or files on your disks. If PC DOS asks you for the date, you see a message like this on your screen:

```
Current date is Fri 8-05-1990
Enter new date (mm-dd-yy): _
```

The Concept of the Cursor

That blinking underscore you see flashing next to the new date request, right after the colon on the second line, is called the *cursor*. The cursor provides a connection between the keyboard and the display. It shows the place on the display where your typing will appear. If you type a new date, the first letter you type appears where the cursor is, moving the cursor forward one space to show you where your next character will appear. Each new character advances the cursor across the screen.

When PC DOS is running, the cursor is present at all times. (When one of your favorite programs is running—such as your word processing program—it provides its own special cursors for your use in entering text or other data.) Whenever the blinking cursor is present, PC DOS is waiting patiently for some sort of response from you. (It waits all night long if you forget to turn off the computer before you leave the office!)

The Concept of Entering a Line of Text

PC DOS is known as a "line-oriented" system. This means that it accepts text that you type a line at a time. As you type, the characters appear at the cursor, and the cursor moves forward. To indicate that you have finished typing on a line, you must press the Enter key.

Once you press the Enter key, there is no going back. Pressing the Enter key is a signal to PC DOS that you have "entered" some kind of information or command. PC DOS accepts whatever you have typed and tries to respond.

As long as you don't press Enter, if you make a typing mistake, you can use the Backspace key to correct your error. The last letter you typed will disappear, and the cursor will move back one space. You can backspace over the entire line, if you wish. Wherever you choose to stop, the cursor will sit patiently blinking, and, until you press Enter, you can retype until you get it right.

The Concept of Default

Automatic actions, such as presenting the date request, are called *default* actions. Understanding the concept of default actions is important. There are many situations in which your PC DOS system takes a certain action automatically, as the default action.

In the previous example, the default action is to accept the current time. If you choose not to change the date, you press the Enter key without typing anything else. PC DOS takes the default action and accepts the displayed date as valid.

In developing your skills, you will learn how to use alternatives to the default action to suit your needs. For instance, if PC DOS did not present a date request, you could use customized instructions for the PC DOS boot process that someone would probably have created as an alternative to the default boot process.

The Concept of Format

In the previous example, PC DOS is expecting you to enter the date in the specific format shown in parentheses as `mm-dd-yy`. If you do not want PC DOS to take the default action (by accepting the date shown in the *Current date* line), you must enter the correct date in the format shown on the screen. For example, if today is June 10, 1990, you type the date as **6-10-1990** and then press the Enter key.

PC DOS doesn't know what the correct date really is, so any date you type—as long as you use the correct format—is accepted as the current date.

Follow the Rules

An important principle to remember in dealing with your computer is that the rules for entering commands and other information are strict. PC DOS can tell if you make a mistake in using the rules, although it cannot tell whether the substance of what you have specified is wrong.

The Concept of Error Messages

If you use a different format, such as typing **August** rather than **8**, PC DOS gives you an error message, `Invalid date`. For now, you shouldn't worry if you get an error message—you can't break anything.

As you learn to use PC DOS, you will encounter error messages—they tend to come in bunches. Error messages may be frustrating, but they are benign. PC DOS uses error messages to indicate a variety of troubles, and how you respond depends on the situation. Part of learning to use a command is to learn what its error messages mean. If you encounter a rainstorm of error messages, take heart: Remember that this means you are learning something new and that very soon, you'll have new powers and the exhilaration that comes with them.

Setting the Current Time: A Review

After you have entered the date successfully, PC DOS presents another, similar message, asking you for the current time. Your screen now looks something like this (assuming you pressed the Enter key without changing the date).

```
Current date is Fri 8-05-1990
Enter new date (mm-dd-yy): 8-05-1990
Current time is 9:32:06.41p
Enter new time:_
```

As with entering the date, if you press the Enter key, you direct PC DOS to take the default action of accepting the current time (9:32:06.41p). If you choose to enter a new time, be sure to type the time in the correct format (as shown). Remember that you can backspace over mistakes if need be—the cursor advances and backs up accordingly—and that when you press the Enter key, PC DOS accepts what you have typed and processes it, updating the time or returning an error message, depending on your typing.

Notice that PC DOS records the time to the nearest hundredth of a second. You can probably live without that kind of accuracy. PC DOS requires only that you enter the current hour, but you probably want to track the minutes, too. As an example, if the correct time is 10:41 in the morning, you can enter `10:41a` without bothering to enter seconds.

Version 4

Older PC DOS Versions Use Military Time
As one of its new features, PC DOS 4 defaults to display the time in the conventional twelve-hour format, using `a` or `p` to indicate morning or afternoon hours, respectively. PC DOS versions 3.3 and earlier use the "military" time format, representing time as a twenty-four-hour day, from 00:00, representing midnight, to 23:59, representing the following evening at one minute to midnight. If you are using PC DOS version 3.3 or earlier, don't include the `a` or `p` when you enter the time.

As you develop your skills, you will find that the date-time stamps help you organize your work, letting you see what is current. Computers enable you to work so fast that sometimes it is easy to generate many versions of your work, and you will discover the importance of discarding or archiving older work.

The System Prompt

After you enter both the current date and time, the screen displays a new message that includes the current version of PC DOS followed by the IBM and Microsoft copyright notices and the *system prompt*. The screen now looks like this:

```
Current date is Fri 8-05-1990
Enter new date (mm-dd-yy): 8-05-1990
Current time is 9:32:06.41p

Enter new time:_

IBM DOS Version 4.00
        (C)Copyright International Business Machines Corp 1981, 1988

        (C)Copyright Microsoft Corp 1981, 1988
C>_
```

The `C>` is the system prompt. It tells you that PC DOS is now fully loaded and awaiting your commands. The system prompt will be with you throughout most of your exploration of PC DOS, so you should become comfortable with its presence.

Version 4

How the Prompt Appears
If you are using PC DOS version 4 or later, the prompt may look slightly different: `C:\>`. If you are using an earlier version of PC DOS, the default presents the prompt as shown in the example, but if your system has been in use for a little while, someone may have customized the way in which the prompt appears. The next

sections of this chapter show you how to use a command to change the prompt. For now, you should consider that `C>` and `C:\>` represent the same thing. The examples in the Quick Primer will continue to use the simpler `C>` style until you learn a few commands.

The Command Line

Notice that the cursor is blinking next to the `C>` prompt. To enter a command, you type its name; the characters you type appear at the cursor, which then advances across the screen. You can backspace over your mistakes and retype your command. When you press the Enter key, PC DOS accepts the line of text you have entered and tries to process it as a command.

Because the system prompt indicates the line on which you enter a command, this line has a special name: It is called *the command line*. The "interface" through which the PC DOS operating system gives you control is called a *command line interface*. By the time you have read all of the Quick Primer, you will understand thoroughly how to use the PC DOS command line to enter commands and provide the correct information in the proper format to make your commands work.

The Current or Default Drive

The prompt gives you a valuable piece of information. By showing a particular letter of the alphabet, it tells you on which disk drive the startup program found PC DOS. This is the letter C if you are booting from a hard disk or the letter A if you are booting from a floppy disk.

Whatever the letter, it also represents the *current drive*. Unless you specify otherwise, PC DOS default action is to search the current drive to look for commands and files that you specify. You can change the current drive to be whichever drive you choose, and you can search for commands on other drives without changing the current drive. The first thing to learn is how to change the current drive.

To try changing the current drive from the C: hard disk drive to the A: floppy disk drive, and to do the exercises in the rest of the Quick Primer, you need to have a formatted disk in drive A:, so insert a floppy disk in the drive now, even if you are using a hard disk. During the exercises, you will learn how to tell whether or not the floppy disk has been formatted. (If you have no hard disk, your PC DOS disk is in drive A: and you should leave it there for now.)

Try this: At the `C>` prompt, type `a:` and press Enter:

```
C>a:
A>_
```

In this example, drive C: (the hard disk) was the current drive. When you typed `a:` and pressed Enter, you changed the current drive to A:, making the floppy disk drive the current drive. To change back, type `c:`. If you want the B: drive to be the current drive, type `b:` and press Enter. Don't forget the colon! If you type a drive letter without its colon, PC DOS will present an error message, `Bad command or file name.` If you type a drive name for a drive that does not exist (for instance, `x:`), PC DOS will present an error message,

`Invalid drive`. (If the disk is not formatted, you see the message `General failure reading drive a:`. Type **a** to abort the command. Then, locate a formatted disk and put it in the drive. You may have to ask someone for a formatted disk, or you can turn to the section *Formatting a Floppy Disk* later in the Quick Primer to see how to do it if help is not available.)

Now change back to drive C:. Type **C:** and press Enter:

```
A>C:
C>
```

What difference does changing drives make in the long run? All the difference in the world! You will see that the operation of many PC DOS commands—and even your own programs—may depend on whether you have made the correct drive current when you try to execute them.

You can tell PC DOS to look for a command or program in more than one place, but it does not do so automatically. PC DOS tries to find a command by looking at the current drive (the one shown in the PC DOS prompt). If PC DOS cannot find it there, you may have to change drives and try again.

Quick Questions

9. When you see a blinking cursor, it means that
   a. you need to set the date and time
   b. PC DOS or a program is waiting for you to enter information
   c. you should turn on the power switch
   d. you should press the Enter key
10. Which of the following is a prompt that indicates your hard disk is the current drive?
   a. C
   b. C>
   c. C:\>
   d. Both b and c
   e. Both a and c
11. An action that PC DOS automatically takes is called
   a. a default
   b. a prerequisite
   c. a command
   d. an option
12. The current drive is the drive where
   a. PC DOS looks automatically for commands and programs
   b. the floppy disk you are using is held
   c. your files are stored
   d. your programs are stored

13. Which of the following is not a valid response to the TIME command?
    a. 12:08p
    b. 00:15:30
    c. 8
    d. 23:59p
    e. 2:31a

Introducing Commands

From this point on, you will begin looking at the commands that are provided by PC DOS. Before learning how to put these useful commands to work, however, you should know about a key distinction that divides PC DOS commands into two separate groups: *internal* and *external* commands.

Controlling PC DOS with Internal Commands

When PC DOS loads into memory, it brings with it a number of tools to help you manipulate files and manage your PC hardware. These are the internal commands. They are always present whenever you see the system prompt (which means that PC DOS has active control of your PC). The terms *internal* and *external* may sound strange to you, but you should not worry about them at this point. Their meanings will become clear enough once you understand what they represent.

Internal commands are very easy to use. At the system prompt, just type the name of the command and press the Enter key. That's all there is to it! You will probably use fewer than ten internal commands regularly in your daily work, and they are designed to be easy to remember. The following are the internal commands.

PC DOS Internal Commands

BREAK	CLS	DATE	ERASE	PROMPT	SET	VER
CHCP	COPY	DEL	MKDIR	RENAME	TIME	VERIFY
CHDIR	CTTY	DIR	PATH	RMDIR	TYPE	VOL

You do not have to worry about what all of these mean. You will get practice using a few of them in the following sections.

External commands are actually programs that are stored on disk. In order for PC DOS to use an external command, the operating system must be able to locate it on the disk where it is stored, so they work in a slightly different way, as you will see in Chapter 3.

Tip

Always Press Enter
After you have typed the name of a command that you want PC DOS to carry out, remember to press the Enter key (the one

marked ↵ on your keyboard. PC DOS usually does not "know" what you have typed until you press the Enter key. In a very few situations—when you are responding to certain prompts from the system, for example—you do not have to press the Enter key. As you work with PC DOS, you will quickly become accustomed to pressing the Enter key to tell the system to carry out your order. The simplest form of entering a command is to type the name of the command and press Enter. Pressing the Enter key directs PC DOS to search the current drive to find a program with that name, then load the program and let it run. When done, the program returns control to PC DOS, which then displays the prompt to let you know you can enter another command.

Clearing the Display Screen with the CLS Command

Your screen can quickly fill up as you work with your computer. Programs may be executed, directories are listed, PC DOS commands may display their results before returning the system prompt. After each execution, the previous command and its output move up toward the top of the screen so that room can be made at the bottom for the next system prompt. The result is that the screen may become cluttered with information you no longer need—garbage.

You can erase the contents of the screen, to get a nice blank slate showing a single system prompt, by using the CLS (clear screen) command.

Try it now: type **data data data** at the system prompt and press Enter. Then clear the screen:

```
C>data data data
Bad command or file name
C>cls
C>
```

What happened? You typed **data data data** and pressed Enter. PC DOS accepted the line as a command and tried to enact it, but there is no such command, so PC DOS returned an error message, **Bad command or filename**, and presented the prompt, ready to accept another command. You entered **cls**, which is a command, to clear the screen and pressed Enter. PC DOS loaded a program named CLS and ran it, clearing the screen. When the CLS command was done, PC DOS took over and displayed the prompt.

Learning More about the DATE and TIME Commands

You have already seen how the DATE and TIME commands work automatically before the copyright notice and your C> system prompt were displayed. You can also run the DATE or the TIME commands any time you wish to see the current date or time displayed, or whenever you want to change them.

The DATE and the TIME commands are internal commands. You can execute an internal command, no matter what the current drive; you do not have to have drive C: as the current drive. For example, you can change the current drive to drive A: and then use the commands:

```
C>A:
A>date
Current date is Sun 8-07-1990
Enter new date (mm-dd-yy):        ←press Enter
A>time
Current time is 8:04:59.74p
Enter new time:                   ←press Enter
```

If the information is correct, you will want to keep the DATE and TIME at the current settings. Pressing the Enter key after each request will tell PC DOS to keep the current settings intact. To change either the DATE or the TIME, enter the correction in the proper format.

Using the DIR Command

Up until now, you have held the PC DOS disk in your hand or watched the blinking light on the hard drive and not had any real idea of what was on the disk. Well, the DIR command is your answer to unraveling that mystery.

DIR stands for directory listing. It tells PC DOS to give you a list of all of the files that are in the current working area of your default drive. This area is called a *directory*. Just as a telephone directory lists the names (and usually addresses) of people in a town, a disk directory contains a list of files on a disk with the important information about them that was mentioned earlier: their size, when they were created, and so on. (A disk can actually have more than one directory, but for now you'll be looking at just one directory on the disk.)

It is time to see for yourself. Make drive C: your current drive (by typing `C:` and pressing Enter). To get a listing of the files that are stored there, do this:

```
C>dir
 Volume in drive C has no label
 Directory of C:\
COMMAND  COM  25307  3-17-87 12:00p
ANSI     SYS   1678  3-17-87 12:00p
COUNTRY  SYS  11285  3-17-87 12:00p
DISPLAY  SYS  11290  3-17-87 12:00p
DRIVER   SYS   1196  3-17-87 12:00p
FASTOPEN EXE   3919  3-17-87 12:00p
FDISK    COM  48216  3-18-87 12:00p
FORMAT   COM  11616  3-18-87 12:00p
                                        ←extra files removed to save space
KEYB     COM   9056  3-17-87 12:00p
KEYBOARD SYS  19766  3-17-87 12:00p
MODE     COM  15487  3-17-87 12:00p
BACKUP   COM  31913  3-18-87 12:00p
CHKDSK   COM   9850  3-18-87 12:00p
EDLIN    COM   7526  3-17-87 12:00p
PRINT    COM   9026  3-17-87 12:00p
RECOVER  COM   4299  3-18-87 12:00p
RESTORE  COM  34643  3-17-87 12:00p
    48 File(s) 18234496 bytes free
```

Depending on how your hard disk is organized, there may be more files than those listed, and you may see different file names. There may also be the names of other directories on the disk, listed with 〈DIR〉 next to them. The first line of the listing proclaims that the `Volume in drive C has no label`. A disk, whether it is one of your floppy disks or the hard disk in the hard disk drive, may be labeled or not. For now, labeling is too complex to explain. You will learn how to label a disk soon, so ignore this line for now. The point is that the DIR command generates a list of files that are specified by a particular disk drive and directory.

Uppercase versus Lowercase
Note that the DIR command does not have to be capitalized. When dealing with files and PC DOS commands, the operating system doesn't care if you use upper- or lowercase. When it interprets your commands, PC DOS translates them into uppercase anyway. So DIR or dir have the same effect. Following common conventions, however, PC DOS commands in this book are capitalized when they are discussed generally, and they are presented in lowercase when they are used to show what you type.

No Hard Disk?
If you don't have a hard disk, your PC DOS system disk is probably still in your floppy drive. You can type `dir` to get a similar listing. Remember that when the discussions or examples mention drive C:, you should use the letter A: instead.

Note that each file listing includes five entries. The first two entries are the file name and extension. Batch files have the extension .BAT, and executable files have the extension .COM or EXE. For now, do not worry about what these extensions mean; you can find out more about them in Chapter 5, "PC DOS Files." The third entry lists the size of each file, and the last two represent the date- and time-stamp information supplied by PC DOS when your files were created or last modified.

At the bottom of the display is a count of the number of files in the working area, or directory, of your current drive as well as the number of bytes of free space left on the disk in that drive.

Being Selective with the DIR Command

Sometimes you may not want a total listing of the files in a directory. Maybe you would like to see only one particular file to find out the day it was last changed, for example, or how big it is. How would you do that using the DIR command?

For example, if you are viewing a listing of your PC DOS files, you can locate an important file called COMMAND.COM by typing a command that looks like this:

```
C>dir command.com
 Volume in drive C has no label
 Directory of C:\
COMMAND COM  37637  6-17-88 12:00p
    48 File(s) 18234496 bytes free
C>
```

Because each file in a directory must have a unique name, if you know the name of the file you are looking for, DOS can quickly locate it, as long as it is in that directory. (There is also a quick way to locate a group of files that have similar names, as you will see later.)

Getting a Printout of the Screen
The Print Screen key (abbreviated PrtSc on older keyboards) provides a handy feature. It sends an exact copy of whatever text is currently on the screen to your printer. You must be sure that your printer is hooked up and working before you try to use PrtSc. Otherwise, you may lock up your entire machine. This may cause you to lose some of your work. Try the Print Screen key. Make sure your printer is connected, turned on, and ready, and then use the DIR command to display the directory of one of your floppy disks. Now press the Print Screen key to print the directory listing. Notice only the text actually visible on the screen is printed.

Using DIR with Different Drives

What if the files you want to see are on a disk in your floppy disk drive, and drive C:, the hard disk, is your current drive? You could change the current drive to drive A: and then get a directory listing:

```
C>a:
A>dir

 Volume in drive A has no label
 Directory of A:\

REVPROC      615 11-25-90  5:01p
CHATF1     12400 11-08-90  4:41p
JS1118      7727 11-18-90  4:50p
COMPET        82 11-22-90  4:00p
NAMES        852 11-25-90  4:59p
SCHEDULE     323 11-25-90  4:59p
PCNOTE1     3784 11-22-90  3:01p
JS1122      3435 11-23-90 10:34a
NETNOTES    6975 11-28-90 12:59p
    11 File(s)   392192 bytes free
```

Of course, what you see depends on what is on your disk.

You don't have to change the current drive to get directory listings for other drives. You can specify another drive, just as you specify names of files. To do this, first type the name of the command, then a space character, then the name of the drive together with your file specification. For instance, if the C: drive is the current drive, and you want to get a directory listing of all variations of file names, beginning with MYFILES, that are on the A: drive, you type `dir a:myfiles.*` as follows:

```
C>dir a:myfiles.*
 Volume in drive A has no label
 Directory of A:\
MYFILES COM    75307 11-09-90  7:50p
MYFILES EXE   148216 11-09-90  7:52p
MYFILES BAT     2048 11-09-90  7:52p
MYFILES SYS     7192 11-09-90  7:52p
    4 File(s)    42857 bytes free
C>_
```

Notice that after you get the directory listing for the A: drive, PC DOS returns the C prompt, to show that the C: drive is the current drive.

You will learn more about the DIR command and about disk directories in the sections ahead, as well as in the next chapter. You can also read more about DIR in Chapter 6, "Managing Your Hard Disk." Finally, remember that you can learn about DIR (or any other command) in exhaustive detail by looking it up in the Command Reference in the last part of this book.

Quick Questions

14. An internal command is one that is
    a. loaded into memory when PC DOS is loaded
    b. stored on disk
    c. only for use with certain programs
    d. erased from memory after it is used
15. To clear the screen, you type
    a. `clear`
    b. `erase`
    c. `cls`
    d. `screen`
16. Which of the following is a valid way to type the DIR command?
    a. `Dir`
    b. `DIR`
    c. `dir`
    d. `diR`
17. To get a directory listing of a disk in drive A: when drive C: is your current drive, you type
    a. `dir c:` and press Enter
    b. `a:` and press Enter; then type `dir` and press Enter
    c. `dir a:` and press Enter
    d. `dira`

Using Files: A Collection of Data

Before you go any further, stop and think about what is going on when you work with files. What is a file? It is nothing more than a collection of data: letters, numbers and other characters—grouped together for a common purpose. Sometimes a file represents some pages of printed text; at other times, a file consists of code (instructions) that make up an executable program. A file may consist of data used to generate a graphic picture. In any event, PC DOS always identifies a file by answering a few important questions:

What is the file called?
How large is it?
When was it created?
Where is it located?

PC DOS assigns to each file the following pieces of information

A file name of up to eight characters
An optional file extension of up to three characters
A file size indicating how many bytes are in the file
A drive location where the file has been stored
A date-time stamp indicating date and time of creation

First, a file has a file name that identifies it. This name may consist of up to eight characters, for example, LETTER1 or SALES. If a file name alone is not enough information to identify a certain file, an added name, called a *file extension*, may also be used and is required for some special kinds of files. A file extension may have up to three characters (and usually does). Extensions are separated from file names by a period (.) when they are used with PC DOS commands. Examples of names with extensions are DRAFT1.TXT and ACCTS.JUL. In these names, the extensions are TXT and JUL, respectively.

More often than not, the type of file you are working with is also identified by its extension. Executable programs, for example, always have an extension of .EXE or .COM after the file name of the program. Batch files must always have the .BAT extension.

In addition, many programs designate a specific file extension to identify work files they have created. Different versions of Lotus 1-2-3, for example, use file extensions of .WKS or .WK1 to mark files created with a unique format. Files created in this type of format are used only by the spreadsheet program when it is running on your system. Other programs, such as WordPerfect, let you choose the file extension for your files—if you want one—whenever you save them to disk.

You cannot use some characters as part of a file name. Chapter 5, "PC DOS Files," explains file-naming rules in detail. You use simple names for the exercises in the Quick Primer.

Copying a File

You often will want to make a copy of a file under a new name so that you can keep the original file intact. You may find yourself wanting to have a copy of a file, but with a different name. Suppose, for example, that you wanted to add some new material to a file named SALES.JAN so that you could use it as the basis for a new report. You want to keep the original SALES.JAN file intact and have a copy of it (called REPORT.NEW) to work with:

```
C>copy sales.jan report.new
1 File(s) copied
C>dir report.new
 Volume in drive C has no label
 Directory of C:\
REPORT  NEW  23014  8-02-90 11:19p
    1 File(s)  5167840 bytes free
C>dir sales.jan
 Volume in drive C has no label
 Directory of C:\
SALES  JAN  23014  8-02-90 11:19p
    1 File(s)  5167840 bytes free
C>_
```

To use the COPY command, you need to have a *source* and *destination*. This fancy wording means simply that you have to have a file to copy, and you have to know the new name you want to give to it. In the example, SALES.JAN is the source, and REPORT.NEW is the destination. When you get a directory listing, you see that both SALES.JAN and REPORT.NEW are present, so you can freely change the contents of the new copy while keeping the original intact.

Caution

Avoid Errors by Using Different File Names

If you are copying files in the same directory and you give the copy of a file the same name as the file itself, you get an error message, `File cannot be copied onto itself`. Always use a different file name for the copy.

Renaming a File with the REN Command

Why would you want to rename a PC DOS file? Perhaps you would like to rename a file that someone gave you on a disk. The current file name might either be hard to remember, or it might not use a naming convention familiar to people in your office.

In any event, changing the name of a file is very easy. You can use the REN (rename) command to change a single file or a group of files. Here are a couple of examples. First, renaming a single file:

```
C>dir sample.fil
 Volume in drive C has no label
Directory of C:\

SAMPLE  FIL  23014  8-02-90 11:19p
    1 File(s) 18167840 bytes free
C>ren sample.fil sample.doc
C>dir sample.doc
 Volume in drive C has no label
 Directory of C:\
```

```
SAMPLE   DOC  23014  8-02-90 11:19p
    1 File(s)  18167840 bytes free
C>dir sample.fil
 Volume in drive C has no label
 Directory of C:\
File not found
C>
```

As the example shows, you used the DIR command to show the name of a file called SAMPLE.FIL. You then use the REN command to change the file extension from .FIL to .DOC. Using the DIR command a second time shows that the file SAMPLE.FIL is now called SAMPLE.DOC, and a third use of DIR proves that the SAMPLE.FIL file no longer exists.

Using Wildcards

This example was easy enough, but it raises an interesting question: If you want to work with a group of files that have very similar names—perhaps to get a directory listing of them, copy them, or rename them—how do you tell PC DOS which group you want to use? Well, it would not be very helpful to type the file name and extension of every file you want to work with. How many people would be using PC DOS if that were the case?

The designers of PC DOS had an easier way in mind. They decided that it would be faster if certain symbols were used to mean: "find me everything" or "find all the names that match this pattern." The symbols for these phrases are the asterisk (*) and the question mark (?). Together, they are called *wildcards*. If you have played Poker or certain other card games, you know that a wildcard is a card that can stand for other cards depending on the situation—one time the wildcard may stand for an ace, but if you have two deuces, you can choose to make it stand for a deuce. In a similar way, a wildcard symbol can stand for a different group of file names or characters within file names, depending on how you use it.

Getting a Directory Listing with Wildcards

How can you use a wildcard to specify the file names that you want? You are in the following situation: You know that the file you are looking for is named MYFILE, but you are not sure what extension you have assigned to it. You can see all the files that are named MYFILE and have an extension by using the * wildcard. The asterisk stands for any number of characters:

```
C>dir myfiles.*    ←press Enter
 Volume in drive C has no label
 Directory of C:\

MYFILES COM    75307 11-09-90   7:50p
MYFILES EXE   148216 11-09-90   7:52p
MYFILES BAT     2048 11-09-90   7:52p
MYFILES SYS     7192 11-09-90   7:52p
      4 File(s) 18193308 bytes free
C>_
```

The pattern you used told PC DOS to find all files that have the file name

MYFILES and any extension. (Remember that the asterisk means "match any.")

Copying All Files
If you want to copy all the files in a directory, issue the command as `copy *.*`. All the files are copied, both the files with and without extensions.

Using the ? Wildcard

The question mark is your other handy wildcard tool. Although the asterisk says "match anything from here to the end of the name" (or, if it is used after the period, the end of the extension), the question mark says "match the corresponding character (but only that character) with any character." For example, suppose that you have a number of files named LETTER.something in a directory, and you know that each name has a number after it. You don't know how many you have, but you want to see them all.

```
C>dir letter?
 Volume in drive C has no label
 Directory of C:\
letter1      45127 11-09-90  7:50p
letter2     108236 11-09-90  7:52p
letter3       4096 11-09-90  7:52p
letter4       7192 11-09-90  7:52p
      4 File(s) 18193308 bytes free
C>_
```

There are some more rules for using wildcards and a few tricky situations to watch out for. When you have completed this Quick Primer, you can read Chapter 6, "Managing Your Hard Disk," for a more complete discussion of the magic of wildcards.

The following PC DOS commands can use wildcards.

PC DOS Commands That Use Wildcards

ATTRIB	COMP	DIR	PRINT	REPLACE
BACKUP	COPY	ERASE	RECOVER	RESTORE
CHKDSK	DEL	FIND	RENAME (REN)	XCOPY

Renaming Files with Wildcards

Suppose that you want to change the extension of a whole batch of files at once. You can do this by using the asterisk wildcard that you just used with the DIR command:

```
C>dir *.fil
 Volume in drive C has no label
 Directory of C:\
SAMPLE1 FIL   3571  3-17-90 12:00p
```

```
SAMPLE2 FIL   3571  3-17-90 12:00p
SAMPLE3 FIL   3571  3-17-90 12:00p
SAMPLE4 FIL   3571  3-17-90 12:00p
SAMPLE5 FIL   3571  3-17-90 12:00p
SAMPLE6 FIL   3571  3-17-90 12:00p
    6 File(s) 18167840 bytes free
C>ren *.fil *.doc
```

Now, run the DIR command again to see the change:

```
C>dir *.doc
 Volume in drive C has no label
 Directory of C:\
SAMPLE1 DOC   3571  3-17-90 12:00p
SAMPLE2 DOC   3571  3-17-90 12:00p
SAMPLE3 DOC   3571  3-17-90 12:00p
SAMPLE4 DOC   3571  3-17-90 12:00p
SAMPLE5 DOC   3571  3-17-90 12:00p
SAMPLE6 DOC   3571  3-17-90 12:00p
    6 File(s)  18167840 bytes free
C>_
```

Again, you see the power of the wildcard: The REN command that you ran said in effect "find all the files that have the FIL extension and give them the DOC extension instead."

Deleting Files with the DEL (or ERASE) Command

Eventually, your disk may become full. You may decide that several of the files are old and are not needed any more. You can get rid of files by using the DEL (delete) or ERASE commands. Both commands are exactly the same: PC DOS understands that files are to be removed from a disk. For consistency, DEL is used for this discussion.

Assume that you want to erase a file called BASKET.CAS

```
C>del basket.cas
C>_
```

PC DOS returns the C> prompt to the screen after the file is erased, but not much else happens. If you use the DIR command to try to find the file, however, you see the following message

```
C>dir basket.cas
 Volume in drive C has no label
 Directory of C:\
File not found
C>_
```

Using the DEL Command with Wildcards

You can use the DEL command with wildcards to erase several files with a single command. For example, if you enter `del myfiles.*`, you are directing the DEL command to erase all files named MYFILE, no matter what their extension. If you enter `del *.doc`, you will erase any and all files that have .DOC as their extension.

The DEL command also works on more than one file at a time. If you specify all files with the wildcard name *.*, PC DOS interprets this as a request to erase all files. If this is your intention, PC DOS is happy to comply with your wish. However, because you are asking for a sweeping action that affects the contents of the entire directory, PC DOS asks you to confirm your request—just to be certain:

```
C>del *.*
All files in directory will be deleted!
Are you sure (Y/N)?_
```

If you have the least doubt, answer N to the question and look through the directory by using the DIR command. Remember that PC DOS is only following directions that you give it. If you tell it to erase every file in a disk or directory, but you did not really mean all of your files, you may be out of luck.

Exploring More Dire Consequences of the DEL Command

You should be careful to think out your actions before using the DEL command when you work with more than one drive. For example, if you intend to erase a file on drive A: while drive C: is your current drive, PC DOS tries to erase that same file on drive C: unless you specify drive A: in your command (so enter `del a:file name`)!

In short, take an extra moment or two to think out your actions before you type them. A few seconds of thought ahead of time can help you avoid hours of pain and frustration. At the same time, acquiring systematic habits will give you more confidence and reduce the likelihood of mistakes.

Quick Questions

18. One of the following does not belong in the description of a PC DOS file. Which one?
    a. date of creation
    b. file name
    c. logical drive location where created
    d. size of file in bytes
    e. amount of RAM required to run
19. To make a copy of a file named ACCOUNTS but have the copy named INVOICES, you would issue the command at the system prompt as
    a. `copy invoices accounts`
    b. `copy accounts invoices`
    c. `copy accounts`
    d. `copy invoices`

20. To rename a file that is currently named CLIENTS so that its new name is CUST.TXT, you would issue the command as
    a. `ren clients`
    b. `copy clients cust.txt`
    c. `ren clients cust.txt`
    d. `copy clients cust.*`
21. To see a directory listing of a group of file names that begin with SALES (but may contain up to three more characters, such as SALES1 or SALES-NEW), and that may or may not have an extension, you would issue the command as
    a. `dir sales.*`
    b. `dir sales*.*`
    c. `dir sales?.*`
    d. `dir sales?.?`
22. To erase a file named SALESSUM on drive A: while drive C: is current, you would issue the command as
    a. `erase c:salessum a:`
    b. `del c:salessum a:`
    c. `del a:salessum`
    d. `erase a: salessum c:`

Organizing Files into Subdirectories

The terms *directory* and *subdirectory* refer to ways to store files. Up until now, all the files presented in this chapter have been contained in one directory. You have used the DIR command to generate a listing of files within a directory.

If you have only a dozen or two dozen files, you have no problem reading a directory listing to find a file. But if you are working with a hundred or a thousand files, storing all those files in one directory would make the job of finding any particular file difficult. The more files you have in a single directory, the more finding one is like finding a needle in a haystack.

PC DOS allows you to organize your files into related groups called subdirectories. PC DOS allows a main directory to contain subdirectories, and subdirectories can contain their own subdirectories. Each subdirectory should contain related files. Thus, you might have one subdirectory for PC DOS files, another subdirectory for your word processor and its related programs, another subdirectory for files that pertain to your clients, and so on.

In PC DOS language, the main directory is called the *root directory*. The *directory structure* refers to the relationships between the root directory and all of its subdirectories and their subdirectories. You can compare the directory structure to the root system of a tree. A real tree, as you know, has an extensive root system underground. At the base of the tree, its main root plunges deep into the earth. Smaller roots branch out from the main root, and still smaller roots branch out from them, with the smallest roots of all ending in fuzzy tips.

The root directory compares with the main root of the tree. The subdirectories compare with the smaller roots. Subdirectories that branch from the root directory are the *first-level* subdirectories. Subdirectories that branch from the first-level subdirectories are *second-level* subdirectories. In this way, a directory system may extend several levels, depending on the detail of the directory structure organization. Figure 2.1 shows a sketch of a real tree and its PC DOS equivalent.

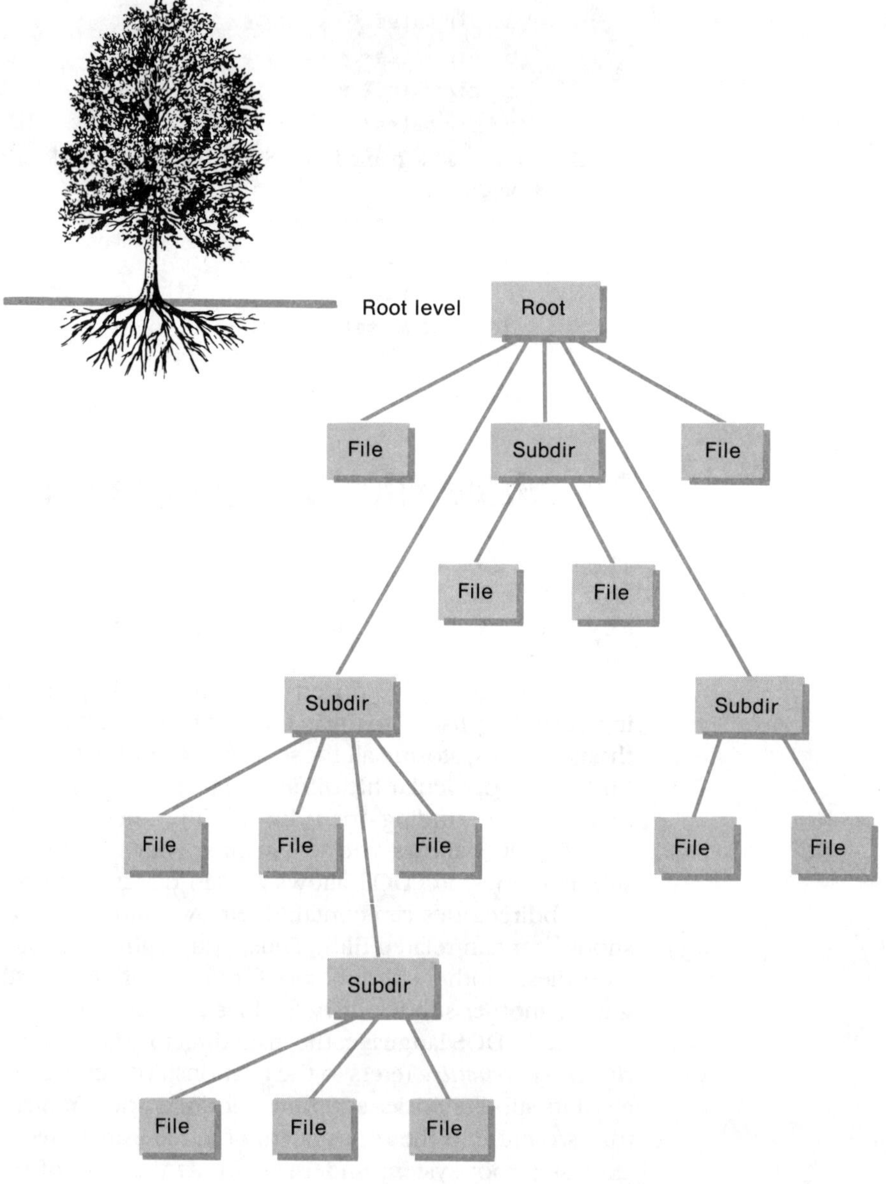

Figure 2.1. ***A tree root and PC DOS analogy.***

The fuzzy tips at the ends of each root branch compare to files. The main root sprouts some fuzzy tips as do each of the root branches. The farther removed from the main root, the more fuzzy tips that a branch is likely to sport. Similarly, the PC DOS root directory contains not only subdirectories, but files, and each subdirectory is likely to contain files as well as other subdirectories, and lower level subdirectories are likely to contain greater numbers of files. Figure 2.2 shows a typical directory tree as it might exist on your hard disk.

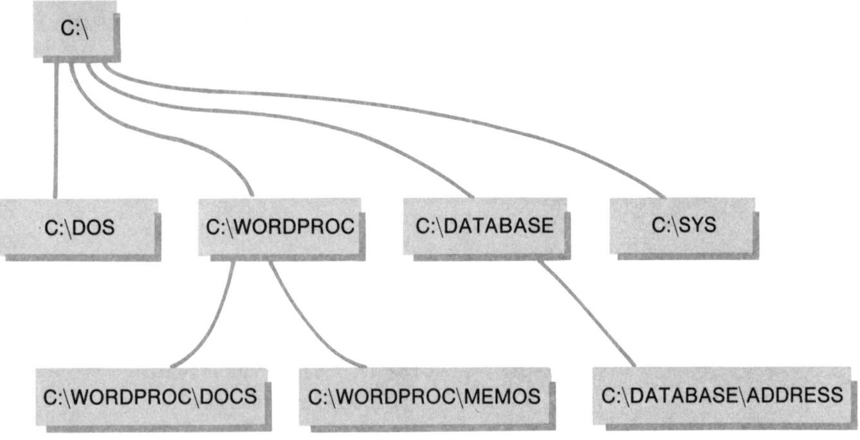

Figure 2.2. *A directory tree on the C: drive.*

Making a Subdirectory with the MKDIR (MD) Command

Unlike the roots of trees, subdirectories don't grow by themselves. You have to create a subdirectory by using the MKDIR command, or its shorter form, the MD command. PC DOS treats the MKDIR command and the MD command exactly the same way as it does the DEL and ERASE commands—two different names for the same program. Nearly everyone uses the shorter form, MD, and so do the examples that follow.

The purpose of making a subdirectory is to store related files together, away from the clutter of the root directory. A well-designed directory structure may contain quite a few subdirectories, each containing its related files. You may be wondering who will create a well-designed directory structure on your PC DOS system.

Probably you, so before you use the MD command to create your first subdirectory, think of what you will store there and then invent a name that will be meaningful not only right now, but a few months from now, when you might have forgotten what files the subdirectory contains. Like a file name, the name for a subdirectory can be up to eight characters in length. A subdirectory name can include an extension, but few people use one. An extension helps only if you have a great number of subdirectories or if the files contained in the subdirectory require the extra letters to help you distinguish them from those in another subdirectory. (For instance, you could use the extensions .OLD and .NEW, or .MAY and .JUN, or some such.)

For your first try, use the MD command to create a subdirectory named WORDPROC.

```
C>md wordproc
C>_
```

Not much happened when you executed the MD command. PC DOS ran the MD program, no doubt, for it did not generate an error message, and it returned the prompt, but it did not give you any visible indication that it created a new subdirectory.

The example below shows a listing for the root directory of the C: drive. To review briefly, the first line of the listing declares the volume label, which, in this case, is none. The second line defines the following listing as "Directory of C:\". That backslash is important—PC DOS uses the backslash to mean "root." So **C:** means "the root directory of the C: drive." The following directory listing, however, now includes an interesting addition.

```
C>dir
 Volume in drive C has no label
 Directory of C:\
.
.
.

WORDPROC      <DIR>      8-11-90   2:45p
    1 File(s)   3023584 bytes free
```

You will find your new subdirectory name somewhere within the directory listing you generate—probably, but not necessarily, near the bottom. Notice that a subdirectory is identified in the listing with the date and time showing its moment of creation, but with <DIR> rather than numbers indicating file size. A subdirectory is not a file, rather it is part of the *filing system*. Figure 2.3 illustrates this concept in a typical filing system.

The Concept of Parameters

The very word, "parameters," looks technical. Well, it is, but that doesn't mean that it is difficult. In fact, it is one of those twenty-five cent words that buys a nickle's worth of meaning.

A *parameter* is represented by some text that you use with a command. When you entered the command **md wordproc**, you used the MD command with the parameter, WORDPROC. In effect you said, "MD, do your thing with WORDPROC."

If you had used the MD command alone, PC DOS would have displayed a message, "Invalid number of parameters." The very idea of using the MD command is that you want to make a subdirectory, and it must have a name. Therefore, the program named MD has been designed to create a subdirectory and give it the name that you specify as a parameter.

The choice of the term, *parameter*, is a little unfortunate, for it smacks of going back to math class. A better term might have been "stuff-that-you-type-for-the-command-to-use." Well, at least the next time that PC DOS returns an error message that reads "Invalid parameters," you'll know what it means.

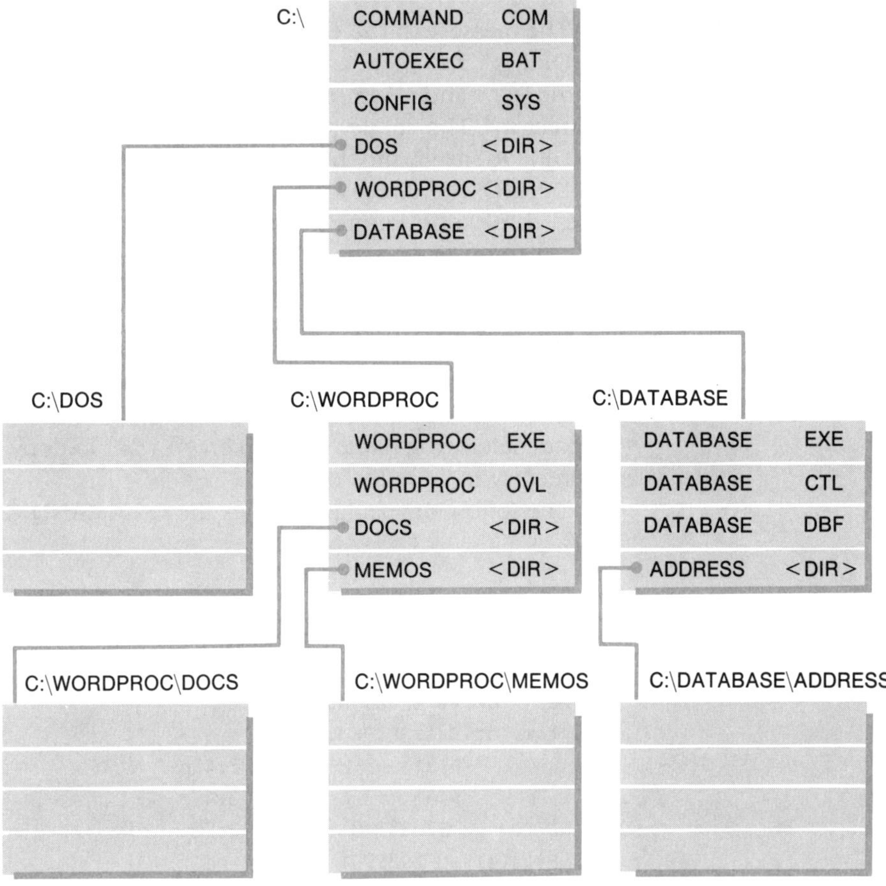

Figure 2.3. ***Using names to identify subdirectories.***

Using the DIR Command to Inspect a Subdirectory

You use the DIR command to generate a list of files in a subdirectory. Why bother, you may ask; if the subdirectory is brand new, it should contain no files.

The new subdirectory certainly does not contain any files, but it is worth a look, just the same. The following example shows how to use the DIR command to get a directory listing for WORDPROC. (Note that you are using the DIR command with the parameter WORDPROC, simply directing the DIR command to do its thing with WORDPROC.)

```
C>dir wordproc
 Volume in drive C has no label
 Directory of C:\WORDPROC
.            <DIR>     8-11-90  2:45p
..           <DIR>     8-11-90  2:45p

2 File(s)    3023584 bytes free
C>_
```

The message at the end of the listing claims there are two files within WORDPROC, and there are two entries, but their names are strange. These two entries, . and .., are called *file pointers*. They exist in every PC DOS subdirectory. The single period represents the subdirectory (in this case, WORDPROC) itself, and the double period represents the *parent directory* of WORDPROC, the directory above (in this case the root directory). If these entries seem exotic, ignore them for now. They exist in every subdirectory, so there they are. Later, you will see how to use them. You have a few more fundamental things to learn first.

Use the COPY Command to Copy a File into a Subdirectory

Copying files into subdirectories is something most users do commonly. It is easy to do. To copy a file into a subdirectory, use the COPY command with two parameters, the name of the file you want to copy, and the name of the subdirectory to store the copy.

The following example copies the COMMAND.COM file into WORDPROC.

```
C>copy command.com wordproc
    1 File(s) copied
C>dir wordproc
 Volume in drive C has no label
 Directory of C:\WORDPROC
.            <DIR>      8-11-90  2:45p
..           <DIR>      8-11-90  2:45p
COMMAND COM     37683  06-17-88 12:00p
    3 File(s)     2985901 bytes free
C>_
```

The Concepts of Delimiters and Syntax

More big words—*delimiter* and *syntax*. Like parameter, both mean something simple.

Notice the spaces between the command, COPY, and each of the parameters, COMMAND.COM and WORDPROC. The space character indicates the end of one word and the beginning of the next; in other words, the space *delimits* each word, hence the space character is a *delimiter*.

When you use a command with one or more parameters, you must use the correct *syntax*. The term syntax means pretty much "the order in which the parameters appear," albeit with a slight twist. The syntax of a command refers to the positions for each word on the command line. The first position is always reserved for the command.

The subsequent positions are defined individually for each command, although most commands use similar syntax.

In the case of the COPY command, the second position is reserved for the *source*, which is the file to be copied. The third position is reserved for the *destination* (sometimes referred to as the *target*), which specifies where the COPY command is to locate the new copy.

When you entered the command in the previous example, PC DOS inspected each character on the line, one at a time. The space character marked the end of the first position on the command line, so PC DOS identified

COPY as the name of the command. PC DOS continued to inspect each character until it found the next space character, which delimited the name of the source parameter, COMMAND.COM, from that of the target parameter, WORDPROC.

How did PC DOS know that WORDPROC was a subdirectory, not a new name you wanted to use for the copied file? PC DOS knew WORDPROC was a directory because it checked for that as part of doing its job. The PC DOS COPY command default is that if you enter the name of a subdirectory as the destination, it will copy the source file into that subdirectory. It is your job to make up a name that is not being used to name another file or subdirectory.

Caution

Don't Type a Subdirectory Name as the Source

Unless you really know what you are doing, be careful not to mix up the parameters for the COPY command. If you enter `copy wordproc command.com`, and if there are any files contained in WORDPROC, the COPY command will copy each file from WORDPROC to the destination file, in this case, COMMAND.COM, one file after another. The meaning of that command is "copy all of the files in WORDPROC to whatever you can find that is named COMMAND.COM."

The effect will be that the command will erase the real COMMAND.COM by copying the first file from WORDPROC over the old COMMAND.COM. Then, the COPY command will repeat the process, copying the second file from WORDPROC over the new COMMAND.COM, and so on. At the end, COMMAND.COM will contain the contents of the last file that the COPY command found in WORDPROC. If you need to use COMMAND.COM, you will be out of luck—it will not contain the original COMMAND.COM contents, but rather the contents of the last file copied to it. Be careful about the syntax for each command.

If this all seems a little too abstract, don't worry. The main thing is that space characters are delimiters that set off commands and their parameters and that the syntax of a command just means you have to type its parameters in the correct order.

Changing the Current Directory with the CD (CHDIR) Command

Always remember that unless you specify some other directory or subdirectory, PC DOS assumes that your commands apply to the current directory. If you have many directories or subdirectories on your disk, only one at a time can be the current directory. Use the CD command to change the current directory.

The ability to specify any directory as the current directory means you can work on the files within a particular directory conveniently, by making that directory the current directory. When you want to work on files in another directory, change directories by using the CD command with the name of the directory or subdirectory you want to be current.

In the examples so far, the current directory has been the root directory. To change directories, you will need a few directories, so use the MD command to create another subdirectory, as the following example shows.

```
C>md subdir01
C>_
```

As you learned, making subdirectories is easy, and PC DOS doesn't even bother to let you know it obeyed your commands. The example above shows the use of the MD command with one parameter, the name of the new subdirectory. But the new subdirectory of what, where? Remember that the current directory is the root directory, and the default is to execute your commands with respect to the root directory. In other words, this last example shows that the root directory is getting another subdirectory named SUBDIR01.

If you use the DIR command, you ought to get a listing of your files that includes the following.

```
C>dir
 Volume in drive C has no label
 Directory of C:\

.
.
.

WORDPROC      <DIR>      8-11-90  2:45p
SUBDIR01      <DIR>      8-11-90  3:15p
    2 File(s)   2985901 bytes free
C>_
```

The following example uses the CD command to change the current directory.

```
C>cd wordproc
C>dir
 Volume in drive C has no label
 Directory of C:\WORDPROC
.             <DIR>      8-11-90  2:45p
..            <DIR>      8-11-90  2:45p
COMMAND COM     37683  06-17-88 12:00p
    3 File(s)    2985901 bytes free
C>_
```

The second line of the listing shows that the listing is the "Directory of C:\WORDPROC." Notice the specification of the current directory begins with the name of the disk drive, followed by the root (backslash), and then the name of the current directory, in this case WORDPROC.

Getting the Root Back

You may feel frustrated if you lose track of the current directory or of its relationships to other directories. As a quick and dirty emergency measure, you can restore order by using the command `cd \` to make the root directory the current directory. You can then use the CD and DIR commands to investigate the lower branches.

The previous example shows that with the command `cd wordproc`, presto! PC DOS quietly makes WORDPROC the current directory. Using the DIR command gives you the listing for the current directory, WORDPROC. Doesn't that seem easy?

If you want to make SUBDIR01 the current directory, you may reasonably guess that you enter the command `cd subdir01`. Get ready for a new concept.

The Concept of a Hierarchical Directory Structure

If the current directory is WORDPROC and you enter the command `cd subdir01`, PC DOS will return an error message, "Invalid directory". Now what? You are entangled with the *hierarchical directory structure*.

You may be catching on to the fact that these PC DOS technical terms are a little like fancy doorknobs—they look ornate, but they do something simple. In this case, though, the window dressing of the term also disguises a feature that can be mildly frustrating.

The word *hierarchy* refers to a precedence, or pecking order. The hierarchical directory structure simply refers to the relationship between subdirectories and their *parent* directories. The root directory is the parent of WORDPROC and of SUBDIR01.

The frustrating part is that you cannot just specify another directory by using its name, because PC DOS uses the current directory as the default for your commands. When PC DOS accepts the command `cd subdir01`, it looks for a subdirectory named SUBDIR01 within the current directory, i.e., WORDPROC. Because WORDPROC does not contain a subdirectory named SUBDIR01, PC DOS returns an error message. The effect, you will see, is that your commands must account for the hierarchical relationships.

The counterpart to a hierarchical directory structure is the "flat-file" structure, in which all files are stored in a single root directory. Because even small-capacity hard disks can store hundreds of files, it is necessary to use a hierarchical directory structure for a hard disk. In the case of floppy disks, though, their capacity is limited, and most people do not fill them nearly to capacity. A flat-file structure is often perfectly adequate for floppy disk use.

Using . and .., the Subdirectory File Pointers

Remember that the directory listing for every subdirectory includes the two weird entries, **.** and **..** and includes them in the total file count. The single period refers to the subdirectory itself, and the double period refers to the parent directory. You can use the period and double period as directory names.

For instance, if the current directory is WORDPROC, you can get a directory listing in three different ways: by entering `dir` or `dir .` or `dir wordproc`. All three mean the same thing, although they "read" a bit differently.

The first reads "generate a directory listing for the current directory" (in this case, WORDPROC); the second reads "generate a directory listing for this subdirectory" (also in this case, WORDPROC); and the third reads as "generate a directory listing for WORDPROC" (which simply uses the name rather than one of the two previous conventions—the default or the single period pointer).

There is not much utility in using the single period, but the double period is quite handy. The meaning of the double period is to specify the parent directory. The command `dir ..` is identical to using the command `dir \`. The first reads "generate a listing of the files in the parent directory" (which in this case, is the root directory); the second reads "generate a listing of files in the root (\) directory" (which says the same thing by using the name of the parent directory rather than the double dot convention).

Similarly, the command `cd ..` directs PC DOS to change the current directory to be the parent directory. Assuming the current directory is WORDPROC, the following example shows how to get SUBDIR01 to be the current directory.

```
C>cd ..
C>cd subdir01
C>dir
 Volume in drive C has no label
 Directory of C:\SUBDIR01
.            <DIR>      8-11-90  3:15p
..           <DIR>      8-11-90  3:15p
    2 File(s)    2985901 bytes free
C>_
```

In this example, the current directory is WORDPROC. Entering the command `cd ..` changes the current directory to the parent of WORDPROC, the root directory.

Entering the command `cd subdir01` changes the current directory to SUBDIR01, as the subsequent directory listing shows. To get from WORD-PROC to SUBDIR01, you use the CD command to change up to a common parent directory (in this case, the root directory) and then use the CD command to change down the other branch to SUBDIR01.

The following example extends the problem and provides a review. The current directory, now, is SUBDIR01.

```
C>md subdir02
C>cd subdir02
C>dir
 Volume in drive C has no label
 Directory of C:\SUBDIR01\SUBDIR02
.            <DIR>      8-11-90  3:37p
..           <DIR>      8-11-90  3:37p
    2 File(s)    2985901 bytes free
C>dir ..
 Volume in drive C has no label
 Directory of C:\SUBDIR01
.            <DIR>      8-11-90  3:15p
..           <DIR>      8-11-90  3:15p
SUBDIR02     <DIR>      8-11-90  3:37p
    3 File(s)    2985901 bytes free
C>dir \
 Volume in drive C has no label
```

```
 Directory of C:\

.
.
.

WORDPROC     <DIR>     8-11-90  2:45p
SUBDIR01     <DIR>     8-11-90  3:37p
    2 File(s)   3023584 bytes free
C>_
```

The first three commands create a subdirectory within SUBDIR01 named SUBDIR02 and then change the current directory from SUBDIR01 to SUBDIR02 and get a directory listing of SUBDIR02. Notice that the second line of that directory listing specifies "Directory of C:\SUBDIR01\SUBDIR02".

Pay particular attention to the two backslashes, the first indicating the root directory of drive C: and the second, between the two subdirectory names, separating the second-level subdirectory, SUBDIR02, from its parent directory, SUBDIR01.

The command `dir ..` generates a directory listing for the parent directory of SUBDIR02, and the command `dir \` generates a directory listing for the root directory.

What command will generate a directory listing for WORDPROC?

The Concept of a Directory Specification

To specify a particular directory in a command, you must name it and all directories above it. The specification for WORDPROC is actually \WORDPROC. Notice the backslash, meaning the root directory, at the beginning.

If the current directory is SUBDIR02, to get a directory listing of WORDPROC, use the command `dir \wordproc`. To change the current directory to be WORDPROC, use the command `cd \wordproc`. No matter what the current directory, you can use a command to operate on any other subdirectory as long as you use its full directory specification. The following example exercises this notion, assuming that SUBDIR02 is still the current directory.

```
C>cd \wordproc
C>dir
 Volume in drive C has no label
 Directory of C:\WORDPROC
.            <DIR>     8-11-90  2:45p
..           <DIR>     8-11-90  2:45p
COMMAND COM     37683  06-17-88 12:00p
    3 File(s)     2985901 bytes free
C>dir \subdir01\subdir02
 Volume in drive C has no label
 Directory of C:\SUBDIR01\SUBDIR02
.            <DIR>     8-11-90  3:37p
..           <DIR>     8-11-90  3:37p
    2 File(s)     2985901 bytes free
C>_
```

Notice the use of the backslash character in both directory listings. If WORDPROC is the current directory, you can make a subdirectory contained within SUBDIR02 by using the command `md \subdir01\subdir02\subdir03` if you wish. The important thing to remember is that you must include a directory specification, or a command will operate with respect to the current directory.

Changing the Prompt with the PROMPT Command

You may have seen the prompt in other forms, perhaps even on your own system, and wondered how you can control it. As usual, it isn't hard to do. You can make the prompt provide a great variety of information, including someone's name, the correct time and date, a line of text, and more.

The place to start is with the basic PC DOS prompt. No matter what state your PC DOS system is in, as long as it shows some form of prompt, the following commands will bring your system into the simple prompt mode with the root as the current directory.

```
C>cd \
C>prompt
C>_
```

The command `cd \` makes the root directory the current directory, and the `prompt` command by itself directs the prompt to take its simplest form, as you can see in the last line. The following commands show you how to use the PROMPT command to make some interesting changes.

```
C>prompt NEW
NEWprompt
C>prompt Carol
Carolprompt
C>prompt I am at your command. What is your wish, Susi?
I am at your command. What is your wish, Susi?_
```

As you can see, each use of the PROMPT command changes the way the prompt appears on the following line. Notice that using the PROMPT command by itself generates the simple "C-style" prompt, which is the default for the PROMPT command.

The Concept of Escape Characters, Options, and Switches

Previous examples in this chapter show how to use parameters with commands. In the case of the PROMPT command, you can type your name, a phrase or sentence, or more, as a parameter. For most text you enter as a parameter, the PROMPT command uses whatever you type as the new prompt.

The next example shows how to get a useful form of the prompt that reflects the current directory specification.

```
C>prompt $p$g
C:\>_
```

Why didn't the prompt become pg, imitating the text as it did in the examples above? The dollar sign is the secret. The dollar sign is a special symbol to distinguish the options used with the PROMPT command.

The dollar sign is an *escape* character that indicates to the PROMPT command that the character following the dollar sign is one of the PROMPT command's *options*. The term option refers to specially designated letters (or sometimes letter combinations) that you can use with a command to modify or expand the way it works. You can look up the options for the PROMPT command in the Command Reference section in Part 3.

If you use the dollar sign with a letter that is not one of the PROMPT options, the PROMPT command will display nothing on the next line—no prompt (as it does if you enter `prompt $`). If you add space characters between different escape and option characters, you may see changes or not, depending on where you put the spaces. You can play with the PROMPT command by using its various options with space characters and dollar sign escape characters.

What is important here is that the PROMPT command, like many other PC DOS commands, has a defined set of option characters that have a specified effect on the way the command works.

The term *switch* is similar to *option* in that it refers to a set of characters to use with a command to modify its behavior. Generally, the term switch refers to a two-character combination that includes a forward slash character and a letter, with no space between. An example of a switch, used with the DIR command, is `dir /w` which directs the DIR command to present a directory listing in "wide" format on the screen. As you become familiar with various commands, you can look in the back of the book for switches that work with them.

The Concept of the PATH

The two option characters that work with the PROMPT command, *p* and *g*, need further explanation. Of the two, the *g* character is straightforward—it stands for "greater-than," which is the name for the symbol (>) and is usually used to separate the prompt itself from the commands you type.

The *p* option introduces the new term, *path*. The effect of the *p* option is to direct the prompt to reflect the *current path*, which includes the current drive and the full specification for the current directory.

Thus, in the previous example, using the pg parameter with the PROMPT command makes the C> prompt change to C:\>. The letter and colon refer to the current disk drive. The backslash is the name of the current directory, in this case, the root. The "greater-than" symbol (>) marks the end of the prompt, pointing like an arrow to the cursor blinking on the command line. Using the prompt to reflect the current directory is a very helpful trick.

Up to this point, this chapter has shown the prompt as C>. In this simplest form, the prompt relects the current drive. If you change the current drive, the prompt changes to reflect the new current drive, but so far, that has been its only trick. This basic "C>-style" prompt is fine when you are dealing with the flat-file, single-level directory structure such as exists on many floppy disks.

As Figure 2.3 shows, however, a hard disk can hold quite a complicated system of subdirectories, and manipulating a large number of files and subdirectories can be like groping in the dark. The prompt provides a light in the form of the current directory. In this mode, whenever you issue a CD command, the prompt reflects the change, just as it does with the drive, but better.

For example, when SUBDIR03 is the current directory, the **$p** option for the PROMPT command will direct the prompt to take the form

```
C:\SUBDIR01\SUBDIR02\SUBDIR03>
```

The prompt form in the example above is somewhat cumbersome, but it shows exactly the state of the current directory. On a hard disk with many subdirectories, this information can really help reveal the hierarchical organization of the disk. Although it may not be apparent to you how useful this information can be, you will see its value in the rest of the exercises in the Quick Primer.

Version 4

The Default Prompt for PC DOS Version 4
If PC DOS 4 is installed in your system, you are probably already looking at a prompt that shows the current directory and current drive. This form of the prompt is the default for PC DOS 4 systems, but not for earlier versions.

For the remainder of the Quick Primer, and throughout most of this book, the PROMPT pg format is adopted in all PC DOS listings and examples.

Removing a Subdirectory with the RD (RMDIR) Command

As you work with your system, you will find that your files and subdirectories tend to grow, filling the storage capacity of your hard disk, increasing the sizes of your directory listings, and generally slowing things down. Making new subdirectories and creating extra files is easy, and the results can remain invisible for quite a while.

Weeding out unnecessary items is a necessary part of computer housekeeping, so you schedule regular times to clean house.

The RD (or RMDIR) command lets you remove a subdirectory, but only if it contains no files or subdirectories (other than its two file pointer directories, . and ..), i.e., if it is an "empty" subdirectory. So to remove a subdirectory, you must first delete all of its files and subdirectories. The following examples show how to remove WORDPROC and SUBDIR01.

Deleting Files to Remove a Subdirectory

In addition to the "dot" and "double dot" file pointers, the subdirectory WORDPROC contains a single file, COMMAND.COM. To remove WORDPROC, you have to make sure it is empty. To empty WORDPROC, you first have to delete COMMAND.COM, as the following example shows.

```
C:\>rd WORDPROC
 Invalid path, not directory,
 or directory not empty

C:\>cd wordproc
C:\WORDPROC>dir
 Volume in drive C has no label
```

```
 Directory of C:\WORDPROC
.            <DIR>      8-11-90  2:45p
..           <DIR>      8-11-90  2:45p

COMMAND COM    37683  06-17-88 12:00p
    3 File(s)    2985901 bytes free

C:\WORDPROC>del *.*
C:\WORDPROC>dir
 Volume in drive C has no label
 Directory of C:\WORDPROC
.            <DIR>      8-11-90  2:45p
..           <DIR>      8-11-90  2:45p
    2 File(s)    3225032 bytes free

C:\WORDPROC>_
```

This example first tries the RD command to remove WORDPROC but generates an error message, `Invalid path, not directory, or directory not empty`. Well, that didn't work.

To find out why the `rd wordproc` command didn't work, use the CD command to change the current directory to WORDPROC and get a directory listing of its contents. The directory listing shows the two file pointers and COMMAND.COM. The command `del *.*` deletes all files.

Notice that PC DOS does not generate a message to let you know that your delete operation is successful. It may feel a bit unnerving to wonder if your command to delete every single file in the target really worked. You will have to get used to it; for PC DOS, the default action is to expect success. Don't you wish you knew more people like that?

The subsequent directory listing shows that WORDPROC contains only its two file pointers, dot and double dot, and no files or subdirectories, which means WORDPROC is empty. The next example shows the next attempts to remove WORDPROC.

```
C:\WORDPROC>rd wordproc
Invalid path, not directory,
or directory not empty

C:\WORDPROC>cd ..
C:\>rd wordproc
C:\>_
```

The first attempt fails because WORDPROC is the current directory (as shown by the prompt), and PC DOS won't let you remove the current directory. In other words, there is no path from WORDPROC to any other file or subdirectory called WORDPROC. If this seems a bit like angels on heads of pins, accept it. This is how you have to think in order to understand computers. (You can always take lunch or do something else as a break.)

The second attempt uses the CD command to make the parent directory the current directory, which is the root. The command `rd wordproc` is successful, for WORDPROC is empty and it is a valid subdirectory of the current directory.

Notice here, too, that like the DEL command, the RD command does not inform you of its success—the ruination of WORDPROC occurred without a murmur. The RD command is supposed to remove subdirectories; that is its default, so it returns error messages only when it fails.

Removing Nested Subdirectories

To remove SUBDIR01, you must empty it. Although SUBDIR01 contains no files, it contains another subdirectory, SUBDIR02, which itself contains a subdirectory, SUBDIR03, as shown in the directory listing below.

```
C:\>dir \subdir01\subdir02
 Volume in drive C has no label
 Directory of C:\SUBDIR01\SUBDIR02
.            <DIR>      8-11-90  3:37p
..           <DIR>      8-11-90  3:37p
SUBDIR03     <DIR>      8-11-90  3:37p
    3 File(s)     2985901 bytes free
C:\>_
```

To remove SUBDIR01, you must first remove SUBDIR03, then SUBDIR02.

```
C:\>rd subdir03
Invalid path, not directory,
or file not empty

C:\>rd \subdir01\subdir02\subdir03
C:\>dir \subdir01\subdir02
          Volume in drive C has no label
  Directory of C:\SUBDIR01\SUBDIR02
.            <DIR>      8-11-90  3:37p
..           <DIR>      8-11-90  3:37p
    2 File(s)     2985901 bytes free

C:\>rd subdir03
```

This example begins by showing the root directory as the current directory. The command `rd subdir03` fails because does not specify a direct path from the current directory (which is the root) to the target—therefore it isn't a *valid command.*

The second try, `rd \subdir01\subdir02\subdir03`, does specify a path connection to the target—it is a valid command—and the lack of any message from PC DOS provides an assurance that the command is successful. The following example shows the task completed.

```
C:\>rd \subdir01\subdir02
C:\>rd \subdir01
C:\>dir
          Volume in drive C has no label
```

```
 Directory of C:\
.           <DIR>     8-11-90  3:37p
..          <DIR>     8-11-90  3:37p
.
.
.

   2 File(s)    2985901 bytes free

C:\>
```

If the RD command has a problem in its mission, it generates an error message. Without an indication of failure, you can assume success, although it is prudent to get a directory listing to keep your bearings, if nothing else.

Rules of Thumb for Subdirectory House Cleaning

Don't ignore older files as you move on to newer ones. If you haven't used files in a particular subdirectory for a while, they are candidates for the archives.

Don't make subdirectories beneath your third-level subdirectories.

Archiving old files on floppy disks helps you clean up your hard disk, but it adds to your floppy disk collection. If you can't make sense of the file name, it's probably safe to erase the file.

Quick Questions

23. Why is the term *root* an appropriate analogy in helping describe how files are organized on a hard drive in PC DOS?
24. The listing of directories in the prompt that shows you where you are in your filing system is called the
    a. prompt
    b. path
    c. option
    d. switch
25. One of the following is not a valid PC DOS command involving the use of subdirectories. Which is it?
    a. md
    b. makedir
    c. rd
    d. chdir
    e. cd
26. To remove a directory, it must be
    a. the current directory
    b. the root directory
    c. empty, except for its directory pointers
    d. all of the above

27. The fastest way to go to the next higher directory in the tree is to type
    a. rd
    b. cd
    c. cd ..
    d. \

Creating Text Files on Disks

As you may have guessed by now, the ability to manipulate files on a disk is an important skill you need to become adept at using PC DOS. The standard COPY and DEL commands play an important role here, but you have a number of additional tools at your disposal.

Creating a File

How do you go about creating a file? After all, the entire structure of PC DOS is geared toward dealing with user files. It is now time for you to learn how to store information in a new file.

Perhaps the easiest way to create a file is to use your word processing program, assuming that you have one and you know how to use it. There are times, however, when you need to rely on the tools that PC DOS makes available.

The first of these is called EDLIN. EDLIN is a program supplied with PC DOS that acts as a line editor. This means that you can enter a line at a time into a file and then save it on disk when you are finished.

Many people believe that EDLIN is a difficult program for a new user. The commands are cryptic, and you need to memorize several of them before you can put them to good use. There is some merit to these arguments, but its saving grace is that EDLIN is fairly easy to learn, it is fast and flexible for working with short text files, and it comes with PC DOS at no extra charge. If you are interested in learning about EDLIN, turn to Chapter 9, "Creating Text Files," for detailed information. For the purposes of this Quick Primer, you learn to use an alternative method that is available.

The second tool is one you can make use of right away. It is a variation of the COPY command that uses a special capability: that of sending lines of data directly from the screen into a file. Remember that the COPY command requires both the source and destination file names for it to work properly. You may find here that the source and destination surprise you. You can substitute a *device* instead of a file for the source. The pieces of equipment that make up your computer system are called devices. The keyboard, for example, is an input device, and the printer is an output device. Each device has a unique name: the keyboard is called CON:, for *console*. (Note that it uses a colon, just like a disk drive.)

If you type `copy con:` followed by the name of a brand new file, you are telling PC DOS to take its input directly from the keyboard and copy it to the new file. If your job is short, and you are a reasonably careful typist, this can be a quick way to produce a file.

The command for creating a file called SAMPLE.TXT looks like this:

```
C:\>copy con: sample.txt
_
```

After you press the Enter key, notice that the blinking cursor is positioned in the first column of the next line of the screen. The DOS prompt—for the time being—has disappeared. This is because you are now in *data input* mode. You can enter data into the SAMPLE.TXT file, line by line:

```
This is a sample file.
It has only two lines in it.
```

You can always use the Backspace key to erase part of a single line while you are typing it. After you press Enter, however, that line is saved in a buffer in memory and the cursor is dropped down to the next line. You can no longer correct the preceding line.

When you finish entering all the information onto the screen, press the F6 key. You will see a Control-Z (^Z) symbol inserted on the next line of the file. The ^Z is known as an *end-of-file-marker* and is always inserted at the end of text files in PC DOS. (You can insert it by pressing the Ctrl and Z key combination if you wish.) The ^Z tells PC DOS that you have finished creating the file, which you named SAMPLE.TXT when you used the COPY command as copy con:.

After the end-of-file-marker is inserted, the contents of the screen are copied into memory. The ^Z disappears from the screen. Next, you see a PC DOS message that confirms the action taken—`1 File(s) copied`. Finally, the PC DOS prompt reappears on the screen.

Here is how the complete sequence for entering your sample file looks:

```
C>copy con: sample.txt
This is a sample file.
It has only two lines in it.
^Z
    1 File(s) copied
C:\>_
```

You will find this technique to be quite handy for creating short text files, bearing in mind that you have only a very limited ability to make corrections. As mentioned earlier, Chapter 9, "Creating a Text File," will give you a much more flexible and easy way to create files.

Looking at the Contents of a File with the TYPE Command

How do you find out what information is actually stored in a particular file? You often need to see the contents of a file. For example, you may want to read certain text files, often called READ.ME files, that are supplied with programs you purchase or disks you exchange with others. You may want to read other special files that help you control your system, called AUTOEXEC.BAT and CONFIG.SYS. As you will see in Chapter 11, "Customizing Your System," you can modify these special files to customize how your system works.

There are two basic ways to see what a text file contains. First, you can use your favorite file editor or word processor to "load" (open) the file. If you don't have access to any of these programs, however, PC DOS can help you with its TYPE command.

The TYPE command (as in "type this letter") is very easy to use. For example, if you want to see the contents of your SAMPLE.TXT file appear on the screen, you type the following command and get the following response:

```
C>type sample.txt    ←press Enter
This is a sample file.
It has only two lines in it.
C>_
```

The TYPE command is a quick and handy command to use when you want to look at short text files. You should keep a few things in mind, however. First, the TYPE command does not let you change the actual contents of a file. You need to use EDLIN, a file editor, or a word processor to do that.

You should also be aware that if you attempt to use the TYPE command to show a file that was created with a word processing program, you will probably find that the text appears along with a number of nontext "special characters" that the word processing program uses to identify underlining, superscripts, paragraph markers, and the like. This makes it difficult to read the file using the TYPE command. In this case, you should use your word processor instead.

Finally, you should note that the TYPE command simply pours the contents of the file on to the screen. Because the output does not pause at the end of each screenful, but continues to scroll up and out of sight, the TYPE command can be hard to use for long files. You can stop the output by pressing Ctrl-S and start it again by pressing any key. Another command (MORE) presents the contents of a long file one screen at a time. You can find out more about it in Chapter 8, "Advanced Use of the Command Line."

Quick Questions

28. How can you create files in PC DOS?
29. The keyboard is a device that PC DOS knows by the name
    a. PRN:
    b. drive E:
    c. CON:
    d. LPT:
30. If you enter the TYPE command and suddenly hear beeps and see strange characters on the screen, what is wrong?

What's Next

Chapter 3 of this Quick Primer explains the external commands and PC DOS 4's new DOS Shell.

Key Concepts and Words

Before you read further, use the following list to test your understanding of the concepts and words in this chapter.

System prompt	Files
The command line	Directories
Internal commands	Subdirectories
Defaults	Wildcards
Options	

Chapter 3

PC DOS has commands stored on disk for special uses. These are called the external *commands. This chapter describes these file-based commands and introduces an important feature of DOS 4, the DOS Shell. You'll learn*

- *How to make directories and backups of your files using external commands*
- *How options make commands more flexible*
- *How the Control key gets you out of trouble*
- *About the DOS Shell*

Before you begin: Read Chapters 1 and 2. If it's been a while since you read them, refresh your memory of their content by browsing through the Quick Questions.

Chapter 3

External Commands and the DOS Shell

Up until now, you have been using only internal commands, but there are external commands to PC DOS as well. These are actually separate utility programs. The name of the file on the disk is the same as the name of the command (although the file names also have an .EXE or .COM extension).

Using External Commands

To run an external command, the appropriate file must be available on your hard disk or on a floppy disk in one of your drives. If PC DOS cannot find the file somewhere on one of your disks, the command cannot be executed, and you receive an error message.

PC DOS External Commands

APPEND	EXE2BIN	KEYB	RESTORE
ASSIGN	FASTOPEN	LABEL	SELECT
ATTRIB	FDISK	MODE	SHARE
BACKUP	FIND	MORE	SORT
CHKDSK	FORMAT	NLSFUNC	SUBST
COMP	GRAFTABL	PRINT	SYS
DISKCOMP	GRAPHICS	RECOVER	TREE
DISKCOPY	JOIN	REPLACE	XCOPY

Getting a List of External Commands
Because external commands have a .COM or .EXE extension, you can get a directory listing of these command files in your DOS directory by typing `dir *.com` or `dir *.exe`.

Making a DOS Directory

To do the exercises in this chapter, you need to make a directory on your disk for your PC DOS files, if you or someone else has not done so already. You then need to use the PATH command to tell PC DOS where these files are.

To see whether a DOS directory already exists, type `cd \dos` at the system prompt. If there is no directory, you need to make one:

```
C:\>cd \
C:\>md \dos
```

You then need to copy the PC DOS files into this directory. See Chapter 12, "Installing a PC DOS System," if this needs to be done on your system.

C:\DOS> Used Automatically in PC DOS 4
If you have installed PC DOS 4 on a hard disk using the SELECT program (described in Chapter 12), you already have a DOS directory with all of your PC DOS command files in it.

Telling PC DOS Where to Find External Command Files

Once you have all your PC DOS files in one directory, you need to tell PC DOS where you have stored them. You do this by using the PATH command so that when you issue one of the external commands, PC DOS searches other directories to find the executable file you want, no matter which directory PC DOS displays. Along with the PROMPT command you learned about earlier, the PATH command is "required learning" for anyone who hopes to use PC DOS successfully on a hard disk.

Checking Your Path
Someone else may have set a path for you. To see if this is the case, type `path` at the system prompt and press Enter. If PC DOS returns a listing similar to PATH=C:\;C:\DOS, your path has been set, and PC DOS knows where to find the external commands.

To tell PC DOS where your new DOS directory is located (assuming that you did not have one before), type

```
C:\>path c:\;c:\dos
```

You can find more information about setting the path in the chapters on customization and installation (Chapters 11 and 12), but for now, look at some other practical examples of when you would need to use the PATH command.

Finding a File with the PATH Command

Suppose that you know in advance that you will be running programs from certain subdirectories nearly all of the time. There may be eight or ten subdirectories on C:\>, but your favorite word processor has been installed in the

the C:\WORDPROC subdirectory. Using the PATH command, you tell DOS to look through the C:\WORDPROC subdirectory and execute your program—despite the fact that the current subdirectory is something other than C:\WORDPROC. In fact, you do not even have to make your hard drive the current drive.

Here is how it works. If you have a program called WORDWRIT.EXE in the C:\WORDPROC subdirectory and try to execute it while you are in the root directory on C:\>, all you get is the standard `Bad command or filename` message. The PATH command, however, lets you run the program no matter what the current directory or drive happens to be. Here is how to use PATH for this situation:

```
C:\>path c:\wordproc
C:\>_
```

Now, the WORDWRIT program runs no matter what the current directory or drive, even from drive A:. You can include several subdirectories in the PATH statement. To add subdirectories to the same PATH command, all you need to do is separate them with semicolons. Many people also include the root directory in the PATH statement. Here is a typical example of the command you might use for this example:

```
C:\>path c:\;c:\dos;c:\wordproc
C:\>_
```

Why the listing of several subdirectories? This happens whenever you want to include more than one subdirectory in the list of directories that is to be searched, which is often called the *search path*. Here, you have included C:\, the root directory (always a good idea), C:\DOS, the PC DOS subdirectory (an absolute must if that is where your PC DOS files have been installed), and the C:\WORDPROC subdirectory that you used for this example. Your PATH statement might also include additional subdirectories for your spreadsheet, database, or other programs.

There are really only two rules that govern the PATH command. First, you must always include a semicolon between each subdirectory in the PATH statement. Second, you should limit the number of subdirectories to those that you use often. This is important because, in order to find a program, PC DOS may have to search through all the subdirectories you place in the search path. The more subdirectory names you include, the slower your PC may respond to your request. If you include every subdirectory on your hard disk, your hard drive could slow down quite a bit as PC DOS tries to find a file in one of the last subdirectories. Don't let your PATH statement exceed the 63 characters that PC DOS allows.

What happens if you forget your path scheme? You don't have to type the entire string again. Just enter the PATH command by itself and DOS shows you the current PATH settings:

```
C:\>path
PATH=C:\;C:\DOS;C:\WORDPROC
C:\>_
```

By the way, the list you have given with the PATH command is not saved by PC DOS once the power to your system is turned off, so you have to type it each time you use your PC. Later, you will be shown how to store your path in a special file so that it is loaded automatically at the start of each session.

Preparing a Disk with the FORMAT Command

The FORMAT command is a good example of an external command. This command is stored as the file FORMAT.COM on your PC DOS startup disk (or on your hard disk if you have installed PC DOS there).

When do you need to use FORMAT.COM? Any time that you want to use a disk fresh out of the box. Before PC DOS can "read" a disk, an invisible series of rings, called *tracks*, must be organized on the disk. This process of organizing a disk for use by PC DOS is called *formatting*. PC DOS disks do not usually come formatted (for an increased price, you can buy already formatted disks, though), so formatting disks is a task that you will routinely do as you work with PC DOS.

To create the format for the disk, you have to run the PC DOS FORMAT command. To format a disk on a system that has PC DOS installed on the hard disk, insert a blank disk into the A: drive. If the disk you have been using in these exercises is a *scratch* disk—that is, if it does not contain any information you want to keep—you can format that disk. Make sure that you use the right capacity disk; use the largest capacity the drive accepts. This means quad- or high-density 1.2M disks for AT-type machines with high-capacity 5.25-inch drives or 360K disks for older PCs. For most PS/2s, use the high-density 1.44M capacity disks. Some models, such as the Model 30, can only use 720K disks. (You can format smaller capacity disks in a high-capacity drive, but discussion of this is deferred to Chapter 7, "All About Floppy Disks.")

Caution

Do Not Accidentally Format Your Hard Disk!

Do not format your hard disk by typing FORMAT C: by mistake! If you do, PC DOS 4 requires that you type the volume label for the hard disk to confirm that you know what you are doing. When you see this question, press the Ctrl key and the C key simultaneously to abort the execution of the FORMAT command. Earlier versions of PC DOS warn you that you are about to erase your fixed (hard) disk. If you see this message, type `n` and press Enter to abort the format. If you continue, you will lose all the files on drive C:. In that event, you will have to reinstall PC DOS and every program that you have loaded onto your hard disk. In practical terms, you should never format your hard drive unless you know exactly what you are doing. Most beginners do not have enough understanding to do this successfully. Chapter 6, "Managing Your Hard Disk," explains when and how to format your hard disk.

Next, type **a:** at the C> prompt. Here is what should happen:

```
C>format a:    ←press Enter
Insert new diskette for drive A:
and strike ENTER when ready_
```

Note that although the "real" name of the command is FORMAT.COM, typing `format` is enough. PC DOS recognizes the names of all external commands without their extensions.

You have already inserted your blank disk in drive A:, so go ahead and press Enter one more time. You begin to hear the write head on the drive laying out the format of the disk. In PC DOS 4, you see a message `5 percent of disk formatted` on the screen and the `percent of disk` increases as the disk format continues. Older versions of PC DOS use more technical measurements, such as the number of *cylinders* or *heads* being formatted.

When the FORMAT command finishes its work, it asks whether you would like to give the disk a *volume label*, a name that you can use to identify this particular disk. You can use up to 11 characters for the volume label; press Enter by itself when you have typed it. If you don't want to supply a volume label, press Enter. You do not have to provide a volume label, but it is a good idea to do so. It can serve as a gentle reminder of why you formatted a given disk. For this example, you can use the volume name SAMPLE.

```
Format complete
Volume label (11 characters, ENTER for none)?sample
```

After you enter the volume label, you see a message similar to the following information about the contents of your disk:

```
  362496 bytes total disk space
  362496 bytes available on disk
    1024  bytes in each allocation unit
     354  allocation units available on disk
Volume Serial Number is 1022-1BC5
Format another (Y/N)?_
```

The first total tells you the full capacity of the disk in bytes. Here, you formatted a regular double-density, double-sided, 5.25-inch disk. The total number of bytes available is equal to 360K. (As mentioned earlier, 1K is actually equal to exactly 1,024 bytes, which is why the number shown is slightly greater than 360,000.)

The next line lists the total bytes available on the disk. It is this total that is used whenever you use the DIR command to ask for a directory listing of your files. When you copy a file to the new disk or create a new file on it, the total number of bytes that the file occupies is subtracted from the total number of bytes available. This leaves the number shown in the `.... bytes free` message that appears at the end of the directory listing.

Version 4

New Information for PC DOS 4

The next two lines of information are new with PC DOS 4. The `1024 bytes in each allocation unit` message tells you that whenever you create a new file, PC DOS assigns one or more "units" of 1024 bytes (1K) each.

Finally, PC DOS 4 generates a random `Volume Serial Number`, which can be helpful to the advanced user who needs to compare the contents of two different disks. For the beginner, however, this information is of little use.

Depending on the size and capacity of the disk you used, you may get numbers that are different from the ones shown here. The FORMAT command, however, reports these numbers in the same way you have seen.

Copying an Entire Disk with DISKCOPY

Formatting a disk is not the only routine chore for which you use an external command. You will often want to copy entire disks—for example, when you purchase an application program or when you want to make a copy of a disk for someone else to use. If you have a disk full of files and want to make an exact duplicate of that disk, use the DISKCOPY command. Assuming that you have two floppy disk drives, with the source disk in drive A: and the destination disk in drive B:, here is the proper command:

```
A:\>diskcopy a: b:
Insert SOURCE diskette in drive A:
Insert TARGET diskette in drive B:
Press any key to continue . . .
```

PC DOS begins copying a "snapshot" of the source disk onto the destination disk. The neat thing about the DISKCOPY command is that you do not even have to format the disk before running it. If PC DOS discovers that the disk in drive B: is unformatted, it formats the disk while data is being transferred onto it.

Caution

Be Careful When Using the DISKCOPY Command

There is, however, one very important detail that you should know about the DISKCOPY command. You should make absolutely sure never to erase the disks by accident—that is, by copying the blank disk in drive B: onto the data-filled disk in drive A:. What happens if you do? Well, instead of getting two copies of your important data, you may well end up with two blank disks. Figure 3.1A and B may help drive this point home.

In short, remember which disk is the source and which is the target. Insert your disks according to the instructions, and you will never have a problem with DISKCOPY.

It may be noted that many PCs come equipped with only one floppy drive. You might ask: How can I use a DISKCOPY command when there is no place for the target disk? Fortunately, PC DOS knows a sneaky way around that problem. On a single-floppy machine, PC DOS lets you use drive A: for both the source and destination. You are asked for the source disk first. PC DOS copies the contents of that disk into RAM memory, and then asks that you replace it with the destination disk in drive A:. PC DOS then transfers all of the data from RAM back onto the destination disk. See Figure 3.2A through E to get a better picture of this concept.

Caution

The DISKCOPY Command Has a Limited Use

You should also be aware that you cannot use the DISKCOPY command to copy disks that are of different sizes or disk capacities.

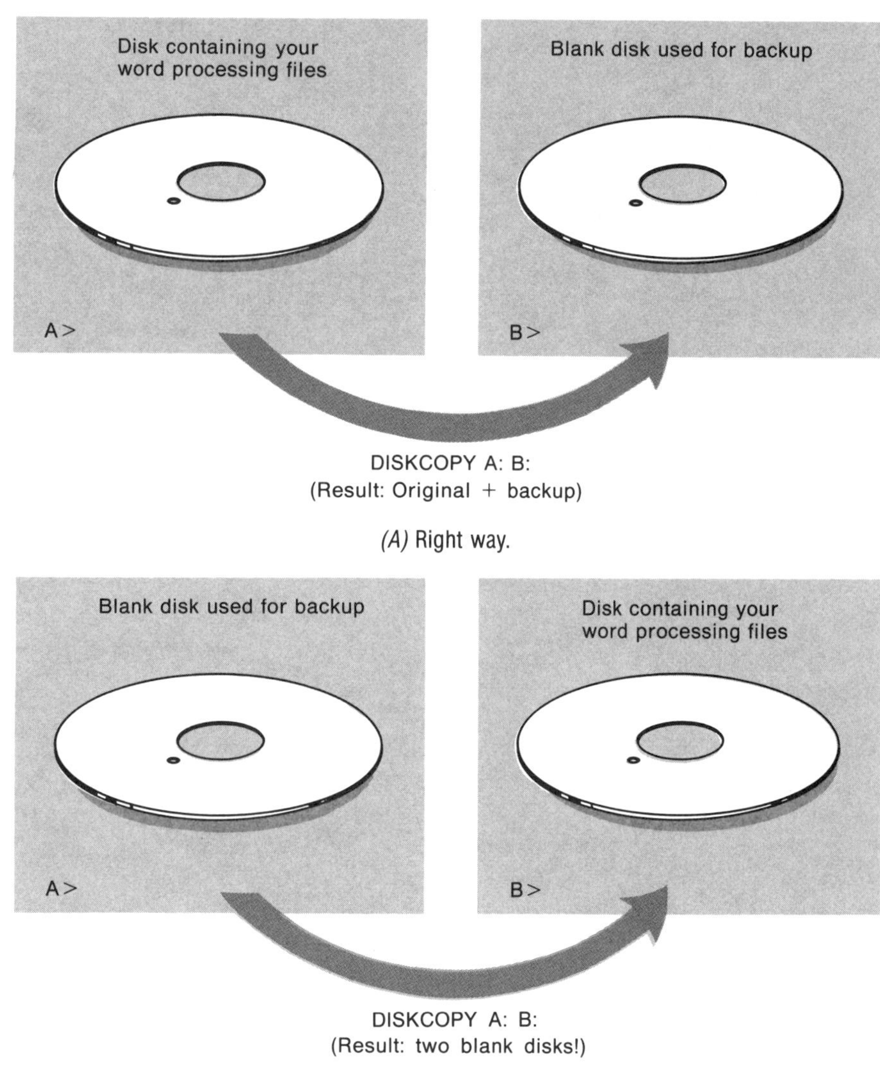

Figure 3.1. ***Right and wrong ways to use DISKCOPY.***

Making Backups

Disks are very reliable when handled properly, following the guidelines given earlier. Even with proper care, however, disks do not last forever. An inexpensive insurance policy against the small but potentially serious risk of unexpected trouble lies in keeping a *backup* of all your important data. More often than not, you will want to keep copies of all your data disks for different applications, such as spreadsheet, word processing, database, and so forth.

Many people have different opinions as to how often they should back up their data disks. The answers are equally varied, but a typical response

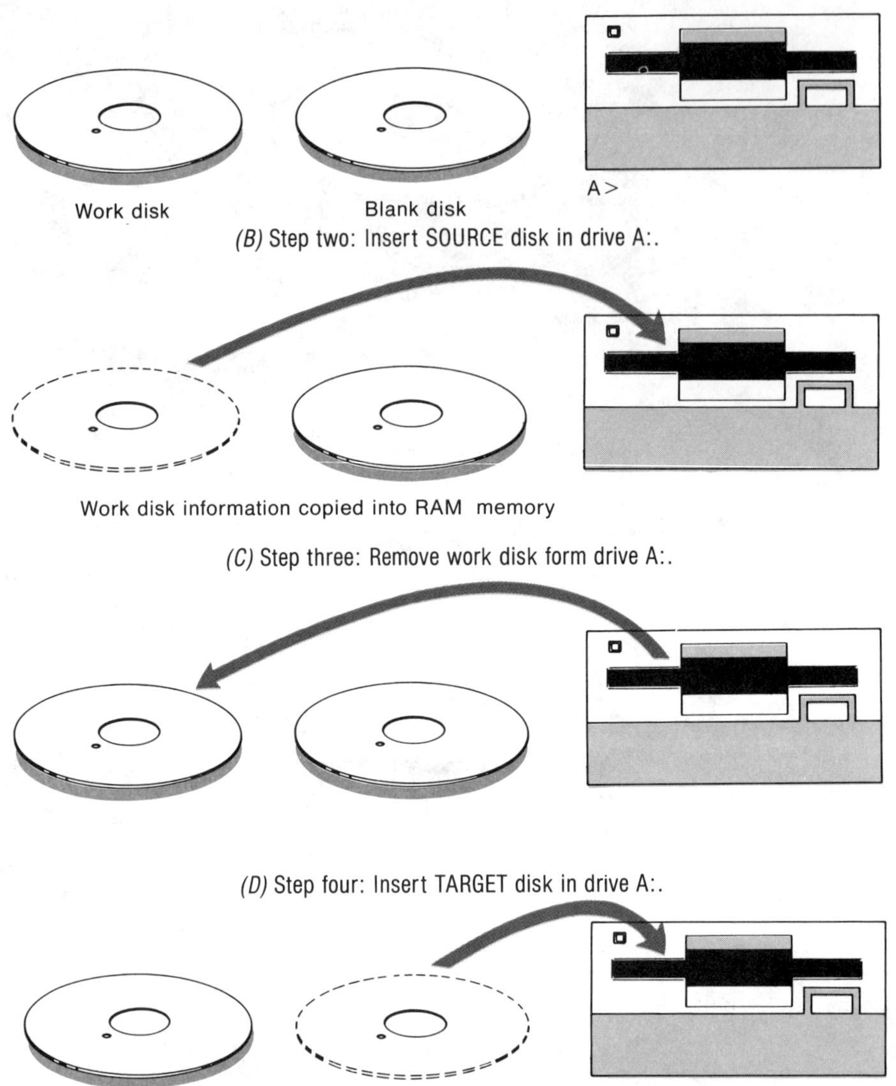
(A) Step one: Type diskcopy a: a:.
Work disk
Blank disk
A>
(B) Step two: Insert SOURCE disk in drive A:.
Work disk information copied into RAM memory
(C) Step three: Remove work disk form drive A:.
(D) Step four: Insert TARGET disk in drive A:.
Contents of RAM memory copied onto blank disk
(E) Step five: Remove target disk. You're finished!

Figure 3.2. ***DISKCOPY using only the A: drive.***

might be anywhere from a few days to a few weeks. If you work in a high-volume area where the data on your PC changes several times a day, backups at the end of each working day are a good idea. On the other hand, if your data changes only a few times a month, there is not much sense in making daily backups. Perhaps the importance of making backups cannot be taught except by experience: Once you have lost valuable files—which happens to everyone sooner or later—you will see why having backups of your important files is so vital.

Making Backups on a Floppy Disk System

If you have a floppy disk system and no hard disk, you will find the DISKCOPY command handy for making backups. You could do the same thing by using the COPY command, but DISKCOPY transfers information much faster than the file-by-file method used by the COPY command.

Making Backups on a Hard Disk System

Many people have come to believe that a hard disk is much safer than a floppy disk. As a result, they tend to ignore repeated warnings to make backup copies of their data files. This is a mistake! Making backups of your data files on a hard disk is just as important as making backups of your floppy disks—in fact, *more* important: If your hard disk crashes, you immediately lose twenty to fifty or more floppy disks' worth of information!

If you have a hard disk, you can use two different external commands: BACKUP and RESTORE. Discussion of these commands, however, is deferred until Chapter 6, "Managing Your Hard Disk." If you are using a hard drive, you need to read that chapter carefully to see how you can protect the valuable data residing on your hard disk.

In either case, making backups of your data files is critically important. You may go for a long time without ever having to rely on backups to recover from a "crashed" hard drive or a bent floppy—but the day probably will come sooner or later. When it does, you will feel much better if you are prepared to recover any lost data on your PC as quickly as possible. It is also likely that your boss will appreciate your efforts as well.

Quick Questions

31. An external command is actually
    a. an executable program
    b. a file extension
    c. a command on a floppy disk
    d. none of the above
32. If your current drive is drive C:, what happens if you use the FORMAT command without specifying the drive, such as A: or B:?
33. Which of the following is a valid PATH command?
    a. `path c:\c:\dosc:\wordpro`
    b. `path c:/;c:/dos;c:/wordproc`
    c. `path c:\c:\dos:c:\wordproc`
    d. `path c:\;c:\dos;c:\wordproc`
    e. `path c:|;C:|dos|c:|wordproc`
34. When is the DISKCOPY command a dangerous tool in the hands of an inexperienced user?

The Command Line: A Review

When PC DOS interprets a command string, it interprets the *syntax* of the command. The syntax of a command is split into two important parts, called the "head" and "tail."

The head is the name of a command or other program that resides as a file on one of your drives. Once PC DOS finds the file, it reads the rest of the command, which makes up the tail. The tail may include any *parameters* (additional pieces of information, such as directory or file names) or *options* (extra features that you can specify) that are needed. (Options are sometimes also known as *switches*.) The entire tail is then fed directly to the program, which then runs.

For example, when you type `dir *.com`, PC DOS begins reading the text string from left to right. It looks for the first space character, which marks the end of the command head and finds D-I-R, a string of characters that matches one of its own internal commands. Thus, DIR represents the "head" of the command syntax.

Next, PC DOS finds the *.COM portion of the command string. It looks to see whether any options follow the target. Seeing none, PC DOS has finished interpreting the "tail" of the command line. The directory listing that you specified is displayed on your screen. (See Figure 3.3 for more details.)

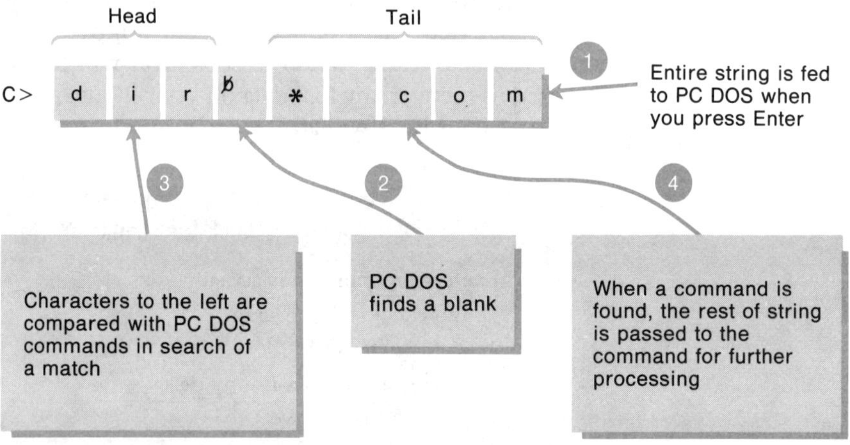

Figure 3.3. ***How PC DOS interprets a string of characters.***

If you type one of the internal DOS commands, or another command or program that is represented by a file on your disk, PC DOS eventually finds the match and makes an honest effort to grant your request.

If you type a bunch of characters that don't match an internal or external command, PC DOS returns an error message.

```
C>shoot the piano player
Bad command or file name
C>_
```

The SHOOT command was not found among the internal commands available to PC DOS, and it could not be found on drive C:.

Even if the command itself is valid and found on the disk, you can still get an error if the tail of the command is invalid:

```
C>type writer
File not found--WRITER
C>_
```

Here, the command, TYPE, is valid. The problem is that no file called WRITER is on the disk. The TYPE command needs the name of a valid, existing file to display its contents on the screen.

To enhance their flexibility, many PC DOS commands include various options. You specify these options by adding them to the basic information that you supply in the command tail. The DIR command serves as a useful example to see how this works. There are two options, or *switches*, that can be used with the DIR command. These are /p and /w.

The /p switch tells PC DOS to pause during a DIR listing whenever the screen fills with new information. The /w switch produces a directory listing that contains only the file names and extensions and lists them in five columns rather than only one. Here is how you might use the DIR command with the /w option:

```
C:\DOS>dir *.com /w
 Volume in drive C has no label
 Directory of C:\DOS
COMMAND COM GRAPHICS COM KEYB     COM MODE   COM DISKCOPY COM
FDISK   COM FORMAT   COM SYS      COM ASSIGN COM BASIC    COM
COMP    COM DEBUG    COM DISKCOMP COM EDLIN  COM LABEL    COM
MORE    COM TREE     COM CHKDSK   COM PRINT  COM SHELLB   COM
    21 File(s)  5605952 bytes free
C:\DOS>_
```

You can type options in either upper- or lowercase.

The commands are described in the Command Reference at the end of this book. If you find yourself wondering whether or not a certain command can perform a task, look it up; you just may find a welcome surprise waiting for you as a useful option.

Getting Out of Trouble

As a new user, you are bound to run into trouble at one time or another. Everyone crosses these bridges of experience as their use of a PC grows into a powerful skill. Even if you are careful while typing commands, a typo or some other error may cause the PC to do something you really didn't want or expect to happen.

Just because mistakes are bound to happen doesn't mean that you are powerless to help correct the error—or at least stop the PC from continuing to run an erroneous command.

Using the Control Key

To give you some control over your PC DOS session, you can use the Control, or Ctrl, key. You saw at the beginning of this Quick Primer where it was located, and you used it in a few of the exercises. By itself, this key is not capable of doing much. When used in combination with other keys, however, it can be a powerful tool to help you control how PC DOS runs a command. For example, the Ctrl-S key combination stops or restarts the scrolling of the screen display during the listing of a very long text file or directory listing.

To Ctrl-S, put your PC DOS system disk (in your floppy drive A: At the C:\> prompt, type `dir a:*.*`. Your PC DOS disk has more files than can be displayed on screen at any one time. When you see the screen filling with directory information, press Ctrl-S (use the lowercase s) to stop the listing from scrolling past the top of the screen.

Then, you can take your time to examine the contents of that portion of the directory. When you are ready to read the next page of text, press any other key on the keyboard to restart the display. You can use Ctrl-S again to stop the scrolling at any time.

The notion of "Ctrl-S to stop, any key to restart" is true for the TYPE command as well. In fact, it is true for almost any PC DOS command or other program that produces text output directly on the screen.

Using Control-Break and Control-C

Ctrl-Break and Ctrl-C basically perform the same function on a PC keyboard. Experienced users know that there are some subtle differences between the two, but the differences are not important for the beginning user. The following examples use Ctrl-C, but if you use Ctrl-Break it works equally well.

If you are in the midst of viewing a long directory listing and would like to stop it completely, press Ctrl-C. Instead of temporarily halting the list, PC DOS aborts it and returns the C> prompt to you. You also see the ^C symbol inserted at the point in the directory listing where you requested the break. The *caret* you see in front of the capital C is the PC DOS representation of a control function. It is likely to show up on your screen like this:

```
 Volume in drive C has no label
 Directory of C:\
COMMAND COM  37637  6-17-88 12:00p
FDISK   COM  60935  6-17-88 12:00p
FORMAT  COM  22923  6-17-88 12:00p
KEYB    COM  14759  6-17-88 12:00p
MODE    COM  23056  6-17-88 12:00p
SELECT  COM   4163  6-17-88 12:00p
SYS     COM  11472  6-17-88 12:00p
ASSIGN  COM   5785  6-17-88 12:00p
BACKUP  COM  31913  6-17-88 12:00p
BASIC   COM   1063  6-17-88 12:00p
BASICA  COM  36403  6-17-88 12:00p
CHKDSK  COM  17771  6-17-88 12:00p
COMP    COM   9491  6-17-88 12:00p
DEBUG   COM  21606  6-17-88 12:00p
DISKCOMPCOM   9889  6-17-88 12:00p
DISKCOPYCOM  10428  6-17-88 12:00p
EDLIN   COM  14249  6-17-88 12:00p
GRAFTABLCOM  10271  6-17-88 12:00p
```

```
GRAPHICSCOM   33 ^C
C>_
```

Notice that PC DOS wasn't very particular about where it put the ^C. It simply interrupted the listing when it detected your keystrokes.

The Ctrl-C combination can be used to help get you out of other types of difficult situations. Many programs that have been written for the PC can be aborted by using the Ctrl-C sequence.

For another example, you can use Ctrl-C to halt processing of the TYPE command. With your PC DOS system disk in drive A:, try to use the TYPE command and display the contents of a program file. The file FORMAT.COM is used for this example.

After you enter `type format.com`, you begin to see all kinds of strange characters. The bell (actually, a beep) sounds several times, and the screen starts to look like a big mess.This happens because FORMAT.COM, like most programs stored on disk, is a *binary* file. A binary file is not in a form that can be read by the TYPE command—its contents represent not readable text, but program instruction codes. This is an ideal situation for the Ctrl-C keystroke. You can abort the TYPE command's execution and prevent it from continuing to produce garbage on the screen and to fill your ears with beeps.

Caution

Using a Program's Exit Command Rather than Ctrl-C

You should not use Ctrl-C in place of a program's normal exit command. Programs, especially those like databases that store and update information on disk, provide a particular command (or menu selection) for exiting the program. You should always use this command or selection rather than Ctrl-C. Before it exits, the program updates the disk file(s) and leaves everything in good order. If you press Ctrl-C, however, the program may not carry out its exit routines properly. Use Ctrl-C only in an emergency.

Using the Control-Alt-Delete Combination

One other key combination is available in times of dire need. Consider this: You have tried everything, but the program you are working with is preventing you from entering any data or even pressing Ctrl-C. In such cases, the system is said to have *crashed* or *frozen up*. If this happens, you can reboot your PC by pressing Ctrl-Alt-Del, all three keys, simultaneously.

You may remember that the process of turning the power switch on and loading PC DOS into your PC was referred to as starting or booting your PC The process is known as a *hard* or *cold* boot. A second method is called a *soft* or *warm* boot and is executed whenever you hold down the Control, Alt, and Delete keys simultaneously and then release them. This combination is known as the *Ctrl-Alt-Del* sequence. You use Ctrl-Alt-Del when a program doesn't run properly. In fact, when you press Ctrl-Alt-Del, you should see your display monitor clear. Your PC then reloads PC DOS and restores the C> prompt. Once in a great while, you may not even be able to use Ctrl-Alt-Del. If that happens, you have to turn the machine's power off, wait a few seconds, and then turn it on again. This restarts everything.

If you are not using a hard drive on your PC, you have to insert a "bootable PC DOS disk (a system disk—one with the files that PC DOS needs to load) in the A: drive before a warm boot if the process is to work correctly. If you accidentally place a nonsystem disk in the A: drive, your PC will tell you so and will ask that you try again with the correct disk.

You will find more detailed information on using these and other special keys in Chapter 9, "Creating Text Files." At this point in the Quick Primer, you have mastered the "basic" basics of using PC DOS. If you have version 4 or later, you also have a program known as the DOS Shell that allows you to use a system of menus and a device known as a *mouse* in place of the keyboard. The DOS Shell is discussed in the following sections.

Quick Questions

35. Which of the following would be part of the "tail" of a PC DOS command string?
    a. dir
    b. copy
    c. *.com
    d. del
36. To enter a command with an option, you precede the option with
    a. a backslash
    b. a forward slash
    c. a period
    d. all of the above
37. To reboot your PC, you use the key combination
    a. Ctrl-Break
    b. Ctrl-S
    c. Ctrl-C
    d. Ctrl-Alt-Del

Using the Shell Interface

PC DOS version 4 has added a new feature known as the *DOS Shell interface*. The DOS Shell lets you view DOS from a full-screen perspective. Instead of typing commands at the PC DOS prompt on the left side of the screen, you can make choices from selections presented over the entire screen by using either a mouse or the directional keys on the keyboard.

Before going into the details of the DOS Shell interface, a bit of history is in order to help you understand the importance of the PC DOS Shell.

Looking at the Past and Present

Ever since its original design, IBM has built the PC to interact with the user in a *command line* environment, the same one used thus far in this book to illustrate the various PC DOS commands. In this environment, the screen simulates a printer—the text printed on the screen continues to *scroll* up toward the top of the screen to make room for the next C:\> prompt. When old commands reach the top, they roll off.

This method of communicating with the user has been successful over the years. Early on, however, users expressed a desire to have a more "user-friendly" environment. A large sector of the PC market was drawn to full-screen user interfaces and their easy-to-use menus. Figure 3.4A and B shows an example of each type of operating environment.

IBM and Microsoft Corporation began joint plans to market a new operating system for the IBM family of equipment. This product, which later became OS/2, was designed with a full-screen interface called Presentation

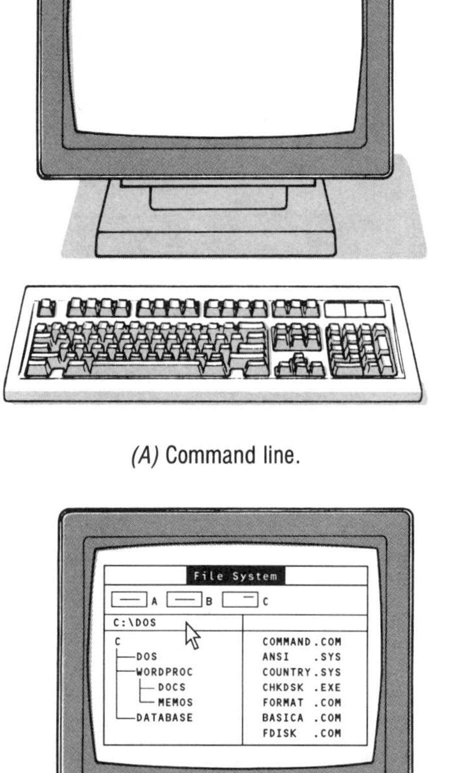

(A) Command line.

(B) PC DOS Shell.

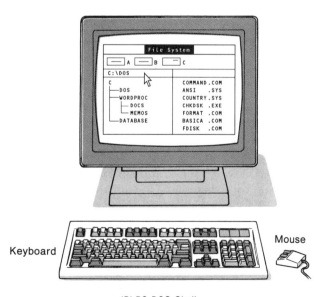

Figure 3.4. ***The command line and Shell environments.***

Manager. It is the OS/2 Presentation Manager that has served as the design model for the DOS Shell that IBM has produced for DOS 4.

Using the DOS Shell: Physical Requirements

In the PC DOS Shell, a specific set of keys becomes important to the user. Figure 3.5 highlights the keys that are used with the Shell. The four directional arrows work along with the function keys to access the various DOS Shell functions. The Tab, Alt, and Esc keys are also used extensively. The Shell program works with most keyboards sold with PC or PS/2 systems.

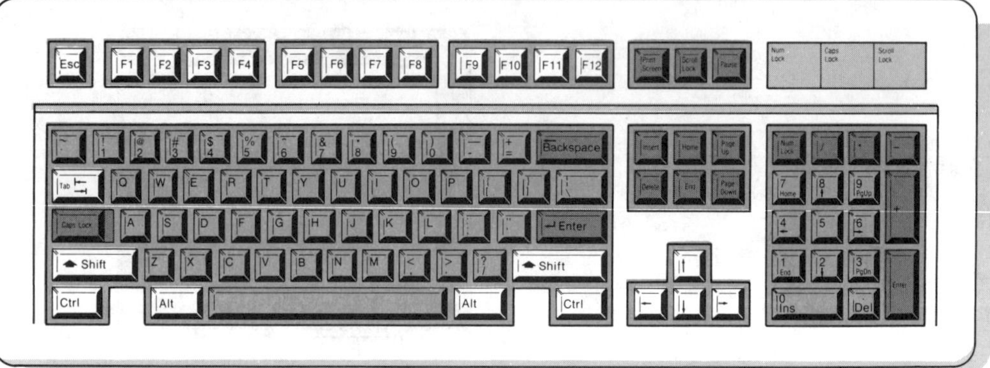

Figure 3.5. ***Important keys used in the DOS Shell.***

More and more often, PCs are being sold with a mouse attached to the system. What is a mouse? A mouse is a pointing device that contains a rolling ball or other sensing device on the bottom. As you move the mouse around your desktop, the movement of the ball causes the arrow pointer to move on the screen. The arrow moves in exactly the same direction that you move the mouse.

Many people use a mouse because they like the precise movement on the screen that a mouse offers. In a high-density graphics environment (which comes standard on the PS/2), the mouse lets the user do things that cannot be done easily with only a keyboard. When it comes to making choices from the Shell menus, a user can squeeze several keystrokes into a few short movements and a *click* or two from the mouse.

The mouse comes equipped with either two or three buttons on top. By positioning the arrow at an item that is highlighted on the screen and clicking the mouse buttons with your fingertip, you can select that item. See Figure 3.6 for an illustration of a mouse and its effect on the screen. The instructions for using a mouse with the PC DOS Shell are given in Chapter 4, "Using DOSSHELL." Here the discussion is confined to the use of the keyboard.

The last physical requirement for the DOS Shell involves a choice of video monitor. Most of the early PCs use either a monochrome (MDA) or color graphics (CGA) type of monitor. The DOS Shell works effectively on these older monitors, but it is displayed in what is known as *text* mode—one which does not provide the high-resolution graphics that are included with the PS/2 machines.

In text mode, the characters look much the same as they do in regular text files. On a color monitor, the colors are present, but they are not very

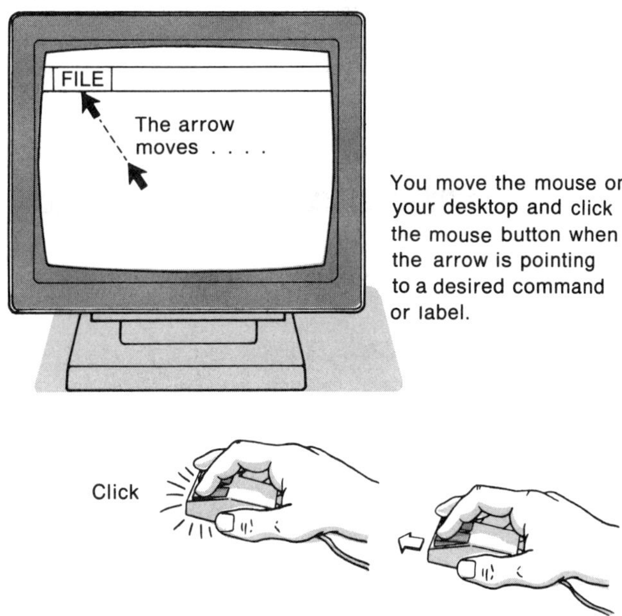

Figure 3.6. ***Using a mouse to select options on the screen.***

well defined or especially sharp in focus. This is due to the limited graphics capabilities of these two monitors. IBM has done the best it could in adapting the Shell for use with these older devices.

Newer monitors have been designed to provide the high-density graphics that are required for sharp, crisp screens in the DOS Shell and other applications. The enhanced graphics adapter (EGA) type of display was offered with the IBM PC/AT when it was first introduced in 1984. Later, IBM improved on that standard by announcing the video graphics array (VGA) and multicolor graphics array (MCGA) monitors with the new IBM PS/2 systems.

When used with these more powerful monitors, the DOS Shell really comes into its own. Horizontal and vertical lines are clean and crisp. Pictures of floppy and fixed drives are displayed so that you can point your mouse to a picture (icon) of the drive to change the current drive.

Starting the DOS Shell

If the SELECT program was used to install PC DOS 4 in your system, the DOS Shell is already installed and ready to use. If this has not been done, turn to Chapter 12, "Installing a PC DOS System," for instructions on how to install PC DOS 4; then, return here.

To start the Shell, type `dosshell` at the PC DOS prompt.

Viewing the Start Programs Screen

When you first start the DOS Shell, you see a screen entitled `Start Programs`. Figure 3.7 shows a snapshot of the Start Programs menu. As configured, the current date and time appear in the first line of the display. The second line lists the groups of actions you can take at this menu: Program, Group, and Exit.

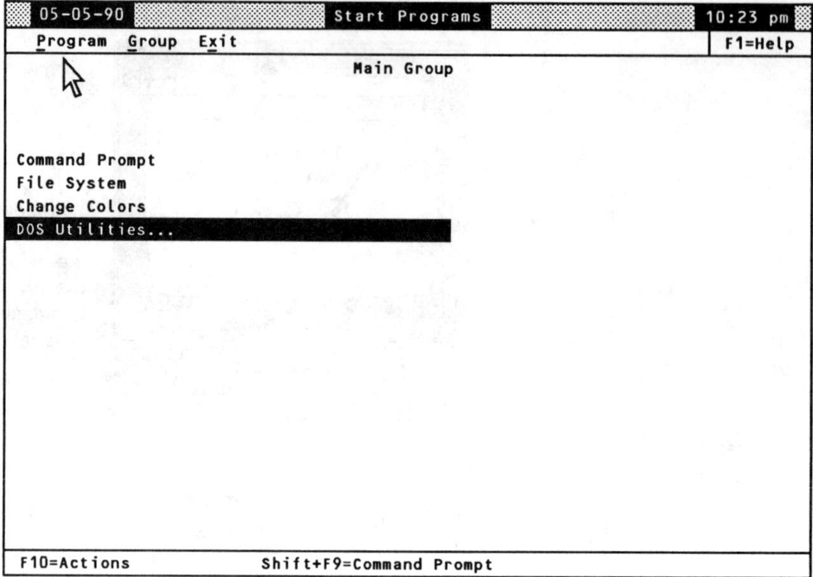

Figure 3.7. ***The Start Programs screen.***

On the same line, you see a reference to the F1 key. This is the universal help key in the Shell. No matter where you are in the DOS Shell, you can always press F1 and find a *help box* that describes the various available options.

The bottom line of the display lists two additional function key assignments that perform special functions. The F10 key activates the action choices in the second line. When you press F10, the Program choice is highlighted. You can then use your directional arrow keys to activate the pop-up window under this or any of the other choices on the second line. The Shift-F9 sequence lets you exit from the Shell and run PC DOS in the familiar command-line environment if you so desire.

The remaining portion of the screen is devoted to the Main Group selections. The first four choices are provided by PC DOS:

Command Prompt
File System
Change Colors
DOS Utilities...

To execute any of these menu choices, you can do one of two things. If you are using a mouse, move the arrow to your choice and click the left button twice. If you are using only the keyboard, there are a few more steps. First, use your arrow keys to highlight your choice. Next, press the F10 key to activate the actions, and then select the Program action. You see a pop-up window with additional choices; pick the `Start` option.

With the exception of Command Prompt, picking one of the menu choices moves you to another screen in the Shell. Command Prompt duplicates the Shift-F9 key sequence and takes you to the command line DOS prompt.

Going to the File System choice takes you to a menu where you can manipulate files on all of your disk drives. Choosing Change Colors leads to a menu that permits those changes if you have a color monitor. The PC DOS Utilities menu offers many of the common PC DOS commands, such as formatting a disk, making a copy of a disk with DISKCOPY, and backing up a hard disk.

Notice that a great deal of open space remains on the Main Group menu. This is done intentionally so that you can add your own menu choices. If you look at the options under both the Program and Group actions, you will see `Add` listed.

Note that in the DOS Shell environment, there is an important difference between a Group and a Program. When you select a Program, you are usually dealing with only a single program or application. A Group, on the other hand, leads you to another screen that may contain many programs which somehow relate to the Group title. For example, all of your communication programs might be installed in a Group called `Communication Programs`. If you establish a number of Groups, you can help end-users find their way through the DOS Shell menu more easily by first identifying the general type of program to be executed.

When you reach the next menu, you can choose between the programs that have been made available by whomever set up the menu.

If you ever "get stuck" looking at an unfamiliar menu, try pressing the ESC key to return to the previous menu. Remember that you can also press F1 for additional help.

Viewing the File System Menu

The File System menu screen is worth some additional discussion. Figure 3.8 shows how the File System menu is displayed.

Ignoring the top and bottom action lines, the menu is divided into three main areas. The horizontal area across the top quarter of the screen shows the available disk drives and lists the current directory (as seen by the File System).

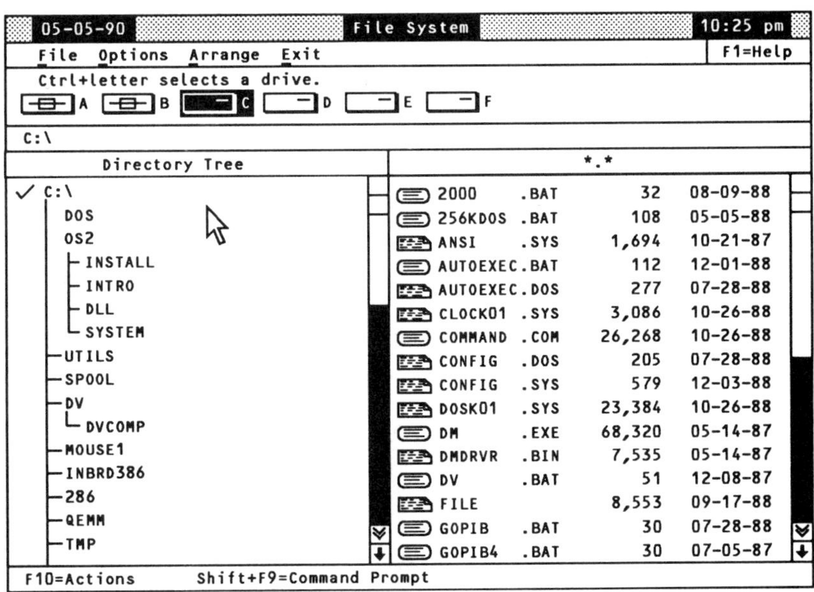

Figure 3.8. ***The File System menu.***

You can change the current logged drive in many ways. The easiest way is to hold down the Ctrl key and type the letter of the new drive. For example, to change to drive A:, you press Ctrl-A. The most difficult way to change drives is to press the Tab and arrow keys until the current drive is highlighted.

After you have selected the current drive, you can select the current subdirectory by choosing it from the directory tree displayed on the left side of the screen. Again, you can use a combination of Tab and arrow keys until the correct subdirectory is highlighted.

When you have chosen the subdirectory, the included files appear on the right side of the screen. Once again, you can use the Tab and arrow method to select a specific file.

When you have a specific file highlighted, you need to select the `File` action offered in the second line of the display. A pop-up menu gives you a number of choices. Two important choices are Open (Start) and View. If the file is a program, you can start it from here by selecting Open. If you have chosen a text file—say a batch file—you can view its contents by selecting the View command.

Always keep in mind that the action lines at the top and bottom of each screen give you a number of choices that you can execute at any time while you are in the current menu.

Summarizing DOS Shell Features

This introduction to the DOS Shell is by no means complete, but is meant to give you a sample look into what the DOS Shell provides. These small glimpses into the DOS Shell may reveal consistent patterns that make up the underlying strength of the graphical environment.

The DOS Shell is extremely easy to use if you have a mouse available on your PC. If not, you can still make effective use of the DOS Shell menus, but you have to concentrate more carefully on how to use the Tab and arrow keys to your advantage.

An advanced PC DOS user can probably expect to learn how to master using the DOS Shell in only a few hours of effort. As a new user, of course, you need an additional amount of time to explore the new environment. You do not have to "master" the DOS Shell in order to begin using it effectively.

What's Next

At this point, you should know the basics of using PC DOS—how to use commands and how the command line works. You should know that internal commands are instantly available when you see the PC DOS prompt and that external commands are stored as files in a particular directory on a disk. You should know how to get listings of files and subdirectories, make copies of files, make and remove subdirectories, and understand generally that the DOS Shell provides a simplified, easy-to-use alternative to using the command line.

Each of the tutorial chapters in Part 2 of this book starts where this Quick Primer leaves off, so you can turn to any chapter that interests you. The chapters in the beginning of Part 2 deal with topics that everyone needs to know; those toward the end of Part 2 deal with more specialized topics.

Each chapter includes complete information on its topic, presenting easier, more fundamental material at first and advanced, more complex material toward the end. You may want to read the first sections of several chapters, and then after you have developed your skills, return to complete those chapters later.

If you are using PC DOS version 4, you may want to read Chapter 4, "Using DOS Shell," to learn how to use the features of this helpful utility. If you still feel uneasy about your understanding, turn to Chapter 5, "PC DOS Files," which presents an especially gentle explanation of files, what they are, and how to work with them. The first sections of Chapter 6, "Managing Your Hard Disk," and Chapter 7, "All About Floppy Disks," include essential reading on how to use these all-important information storage devices.

Key Concepts and Words

Before you read further, use the following list to test your understanding of the concepts and words in this chapter.

External commands	Rebooting
DOS Shell	DOSSHELL

Answers to Quick Questions

1. b. The CPU is mounted inside the base unit of your PC. This is true no matter what IBM model you have.
2. d
3. PC DOS stands for Personal Computer Disk Operating System.
4. d
5. d. The startup program (also known as the Power On Self Test) always checks the integrity of the memory chips inside the base unit. If an error occurs, you see a message on the screen.
6. c
7. A bootable disk is one that has been formatted with part of the PC DOS operating system already installed on it. This permits you to start a floppy-drive-only PC without having to use the original copies of your PC DOS system disks, which can be useful if you want to use a single program on your PC. In this way, you may be able to fit both the boot files from PC DOS and your favorite word processing program on the same disk.
8. a
9. b
10. d
11. a
12. a
13. d. 23:59p represents a logical conflict. The fact that you have entered 23 as the hour indicates that you are using military time to enter the correct time. If you use military format, you cannot include the p to represent P.M.
14. a
15. c
16. d
17. d
18. e. If a file is a program, you can't tell how much RAM will be needed to execute it under PC DOS. The other choices are all valid pieces of information that are recorded whenever you create a PC DOS file.
19. b
20. c
21. b
22. c
23. The root system of a tree comes very close to describing how files are manipulated in directories on a hard drive. In the root directory, at the "top" of the analogy, the labels of other subdirectories appear. On a real tree's root system, the main root branches forth into several smaller roots. In turn, these roots can branch into still smaller roots (additional subdirectories) or tiny nibs (individual files).
24. b
25. b

26. c
27. c
28. Many people find that a professional file editor does the best job for their needs. PC DOS provides at least two ways of creating files when a file editor is not available. The first, EDLIN, is a line editor that can be difficult for the beginner to use. The second, COPY CON:, is easy to use and can be helpful if your task is to create short text files.
29. c
30. You probably used the TYPE command to display the contents of a binary file. There is no need to fear if this happens to you, because typing the contents of a binary file does not damage the file. On the other hand, it won't be enlightening either.
31. a
32. You will reformat the entire C> drive! Make sure you know what you want to format when using the FORMAT command, or you will live to regret the error. Fortunately, however, PC DOS does a good job of warning you that you are about to reformat your hard drive whenever it detects an action on the C> drive. Because you were logged onto C> and specified no other drive in the command string, PC DOS did the only thing it could do under the circumstances: assume that you meant to FORMAT C:.
33. d. The remaining choices have syntax errors that would result in an error. Make sure that you separate each of your search paths with a semicolon.
34. Whenever you confuse the disk you are backing up with the blank disk being used for backup purposes. If you are doing a `diskcopy a: b:`, make sure that the source disk in A: is your work disk. Otherwise, you end up with two very clean disks and perhaps several weeks of work to make up for the lost data!
35. c. The *.com is likely to appear after the other choices, which are all valid PC DOS commands. PC DOS searches for a valid command (the head), and then passes the remainder (the tail) to the command itself for further processing.
36. b
37. d. Ctrl-C can be used to "break out" of the execution of many PC DOS commands and user programs. Ctrl-S is often used in the DIR and TYPE commands to suspend their execution and then restart them. The Ctrl-Alt-Del sequence can be used to save wear and tear on your PC. Turning your PC on and off frequently places stress on the electrical components inside the base unit. When you need to reboot, you can extend the life of your machine by using this warm boot combination.

Part 2
Tutorials

The chapters in this part are in-depth tutorials on the major topics of PC DOS use. You'll learn all the details of managing files and directories on your hard disk, using the DOS Shell to simplify PC DOS, customizing PC DOS for your own uses, and more.

Each chapter discusses one topic in detail, beginning with a quick review of basic concepts and terms. Carefully sequenced examples then show exactly how to use PC DOS commands and features. Examples early in each chapter treat the easiest or most common problems you'll encounter. Later examples focus on less common, more difficult problems and more complex solutions and techniques. Each chapter ends with suggestions for related chapters.

Within this part, the chapters are organized roughly from the simplest to the most advanced. But if you've read and understood the material in the Quick Primer, you're ready to read the chapters in Part 2 in any order that interests you.

Chapter 4

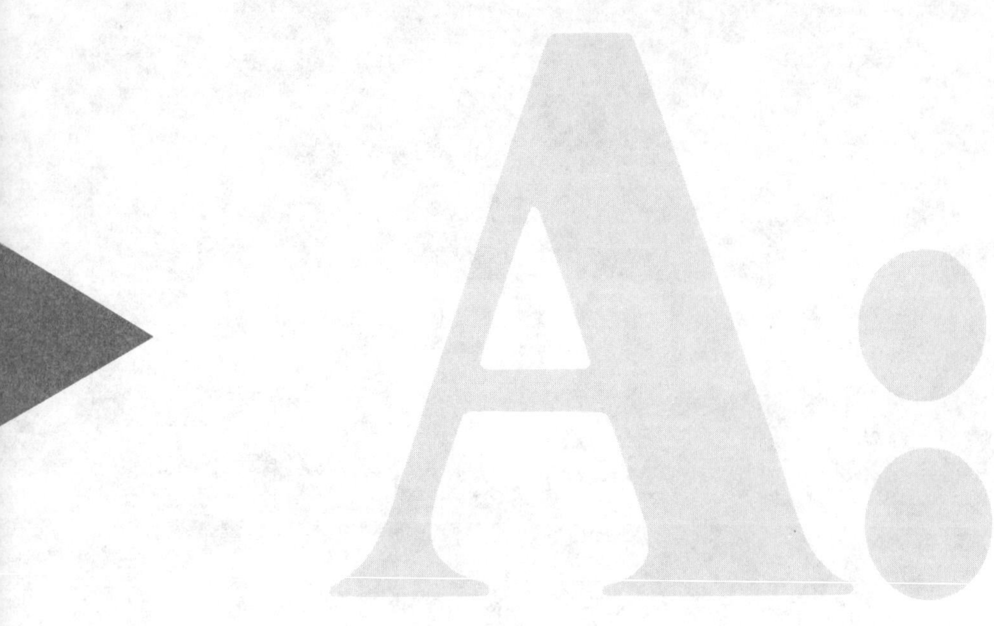

The DOSSHELL's graphic interface lets you use either a keyboard or a mouse with PC DOS. It streamlines many routine operations by letting you point and choose on screen instead of typing whole commands. In this chapter, you'll learn to

- *Select options from pull-down menus*
- *Run commands and application programs automatically when you select them in the shell*
- *Customize the shell with your own menus and start-up options*
- *Group files with their programs for instant start-up*

Chapter 4
Using DOSSHELL

You may be wondering why all this fuss about DOSSHELL? After all, you may have been perfectly happy typing `dir wordproc` to get a quick listing of the files in your `wordproc` directory. You also know that it's not hard to use the COPY, DEL, and TYPE commands to work with the files in your directory. Why bother to load a shell program like DOSSHELL? Why learn how to navigate through a series of menus and windows to do something as simple as `del letter1`?

These are good questions. A graphic interface such as DOSSHELL has some real advantages, as you will see, but it isn't the best tool for every kind of PC housekeeping task. In fact, DOSSHELL provides you with quick access to the traditional command-line prompt for those occasions when it is easier to use the command-line prompt. The following review of the basic command-line interface will help you find out where DOSSHELL fits into your work.

Command-Line Limitations

Traditionally, PC DOS users sit in front of a prompt such as `C:\>`. They type commands such as `copy letter a:letter.bak` or `format a: /f:720` at this prompt. After the Enter key has been pressed, PC DOS responds by listing the directory, copying the file, or whatever else has been requested.

Part 3 of this book, the Command Reference, gives a variety of examples of such commands. The advantage of typing commands directly at the command line is that PC DOS will do exactly what you tell it to do, and do it immediately, without requiring a series of menu selections. You can also put commands, one per line, in a batch file to have them executed automatically. (See Chapter 10, "Batch Files," for more about this powerful feature.)

The disadvantage of working at the command prompt is that you must know *exactly* how to tell PC DOS what you want to do. If you make a mistake, you may get a not-very-helpful error message such as "too many parameters." If the command you typed has a potentially irrevocable effect (such as deleting all the files in a directory or formatting a disk), you are given a warning ("do you really want to do this?"). At other times, your command may be in an acceptable form, but the result may not be what you intended. In such cases, PC DOS will do what you told it to do rather than what you really wanted it to do. Learning to use the command line effectively requires becoming familiar with the syntax and rules for using a variety of PC DOS commands. This can be a tedious process, and, until version 4, PC DOS provided no on-line help for commands and other features. (Some third-party products are available for plugging in an on-line help facility.)

A related problem is that often you don't have easy access to the information you need for the next step. Suppose, for example, you want to back up the file LETTER1 from your hard disk to a floppy. Fine, but where *is* LETTER1? Is it in the WordPerfect directory? The customer contacts directory? The accounting directory? Before you can copy the file, you often have to issue a series of DIR commands, find the file, and then issue the COPY command. This lack of easily accessible information about directories and files frustrates many beginning PC DOS users.

With DOSSHELL, the information you need to complete your tasks will usually be right there on the screen when you need it. When you want to copy a file, for example, there will be a list of directories and files that you can browse through until you find the file you want. You don't have to try to think of all the directories the file might be in and type a DIR command to look at each one. Other information about your files and directories will be available by selecting reports from a menu.

When DOSSHELL asks you for something and you're not sure what it wants, a key-press brings up a help box. Many frequently used PC DOS commands, such as COPY, DISKCOPY, and DEL, are already packaged for you into menu selections. You don't have to remember the exact name of the command that you need.

Not Just for Beginners

Those of you who are experienced PC DOS users may not be worried about the problems that face beginners. You have learned how to type long path names to search distant directories. You already know most of the basic techniques for working with PC DOS, and some more advanced tricks besides. Indeed, one of the main purposes of this book is to build on your knowledge and help you learn to use PC DOS commands in depth, and then help you to bring together the commands and settings you need to configure your system.

In many situations, however, you will be working with users who know little or nothing about PC DOS. You can give such users "recipes" that they can refer to by rote for tasks such as backing up the hard disk. If they make mistakes, however, they're stuck, often without ready access to help. Ideally, you want to provide users with a standard way of performing such tasks as selecting programs from menus, viewing and managing their disk files, and carrying out other utility functions. You want context-sensitive on-line help to be available each step of the way, and you want the ability to customize program start-up options and user prompts to suit various work situations.

Programs such as Microsoft Windows or OS/2 Presentation Manager provide all of these features, and more besides. Their drawback is that they require a fast 286 or 386 processor and a megabyte or more of additional memory (several megabytes for OS/2), not to mention a good EGA or VGA display. PC DOS 4, through the DOSSHELL user interface, offers an alternative that works with just about any hardware configuration. Working with either text or graphics-based systems, DOSSHELL has the following features:

- Mouse or keyboard operation
- Menus that can be customized for running programs
- The ability to group related applications
- Program start-up options and prompts that can be customized to obtain information from the user
- Context-sensitive on-line help, both built-in help and help that you can customize
- The ability to link programs and their data files (such as word processing documents, spreadsheets, or database files) so that selecting a file runs the appropriate application
- Menu-driven access to the most frequently used PC DOS utilities, such as DISKCOPY, BACKUP, and FORMAT
- A facility that lets you browse through the file system on a hard disk, selecting individual files or groups of files to be copied, moved, or otherwise manipulated
- Easy access to the standard command-line prompt when you need to perform functions not provided by DOSSHELL

With DOSSHELL, you can provide both yourself and the beginning user with most of the advantages of Presentation Manager for OS/2 or Microsoft Windows at a fraction of the cost of supporting hardware. The only major feature you will lack is *multitasking*—the ability to run more than one program at a time. As a bonus, however, users who are familiar with DOSSHELL are well prepared for moving up to the Presentation Manager.

Anatomy of DOSSHELL

Now that you're aware of the reasons for using DOSSHELL, you're ready to look at the anatomy of DOSSHELL. Where does it live and how does it work? How do the facilities offered by DOSSHELL fit into the structure of standard PC DOS? How is DOSSHELL installed into your system?

DOSSHELL and COMMAND.COM

Most users think that the command prompt (such as C:\>) is part of PC DOS itself. Actually, this user interface is a separate program. If you are familiar with earlier versions of PC DOS (or MS-DOS), you know that this interface program, the one that prompts you for commands, is called COMMAND.COM. Basically the COMMAND.COM program allows you to do three things:

- Run internal PC DOS commands, such as DIR to list directories or COPY to copy files
- Run external PC DOS commands or utilities, such as CHKDSK to get a summary of disk usage or FORMAT to prepare a disk
- Run other programs, such as Lotus 1-2-3 or a PC DOS batch file

It is important to remember that COMMAND.COM is an ordinary program, run by PC DOS in the same way as the utility FORMAT.COM or the application program WordPerfect. Because the user interface program isn't "special," other user interfaces can be run instead of COMMAND.COM simply by specifying them in a SHELL statement in the CONFIG.SYS file. In other words, PC DOS allows for interchangeable, "snap-in" user interfaces.

There are two ways you can add a new user interface to PC DOS. One way is to *replace* COMMAND.COM with a new shell by using the SHELL command. While this has been done occasionally, there is a disadvantage in that the new program must duplicate all the functionality of COMMAND.COM, in addition to providing its enhanced interface.

The new PC DOS user interface, DOSSHELL, takes a different approach. Rather than replacing COMMAND.COM, it runs as a separate program over it, providing menus, dialog boxes, and window displays and calling upon COMMAND.COM or external PC DOS commands to carry out the operations you select. In this way it provides all the functions of COMMAND.COM and many of the PC DOS commands, but it does not require you to memorize the syntax or details of usage required by the traditional command line. *Note*: Although DOSSHELL is available only with PC DOS 4, a variety of third-party shell programs provide a similar range of functions to users of earlier PC DOS versions.

How DOSSHELL Runs

Since DOSSHELL is a regular PC DOS program, you can run it automatically on start-up by placing the name DOSSHELL in the AUTOEXEC.BAT file, or you can type `dosshell` at the regular command prompt. The PC DOS 4 installation program, SELECT, provides the appropriate AUTOEXEC.BAT settings for you, according to your disk configuration and your responses to the questions it has asked you about how you want to run the shell. (If you have not yet installed PC DOS 4 and DOSSHELL, please read the section on PC DOS 4 in Chapter 12, "Installing a PC DOS System." After you have installed the shell, continue here. You will get more out of this chapter if you can try out the DOSSHELL features and commands on your own PC.)

DOSSHELL is actually the name of a batch file called DOSSHELL.BAT, which typically looks like this:

```
@C:
@CD C:\DOS
@SHELLB DOSSHELL
@IF ERRORLEVEL 255 GOTO END
:COMMON
```

```
@BREAK=OFF
@SHELLC /MOS:PCIBMDRV.MOS/TRAN/COLOR/DOS/MENU/MUL/SND/MEU:
     SHELL.MEU/CLR:SHELL.CLR/PROMPT/MAINT/EXIT/SWAP/DATE
:END
@BREAK=ON
```

Don't worry about understanding this file now. In general, this batch file runs two programs, SHELLB.COM and SHELLC.EXE, which contain the bulk of the shell's program code. The long line of options following the SHELLC statement contains the current settings for the mouse driver, colors, memory usage, and other variables (these may be different on your system, depending on the hardware you have and how you answered the setup questions). At the end of this chapter, you will learn how to change these start-up options.

Overview of the DOSSHELL Menu System

From the user's point of view, the DOSSHELL program has a *hierarchical*, or layered, menu system. This simply means that you start with general menus and, as necessary, make more specific selections from successive submenus or pop-up boxes until you have selected the actual task that you want to perform.

The highest-level menu, the Start Programs screen, enables you to set up or revise menus of programs that can be run from the shell. Related programs, such as a word processor, printer control program, file converter, and spelling checker, can be grouped together, and you can switch back and forth among these program groups (see Figure 4.1). It's important to realize, however, that only one program can actually be run at a time: DOSSHELL does not provide multitasking.

The default list of programs shown on the Start Programs screen is called the *Main Group*. It is special in that it can contain other groups as well as programs, just as a directory can contain subdirectories. The Main Group is the only group that can contain other groups, which are also called *subgroups*.

In Figure 4.1, the application programs WordPerfect, Lotus 1-2-3, and dBASE IV have been added to the Main Group menu. You will learn later how to add your applications to the program selection menus.

The Main Group also contains some built-in groups and programs, including a group of PC DOS Utilities (time, date, copy, compare, backup/restore, and format), a program that you can use to change the colors used by the shell, and the program COMMAND.COM (described as "Command Prompt,"), which gives you access to the traditional PC DOS command line.

One of the options under Main Group is a program called "File System." This in turn provides a set of menus enabling you to manipulate files, control the way file information is displayed, and set various options. Figure 4.2 shows how the supplied and user-defined groups and programs fit together in DOSSHELL's Main Group structure. In the figure, "Command Prompt," "File System," and "Change Colors" are programs supplied with the shell. "DOS Utilities," also supplied with the shell, is a subgroup of the Main Group. (You can tell that it is a subgroup rather than a program because it ends in an ellipsis.) The subgroups "Spreadsheet," "Database," and "Writing" are user-defined subgroups containing application programs.

A Guided Tour of DOSSHELL

The following section gives you a quick tour of DOSSHELL. Here you will see how to start and exit the shell, obtain context-specific help, make menu selections, run a PC DOS utility command, manage your files, and install a program and a program group in the menu system.

Starting and Exiting DOSSHELL

How you start DOSSHELL depends on how you have installed it. In Chapter 12, "Installing a PC DOS System," you will find a discussion of the different configurations that are possible. Recall that DOSSHELL can be run in one of two ways. In the first way, you place a line with the word "DOSSHELL" in your AUTOEXEC.BAT file, and DOSSHELL runs automatically when the system is started from the hard disk. (For some floppy-based configurations, you will have to boot from a system disk and then insert the DOSSHELL disk.) In the second way, you can run DOSSHELL from the regular PC DOS command line by typing the command `dosshell`. Whichever way you start it, you will know DOSSHELL is running when you see a Start Programs screen such as that shown in Figure 4.1.

When you are running the shell, you can exit from it in two ways: you can press F3, or you can select "Exit" from the action bar at the top of the Start Programs screen (see Figure 4.1) and then select "Exit Shell F3" from the pull-down menu that appears. You will learn all of the methods for selecting items in the shell shortly.

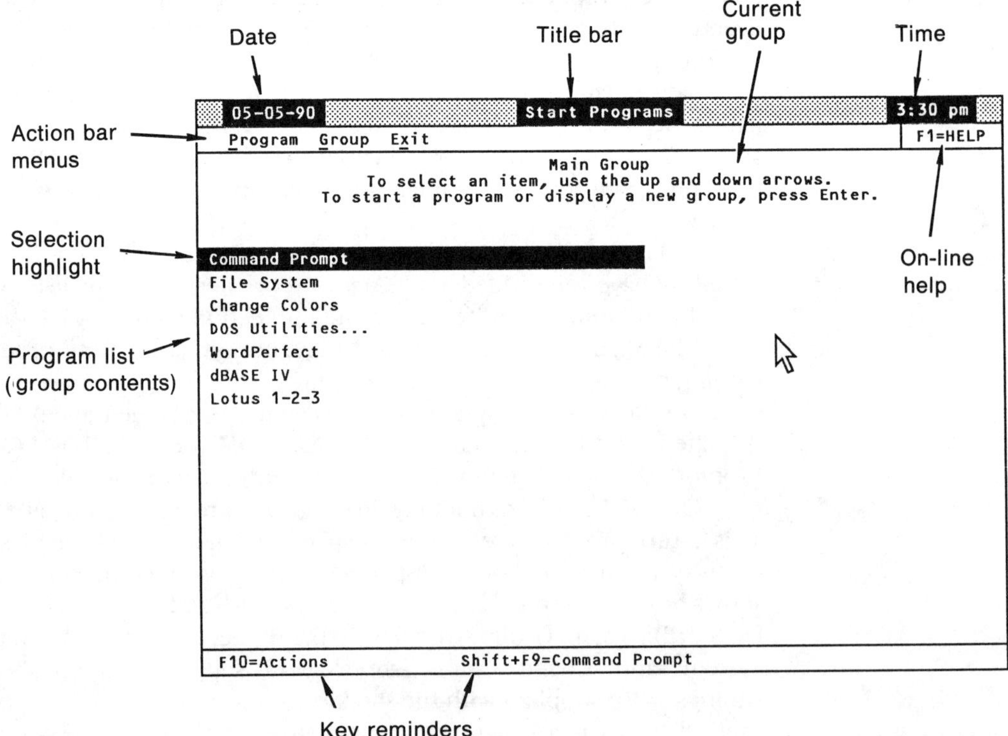

Figure 4.1. ***The Start Programs screen.***

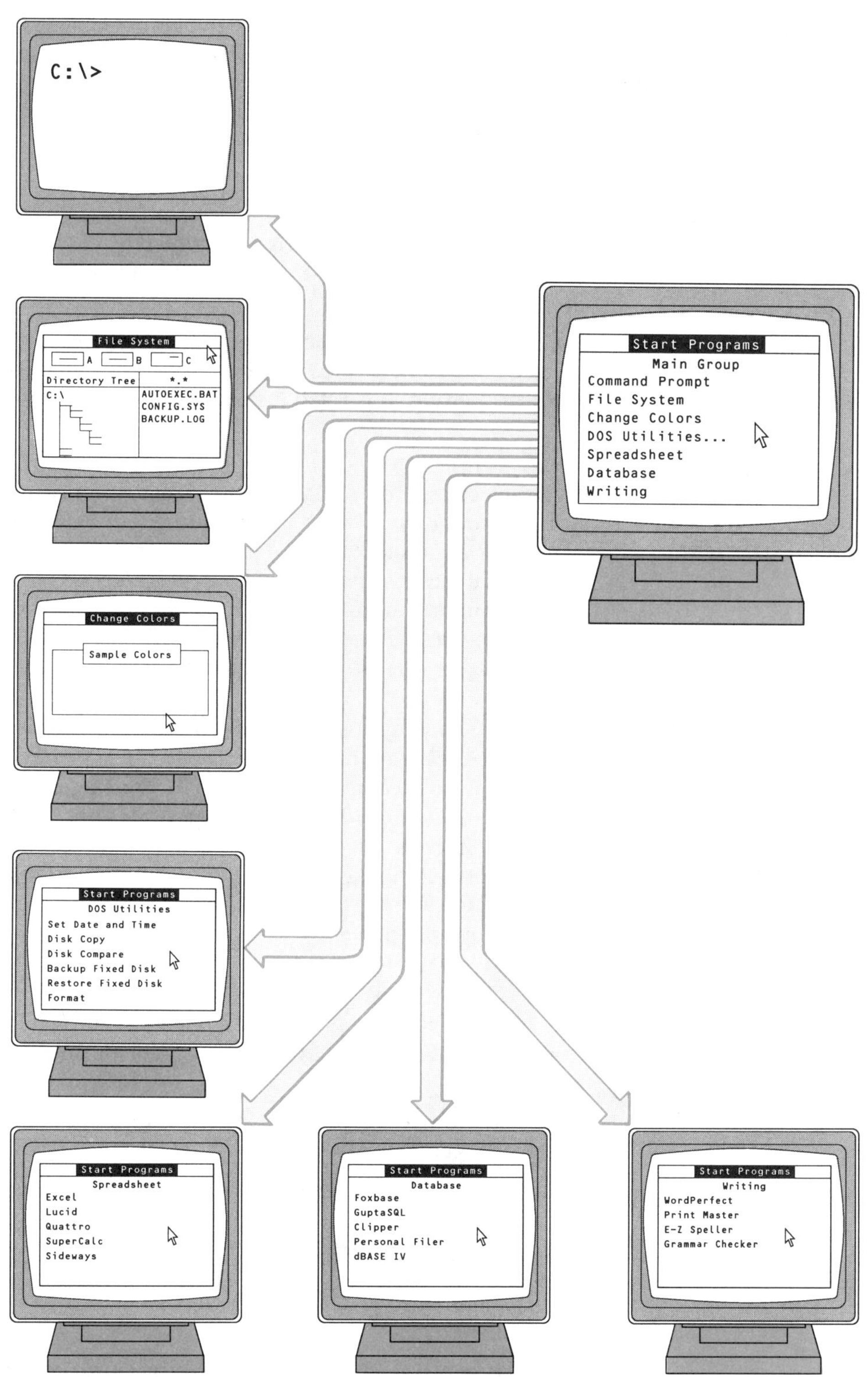

Figure 4.2. ***Structure of DOSSHELL.***

The Start Programs Screen

At this point, if you haven't done so already, start DOSSHELL. You should be looking at a screen similar to that shown in Figure 4.1. This figure shows the graphics-mode screen, but the text-mode screen is very similar. Any small differences will be pointed out as they arise.

Note the important parts of this screen:

- The *title line*, with Start Programs at the top center. The current date appears at the left end of the title line; the current time at the right end.
- Just below this line on the left is the *action bar*, a menu from which you can make selections. In this case it consists of three selections: Program, Group, and Exit.
- The main part of the screen shows the group of programs currently selected. Normally, as shown here, this is the Main Group. When you select a subgroup, it is listed instead of the main group.

Tip

Pop-ups and Pull-downs

If you select an item from the action bar, a pull-down menu appears. A *pull-down menu* is a list of further choices that you can make after selecting an item from the action bar. Some menu choices will present a pop-up box. A *pop-up box* is used to request additional information about an item in a pull-down menu. If you see an ellipsis (. . .) next to a menu choice (as in "DOS Utilities . . . " in Figure 4.1), you know that a pop-up will appear.

Making Selections from the Keyboard

To select a program or group from a list by using the keyboard, move the selection cursor (the highlighted bar over a line of text) up and down with the arrow keys and then select the desired item by pressing Enter. On the action bar, you can use the Left Arrow and Right Arrow keys to move the highlight, and then press Enter to select the highlighted item. Alternatively, you can press the key corresponding to the underlined letter in the item you want. Use the F10 key to switch between the program list and the action bar.

Try running a program:

1. When the Start Programs screen comes up, the selection cursor (a shaded bar) will highlight the Command Prompt selection. Use the Down Arrow key to move the selection cursor until it is over Change Colors.
2. Press Enter to run the Change Colors program. (You will learn how to use this program later.)
3. Press Esc. The Escape key generally returns you to where you were before you made the last selection. In this case, it returns you to the Main Group on the Start Programs screen.

Try selecting a group:

1. Move the selection cursor with the Up or Down Arrow key until it is over DOS Utilities.

2. Press Enter, and the list of programs in the DOS Utilities group will be shown. You can run any of these programs by using the arrow keys to move the cursor onto the desired program and then pressing Enter.
3. For now, press Esc, and you will be returned to the Main Group on the Start Programs screen. You will learn how to use the DOS Utilities program later.

Try a pull-down menu:

1. Press F10 to switch the selection cursor from the list of items in the Main Group to the row of items on the action bar: Program, Group, and Exit. (F10 is a *toggle*: typing it again returns the selection cursor to the list of items in the center of the screen.)
2. You can now move the selection cursor from left to right and back again by using the Left Arrow and Right Arrow keys. Use the Right Arrow key to move the cursor over the Exit item.
3. Press Enter to select Exit. The pull-down menu shown in Figure 4.3 will appear. For now, press Esc to return to the action bar.

Try the alternative method:

1. With the cursor on the action bar, type `x`.
2. The Exit menu will appear. Press Esc to return to the action bar.

On pull-down menus, items that are not applicable to your work appear dimmed (in graphics mode), or the first letter appears as an asterisk (in text mode). For example, if the highlight is on one of the built-in programs (such as DOS Utilities) and you select the Program menu, you'll find that the Delete, Change, and Copy selections are dimmed. This is because you can't change a built-in program.

Making Selections with a Mouse

With a mouse, making selections is even simpler. On text-mode screens, a small shaded rectangle represents the mouse position. On graphics-mode screens, an arrow-shaped pointer is used, as shown in Figure 4.3.

Try running a program:

1. Move the mouse until the mouse pointer (the arrow or small shaded box) is over Change Colors.
2. Press the mouse button twice in rapid succession. (This is called *double clicking*.) The Change Colors program will run. (You will learn how to use the Change Colors program later.)
3. Move the mouse pointer until it is in the small rectangle marked "Esc=Cancel". Press (click) the mouse button once. You will be returned to the Start Programs screen. Note that you can also press the Escape key to cancel the program. In general, you can mix mouse and keyboard commands, using whichever method is most convenient.

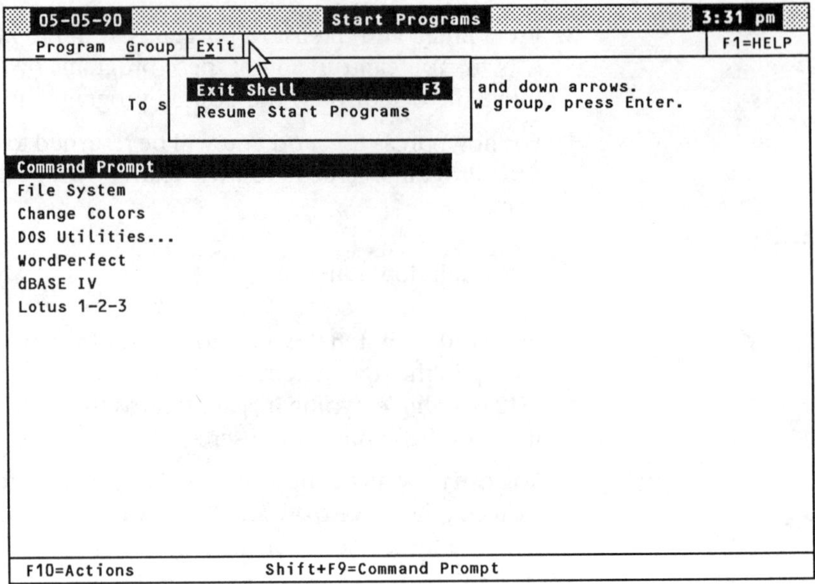

Figure 4.3. ***Pull-down menu.***

Try selecting a group:

1. Move the mouse pointer until it is over DOS Utilities.
2. Double-click, and the list of programs in the group will be shown. You can run any of these programs by double-clicking on its name.
3. For now, click in the Esc=Cancel rectangle (or just press the Escape key) and you will be returned to the Main Group on the Start Programs screen. (You will learn how to use the DOS Utilities programs later.)

Try a pull-down menu:

1. Move the mouse pointer to Exit on the action bar (with the mouse, you do not need to use F10 to switch from the program list to the action bar).
2. Click once, and the Exit menu will drop down.
3. Move the pointer to Resume shell and click (or press the Escape key) to return to the Start Programs screen.

Tip

Just Say No
To exit from a pull-down menu without choosing anything from it, press Esc or click with the mouse anywhere outside the menu.

Getting Help

When you're running DOSSHELL, help is only a keystroke or mouse-click away:

1. Move the selection cursor over File System, or click once with the mouse to highlight this item.
2. Press the F1 key, or click with the mouse over the F1=Help rectangle.

You will see the help window shown in Figure 4.4. This help text describes the File System (which you will be working with in detail later).

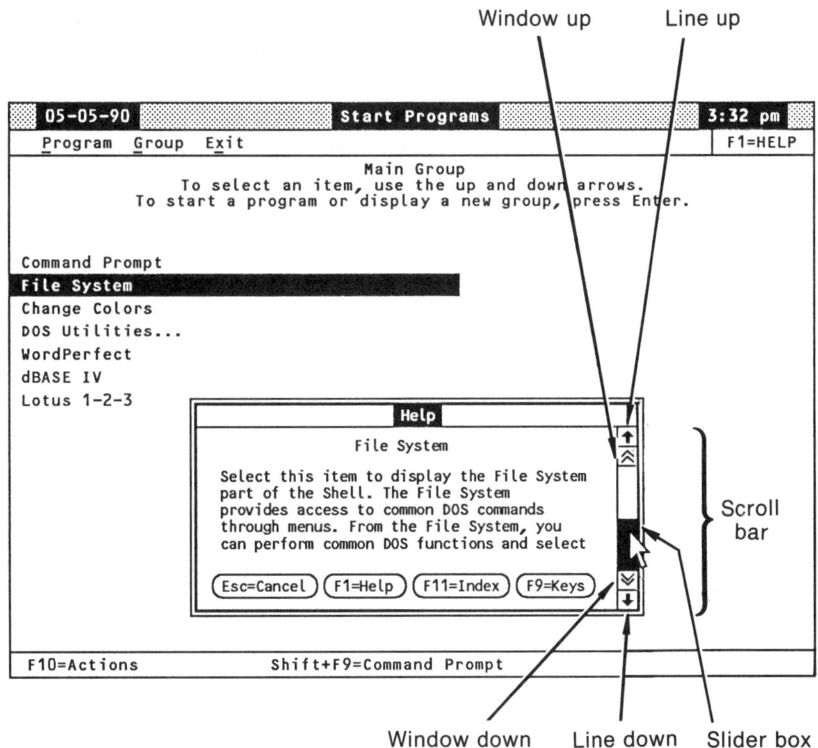

Figure 4.4. ***Context-sensitive help window.***

Scrolling Text in Windows

Only a small part of the help text is visible in the window. To continue reading, you can use the keyboard as follows:

1. Press the Up and Down Arrow keys to scroll the text up and down one line, or click on the Up and Down Arrow symbols with the mouse.
2. Press the PgUp and PgDn keys to scroll the text up and down a window at a time. The arrows will appear shaded when no more scrolling in either direction is possible.

Or, if the shell is in graphics mode and you have a mouse, you can use the scroll bar features on the right side of the window as shown in Figure 4.4:

1. Click on the single arrows at the top and bottom of the bar to scroll the text up or down by one line.
2. Click on the double arrows just inside the single arrows to scroll the text up or down by one window.
3. Place the mouse pointer over the shaded rectangular *slider box*, hold down the mouse button, and drag the box up or down to scroll the

window text. When you move the slider box, the text is moved relative to the position of the slider. For example, if you drag the slider until it is three-fourths of the way toward the bottom of the scroll bar, the text will scroll to a position aproximately three-fourths of the way to the end. (When an arrow is shaded, it means that you cannot scroll in that direction.)

Practice scrolling the text with the keyboard and mouse. Note that although you can use all of the mouse selection methods when the shell is in text mode, the scroll bar feature does not appear, so you must use the keyboard methods for scrolling text in windows.

In using the shell, you will encounter many windows of text. The keyboard scrolling, scroll bar, and slider techniques are applicable to any window that has more text than can be displayed at once.

Indexed Help Display

Notice that the help window shown in Figure 4.4 offers, in addition to the Escape option, the options F1=Help, F11=Index, and F9=Keys. Here, the F1 option provides "help on help"; that is, it brings up a help window that describes the use of the help facility itself.

If you press F11 (or click it with the mouse), you will see another type of help window called "Indexed Help Selections," shown in Figure 4.5. The previous help window (Figure 4.4) was context-specific; that is, it referred to the currently selected item (in that case, the File System). Indexed Help, on the other hand, allows you to get help on any topic. Simply select the appropriate topic with the selection cursor or mouse. The window shows only the first five topics. To see more, scroll by using any of the methods discussed earlier.

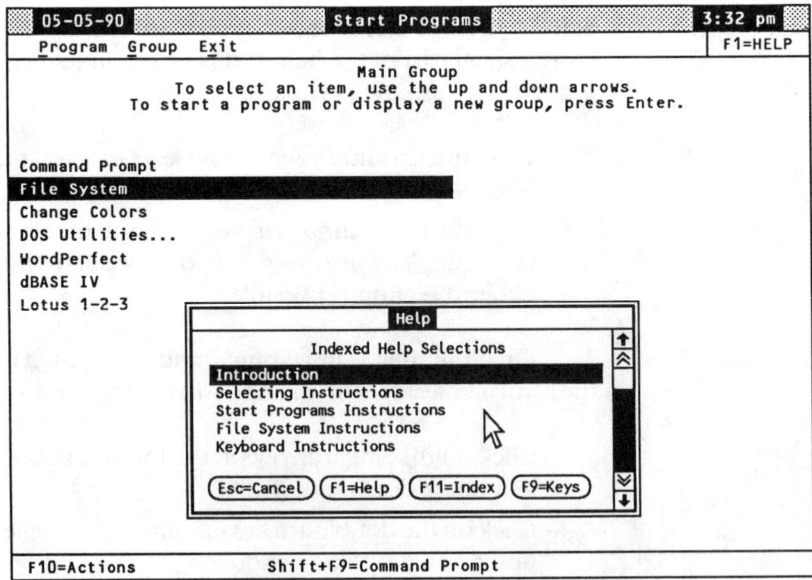

Figure 4.5. ***Indexed help window.***

Key Assignments Help

If you press F9 (or click it with the mouse), you will see yet another type of help window, shown in Figure 4.6, that describes each of the keys having special meaning to DOSSHELL. Again, you can scroll to see the rest of the list.

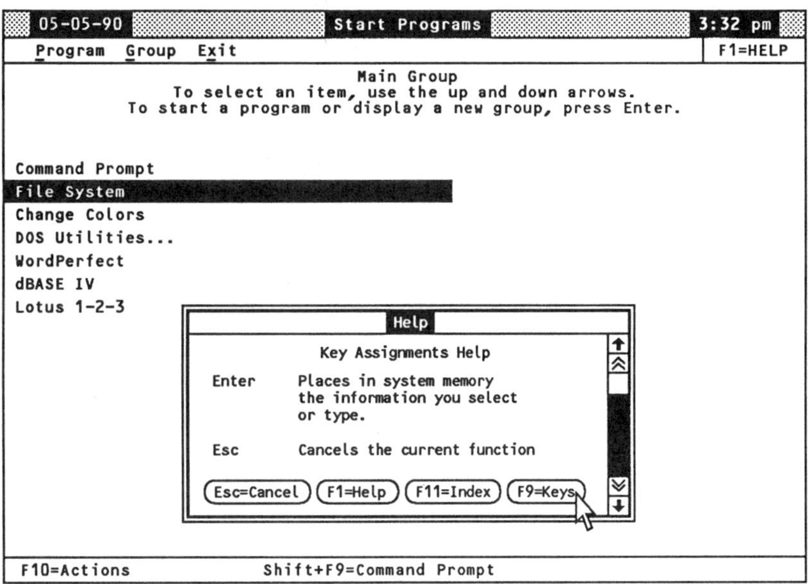

Figure 4.6. ***Key assignments help window.***

To close the help window and resume operations, press the Escape key or click Esc=Cancel with the mouse.

Table 4.1 summarizes the special functions that the shell assigns to certain keys to help you manipulate the menus and the information on the screen. It lists some techniques that you have not seen yet—such as moving through the File System screen and selecting files there—but you will see how to do this when the File System is discussed. Also, remember that you can use the mouse, if you have one, to make selections instead of using these special keys.

Running Utility Programs

Now that you know how to get on-line help and how to move around in windows, you can use DOSSHELL to perform a common task—copying a disk. Suppose you have a disk in drive A, and you need to copy it to a disk in drive B. (If you have a disk handy for copying, and a blank or unneeded disk to copy to, try the steps as you read.)

1. From the Start Programs screen, select "DOS Utilities." Remember that you can use either the cursor bar or the mouse to make selections from the current list of programs or groups in the center of the screen.

Figure 4.7 shows the DOS Utilities group. Notice that there is a new list in the center of the screen, showing the programs available in this group.

2. Select "Disk Copy."

The Start-up window for the Diskcopy Utility pops up. This window, shown in Figure 4.8, is the equivalent of the command line: it allows you to provide the information needed to complete the command. Unlike the command line, however, the most commonly needed information is already provided. In this case, the source drive is specified as **a:**, and the destination drive as **b:**.

Table 4.1. ***Using Special Keys in the Shell***

Key	Function
Enter	Make a selection
Highlighted letter keys	Make a selection
F10	Switch to action bar
Arrow keys	Move the cursor
F1	Get help
F9	Get help on key assignments
F11	Get indexed help
Esc	Back out of a menu or close a window
F3	Exit from the shell or return to Start Programs
Arrow keys, PgUp, PgDn	Scroll information
Shift-F9	Get command-line prompt
Tab, Shift-Tab	Move around the File System screen
Space bar	Select and deselect a file in the File System

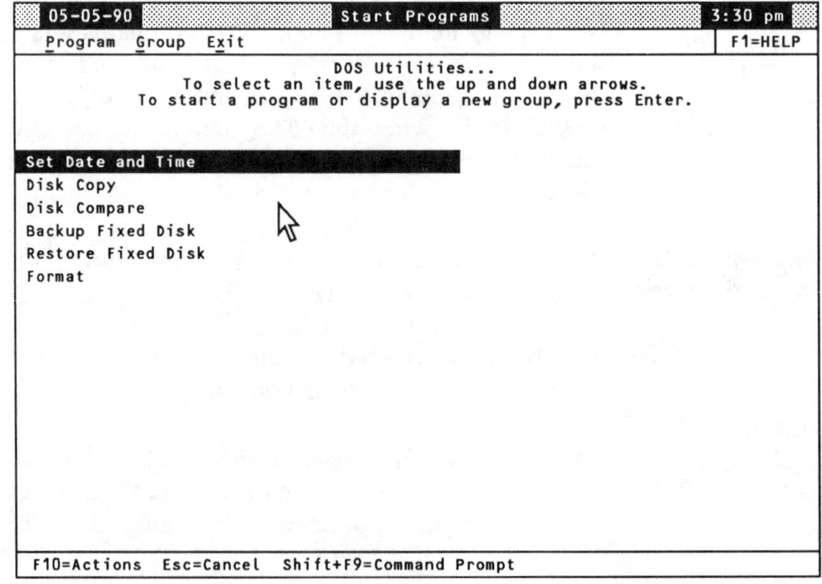

Figure 4.7. ***The DOS Utilities program group.***

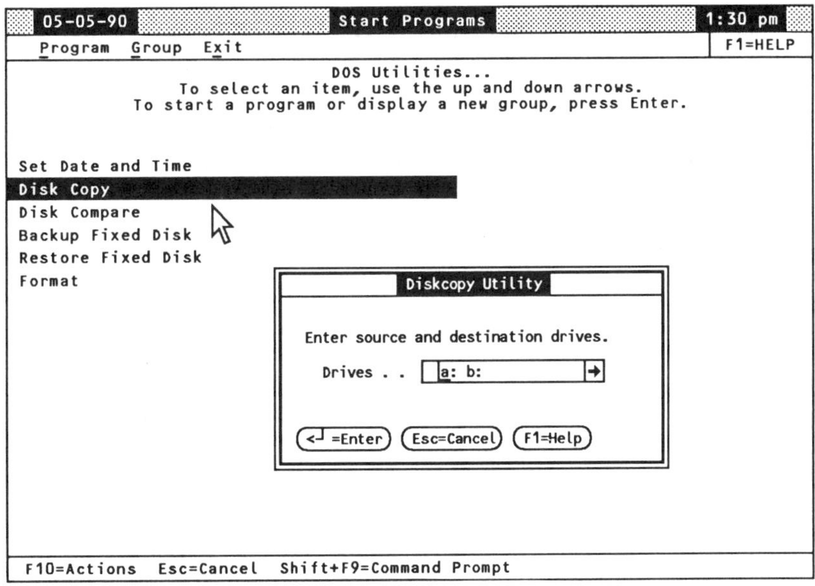

Figure 4.8. ***The Diskcopy program prompt window.***

Suppose you want to switch drives, copying B to A. Just use the Right Arrow and Left Arrow keys to move the cursor to the part of the command line you want to change (in this case, the names of the source and destination drives), and type the appropriate drive letters. Note that the mouse cannot be used to move the insertion point. You must use the arrow keys or simply start typing at the current cursor location.

Suppose you don't know what to do next? For example, you may not be sure how to specify the drive letters. To invoke the ever-present help, type the F1 key (or click the F1 box with the mouse), and a help window will pop up. This help is context-specific, giving the information you need to complete your data entry. Here, it briefly explains the purpose of the DISKCOPY command and tells you how to specify the drive letters. (Note that these help screens don't describe all the options that can be used with each command. They refer you to the PC DOS 4 manual, *Using DOS*. Also see the Command Reference in Part 3 of this book for complete explanations of all PC DOS commands.

3. To execute the disk copy (`diskcopy a: b:`), press Enter or click the word Enter with the mouse. You do not have to type the words "diskcopy a: b:".

When the DISKCOPY command runs, the screen will be switched to text mode, and you will see the same messages and prompts that you would if you were running the command from the command line. In the case of this DISKCOPY command, you will be prompted first to insert the source disk in drive A and press a key and then to insert the destination disk in B and press a key to begin the copy.

When the command is completed, you will be prompted to press a key once more. After you do this, you are returned to the program group where you began, in this case, DOS Utilities.

Tip

Escaping from Your Actions

Remember that up to the time you are actually running the DISK-COPY command, you can back out of what you are doing by pressing the Escape key or, if the word "Esc" is shown, by clicking it with the mouse. For example, if you selected Disk Copy and then realized that what you wanted was Disk Compare, all you have to do is press Esc to get back to the DOS Utilities group and then select "Disk Compare."

If you keep pressing Esc, you eventually end up at a top-level screen such as the File System screen. From such a screen, select "Exit" to return to the highest-level screen, Start Programs. From there, F3 or Exit will allow you to exit the shell itself.

However, once a command such as DISKCOPY has started to run, you cannot get out of it by pressing Esc. Press Ctrl-C instead, once for each disk insertion prompt. When you are asked `Terminate Batch File (Y/N)?`, type `y`.

Housekeeping in the File System

In the traditional command-line mode, it is hard to visualize the full structure of your file system, particularly on a hard disk. By using one of the more informative versions of the PC DOS prompt (such as `prompt $p$g`, which shows the current drive and directory) or by issuing the CD command by itself, you can determine the current directory. You can use the DIR command to view the current directory, listing files and subdirectories. You can also use it to view another directory, but only if you know the correct path name. The TREE command can be used to get a complete listing of the file system structure, but you can't scroll around in the resulting list or make selections from it directly.

In contrast to the traditional command-line mode, DOSSHELL gives you an active, movable window on your file system. To see how it works, select "File System" from the Main Group. There will be a pause while DOSSHELL loads your directory and file structure into memory. You will see a display similar to that of Figure 4.9. (The directories and files listed will of course be different.)

Notice that the screen is divided into the following areas:

- The *title line* (here, it displays "File System").
- The *action bar*, with the menus File, Options, Arrange, and Exit.
- The *drive selection* area for selecting the current drive. You can select the drive with the mouse or you can press Ctrl plus the key corresponding to the drive letter.
- The *path* area, showing the current path—in this case, `C:\`, which represents the root directory of drive C. (For more on path names, see Chapter 6, "Managing Your Hard Disk.")
- On the left side of the main part of the screen, the *Directory Tree* appears. This listing shows the directories and subdirectories (here, those on drive C), with subdirectories indented under their parent directo-

ries. Thus, you can see at a glance that SYS is a subdirectory of INCLUDE, which in turn is a subdirectory of TC.

- On the right side of the main part of the screen is a listing of the files in the currently selected directory. This area is called the file name area, or simply the *file list*.

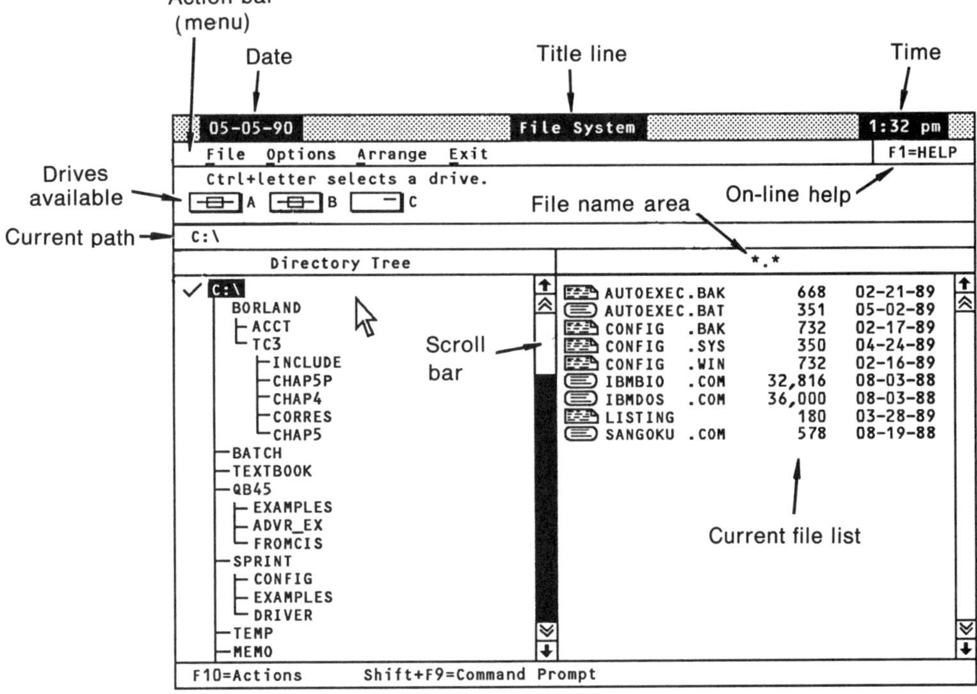

Figure 4.9. ***File system default display.***

Press the Tab or Backtab (Shift-Tab) keys to move among the action bar, the drive selection area, the Directory Tree, and the file list. Or, with the mouse, just move the pointer directly to the area where you want to make a selection. Press F10 at any time to make a selection from the action bar.

You can scroll through both the Directory Tree and the file list portions of the window independently, using the same methods discussed earlier in connection with Help text windows. Use the Up or Down Arrow keys or the PgUp or PgDn keys. With the mouse, click on the Up or Down Arrow key or, in graphics mode, use the various scroll bar features.

Copying a File

Now you can practice copying a file in the File System:

1. If you need to change disk drives, press the Ctrl key. While holding it down, press the key corresponding to the new drive. For example, press Ctrl-A to make drive A the current drive. Or, with the mouse, simply

click on the icon representing the drive you want. The shell will load the directory structure for the selected drive into the Directory Tree window.

2. Move (using the Tab or Backtab key or the mouse) to the Directory Tree window.
3. Move the selection cursor or the mouse pointer to the name of a directory containing a file that you wish to copy. If necessary, use one of the scrolling methods to move quickly through the directory list.
4. Press Enter or click the mouse to select the highlighted directory. The files in that directory will be listed in the window on the right side of the screen.
5. Use the Tab key or the mouse to move to the file list window. Move the selection cursor or mouse pointer to the name of the file you want to copy. Press the space bar or click the mouse once to select the file.
6. Move to the action bar by pressing F10 or using the mouse. Select the File option. When the menu drops down, select "Copy."
7. A window appears with the name of the source file already filled in. You are prompted for the destination file name. Type the file name (or a full path name if you are copying to another directory).
8. Press Enter or click the Enter box, and the file will be copied.

This same technique is used for the other options that manipulate files, such as deleting a file, viewing a file, or printing a file. Try out some of these options, using a file that doesn't contain important data—just in case you make a mistake.

Tip

Selecting Multiple Files

When you are in the file list, you can select more than one file simply by repeatedly pressing the space bar or by clicking with the mouse on each file. Each file you select is marked by a symbol placed in front of its name: a check mark in graphics mode or a > in text mode.

Running a Program from the File System

If a file in the file list is an executable program (if its extension is .COM, .EXE, or .BAT), you can run it by moving the selection cursor to it (or moving the mouse pointer), and either pressing Enter or double-clicking with the mouse. An "open file" window will pop up, allowing you to specify any options or file names that the program needs. Pressing or clicking on Enter runs the program.

You can try this by finding one of your favorite programs in the file list and pressing Enter or double-clicking on the program name. When you have exited the program in the usual way, you will be returned to the File System screen.

You can also run an application program by opening one of its data files. To do this, press Enter or double-click on the file name. For this technique to work, you must have used the Associate function to associate an application program with a particular file extension. For example, .WKS can be associated with Lotus 1-2-3. For details on how to set this up, see the later discussion of the Associate function in the section "Selection from the File System Menu."

Getting a PC DOS Command Prompt

If you wish to use the traditional methods for working with files or running programs, you can press Shift-F9 at any of the shell's main screens. This option switches the system into text mode and provides a standard PC DOS prompt—the basic command line you saw in the Quick Primer. The facility for easy access to the standard prompt is useful when you need to perform PC DOS commands that are not presented as menu items in DOSSHELL—such as MODE or XCOPY. You can also run any program from the command prompt as usual, as long as there is enough memory. (Remember that the shell is still reserving some memory for itself.) When you are ready to return to DOSSHELL, type `exit` at the PC DOS prompt and then press Enter.

Creating a Custom Menu Selection

As you have seen, you can run programs either by selecting them in the File System or by getting a PC DOS prompt and typing the program's file name there. The easiest way to run applications, however, is for you to provide them as menu selections in the Main Group or another program group.

You should now be back at the Start Programs screen. If you are in the File System screen, use the Exit option from the action bar to return to Start Programs.

1. From the action bar, select "Program" and then "Add." (By now you should know how to select items, so the gory details will no longer be repeated.)

A box appears requesting information about the program to be installed (see Figure 4.10). This box is an example of a pop-up box that accepts data entry into several fields. You will find that these boxes are used to configure programs, groups, and other items that require extensive information. Use the Tab or Backtab keys to move among the fields, or use Enter to move to the next field. You can also click the mouse on a field to insert data in it.

Tip

Making Entries in Pop-up Boxes
If a field has solid ends, or brackets ([ ]) in text mode, you are limited to a fixed amount of space for entry. The Password field is an example here. The other data entry fields in this pop-up box have arrows (> in text mode) at the end. The arrow means that the fields will scroll as you enter data.

At this point you are ready to install your word processor or text editor. The example will use WordPerfect, but you can substitute the name and appropriate start-up command for another program.

2. DOSSHELL prompts you for a program title. Type a name that describes the program. In Figure 4.10, the name `Word Processor` is shown typed into the Title entry field.

```
 05-05-90              Start Programs                      4:24 pm
 Program  Group  Exit                                      F1=HELP
                           Main Group
              To select an item, use the up and down arrows.
          To start a program or display a new group, press Enter.

 Command Prompt
 File System            ┌──────── Add Program ────────┐
 Change Colors          │
 DOS Utilities...       │ Required
 WordPerfect            │  Title . . . . [Word Processor   →]
 dBASE IV               │  Commands  . . [wp /r            →]
 Lotus 1-2-3            │ Optional
                        │  Help text . . [This runs WordPerfect→]
                        │  Password  . . [_    ]
                        │
                        │ (Esc=Cancel) (F1=Help) (F2=Save)
                        └─────────────────────────────┘

 F10=Actions            Shift+F9=Command Prompt
```

Figure 4.10. ***Add Program box.***

Tip

Editing Text in Pop-up Boxes

Within a data entry field like the Title field shown in Figure 4.10, you can use the Left and Right Arrow keys to move the insertion point. If you want to insert characters in front of existing text, press the Insert key and type the new characters. Use the Delete key to delete existing characters that are no longer wanted.

3. Move to the Commands field. Here you give the actual command used to run the program from the command line. In the case of WordPerfect, the command `wp /r` is used. Note that you can add whatever command-line options the program ordinarily accepts. In this case, the `/r` option tells WordPerfect to use expanded memory.
4. Move to the Help text field. Here you enter the text that will be displayed if the user types F1 to ask for help.
5. You can also move to the Password field. In this example, no value was supplied for a password, so you are not asked for one.
6. Press or click on F2 to save the new program specifications.

You are now back at the Main Group screen. A new item with the name you have given (`Word Processor` in this example) appears at the end of the list of programs and groups in the Main Group. You can now select this application and run it in the same way as, for example, the File System menu.

Creating a New Program Group

Recall that several program groups can reside within the Main Group (see earlier Figure 4.2). You have just added the WordPerfect program (or another program of your own choice) to the Main Group. But suppose that you use your system for three different areas of activity: writing, database, and spreadsheet. The logical thing to do is to create three program groups within the Main Group, one for each area. This is easy to do. Adding a group requires information similar to that used for adding a program, as you will see in the following steps:

1. From the Group menu, select "Add."
2. Type a descriptive name for the group into the Title field.
3. In the Filename group, give the name of a data file that PC DOS will use to contain information about the group. DOSSHELL will create this file with the extension .MEU (for menu).
4. Type some descriptive text into the Help text field. This text should explain the purpose of the program group that you are installing.
5. Optionally, type a password into the Password field. The user will now have to enter a password to use the program group.
6. Press or click on F2 to save the new group.

Suppose that you've created a new program group called "Writing." It would be logical to have the word processor (such as WordPerfect in the example) in the Writing group rather than in the Main Group, which is cluttered with built-in programs like File System.

1. Select the program file "Word Processor" from the Main Group. Use the arrow keys to move the highlight over the name of the program, or click *once* with the mouse. (Don't press Enter or click twice—you want to select the program, not run it.)
2. Select "Copy" from the Program menu.
3. Select the new group "Writing." Press or click on F2. Your word processing program will now be copied to the Writing group.
4. Select "Delete" from the Program menu to remove the Writing program from the Main Group.

As you can see, you have the flexibility to set up menus for each kind of work you do. If several people use the system, each person could have his or her own menu by creating a group with the person's name as the title. If you wish, you could provide a password for each group so that only the rightful owner could access it.

Reference Guide to DOSSHELL Functions

Now that you've sampled DOSSHELL's functions, here is a concise description of all of the functions provided in the various DOSSHELL menus. These functions are also given in Table 4.2, which describes the various tasks and the steps needed to perform them with DOSSHELL.

The second column of Table 4.2 lists the steps involved in carrying out the functions. These steps can include

- **Menu items and submenu items**. For example, "Program/Start" means to select "Program" from the action bar in Start Programs and then select "Start" from the pull-down menu that appears. Items are given in the order in which you encounter them as you work your way down from the Start Programs screen.
- **Keystrokes**, such as F1. "Shift-F1" means that you hold down the Shift key and, while doing so, press the F1 key. "F1/F9" means that you press the F1 key, release it, and then press the F9 key.
- **Select instructions**. "Select" means to use the appropriate selection method (arrow keys, mouse, and so on) to select an appropriate item. Italics are used to distinguish selections that you make in a program or file list from items selected in the action bar or a pull-down menu.For example, *Select file name* means to select a file name from the list. Depending on the function you will be using, you may be able to select several files at once.

Table 4.2. *DOSSHELL Functions*

Function	Steps
Add a directory	Main Group/File System/File/Create Directory
Add a program group	Group/Add
Add a program to a group	*Select group*/Program/Add
Associate a data file with an application program	Main Group/File System/*Select file*/File/Associate
Back up a hard disk	Main Group/DOS Utilities/Backup Fixed Disk
Change a program group	Group/Change
Change colors used by the shell	Main Group/Change Colors
Change file attributes (hidden, etc.)	Main Group/File System/*Select file*/File/Change attribute
Change how a program is run	*Select Group/Select Program*/Program/Change
Change the name of a directory	Main Group/File System/*Select directory*/File/Rename
Change the name of a file	Main Group/File System/*Select file*/File/Rename
Change the order of programs in a program group	Group/Reorder
Command-line prompt	Shift-F9
Compare two disks	Main Group/DOS Utilities/Disk Compare
Confirm all file deletions	Main Group/File System/Options/File options/Confirm on Delete
Confirm all file replacements	Main Group/File System/Options/File options/Confirm on replace
Copy a disk to another disk	Main Group/DOS Utilities/Disk Copy
Copy a program to a group	Select Group/*Select program*/Program/Copy/*Select group*
Copy one or more files	Main Group/File System/Select Directory/*Select file(s)*/File/Copy

Table 4.2. ***(cont.)***

Function	Steps
Exit the shell	F3 or Exit/Exit shell
Format a disk	Main Group/DOS Utilities/Format
Help, context-sensitive	F1
Help, select a topic	F1/F11
Help, list important keys	F1/F9
List all files on disk, in file name order	Main Group/File System/Arrange/System file list
List files in current directory	Main Group/File System/Arrange/Single file list (this is the default)
List files in two directories at once	Main Group/File System/Arrange/Multiple file list
Make a file "archive" so that it will be backed up by BACKUP	Main Group/File System/File/Change attribute/*Select archive*
Make a file "hidden"	Main Group/File System/File/Change attribute/*Select hidden*
Make a file "read-only"	Main Group/File System/File/Change attribute/*Select read-only*
Move a file	Main Group/File System/*Select file*/File/Move
Print a file	Main Group/File System/*Select file*/File/Print
Remove a directory	Main Group/File System/*Select directory*/File/Delete
Remove a file	Main Group/File System/*Select file*/File/Delete
Remove a program from a group	Select Group/*Select program*/Program/Delete
Remove a program group	Group/Delete
Remove file selections	Main Group/File System/File/Deselect All
Restore from a backup disk	Main Group/DOS Utilities/Restore Fixed Disk
Run a program from command line	Shift + F9/*Type program name*/Enter
Run a program from File System	Main Group/File System/File/Open
Run a program from file list	Main Group/File System/*Select program file*/Enter or double-click on name
Run a program from a program group list	*Select group*/*Select title*/Enter or double-click on title
Select all files in file list	Main Group/File System/File/Select All
Select files across directories	Main Group/File System/Options/File options/Select Across Directories and *then select as usual*
Select files to be displayed by using wildcards	Main Group/File System/Options/Display options/*Use wildcards in name field*
Set date	Main Group/DOS Utilities/Set Date and Time
Set time	Main Group/DOS Utilities/Set Date and Time
Show information about selected file	Main Group/File System/*Select file*/Options/Show information

Table 4.2. *(cont.)*

Function	Steps
Sort files by date	Main Group/File System/Options/Display Options/Sort by date
Sort files by disk position	Main Group/File System/Options/Display Options/Sort by disk order
Sort files by extension	Main Group/File System/Options/Display Options/Sort by extension
Sort files by name	Main Group/File System/Options/Display Options/Sort by name (default)
Sort files by size	Main Group/File System/Options/Display Options/Sort by size
View contents of a file	Main Group/File System/*Select file*/File/View

Selections Available from the Start Programs Screen

The Start Programs screen is the first screen shown when the shell is started. It is also the highest-level screen: exiting from the File System screen returns you to the Start Programs screen. The Exit option on the Start Programs action bar exits the shell and gives you a standard PC DOS prompt.

Program Menu

Start Runs the program highlighted on the list of programs for the currently selected group. You can also run the selected program by pressing Enter while in the program list area. You can select and run a program in one step by double-clicking its name with the mouse. If the program has a password, you will be asked to supply it before the program is run.

Add Adds a program to the list for the currently selected group. The pop-up box has data entry fields for the following:

Title The descriptive title that you wish to assign to the program. The title can have up to 40 characters.

Commands The actual commands that run the program. At minimum you need the program's file name. You can include options and other file names, just as you would type them on the PC DOS command line. You can also include special commands to obtain more information from the user and otherwise customize the running of the program. These commands are discussed in the section "Customizing with Special Program Start-up Commands" found later in this chapter.

Help text Text that you want to be displayed when the user presses or selects F1 for help. Write this text to remind yourself or another user about important aspects of using the program. You can use up to 478 characters.

Password A password of up to 8 characters that the user must type before gaining access to the program. Note that the password isn't a heavy-duty security feature—it doesn't prevent users from executing the program outside DOSSHELL, or even from the PC DOS prompt within DOSSHELL. It only prevents the program from being run from the program list or Program/Start without the correct password. Once a password is assigned, it must be supplied before any of the other Program commands (Change, Delete, or Copy) can be used with that program.

Press F2 to save the completed program start-up specifications. The program will now appear on the list of programs for the current group.

Change Displays the same pop-up box as used for Add. It allows you to change any of the program start-up specifications. If the program has a password, you will be asked to type it first.

Delete Deletes the currently selected program from the program list for the current group. If the program has a password, you will be asked to type it first. This function does *not* actually remove the program from disk.

Copy Copies the currently selected program to another group. If the program has a password, you wil be asked to type it first. DOSSHELL then prompts you to select the group to which the program is to be copied. After selecting the group, press the F2 key or select the F2 box to copy the program to it. The program is not deleted from the old group; use **Delete** for this purpose.

Group Menu

Add Adds a group to the list of groups in the Main Group. The pop-up box has data entry fields for the following:

Title The descriptive title that you wish to assign to the group. You can use up to 37 characters.

Filename The file name for the group information file. Do not use an extension. DOSSHELL will create this file and supply the .MEU extension.

Help text Text that you want to be displayed when you or other users press or select F1 for help. This text can remind you and others about important aspects of using the group. You can use up to 478 characters.

Password A password of up to 8 characters that the user must type before gaining access to the group and running programs from its list. Note that the password provides only minimum security. It doesn't prevent users from executing programs in the group outside DOSSHELL, or even from executing programs at the PC DOS prompt within DOSSHELL. It only prevents the group from being accessed from the group list without the correct password. Once a password is assigned, it must be supplied before the Change or Delete commands can be used with that group.

Press F2 to save the completed Add Group specifications. The group will now appear on the list of groups for the Main Group.

Change Displays the same pop-up box as used for Add. It allows you to change any of the group specifications. If the group has a password, you will be asked to type it first.

Delete Deletes the currently selected group from the group list for the current group. If the group has a password, you will be asked to type it first. This function does *not* actually remove the group from the disk.

Reorder Changes the order in which groups or programs are listed in the Main Group, or the order in which programs are listed in another selected group. First, select the item you want to move; then select Group/Reorder. Use the selection cursor or mouse to indicate the item *after* which the moved item is to be placed, and press Enter. If you select the *first* item as your destination, the moved item will be placed *before* it. Also, you can move the item *before* the selected destination item by double-clicking on the destination with the mouse, rather than moving the cursor and pressing Enter.

Exit Menu

Exit shell Exits DOSSHELL and goes to the PC DOS prompt. To run the shell again, type `dosshell` at the PC DOS prompt.

Resume Start Programs Aborts your exit from the shell and returns you to the Start Programs screen.

Selections Available from the Main Group Screen

The following selections are always available when the Main Group screen is displayed. (The Main Group appears when the Start Programs screen is first accessed.) In addition to these built-in groups and programs, you may supply your own custom groups and programs by using the functions on the Program and Group menus.

DOS Utilities This is a built-in program group. When it is selected, the following program list is displayed:

Set Date and Time Executes the PC DOS DATE and TIME commands, and allows you to set a new system date and time. Note, however, that some systems require that you run a special utility to actually update the internal clock.

Disk Copy Runs the PC DOS DISKCOPY command, which allows you to copy the entire contents of one disk to another disk. The contents of the destination disk, if any, are lost.

Disk Compare Runs the PC DOS DISKCOMP command, which allows you to compare the contents of one disk with that of another disk. Reports any differences.

Backup Fixed Disk Runs the PC DOS BACKUP command, which enables you to copy all or part of the contents of your hard disk to multiple floppy disks.

Restore Fixed Disk Runs the PC DOS RESTORE command, which is used to copy files from a backup disk to your hard disk.

Format Runs the PC DOS FORMAT command, which is used to prepare a new disk for receiving data.

Note that you can press the F1 (Help) key to receive useful advice while running any of these commands. These commands, particularly BACKUP and FORMAT, have many options. For extensive discussion of these commands, see the appropriate entry in the Command Reference.

Change Colors Allows you to choose one of four sets of colors for the screen background and the various pop-up boxes. Use the Right Arrow or Left Arrow key to cycle through the selections. Press Enter to save the currently displayed color set, or press Esc to exit from the Change Colors menu without making a selection.

Command Prompt This program is in fact COMMAND.COM. When you select it, the screen will change to text mode and you will see the regular PC DOS prompt:

```
When ready to return to the DOS Shell, type EXIT then press enter.

IBM DOS Version 4
     (C)Copyright International Business Machines Corp 1981, 1988
     (C)Copyright Microsoft Corp 1981-1986

C:\DOS>
```

The message at the top of the screen (which is actually highlighted) reminds you to type `exit` when you are ready to return to the shell. While at the PC DOS prompt, you can type anything that can be entered on the regular command line, including PC DOS commands, other programs, or batch files. You can use this facility to run applications that have not been installed in the shell's menu system, or to run PC DOS commands (such as MODE or XCOPY) that are not accessible through the menus.

File System Runs a program that allows you to view and manipulate your files in a variety of ways. The File System is discussed next.

Selections Available from the File System

The options in the File System will be discussed in the order in which their menu selections appear in the action bar. Remember that each function appears as an item in the pull-down menu. For example, to select Associate Files, you would select "File" from the action bar and then "Associate" from the pull-down menu.

File Menu

The File menu bar selection provides functions for running programs and managing your files. Of particular interest is the Associate function. This function allows file extensions to be associated with a specified application that will be run automatically for these files. Selections on the File Menu also allow you to move files without having to copy and then delete them, and allow you to print, move, copy, or delete many files at once. In most cases, you must select one or more files from the file list area before selecting a function to work with them. (The Select All function on this menu allows you to select *all* the files in the file list.) When File is selected from the menu bar, the following functions are available on the pull-down menu:

Open (start) Runs a program. Before selecting this function, you must have selected a program from the file list. The pop-up box appears and gives the name of the program and any associated data file (see the following explanation of Associate). A cursor appears in the Options field. Type any options and/or data file names needed by the program, just as you would on the command line. Do not repeat the name of the program, however. Press or select Enter to run the program. When you have exited the program, you will be prompted to press Enter to return to the File System.

Print Prints the selected file(s) using the PC DOS PRINT command. For this function to be enabled, you must first run the PRINT command. Do this by using File/Open after selecting PRINT.EXE from your PC DOS directory, or by typing `print` from the PC DOS command line, or by using any other method for running programs. You can now print any selected file(s) for the rest of the session. For information on setup and options for the PRINT command, see the Command Reference.

Associate Allows you to associate a program with all files having a specified extension. First select the program from the file list and then select the Associate function. A pop-up box will ask you for the file extensions you wish to associate. Type just the extensions, without wildcards or periods. For example, having selected Lotus 1-2-3, you can select Associate and type `wks` in the Extensions field. The next pop-up queries whether you want a prompt box to ask for program options when the program is run. (See the documentation for your program to determine whether options might be needed.) Now, whenever you select a file with the .WKS extension from the file list (by highlighting and pressing Enter, or double-clicking with the mouse), the Lotus 1-2-3 program will be run with that file as the data file. In other words, the effect is the same as if you had typed `123 filename` on the command line. You can associate a total of 20 different extensions with programs. Of course, you can't associate the same extension with two different programs.

Move Moves the selected file, or files, to a destination directory. When the pop-up box appears, type the path (up to 63 characters) for the directory to which the file is to be moved. The current directory is shown initially. (For more on paths, see Chapter 6, "Managing Your Hard Disk.") The file is deleted from the original directory. In other words, Move combines the Copy and Delete functions. If you want a file to have a different name in the destination directory, add the desired file name to the destination path. Note that if you want to move multiple files to a directory, you should not specify a file name in the destination directory.

Copy Copies the selected file, or files, to a destination directory. When the pop-up appears, type the path (up to 63 characters) for the directory to which the file is to be copied. The current directory is shown initially. Unlike Move, Copy does not delete the original files. (For more on paths, see Chapter 6, "Managing Your Hard Disk.") If you want a file to have a different name in the destination directory, add the desired file name to the destination path. Note that if you want to copy several files to a directory, you should not specify a file name in the destination directory.

If you have previously selected "Select across Directories" from the Options/File menu, you can use the keyboard or mouse to specify both the source files and the destination directory. First, select the files to be copied from the file list. Next, move to the Directory Tree area and select the destination directory. Select "File/Copy," and the pop-up will show both the files to be copied and the destination directory. Press or select Enter to complete the copy. (The "Select across Directories" option is discussed later under the File/Options menu.)

Delete Deletes the selected files or directories. The first pop-up lists the files or directories that are to be deleted. Press or select Enter to continue. For each file, a pop-up asks whether you want to delete the file or skip the file and continue. (This prompting can be turned off; see the Start-up Options section.) Note that a directory cannot be deleted unless it is empty—does not contain any files or directories.

Rename Allows you to rename selected files or directories. This is handy, since renaming a directory cannot be accomplished with a regular PC DOS command. A pop-up appears for each file or directory selected. Type the new name *without* any path.

Change Attribute Allows you to change certain attributes (sometimes called "permissions") that determine what may be done with a file. The first pop-up asks whether you want to change the attributes for all selected files or change the files one at a time. The latter is useful if the files need to have different attributes. (In early versions of DOSSHELL, a bug causes this pop-up to appear even when only a single file has been selected.)

Next comes either one or a series of pop-ups, depending on your response to the previous question. The pop-up allows you to select one or more of the following three attributes (selecting the attribute means it should be set):

> **Hidden** The file will no longer appear in directory listings. This is the default for system files such as IBMDOS.COM and IBMBIO.COM.
>
> **Read Only** The file can no longer be changed or deleted.
>
> **Archive** The file is marked so that it will be automatically backed up the next time the BACKUP command is run.

View Permits you to view a selected file. Only a single file may be selected. The pop-up displays the text of the selected file. Use the PgUp and PgDn keys to scroll the display. Files to be viewed should be in straight ASCII text format, rather than binary (program) files or files in special word processing formats. (See Chapter 9, "Creating Text Files," for a discussion of ASCII files.)

Create Directory Creates a new subdirectory in the current directory. The pop-up prompts for the directory name. Since you cannot use paths, you must select the parent directory before selecting Create Directory.

Select All Selects all the files in the file list. Normally, you select files by using the selection cursor and space bar (or the mouse) in the file list window of the File System screen. This option provides a shortcut by selecting all the files in the file list window, including those not in the visible portion.

Deselect All De-selects all files in the file list. Normally, you can de-select a selected file by selecting it again, that is, by using the cursor and space bar again or by clicking with the mouse. This shortcut de-selects all files in the file list, including those not in the visible portion. If you use this option to remove any existing selections before you select files to be deleted, you will avoid inadvertent deletions.

Options Menu

The Options menu lets you control which files will be shown in the file list and how they will be sorted, and whether safety prompts will be used with potentially dangerous file options. You can also get a status report on the currently selected drive and directory.

Display Options This function has two parts, as shown in the pop-up in Figure 4.11. First, it allows you to use a name with wildcards to select files from the current directory to be shown in the file list. Second, it gives you control over the order in which the files in the file list will be displayed. In the example, the wildcard *.TXT was used so that all files in the currently selected directory (C:\) having the .TXT extension would appear in the file list. The Date option was then selected to sort them by date.

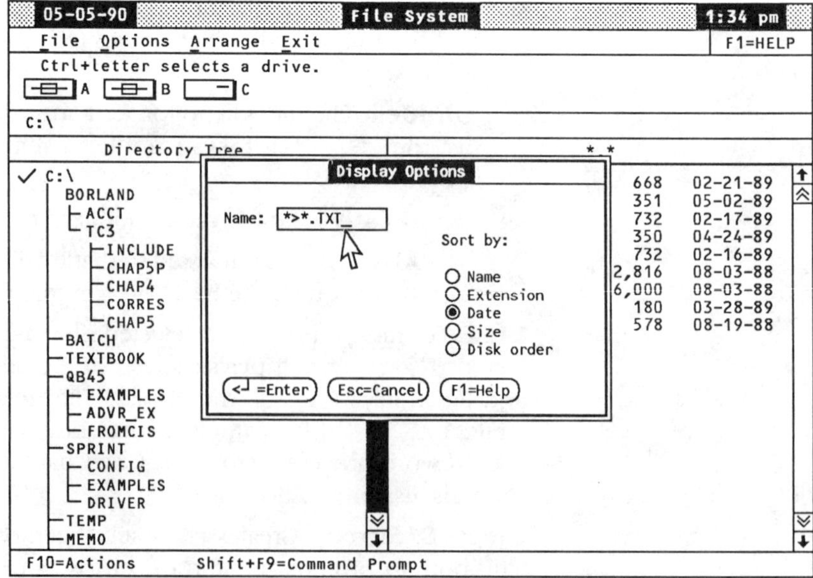

Figure 4.11. ***File Display Options box.***

Files can be sorted by

- **Name**. Alphabetical order by name (the default).
- **Extension**. Alphabetical order by extension. The files are not alphabetized by name within each extension group, however.
- **Date**. In order of date, from most recent to oldest. The date used is the date the file was created or last modified.
- **Size**. From largest (in number of bytes) to smallest.
- **Disk order**. The actual order in which the files appear on the disk. Note that sorting a large directory by this method can speed up shell operations with the files.

Files are sorted only in the buffers that the shell uses to keep track of directory and file information. The actual directory on disk is not affected by any of these operations.

Press or click on Enter to confirm the name selection and sorting option. Until you restart the shell or change the specifications, all file lists will be displayed in the way you selected, even if you select a different directory.

File Options Displays a pull-down menu with three items:

Confirm on Delete Selecting this option causes a pop-up to appear before any operation takes place that would delete a file. The pop-up allows you to either delete the file or abort the deletion and continue. This setting is turned on by default; you must turn it off during each session if you don't want to be prompted for deletions.

Confirm on Replace Selecting this option causes a pop-up to appear before any operation takes place that would replace an existing file (such as copying a file to a file of the same name). The pop-up allows you to either proceed with the operation and replace the existing file, or to abort the operation and continue. This setting is turned on by default; you must turn it off during each session if you don't want to be prompted for replacements.

Select across Directories Selecting this option allows you to select files on the file list for the currently selected directory, select a new directory, and continue selecting files on the new file list. By default, this setting is off, meaning that you lose all file selections when you select a new directory. As noted earlier under File/Copy, this option allows you to specify both the source and the destination for a copy without having to type path names.

Show Information Displays information about the currently selected file, drive, and directory. If you select the System File List display under the Arrange option, the Show Information display for the currently selected file is provided automatically at the left (see Figure 4.13 later on in this chapter). The following information is displayed:

The last file selected and its attributes (*a* is archive, *r* is read-only, *h* is hidden)

The currently selected drive

The number of files selected and their total size

The currently selected directory, the total number of files in it, and the total size of the files in the directory

The currently selected disk volume name, the total capacity of the disk, the total amount of unused storage, and the total number of files and directories on the disk

Arrange Lets you control how the file lists on the right side of the screen will be displayed. There are three selections:

Single File List Shows a single list of all files in the current directory (as modified by any display options set). This is the default that has been shown in the examples.

Multiple File List Shows two file lists, one for each of the two most recently selected directories. Figure 4.12 shows one use for this option. Here you can view the contents of the \TWG \PCDOSBIB\NOTES directory on drive C. Then, by selecting drive A and the NOTES directory, you can also display the list for A:\NOTES to see if you have backed up everything to the floppy.

System File List Shows every file on the selected disk (see Figure 4.13). This is useful because you can then use Options/Display Options, type the name of a file, and find the file regardless of where it is on the disk. Note that the Show Information display discussed earlier is automatically given for the last selected file.

When you next start the shell, the default Single File List is restored.

Exit Allows you to exit the File System. Selections are

Exit File System Leaves the file system and returns you to the Start Programs screen.

Resume File System Aborts the exit and returns you to the File System screen.

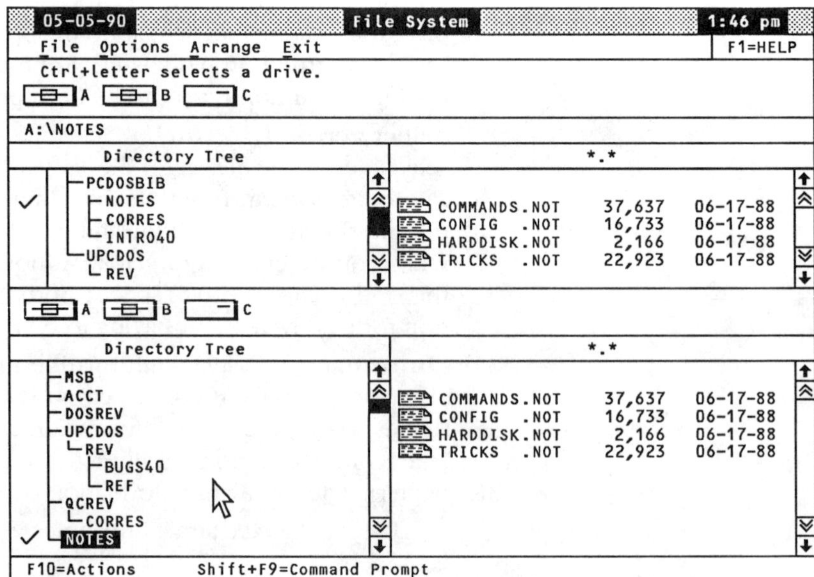

Figure 4.12. ***Multiple file lists.***

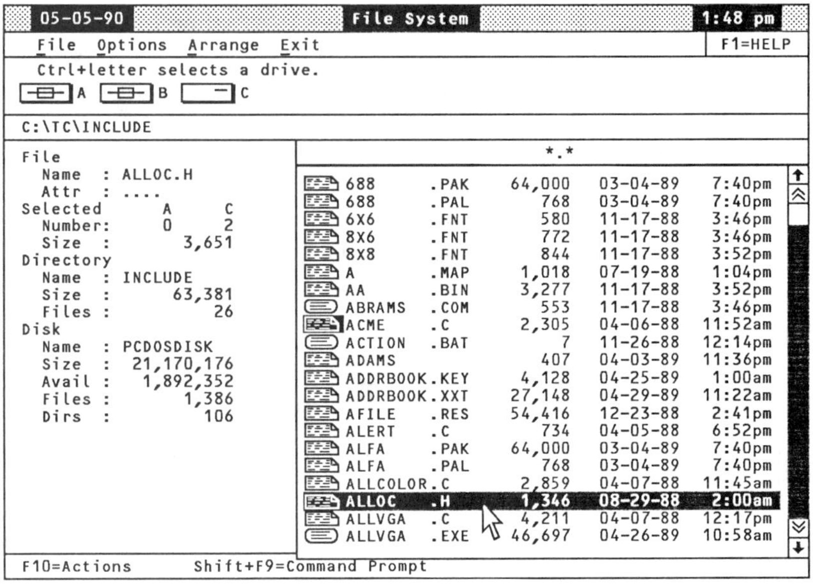

```
05-05-90                    File System                         1:48 pm
 File  Options  Arrange  Exit                                   F1=HELP
 Ctrl+letter selects a drive.
 A  B  C
C:\TC\INCLUDE
File                          *.*
  Name  : ALLOC.H          688      .PAK   64,000  03-04-89   7:40pm
  Attr  : ....             688      .PAL      768  03-04-89   7:40pm
Selected    A     C        6X6      .FNT      580  11-17-88   3:46pm
  Number:   0     2        8X6      .FNT      772  11-17-88   3:46pm
  Size  :      3,651       8X8      .FNT      844  11-17-88   3:52pm
Directory                  A        .MAP    1,018  07-19-88   1:04pm
  Name  : INCLUDE          AA       .BIN    3,277  11-17-88   3:52pm
  Size  :     63,381       ABRAMS   .COM      553  11-17-88   3:46pm
  Files :         26       ACME     .C      2,305  04-06-88  11:52am
Disk                       ACTION   .BAT        7  11-26-88  12:14pm
  Name  : PCDOSDISK        ADAMS              407  04-03-89  11:36pm
  Size  :  21,170,176      ADDRBOOK.KEY     4,128  04-25-89   1:00am
  Avail :   1,892,352      ADDRBOOK.XXT    27,148  04-29-89  11:22am
  Files :      1,386       AFILE    .RES   54,416  12-23-88   2:41pm
  Dirs  :        106       ALERT    .C        734  04-05-88   6:52pm
                           ALFA     .PAK   64,000  03-04-89   7:40pm
                           ALFA     .PAL      768  03-04-89   7:40pm
                           ALLCOLOR.C       2,859  04-07-88  11:45am
                           ALLOC    .H      1,346  08-29-88   2:00am
                           ALLVGA   .C      4,211  04-07-88  12:17pm
                           ALLVGA   .EXE   46,697  04-26-89  10:58am
F10=Actions        Shift+F9=Command Prompt
```

Figure 4.13. ***System file list.***

Customizing with Special Program Start Commands

Earlier, you learned how to add your own program to the program list for a group. To do so, you specified a descriptive title, commands, and, optionally, help text and a password. Such customizing is one of the special features of DOSSHELL. In fact, DOSSHELL allows you to add special Program Start Commands to the commands field so that you can control quite extensively how the user will interact with the program. You can ask the user for additional information (such as program options or file names). You can even use all of the batch file commands except GOTO. You can display a message (the ECHO command), pause for insertion of a disk (the PAUSE command), and so on. For more information on the use of batch file commands, see their entries in the Command Reference, and also refer to Chapter 10, "Batch Files."

The next two sections summarize the Program Start Commands and provide examples of how to use them.

Summary of Program Start Commands

This summary divides the special Program Start Commands into categories by function. Text in `monoface font`, such as commands that you enter, should be typed exactly as given. For example, `/T"` means to type a slash sign, a *T*, and double quotes. Note that you can use either uppercase or lowercase for the letter following the slash: `/T"` or `/t"`. Text in *`italic monoface`*, such as *`file name`*, signifies information you should provide. That is, you don't type the word "file name"; you type an actual file name.

The Prompt Panel: Getting Information from the User

The following command allows you to specify options or file names appropriate to your program. It does not in itself provide help text, but you can add help and descriptive information by using it and the other Program Start Commands.

[] Typing a set of brackets with no parameters causes the Program Parameters prompt panel, shown in Figure 4.14, to be displayed when the program is selected.

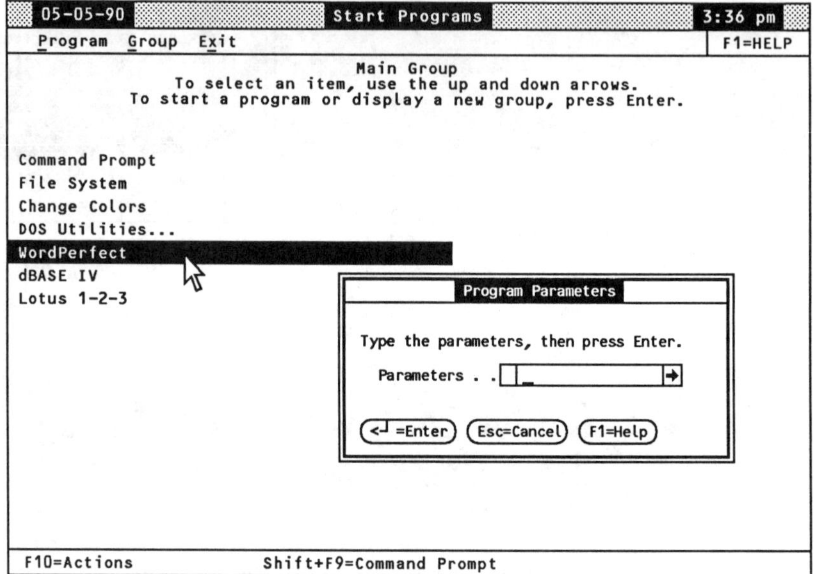

Figure 4.14. ***Program Parameters prompt panel.***

The next commands can be entered within one set of brackets in the Command field. They control the text displayed by the prompt panel and the way that the user can enter text at the prompts.

/T"*title text*" Adds a title to the prompt panel, for example, /T"Field Results Tabulation Program". The maximum length of the title is 40 characters.

/I"*instruction text*" Adds a brief instruction telling the user what information is requested, for example, /I"Enter name of file to be edited". The maximum length of the instruction is 40 characters.

/P"*prompt text*" Adds a prompt for the data entry area, for example, /P"Name:". The maximum length of the prompt is 20 characters.

/%*n* Saves what the user enters as a command-line parameter. For example, if you use /%1, your program or batch file can refer to the information entered by using the *%1* command-line parameter, as if it had been entered on the command line.

/D"*default value*" Displays the specified value in the data entry field as the default. When running the program, the user can change it by typing over it and deleting any remaining characters, for example, `/D"LOG.TXT"`. The maximum length of the default value is 40 characters.

`/D"%n"` Displays a default value previously entered as a parameter. For example, `/D"%2"` displays a previously entered value that was stored in the `%2` parameter.

`/R` Clears any default value if the user presses any key other than a cursor-movement or editing key.

`/L"length"` Sets the maximum length of the data entry field to fewer than 127 characters, which is the absolute maximum, for example, `/L"40"`.

`/M"e"` Allows only the names of existing files to be specified by the user. If a nonexistent file is specified, the user is given a message and the prompt panel is repeated.

`/C"%n"` Uses any existing value of the parameter specified. For example, `/C"%1"` allows the use of a file name specified earlier in the `%1` parameter.

`/F"file name"` Checks for the existence of the file whose name is specified.

Commands That Substitute Values

These commands must be entered outside of the brackets. They do not affect the prompt panel.

`%n` Uses a value that has been entered by the user. For example, `print %1` will print the file whose name was entered into the parameter `%1`.

`/#` Inserts into the stream of commands the drive letter of the drive from which the shell was started.

`/@` Inserts into the stream of commands the path from the root directory of the drive from which the shell was started, to the current directory.

Examples of Program Start Commands

When you enter commands in the command entry field on the Add Program (or Change Program) pop-up, you separate them by pressing the F4 key. This generates a double bar symbol (||). Do not use the Enter key. You can use up to 500 characters for the commands in the command field. The field will scroll as you type. In the following examples, some commands are shown on several lines, but you should type them as all one line in the command field. Where a double bar (||) is shown, press the F4 key.

Example 1. Change directory and run a program:

```
c:||cd \word||write
```

It is often convenient to change directories before running a program, especially if the program expects to find certain files in the current directory. To do this, add the CD command before the program name. Here, the current drive changes to C, the current directory changes to \WORD, and then the program WRITE is run.

Example 2. Display a default prompt box:

```
wp []
```

The program `wp` (WordPerfect) is run. The empty brackets ([ ]) specify that a default program prompt box be shown (Figure 4.14). The user can enter any desired options and file names into this box, and then press or click on Enter to run the program.

Example 3. Supply descriptive titles and help text:

```
wp /r [/T"Edit a document"/I"Enter name of existing file if any.
"/P"Filename:"]
```

The `/T` is followed by the text `Edit a document`, which will appear as the title of the program prompt box. The `/I` is followed by the text `Enter name of existing file if any.`, which will appear above the data entry field. Finally, the `/P` specifies that the prompt `Filename:` appear just before the data entry field. The complete program prompt box is shown in Figure 4.15.

Example 4. Add help text to the preceding example:

```
Run WordPerfect with the file you have specified. If you don't
specify a file, WordPerfect will be started with an empty file.
Exit WordPerfect normally to return to the shell.
```

The user types the desired text into the Help text field in the Add Program or

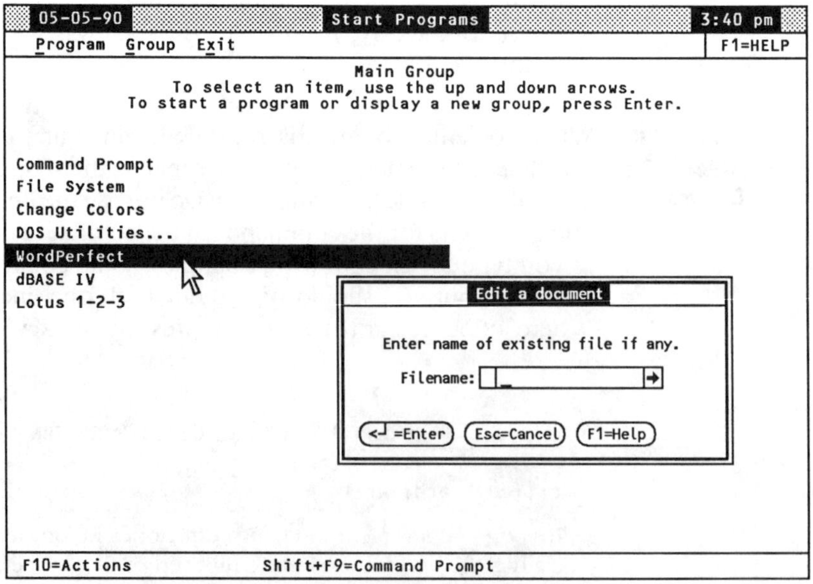

Figure 4.15. ***Program prompt box for Example 3.***

Change Program box. Again, this is a scrolling field, so type the desired text in a single line.

When the user runs the program, the program prompt box will pop up. If the user needs help and presses or selects F1, the pop-up help box, shown in Figure 4.16, will appear.

Example 5. Run a batch file before running the program:

```
call setup||dtp []
```

First, the batch file SETUP.BAT is run. This file can contain MODE commands, APPEND commands, graphics setup, loading of fonts, or whatever else is needed. Notice that the CALL command is used. This command causes execution to return to the current batch file (here, the series of program start-up commands) after the batch file SETUP.BAT has run. Always use CALL when running a batch file from a program start-up command list. (See the entry for CALL in the Command Reference.) Finally, a default program prompt box is presented, and the DTP (desktop publishing) program is run.

Example 6. Create an automatic time-logging system:

```
call start ||wp /r [%1]||call end %1
```

The idea behind this example is that you can capture the output of the PC DOS TIME command before and after running a particular program. This will make a record of how long the work session lasted, which might be useful for billing or tax purposes. Here the WordPerfect program will be run. The `[%1]` command does two things. First, the brackets specify the default program prompt so that the user can specify a file to edit. Second, the `%1` saves any file name that the user types in the prompt box into the parameter `%1`, where it can be used later.

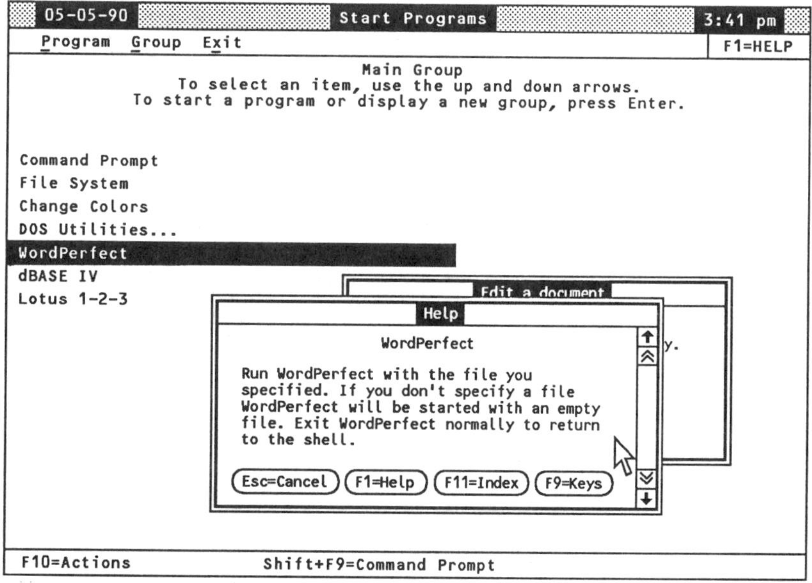

Figure 4.16. ***Custom help box.***

Before WordPerfect is run, the current time has to be saved into a file. Unfortunately, you can't just run the TIME command by itself, since this command not only displays the current time but also demands that a new time be typed in, or at least that the Enter key be pressed to keep the existing time.

How do you feed the Enter key-press to TIME within a batch file? One way is to create a file (called CR here) that consists of just a carriage return (equivalent to pressing Enter):

```
copy con: cr
                         ←press Enter
                         ←press F6 or Ctrl-Z
^Z
      1 file(s) copied
```

The file START.BAT does the time-stamping as follows:

```
@echo off
type cr | time >>log
```

The command `type cr | time >>log` sends the output of the TYPE command (the Enter keystroke in the CR file) to TIME. The TIME command displays the time, sees the Enter key, and exits. Finally, the redirection `>>log` puts the output (that is, the current time) into the LOG file, adding it to whatever is already there. (If there is no LOG file, that is all right—the file will be created for you.)

After the user exits WordPerfect, the ending time must be added to the LOG file. The batch file END.BAT is called upon to do this as follows:

```
@echo off
echo edited %1 >>log
echo session ended >>log
type cr | time >>log
echo ========== >>log
```

The line `echo edited %1 >>log` puts into the LOG file a message with the name of the file the user has edited (which had been stored in `%1`). Next, the command `type cr | time >>log` is again used to stamp the ending time into the LOG file. The final ECHO statement puts a line of = characters to space the entries in the LOG file. A complete entry to the LOG file looks like this:

```
Current time is  1:18:11.13p
Enter new time:
edited start.bat
session ended
Current time is  1:42:22.06p
Enter new time:
==========
```

While it would be nice to get rid entirely of the `Enter new time:` prompt from the TIME command, you still have a serviceable time logger. If you wish, you can add titles, prompts, and instructions within the bracketed part of the command, as was done in the earlier examples.

As you have seen, program start-up commands offer considerable power and flexibility for customizing: in the presentation of menus, in the way programs will be started, and in pre- and postprocessing for a user session. You can also customize many of DOSSHELL's own features. The next section will explain the DOSSHELL start-up options.

Configuring DOSSHELL Start-up Options

Earlier in this chapter you saw a listing of the file DOSSHELL.BAT, which runs the DOS shell. This file includes a number of start-up options, following the name `SHELLC`, that can preset characteristics of the shell. These characteristics include the display mode, how the shell will use memory and the disk, and which shell facilities will be made available to the user. When you install PC DOS 4 via the SELECT command, a screen appears, showing you the defaults for many of these options and allowing you to change them. Since you don't want to run SELECT (which does a complete PC DOS installation) every time you want to change a shell start-up option, you can instead pass options to the shell by including them in the line beginning `@SHELLC` in the DOSSHELL.BAT file. Here is a list of the DOSSHELL options, grouped by function.

Display Mode Options

The display mode options for the shell are text mode, three graphics modes, color mode, sound mode, and a date/time display. Note that during PC DOS installation the SELECT program automatically selects the highest resolution and largest number of colors allowed by your display hardware. However, by editing DOSSHELL.BAT, you can tell the shell to use a different mode, perhaps to accommodate a new video display.

`/text` Runs the shell in text mode. This can provide faster operation on slower machines (such as PC or XT clones). It can also provide easier access to some terminate-and-stay-resident (TSR) programs. Some TSR programs cannot be accessed from the shell in graphics mode, though you can get a text-mode command prompt (by selecting Command Prompt or pressing Shift-F9) and you can activate the TSR program from there.

`/co1` Runs the shell in 16-color EGA, 640 x 350 graphics (mode 10).

`/co2` Runs the shell in 2-color VGA, 640 x 480 graphics (mode 11).

`/co3` Runs the shell in 16-color VGA, 640 x 480 graphics (mode 12).

`/color` Allows you to use the Change Colors option while in the shell.

`/clr:`*`color settings file`* Identifies the name of the file containing your color setup selections. The default is SHELL.CLR.

`/snd` Activates the use of sound in the shell (for warnings or other purposes).

`/date` Maintains a date and time display in the shell.

Mouse Driver Options

The following options are used with the mouse driver:

`/mos`*`driver-name`* Identifies the mouse driver to be used by the shell. Several mouse drivers come with PC DOS 4. If possible, use either the Microsoft serial mouse (PCMSDRV.MOS), the Microsoft parallel mouse

(PCMSPDRV.MOS), or the IBM PS/2 mouse (PCIBMDRV.MOS). If you haven't installed your mouse yet or aren't sure which kind of mouse you have, see Chapter 12, "Installing a PC DOS System," for details.

`/com2` Allows a serial mouse to be used in the second serial port (COM2:) instead of the default COM1:.

`/lf` Sets up the mouse for left-hand use. This setting simply reverses the function of the two mouse buttons so that you click and double-click with the right instead of the left button.

Memory and Disk Use Options

The following options specify memory and disk use:

`/tran` Frees memory by running the shell in *transient mode*. This means that the shell will load from disk those parts of its program code that are needed, rather than keeping the program code in memory. This setting is recommended for hard disk users. Floppy-only users may wish to remove it so that the entire shell will remain in memory at all times. This technique eliminates disk swapping but uses a lot of memory, depending on shell configuration.

`/swap` Allows the shell to save the file system directory and file information to a disk file while running other commands or programs. This option speeds up performance by making recently used information continually accessible. It is recommended for hard disk systems.

`/b:`*`kilobytes`* Specifies the number of kilobytes of memory to be used for the shell's File System *buffer*—the space used to store your directory and file information for access in the Directory Tree and file list windows. If you are running the shell in resident mode or are otherwise short of memory, you may want to use this setting with a small number (for example, `/b:5`).

`/mul` Allows multiple directory and file buffers in the File System facility. This option improves performance, though at some cost in memory.

Controlling and Specifying Available Shell Options

These options can be used to make a restricted subset of shell functions available. They can prevent the user from exiting the shell level, for example. However, you should not consider them to be a full-fledged security system, since knowledgable users can easily get around the restrictions.

`/menu` Allows the Start Programs option in the shell.

`/meu:`*`menu-file`* Specifies the name of the file containing the Main Group structure for the Start Programs screen. The default is SHELL.MEU. Multiple menu configurations can be used for different nodes in a network.

`/maint` Allows changes to the menu structure displayed in the Start Programs screen.

`/dos` Allows use of the file system (file viewing, copying, deletion, etc.) in the shell.

`/prompt` Allows access from within the shell to the PC DOS command prompt.

Let DOSSHELL Work for You

As you have seen, DOSSHELL is a versatile interface that gives easy access to your files and programs and provides powerful housekeeping functions. In addition, DOSSHELL can provide a friendlier working environment for less-experienced users.

To make DOSSHELL work for you, start by setting up program groups based on your main work activities. Then install your favorite application programs with appropriate options. If other people also use the machine, you can set up groups and program lists for them. You can even use DOSSHELL on a network. (For a discussion of this, see the IBM manual *IBM Getting Started with Disk Operating System Version 4*, beginning with page 117.)

You will need to experiment with DOSSHELL in order to find its appropriate use in your work. Review the start-up options given earlier, and experiment to determine the trade-offs between the ease of use and the speed and efficiency of operation.

If you are an experienced user, you may find in the end that all the menus and boxes get in your way—so be it. You will still have learned how to provide greater ease of use for the casual or less experienced user. Reducing the intimidation factor in your workplace is no small thing.

What's Next

Chapter 5, "PC DOS Files," offers tricks and tips for creating and using files. Chapter 6, "Managing Your Hard Disk," contains a complete tutorial on using a hard disk. Chapter 10, "Batch Files," explains how to use batch files.

Key Concepts and Words

Before you read further, use the following list to test your understanding of the concepts and words in this chapter.

Shell	File System screen
Graphic interface	Main Group screen
Hierarchical menu system	Program Start commands
Start Programs screen	DOSSHELL customization

Chapter 5

Everything in PC DOS—commands, directories, operating system control data, everything!—is stored on disk and manipulated in memory as a file. If you understand the basics of files, a great deal of PC DOS becomes clear. This chapter defines files and their parts and uses simplified examples to illustrate how file-related commands work. You'll learn

- *How to create, organize, name, and rename files*
- *How to view a file's contents*
- *The differences among kinds of files—ASCII, binary, and program*
- *How to control access to files*
- *How to maximize file usage*

Chapter 5
PC DOS Files

PC DOS uses files to hold information. This includes everything from stray facts about schedules and your tax records to the programs that actually do the work on your PC. As a matter of fact, PC DOS itself is stored in files.

Computers, like humans, cannot keep track of all the information in the universe. For instance, humans keep as much as they can in their heads and go to the library to get the rest. Computers act in a similar manner. They can act only on information that resides in their memory (most PCs today have 640K of memory). This means that any other data your PC might want needs to be kept in storage somewhere else. The storage place is the disk, and the containers that hold the data are called *files*. With this in mind, it seems as though DOS, which stands for Disk Operating System, is not such a silly name after all.

DOS Shell

Command-Line Prompt

Most of the examples in this chapter are designed to be used at the command line. If you are running DOSSHELL, you can exit the shell by pressing F3 at the Start Programs screen—this gives you a PC DOS command-line prompt. Alternatively, you can get a command-line prompt from within DOSSHELL by pressing Shift-F9.

DOSSHELL techniques for performing some of the commands discussed in this chapter will be provided in inserts like this one.

A file in your PC DOS system has many of the characteristics its ancestors had, and still have. The ancestor of the file? Why, yes, the proverbial manila folder which is still prevalent in all but the most modernized offices. The manila paper folder and a computer file have characteristics in common. Both are named, and both are stored somewhere, ideally in some organized manner. Both can be created, opened, added to, deleted from, closed, hidden, destroyed, moved, copied, and archived. This little comparison is by no means exhaustive, but it does demonstrate that almost anything that can be done to a manila folder and its contents can also be done to a PC DOS file, only more efficiently.

Files and the Disk

When PC DOS stores a file on disk, or reads it from disk, it makes no difference what kind of file it is. From a storage point of view, each file is simply a sequence of bytes to be stored and retrieved.

Figure 5.1 depicts some PC DOS files. Note that each file is shown as a box. PC DOS, just like UPS, does not need to know what is in the box in order to do its work. PC DOS does not care: it treats all the boxes the same. What PC DOS does care about is the information represented by the stickers on the outsides of the boxes, such as the file names, date and time, and other statistics. Keep in mind this idea of files as boxes while you read about the characteristics of PC DOS files.

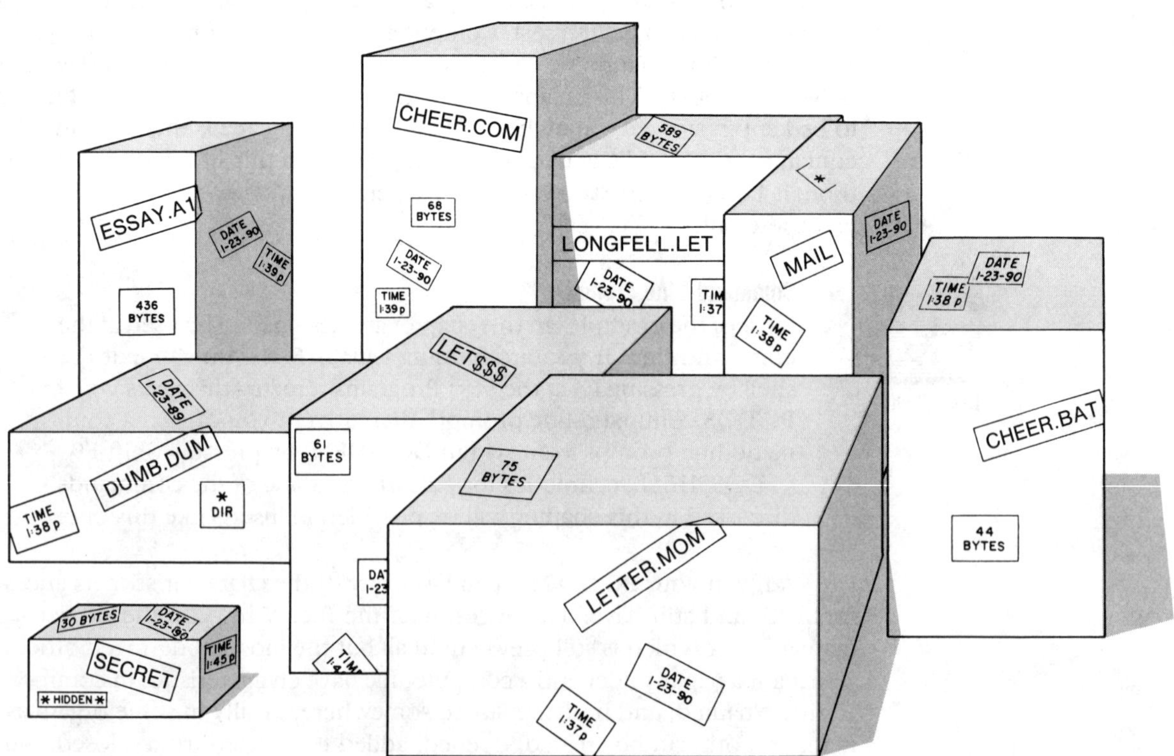

Figure 5.1. ***How PC DOS thinks of files.***

The contents of any file are not known until it is open. Some PC DOS commands will let you see the inside of a file, such as TYPE and MORE. Others, such as EDLIN, let you see the contents and also let you change them. The COPY command moves the files around, and the RENAME command simply changes the name-label on the outside of the file. Application programs (programs that are not part of PC DOS, such as Lotus, WordStar, etc.) can do many of the same things to files that PC DOS can.

As you read on, you should be able to come up with more similarities between files and boxes. Actually, some of them correspond quite accurately to the detailed workings of PC DOS, which is a good sign that there is not really any insurmountable mystery to the way your computer works.

Getting a Directory Listing

Recall from the Quick Primer that PC DOS uses the information on the "outside" of a file to help keep track of your files. One way to get a quick listing of this kind of information is to use the DIR command. The following is a typical output from a DIR command:

```
C:\>dir
 Volume in drive C is DISK1_VOL1
 Directory of  C:\
.               <DIR>      1-23-90    1:36p
..              <DIR>      1-23-90    1:36p
LETTER   MOM          75   1-23-90    1:37p
ESSAY    A1          436   1-23-90    1:39p
LET$$$                61   1-23-90    1:40p
LONGFELL LET         589   1-23-90    1:37p
DUMB     DUM    <DIR>      1-23-90    1:38p
MAIL            <DIR>      1-23-90    1:38p
CHEER    BAT          44   1-23-90    1:38p
CHEER    COM          68   1-23-90    1:39p
     10  File(s)  15873792 bytes free
```

The first two lines after the word `dir` are the standard header of any directory listing. They contain the disk volume label and the name of the directory containing the files listed. Every directory listing includes `.` and `..`. These are files also, but they are special subdirectory files (notice the `<DIR>`) and refer to the current directory and the parent subdirectory, respectively. Notice that the last line, which lists the number of `bytes free`, pertains to the entire C disk, not just the directory.

The first two columns are the file name and the extension. Since these are created by you, the user, the rules for creating them need to be covered. But first the other parts of the DIR listing will be explained.

The number to the left of the date column tells you exactly how many bytes each file contains. This number does not include the number of bytes for the information on the "outside" of the file; it refers only to the contents of the file.

The column that sometimes contains <DIR> is used to signify that the particular file name (DUMB.DUM in this case) is a subdirectory of the current directory. Note that if a file is a subdirectory, PC DOS will not tell you the length of the file, since the length of a subdirectory file does not have much meaning to anyone but PC DOS.

The date column and the time column to the right of it give you the time stamp of the file. The *time stamp* tells you when the file was last modified. Note that "modified" does not necessarily mean that the contents have changed, but only that the file has been written to. An example of changing the time stamp of a file, but not changing the contents of it, is loading a file into your editor (or word processor) and then immediately saving it by writing it back to disk before any changes are made.

DOS Shell

Selecting Directories and Files

When you are on the File System screen in DOSSHELL, the current Directory Tree structure is always shown in the left window. Select a directory by using the Up and Down Arrow keys and pressing Enter, or use the mouse and arrow boxes or scroll bar, and click once on the directory name. In the right window, you can see the list of files for the currently selected directory window. Use the Tab key to switch between the two windows, and scroll through the file list using the Up and Down Arrow keys. Select the currently highlighted file by pressing the space bar or use the mouse. Select "Show Information" from the Options menu to see a window containing more information about the selected file.

Caution

A Time Stamp Quirk

You might think that copying FILE1 to a brand new file FILE2 would change the date for FILE2, since FILE2 would be created anew. This is not the case, as you will see in the following example where the COPY command has been used to create a new file named LETTER.DAD:

```
C:\>dir letter.*
C:\>copy letter.mom letter.dad
C:\>dir letter.*

 Volume in drive C is DISK1_VOL1
 Directory of  C:\

.               <DIR>      1-23-90  12:33a
..              <DIR>      1-23-90  12:33a
LETTER    MOM         75   1-23-90   1:37p
LETTER    DAD         75   1-23-90   1:37p
      4 File(s)  19879936 bytes free
```

Observe that both files, LETTER.MOM and LETTER.DAD, have the same time stamp.

Rules for Naming Files

If you want to keep things organized in your filing system, you have to use meaningful names. The habits you develop in assigning names to files go a long way toward creating order (or chaos) on your disk.

The key points to consider when creating a file name are

- The number of characters allowable
- The characters themselves
- Potential conflicts with names reserved by PC DOS
- Any attributes that you would like assigned to the file (such as read-only, hidden, etc.—you will learn about these later)

How Long Can a File Name Be?

PC DOS permits you to give each file a name of up to 8 characters plus an optional 3-character extension. Looking back at the output of the DIR command in the previous example you can see that the first column of information is the file name and the second column is the file extension, if one is used. For now, think of the extension as another 3 characters that you can use to add to a file name. The upcoming section on organizing files will provide examples of efficient use of the extension. In this example, the third file, `LET$$$`, does not have an extension. Also, the second file, `ESSAY.A1`, has an extension of only 2 characters. Fine, no problem; these matters are up to the creator of the file.

Keep in mind that, although PC DOS requires you to use a period between your file name and extension when issuing commands, the output of the DIR command does not include any such period. The makers of PC DOS simply decided not to clutter the output of the DIR command with something that is taken for granted.

Which Characters Can You Use in File Names?

While you are looking at the DIR listing, consider what the allowable characters for making a file name are. In general, the legal characters are the letters of the alphabet, the numbers, and certain symbols. The symbols that you cannot use are

. " / \ [ ] : | < > + = ; , * ?

The reason these are illegal characters is that most of them already have a special meaning to PC DOS.

The following names are legal:

BOSS_1.MEM, 123.DAT, BOSS-2.MEM, 123.$$$

Some illegal names are

BOSS+1.MEM, 123:DAT, BOSS|2 MEM, 123....

Tip

Reminder
Do not forget that PC DOS converts all commands to uppercase letters. This means that letter.mom is the same as LETTER.MOM.

Make a Test Directory

The rest of the examples for this chapter will take place in a subdirectory called TEST. If you need to review subdirectories, go back to the Quick Primer or see the more detailed information in Chapter 6, "Managing Your Hard Disk."

```
C:\>md test
C:\>copy *.* test
C:\>cd test
```

DOS Shell

Creating a New Directory
To create a new directory, select "File System" from the Main Group on the Start Programs screen. Select "Create Directory" from the File menu. You will be prompted for the path of the new directory.

Tip

Making a Test Directory
Make your own test directory to test commands you aren't quite sure of. That way you can avoid wiping out data files with an errant command.

The File Name versus the File Specification

What good is a file name if you are never sure which file someone is talking about? Think of it this way: files, like people, have names. Like people, some files are given the same names. The phone book might list three Bill Sedgewicks, which is confusing. But, by looking at their addresses, you can keep separate the various Bill Sedgewicks. Files having the same names pose a similar dilemma. By knowing their addresses—or file specifications—you can tell PC DOS where to find them. In the next few sections you will see how PC DOS uses directories as addresses. This directory concept enables PC DOS to differentiate between files with the same name.

First you will be introduced to file names and the current directory, with a slight detour to talk about naming directories. Next will be some rules for specifying the exact whereabouts of a file.

Naming Files within a Directory

The *current directory* is the directory that PC DOS is currently in, or pointing to. If your prompt is set up to reflect the current directory (and it is for all the examples in this chapter), then you always know what your current directory is. Figure 5.2 shows a way to think of the TEST directory. This directory will be used for the rest of the examples in this chapter.

There are a number of things to point out in Figure 5.2. Notice the sign (C:\TEST) above the building. This is the complete file specification for the directory. On the outside wall of the building is a sign listing the contents of the building. By looking through the cutaway in the wall, you can see that the

Figure 5.2. ***A directory as a warehouse of files.***

boxes listed on the outside of the building physically exist within. Inside this building, all boxes must have different names; otherwise PC DOS will get confused. The following example illustrates how PC DOS reacts to an attempt to rename LETTER.MOM to the already existing file CHEER.BAT. C:\TEST is assumed to be the current directory.

```
C:\TEST>dir

 Volume in drive C is DISK1_VOL1
 Directory of  C:\TEST

.            <DIR>       1-23-90   1:36p
..           <DIR>       1-23-90   1:36p
LETTER   MOM           75  1-23-90   1:37p
ESSAY    A1           436  1-23-90   1:39p
LET$$$                 61  1-23-90   1:40p
LONGFELL LET          589  1-23-90   1:37p
DUMB     DUM  <DIR>        1-23-90   1:38p
MAIL          <DIR>        1-23-90   1:38p
CHEER    BAT           44  1-23-90   1:38p
CHEER    COM           68  1-23-90   1:39p
```

```
     10 File(s)  19873792 bytes free

C:\TEST>rename letter.mom cheer.bat
Duplicate file name or File not found
```

PC DOS prevents you from doing something that could lead to confusion—creating two files with the same name within the same directory.

DOS Shell

Renaming a File

To rename a file using DOSSHELL, select "File System" from the Main Group on the Start Programs screen. Then use the arrow keys and Enter key, or mouse in the left window, to select the directory containing the file to be renamed. Then use the arrow keys and space bar, or mouse in the right window, to select the file to be renamed from the file list. Finally, select "Rename" from the File menu, and follow the prompts.

Now look at Figure 5.2 again, and check out some more subtle points. Notice that the file SECRET is physically in the directory, even though it is not listed as such on the outside. This is because SECRET is a "hidden" file. *Hidden files* are exactly the same as other files except that their *hidden attribute* is set. You can think of the hidden attribute setting as one of the stickers on the outside of the file. When it is clear, it has no effect; when it is set, it instructs PC DOS not to display the file's name in a directory listing. In this way you can hide a file from the casual observer.

Another oddity in Figure 5.2 is that DUMB.DUM and MAIL are listed on the outside of the directory (with the 〈DIR〉 symbols where their byte sizes should be), but they are not boxes like the other files. Instead, they are shown as doors leading out of the TEST directory. Well, as you probably know from previous examples, DUMB.DUM and MAIL are each a subdirectory of TEST and as such are files that cannot be edited or modified by you except with the MD and RD commands.

Figure 5.2 shows a directory listing on the doors leading to the subdirectories. This listing shows how PC DOS can get the contents of the DUMB.DUM directory without having to physically go to the DUMB.DUM directory and look through the files one by one.

By the way, the reason for DUMB.DUM's name is that most people do not put extensions on their directories. And that can be a smart thing to do. If you don't use extensions, you can get an exclusive DIR listing of all subdirectories by issuing the DIR command as `dir *.`.

```
C:\TEST>dir *.

 Volume in drive C is DISK1_VOL1
 Directory of  C:\TEST

.            <DIR>       1-23-90   1:36p
..           <DIR>       1-23-90   1:36p
LET$$$            61     1-23-90   1:40p
```

```
MAIL          <DIR>      1-23-90   1:38p
     4 File(s)  19879936 bytes free
```

Notice that the preceding listing does not reflect the existence of the directory DUMB.DUM. However, if you had typed the command as `dir *.dum`, you would have seen only DUMB.DUM. So with this in mind, read the following tip.

Tip

Be Consistent!
There is nothing wrong with using an extension on a directory name as long as you are consistent (e.g., use ".DIR" for all directory extensions). If, however, you give your subdirectories random extensions, it is hard to use the DIR command to get a quick listing of a directory's subdirectories without distracting information filling the screen.

Finding the Path to a File

Now that you can handle file names within a directory, how about all those other directories? What about other drives (like the floppy drives)? No problem. PC DOS keeps track of all these things. Look at Figure 5.3. Notice how all the directories stem from the topmost directory, C:\. This type of arrangement is called a *tree*. Directories conform to an upside-down tree structure with the root of the tree at C:\. In fact, many people call "C:\" the *top* of the (disk) drive, or the *root directory*. Because of the letter *C*, you know that this is an example of a hard disk, but the example applies equally to your *A* floppy drive. Just change C:\ in the figure to A:\.

PC DOS uses the concept of a path to find a file. *Path* refers to the route you take to get from the root directory to the file in question. Although you as a person do not walk around in your hard drive, PC DOS does. For example, if, in Figure 5.3, you wanted to copy the file FINANCE.WKS, located in directory C:\TEST\ACCOUNTS, to a floppy in the A drive, PC DOS would have to start by looking at the contents of C:\. After it found a subdirectory named TEST, it would then look through the contents of TEST for a subdirectory of TEST called ACCOUNTS. After finding ACCOUNTS, PC DOS would see if FINANCE.WKS existed within ACCOUNTS. This tortuous trail that PC DOS followed in tracking down the long file name C:\TEST\ACCOUNTS \FINANCE.WKS is called the path of FINANCE.WKS.

Besides being important to PC DOS, the concept of a path is also important to human beings. Pretend you have a file named FINANCE.WKS in the ACCOUNTS directory shown in Figure 5.3. You want to tell your friend Bert how to get a copy of FINANCE.WKS. You cannot just say, "Bert, copy my FINANCE.WKS file." Bert will look at you and say, "Where is it?" When you reply, "It's in my ACCOUNTS directory," Bert won't change his expression. He'll say "That's great, but where is your ACCOUNTS directory?" Do you get the drift? Bert does not want to spend all day poking around on your machine, trying to find out which disk drives and which directories contain FINANCE.WKS. And what if you have this file in two different directories? How does Bert know that he found the right one? What you really need to do is tell Bert exactly where the file is—give him the path. This means three items: the drive letter, any and all subdirectories involved, and the file name and extension. The complete path or file specification is as follows:

Drive letter	C:
Subdirectories that are traversed	\TEST\ACCOUNTS
File name	FINANCE.WKS

Now Bert can get the file you are talking about. Keep in mind that you could have a file called FINANCE.WKS in every directory on your C drive and Bert, given the complete file specification, would still have grabbed the right one. This is the beauty of a file specification.

Finding a File

In DOSSHELL, you can find a file anywhere on a disk, regardless of the current directory. Select "File System" from the Main Group on the Start Programs screen. Next, select the Arrange menu, and select the System file list. A list of all files on the current drive will be shown in the right window. Select "Display Options" from the Options menu. Type a file name in the Name: field in the pop-up window. You can use the * and ? wildcard characters. All files matching your specification will be listed in the right window. You can now select options from the File menu to perform functions such as renaming or copying files.

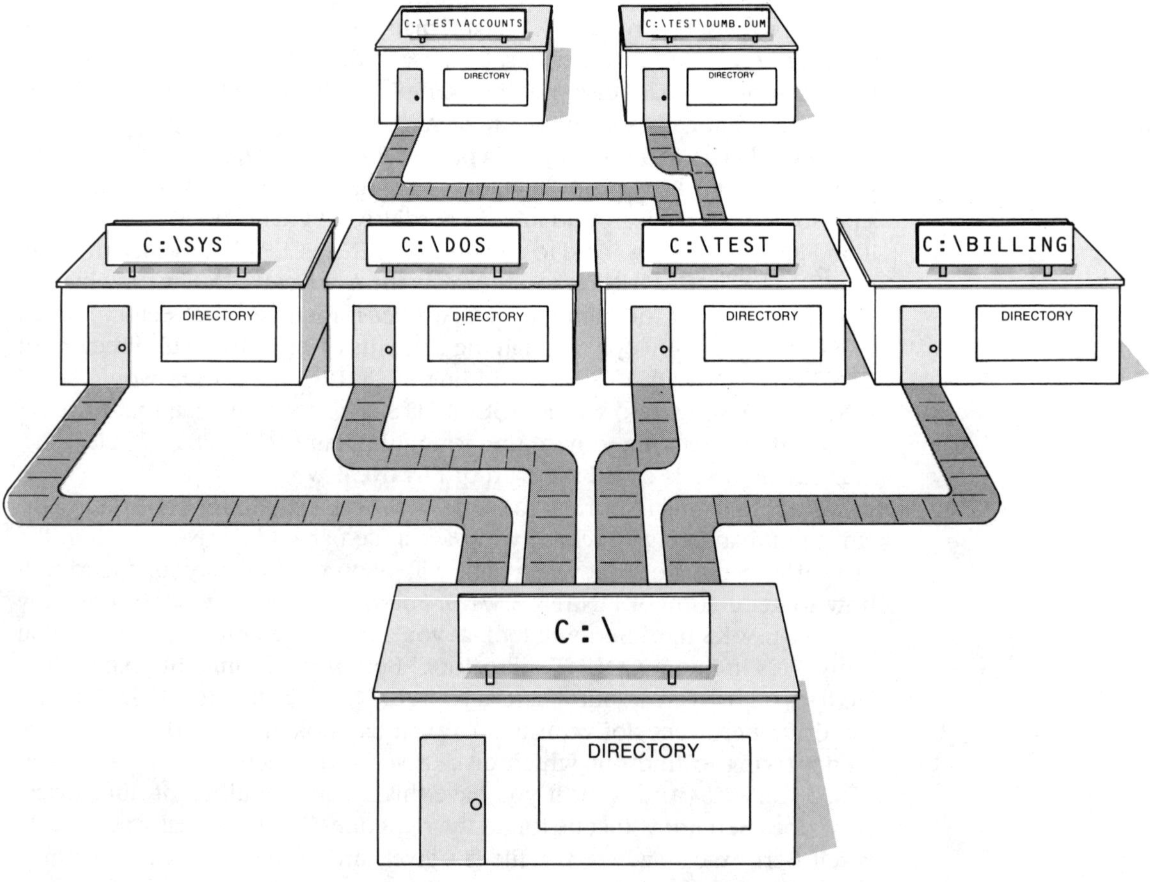

Figure 5.3. ***Some PC DOS directories.***

The 63-Byte Limit

For you fans of subdirectories, here is something to keep in mind. Because of the way PC DOS remembers file specifications, PC DOS is incapable of keeping track of a specification more than 63 bytes long. Remember the drawing earlier in this chapter (Figure 5.2) showing a warehouse with boxes inside and a billboard on the roof? The billboard is where the file specification is stored, and it is what cannot hold a specification longer than 63 characters. This includes the file names, the extensions, the dots in-between, and the backslashes. The sum total of the file specification cannot be over 63. Remember this limit when you name subdirectories.

Avoid Error Messages: Use the Rules Correctly

Now that you know the rules for file-naming, you can check out the following examples. The first one concerns the case of an invalid parameter and the second one involves an uncaring PC DOS.

The Case of an Invalid Parameter

Remember how the DIR command's output omits the period before the extension? This little quirk can be used as an example of how PC DOS thinks and how certain error messages can occur. What if you had a lot of files and you wanted only to check on the date for LETTER.MOM? A way to do this would be to type `dir letter.mom`. In the following listing, the first DIR is entered correctly, and the second one is missing a period between the file name and its extension.

```
C:\TEST>dir letter.mom

 Volume in drive C is DISK1_VOL1
 Directory of  C:\TEST

LETTER    MOM  75   1-23-90   1:37p
       1 File(s)  19873792 bytes free

C:\TEST>dir letter mom
Invalid parameter
```

This is a good example of how PC DOS responds to commands in general, and how and why PC DOS might send error messages back to you. Suppose you type `dir test/p`. PC DOS grabs the first word on the line and tries to match it against its list of PC DOS commands. It finds `dir` and then makes a managerial decision. PC DOS gives control to the program that handles the DIR stuff, and it also gives this program the rest of the words on the command line. This makes sense because the DIR program needs to know which files are being looked for and which parameters apply. *Parameters* are the mnemonics that tell a command to act a special way. For instance, the first part of the command, `dir test`, tells PC DOS to look for a file or subdirectory named TEST. The `/p` parameter says to pause after each screen-full of output.

When PC DOS gave `letter mom` to the DIR program, the DIR program thought that `letter` was the file name to be listed and that `mom` was a parameter telling DIR how to do its job. This is when the problems happened. DIR looked at `mom` and tried to match it with its list of parameters. When it could not find a match, it sent you the message `Invalid parameter`, and then it aborted the entire DIR operation.

When PC DOS Does Not Care

Take a look at the directory listing for LONGFELL.LET, which presumably is a letter to a certain Mr. Longfellow.

```
C:\TEST>dir longfellow.let

 Volume in drive C is DISK1_VOL1
 Directory of  C:\TEST

LONGFELL  LET  589  1-23-90   1:37p
       1 File(s)  19873792 bytes free
```

PC DOS ignores all letters past the first eight of a file name. It also ignores all letters past the first three of a file name's extension. You can play with this little phenomenon yourself by trying such things as

```
C:\TEST>dir longfelloweldersta tesmanandscholaratlarge.letter
```

Device Names Reserved by PC DOS

Certain file names have a special meaning to PC DOS. These are the PC DOS *device names*. Devices are hardware items like printers, modems, the screen, the keyboard, etc. "Doesn't PC DOS know the difference between a piece of hardware and a file on a disk?" you may ask. The problem has to do with operating system design. For purposes of writing and reading to the hardware, it is easier for PC DOS to pretend that a piece of hardware is a file. You can "open" a modem, "write" to it, "read" from it, and, when your file transfer is done, "close" the modem. In this way, the modem is thought of as a file, and the same parts of PC DOS that deal with files on disk can be used to deal with modems and printers and such. There is more to it than this, of course, but that is the general idea.

To get back to your question, the reason PC DOS device names should not be used for just any disk file name is that PC DOS thinks of devices as files and consequently is on the lookout for certain file names corresponding to the actual hardware on your computer. This does not mean that you can never use these device names with a PC DOS command. Just remember that when you give a command like `copy con: letter.irs`, there is no file named `CON:`. Instead, you are sending the output of the keyboard into the file LETTER.IRS. Table 5.1 shows the device names reserved by PC DOS.

Device names can come in handy when strange things happen. Say, for instance, you have just returned from vacation and find that someone has changed the way your computer is set up. Your disk is hopelessly disorganized, and your PATH is also all wrong. You need to print a file called

Table 5.1. *Reserved Device Names*

Device Name	Description
CON:	Stands for console and refers to the screen or the keyboard, depending on whether it is an output device or an input device, respectively. If CON: is used as an input device, all input will come from the keyboard until an end-of-file (EOF) mark is entered. To enter an EOF, press F6 and the Enter key, or press Ctrl-Z and the Enter key.
AUX: or COM1:	Refers to the first asynchronous communications port, COM1. Can be used as an input or an output device.
COM2:	Refers to the second asynchronous communications port. Can be used only as an input or an output device.
LPT1: or PRN:	Refers to the first parallel printer port. Can be used only as an output device.
LPT2: and LPT3:	Refers to the second and the third parallel printers, respectively. Like LPT1:, these can be used only as output devices.
NUL:	Refers to a nonexistent device, thought of as a dummy device. The dummy device can be used to send unneeded screen output to a non-existent file. This will speed up the program that is running, since the output will bypass the screen. It is almost always faster to write to a file than you can write to the screen or console.

SUM.OUT, and you do not have time to straighten out your mess. When you enter the PRINT command, PC DOS does not recognize it.

```
C:\>print sum.out
Bad command or file name
```

Now, if you have been paying attention, you know that this error message means one of two things. Either the PRINT program (PRINT.COM) is actually missing on your disk, or your PATH is no longer correct. Instead of panicking, you could simply TYPE the file and redirect its output to the device LPT1:. You type `type sum.out > lpt1:`. This is a handy solution to a common office scenario.

Creating and Organizing Files

This section explains how files are created by PC DOS and application programs, and then it illustrates some common approaches to organizing a sample filing system.

In general, a file is created with the following points in mind. Under the supervision of PC DOS, a program desiring to create a file asks PC DOS to check on such details as the legality of the file name and whether that file name is already being used. Then the program asks PC DOS to find an unused spot for the file on the disk. The program writes to the file. When the program has finished writing, it closes the file. If these actions occur in an orderly fashion, the file will reside on your disk and will show up later when you use the DIR command.

What if things do not proceed so routinely? PC DOS will send you error messages. Don't be afraid of error messages; they are only trying to give you helpful information. They are messengers from PC DOS to you. In the next examples you will see some of the more common error messages from PC DOS.

Creating Files

PC DOS commands are quite capable of creating files. Usually, people fill up more of the disk with the COPY command than with the other PC DOS commands combined. The standard output redirection symbol (>) is also good at creating files.

It is assumed that you know how to use the COPY command and that you are familiar with the concept of redirection. If not, read the entry for the COPY command in Part 3, the Command Reference, and also read Chapter 8, "Advanced Use of the Command Line," for details about the redirection operators.

Creating a File with the COPY Command

Suppose that you have a floppy in the A drive that contains a number of files, all of which you want to copy to C:\TEST, which is also your current directory. Suppose also that C:\TEST already has some files in it. Assuming your current directory is C:\TEST, the command that you decide to use is `copy a:*.*`, since you know that it is shorter to type than the equivalent command `copy a:*.* c:\test`.

But first you ask yourself, "What are the implications of such a COPY maneuver?" Glad you asked . . .

Caution

A Fundamental Rule

Most commands that create new file names on the disk follow this fundamental rule: If the target file (the file you are copying to) does not exist, it is created. If the target file does exist, it is overwritten. File destruction goes hand in hand with file creation.

DOS Shell

Moving a File

DOSSHELL allows you to move a file without having to copy it and then delete the original. To move a file, select "File System" from the Main Group on the Start Programs screen. In the left window, select the directory containing the file to be moved, using the arrow keys and Enter key, or the mouse. Then select the file from the file list in the right window, using the arrow keys and space bar, or the mouse. Finally, select "Move" from the File menu. You will be prompted for the path and name for the destination.

By default, DOSSHELL warns you if a copy or move operation would replace an existing file. You are asked whether you want to continue with the operation. You can turn off this warning and confirmation by selecting "Options" from the File System main menu, and then selecting "Confirm on Delete" or "Confirm on Replace." Selecting these features when they are on will turn them off, and vice versa.

The following listing shows the files on the floppy and then the contents of the C:\TEST directory before and after the COPY operation:

```
C:\TEST>dir a:

 Volume in drive A is FLOPPY
 Directory of  A:\

ADRIAN          68  11-15-89 4:33p
LETTER   MOM   334  11-15-89 4:34p
FRANK           79  11-15-89 4:34p
     3 File(s)  1212416 bytes free

C:\TEST>dir

 Volume in drive C is DISK1_VOL1
 Directory of  C:\TEST

.               <DIR>      1-23-90   1:36p
..              <DIR>      1-23-90   1:36p
LETTER    MOM         75   1-23-90   1:37p
ESSAY     A1         436   1-23-90   1:39p
LET$$$                61   1-23-90   1:40p
LONGFELL  LET        589   1-23-90   1:37p
DUMB      DUM   <DIR>      1-23-90   1:38p
MAIL            <DIR>      1-23-90   1:38p
CHEER     BAT         44   1-23-90   1:38p
CHEER     COM         68   1-23-90   1:39p
    10 File(s)  19873792 bytes free

C:\TEST>copy a:*.*
C:\TEST>dir

 Volume in drive C is DISK1_VOL1
 Directory of  C:\TEST

.               <DIR>        1-23-90  1:36p
..              <DIR>        1-23-90  1:36p
LETTER    MOM          334  11-15-89  4:34p
ESSAY     A1           436   1-23-90  1:39p
LET$$$                  61   1-23-90  1:40p
LONGFELL  LET          589   1-23-90  1:37p
DUMB DUM        <DIR>        1-23-90  1:38p
MAIL            <DIR>        1-23-90  1:38p
CHEER     BAT           44   1-23-90  1:38p
CHEER     COM           68   1-23-90  1:39p
ADRIAN                  68  11-15-89  4:33p
FRANK                   79  11-15-89  4:34p
       12 File(s)   19671040 bytes free
```

Notice how the file LETTER.MOM already existed in the C:\TEST directory before the COPY operation. You can see that A:\LETTER.MOM overwrote it by observing that the file size of C:\TEST\LETTER.MOM and its date are different before and after the files were copied from drive A. On the other hand, the files FRANK and ADRIAN did not exist in C:\TEST (the target directory) before the copy operation and so were created by the COPY command.

Caution

A Double-Edged Sword
This example of COPY operation was not meant to be very tough, but it does illustrate the whole idea behind file creation and its flip side—file destruction. In short, the command `copy a:*.*` saw that LETTER.MOM already existed within the C:\TEST directory and so it had no other choice but to overwrite it with A:\LETTER.MOM—which is file destruction.

Creating a File by Redirection

As a general rule, any command that sends output to the screen can be made to redirect this output into a file. If you use the > symbol, PC DOS will create or overwrite the file name. In file creation, the > operator behaves like the COPY command.

If the >> symbol is used, then PC DOS simply appends the output to an existing file, or creates a new file if one does not exist. An easy example is

```
DIR *.* > DIR.LST
```

Here, the output from the DIR command is sent to DIR.LST. If DIR.LST did not exist, it would be created. If it already existed, it would be overwritten. This is another example of the double-edged sword of file creation/file destruction. (If you are interested in more details about redirection, see Chapter 8, "Advanced Use of the Command Line.")

Renaming Is Not Creating

The RENAME command seems at first to work like the COPY command. But it does not. The RENAME command simply manipulates the stickers on the outside of the file. The contents of the file do not even enter into the picture. This is fine, since who wants to wait while PC DOS copies FILEA to FILEB and then deletes FILEA? The bad news is that the RENAME command will not rename FILEA to FILEB if FILEB already exists. Also, RENAME won't let you rename a file to a file name in another directory. Observe the next few attempts at doing things the RENAME command is not meant to do.

```
C:\TEST>rename essay.a1 letter
Duplicate filename or File not found
C:\TEST>rename essay.a1 c:\essay.a2
Invalid number of parameters
C:\TEST>rename dumb.dum smart
Duplicate filename or File not found
```

Managing Files Created by Application Programs

Although all programs are different, and it is hard to mention anything but the generalities, file creation by programs other than PC DOS should not be ignored. You as a user can only strive to become as familiar as possible with the programs you use. After using a program for a while, it is easier for you to estimate the size of the data files you are creating. For example, after working with Lotus 1-2-3 for a time, you can accurately guess how big a particular spreadsheet is likely to be when you save it (write it out to the disk).

So why do you care? Besides being a conscientious PC user, you need to know these things for the day a program tries to write to a file when the disk is full. Some programs (the well-written ones) will report this condition to you, but others will say nothing while trying to store more bytes onto a full disk. One way to tell whether the latter is happening is to observe whether your program is taking forever to finish. The disk light may be blinking but nothing will be happening in your program. You need to stop the program (use the program's Cancel key if there is one, or press Ctrl-Break, or reboot only if all else fails) and then delete some files to make room for what you want to do.

Tip

When Your Disk Is Full
Should you find yourself in a disk-full situation, here is a tip that may help. If you know the names of some of the files on the full disk and you know that you no longer need them, save the file you are trying to save under the name of one of these outdated files. That way you do not have to exit to PC DOS, delete some unwanted files, and then go back into your program and save the file again. Just remember the name you used so that you can rename the file later.

Organizing Files

Think of a directory as a dresser drawer. Do people buy dressers with just one drawer or with many drawers? And how many drawers are too many? If you are a knick-knack kind of person, you cannot have too many directories. File organization, like most attempts at tidiness, is a personal thing. Although directories are usually your main method of organizing, much can be achieved towards the same goal by using file name extensions efficiently. This helps when you have a lot of files in your directory but do not want to make another subdirectory. Perhaps you are already so far down in your directory hierarchy that the prompt is halfway across the command line, as in `C:\CORRESP\FAMILY\COUSIN\ROBBIE>`.

You may be surprised to discover that strategies for organizing files on floppy and hard disks differ (see Chapters 6 and 7). Here in this chapter you can look at basic techniques for organizing your files and directories, but be sure to see the other chapters for specific recommendations, depending on which type of disk—floppy or hard—you are using.

Basically, the idea is simple enough; just keep similar things together. For example, assume you are in charge of a software consulting company and have three programmers working for you. Their names are Bill, Jenny, and Lou. Each time one of them finishes a job, you send an invoice to the client. Assume also that you would like to keep track of which person on the programming staff did the work, who is being billed, and which billing notice is being sent.

This section will show two ways to organize the above scenario, one by using several directories, and the other by careful choices of file names and extensions within a single directory.

Organizing Files into Directories

One way to organize these files using multiple directories is to create a separate directory for each programmer, and then a subdirectory for each company that the programmer worked for. Figure 5.4 shows this type of arrangement.

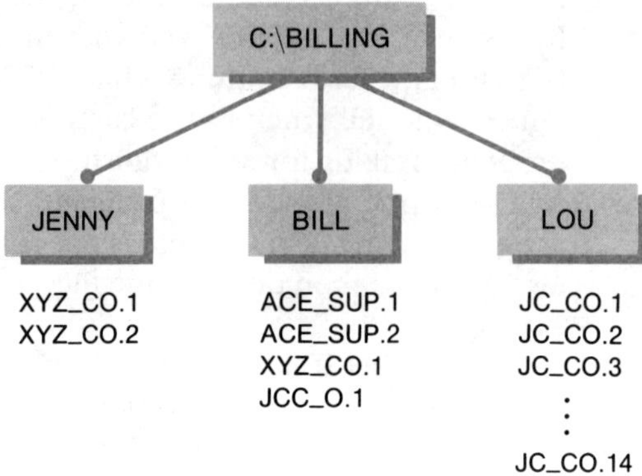

Figure 5.4. ***The directory solution.***

While you may find it frustrating sometimes to navigate the extra directories, this approach does not require that you be very disciplined when you give files their names. For instance, all you need to embed in the file name is the name of the company. The file extension is used for the billing number.

Organizing Files by Using Extensions

This approach requires more thinking on your part. Figure 5.5 shows a solution using file extensions. In Figure 5.5, you can see that these file names hold more information than their Figure 5.4 counterparts. If you wanted to see all of Jenny's bills, you would use

```
C:\BILLING>dir j*.*
```

Figure 5.5. ***The extension solution.***

If you wanted to see Lou's first nine bills, you would use

```
C:\BILLNG>dir l*.00*
```

Note, however, what would happen if the file name extensions were not padded with zeros. For example, if `L_JC.001` were `L_JC.1`, you could not get Lou's bills so neatly, since the command `dir l*.1*` would list all of Lou's files, not just the first nine. Or what about adding another person named Jake? Then you would have to decide how to tell his files from Jenny's. Things like that.

This is a good example of how you need to be a little more careful with your file names when you throw them all in one directory.

How PC DOS, Programs, and Data Interact

This section discusses the different kinds of PC DOS files. How many different kinds of files are there? Not too many, though at times it can seem as though there is a different kind of file for every office guru in corporate America. As usual, it boils down to how you look at things. If you look at files from the disk's point of view, they all behave pretty much the same. If you consider the effect a file has on the computer as a whole, "program" files definitely act differently from "data" files. On the other hand, if you judge a file only by what it does when you TYPE it on the screen, that's another category. The rest of this section will more fully examine files from these different perspectives.

ASCII versus Binary Files

There has always been much misunderstanding among computer users over the difference between *ASCII* files (sometimes called text-only files) and *binary* files (the ones with the 0s and the 1s). Is an ASCII (American Standard Code for Information Interchange) file something that comes out as text when you TYPE it? Is a binary file something that produces incomprehensible characters on the screen when you use the TYPE command to see what it contains? Roughly speaking, this is how most people would define the difference between the two types of files, and, as a rule of thumb, it works out all right. However, the difference between ASCII and binary files is not so straightforward. As usual, with "naming" problems, the crux of the issue lies in the definition of the terms involved.

From the beginning then: The computer sees everything as a stream of bits. A *bit* can be either a 1 or a 0, that is, binary. A *byte* is a group of 8 bits and so can be thought of as a binary number. A *file* is simply a sequence of bytes. From this standpoint, all files are really binary files. So why don't you see 1s and 0s when you TYPE a file? One reason is that no one could make any sense out of an endless stream of 1s and 0s. Humans want to see letters and decimal-based numbers. This is why the set of ASCII codes was created. ASCII refers to a special set of codes that translates binary numbers into printable characters that users can read. For more information about ASCII files, see Chapter 9, "Creating Text Files."

Figure 5.6 shows the TYPE command as a box with a window through which you can view the insides of a file. The TYPE command shows only the

ASCII representations of the file. When you use the TYPE command, as in the following example, the program that is invoked to type the file reads each byte of CHEER.BAT. Each byte is a binary number, and the program finds the ASCII character representing that number. Then this character is output to the screen. Thus, an ASCII file contains text that appears on the screen in a meaningful way.

```
C:\TEST>type cheer.bat
```

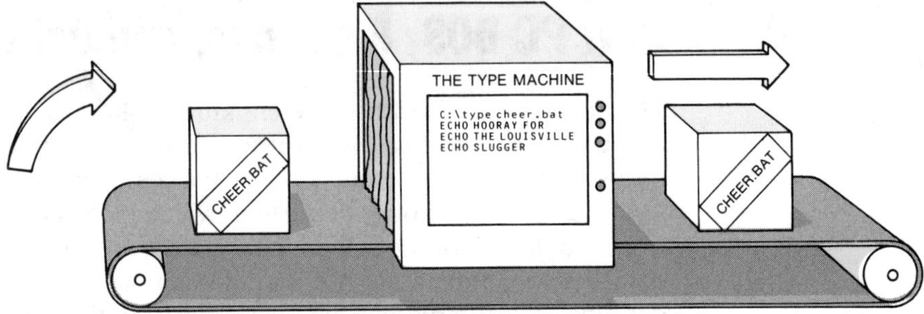

Figure 5.6. ***TYPEing an ASCII file.***

Now, what about binary files? Most people have typed an executable file (one that ends in .EXE) at some point in their life and know that the screen display looks like garbage. Figure 5.7 shows the same TYPE command converting the contents of CHEER.COM into its ASCII representation.

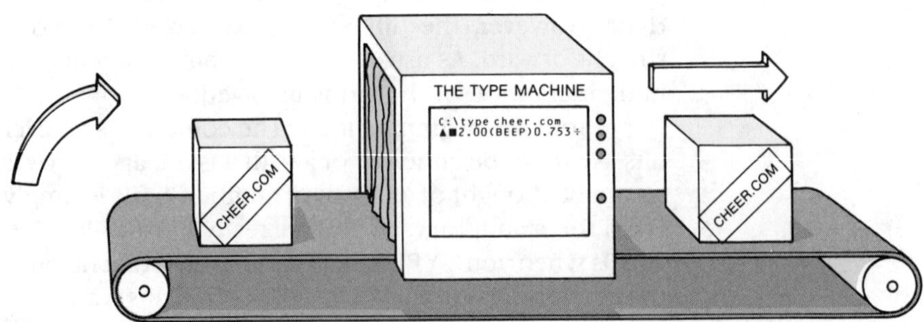

Figure 5.7. ***TYPEing a binary file.***

The way the TYPE command works is to convert each byte of a file into its ASCII equivalent. Byte values less than 32 represent control characters.

Those between 32 and 127 represent punctuation, numerals, and alphabetic characters (the characters of the typewriter keyboard). Those from 127 to 255 represent various graphic and other special characters. The bytes in an executable file were never intended for such a conversion. Rather, they represent instruction codes for the microprocessor chip in the machine.

DOS Shell

Viewing a File

To view a file while using DOSSHELL, select "File System" from the Main Group on the Start Programs screen. In the left window, select the directory containing the file to be viewed, using the arrow keys and Enter key, or the mouse. Then select the file from the file list in the right window, using the arrow keys and space bar, or the mouse. Finally, select "View" from the File menu. The file is shown on a full-screen display, and you can use the PgUp and PgDn keys to scroll back and forth through it, which you can't do with the TYPE command. Binary files are displayed as the equivalent ASCII characters where possible. You can also press the F9 key to switch between ASCII and hexadecimal formats.

Famous ASCII and Binary Files

Probably the most common ASCII (or text) file is AUTOEXEC.BAT. It is usually present on the boot disk. It is always pure ASCII.

Common binary files are the external PC DOS commands that come with your version of PC DOS. This includes files like FORMAT.COM, BACKUP.COM, SORT.EXE, JOIN.EXE, MODE.COM, MORE.COM, etc.

Other System Files

You will run across files with the .SYS extension. These files contain programs called *device drivers*. Device drivers help PC DOS send commands to the screen, a disk drive, a mouse, or other device. For example, ANSI.SYS allows programs or batch files to control the screen appearance and to redefine keys on the keyboard.

Another extension you might see is .CPI, which stands for *code page information*. It is used to support foreign language character sets. See Chapter 13, "International Language Support," for details.

Some users move the .SYS and .CPI files into a separate directory to reduce clutter in the DOS directory. If you do this, be sure to change any paths for these files in your CONFIG.SYS and AUTOEXEC.BAT files so that they reflect the new location.

Other extensions you might encounter are .CHK and .LOG. The CHKDSK command sometimes saves orphaned disk clusters as files, giving them a file name of a four-digit number with a .CHK extension.

The BACKUP command uses a default file name of BACKUP.LOG for the names of backed-up files (although you can override this default and use another file name of your choice).

Program Files

The purpose of this discussion of program files is to give you an idea of what happens when you tell PC DOS to run a program and of how file extensions come into play. Recall that PC DOS is really a program. If you wanted to, you could write your own program to boot up in place of PC DOS. The point is that, although PC DOS runs the hardware, it is stored in files just like everything else. So how do other programs run with PC-DOS? When you type 123 at the keyboard, you are telling PC DOS to run another program that basically will elbow PC DOS aside and take over your computer.

This situation is analogous to having a pilot named PC DOS. You get into your Lear Jet and tell PC DOS that you want your friend, Lotus 1-2-3, to fly the plane. PC DOS does not mind; it has no ego. So it moves over to the copilot seat and tells 1-2-3 to take the controls. Lotus 1-2-3 gets into the captain's chair and takes off. Keep in mind that PC DOS hasn't bailed out of the plane; it is still there to help 1-2-3 fly the plane. The bottom line, however, is that whoever (or whatever) is in the captain's chair has ultimate control over the flight. If 1-2-3 makes a serious error, there is nothing that PC DOS can do to prevent a crash. What usually happens, of course, is that 1-2-3 successfully takes you where you want to go and then relinquishes control of the computer to PC DOS. You are now responsible for giving instructions to PC DOS.

Anyway, back to the facts. PC DOS recognizes three types of program files. To keep things straight, PC DOS requires that there be a particular extension for each type. These extensions are .EXE, .COM, and .BAT. Of course, you can give any name you want to any file—within the legal limits—but if you want PC DOS to recognize your programs and batch files for what they are, you need to give them the proper extension.

As a user, you will be concerned mostly with .BAT files. Programmers are the ones who create .COM and .EXE files, and they know the rules for giving their programs the proper extensions.

In any case, PC DOS searches for the commands with these extensions in the following order: .COM, .EXE, and .BAT. What? Who said anything about PC DOS searching for anything? Suppose you had a batch file named PRINT.BAT. How does PC DOS decide whether to run your batch file or its own PRINT.COM? The rules for these kinds of decisions have to do with the PATH command and the search path.

It is time to digress a bit and talk about this "search path." Then you can continue to review the different program files.

How PC DOS Executes Commands

When you want to run a program or batch file, you simply type the name of the file at the PC DOS prompt. The extension is not needed. This brings up a question. If PC DOS demands that all program files have one of the three previously mentioned file name extensions, then why don't you have to include the extension at the command line? Anytime you type something at the PC DOS prompt and press Enter, PC DOS checks the first word of the command against its list of internal commands (CD, COPY, DIR, and so forth). If PC DOS cannot find a match, it decides that the command refers to a program or a batch file.

Setting a Path for PC DOS to Follow

At this point, PC DOS needs to find a file with one of the three aforementioned extensions (.COM, .EXE, and .BAT). Does PC-DOS look through all the files on your disk? That could take longer than you probably want to spend. Instead, PC DOS encourages you to be organized. By putting all your programs in a few selected directories, you can run any of them from any directory simply by setting the PATH variable to a list of your program directories.

Pretend you have a directory called C:\TEST2 and that this directory holds only two files. The first file, CHEER.BAT, is a batch file containing a cheer for the Louisville Slugger. The second file is a letter to a company that makes laundry detergent. Suppose you type the DIR command `dir cheer.*` to get a directory listing of all the files named CHEER:

```
C:\TEST2>dir cheer.*

 Volume in drive C is DISK1_VOL1
 Directory of  C:\TEST2

.            <DIR>      11-27-89  12:33a
..           <DIR>      11-27-89  12:33a
CHEER     BAT        44   1-23-90   1:38p
CHEER     LET        28  12-22-89   6:16p
     4 File(s)  19720192 bytes free

C:\TEST2\cheer
```

PC DOS performs the following tasks. First, PC DOS looks for a PC DOS command that is named CHEER. There is no PC DOS CHEER command (if you do not believe this, look through your PC DOS manual). Upon this discovery, PC DOS assumes that CHEER is a program that you want to run. PC DOS then looks for CHEER.COM in the current directory. If it cannot find CHEER.COM, it looks for CHEER.EXE. If it cannot find CHEER.EXE, it looks for CHEER.BAT. Upon finding CHEER.BAT, it executes the commands within the batch file, one at a time, until it hits the end.

If PC DOS cannot find the proper file name in the current directory, it performs a similar search through all the other directories specified in PATH. The following example sets the path variable to two directories: C:\DOS and C:\BIN. Notice that a semicolon separates each two paths on the command line.

```
C:\>path c:\dos;c:\bin
```

Now, if PC DOS decides that a command is not an internal PC DOS command, and the command cannot be found in the current directory, PC DOS will go through the same kind of .COM, .EXE, and .BAT search in each of the directories specified in the PATH command.

If you want to see what the PATH variable is currently set to, simply use the SET command, or the PATH command with no arguments. If you would like to set the PATH variable to nothing, type `path;`. Here are some examples:

```
C:\TEST>path c:\dos;c:\bin
C:\TEST>path
PATH=C:\DOS;C:\BIN
C:\TEST>set
COMSPEC=C:\COMMAND.COM
PROMPT=$p$g
PATH=C:\DOS;C:\BIN
```

```
C:\TEST>path;
C:\TEST>path
No Path
```

Notice that the SET command reports on the environment, of which the PATH and PROMPT variables (set by the PATH and PROMPT commands) are a part.

Caution

The Right Order
The order of the directories in the PATH command is very important. PC DOS searches the directories just as they are entered—from left to right. In the preceding example, C:\DOS would be searched before C:\BIN.

Executable Files: .COM and .EXE Files

Both .COM and .EXE files contain instructions for the CPU of your computer. Neither acts very civilized when being TYPEd or PRINTed, which indicates that you cannot edit them without a special binary editor. Both of these files are binary files. Besides the fact that PC DOS will look for the .COM file first, the differences between a .COM and an .EXE file are of concern only to programmers. In general, though, .COM files are smaller than their equivalent .EXE cousins. They are also a little quicker at getting started when they are loaded into memory (remember the captain's chair?).

Tip

Editing Binary Files
PC DOS provides a utility program called *DEBUG*, which you can use to edit binary (program) files if you are careful. See Chapter 11, "Customizing Your System."

Batch Files

A *batch file* is simply a text file containing PC DOS commands. The contents of a batch file are generally the same sort of PC DOS commands that you yourself might type at the PC DOS prompt. Another property of batch, or .BAT, files is that they are ASCII files. This refers to the fact that they can be edited, TYPEd, or PRINTed. You can find out more about .BAT files in Chapter 10, "Batch Files."

A Famous .BAT File (AUTOEXEC.BAT)

The AUTOEXEC.BAT file is no different than any other .BAT file except that PC DOS looks for it in the boot directory (usually C:\ if you have a hard disk), and if it finds the file, it executes it before giving you the prompt. This is why the AUTOEXEC.BAT file is the ideal place for such commands as `prompt $p$g`. (Chapter 11, "Customizing Your System," will show you how to set up your own AUTOEXEC.BAT file.)

Tip

Start-up Files: CONFIG.SYS and AUTOEXEC.BAT
When you boot up PC DOS on your machine, PC DOS follows a standard boot procedure before giving you the PC DOS prompt. Basically, PC DOS reads special files: the CONFIG.SYS and AUTOEXEC.BAT files. This chapter will not go into details on how

to set up and use these two files. That information can be found in Chapters 11 and 12.

Freedom of Extension versus PC DOS Abuse

Recall that PC DOS follows a particular order in searching for commands with extensions. For example, if a file name such as DBASE is used as a command, PC DOS looks for DBASE.COM, then DBASE.EXE, and finally DBASE.BAT. As soon as PC DOS finds something, it uses the extension to tell it whether to load the file in memory for the CPU (DBASE.COM and DBASE.EXE) or to interpret the file command-by-command (DBASE.BAT).

As mentioned before, you are free to give any file any extension you wish. This means that you can give any file a .COM, .EXE, or .BAT file extension whether it needs it or not. PC DOS doesn't care. Be advised, however, that this is not a good idea. The reason for avoiding such a practice is simply that PC DOS believes what you tell it. Thus, if you rename LETTER.MOM to LETTER.BAT and then type the next command shown, the computer will find LETTER.BAT and then start spitting `bad command or filename` at you for each carriage return or line feed in the file. The computer thinks that LETTER.BAT is a bona fide batch file with bona fide batch commands, as opposed to a letter to your mom.

```
C:\TEST>letter
```

To take such abuse one step further, copy LETTER.BAT into a LETTER.EXE file. Then, if you are prepared to reboot your machine, type the next command (if you don't want to reboot, just follow along):

```
C:\TEST\letter
```

The reason your machine froze is that PC DOS found LETTER.EXE in addition to LETTER.BAT. Since .EXE files take priority, PC DOS thought you wanted it to run LETTER.EXE. Now wait, there's one more consideration. Since the chosen file name extension was .EXE, PC DOS made the additional assumption that LETTER.EXE was a binary file fit for delivering straight to the CPU, rather than the batch file it really was.

.COM Files Come First

What would happen if you replaced AUTOEXEC.BAT (in the root directory) with AUTOEXEC.COM, and then rebooted your machine? (Be sure to copy a legitimate .COM file into AUTOEXEC.COM, or AUTOEXEC.COM will not be a proper .COM file and will freeze the machine.) As it turns out, PC DOS is apparently smart enough to insist on AUTOEXEC.BAT during the boot sequence, regardless of what other AUTOEXEC.* file names there are. But once the boot process is over, PC DOS always looks for the .COM (and takes it, if it is there).

When would you need to know this type of information? Admittedly, not too often, but sometime you may find yourself in a directory with a large number of files in it, trying to run a program that you know is in the directory. Instead of the program you want to run, you discover that a strange program is running. What you might not know, however, is that buried in the directory is another program with the same name, but a different extension. Knowing that PC DOS chooses a file with a .COM extension over other files may help you figure out the problem of the strange program.

Files Used by Programs—Data Files

There is not much mystery about a data file. A data file is simply a collection of data. It is important to realize that a data file associated with one program is not going to mean much to another program. This is because data files created by commercial software packages are set up to solve a particular programming problem, and the solution that each programmer comes up with is, to some degree, a personal issue.

A particular program's data file extensions become the earmark of that program. Typically, a commercial program will try to control the extension and let the user dictate the name of a file (the first 8 characters). For instance, dBASE programs use .DBF as the recognized extension to identify dBASE data files. Most other commercial programs have similar file extensions that you should avoid when creating your own file names and extensions.

Examples of Mixed Data Files

Some files are pure ASCII, or *text* files. Others are *binary* files containing codes that aren't meant to be meaningful to the average PC user. In between these two types is a third type—*mixed* files, files that are combinations of the two extremes. These types of files, which are often produced by commercial programs, are not readily classified as either ASCII or binary.

An example of a mixed file is a dBASE .DBF file. Each .DBF file has a header containing the field information, followed by the actual data to be stored in the file. When you TYPE the file, the field information comes out first, quite possibly making beeping noises; then the data comes out on the screen. Since dBASE stores all data in ASCII form, this data is readable if you know what you are looking for. Of course, to make sure, you should run the dBASE program and view the .DBF file from within dBASE.

For example, the many word processors on the market today employ different schemes for storing their documents. Each word processor must keep track of how to format, to highlight, to print, etc., a document. This information can be kept in a separate file, can be embedded within the document itself, or can be placed in a group at the beginning or end of a document. In practice, all of these techniques are used among the different word processing packages. If, for some reason, you wanted to guess at how a word processor stored its information, you could TYPE one of its files. If a lot of binary gibberish is displayed at the beginning of the file, and then the file settles down to plain ASCII, a header is probably being used.

Tip

Shared Formats

Many commercial programs have the capability to "export" and "import" files in formats other than their native one. Many word processors can convert files from and to the formats of other popular word processors. (There are also stand-alone conversion programs that you can buy.) Many spreadsheet programs understand the Lotus 1-2-3 format, since 1-2-3 is an industry standard. Likewise, many database programs can read or create dBASE files. Others can create files in a text format with the data items separated by commas. These files can be read by other programs and converted to their own format. You may have to read carefully the documentation for two programs in order to find out which formats, if any, they have in common.

File Attributes

The term *file attributes* refers to certain properties of a file. As a casual user, you do not have to worry about the attributes of a file. However, a time may come when you need to know how to set and/or reset file attributes to suit your needs. Before looking through the file attributes listed in Table 5.2, keep in mind that the majority of attributes are accessible only through a programming language, and that depending on your version of PC DOS, only one or two may be manipulated from the PC DOS prompt. These two PC DOS prompt-accessible attributes are: for PC DOS 3.0 and above, the *read-only* attribute; and for PC DOS 3.2, the *archive* attribute. Use the PC DOS command ATTRIB to view these attributes or set them.

Table 5.2. ***PC DOS File Attributes***

Attribute	Description (Attribute Is "On")
Read-only	File cannot be erased.
Hidden	File is excluded from *normal* directory searches (*normal* means the DIR command). Many file utility packages such as Norton Utilities have the ability to manipulate hidden files.
System	File is a system file, such as those used to boot the system.
Volume label	Tells PC DOS that the file name is to be used as a disk drive volume label. Consequently, the file name won't show up with the DIR command.
Subdirectory	File refers to a subdirectory and contains directory information for that particular subdirectory.
Archive	File has been opened and closed. Can be used by file archival systems to see if a file needs backing up. This implies that after a file has been backed up, the backup program would reset the file's archive attributes to "off," or to 0. That way the file won't be backed up again unless it has been opened and closed in the meantime.

Here is a simple example of using the ATTRIB command to make a file read-only. A read-only file cannot be deleted or copied. For more information about file attributes, see Chapter 6, "Managing Your Hard Disk."

```
C:\TEST>attrib +r letter.mom
C:\TEST>del letter.mom
```

Setting File Attributes

To set file attributes from DOSSHELL, first select "File System" from the Main Group on the Start Programs screen. Next, select the file by using the directory and file list windows. Select "Change Attribute" from the File menu. Then select the attribute you want to set: hidden, read only, or archive.

What's Next

Chapter 6, "Managing Your Hard Disk," discusses managing hard disks with multimegabyte capacities. Chapter 7, "All About Floppy Disks," shows how to use floppy disks. Chapter 9, "Creating Text Files," explains text files. Chapter 10, "Batch Files," shows how to use batch files.

Key Concepts and Words

Before you read further, use the following list to test your understanding of the concepts and words in this chapter.

Hierarchical directory system	ASCII and binary files
Paths	File attributes
File names	Devices as files
Path names	Reserved device names
Data files	File name extensions
Program files	Parameters
Start-up files	File specifications

Chapter 6

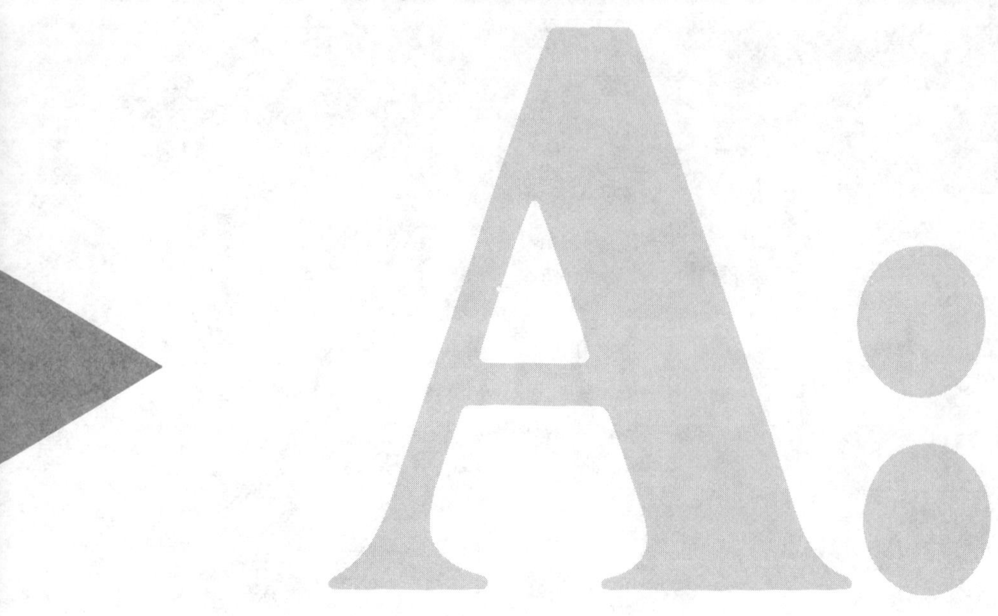

Hard disks provide a tremendous amount of storage, but storing a tremendous amount of data presents organizational problems. You'll get more out of your hard disk if you know more about how to organize and manage the information you store on it. This chapter shows how to

- *Organize files, directories, and subdirectories*
- *Back up and restore files*
- *Speed hard disk operation*
- *Set up your system security with easy techniques*
- *Partition your hard disk with FDISK*
- *Prepare your hard disk with proper formatting and partitions*

Chapter 6
Managing Your Hard Disk

The complexity and the diversity of today's PC applications have outgrown the space limitations of floppy diskettes. As a result, many PC users are upgrading to a faster disk that provides much greater storage capacities: the *hard disk*. The most common PC configuration today has a hard disk and a floppy drive as shown in part B of Figure 6.1.

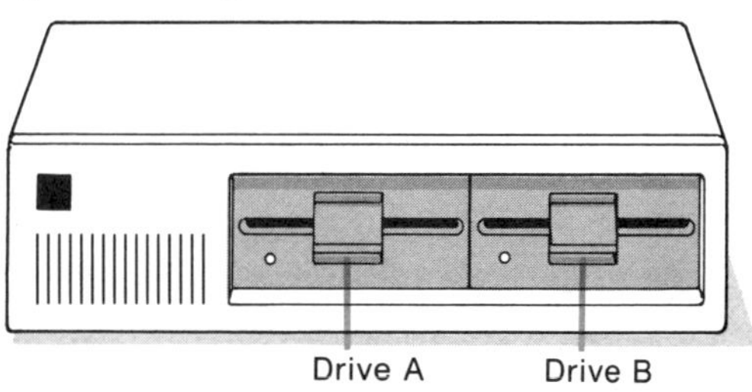

(A) Dual floppy drives.

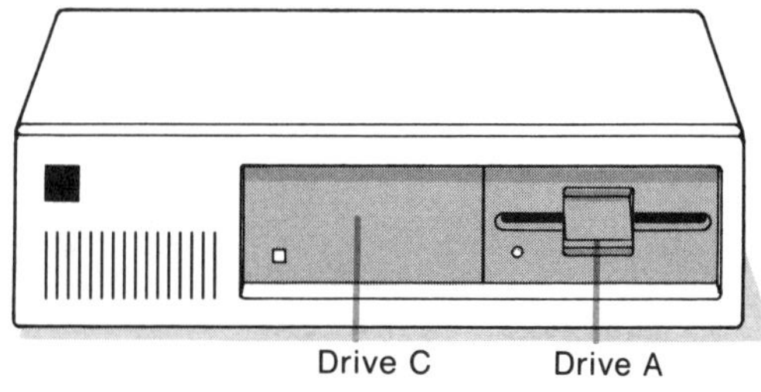

(B) One hard disk and one floppy drive.

Figure 6.1. ***Personal computer configurations.***

Storage capacities of hard disks range in tens of megabytes; for example, a typical PC AT may have a hard disk with a capacity of 20 to 100 megabytes. With such enormous storage capacities, hard disks can store thousands of files. When you have a large number of files, you need a means of organizing them. Without a means of organization, you will find it very hard to locate the information you want. The problem becomes clear when you compare files in a disk to books in a library. All books in a library are classified and arranged according to their subjects. It is easy to locate the book you want. But, suppose that the librarian placed books in no particular order. Patrons would have a lot of difficulty finding books.

There are a number of techniques for organizing files into a workable arrangement on the hard disk. The most important of these is the use of *subdirectories* to create segregated work areas on the hard disk. Segregated work areas allow each computer user to keep track of his or her own files without having to worry, or even know about, the files of the other users. Even if you are the only user of your hard disk, you will find the use of separate work areas beneficial because you can separate your application programs and data files into individual subdirectories.

Subdirectories are subgroups of files within the hard disk. Each subdirectory acts as a separate directory of files. The directory functions in much the same way as a table of contents for a book; it contains information about the files, such as name, size, and other attributes. Designing a directory structure suitable for the needs of hard disk users is an important skill that every hard disk user has to master.

File Organization in a Hard Disk

In setting up a hard disk, PC DOS initially creates only a root directory. You will find some important system files used by PC DOS, such as CONFIG.SYS, COMMAND.COM, etc., in the root directory. As you create new files, you can store them in the root directory itself, using a *flat file* organization. In flat file organization, as shown in Figure 6.2, the storage volume (hard disk) lists all file names in the root directory. The root directory is the only directory on the disk.

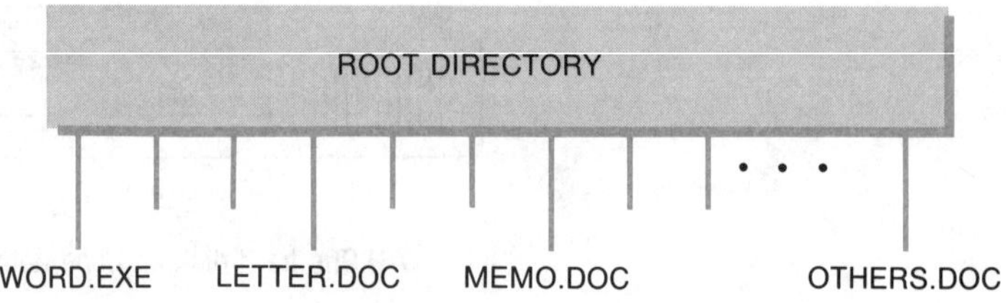

Figure 6.2. ***Flat file organization.***

In a hard disk, where you have a large number of files, using a *tree-structured* file organization is more appropriate than a flat file organization.

In this section, you will learn the basic concepts of tree-structured file organization and how to manage your tree-structured files.

Getting a Directory Listing

You can use the DIR (directory) command to display the file names in a directory:

```
C:\>dir

 Volume in drive C has no label
 Directory of  C:\

COMMAND  COM    23791  12-30-85  12:00p
AUTOEXEC BAT      404  11-07-88  10:32a
     ...
     ...  (more files)
     ...
ANSI     SYS     1651  12-30-85  12:00p
CONFIG   SYS       99   7-12-88   2:22p
VDISK    SYS     3307  12-30-85  12:00p
       17 File(s)   18031040 bytes free
```

Since most of the examples involve a hard disk, there is no volume label. (Volume labels are used mainly to identify removable disks and are discussed in Chapter 7, "All About Floppy Disks.") If you are using PC DOS 4, you may find a disk serial number listed, but the serial number is not important for this discussion.

Following the directory name (C:\ in this case), each line in the output describes one file, and the information is arranged in five columns. The first two columns have the file name and extension. The next column gives the size of the file, and the last two columns have the date and the time when the file was last created or modified.

Caution

Correct Date and Time
The date and time information that the DIR command displays for a given file will be correct only if the system clock was set to the proper date and time when you created (or last modified) the file.

At the bottom of the directory listing, PC DOS indicates the number of files contained in the directory and the amount of space that remains on the disk. When you add a new file, PC DOS adds the new entry to the directory. The new file takes up space on the hard disk, reducing the amount of available space. In adding new files, you are limited both by the amount of free space on the disk and by the number of file names that a directory can hold.

DOS Shell

Selecting a Directory and Files
When you are on the File System screen in DOSSHELL, the current Directory Tree structure is always shown in the left window. Select a directory by using the Up and Down Arrow keys and pressing Enter, or use the mouse and arrow boxes or scroll bar, and click once on the directory name. The list of files for the currently selected directory is shown in the right window. Use the Tab key

to switch between the two windows, and scroll through the file list by using the Up and Down Arrow keys. Select the currently highlighted file by pressing the space bar. Alternatively, use the mouse as you did with the directory tree window. Select "Show Information" from the Options menu to see a window containing more information about the selected file.

The number of files that a directory can hold depends on the amount of disk space that PC DOS sets aside for storing the directory file itself. The *sector* is the basic unit in the disk that PC DOS uses for allocating space for files. Each file entry in a directory occupies 32 bytes. In a single sector, which is 512 bytes long, 16 file entries can be stored ($512 \div 32 = 16$). A double-sided diskette formatted under PC DOS 2.xx or later versions has 7 sectors allocated for a directory, resulting in a maximum of 112 file entries ($16 \times 7 = 112$) in a directory. The size of a directory on a hard disk depends on the partition size. In the case of PC ATs, the root directory is 32 sectors long, allowing up to 512 file entries. (You will find more information about sectors later in this chapter and in Chapter 7.)

Displaying Long Directory Listings

When you display the directory listing of a long directory, you will often find that the file names displayed at the top of the list scroll off the screen. In hard disks, there may be hundreds of files in a directory. The problem is to display such a directory listing so that you can inspect all the files. There are two options in the DIR command for getting around this problem: the *wide display* option and the *pause* option. (These options are also known as *switches* or *parameters*.)

The wide display option is employed by adding a slash and a *w* to the DIR command as follows:

```
C:\>dir /w

 Volume in drive C has no label
 Directory of  C:\

TMP          ANSI     SYS COMMAND  COM HISTORY  SYS RMXR3
AUTOEXEC BAT AUTOEXEC BAK JOHN         SPRINT   COM MSPROJ
MOUSE        AEDIT        MSWORD       ICEDIR       PCLINK2
ETC          CONFIG   SYS VDISK    SYS UTILS        PERSONAL
LANG         SYSTEM       USR          MSTOOLS
       24 File(s)   3022848 bytes free
```

The DIR command now displays the file names across the screen in five columns. The /w option allows up to five times as many files to be displayed in a single screen. However, additional information such as the file size and the date and time stamps is not displayed.

You can use the pause option of the DIR command to display the directory listing one screen at a time:

```
C:\>dir /p
```

The DIR command displays as many files as will fit in one screen and then displays the message `Strike a key when ready ...` at the bottom of the screen. The next screen-full of file names shows up on the screen when you press a key on the keyboard. The screen-by-screen display of the directory continues until the entire directory has been displayed.

Tree-Structured File Organization

In the days when floppy diskettes were used mainly for storage, the flat file organization was sufficient for most purposes. Because of their limited storage capacity, floppy diskettes contained relatively small numbers of files and the directories were short. It was easy for the user to locate files in such directories. When using a hard disk, however, the flat file organization is a poor scheme. A hard disk's large storage capacity allows thousands of files. If all files were contained in a single directory, it would be difficult to locate a particular file.

The *tree-structured file organization* handles a large number of files by grouping files in subdirectories. In a tree-structured file system, the root directory contains not only files but also other subdirectories. These subdirectories in turn contain more files and even more subdirectories. Typically, a directory contains files that logically belong together. In a directory tree, each subdirectory has a portion of the tree; so directory listings tend to be short, letting you quickly locate the file you want. Because the tree structure allows subdirectories to have their own subdirectories, the tree is easily expanded by creating additional subdirectories.

Figure 6.3 shows an example of a tree-structured file organization. In the example, the root directory contains the subdirectories DOS\, SYS\, PLAN\, WP\, PERSONAL\, and CLIENTS\. Notice that each subdirectory name ends with a backslash (\) indicating its status as a subdirectory name. The PERSONAL directory contains some other subdirectories, three of which (PETS\, REPORTS\, and BUDGETS\) contain more subdirectories.

Designing Your File System

In designing your directory structure, you should organize it based on the way you use your computer and not on the programs you use. Suppose you use a word processing program. If you organized your directory structure based on your programs, then you would probably place all your document files in the same directory as the word processor. The danger is that this directory may become full of unrelated files. Such a directory structure is called *application-oriented.*

A better way to organize your documents is to create separate subdirectories by category of use and to place related documents in those subdirectories. For example, you might classify documents as internal correspondence, external correspondence, memos, and so on. Place each of these document classes in the appropriate subdirectory. Such a file organization method is called *project-oriented.*

A project-oriented directory structure reflects the way you work, and each subdirectory represents a complete project. For example, in a legal office, a single client's case could be a project, and related files would be stored in a single subdirectory. In a construction company, each construction contract might be considered a project, divided into its own subdirectory. If you create your directory structure around your projects, you will maintain the logical relationship between files.

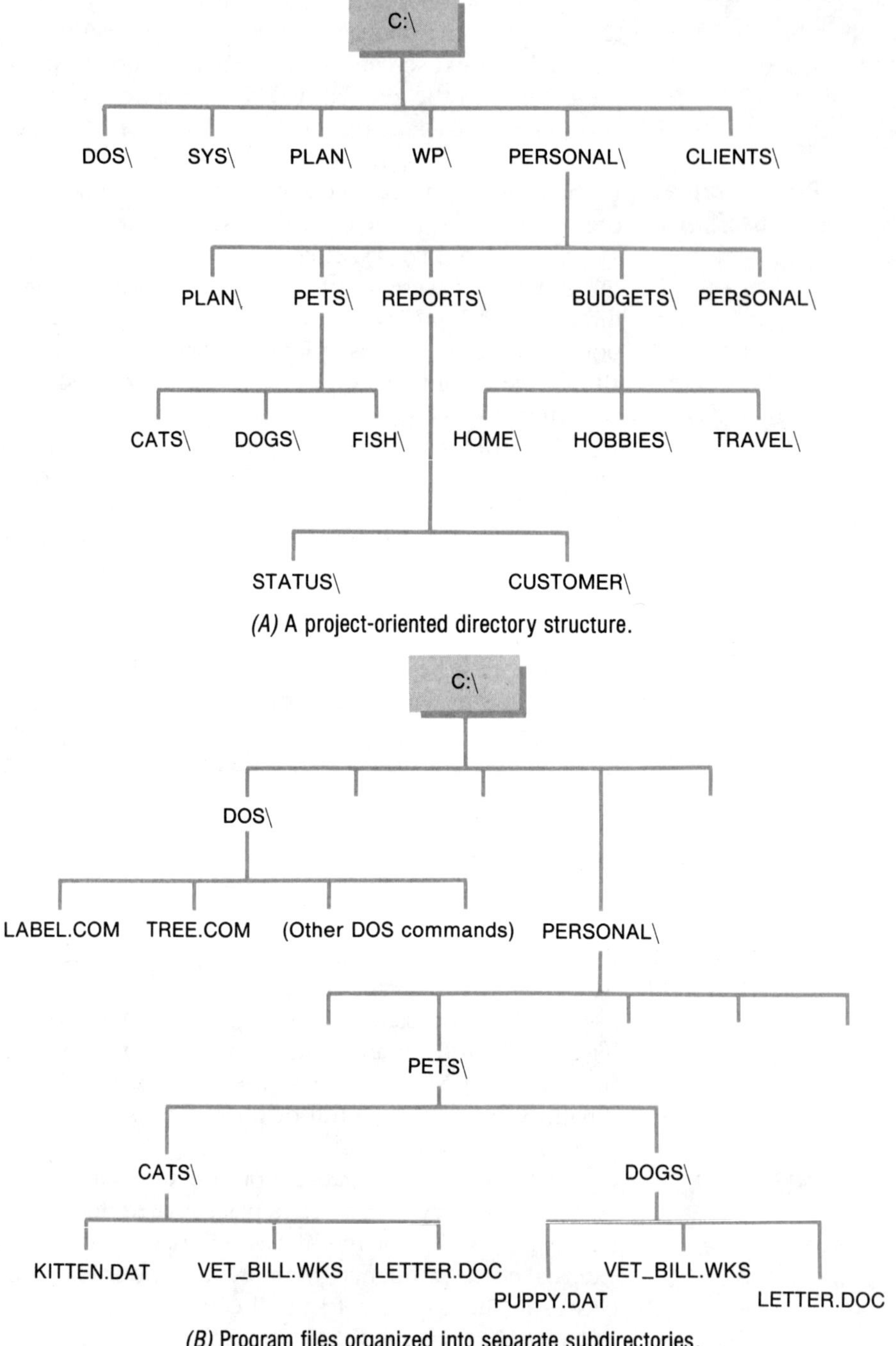

(A) A project-oriented directory structure.

(B) Program files organized into separate subdirectories.

Figure 6.3. *Tree-structured file organization.*

Figure 6.3 is a project-oriented directory structure. For example, part B of the figure shows that the C:\DOS subdirectory contains all PC DOS commands. Word processor and spreadsheet programs are in their subdirectories.

Data files and document files created by using a word processor or spreadsheet are organized in separate subdirectories, depending on their projects. You can see that the PETS subdirectory has subdirectories (CATS\, DOGS\) that relate to PETS.

In designing a file structure, you must first plan how you, and possibly others, will be using the file system. If you are using just a few applications, then designing your directory structure will not be hard. If you will be using many applications and working on many files, you will want to plan the directory structure carefully to allow for future expansion.

The Current Directory

You can locate a file in the tree structure by using a *path name*. A path name reflects the hierarchy of directories that leads to a file or to a directory. The term *file specification* refers to the path name of a file, and it is discussed in detail in Chapter 5, "PC DOS Files." For now, all that you have to keep in mind is that the names of directories in a path name are separated by the backslash (\) character. Looking at part B of Figure 6.3 again, you can identify the path for a file that stores details of your kitten as C:\PERSONAL\PETS \CATS\KITTEN.DAT. Notice in part A of the figure that the name PERSONAL appears twice. The subdirectory C:\PERSONAL is thus different from C:\PERSONAL\PERSONAL because each is a unique path name. Similarly, there are two PLAN directories. One is specified by the path name C:\PLAN, and the other by C:\PERSONAL\PLAN.

In order to access a file, you have to specify its unique path name, but this can be cumbersome. For instance, if you want to use the TYPE command to access a file named JAN89.BIL in your TRAVEL directory, you would have to enter `type \personal\budgets\travel\jan89.bil`. But such long file specifications are not necessary if you are working in a project-oriented directory structure. You can set any directory in your file tree as the current directory by using the CD command. If you are working in BUDGETS, set that as the current directory:

```
C:\>cd \personal\budgets
C:\PERSONAL\BUDGETS>type travel\jan89.bil
```

The current directory is now C:\PERSONAL\BUDGETS, and you can specify the path name for the file as TRAVEL\JAN89.BIL. Thus, having specified a current directory, you can specify the location of a file relative to your current directory rather than the root directory. The longest path name that you can specify is 63 characters.

Absolute and Relative Path Names

The path name for a file can be either *absolute* or *relative* to the current directory. The absolute path name starts from the root directory and continues all the way up to the file or directory in question. A path name with a backslash (\) after the drive name indicates that it is an absolute path name. For example, C:\PERSONAL\REPORTS\CUSTOMER\SMITH.DOC is an absolute path name from the root directory.

The relative path name specifies the path name for a file relative to the current directory. If your current directory is C:\PERSONAL\REPORTS, then C:CUSTOMER\SMITH.DOC is a relative path name to the same file. Note that there is is no leading \ after the drive name in a relative path name. However, if you do include a leading backslash in a relative path name, PC DOS interprets it as an absolute path. For example, if you specify the path name C:\CUSTOMER\SMITH.DOC from the current directory C:\PERSONAL \REPORTS, PC DOS will try to locate the file SMITH.DOC in the subdirectory CUSTOMER under the root, which does not exist.

```
C:\>PERSONAL\REPORTS>type \customer\smith.doc
File not found
```

The . and .. Directories

Two special relative paths serve as shorthand notations for files in subdirectories located immediately above or below your current directory. They are the "**..**" and "**..**" directories. The **.** represents the current directory, and the **..** represents the parent directory. The *parent directory* is the directory that contains the file or directory. For example, if the travel budget for the month of December is available in the specified path C:\PERSONAL\BUDGETS \TRAVEL\DEC88.BGT, then the parent directory for the file DEC88.BGT is TRAVEL (C:\PERSONAL\BUDGETS\TRAVEL). The parent directory for the directory TRAVEL is BUDGETS (C:\PERSONAL\BUDGETS). So if your current directory is C:\PERSONAL\BUDGETS\TRAVEL, then **..** in that current directory refers to the parent directory, C:\PERSONAL\BUDGETS. In the current directory, C:\PERSONAL\BUDGETS, **..** refers to the parent, C:\PERSONAL. In other words, **..** in any directory denotes a directory one level above the current directory.

You can use the **..** directory to indicate relative path names of the parent directory. For example, if your current directory is C:\PERSONAL\REPORTS, then to access a temporary file in the C:\PERSONAL directory, the path name **..**\TEMP.FIL is sufficient (see Figure 6.3A). From the same current directory, C:\PERSONAL\REPORTS, the path name to specify a home budget file will be **..**\BUDGETS\HOME\MISC.BGT.

By using the **..** names in series, you can refer to directories above the current directory in the tree structure. For example, if your current directory is C:\PERSONAL\REPORTS\STATUS, you can use **..** to refer to C:\PERSONAL\REPORTS. If you use two **..** names serially, say **..\..**, you can refer to the directory two levels up in the tree, which is C:\PERSONAL. In the same current directory, C:\PERSONAL\REPORTS\STATUS, the path **..\..\..** denotes a directory three levels up in the tree, which in this case is the root directory.

Creating Tree-Structured Subdirectories

PC DOS automatically creates the root directory when it is loaded in the hard disk. To create tree-structured subdirectories, use the MD (make directory) command:

```
C:\>md c:\dos
```

This command creates a directory named DOS under the root directory. Now use MD to create other directories under the root, as shown in Figure 6.3A.

```
C:\>md c:\sys
C:\>md c:\plan
C:\>md c:\wp
C:\>md c:\personal
C:\>md c:\clients
```

You can then proceed to create directories under the C:\PERSONAL directory:

```
C:\>md c:\personal\plan
C:\>md c:\personal\pets
C:\>md c:\personal\reports
C:\>md c:\personal\budgets
C:\>md c:\personal\personal
```

You can use the same procedure for creating the remaining subdirectories under C:\PERSONAL. However, specifying paths from the root, such as C:\PERSONAL\REPORTS\STATUS, may be difficult. By changing the current directory to C:\PERSONAL, you can use shorter relative paths for creating the rest of the tree structure:

```
C:\>cd c:\personal
```

DOS Shell

Creating a New Directory
To create a new directory, select "File System" from the Main Group on the Start Programs screen. Select "Create Directory" from the File menu. You will be prompted for the path of the new directory.

After changing the current directory to C:\PERSONAL, you can use a combination of the CD and MD commands to create the rest of the directory structure. Notice the use of **..** in the CD commands of the following example:

```
C:\>cd pets
C:\>md cats
C:\>md dogs
C:\>md fish
C:\>cd ..\reports
C:\>md status
C:\>md customer
C:\>cd ..\budgets
C:\>md home
C:\>md hobbies
C:\>md travel
```

Any time that you want to know what your current directory is, simply type **cd**:

```
C:\>cd
C:\PERSONAL\BUDGETS
```

DOS Shell

The Current Directory

In the File System in DOSSHELL, selecting a directory from the left (Directory Tree) window automatically makes it the current directory.

Changing the Prompt

You may recall that if you use the command `prompt $p$g`, PC DOS shows the current directory as part of the prompt. (This is the standard prompt used in most of this book.)

PC DOS allows you to modify the prompt in your system. The default prompt C:\>, C>, or A> may be replaced with any text you choose, such as "Next command please:" or "What can I do for you?". To change the prompt, type `prompt` followed by the text for the new prompt:

```
C:\>prompt Next Command Please:
Next Command Please:
```

In addition to text, you can embed other information in the prompt, such as date, time, current directory, current drive, or PC DOS version number. To include such information, specify a dollar sign ($) followed by a lowercase character representing the information. Table 6.1 shows the options available.

Table 6.1. ***Additional Information in Prompt***

Characters	What the Prompt Displays
$t	Current time
$d	Current date
$p	Current directory in current drive
$v	Version number
$n	Current drive
$g	Greater-than sign (>)
$l	Less-than sign (<)
$b	Vertical bar sign (|)
$q	Equal sign (=)
$h	Backspace character
$e	Escape character
&_	New line in prompt

With the characters listed in Table 6.1, you can create useful prompts, like the one you created with `$p$g`. Try the following command:

```
C:\>prompt $d $t $_$n$g
Sun 12-04-1988 23:12:34.12
C>
```

Note that `$_` causes the prompt to continue in the next line. If you don't want the time in the prompt to be accurate up to one hundredth of a second, type the **$h** (backspace character) to backspace over the unwanted portions of the prompt:

```
Sun 12-04-1988 23:12:34.12
C:\>prompt $d $t$h$h$h$h$h$h $_$n$g

Sun 12-04-1988 23:15
C>
```

Version 4

Current Drive and Directory

If you have installed PC DOS 4 by using the SELECT program and you have a hard disk, the statement **prompt pg** was put in your AUTOEXEC.BAT file. Your prompt will therefore always show the current drive and directory.

Getting Directory Listings in Subdirectories

You can get directory listings for directories other than the current directory. Use the DIR command and enter the path name of the directory whose contents you want displayed. As an example, change the current directory to the root; then display the file names in C:\PERSONAL\REPORTS by typing

```
C:\>dir c:\personal\reports

 Volume in drive C has no label
 Directory of  C:\PERSONAL\REPORTS

.               <DIR>  01-05-90   2:34p
..              <DIR>  01-05-90   1:40p
STATUS          <DIR>  01-05-90   2:37p
CUSTOMER        <DIR>  01-05-90   2:40p
        4 File(s)   17871040 bytes free
```

Now change the current directory to C:\PERSONAL\REPORTS. Use the DIR command to get the directory listing of the STATUS directory that is below the current directory:

```
C:\>cd c:\personal\reports
C:\PERSONAL\REPORTS>dir status

 Volume in drive C has no label
 Directory of  C:\PERSONAL\REPORTS\STATUS

.              <DIR>  01-06-90  10:34a
..             <DIR>  01-06-90   9:40a
        2 File(s)   17871040 bytes free
```

The DIR command accepts the parent directory notation **..** in a path name. For example, to get the listing of the BUDGETS directory, type

```
C:\PERSONAL\REPORTS>dir ..\budgets

 Volume in drive C has no label
 Directory of  C:\PERSONAL\BUDGETS

.               <DIR>   01-05-90    3:48p
..              <DIR>   01-05-90    1:56p
HOME            <DIR>   01-05-90    4:37p
HOBBIES         <DIR>   01-05-90    4:59p
TRAVEL          <DIR>   01-05-90    5:34p
        5 File(s)   17871040 bytes free
```

You can get the parent directory listing by typing `dir ..`. To get the listing of a directory two levels above the current directory, type `dir ..\..`, which in this case is the root directory.

Recording a Directory Listing

You can use the redirection facility of PC DOS to redirect the output of the DIR command to a printer or to a file (see Chapter 8, "Advanced Use of the Command Line"). Having a directory listing in a file is a helpful tool for directory reorganization because, after storing the directory listing in a file, you can edit the file with a text editor and include your comments and notes about those directories in that file. Having a printed directory listing is handy when you want to consult the directory listing while executing a program that does not allow you to obtain directory listings unless you exit the program.

To redirect the output of the DIR command to a file, type

```
C:\>dir > rootdir.lst
```

Now you can see the contents of the file by typing `type rootdir.lst`. To print directory listings, redirect the DIR command output to a printer as follows:

```
C:\>dir > prn:
```

The device name `prn:` stands for the printer. Before issuing this command, make sure your printer is ready to print. If the printer is not ready, the computer waits forever for a response from the printer. You may not be able to execute any other command unless you restart your computer. Even typing Ctrl-C:\ or Ctrl-Break will not bring back the system prompt.

Finding a File

By using the path for a file as input to the DIR command, you can determine whether the file exists in the directory:

```
C:\PERSONAL\REPORTS>cd status
C:\PERSONAL\REPORTS\STATUS>dir temp.doc
File not found
C:\PERSONAL\REPORTS\STATUS>dir jun88.doc
```

```
 Volume in drive C has no label
 Directory of  C:\PERSONAL\REPORTS\STATUS

JUN88    DOC     3791  12-03-88   4:52p
        1 File(s) 17871040 bytes free
```

You can use other drive names (such as A: or B:) or wildcard characters (such as ? and *) in path names also. You may recall that the wildcard * stands for more than one character in a file name; the character ? indicates one character. Assuming that you have three files, JUN88.DOC, JUL88.DOC, and AUG88.DOC, in the current directory, the following example illustrates the use of wildcard characters:

```
C:\PERSONAL\REPORTS\STATUS>dir *.doc

 Volume in drive C has no label
 Directory of  C:\PERSONAL\REPORTS\STATUS

JUN88    DOC     3791  08-03-88   4:52p
JUL88    DOC     4562  09-04-88   5:23p
AUG88    DOC     2387  10-07-88   8:45a
        3 File(s)   17871040 bytes free

C:\PERSONAL\REPORTS\STATUS>dir j??88.doc

 Volume in drive C has no label
 Directory of  C:\PERSONAL\REPORTS\STATUS

JUN88    DOC     3791  08-03-88   4:52p
JUL88    DOC     4562  09-04-88   5:23p
        2 File(s)   17871040 bytes free

C:\PERSONAL\REPORTS\STATUS>dir a*.*

 Volume in drive C has no label
 Directory of  C:\PERSONAL\REPORTS\STATUS

AUG88    DOC     2387  10-07-88   8:45a
        1 file(s)   17871040 bytes free

C:\PERSONAL\REPORTS\STATUS>
```

DOS Shell

Finding a File

In DOSSHELL, you can find a file anywhere on your hard disk, regardless of the current directory. Select "File System" from the Main Group on the Start Programs screen. Next, select the "Arrange" menu, and select "System" file list. A list of all files on the current drive will be shown in the right window. Select "Display Options" from the Options menu. In the pop-up window, type a file name in the Name: field. You can use the * and ? wildcard characters. All files matching your specification will be listed in the right window.

Removing a Directory

Removing a directory may become necessary when you want to reorganize your directory structure. After a project has been completed, you may want to archive the project's files and remove its subdirectory(ies) to free space on the hard disk to make room for new project files. Removing a subdirectory is also necessary when you want to give it a different name.

You can remove unwanted directories by using the RD (remove directory) command. Note that the DEL command cannot be used for removing a directory. The directory has to be empty before you can delete it. Make a copy of any valuable information in the directory, delete all files present in it, and remove the directory by using RD. If you attempt to delete a nonempty directory, PC DOS displays an error message:

```
C:\>rd c:\personal
Invalid path, not directory,
or directory not empty
```

DOS Shell

Deleting a Directory or File

To remove a directory using DOSSHELL, select "File System" from the Main Group on the Start Programs screen. In the Directory Tree window on the left, select the directory you wish to delete. Next, select "Delete" from the File menu. Note that the directory must be empty before you can delete it.

To delete a file, select the file in the file list window on the right and then select "Delete" from the File menu. You can select more than one file with the keyboard or mouse before selecting the Delete menu item.

Reorganizing Subdirectories

As you continue to work with your PC, you will sometimes want to reorganize your system of directories and subdirectories. Suppose that you have a directory called NEWTOOLS, which is a subdirectory of the directory PERSONAL on drive C. In turn, the NEWTOOLS directory has two subdirectories called TEXT and NUMBERS, indicating tools used for word processing and spreadsheet analysis, respectively.

You decide that you want to move the contents of the NEWTOOLS directory, including its files and its subdirectories TEXT and NUMBERS, to a new directory called UTILS. How do you get the contents of C:\NEWTOOLS, C:\NEWTOOLS\TEXT, and C:\NEWTOOLS\NUMBERS to your new directory C:\UTILS?

One approach is to first make the target directories and then use the COPY command to copy each source directory to the corresponding destination directory:

```
C:\>md utils
C:\>md utils\text
C:\>md utils\numbers
C:\>copy c:\newtools utils
```

```
C:\>copy c:\newtools\text utils\text
C:\>copy c:\newtools\numbers utils\numbers
```

This is a lot of typing, and you have to get all of the path names right. Even if you use the CD command as appropriate to simplify the path names, it is still a lot of work.

Users of PC DOS 3.2 and later have an alternative—the versatile XCOPY command. XCOPY reads as many files to be copied into memory as possible and then writes them all to the destination. Some people have claimed that because of this the XCOPY command is much faster than the COPY command. In fact, XCOPY is only slightly faster. Its real advantages lie in its flexibility, partly reflected by its many options.

Unlike the COPY command, the XCOPY command has a variety of options you can use to select which files are to be copied.

Table 6.2. *Summary of XCOPY Options*

Option	Explanation
/a	Copy only archived files; do not reset archive attribute
/d	Copy only files modified after a certain date
/e	Copy empty subdirectories
/m	Copy only archived files; do reset archive attribute
/p	Prompt before copying each file
/v	Verify that the copy is correct
/w	Allow multiple diskettes for source files

As you can see in the following example, the XCOPY command does the whole job with a single command. The */s* option at the end of the first line directs XCOPY to copy all subdirectories and their contents, as well as all files in the source directory. If necessary, XCOPY will create the subdirectories before copying the files. The d at the end of the last line is not an option but a response to the XCOPY query. The d directs XCOPY to assume that TEXT is the name of a directory not a file. That little d is important!

```
C:\>xcopy newtools\text /s
Does TEXT specify a file name
or directory name on the target disk d
```

Because the name TEXT could refer to either a file or a directory, XCOPY is designed to ask you which you mean. Always specify a directory as the destination, so type d. XCOPY copies the files:

```
Reading source file(s)
...names of files copied...
```

Caution

Get the Destination Right

Never use a file name as the destination for an XCOPY command, nor tell XCOPY that the destination is a file. If you do, XCOPY will copy all the source files, one at a time, to the destination file, letting each new copy overwrite the previous file. The result is that the destination file contains a copy of only the last file copied to it. The preceding example (`xcopy newtools\text /s`) showed the XCOPY query message. Always enter `d` to indicate that your destination specification is a directory.

Setting a Search Path for Commands

When you execute an external PC DOS command (like LABEL, CHKDSK, FORMAT, etc.) or execute a program (such as a word processor, spreadsheet, etc.), PC DOS expects a copy of the program file (with an .EXE, .COM, or .BAT extension) to be in the current directory. For example, try the LABEL command from a directory while the program file LABEL.COM is in a different directory:

```
C:\PERSONAL>dir \dos\label.*

 Volume in drive C has no label
 Directory of  C:\DOS

LABEL    COM     2346  12-30-85  12:00p
        1 file(s)   17834676 bytes free
C:\PERSONAL>label
Bad command or file name
```

The LABEL command did not work because PC DOS could not find a copy of the program file in the current directory. You can use the PATH command to specify one or more directories from which programs will be executed. If you have all PC DOS external-command program files under the C:\DOS directory, you can use the PATH command as follows:

```
C:\PERSONAL>path c:\dos
C:\PERSONAL>label
Volume in drive C has no label
Volume label (11 characters, ENTER for none)?   ←press Enter
```

In the preceding example, note that the command file LABEL.COM is in a directory (C:\DOS) different from the current directory (C:\PERSONAL). But the LABEL command still worked because the PATH command directs PC DOS to search additional directories, which in this case is the C:\DOS directory. Thus, the PATH command allows you to execute programs in one of the specified directories from any other directory.

The PATH command works as follows. The paths entered along with the PATH command are retained in memory. Whenever a command name is entered at the PC DOS prompt, PC DOS first checks the current directory to find a file with the same name and the .COM, .EXE, or .BAT extension. If none is found, PC DOS next checks the first directory specified in the PATH command. If the file is not found there, PC DOS proceeds to the next and subsequent directories given in the PATH command until it finds the file or until all search directories are examined. If the file is found in one of the directories, it will be executed. Otherwise, PC DOS displays an error message `Bad command or filename`.

More than one search path for the PATH command can be specified by delimiting them with semicolons, as shown here:

```
C:\PERSONAL>path \;\dos;\wp;\tools;\personal\tools
```

The preceding command replaces the existing search path with the directories given in the command. Once executed, the PATH command remains in effect until the system is rebooted. Later, if you want to know what the path is, you can simply type `path` in the command line:

```
C:\PERSONAL>path
PATH=\;\DOS;\WP;\TOOLS;\PERSONAL\TOOLS
```

To cancel the effect of the PATH command, type `path` followed by a semicolon, as shown here:

```
C:\PERSONAL>path;
```

The preceding command removes all search directories specified earlier with PATH.

Using APPEND to Set a Search Path for Data Files

Recall that the PATH command establishes a list of directories for PC DOS to search when a file is not in the current directory. Unfortunately, the PATH command is useful for commands and batch files only, namely, those files with the extension .EXE, .COM, or .BAT. If your program needs a data file that is not in the current directory, then having specified a search path using the PATH command will not be of much help. The APPEND command introduced in PC DOS version 3.3 corrects this deficiency by allowing nonexecutable files to be included in a directory search path.

For example, consider a word processor program contained in the file WP.EXE. It uses four nonexecutable files, WPMSG.TXT, WPSYSD.SYS, WPHELP.TXT, and WPQUE.SYS, for displaying help and other types of messages on the screen. Assume that all five files are stored in the C:\WORD directory. While executing WP.EXE from a different directory, if you request a help message, it may be read from WPHELP.TXT. In the absence of the APPEND command, however, WP.EXE cannot open and read WPHELP.TXT unless it is in the current directory. If you use the APPEND command to tell PC DOS that it has to search the C:\WORD directory also (in addition to the current directory), then WP.EXE can locate the file WPHELP.TXT from any other current directory.

Many programs, particularly word processors, have overlay files. The primary executable file does not contain the entire program. Instead, the program is distributed in two or more files. Prior to introducing the APPEND command, there was no way to locate these overlay files unless they were in the current directory. With the APPEND command, PC DOS can locate all files regardless of their extensions. The APPEND command accepts one or more paths as input parameters.

Assume that your current directory is C:\PERSONAL and that you have a file SMITH.DOC in the C:\CLIENTS directory. Try the following command:

```
C:\PERSONAL>type smith.doc
File not found
```

The command did not work because the file SMITH.DOC is not in the current directory, C:\PERSONAL; it is in C:\CLIENTS. You can now use the APPEND command to specify a search path as follows:

```
C:\PERSONAL>append c:\clients
C:\PERSONAL>type smith.doc
Client Name: John Smith
Company     : Somecompany, Inc.
Address     : 1234 56th Ave,
              Smallville, TX 98765.
```

Once you execute the APPEND command, PC DOS searches the additional directories specified by the APPEND command. When you invoke the APPEND command, PC DOS retains the search path in the computer's memory until the system is rebooted. APPEND takes multiple paths for searching data files, each of them separated by semicolons, as follows:

```
C:\PERSONAL>append c:\clients;c:\plan;c:\personal\tools
```

Like the PATH command, APPEND can be used to display, change, or delete the search path. When you type `append` with no parameters in the command line, it displays the current data file search path:

```
C:\PERSONAL>append
APPEND=C:\CLIENTS;C:\PLAN;C:\PERSONAL\TOOLS
C:\PERSONAL>append c:\personal\budgets
C:\PERSONAL>append
APPEND=C:\PERSONAL\BUDGETS
```

To cancel a data file search path, type `append` followed by a semicolon, as shown here:

```
C:\PERSONAL>append;
C:\PERSONAL>append
No appended directories
```

DOS Shell

Running an Application Automatically

Using DOSSHELL, you can have an application run automatically whenever a data file with a particular file name extension is selected. Select "File System" from the Main Group on the Start Programs screen. Select any file having the extension you wish to associate. Now select "Associate" from the File menu. You will be prompted for the name of the application to associate. From now on, every time you select any file with that extension, the associated application will be run using that file as its working file.

How Programs Use the APPEND List

Programs access a file in PC DOS by different methods. Some of them open, read/write, and close files by using simple internal PC DOS functions. Examples of such programs are word processors, which look for a specific file to read help messages (WP.EXE opens and reads WPHELP.TXT for help messages). The normal APPEND command works for such programs; that is, if a program uses simple PC DOS functions to access files, then executing the APPEND command will help in locating the file even if it is not in the current directory.

Some programs use more advanced PC DOS internal functions for accessing files. An example is the COPY command. If you use the COPY command with a wildcard specification, such as COPY *.DAT \DATA*.DAT, then the program COPY.COM does not know the complete name of the file it wants to open. So it uses one of the advanced PC DOS functions, which will search the directory and open any file that meets the wildcard condition. If a program uses these advanced PC DOS functions to access a file, the normal APPEND command does not help in locating files in directories other than the current directory.

To expand the effect of APPENDed directories to all programs using the advanced PC DOS functions, use the */x* switch with the APPEND command before you invoke it for the first time:

```
C:\PERSONAL>append /x
C:\PERSONAL>append c:\clients
```

However, you won't know whether a program uses simple PC DOS functions or advanced functions. Thus, you can't really determine when to use the /x switch with the APPEND command. A simple rule is: use the normal APPEND command first; if it doesn't work the way it is supposed to, reboot the system and use the /x switch with APPEND. (What happens when you use the /x switch with APPEND is beyond the scope of this chapter. Interested readers can refer to other references in this area.)

Tip

Helping Programs Use APPEND

PC DOS maintains a list of information called the *environment*, which it automatically supplies to each program when it is loaded. Normally, APPEND doesn't put its list of paths in the environment. However, if you use the */e* option, APPEND also puts its list of paths in the environment. Since some programs search their environment for information about files and directories, this option can help APPEND work with certain programs. The /e option can be combined with other options such as */x*, but it must be used before APPEND is involved with a path list, for example:

```
append /x /e
append c:\wp;c:\db4
```

There is good news and bad news about the APPEND command. The good news is that destructive commands like DEL do not operate on files that are not in the current directory. For example, even if the DEL command locates files using the APPENDed directory, it does not delete the file:

```
C:\PERSONAL>
del smith.doc
Access denied
```

The bad news is that when a data file, located in one of the data file search paths, is written back to the disk by a program, it is written to the current directory. For example, after you save the file PHONE.BIL, which is not in the current directory, the file is written to the current directory, and the original copy of PHONE.BIL is unaffected. The reason behind this feature is to protect files from inadvertent destruction.

Version 4

The /x and *Path* Options

In PC DOS 4, APPEND automatically supports the advanced directory search functions used by many programs. Therefore, the */x* option has a different meaning: it tells APPEND to find executable files (programs) in a way similar to that used by PATH. Unlike the latter, APPEND used with /x will even find executable files that don't have the .COM, .EXE, or .BAT extension. You can turn off this option at any time by typing `append /x:off`.

PC DOS 4 also adds the */path* option. This tells APPEND to search for a file even if a full path (such as C:\WP\WP.EXE) was specified. Normally, if you give the full path, PC DOS will search only that specific path. To turn on this function, use the `/path:on` option. To turn it off, use `/path:off`.

Both the /x and the path options can be used at any time, not just prior to giving the first APPEND path list of the session.

Caution

ASSIGN Used with APPEND

If you use the ASSIGN command and also wish to use APPEND, your first APPEND command must come before the ASSIGN command.

Displaying the Tree Structure

Unless the directory structure in your hard disk is very simple, it may be difficult to get an idea of the entire directory structure. For a new user, a display of the entire tree structure of directories is a helpful way to become familiar with the system. You can use the TREE command to list all the subdirectories in the hard disk:

```
C:\>tree
DIRECTORY PATH LISTING
Path: \DOS
Sub-directories:  None
Path: \SYS
Sub-directories:  None
Path: \PLAN
```

```
Sub-directories:  None
Path: \WP
Sub-directories:  None
Path: \PERSONAL
Sub-directories:  PLAN
                  PETS
                  REPORTS
                  BUDGETS
                  PERSONAL
Path: \PERSONAL\PLAN
Sub-directories:  None
Path: \PERSONAL\PETS
Sub-directories:  CATS
                  DOGS
                  FISH
Path: \PERSONAL\REPORTS
Sub-directories:  STATUS
                  CUSTOMER
Path: \PERSONAL\BUDGETS
Sub-directories:  HOME
                  HOBBIES
                  TRAVEL
Path: \PERSONAL\PERSONAL
Sub-directories:  None
       ... <more of such display> ...
```

When you execute the TREE command, you will see a display of all subdirectories and their paths. You can display the files as well by using the */f* option of the TREE command:

```
C:\>tree /f
```

Most of the time, TREE's output display scrolls off the screen too fast to be of much use. To display the entire tree structure screen-by-screen with the TREE command, use the MORE command:

```
C:\>tree /f | more
```

Another trick is to redirect the output of the TREE command to the printer. Before issuing the command, make sure that the printer is ready to print:

```
C:\>tree /f > prn:
```

The TREE command of PC DOS is rather limited in its features and usefulness. A number of commercial programs extend and enhance the TREE command. One of the best-known is XTREE. This program provides a graphic display of your disk and simultaneously shows files in each directory. You can inspect the display by using the cursor keys. XTREE also allows mass copying, deleting, and renaming of files. It is a menu-driven, user-friendly program helpful in dealing with many file organization problems.

Version 4

TREE Displays

In PC DOS 4, using a path name after the word `tree` will cause TREE to display the tree structure starting from a specified directory. For example, the following command will display all subdirectories in the C:\ACCOUNT directory, any subdirectories in these subdirectories, and so on:

```
C:\>tree c:\account
```

In the preceding command, files as well as subdirectories can be listed by following the path name with /f.

PC DOS 4 also uses graphics characters to display a more tree like tree structure, for example:

```
Directory PATH listing for Volume PCDOSDISK
Volume Serial Number is 1454-3E20
C:\
+---DOS
+---TOOLS
+---PLAN
+---WP
+---PERSONAL
|   +---TRAVEL
|   +---TOOLS
|   \---PETS
        ... and so on ...
```

Subdirectories are shown indented under their parent directories. This display was made by specifying the */a* option. Without that option, TREE will use special graphics characters that make solid lines on the screen and are not printable on all printers.

Setting Up Logical Drives

If you use programs that don't recognize the tree-structured file organization, such as WordStar, you may find that you need to replace the path name for a file with an imaginary drive name. For example, the file C:\CLIENTS \SMITH.DOC could be referred to as E:SMITH.DOC if the directory C:\CLIENTS is given the *logical drive* name of *E:*. Another use for setting up a logical drive is to save you some typing when you are using files located deep in the directory structure. If you have been following the tree-structured file organization faithfully, it will not take much time for you to create paths like C:\CLIENTS\SALES\FOURTH.QTR\DECEMBER\HARDWARE.RPT. In such a situation, you can use the logical drive name *E:* to represent the path C: \CLIENTS\SALES\FOURTH.QTR\DECEMBER. The path for the file you want is then simply E;HARDWARE.RPT.

A logical drive is given a drive name, just as the floppy drive or the hard disk drive is given one. PC DOS normally uses the drive names *A:* and *B:* for referring to floppy drives, while *C:* is reserved for the hard disk drive. *D:* is used for a second hard disk or a second partition. By default, PC DOS can recognize drive names only up to *E:*, which doesn't leave many names for use in logical drives.

However, you can use the LASTDRIVE command to configure PC DOS so that it recognizes more drives. Specify a letter as the name of the last drive in the LASTDRIVE command found in the CONFIG.SYS file. If you want to see what the current last drive name is, you can examine the CONFIG.SYS file by typing `type \config.sys`. For configuring more drive names, you must modify the LASTDRIVE command in the CONFIG.SYS file. If you don't see the LASTDRIVE command in the CONFIG.SYS file, you will have to add the following line:

```
LASTDRIVE=M
```

Remember, LASTDRIVE can be specified only in the CONFIG.SYS file. After changing the CONFIG.SYS file, you must reboot the computer in order to put the change into effect.

The SUBST command (substitute) allows you to set up logical drives for any of your directories. In other words, you can refer to a directory in the tree-structured files by a drive name, such as *E:*. To use the SUBST command, type the name of the logical drive and the path name that you want to call by that logical drive name. After substituting, manipulate the files and directories under the substituted path as though they were in the logical drive:

```
C:\>dir \clients\sales\fourth.qtr\december

 Volume in drive C has no label
 Directory of C:\CLIENTS\SALES\FOURTH.QTR\DECEMBER

.            <DIR>     08-30-90  12:34p
..           <DIR>     09-12-90   3:56p
HARDWARE RPT     8404  11-07-90  10:32a
PROJECTS     <DIR>     12-02-90   9:10a
     4 File(s)       3167289 bytes free

C:\>subst e: \clients\sales\fourth.qtr\december
C:\>dir e:

 Volume in drive E has no label
 Directory of  E:\

.            <DIR>     08-30-90  12:34p
..           <DIR>     09-12-90   3:56p
HARDWARE RPT     8404  11-07-90  10:32a
PROJECTS     <DIR>     12-02-90   9:10a
     4 File(s)       3167289 bytes free

C:\>dir e:projects

 Volume in drive E has no label
 Directory of  E:\PROJECTS

.            <DIR>     08-30-90   2:45p
```

```
..           <DIR>       08-30-90  12:34p
     2 File(s)  3167289 bytes free
```

Caution

Using Other Commands during a Substitution

Do not use the following commands when a substitution is in effect: ASSIGN, BACKUP, DISKCOMP, DISKCOPY, FDISK, FORMAT, JOIN, LABEL, and RESTORE.

You can use the CD, MD, RD, and PATH commands with substitution in effect, but make sure you know the real (physical) path location that will be affected.

SUBST allows you to substitute more than one directory by using different logical drive names. Later, if you want to display the current logical drives and the directory paths they represent, type `subst` at the command line:

```
C:\>subst f: \personal\reports\status
C:\>subst
E: => C:\CLIENTS\SALES\FOURTH.QTR\DECEMBER
F: => C:\PERSONAL\REPORTS\STATUS
```

To delete a logical drive, use the */d* switch with SUBST:

```
C:\>subst e: /d
C:\>dir e: Invalid drive specification
```

The name of the logical drive cannot be the drive of the directory being substituted. In other words, you can't use logical drive name *C:* for a directory in *C:*.

If you use early versions of some programs that do not recognize a hierarchical directory structure, you can use the SUBST command to tell PC DOS that a subdirectory on drive C is to be treated as if it were floppy disk drive A. This technique is discussed in greater detail in Chapter 5, "All About Floppy Disks."

Viewing a Disk as a Subdirectory

Sometimes you may want to do just the opposite of what the SUBST command does: reference a drive as though it were part of another directory structure. If you have files located on several disks and you want to access them without changing your current drive, you can use the JOIN command. JOIN allows you to create a logical link between a disk drive and a subdirectory in another disk. For example, you can refer to your floppy drive (A:) as one of the subdirectories in the hard disk (C:).

Caution

Using Other Commands during a Join

Do not use the following commands when a join is in effect: BACKUP, DISKCOMP, DISKCOPY, FORMAT, and RESTORE.

Neither of the two drives used in a JOIN command can be currently specified in an ASSIGN or a SUBST command.

JOIN will create a subdirectory if the specified one does not exist. The subdirectory must be empty and must exist exactly one level below the root directory.

Suppose that a floppy diskette in drive A has the files PARTS.DOC, BILLS.DOC, and INVOICE.DOC, as shown in Figure 6.4A. Use the JOIN command to access drive A as part of your hard disk directory structure:

```
C:\>join a: c:\drive_a
C:\>dir \drive_a

 Volume in drive C has no label
 Directory of  C:\DRIVE_A

BILLS    DOC      1267  11-30-90  10:24p
INVOICE  DOC      4509  12-06-90   3:39p
PARTS    DOC      4454  11-05-90  11:45a
     3 File(s)    2147782 bytes free
```

After the join is in effect, your hard disk directory structure will look like the one in Figure 6.4B.

Caution

No Direct Access to Drive

After JOINing a disk drive with another directory structure, you cannot access the drive directly. For example, after issuing the JOIN command as in the preceding example, try the following command:

```
C:\>dir a:
Invalid drive specification
```

More than one drive can be joined to the hard disk by using the JOIN command. If you want to display the joins currently in effect, type `join` with no parameter. To delete a join, use the */d* switch:

```
C:\>join b: c:\drive_b
C:\>join
A: => C:\DRIVE_A
B: => C:\DRIVE_B
C:\>join a: /d
C:\>join b: /d
C:\>join
C:\>
```

Getting Information about Your Hard Disk

When you use the DIR command, PC DOS provides certain information about your hard disk. For example, when you use the DIR command in the root directory, you will see a display similar to the following:

```
C:\>dir

 Volume in drive C is JULIE
 Directory of  C:\
```

```
COMMAND  COM     23791  12-30-85  12:00p
AUTOEXEC BAT       404  11-07-88  10:32a
     ...
     ...     (more files)
     ...
ANSI     SYS      1651  12-30-85  12:00p
CONFIG   SYS        99   7-12-88   2:22p
VDISK    SYS      3307  12-30-85  12:00p
       17 File(s)   18031040 bytes free
```

Besides listing the file names in a directory and their sizes and date of creation or alteration, the DIR command displays some information about the hard disk, such as the name of the hard disk and the amount of free space

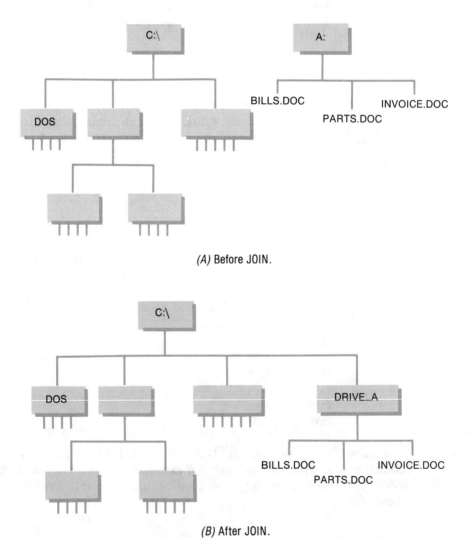

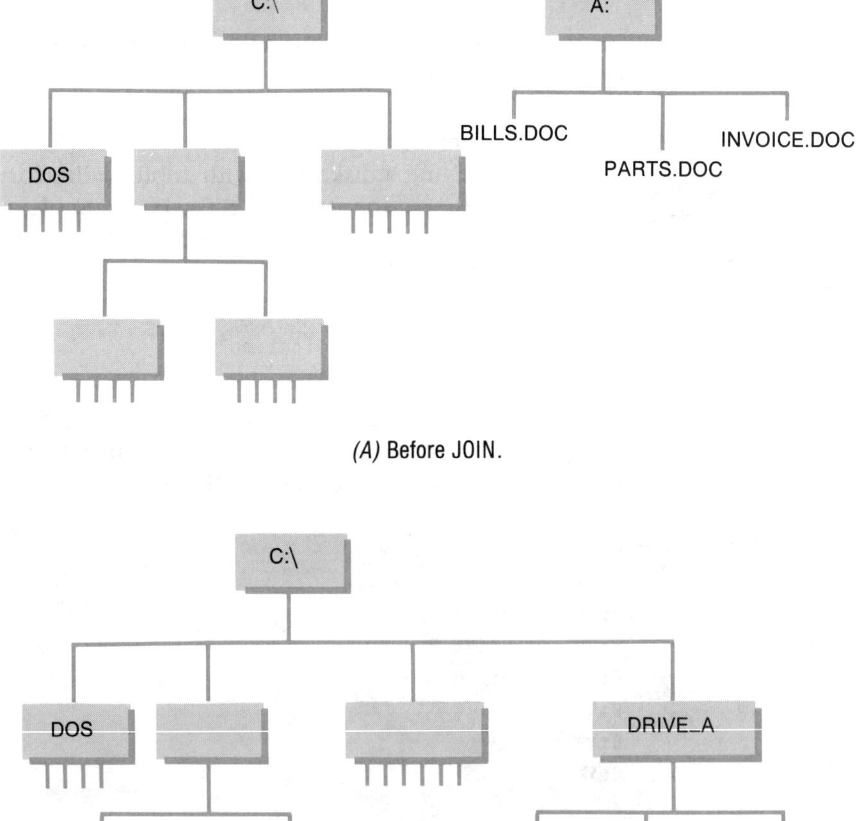

Figure 6.4. ***Drive joined in a directory structure.***

available. However, the DIR command does not provide a complete picture of what is on the hard disk. Suppose that you need to find out such information as the total number of files on the hard disk, the total number of directories, the space occupied by hidden files, or the number of bytes located in bad sectors? In these cases, the DIR command is of little help. Instead, you can use the CHKDSK command (CHECK DISK) to get such additional information about the disk.

Checking Your Disk with the CHKDSK Command

Here is what happens when you use the CHKDSK command:

```
C:\>chkdsk

 Volume JULIE       created Mar 31, 1990 3:01p

 21309440 bytes total disk space
    45056 bytes in 3 hidden files
   296960 bytes in 138 directories
 17840128 bytes in 1760 user files
    81920 bytes in bad sectors
  3041280 bytes available on disk

   655360 bytes total memory
   596960 bytes free
```

Error Message with CHKDSK

If PC DOS can't find the command file when you use the CHKDSK command, it displays the message `Bad command or file name`. If this happens, either copy CHKDSK.COM to the current directory or set up a search path using PATH.

First, CHKDSK displays the hard disk volume label and the date on which the volume label was assigned to the disk: in this case, the volume name is JULIE, created on March 31, 1990 at 3:01 PM. (You may recall that you can use the LABEL command to display and change the volume label.) Next, CHKDSK displays the total storage capacity of your disk: in this case, 21309440 bytes.

But what are the three "hidden" files? Each time you create a bootable PC DOS disk (with the command `format /s`), PC DOS creates on the disk two hidden system files that it uses during system initialization. Since these files do not appear in your directory listings, they are called *hidden files*. PC DOS makes them hidden to prevent you from inadvertently deleting or renaming them. When you assign a volume name to a disk, PC DOS creates a third hidden file. All these files show up in the output of the CHKDSK command:

```
45056 bytes in 3 hidden files
```

CHKDSK then displays the total number of subdirectories and files that reside on your hard disk:

```
 296960 bytes in 138 directories
17840128 bytes in 1760 user files
```

In addition to the number of directories, the CHKDSK command shows the amount of storage occupied by the subdirectories themselves. The directory files use this space to store information about files such as file names, their attributes, and their location in the hard disk. The CHKDSK command then displays the total number of files and the total space used by all of them.

If the FORMAT command locates damaged sectors in your disk, it marks them as bad to prevent their use by PC DOS. If damaged sectors exist in your disk, CHKDSK will display the number of bytes of damaged disk space:

```
81920 bytes in bad sectors
```

Next, CHKDSK displays the amount of space available on the disk:

```
3041280 bytes available on disk
```

To determine the amount of disk space that you are actually using, subtract this value from the total disk space:

Actual space used = total disk space − bytes available
= 21,309,440 − 3,041,280
= 18,268,160 bytes

Finally, CHKDSK displays the memory utilization in your computer:

```
655360 bytes total memory
596960 bytes free
```

The first number tells you the amount of memory present in your system. When PC DOS starts running, it occupies a certain amount of memory. In addition, if you install some memory resident programs, such as the APPEND command, they too occupy memory space. That is why the amount of free memory in the second line is less than the first amount.

Version 4

Volume Serial Number and Allocation Amounts

In PC DOS 4, the CHKDSK command includes the volume serial number for the disk. It also displays the size of each allocation unit used on the disk. This is the smallest amount of space that can be used for a file. The total number of allocation units on the disk, and the total available are also displayed, for example:

```
C:\>chkdsk

 Volume PCDOSDISK   created 10-20-1990 11:11a
 Volume Serial Number is 1454.3E20

  21170176 bytes total disk space
```

```
   71680 bytes in 3 hidden files
  192512 bytes in 83 directories
18051072 bytes in 1242 user files
   71680 bytes in bad sectors
 2783232 bytes available on disk

    2048 bytes in each allocation unit
   10337 total allocation units on disk
    1359 available allocation units on disk

  655360 total bytes memory
  519696 bytes free
```

Backing Up Your Hard Disk

Hard disks are usually very reliable, but problems can still occur. Vibrations or power fluctuations can cause the read/write head in the disk to crash onto the platter and damage the data on the disk. Unforeseen catastrophes, such as fire or theft, may destroy your hard disk. Before such a problem happens to you, consider the amount of time and money that has gone into your hard disk. Apart from the money invested in hardware and installation, you have probably spent a lot of time in preparing the data and programs that the hard disk contains. All this time and money is at risk if your hard disk becomes unusable. You must have a way to reconstruct programs and data as they existed before the hard disk failure. Even if you don't have an exact copy of everything on your hard disk, even a close copy would save you a lot of time, money, and frustration. Backing up your hard disk regularly ensures the reliability of the software on the hard disk.

Backing up the hard disk means making a duplicate copy of the information that is on it. You can make the duplicate copy on another hard disk, on a set of floppy disks, or on a digital cassette tape. If anything happens to your hard disk after you back it up—say a hardware failure or a disk crash—you would still have a copy of your valuable data.

There are several ways to make backups. The one you choose depends on the time you can afford to spend backing up your hard disk, the amount of money you can spend to buy new hardware or software for doing backups, and the extent of backup work that needs to be done. You can back up your hard disk by using the PC DOS commands BACKUP and RESTORE, or you can buy commercial software that does the backup easier and faster than these PC DOS backup commands. In addition, you may want to purchase a streaming tape drive backup system that will back up your entire hard disk on a digital cassette tape.

The success of your backup scheme lies in the regularity and strategy of making backups. Unless you develop a strategy for making regular backups and follow it diligently, you may find yourself left without a backup after a hard disk failure.

Devising a Backup Strategy

A general strategy for backing up your hard disk usually involves two steps: making a *master* backup of the entire hard disk periodically—say, at the end of every week—and making *intermediate* backups of daily files at the end of the day.

As an example, you may choose to make master backups every Friday afternoon, as you are wrapping up your business week. Use the BACKUP command to make the master backup on disks. You can make intermediate backups at the end of each day by using one of the following strategies: back up only those files modified on that day; if you use only a particular directory, back up only that directory; or, back up those files whose date stamp is later than the last backup. You can make the intermediate backups by using one of the PC DOS commands: BACKUP, XCOPY, or COPY.

Having weekly master backups and daily intermediate backups will help in reconstructing your data after a hard disk failure. For example, if a hard disk failure occurs on Monday morning, the master backup of the previous Friday will provide a complete replacement of data. If the hard disk fails on Wednesday, you can restore the data by using the master backup of the previous Friday and then using the two daily intermediate backups you made on Monday and Tuesday.

The interval between master backups depends on the extent to which you use your computer. If you use your computer extensively—say you use it to keep track of inventory in your retail store—you may have to record transactions on a daily basis. Each day's sales have to be entered in the computer as well as the new products that you have stocked. In such cases, you can follow a weekly master backup plan with intermediate backups taken at the end of every day. On the other hand, if you don't use the computer extensively—say you use the computer only a few times a week—you can follow a monthly backup plan with weekly intermediate backups. For example, suppose that you use the computer for storing management information, such as employee files, payrolls, and accounting information. Transactions will not take place very often, so a monthly master backup plan will be sufficient.

The way you make the backups also depends on how you use your computer. If you are the only one using the computer, you may want to back up the entire hard disk during master backups. In intermediate backups, you can back up individual subdirectories or only files that have been modified. If you are sharing the computer with other users, each user will need a separate workspace that has been created by a subdirectory. In such cases, one user may take care of master backups, while each user makes intermediate backups of his or her own subdirectory.

A vital part of your backup strategy is what you do with the floppy disks or tapes after you have backed up the hard disk onto them. You can store intermediate backup floppy disks in your office desk for making daily backups. If you store master backup disks in a place other than your office, you have a chance of saving them in case of a fire or other disastrous event.

You can use the same floppy disks over and over for making master and intermediate backups. However, floppy disks wear out after being in use for some time, so you should replace your backup disks with a new set once every six months or a year.

A Master Backup Procedure with Floppy Disks

You can use the BACKUP command for making the weekly master backup. The BACKUP command copies the specified information from the hard disk to another medium, such as floppy disks or another hard disk. When one floppy disk fills up, the BACKUP command asks you to insert another disk. If a file cannot fit on one floppy disk, then BACKUP splits the file between two disks. The BACKUP command is not the same as the COPY command. It not only copies files but also stores them in a special archival format. The files contain some extra information that only the RESTORE command can interpret. Thus, the backed-up files are not the same as their originals, and you can't simply copy them to use them.

Before starting the backup process, you need to know how many floppy disks your hard disk backup will need. To determine the number of disks, use the CHKDSK command to find out the number of bytes currently in use:

```
C:\>chkdsk

 Volume JULIE       created Jan 15, 1990 5:10p

 21309440 bytes total disk space
    45056 bytes in 3 hidden files
   165888 bytes in 79 directories
 13277184 bytes in 1466 user files
    81920 bytes in bad sectors
  7739392 bytes available on disk

   655360 bytes total memory
   595536 bytes free
```

To determine the number of bytes currently in use, use the following formula:

$$\begin{aligned}\text{Bytes in use} &= \text{total disk space} - \text{bytes available}\\ &= 21{,}309{,}440 - 7{,}739{,}392\\ &= 13{,}570{,}048 \text{ bytes}\end{aligned}$$

To determine the number of floppy disks needed, divide the number of bytes in use by the storage capacity of each disk. Table 6.3 provides a quick summary of the storage capacities of floppy disks.

Table 6.3. ***Storage Capacities of Floppy Disks***

Disk Type	Storage Capacity
Single-sided	184,320 bytes (180K)
Double-sided, double-density	368,640 bytes (360K)
Double-sided, high-density	1,228,800 bytes (1.2M)
3.5″ Double-sided, double-density	737,280 bytes (720K)
3.5″ Double-sided, high-density	1,474,560 bytes (1.4M)

Using a 360K disk as an example, the number of disks becomes

Number of disks = bytes in use ÷ storage capacity
= 13,570,048 ÷ 368,640
= 36.8
= 37 disks

After you have determined the number of disks needed for the backup, make sure that all disks are formatted in PC DOS. Although the improved BACKUP command formats disks in PC DOS version 3.3, you will save time if you format all your floppy disks before starting the backup process.

Caution

PC DOS Versions Earlier Than 3.3 and Copy-Protected Programs
In PC DOS versions earlier than 3.3, the BACKUP command will not format floppy disks. If you interrupt the backup to format disks, you must start the backup all over again. Therefore, be sure to format the required number of floppy disks **before** you start the backup.

If you have installed copy-protected programs in your hard disk, it may be necessary to "uninstall" those programs before starting the backup. Copy-protected programs may become unusable after a backup. Consult the user manual that comes with each copy-protected program.

You also may need some additional materials, such as a storage box for storing all the floppy disks, a set of disk labels, and a soft-tipped pen for writing the serial number of the disk on its label. When you have all your materials ready, issue the BACKUP command as follows:

```
C:\>backup c:\*.* a: /s

Insert backup diskette 01 in drive A:

Warning! Files in the target drive
A:\ root directory will be erased
Strike any key when ready
```

In this case, you are using the BACKUP command to back up the entire hard disk (C:) to the floppy disks in drive A. The */s* switch tells PC DOS to copy all files, including those in all the subdirectories. Keep in mind that BACKUP is an external command, so a copy of the program file should be made accessible to PC DOS. Otherwise, you will see the message `Bad command or filename`. Insert a formatted disk in drive A and press any key. The BACKUP command will start archiving files to drive A, as shown here:

```
** Backing up files to drive A: **
Diskette number: 01
```

BACKUP numbers the backup disks sequentially. The serial number of each disk appears on the screen (01 in the example). As BACKUP archives each file to the disk, its name will appear on the screen. If the current disk becomes full, PC DOS will instruct you to insert another disk. Remove the disk from drive A and write its serial number on its label. Insert the next disk in drive A and continue to back up files.

Once you complete the backup process, arrange the disks in order of their serial numbers and place them safely in the storage box. Keep the backup disks in a location different from your computer. That way, if your computer is damaged by fire, smoke, spills, etc., your backup disks are not also damaged. You may use the same disks for your next master backup.

Caution

To start a backup from DOSSHELL, select DOS Utilities from the Main Group and then select "Backup Fixed Disk." In the pop-up window you can give any options that you would use on the command line. Whether you use DOSSHELL or the command line, your backup floppies do not need to be formatted ahead of time: you need not use the */f* option.

Making Master Backups on a Hard Disk or Tape

If you have a second hard disk or if you have purchased a tape backup system, you may want to make your backups on these media. The procedure for making a master backup on another hard disk is very similar to that for a floppy disk backup. You have to make sure that the second hard disk is large enough to hold all the backed-up files. If your second hard disk is known as *D*, you can back up files to drive D with the command

```
C:\>backup c:\*.* d: /s
```

Backing up files to a tape backup system depends on the specific system that you use. Consult the user's manual of your tape backup system for instructions.

Intermediate Backup Procedures

Intermediate backups are those that take place between master backups. How often you perform intermediate backups depends on how you use your computer. If you use your computer daily and you make master backups at the end of each week, you can perform intermediate backups at the end of each day. Four switches are helpful in making intermediate backups, and these are discussed next.

Backing Up Modified Files with the */m* Switch

Suppose you want to back up only the files that have been changed since the last backup. If you have a lot of files on your hard disk, this could save you time because you would not have to back up all the files. The BACKUP command will let you do this.

Every file on the disk has an attribute called the *modified* attribute. When PC DOS creates a file, it sets this attribute to 1. Later, when a file is backed up, the BACKUP command sets this attribute to 0. When you modify the file with any other command, PC DOS sets this attribute to 1. If you use the BACKUP command with the */m* switch, BACKUP will back up only those files with the modified attribute set to 1.

Adding Files to an Existing Backup Disk with the */a* Switch

Suppose you want to add files to a floppy disk that already has backup files on it. Normally the BACKUP command erases files in the target drive before backing up new files. However, if you use the */a* switch with the BACKUP command, files in the target drive will not be erased. Instead, the BACKUP command will simply add new files to the existing files in the target drive. Practically speaking, this means that you can make the first intermediate backup after a master backup without the /a option. You can then make the subsequent intermediate backups with both the /a and /m options, which can be combined, as explained in the next example.

Using a weekly master backup plan, you would make your master backup on Friday evening. On Monday evening, you would make the first intermediate backup. The previous intermediate backups can be considered obsolete, since you just performed a master backup. The first intermediate backup thus will not require the use of the /a option:

```
C:\>backup c:\ a: /s /m
```

On Tuesday evening, the second intermediate backup takes place. There may be some files that have been modified since Monday. Their modified attribute will be set. If you copy over Monday's intermediate disks, you will destroy Monday's files. So you must use the /a option to perform Tuesday's backup. Note that you can continue to use Monday's intermediate backup disk as long as free space is available. Since you used the /a option, BACKUP adds files to the disk:

```
C:\>backup c:\ a: /s /m /a
```

Every day the intermediate backup set becomes larger and larger because all versions of new or modified files are backed up. You can use the same floppy disk the next day for the next intermediate backup. Because the /a switch is used, PC DOS will add new files to the disk every day. If a disk becomes full during an intermediate backup, PC DOS will display a message such as

```
Insert backup disk 02 in drive A:
Warning! Files in the target drive
A:\ root directory will be erased
Strike any key when ready
```

You can remove the current backup disk from the drive, write its serial number on its label, and keep it in a safe place. Insert a new disk in the drive, and continue the backup. The second disk will also become full after some intermediate backups, at which point PC DOS will again display the preceding message. Remove the disk from the drive, write its serial number on its label, use another disk, and continue to collect intermediate backup disks in this manner until the next master backup. When you restore the files to the hard disk (if you should ever need to), each disk in the intermediate backup set is restored in order; newer files copy over older versions during the restore.

Backing Up Subdirectories with the */s* Switch

Instead of backing up an entire hard disk or specifying only the files that have been changed, you can back up only the files in one directory and its subdirectories. As an example, assume that you have all your data files in a directory named C:\DATA and that subdirectories within that directory store data files for individual applications. On any given day, you typically would modify only files in one of the subdirectories of C:\DATA. Your daily intermediate backup can copy files from only the C:\DATA directory:

```
C:\>backup c:\data a: /s
```

Note that the */s* switch in the preceding command directs PC DOS to back up subdirectories also. If you had followed the project-oriented directory structure, you would have organized all your data files in separate subdirectories under C:\DATA. In such cases, using the /s switch ensures that data files in subdirectories are also backed up. You can combine the /m and /a options with backing up subdirectories to save more intermediate backup space and time.

Backing Up Files by Date

If you regularly modify only a particular set of files, making intermediate backups with the /m and /a switches (as described earlier) will make multiple copies of the modified files on the backup disks. Because files are added to backup disks every day, newer versions of files don't replace older versions; instead, they occupy additional space on backup disks. (It will take longer to restore these backup disks because multiple versions of the same files have to be restored.) In such cases, backing up by date using the */d* switch is more efficient than using the /m switch.

The /d switch backs up only those files that have been created or modified after a certain date. The date you select is typically the date after your last master backup. With this daily strategy, you back up all files created or modified since the date of the last master backup onto a set of floppy disks, erasing the existing files on the disk. Thus, if you modify the same set of files every day, newer versions replace the older versions on the backup disks. The existing older files are no longer needed because the most recent files are being copied. You do not need to use the /a option when using the date option in intermediate backups. Since only the most recent versions of the files are contained in backup disks, restoring them takes much less time:

```
C:\>backup c:\ a: /s /d:12-28-90
```

The preceding command backs up all files in the hard disk that have been created or modified after December 28, 1990. Note that the /s switch directs PC DOS to back up files in all the subdirectories having date stamps later than the specified date.

Tip

Backup Enhancements in PC DOS 3.3 and Later

Suppose that in the middle of a backup you find that you don't have a sufficient number of formatted disks. If you are using PC DOS versions earlier than 3.3, you will have to abort the backup, format more disks, and start over. To alleviate this frustration, PC DOS version 3.3 has introduced the */f* switch. The /f switch allows you to use unformatted disks during BACKUP. If you use the BACKUP command with the /f switch, BACKUP will format a disk if necessary. The program file FORMAT.COM should be accessible to PC DOS from the current directory.

After making a backup, you may want to keep a record of the contents of the backup disk. Such a record will be useful at the time of a restore operation. If you erase a file accidentally and you want to restore it selectively from a set of backup disks, you will need a list of the files that are on the backup disks. Using the DIR command on the backup disk won't help because backup disks store files in a special archival format. To prepare a list of backed-up files during a backup, PC DOS has added the */l* switch in PC DOS version 3.3. The /l switch specifies a LOG file to be prepared during backup. The LOG file is a text file that is stored in the path specified with the /l option. It contains the date and time when the backup was made and a list of the files that have been backed up. The format for specifying the path for the LOG file in the /l switch is `/l:c:\backup\backup.log`. If no path is specified, then the BACKUP command assumes a default path of \BACKUP.LOG for the LOG file.

Backing Up Files with the XCOPY Command

After using the BACKUP command for backing up files to a disk, you must use the RESTORE command before the files on the backup disk can be accessed. This can be inconvenient when you want to access files on a backup disk directly. For example, suppose you want to distribute a set of files to someone. You may not want this person to use the RESTORE command before accessing the files. Or, if your hard disk goes down and you don't have access to another hard disk, you may want to get to the files on the backup disks quickly without doing a restore. You can use the XCOPY command as an alternative to BACKUP in these cases.

The XCOPY command is a unique hybrid of the BACKUP and COPY commands. XCOPY has features of the BACKUP command: it allows you to copy single files, groups of files in one directory, or files under all subdirectories. XCOPY's option switches are also similar to many of BACKUP's. However, in copying files, XCOPY is more like the COPY command than the BACKUP command because the copied files are not stored in a special archival format; rather, they retain their conventional PC DOS format. The advantage of XCOPY is that files copied by XCOPY can be used directly, whereas files backed up by BACKUP can be interpreted only by the RESTORE command.

Another difference between XCOPY and BACKUP is that while you are copying files to a floppy disk, XCOPY can copy only as many files as one disk can hold; it can't copy files to sequentially numbered disks like BACKUP can. Thus, if the files to be backed up require more disk space than the capacity of one floppy disk, XCOPY can't be used for copying all of them. You can get around this problem when you are copying only changed files, as you will see in a moment.

When should you use XCOPY and when BACKUP for intermediate backups? If you can store all the files to be backed up on a single floppy disk, then using XCOPY is faster and easier than using BACKUP. Another situation in which XCOPY is more useful than BACKUP is when your directory structure is organized in such a way that XCOPY can be used for backing up individual subdirectories (files in each directory should occupy less space than a floppy disk's capacity). In this case, you can selectively use XCOPY for only those directories whose files are modified. If you can't predict the size of the files to be backed up, or if your directory structure is not very convenient for using XCOPY, you must use the BACKUP command for intermediate backups.

If you want to make your intermediate backup of the modified files using XCOPY, you can use the */m* switch. Using this switch will cause XCOPY to copy only those files for which the archive attribute has been set to 1. PC DOS sets the archive attribute to 1 when a file is first created and any time later when it is changed, such as by the addition of text to a word processing document. After XCOPY, the attribute will be set to 0. You can use the */s* switch along with the /m switch to copy files in subdirectories also. This is the same /s switch used for BACKUP and RESTORE. To make an intermediate backup of modified files on the hard disk, type

```
C:\>xcopy c:\ a: /m /s
Reading source file(s) ...
```

After reading files into memory, XCOPY copies them to the target, displaying the file names as they are being copied.

As XCOPY copies the files, it resets their archive attribute to 0. This means that they will not be copied by a future XCOPY /m command, unless the file has been changed in the meantime.

The advantage of using XCOPY with the /m option is that if the files to be copied don't fit on a single floppy, you can just keep repeating the command until all of the files are copied. (Remember that you can repeat the last command by pressing the F3 key.) The only file that cannot be copied is a file that by itself is larger than the maximum capacity of a floppy disk.

Tip

Use the ATTRIB Command with XCOPY

You can also force XCOPY to include a particular file in an XCOPY /m copy. To do this, use the ATTRIB command with its *+a* option to set the archive attribute of the specified file or files to 1. Then use XCOPY /m to copy those same files, for example:

```
C:\>attrib +a *.txt
C:\>xcopy *.txt target /m
```

Using ATTRIB with the +a option sets the archive attribute for all files ending in .TXT to 1.

To copy all files within all subdirectories of the source directory, use the /s option with ATTRIB. This will set the archive bit for all *matching* files in all subdirectories of the specified directory, for example:

```
C:\>attrib +a newtools\*.* /s
```

Using the /s option will set the archive attribute for all files in the NEWTOOLS directory as well as those in the TEXT and NUMBERS subdirectories. *You must always specify the wildcards* *.* *after the directory name for this to work.*

While making intermediate backups, you may find that multiple versions of modified files are backed up if you use the /m switch. In this case, you can back up files by date in your intermediate backup. Use the /d:*mm-dd-yy* switch to copy only files that have been created or modified after the specified date. For example, you can use

```
C:\>xcopy c:\ a: /s /d:12-28-90
```

to copy only files that have been modified after 12/28/90. The /s switch also copies files in the subdirectories that meet this condition.

Restoring Files

After backing up your files, you should store the backup disks in a safe place. It is hoped that you won't have any use for the backups; they are just for insurance. But, if anything does happen—say you inadvertently delete some files from your hard disk—you can use the RESTORE command to selectively restore files from the backup disks. The RESTORE command is simpler to use than the BACKUP command. There is no planning required. You simply use RESTORE whenever you want to restore files to the hard disk.

Restoring Selected Files and Subdirectories

If you delete a file inadvertently, you can use the RESTORE command to restore that individual file from a backup set. For example, to restore a file named C:\DOCS\CLIENTS.DOC, type

```
C:\>restore a: c:\docs\clients.doc

Insert backup diskette 01 in drive A:
Strike any key when ready ...
*** Files were backed up 12-28-1990 ***
*** Restoring files from drive A: ***
Diskette: 01
\DOCS\CLIENT.DOC
C:\>
```

The RESTORE command searches the backup disks one by one after prompting you to insert them in sequential order. Once the specified file is found, the RESTORE command copies it to the hard disk. To restore an entire directory, simply specify the destination directory in the RESTORE command. To copy all subdirectories of the specified directory, use the /s switch:

```
C:\>restore a: c:\document /s
```

DOS Shell

Starting a Backup

To start a backup from DOSSHELL, select "DOS Utilities" from the Main Group; then select "Restore Fixed Disk." In the pop-up window you can give any options that you would use on the command line.

Preventing Changed Files from Being Overwritten by RESTORE

While restoring files in subdirectories, you may not want to restore any files that have been modified since the backup. Because you have modified these files after making the backup, restoring over them would cause newer versions of the modified files to be lost. In such cases, using the */p* switch with the RESTORE command will cause it to check to see whether the file being restored has been modified since the last backup. If so, a warning message will be displayed and RESTORE will ask your permission to overwrite the file. For example, suppose you have modified the file CLIENTS.DOC after making the backup and you use the RESTORE command with the /p switch, as shown in the following example:

```
C:\>restore a: c:\docs\clients.doc /p

Insert backup diskette 01 in drive A:
Strike any key when ready ...
*** Files were backed up 12-28-1990 ***
*** Restoring files from drive A: ***
Diskette: 01

Warning! File C:\DOCS\CLIENTS.DOC
Was changed after it was backed up.
Replace the file (Y/N)?y
\DOCS\CLIENT.DOC

C:\>
```

If you respond y, then RESTORE will overwrite the file; otherwise, RESTORE leaves the newer version of the file unaffected.

Restoring the Entire Hard Disk

To restore your entire backup set, obtain your latest master backup floppy disks and type

```
C:\>restore a: c:\  /s

Insert backup diskette 01 in drive A:
Strike any key when ready ...
*** Files were backed up 12-28-1990 ***
*** Restoring files from drive A: ***
Diskette: 01
```

In the preceding command, backed-up files from drive A are restored to the hard disk drive C. The RESTORE command will start restoring files at the root directory and will also restore all subdirectories. If all files from the current disk have been restored, PC DOS will instruct you to insert the next disk:

```
Insert backup diskette 02 in drive A:
Strike any key when ready ...
```

Because you have used the /s switch, PC DOS will also restore files in subdirectories. If subdirectories do not exist on the hard disk, the RESTORE command will create them and restore files in them. At the end of the restore, the RESTORE command will create the tree structure of directories on the hard disk as it existed at the time of making the backup.

Caution

Error Message from RESTORE

After restoring the entire hard disk, the RESTORE command may display the message

```
System files restored
The target disk may not be bootable
```

The message means that older versions of the system files IBMBIO.COM and IBMDOS.COM have been restored to the hard disk from the floppy disks. As a result, the hard disk may contain older PC DOS system files. If this message is displayed, then use the SYS command to copy the correct version of the system files from your PC DOS master disks. However, in PC DOS versions 3.3 and later, the RESTORE command does not restore the hidden system files; so you will not have this problem if you use PC DOS 3.3.

Optimizing Storage on a Hard Disk

As you use your hard disk, PC DOS eventually distributes parts of files all over it. Over time, the hard disk tends to become slower and slower because PC DOS has to spend more time in assembling the individual pieces of files so it can access them. Since speed is one of the major advantages of the hard disk, getting the highest performance out of your hard disk is very important. Understanding how and why the performance of the hard disk degrades over time will help you keep it running at top speed.

Formatting and Space Allocation

When PC DOS formats a disk, it lays down a series of concentric circles called *tracks*. Each track consists of several arcs of circles, called *sectors*. These sectors and tracks define the space for storing programs and data on the hard disk, much as lines painted in a parking lot encourage orderly use of the space. The number of tracks on the surface of the disk and the number of sectors per track are determined by the version of PC DOS and the size of your disk drive.

As part of the formatting process, PC DOS sets up sectors into groups called *clusters*. A cluster in a hard disk consists of 8 sectors in PC DOS version 3.1 and 4 sectors in PC DOS version 3.2. This means that even if you have a small file, for instance a file 43 bytes long, PC DOS will allocate 4 sectors (2048 bytes) to store the file. The DIR command shows the actual size of the file, but the free space information at the end of the DIR display shows that the total space left on the disk has decreased by one cluster. You can see this in the following example:

```
C:\PERSONAL\TEMP>dir

 Volume in drive C is JULIE
 Directory of  C:\PERSONAL\TEMP

.            <DIR>   12-30-90  12:34p
..           <DIR>   12-30-90  10:32a
        2 File(s)   18031040 bytes free

C:\PERSONAL\TEMP>copy con: small.fil
This is a small file
<F6>
1 file(s) copied

C:\PERSONAL\TEMP>dir

 Volume in drive C is JULIE
 Directory of  C:\PERSONAL\TEMP

.            <DIR>    12-30-90  12:34p
..           <DIR>    12-30-90  10:32a
SMALL.FIL          22  12-30-90   1:42p
        3 File(s)   18028992 bytes free
```

In the example, when you executed the first DIR command, PC DOS showed that 18,031,040 bytes were free on the disk. With the COPY command, you created a small file, only 22 bytes long. But since PC DOS had allocated one cluster (2048 bytes) for this file, the free space was reduced by one cluster size, as you can see by executing the DIR command again (18,031,040 − 2048 =18,028,992 bytes free).

File Fragmentation

When PC DOS initially formats a disk, most sectors in the disk are free for storing files. A few sectors are reserved for special purposes, as shown in Figure 6.5. When you store a file on the hard disk, PC DOS allocates one or more clusters depending on the size of the file. During the initial stages of hard disk use, all files will be in contiguous sectors (next to each other) because most areas of the disk are available for storage. When files are available in contiguous sectors, PC DOS reads the first sector and then has to wait only a short time before the second sector comes under the read/write head. This means that PC DOS is able to read files in contiguous sectors faster than those in noncontiguous sectors.

After a disk has been in use for some time, new files will have been added and existing files deleted. The sizes of your files increase and decrease as you modify them. The tracks and sectors used by erased files become available for storing new files. If this process continues for some time, the free space in the disk is not available in one contiguous block. Instead, the entire disk contains free space in small fragments, as shown in Figure 6.6. So when

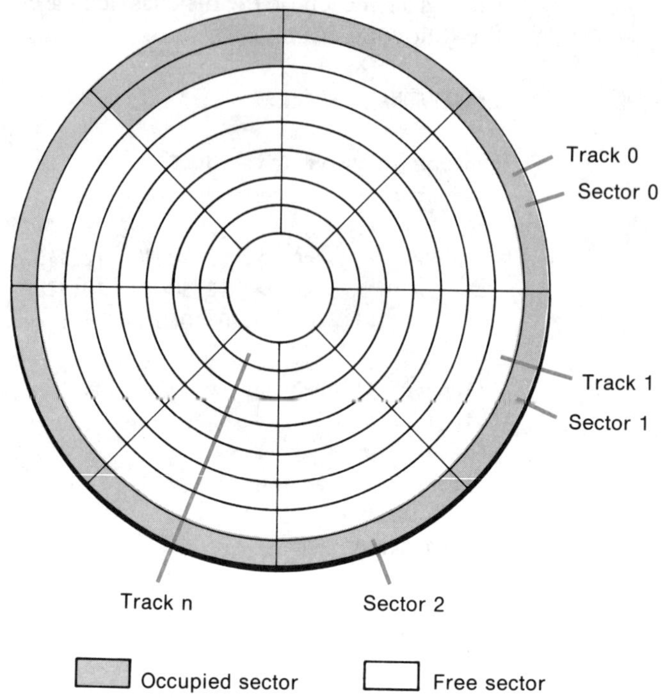

Figure 6.5. ***Newly formatted disk with a majority of free sectors.***

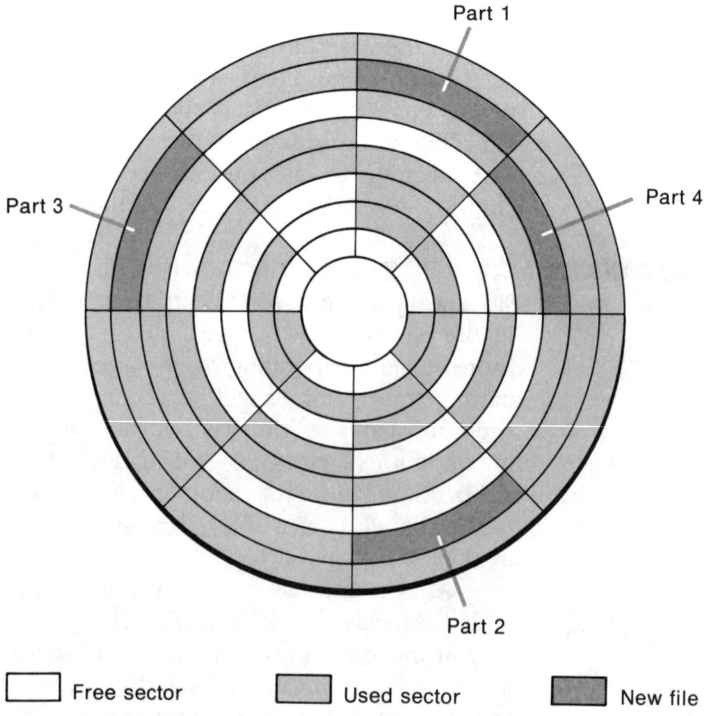

Figure 6.6. ***Free sectors in a disk.***

PC DOS writes a file to the disk, it stores the file in the first free cluster it locates. Subsequent parts of the file are stored in additional free clusters wherever they are. As a result, sectors that store a new file are now widely dispersed about the disk. As you alter files, a single file can become scattered all over the disk. This problem is known as *fragmentation* of files on the disk.

You can understand file fragmentation easily by means of the following example. Say you have three files on your disk: file A, file B, and file C. Figure 6.7 shows a linear representation of the clusters occupied by files A, B, and C. File A occupies 4 clusters; file B, 3 clusters; and file C, 2 clusters. All files were initially in contiguous sectors, as shown in Figure 6.7A. Suppose you reduce the contents of file A by one cluster, leaving a free cluster between files A and B, as shown in Figure 6.7B. Now if you add some material to file C, its contents expand by one more cluster, the new cluster of file C occupying the free cluster between files A and B, as shown in Figure 6.7C. Assume that files A, B, and C each expand by one more cluster. The new clusters will occupy free clusters as shown in Figure 6.7D. After seeing how just three files can become

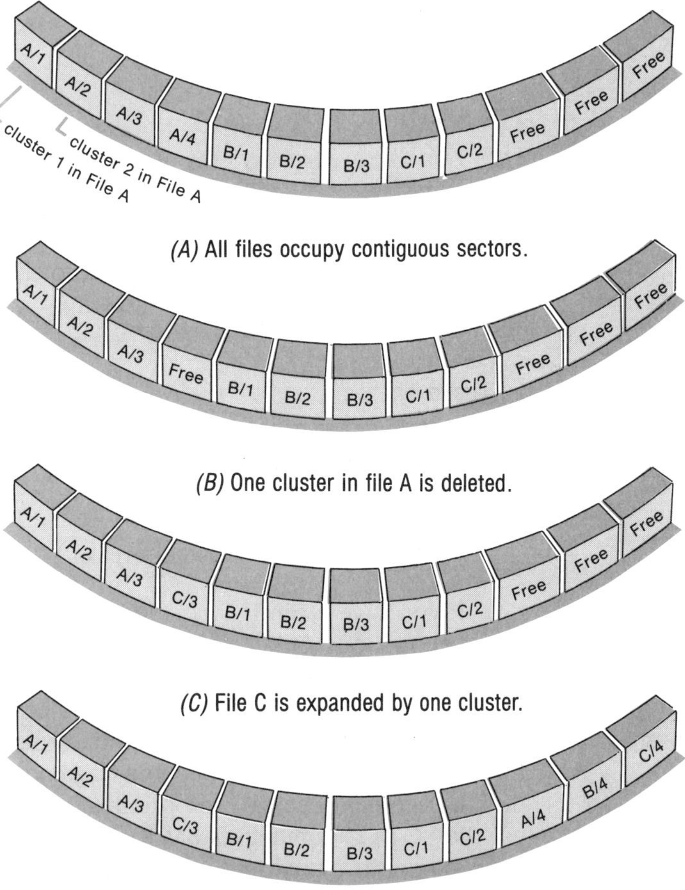

Figure 6.7. ***File fragmentation.***

fragmented, you can understand how severe the problem of file fragmentation becomes in a hard disk with thousands of files.

The greater the fragmentation of files, the more the hard disk performance drops, and the slower it gets. For reading or writing to a file, the read/write head has to move to all the tracks in the disk where pieces of the file are stored. This additional movement increases the access time and slows down the overall system performance. You can diagnose the problem of file fragmentation by observing that the time PC DOS takes for loading and executing programs is longer than normal. You can also note that your database search programs and spreadsheets take longer to read data files. To see whether files are fragmented, use the CHKDSK command.

Checking for Fragmented Files with CHKDSK

To see whether a file, say HDDSK.DOC, is stored contiguously, use the name of the file with the CHKDSK command:

```
C:\>chkdsk hddsk.doc
All specified file(s) are contiguous
```

If the file is contiguous, CHKDSK displays the preceding message. If the file is fragmented, that is, stored in two or more noncontiguous clusters, PC DOS will display a message such as

```
C:\>chkdsk hddsk.doc
C:\HDDSK.DOC
     Contains 5 non-contiguous blocks
```

To inspect the contiguity of more than one file, use wildcard characters in the place of file names. For example, to check contiguity of all the files in the current directory, type the following:

```
C:\>chkdsk *.*
C:\CUSTOMER.DOC
     Contains 3 non-contiguous blocks
C:\SALES.DOC
     Contains 2 non-contiguous blocks
C:\EMPLOYEE.DAT
     Contains 2 non-contiguous blocks
```

If you have recently formatted your hard disk, then all files will probably be contiguous. Otherwise, you will see that some files are in noncontiguous areas. Although CHKDSK reports on the noncontiguity of files in the disk, it does nothing to remedy the problem.

There are several ways to optimize your hard disk filing system. Since files on a hard disk tend to become fragmented over normal use of the hard disk, it becomes necessary to optimize the storage on the hard disk. You can use the PC DOS commands BACKUP and RESTORE for optimizing storage. As an alternative, you can buy commercially available hardware and software to make the process easier and automatic. A number of disk optimizing products are now available in the market. Some of the hardware solutions for disk optimization are Konan KXP-230Z Drive Maximizer from Konan Corp and Awesome I/O board from CSSL. Whenever a file is written to the disk, these hardware products automatically make the clusters of each file logically contiguous. On the software side, you can use Disk Optimizer from SoftLogic Solutions, Norton Utilities, or Mace Utilities. When these programs are used, they rearrange each file's clusters so that they are next to each other.

Version 4

Disk Utility Programs
Because PC DOS 4 has changed certain parts of the FAT structure, some disk utility programs may not work with PC DOS 4. Most of these programs will be available in revised versions by the time you read this, however. Check with the vendor or manufacturer.

Optimizing Disk Performance with BACKUP and RESTORE

When you optimize a disk, you "unfragment" the files that are stored on it. That is, if a file occupies noncontiguous sectors, it is copied to contiguous sectors. Rather than buying additional software and hardware, using BACKUP and RESTORE commands is an inexpensive way of optimizing your hard disk.

This optimization method involves backing up your entire hard disk, formatting the disk, and then restoring all of the files. Recall that PC DOS places files in contiguous sectors in a freshly formatted disk, thus improving the performance of the hard disk. The earlier discussion on the BACKUP and RESTORE commands suggested that to prevent accidental loss of data, you should back up your hard disk regularly. You can add to the payoff if you include the step of optimization in your regular weekly or monthly backup sessions. *Optimization* involves formatting the disk and restoring the backed-up files.

The difference between the backup procedures described earlier and the optimization method is that the earlier backup procedure did not involve formatting the hard disk and then restoring the files. In a normal backup, files on the hard disk are copied to a set of floppy disks. Unless the drive goes down, formatting the hard disk and restoring the files are not part of the backup process. But if you want to optimize the hard disk, you must format the disk so that the entire disk becomes free and then you must restore the files so that they are stored in contiguous clusters.

Tip

Delete Unwanted Files before a Backup
Before starting a backup, delete unwanted files from the hard disk. Scan the directory structure and erase all those files that are not necessary, such as the .BAK backup files created by text editors and word processors and files that are already archived in another place. Getting rid of these unwanted files will decrease the time and the number of floppy disks it takes for the backup. You also should uninstall any copy-protected software.

Turn on the VERIFY feature before the backup to make sure that data on the disks is valid. Using the VERIFY command may slow down the backup, but, since you are going to reformat the hard disk, you should ensure that the backup set is good.

```
C:\>verify on
C:\>verify
VERIFY is on
C:\>backup c:\*.* a: /s
```

```
Insert backup diskette 01 in drive A:
Warning! Files in the target drive
A:\ root directory will be erased
Strike any key when ready    ←press Enter

** Backing up files to drive A: **
Diskette number: 01
```

Note that the /s switch directs PC DOS to back up files in all subdirectories. When PC DOS fills up the current disk, remove it from drive A, write its serial number on its label, and insert a new disk into drive A. Continue the backup until all files are backed up to floppy disks. You can then type `verify off` to shut off the VERIFY feature.

Reset the system and insert the PC DOS disk in drive A before starting the computer again. Now the computer loads PC DOS from drive A, and it will be the default drive. Format the hard disk using the FORMAT command, and use the /s switch to transfer system files at the end of formatting:

```
A>format c: /s

WARNING, ALL DATA on NON-REMOVABLE DISK
DRIVE C: WILL BE LOST!
Proceed with Format (Y/N)?
```

Answer `Y` to the above question. In PC DOS versions 3.3 and later, PC DOS requests that you enter the volume label of the hard disk. Only if you enter the correct volume label will PC DOS proceed with the formatting. Otherwise, the format process will be aborted. After completing the format, PC DOS displays

```
Format Complete
System Transferred
```

The format process clears all files and directories that were present in the hard disk before the backup. The free space on the disk is now contiguous. Reset the system and start the computer using the copy of PC DOS on the hard disk. Copy all command files from the PC DOS disk.

Now you can restore all files using the backup disks. Use the /s switch of the RESTORE command to include subdirectories in the restore.

```
C:\>restore a: c:\  /s

Insert backup disk 01 in drive A
Strike any key when ready
```

PC DOS now stores files in your freshly formatted hard disk, with all files in contiguous sectors. Place the backup disks in a safe place.

Increasing Optimization by Reorganizing Subdirectories

One way to further increase optimization is to reorganize your directory structure so that program files and data files are stored in separate directories. Then you can back up programs and data onto two different sets of floppy disks. When you restore files, restore program files first and data files next. This technique groups all infrequently modified programs in the outer tracks of the hard disk. All data files, which are subject to frequent changes, are stored in the inner tracks. The read/write head movement is thus restricted to inner tracks most of the time, resulting in better access times for your data files.

Optimizing Disk Performance by Changing the Interleave

Earlier you saw that files can be unfragmented and disk performance optimized by formatting the disk and restoring the backed-up files. Aside from unfragmenting files on disk, there are certain formatting techniques to optimize disk performance. One of them is to change the *interleave factor*. The interleave factor refers to the amount of physical separation between logically sequential sectors. The proper value for the interleave depends on the speed of your computer and your hard disk controller board. Choosing the proper interleave value may optimize your disk performance.

Recall that when PC DOS formats a disk, it forms concentric circles of tracks on the surface of the disk, each divided into a number of sectors. Tracks have sequential numbers starting from the outside, with the outermost track being track 0. The next track will be track 1, and so on, with the innermost track being the highest-numbered. Sectors on a track, however, are not numbered sequentially; that is, sector 1 is not necessarily physically adjacent to sector 0. Sectors are numbered in a specific pattern, according to the *interleave factor*.

For example, if you consider the sectors in a single track of a 360K disk, they are not numbered sequentially like the numbers on a clock face. Instead, the sectors interleave in their physical location, as shown in Figure 6.8A. The next numbered logical sector is physically 6 sectors away. This is referred to as a 1:6 interleave. The IBM PC AT's disk drive uses a 1:3 interleave as in Figure 6.8B.

The interleave factor is used to match the speed of reading data to the speed of the rotating disk. Whenever the computer needs information from the disk, it sends a request to the disk controller board. The hard disk is rotating continuously, so the disk controller waits until the specified sector comes under the read/write head. After the data in a sector is read from the disk, the disk controller has to check to see whether it has committed any error while reading. It does this by performing some binary arithmetic operations using all the bytes that have been read and calculating a value known as the *Cyclic Redundancy Code* (CRC). The disk controller compares this CRC value with the CRC value in the disk stored at the time of writing the data. If the CRC values match, then the data read is correct; otherwise, the disk controller returns an error to PC DOS.

Remember that while the disk controller is computing the CRC, the disk continues to spin. Suppose that the disk were not interleaved. By the time the CRC for the sector had been verified, the next sector would have passed the read/write head, and the read/write head would have had to wait for almost one revolution to read the next sector. To prevent this waiting, disk sectors are interleaved. While the CRC for a sector is being verified, the adja-

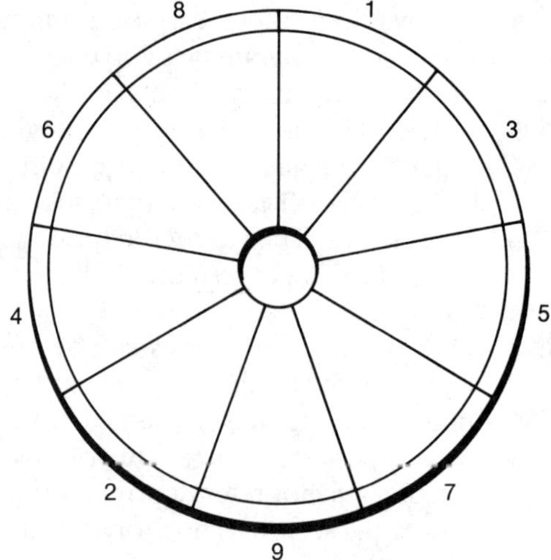

(A) A 1:6 interleave.

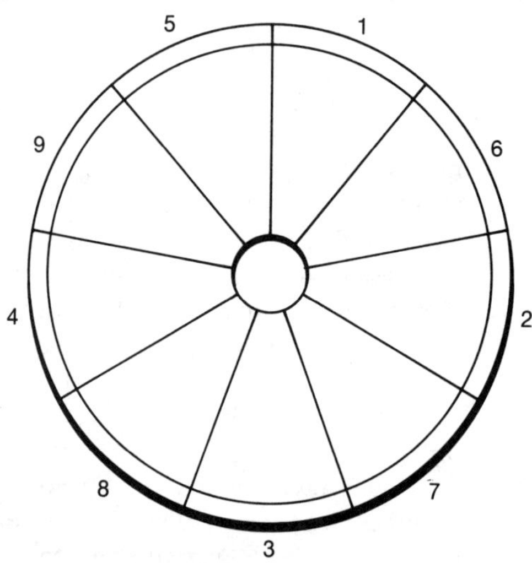

(B) A 1:3 interleave.

Figure 6.8. *Interleave factors.*

cent, nonsequential interleaved sectors pass the read/write head. When the CRC checking is complete, the next sequentially numbered sector has come under the read/write head just in time, with a minimum waiting period.

The interleave factor is transparent to PC DOS and its programs. The disk controller board, which monitors the disk activity, maintains the interleave. When PC DOS reads files from the disk, the disk controller is responsible for reading the next block of data, including the calculation of the CRC and management of the interleave factor. The potential problem with the interleave factor is that it has to match closely the performance of the disk controller with the speed of rotation of the disk. If the interleave factor is too large, then the disk controller will wait unnecessarily to read the next sector.

If it is too small, the disk controller will miss the next sector and wait for an entire extra revolution to read it.

Several commercially available programs optimize your disk's interleave factor. The Advanced Hard Disk Diagnostics from Paul Mace Software contains two programs for optimum interleave performance: HOPTIMUM and HFORMAT. HOPTIMUM analyzes hard disk performance. It times the disk drive in a number of situations and determines the most efficient interleave factor. This information can be used by the second program, HFORMAT. HFORMAT performs a thorough, *low-level formatting* of the hard disk based on the optimum interleave factor provided by HOPTIMUM. Performing a low-level format on a hard disk will rearrange the magnetic markers of the disk so that every byte is redefined. This process overwrites all bytes on the disk with dummy data bytes.

The drawback of this kind of optimization is that the low-level formatting process erases everything on the hard disk. Thus, it is necessary to back up the entire hard disk before formatting. You can restore the files later.

Optimizing Disk Performance by Using Disk Buffers

Computers store data and programs on disks in order to be able to access the data and programs later on. Because disk drives are mechanical, they are inherently slow. The computer's memory, on the other hand, is completely electronic and thus is faster than the disk. Access optimization methods load as much information as possible into the computer's memory so that the number of slow disk accesses is minimized. Because the information is available in memory, system performance is maximized. This is the idea behind using large regions of memory as disk buffers.

A *disk buffer* is a small area of memory that stores 512 bytes of data, which is equal to the size of one sector in the disk. The buffer is used to hold one sector's worth of information read from disks. When PC DOS reads from, or writes to, the disk, the smallest amount of information that PC DOS can transfer is 512 bytes, one sector's worth. Whenever PC DOS reads anything from a file, it reads at least one complete sector and stores that information in one disk buffer. For subsequent read operations, the data from that sector is now available in memory.

Assume, for example, that a database or accounting program reads data records one by one from the disk and that each record is 128 bytes long. When the program requests the first record, PC DOS reads the entire 512 bytes from the appropriate sector (which includes the 128 bytes that the program requested and also the next three records). Thus, not only the first record but the first four records are stored in a disk buffer. When the program later asks for the second record, PC DOS doesn't have to read the disk again—it already has the information in memory. This is true for the third and fourth records as well. In this example, the number of disk read operations drops from 4 to 1.

Whenever any program asks for some data to be read from the disk, PC DOS checks to see whether the information is already available in memory. If the data is in one of the disk buffers, then PC DOS returns the information to the program. If the data is not available in one of the disk buffers, PC DOS reads the entire disk sector containing the requested data into a disk buffer.

The number of buffers that PC DOS assigns by default depends on the amount of memory in your system. For a system with more than 512K of

RAM, 15 buffers are allocated. Whether this is enough depends on three factors. First, buffers are useful mainly when an application reads a series of consecutive records from the disk (this is called *sequential access*). In such an application, several records (or parts of a text file) will be stored in each disk sector, and each sector can be stored in a buffer and then reread from the buffer repeatedly to fetch each record. Other applications, such as many databases, use *random access*. This means that one record might be in sector 12, another in sector 87, and another in sector 99. Since a sector is usually not needed again once a record has been read from it, there is no advantage in storing the sectors in buffers. In fact, there is a disadvantage: it takes time to search the buffers in memory to see if one of them has the needed sector. If there are many buffers (say more than 50), this can slow down disk access—as well as use up at least 26K of memory at about 0.5K per buffer.

The speed of the CPU also has an effect: a PS/2 with an 80386 processor can search through memory considerably faster than a PC with an 8088 processor. Finally, the access speed of the disk itself helps determine how much time is saved by using buffers. Floppy disks are slow, so using buffers can make quite a difference. With a fast (28-ms) hard disk, the speedup resulting from using buffers will be less noticeable, though it still can be worthwhile.

You can configure the number of disk buffers by using the BUFFERS command in the CONFIG.SYS file, for example, `buffers=20`. Each time you boot the system, PC DOS reads this entry and reserves space for 20 buffers in the memory. You can set the number of buffers from 2 to 255. Most users achieve best performance by using 20 to 25 buffers. The larger the number of buffers, the less memory available for your programs. Moreover, PC DOS will take longer to search through all the buffers each time that an application needs information from the disk. See Chapter 11, "Customizing Your System," for more details on the CONFIG.SYS file.

Version 4

Buffers

PC DOS 4 lets you have up to 10,000 buffers if you use expanded memory. To use expanded memory, you must have installed the appropriate device driver (see Chapter 12, "Installing a PC DOS System"). For example, the following statement uses about 50K of expanded memory to store a maximum of 100 sectors of recently read disk data:

```
buffers=100 /x
```

PC DOS 4 also adds a second, optional number to the BUFFERS command. This specifies the number of *look-ahead buffers* that can be stored. Look-ahead buffers are an extension of the basic buffers idea. If an application is reading data sequentially from a file, and the application starts by reading a sector, it is likely that the next sector in sequence will soon be wanted—and then the one after that, and so on. Most of the overhead involved in reading data from the disk lies in the initial positioning of the head and the wait for the sector to arrive under the head—it takes only a few more milliseconds to read additional sectors. These sectors are put in look-ahead buffers. Now when the program asks for more data, the next several sectors are already there, waiting in memory.

The following CONFIG.SYS setting specifies that the first sector read from up to 20 files will be stored in memory, and that when a sector is read, the next 4 sectors will be read as well:

```
buffers=20,4
```

Optimizing Disk Performance by Using the FASTOPEN Command

Before a program can access a file on a disk, either to read or to write information to it, PC DOS must determine whether the file exists on the disk and whether the file has access for the specified operation. For example, PC DOS will not allow a read-only file to be written to. If the file exists and has the access for the specified operation, then PC DOS allows your program to access the file.

To determine the access for the file and also the starting location of the file in the disk, PC DOS must first read several pieces of information from the disk. As you know, disk read operations are very slow. To reduce the amount of overhead associated with accessing your commonly used files, PC DOS version 3.3 provides the FASTOPEN command. Once you invoke FASTOPEN, PC DOS keeps the necessary access information (the location in the disk, access type, etc.) in memory for a number of the most recently opened files. When PC DOS needs to open one of those files, the information is already in memory, and thus your system performance is improved.

To keep track of your 30 most recently opened files in drive C, you can use the command

```
C:\>fastopen c:=30
```

(Note that normally you would put this command in your AUTOEXEC.BAT file so that it would be executed automatically at start-up.) FASTOPEN can keep track of up to 999 files.

How do you determine the number of FASTOPEN buffers to reserve? If the number is too large, memory will be wasted. If the number is too small, PC DOS won't have enough room for information about all your files, and it will have to reread the directory entries and the FAT when you want to reopen a file that hasn't been used for a while.

To determine the first number, look at your applications and estimate how many different files you open in a given session. Then add 10 to 20 more to be generous. (For example, if your word processor uses 5 files for its programs and initialization and makes a backup of each file you edit, and you edit an average of 10 files per session, the total comes to 5 + (10 × 2), or 25 files. But suppose that you run SideKick on about 10 other files, and you run a communications program that uses another 5 files. Now you are up to 25 + 15 for SideKick, plus 5 files for the communications program. Add 10 for good measure, and you are up to 55 files, or `fastopen c:=55`. Most users find a value of 30 to 50 files for FASTOPEN to be most efficient (which requires from 1200 to 2000 bytes of memory).

You can specify FASTOPEN for additional hard disk drives too. If you have a hard disk drive installed as D, then you can use the FASTOPEN command to specify files for both the drives:

```
C:\>fastopen c:=30 d:=30
```

If you specify several disks in this manner, the total number of such file entries (for all disk drives) should not exceed 999. Because floppy disks are removable, keeping track of file information in memory for floppy disks is unpredictable, so FASTOPEN does not support floppy drives:

```
C:\>fastopen a:=30
Cannot use FASTOPEN for drive A:
```

Once you invoke FASTOPEN, the number of file entries is retained in memory until the system is shut down. If you want to change the value of FASTOPEN, you have to reboot your system.

Version 4

FASTOPEN Features

PC DOS 4 adds two features to the FASTOPEN command. First, you can add the */x* option to tell FASTOPEN to store its directory and file information in expanded memory. If you have expanded memory, doing this saves memory in the first 640K for your applications.

Next, FASTOPEN in PC DOS 4 allows you to specify an additional number. PC DOS must consult a cluster list in order to find out where the next chunk of the file is stored. The second number tells PC DOS to reserve memory to store the cluster list for each file that has been used so far in the session. This speeds up access to the file as your application requests different parts of it. A typical FASTOPEN command for PC DOS 4 would look like this:

```
install=c:\dos\fastopen.exe c:=(50,250) /x
```

FASTOPEN is one of the commands supported by the PC DOS 4 INSTALL command, and it is recommended that you use INSTALL for more efficient memory allocation. The INSTALL statement goes in CONFIG.SYS, not AUTOEXEC.BAT, and it must give the full path name, including the .EXE extension. The example statement tells FASTOPEN to reserve memory for up to 100 directory or file locations and for up to 400 file cluster locations, and to use expanded memory. The default for the number of file locations is 34, and the maximum (for all drives specified) is 999.

The value for the second number (cluster list buffers) depends mainly on how fragmented your hard disk is (the more files scattered around the disk, the more cluster number entries needed to keep track of them). A rough rule of thumb is to multiply the first number (the number of directories and files) by 5 to get the second number. If you are working with 55 files, then, the second number is 275 (`fastopen c:=(55,275)`).

Optimizing Disk Performance by Using Disk Caches

You can improve the speed of a hard disk by using a *disk cache*. A disk cache optimizes the disk performance by closely monitoring the disk activity and maintaining copies of data in computer memory. The disk buffers configured in CONFIG.SYS using the BUFFERS= entry are very similar in concept to a disk cache. The disk cache consists of two components: an area of memory called the *cache memory* and *cache software*. The cache memory acts as a buffer between the disk and the computer. The cache software logs all reads and writes to the disk and then keeps a copy of what goes to, or comes in from, the disk in the cache memory. Whenever your computer makes a request to read information from the disk, the cache software intercepts the disk request and provides information that is already available in the cache memory. In this way, a time-consuming disk read or write operation is avoided.

The cache software manages the data transfer between the computer's memory and the disk. As soon as any information is changed, the cache software writes that modified information to the disk, maintaining a copy of the information in memory. This aspect makes a disk cache different from a RAM disk. Changes made to the information in a RAM disk are not automatically saved to the physical disk: you must save everything explicitly.

A disk cache is a very useful disk speedup tool. It can improve performance considerably in the case of programs using overlays, disk-intensive applications like databases (that access many files on various parts of the disk), and word processing applications. Programs using overlays often load their various modules into memory as they are needed. When a disk cache is in operation, it monitors the overlays loaded and keeps a copy of each of them in its cache memory. When the program asks for an overlay from disk and that overlay is already in cache memory, the cache software intercepts the disk request and automatically supplies the overlay into memory.

In databases, each record is read from the disk as it is individually called up. Using a disk cache, database operations such as searching and sorting records can be accelerated because records will be supplied from cache memory most of the time.

Many varieties of disk cache software are available commercially. Mace Utilities offers VCACHE, a disk cache program available in three versions: CACHE for conventional memory, CACHE-AT for the extended memory of AT, and CACHE-EM for the EMS memory. To install CACHE, invoke the CACHE command at the PC DOS prompt. Another cache program available from the Personal Computer Support Group is LIGHTNING. LIGHTNING is configurable to any disk drive, and it can use up to 1.5M bytes of expanded (EMS) memory. LIGHTNING is memory resident and typically invoked by AUTOEXEC.BAT.

Using DISKCACHE on the IBM PS/2

Owners of PS/2 Model 50 or higher get a free cache program called IBMCACHE. The cache itself is a hidden file on the Reference Diskette. To install the cache, start the system from the Reference Diskette (or change to the drive containing the Reference Diskette) and type `ibmcache`. Select item 1 from the menu to install the cache on your hard disk. IBMCACHE automatically makes a backup copy of your CONFIG.SYS file and creates a new one with the following statement in it:

```
device=\ibmcache.sys 64 /ne /p4
```

In this statement, `64` is the number of kilobytes reserved for the cache, and `/ne` means "not extended" memory—in other words, the lower 640K of memory. The `/p4` means that a total of 4 sectors should be read at a time (that is, the desired sector and 3 more "read-ahead" sectors).

To tune this setting, select item 3 (change disk cache settings) from the IBMCACHE menu. Use the arrows to move between the three items (cache size, type of memory, and number of sectors to read at a time). For the total cache size, 16K is the minimum and 512K the maximum. (The maximum is 15,360K, i.e., over 15MB, if you use extended memory. Of course, you are unlikely to have that much memory available.) To toggle between regular and extended memory, press the F5 or F6 key while positioned at that field. For page size, you can use the F5 and F6 keys to step through the valid values (2, 4, or 8 sectors). Alternatively, you can simply edit the `device=\ibmcache.sys` statement in your CONFIG.SYS file to specify the desired values.

The cache runs faster when it is in regular memory (`/ne`), but regular memory is likely to be scarce and your cache would have to be only 64K or so. Of the 1MB minimum memory that comes with the PS/2 Model 50 or higher, 640K is standard memory, and the rest is configured automatically as extended memory. This means that you have at least 384K of extended memory, and few applications are designed to use this memory (as opposed to *expanded* memory over 1MB). Thus, you lose little by allocating all 384K of extended memory to the cache, even though data is transferred a bit more slowly in and out of extended memory. (If you do this, the IBMCACHE.SYS driver still needs about 16K of your lower 640K, however.)

The last number (look-ahead sectors) works the same way as for the look-ahead specification in BUFFERS of PC DOS 4. Four is a good value for most applications, but you can experiment with 8 if you do a lot of word processing or other sequential data access.

A typical setting for a PS/2 Model 50 would be

```
device=\ibmcache.sys 384 /e /p4
```

The `/e` means to use extended memory.

Disk Layout and File Recovery

Files can be deleted in many ways. You can delete files yourself by using the DEL or ERASE commands. Files can also be deleted by a program running in your system. Word processors, spreadsheets, and other application programs can be directly or indirectly instructed to delete files. When a file is deleted inadvertently by one of these methods, you may want to restore the contents of that file. The PC DOS file system has been designed so that recovering deleted files under certain conditions is not very difficult. As a result of this design, several commercial utilities have been developed to recover deleted files. Norton Utilities and Mace Utilities are popular examples of such utilities.

In this section, you will learn about the general methods of recovering erased files. The material contained in this section is not necessary for the routine use of PC DOS. It is included for those readers who want a further understanding of how PC DOS stores and retrieves files.

Structure of PC DOS Disks

Before you learn about methods of file recovery, you need a clear picture of how files are stored on the disk. Hard disks have one or more *platters*, each platter consisting of two sides. Recall from an earlier discussion that PC DOS divides the surface of the platters into *tracks* and sectors. The outermost track is numbered track 0, the next inner one is track 1, and so on. Each track is divided into arcs of circles called *sectors*. Like tracks, sectors are also sequentially numbered. The first sector in a track is sector 1, the second is sector 2, and so on. All tracks having the same radius form a *cylinder*. Thus, the combination of each track 0 of all the sides of all the platters forms cylinder 0. The combination of each track 1 of all sides forms cylinder 1, and so on.

Consider a hard disk with two platters, each platter having two sides. Each side of each platter has a corresponding track. Thus, there are a total of four tracks for each position (e.g., there are four of track zero). A standard 10MB hard disk has 306 cylinders, 4 tracks per cylinder, and 17 sectors per track. The total number of tracks on the disk is 1,224 (306 cylinders × 4 tracks per cylinder). The total number of sectors is 20,808 (1,224 tracks × 17 sectors per track). The total storage capacity is 10,653,696 (20,808 sectors × 512 bytes per sector).

In constructing tracks and sectors with the FORMAT command, PC DOS reserves certain sectors for its internal functions, such as tracking space allocation for files. In the following discussion you will learn more about those sectors that PC DOS uses for file and space management functions on the disk.

Control Sectors and Data Sectors

PC DOS uses the first few sectors on a disk to control how files are stored on the disk. All other sectors following these *control sectors* store the actual data, and these other sectors are called *data sectors*. The control sectors fall into three major groups: the boot sector, the file allocation table sectors, and the directory sectors.

The Boot Sector

The first sector on every disk formatted under PC DOS is defined as the *boot record*. The boot record is always found in sector 1, track 0, side 0. It consists of a short program that loads the operating system into the computer's memory and also a table containing information about the format of the disk.

The boot program is automatically loaded into the computer's memory when the computer is turned on. This program instructs the computer where to look on the disk for the system files, IBMBIO.COM and IBMDOS.COM, that contain PC DOS. The FORMAT command transfers these two files to the disk when the disk is formatted as a *boot disk* or the *system disk* using the */s* switch. Once the two hidden system files are found, the boot program loads them into the computer's memory and then loads COMMAND.COM, the PC DOS command interpreter. (COMMAND.COM is the program that responds to the invocation of commands such as DIR, CD, CLS, COPY, and so on.) The boot record containing the boot program is always stored in the first sector of the disk, regardless of whether or not the disk is designated as a boot disk.

The first 3 bytes of the boot record contain an instruction for the computer, telling the computer where to find the boot program. A table containing information about the format of the disk is stored immediately following the first 3 bytes. The table contains details about the format of the disk, such as bytes per sector, sectors per cluster, number of directory sectors, sectors per track, number of heads, etc. The actual boot program is stored after the table.

The File Allocation Table

Following the boot record, several sectors store the *file allocation table* (FAT). The FAT provides a map of the disk, helping PC DOS determine the locations on the disk of each part of every file. When a disk is formatted, the FORMAT command reserves the sectors for the FAT. A FAT consists of *FAT entries*. Each FAT entry controls one unit of space allocation on the disk, namely a cluster.

FAT refers to files in terms of *clusters*. A file always occupies at least one cluster, and larger files are stored in several clusters. A cluster is a group of one or more sectors. In double-sided diskettes, one cluster contains two sectors.

When 10MB hard disks were introduced, a cluster contained 8 sectors. In 20MB hard disks in PC ATs, one cluster contains 4 sectors. The entire remaining area of data sectors that follows the FAT sectors (except the boot, FAT, and directory sectors) is divided equally into clusters. Each cluster is numbered sequentially starting from 2.

Disk Structure Differences in PC DOS Versions

PC DOS versions 2.0 through 3.2 support only one PC DOS partition per hard disk, whereas version 3.3 supports several PC DOS partitions per hard disk, each with a maximum size of 32MB and each assigned a different drive name. PC DOS 4 supports extended-size partitions that may be as large as 512MB. Extended-size partitions are optional under PC DOS 4: a large disk can still be formatted with several PC DOS partitions that are 32MB or smaller in size. Note that 32MB or smaller partitions use 16-bit sector numbers, and extended-size partitions use 32-bit sector numbers. This can cause incompatibility problems with many applications that reference a disk's FAT and that reference sectors with 16-bit values. (See *The Waite Group's MS-DOS Developer's Guide*, second edition, #22630, published by Howard W. Sams, for more details.)

The entire range of clusters is mapped by the FAT, and each FAT entry gives the state of the correspondingly numbered cluster. The FAT entries numbered 0 and 1 are used for identifying the disk format, which is why cluster numbers start at 2. Table 6.3 gives the location of FAT sectors in relation to other control sectors. Figure 6.9 shows how clusters are numbered in a hard disk.

The number of sectors that the FAT occupies depends on the storage capacity of the disk. Diskettes with the 9-sector-per-track format have a 2-sector FAT. The FAT in high-density diskettes consists of 7 sectors. Ten-megabyte hard disks have an 8-sector FAT. As you can see from Figure 6.9, PC DOS maintains two copies of the FAT on each disk. The FAT is so important in accessing files that a second copy is available should the first be damaged.

A linked list describes the chain of clusters belonging to each file. Here's how it works. Each cluster corresponds to a FAT entry: cluster 2 corresponds to FAT entry 2; cluster 3 corresponds to FAT entry 3; and so on. The contents of the FAT entry normally represent the number of the next cluster occupied by a file, as shown in the sample FAT of Figure 6.10. To access a file, PC DOS gets the number of the file's first cluster from its directory entry. The FAT entry corresponding to the first cluster indicates the second cluster number; the FAT entry for the second cluster shows the third cluster number; and so on. The FAT entry for the file's last cluster stores an end-of-file marker.

Table 6.4. ***Location of Boot, FAT, and Directory Sectors***

	8-Sector/Track Diskettes	9-Sector/Track Diskettes	10MB Hard Disk
Boot Record	Sector 1 Track 0	Sector 1 Track 0	Sector 1 Track 0 Side 0
FAT, 1st copy	Sector 2 Track 0	Sectors 2–3 Track 0	Sectors 2–9 Track 0 Side 0
FAT, 2nd copy	Sector 3 Track 0	Sectors 4–5 Track 0	Sectors 10–17 Track 0 Side 0
Directory	Sectors 4–7 Track 0	Sectors 6–9 Track 0	Sectors 1–17 Track 1 Side 0 Sectors 1–15 Track 2 Side 0

At the time of formatting the disk, if PC DOS finds a damaged cluster that is unusable, it marks the corresponding FAT entry as bad so that the cluster does not get allocated for any file. The possible values for a FAT entry and their meanings are as follows:

FAT Entry (Hex)	Meaning
000	Cluster is free and available for storage
FF0 through FF6	Reserved cluster (not available for normal file storage)
FF7	Bad cluster (not used for file storage)
FF8 through FFF	Last cluster occupied by a file
XXX	Any other value indicates the number of the next cluster occupied by a file

The way in which information is stored in the FAT is not so straightforward as one would expect. Because the FAT serves as the complete road map of the disk, storage and retrieval of information is complex. As much information as possible about the disk is packed into the FAT. Interpreting or decoding the contents of the FAT is beyond the scope of this book. However, the interested reader is referred to *The Waite Group's MS-DOS Developer's Guide*, second edition (#22630, Howard W. Sams) and other references on the subject.

The Directory Sectors

The directory sectors store the directory information for all files on the disk. The DIR command displays the information retrieved from the directory sectors. The directory entry for a file consists of the file name, its attributes, size, and other information. Each directory entry occupies 32 bytes, so one sector can store 16 directory entries. The total number of directory entries for the entire disk depends on the number of directory sectors. In a 40-track double-sided diskette, 7 directory sectors allow up to 112 directory entries. For hard disks, the number of directory sectors depends on the storage capacity of the disk (or the size of the PC DOS partition). Most hard disks use 32 directory sectors, which will allow up to 512 directory entries.

Each directory entry corresponds to a file present in the directory. The directory entry contains the following information as shown in Table 6.5.

The first 11 bytes of the directory entry contain the file name and extension, each byte representing one ASCII character (8 characters for the file name and 3 characters for the extension). Subdirectories are treated as files, so you can find entries for subdirectories also in the root directory.

As shown in Table 6.5, the first byte in a directory entry can represent the first character of the file name or the file status. When a disk is formatted, this first byte is set to 00, and the rest of the directory entry is filled with the hexadecimal value of F6. When a new file is created, this first byte is changed to represent the first character of the file's name. Later, when a file is erased, the first byte of the corresponding directory entry is changed to a hexadecimal value of E5. The rest of the information in the directory entry is left intact. Thus, by reading only the first byte of a file's directory entry, PC DOS determines whether the directory entry is free.

Sector \ Track	0	1	2	. . .	39
1	Boot	Cl.3	Cl.11	. . .	. . .
2	FAT1	Cl.4	Cl.12	. . .	. . .
3	FAT2	Cl.5	. . .	. . .	Cl.309
4	Dir	Cl.6	. . .	. . .	Cl.310
5	Dir	Cl.7	. . .	. . .	Cl.311
6	Dir	Cl.8	. . .	. . .	Cl.312
7	Dir	Cl.9	. . .	. . .	Cl.313
8	Cl.2	Cl.10	. . .	. . .	Cl.314

(A) Cluster numbers in 8-sector/track diskettes.

Sector \ Track	0	1	2	. . .	39
1	Boot	Cl.2	Cl.11	. . .	. . .
2	FAT1	Cl.3	Cl.12	. . .	. . .
3	FAT1	Cl.4	Cl.13	. . .	. . .
4	FAT2	Cl.5	. . .	. . .	Cl.347
5	FAT2	Cl.6	. . .	. . .	Cl.348
6	Dir	Cl.7	. . .	. . .	Cl.349
7	Dir	Cl.8	. . .	. . .	Cl.350
8	Dir	Cl.9	. . .	. . .	Cl.351
9	Dir	Cl.10	. . .	. . .	Cl.352

(B) Cluster numbers in 9-sector/track diskettes.

Figure 6.9. ***Cluster numbers in diskettes and hard disks.***

Table 6.5. *Information Found in the Directory Entry*

Offset	Description	Size in Bytes	Format
0	First character of file name or file status	1	ASCII
1	Rest of file name	7	ASCII
8	File extension	3	ASCII
11	Attribute	1	Bit-coded
12	Reserved	10	Unused
22	Time stamp	2	Word
24	Date stamp	2	Word
26	Starting cluster number	2	Word
28	File size	4	Integer

The *attribute* byte contains information about the storage attributes of a file. Each bit in the byte represents one specific attribute and is set to 1 when the attribute is assigned to the file. Attributes control the way PC DOS interprets the contents of a directory entry. Table 6.6 shows the definitions of each attribute and the respective hexadecimal values for the attribute byte.

Recovering Files

When a file on a disk appears to be damaged, there are three basic ways to recover it. The first way is to use one of the PC DOS commands, CHKDSK or RECOVER. These commands can read the damaged areas of a file, allowing you to recover some or all of it.

The second way is to use the DEBUG program to read the control sectors of a disk. You can then interpret these control sectors by using the princi-

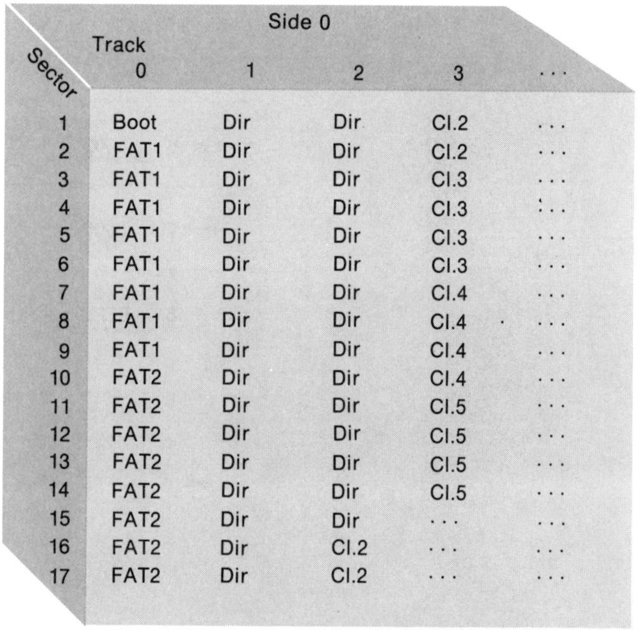

Side 0

Sector \ Track	0	1	2	3	...
1	Boot	Dir	Dir	Cl.2	...
2	FAT1	Dir	Dir	Cl.2	...
3	FAT1	Dir	Dir	Cl.3	...
4	FAT1	Dir	Dir	Cl.3	...
5	FAT1	Dir	Dir	Cl.3	...
6	FAT1	Dir	Dir	Cl.3	...
7	FAT1	Dir	Dir	Cl.4	...
8	FAT1	Dir	Dir	Cl.4	...
9	FAT1	Dir	Dir	Cl.4	...
10	FAT2	Dir	Dir	Cl.4	...
11	FAT2	Dir	Dir	Cl.5	...
12	FAT2	Dir	Dir	Cl.5	...
13	FAT2	Dir	Dir	Cl.5	...
14	FAT2	Dir	Dir	Cl.5	...
15	FAT2	Dir	Dir	...	...
16	FAT2	Dir	Cl.2	...	...
17	FAT2	Dir	Cl.2	...	...

(C) Cluster numbers in a hard disk.

Figure 6.9. ***(cont.)***

Table 6.6. ***Attribute Definitions and Corresponding Byte Values***

Attribute	Value (Hex)	Value (Decimal)	Bits 7 6 5 4 3 2 1 0
Read-only	01	1	0 0 0 0 0 0 0 1
Hidden	02	2	0 0 0 0 0 0 1 0
System	04	4	0 0 0 0 0 1 0 0
Volume label	08	8	0 0 0 0 1 0 0 0
Subdirectory	10	16	0 0 0 1 0 0 0 0
Archive	20	32	0 0 1 0 0 0 0 0
Not used	40	64	0 1 0 0 0 0 0 0
Not used	80	128	1 0 0 0 0 0 0 0

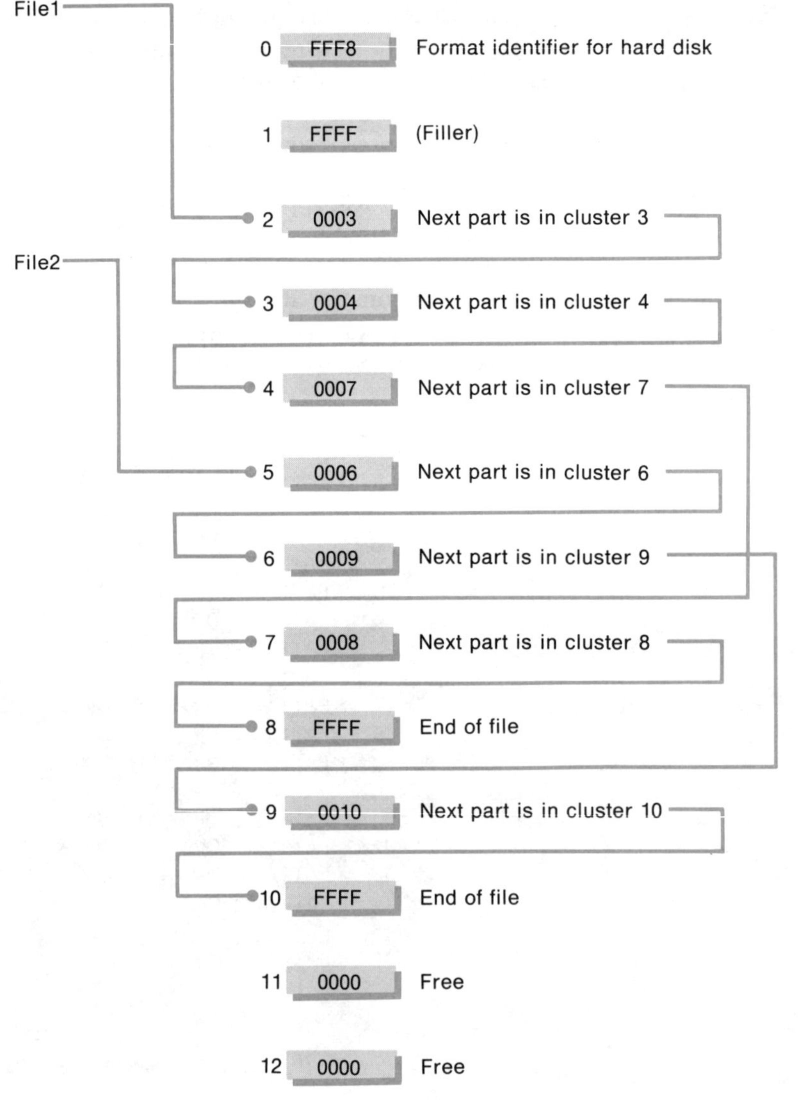

Figure 6.10. ***A sample FAT.***

ples of file storage discussed earlier. With your knowledge of how PC DOS stores files on a disk, and the information obtained by reading the FAT and directory sectors, you can attempt to reconstruct the damaged file. This same approach can be used to write your own program to recover files.

The last way is to use a commercially available utility, such as Norton Utilities or Mace Utilities. These utilities provide various capabilities, including decoding the FAT, inspecting individual sectors of a disk, repairing damaged files, and restoring erased files.

Recovering Damaged Files Using CHKDSK and RECOVER

If you repeatedly get disk errors when you attempt to access a file, the file may occupy one or more damaged sectors. For example, if the file ADDRESS.LST occupies some damaged sectors, you may see the following error:

```
C:\CLIENTS>type address.lst

Data error reading drive A
Abort, Retry, or Ignore ?r

Data error reading drive A
Abort, Retry, or Ignore ?a

C:\CLIENTS>copy address.lst addrlist.tmp

Data error reading drive A
Abort, Retry, or Ignore ?a
```

As the preceding example shows, copying the file will not alleviate the problem. The COPY command will not be able to read the rest of the file beyond the bad sectors. In this situation, you can use the RECOVER command to extract as much data belonging to the file as possible. RECOVER makes a copy of the original file as far as possible and writes the file in new sectors. Unlike COPY, it continues to read the file even after it encounters a bad sector. Thus, it may leave gaps between parts of the file, where the original file occupied bad sectors. In this process, RECOVER automatically marks all the bad sectors it encounters in the FAT so that these bad sectors do not get allocated to other files in the future. If you are recovering a text file, you can use a word processor or text editor to see whether any data has been lost. For other types of files, use the corresponding tool to see if you have lost data (e.g., use the spreadsheet program for inspecting spreadsheet files).

For example, if the file BADFILE.TXT occupies bad sectors, use RECOVER as follows:

```
C:\>recover a:badfile.txt
Press any key to begin recovery of the
file(s) on drive A:

872 of 1435 bytes recovered
```

Since RECOVER is an external command, a copy of RECOVER.COM

must be accessible by PC DOS, either in the current directory or through the use of PATH. After RECOVER starts executing, it waits until you change disks in the specified drive, if necessary. Then it displays the number of bytes recovered for the file. After recovering a file, you can copy it elsewhere, modify its contents, or use it as a normal file.

Caution

RECOVER Destroys the Directory Tree Structure

Do not use RECOVER for recovering all files in a disk. Even though you can use RECOVER to recover all files in a disk by simply giving the drive name, using RECOVER for this purpose will destroy the tree structure of directories in the disk. Because RECOVER cannot distinguish between a damaged sector and an undamaged sector, it recovers all files. It removes all subdirectories from the root and places the recovered files under the root. Do not, under any circumstances, use a command such as `recover c:`.

If you execute such a command, the tree-structured directory organization on the disk will be completely lost, and all you will see is a flat directory of recovered files. The first recovered file gets the name "FILE0001.REC", the second file "FILE0002.REC", and so on. The recovered files may contain the information that was present in the files before the recovery. The hardest part is that RECOVER deletes all subdirectories and places them as recovered files under the root directory. After this disaster, the only way of getting back your directory structure is to restore the files from a recent backup set.

Recall that the FAT details which disk clusters (basic units of disk space allocation) are allocated to which files. A file usually gets a chain of clusters, with pointers from one cluster to another. However, certain actions, such as restarting PC DOS or turning off your system while a program is running, or terminating a program with Ctrl-Break, can cause a link in this cluster chain to be broken. If this happens, the pointer to the cluster chain will be lost, and the data in these clusters will be unavailable to you. To recover the file and to fix the FAT, use the CHKDSK command with the */f* option. CHKDSK checks the FAT to see if there are any lost clusters. Usually there are not, in which case CHKDSK displays the hard disk statistics.

If CHKDSK discovers some lost clusters, it will display a message such as

```
C:\>chkdsk /f
009 lost clusters found in 003 chains
Convert lost clusters to files (Y/N) ?
```

CHKDSK has no way of knowing which files those lost clusters originally belonged to. Thus, it cannot replace the clusters to their original files. If you type `y` in answer to CHKDSK's question, CHKDSK will convert these lost clusters into separate new files and place them under the root directory. Each cluster replaced by CHKDSK will be identified as a file with the name FILE*nnnn*.CHK under the root directory. The first cluster is named "FILE0000.CHK," the next one "FILE0001.CHK," and so on. If you already have files with similar names under the root directory (e.g., if you have

FILE0001.CHK and FILE0002.CHK under the root), CHKDSK will start naming files from the next number onward.

Later you can inspect these files with the TYPE command or other method, and if the information is important, you can save those files. At worst, you can simply delete the files, thus reclaiming the storage space occupied by the lost clusters.

Recovering Erased Files

If you delete a file unintentionally, it is fairly easy to "undelete" the file under certain conditions. When the ERASE or the DEL command is used to delete a file, two things happen to the disk. The first character of the file's directory entry changes to a hexadecimal E5, indicating that the directory entry is free. All FAT entries corresponding to the clusters occupied by the deleted file are zeroed; this means that these clusters are now available for storage.

Everything else remains intact, including the remaining information in the file's directory entry and the contents of the file's data clusters. This is true only until PC DOS writes a new file to the disk. While storing a new file, PC DOS will allocate these free clusters for the new file, thus overwriting the deleted file's data. So, as long as no new file is written to the disk, you can undelete a file.

You can use the DEBUG program for reading the directory and FAT sectors of the disk. Begin the recovery process by looking at the directory entries that start with a hexadecimal value of E5. When you find a free directory entry (starting with hexadecimal value E5), look at the remaining characters of the file name in the directory entry. If the remaining characters of the file name match the file name you want to recover, you can replace the E5 in the directory entry with the first character of the file name. By examining other fields of the directory entry, you can get the number of the first data cluster. Now you have to inspect the FAT for free data clusters because PC DOS marks the data clusters of a deleted file as free. By examining the contents of the free data clusters one by one, you can reconstruct the FAT entries to reflect the chain of data clusters that were originally allocated to the file. The actual process of recovering a file using this method is beyond the scope of this chapter. Using commercial software, such as the Norton Utilities and Mace Utilities, is a more comfortable and effective method of recovering erased files.

Hard Disk Security

The problem of data security has become more prominent as the capacity of hard disks has become larger. In most organizations, the concept of data distribution—placing data close to the user—has caused the transfer of information from mainframes to personal computers. In addition, technological advances like local area networks (LANs) and large-capacity hard disks have made it easier to store and retrieve large quantities of data. These conditions have given rise to data security problems such as illegal access, data tampering, and unauthorized modifications. Data security is also important in noncriminal situations, such as inadvertent data corruption from unintended overwrites, storage of files in bad sectors, and electrical and mechanical failures that cause files to be lost.

Data security is the process of controlling access to data on the hard disk, limiting access so that only authorized people or programs make use of the data and ensuring overall data integrity. The data security problem in PC DOS can be handled in three basic ways:

- Change the file attributes so that files cannot be modified.
- Store the contents of the file in encrypted form; unless a user has the key to decrypt the data, he or she cannot make use of the data.
- Use passwords to control access to files, directories, or the computer itself.

A brief discussion of each data protection method follows.

Changing File Attributes

Recall from the earlier discussion of the directory sectors that every file in a directory has an attribute byte associated with it. PC DOS stores the attribute byte in the directory entry of the file along with other directory information. Inside this byte are 8 bits that give PC DOS some information about the file. The bits in the attribute byte are as follows:

Attribute	Bit Position
Read-only	0
Hidden	1
System	2
Volume label	3
Subdirectory	4
Archive	5
Not used	6
Not used	7

Protecting Files by Using the Read-Only Attribute

Normally there is no reason to change any of the attribute values for files. PC DOS assigns them as needed. However, to add a level of file security, you can change the read-only attribute by using the ATTRIB command. If the read-only attribute is not set ("clear" or equal to 0), the contents of the file may be changed. Generally, this attribute is not set. Setting the read-only attribute bit (set to 1) of a file gives you protection against accidental deletion or modification. The ATTRIB command also allows you to modify the archive attribute of a file. Typing `attrib` followed by the file name displays the current values of these attributes. In the following example, the ATTRIB command displays all files in the current directory and their read-only and archive attributes.

```
C:\WORDP>attrib *.*
R        C:\WORDP\LETTER
R        C:\WORDP\TEST1.DOC
R        C:\WORDP\TEST2.DOC
A        C:\WORDP\HARDDISK.DOC
A        C:\WORDP\HARDDISK.BAK
A        C:\WORDP\CARDS.TXT
```

Files with an R by them have their read-only attribute set. Any attempt to delete, rename, or modify those files results in an error, as in the next example:

```
C:\WORDP>del test1.doc
Access denied
```

To change the attribute of any file, you can use the *r* or *a* switch with a + or − sign in the ATTRIB command. The following example shows how to protect all files *.DOC with read-only status:

```
C:\WORDP>attrib +r *.doc
```

This command sets the read-only attribute for all files specified in the command—in this case, all files with a .DOC extension are given the read-only status. These files can no longer be deleted, renamed, or modified. They can, however, be looked at, or read.

Later, if you want to remove the read-only attribute of a file, you can type -r in the ATTRIB command:

```
C:\WORDP>attrib -r test1.doc
```

This command removes the protection offered by the read-only attribute. You can remove the read-only attribute for all files in the current directory with the following command:

```
C:\WORDP>attrib -r *.*
```

Another way of providing security for a file is to mark it as a hidden file. To do this, you must set the hidden attribute. PC DOS protects its system files, IBMDOS.COM and IBMBIO.COM, by making them hidden in the root directory. When a file's hidden attribute is set, its name does not show up in normal directory searches, and for all practical purposes the file is not seen by a normal user. Thus, the file is protected from unauthorized access. However, if you use the CHKDSK command with the */v* switch to display the tree structure, the result displays the hidden files also. Additionally, PC DOS does not provide any direct method for making a file hidden. Thus, you have to use commercially available utilities (or the DEBUG utility) to hide files.

DOS Shell

Setting File Attributes

To set file attributes from DOSSHELL, first select "File System" from the Main Group on the Start Programs screen. Next, select the file using the directory and the file list windows. Select "Change Attribute" from the file menu. Then select the attribute you want to set: Hidden, Read Only, or Archive.

Hiding Files by Using Nonstandard Names

PC DOS allows certain special characters to be used in naming files. Although the PC DOS manual does not state that these characters can be used in file names, PC DOS accepts them and they serve as a good method of file security.

Except for the control characters (such as ^A, ^C, etc.) and some special characters having specific meanings to PC DOS (such as \ | < > = : [ ] " etc.), a wide variety of characters available on the keyboard can name files. These characters include the *extended ASCII characters*, which can be typed by holding down the Alt key and pressing numbers from your keyboard's numeric keypad.

For example, the extended ASCII character number 219 is a solid block. To type this character, hold down the Alt key and type **219** on the numeric keypad. When you release the Alt key, the solid block appears on the screen.

The extended ASCII character set contains a variety of characters that you can use in file names. However, character 255 appears as a blank. If you rename a file to this character, PC DOS displays it as a blank in the directory listing. Note that the ASCII character 255 is not the same as a blank. PC DOS will not accept the blank character as part of a file name. Suppose you have a file TEST1 on the hard disk. You can rename TEST1 to the extended ASCII character 255 by using the REN command and typing the ASCII character 219 (hold down the Alt key and type **255** on the numeric keypad).

```
C:\>ren TEST1 [255]
C:\>dir

 Volume in drive C has no label
 Directory of C:\

                134    12-28-90        6:23p
TEST2           128    12-28-90        6:29p
TEST3           149    12-28-90        6:47p
```

The file named [255] appears in the directory listing as a blank. Unlike a hidden file, [255] is listed. Its name is blank, but the size and date show up. You can rename other files in this directory also. TEST2 can be renamed to [255] [255], TEST3 can be renamed [255] [255] [255]. You can have up to 32 file names in a single directory using the [255] character alone. However, if you have too many files named with the [255] character in a single directory, you yourself may get confused about their contents.

Data Encryption

Data encryption refers to the systematic scrambling of information in a file, making that information unreadable. Because the information scrambling takes place systematically, or according to a specific pattern, you can unscramble and return it to its original form. *Encryption* is the method of scrambling information in this manner; unscrambling is referred to as *decryption*.

The simplest encryption method is substitution, where each character is substituted by another one, in a specific pattern. For example, using the following substitution, you can transform the text HELLO WORLD into an encrypted form, WTAAD LDGAS:

```
ABCDEFGHIJKLMNOPQRSTUVWXYZ
PQRSTUVWXYZABCDEFGHIJKLMNO
```

The decryption of the text requires knowledge of the transformation pattern, which is called the *key*. In its simplest form, an encryption program adds or subtracts every character in a file by a key value. Such simple encryption methods are easy to break, so most commercially available data encryption programs use schemes much more complicated than this.

The most popular encryption scheme is called the *Data Encryption Standard* (DES) and is defined by the National Bureau of Standards. DES is so powerful that federal departments and agencies use it to protect all sensitive computer data. The encryption algorithm of DES is very complicated and beyond the scope of this book.

One commercially available encryption program is Borland's SuperKey. SuperKey supports two modes of data encryption: text mode and nontext mode. Both modes can use either the DES algorithm or a special encryption scheme developed by Borland. The nontext mode takes the information in a file and scrambles it according to a keyword 30 characters long. The resulting file has the same length as the original, and only those who know the keyword can unscramble the file. In text mode, the encrypted information is placed in a file composed of only uppercase alphabets. Such a text file is ideal for transmitting over a modem, without the fear of someone tapping the data.

Password Protection

If you are the only person using the computer, you may want to set up a password to prevent others from using your system. If more than one person uses the computer, you may want to restrict the access of certain users to certain subdirectory areas or to certain files. You can implement a simple password scheme by using PC DOS's batch file commands or by using BASIC language. Designing such a password scheme with batch file commands is explained in Chapter 10.

Preparing a Hard Disk for PC DOS

The last section of this chapter gives instructions for a task you won't need to do very often—prepare a brand new hard disk for use with PC DOS. Before performing the procedures described here, however, read about preparing the hard disk in Chapter 12, "Installing a PC DOS System." That will help you determine which procedures you will need to perform.

Low-Level Formatting

Caution

Before You Begin

Low-level formatting destroys any existing data on the disk. If there are files on your hard disk, it is already formatted, and you don't need (or want) to do a low-level format. The exceptions are situations in which there is serious damage to the disk or you want to change the interleave. In those cases, you should attempt to back up as many files as possible before beginning the low-level format.

Low-level formatting has traditionally been done at the factory or by the dealer. Systems shipped by IBM with a hard disk already have low-level formatting. At the time of this writing, more and more users who buy from mail order and discount outlets find that they have to do it themselves. How can you tell?

If you have PC DOS 4, refer to Chapter 12 and run the SELECT program. If SELECT doesn't recognize the existence of any drive C or if it gives you an error message such as `Drive not ready`, then the disk does not have a low-level format. Press Esc and F3 to exit SELECT, and return here. If SELECT recognizes your drive, it will lead you through partitioning and high-level formatting if necessary.

If you don't have PC DOS 4, type

```
A>fdisk
```

to run the FDISK utility. (If this program isn't on your start-up disk, use the DIR command on successive disks until you find the PC DOS disk that has it.) If FDISK recognizes your drive, you can advance to the section in this chapter titled "Partitioning the Disk with FDISK"; if not, continue here.

How to Do a Low-Level Format

How do you accomplish low-level formatting? If you have a PS/2 or AT, check your system documentation: the Reference or Utility disk for many of these models has an option called "Prepare fixed disk for DOS" or something similar. Run this option to take care of your low-level formatting. Other systems may also come with a low-level format utility. If you have bought a mail-order clone or if you are installing a hard disk in an existing system, look for documentation accompanying the system or hard disk. You may have to call your dealer.

In some systems, the low-level formatting is performed automatically by a ROM (program in permanent memory) on the controller. If you suspect that this is the case, remove any diskette from your floppy drive and restart the system. When the hard disk comes on, the display will indicate that low-level formatting is in process. When it is over, you will have to restart the system from your PC DOS floppy, since the hard disk won't be partitioned nor will a high-level format have been done yet.

Using DEBUG to Do Low-Level Formatting

The last resort is to do low-level formatting by using the DOS utility DEBUG to call the routine built into the controller ROM. You will need to know the manufacturer and the model of the disk controller. The command that you type in after invoking DEBUG depends on the manufacturer and model of the disk controller. For example, the keyboard command `G=C800:5` is used for the following controllers:

Western Digital WD1002 WX2

Western Digital WD1002 WX1

Western Digital WD1002 27X

Seagate ST01

Seagate ST10

Seagate ST11R

(If you are not familiar with DEBUG, see Chapter 11, "Customizing Your System," for a brief tutorial.)

The following tutorial assumes that you have one of the preceding controllers. If you have another controller, find the appropriate substitute for the `G=C800:5` command. To start the process, type

```
A>debug
```

The monitor will display a dash

```
-
```

Type `G=C800:5` and press Enter, or the equivalent if you are using another controller. The low-level format routine will request the technical data for your hard disk, such as the number of cylinders, number of heads, reduced write current, write precomp., and ECC correction span. Most of the information required is very technical and beyond the scope of this book. You simply enter the value supplied with your disk controller and/or drive documentation. The interleave factor, however, is variable and can have an important effect on the performance of your hard disk. (See the earlier discussion "Optimizing Hard Disk Performance by Changing the Interleave.")

Partitioning the Disk with FDISK

Partitioning a hard disk means that you set up one or more areas of the hard disk, each of which is treated as an independent logical drive by PC DOS and is referred to by using drive letters such as C or D.

Why would you want to do this? One reason is size. The versions of PC DOS prior to 4 don't allow a partition larger than 32MB. If you have a hard disk with a capacity of 40MB, 60MB, or even more, and you are using a version of PC DOS prior to 4, you must set up multiple partitions if you want to use all of your disk. (Of course, this is a good reason to consider upgrading to PC DOS 4.)

A second reason for partitioning a hard disk is to allow for use of another operating system in addition to PC DOS. While OS/2 can share partitions with PC DOS, other operating systems such as XENIX and CP/M86 cannot, so each operating system must have its own partition.

Version 4

Partitions

PC DOS 4 allows partitions of virtually unlimited size. You must create at least one partition on your hard disk, but you may create up to four separate partitions. The first partition is called the *primary* DOS partition. The PC DOS operating system starts up from this primary partition when you turn on the power. Additional partitions are called *extended* partitions.

With PC DOS versions 3.3 and earlier, the largest allowable partition size is 32 megabytes because this is the most disk space that can be mapped by the standard DOS file allocation table (FAT) in 2048-byte clusters. Systems using larger hard disks under these versions of PC DOS can do one of three things: partition the hard disk so that each partition is no greater than 32MB, devote more disk space to the FAT (containing the list of disk clusters used by each file), or increase the cluster size.

A 100MB hard disk could, for example, be partitioned into three partitions of 32MB each, and another partition of 8MB. The disadvantage is that any single file is still limited to a maximum length of 32 megabytes. (For some large databases, this may not be enough!) Moreover, with PC DOS versions 3.1 and earlier, only one partition can be a DOS partition.

Increasing the size of the FAT requires using a customized version of PC DOS. This custom version is supplied by some system or hard disk vendors. The modification would not interfere with most programs because the modified DOS would intercept requests for the disk and translate them appropriately. However, special utilities that recover files or otherwise maintain the hard disk would probably not work. Further, you might be locked into an older version of PC DOS if the vendor doesn't provide later versions.

Clusters can be enlarged beyond 2048 bytes either by increasing the size of each of the standard four sectors per cluster beyond 512 bytes, or by using more than four sectors per cluster. Sector size is set automatically by low-level formatting, but it is also limited by data density and the speed of revolution of the hard disk. The number of sectors per cluster is determined by PC DOS and can be more easily modified. The disadvantage of increasing the cluster size is increased waste of the storage space, since the cluster is the minimum allocation of space for a given file—even the smallest file must use one cluster. The larger the cluster size is, the more space is wasted if you have many small files.

Since each of the approaches just mentioned has disadvantages, it is recommended that you upgrade to PC DOS 4, eliminating the partition size limitation. There are very few programs that won't run under PC DOS 4, and upgraded versions of most of them will be available.

How to Run FDISK

Caution

Changing Existing Partitions

If you run FDISK on a hard disk that is already partitioned, and you try to delete or change a partition, you will be warned that doing so will destroy any data in that partition. If you wish to repartition your hard disk, be sure to first back up its data (see the earlier discussion "Backing Up Your Hard Disk").

If you have PC DOS 4 and your hard disk has been low-level formatted but not partitioned, put your Install diskette in drive A and restart the system. The SELECT program will run FDISK for you. You should still read this section for general advice, but you can also get help from SELECT at any time by pressing the F1 key. (See Chapter 12 for more information on SELECT.)

If you have an earlier version of PC DOS, or if you have already partitioned your hard disk and need to change the partitions for some reason, you must run FDISK correctly. Here is how to partition a blank, low-formatted hard disk using the FDISK utility, which is one of the PC DOS external commands. (For a complete summary of FDISK, see the Command Reference in this book.)

Use DIR to locate FDISK.COM on one of your PC DOS operating system floppy diskettes. Load FDISK into your machine by typing

```
A>fdisk
```

PC DOS will load FDISK into memory and FDISK will present its first screen. Here is the FDISK screen for PC DOS version 4:

```
IBM DOS Version 4
Fixed Disk Setup Program
(C) Copyright IBM Corp. 1983, 1988
FDISK Options
Current fixed disk drive: 1
Choose one of the following:
    1. Create DOS Partition or Logical DOS Drive
    2. Set Active Partition
    3. Delete DOS Partition or Logical DOS Drive
    4. Display Partition Information
    5. Select next fixed disk drive
Enter choice: [ ]
Press Esc to exit FDISK
```

The first choice lets you create a DOS partition or create a logical DOS drive. Don't worry about what "logical DOS drive" means for now. Since you want to create a DOS partition so that you can use your blank hard disk, enter `1` as your choice. FDISK will present this next screen:

```
Create DOS Partition or Logical DOS Drive
Current fixed disk drive: 1

Choose one of the following:

1. Create Primary DOS Partition
2. Create Extended DOS Partition
3. Create Logical DOS Drive(s) in the Extended DOS Partition

Enter choice: [  ]
```

Because your hard disk is completely blank, you want to create a primary DOS partition. The primary DOS partition is the one that the system will use when it starts up. It may be the only partition that you will use. Enter `1` as your choice. FDISK will present this screen:

```
Create Primary DOS Partition
Current fixed disk drive: 1

Do you wish to use the maximum available size for a Primary DOS
Partition and make the partition active? (Y/N).......? [ ]
```

You can choose either **Y** (yes) or **N** (no). If you choose **N**, FDISK will let you set up part of your hard disk as the primary DOS partition and also let you create up to three additional extended partitions. Unless you are going to be using a non-DOS compatible operating system, there is little reason to do this with PC DOS 4. All you need to do is create one partition that includes the entire hard disk space, so type y as your choice. FDISK will present its last screen.

FDISK with PC DOS 3.3

If you are using PC DOS 3.3 with a hard disk having a capacity of 30MB or less, you can follow the same procedure as above. If you are using a 40MB or higher-capacity hard disk, however, you will have to create multiple PC DOS partitions, since no one partition can be larger than 32MB. On the first FDISK screen, choose 1 (Create DOS Partition) and then 1 again (Create Primary DOS Partition). Then, when you see the following screen, type n.

```
Create Primary DOS Partition
Current fixed disk drive: 1

Do you wish to use the maximum available size for a Primary DOS
Partition and make the partition active? (Y/N).......? [ ]
```

You can then set the size of your primary and extended partitions up to the total capacity of your disk:

```
Create Primary DOS Partition
Current Fixed Disk Drive: 1

No partition defined

Total disk space is  305 cylinders.
Maximum space available for partition
is  305 cylinders.

Enter partition size...........:[     ]

Press ESC to return to FDISK options
```

The number of cylinders available will vary with the capacity of your hard disk. You don't have to worry about how large a cylinder is; just divide the total number of cylinders by the number of partitions you want. Thus, if you have a 40MB hard disk that you want to divide into two equal 20MB partitions, type in half the maximum number of cylinders—152. Now press Esc to return to the main FDISK menu and choose item 2 (Change Active Partition) to make this your active partition. You can then go back and repeat the process to create your second partition. This time when asked for the number of cylinders, you can just press Enter to automatically allocate all of the remaining cylinders. Remember that you don't make the second partition active; there can be only one active partition.

FDISK with PC DOS 3.2 and Earlier

For PC DOS versions 3.2 and earlier, there are no "extended DOS partitions." Here is the FDISK screen for PC DOS 3.20:

```
IBM Personal Computer
Fixed Disk Setup Program Version 3.20
(C) Copyright IBM Corp. 1983,1986

FDISK Options

Choose one of the following:
    1. Create DOS Partition
    2. Change Active Partition
    3. Delete DOS Partition
    4. Display Partition Data
Enter choice: [ ]

Press Esc to return to DOS
```

To create a DOS Partition, choose item 1. The remainder of the partitioning process is similar to that for version 4 already described.

Once you have left FDISK, you will get the following message:

```
You must restart your computer to continue
Press Ctrl+Alt+Del to continue with DOS installation
```

Make sure that your PC DOS start-up disk (or the Install disk if you are using PC DOS 4 and running SELECT) is in drive A, and press Ctrl-Alt-Del. The computer will now reboot. After it has rebooted, it will recognize the hard disk as your system's C drive.

High-Level Formatting

Caution

Using FORMAT

Running the FORMAT command destroys all existing data. PC DOS will warn you of this fact. Normally you should not have to format a hard disk that already has data. Back up any existing valuable data before doing a low-level format, changing a partition with FDISK, or running the FORMAT command.

Do not run FORMAT on a hard disk that has no existing partition. Create the partition(s) first with FDISK. FORMAT will not recognize a hard disk that is not partitioned, and it will instead attempt to format the *next* hard disk if any.

The last step in preparing your hard disk for PC DOS is to do the high-level format.

Version 4

High-Level Format

If you are using PC DOS version 4, the high-level format will be done automatically by the SELECT program. See Chapter 12, "Installing a PC DOS System," for more information on SELECT.

Formatting a Hard Disk

You can also format a hard disk from DOSSHELL by selecting the Main Group, DOS Utilities, and then Format.

If you have an earlier version of DOS, you will have to do the formatting manually. To do so, put your PC DOS distribution disk in drive A and type

```
A>format c: /s
```

PC DOS will display the following message:

```
WARNING, ALL DATA ON NON-REMOVABLE DISK
DRIVE C: WILL BE LOST!
Proceed with Format (Y/N)?  y
```

PC DOS will proceed to format the hard disk. The task is completed when the screen displays

```
Format complete
System transferred
xxxxxxxxx bytes total disk space
xxxxxxxxx bytes available on disk
```

(The numbers shown will depend on the capacity of your hard disk. The second number will be a bit smaller than the first, since some space will have been taken by the system files.)

Your hard disk is now ready for PC DOS installation. See Chapter 12 for instructions on how to install PC DOS 4 and earlier versions.

What's Next

All that you need and want to know about floppy disks is covered in Chapter 7, "All About Floppy Disks." Find out more about files in Chapter 9, "Creating Text Files," and Chapter 10, "Batch Files." Learn about optimizing PC DOS in Chapter 11, "Customizing Your System."

Key Concepts and Words

Before you read further, use the following list to test your understanding of the concepts and words in this chapter.

Sectors	Parent directory	Interleave
File fragmentation	File search paths	Disk cache
Buffers	Logical drives	Data protection
File allocation table	Subdirectory linking	Format
Attribute byte	Backing up	Partition
File organization	Restore	Encryption
Redirection		

Chapter 7

Floppy disks are the coin of the PC DOS realm, used to transfer programs and data between machines, to back up data, and to archive outdated information. Floppies come in several sizes, shapes, and formats—all of which are described in this chapter. You'll learn to

- *Handle and store floppies*
- *Copy files and entire disks*
- *Back up data from another disk drive*
- *Organize floppies with directories and subdirectories*

Chapter 7
All About Floppy Disks

Knowing how PC DOS deals with information stored on floppy disks is vital to your work. If you aren't comfortable using floppies, you may become frustrated with your computer and find that your filing system becomes more of a hindrance than a help.

Get out a couple of floppy disks now so that you can practice the tutorials in this chapter.

Types of Floppy Disks

There are two basic types of floppy disks: the *5¼-inch floppy disks*, which are also called "soft-shell floppies" or "minifloppies," and the *3½-inch hard-shell disks*, which are sometimes called "microfloppies." Figure 7.1 illustrates both types of disks.

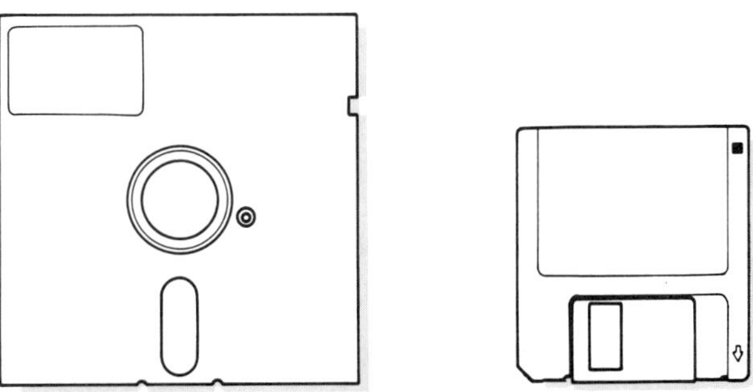

Figure 7.1. ***5¼-inch soft-shell disk and a 3½-inch hard-shell disk.***

Each type of disk is available in two different capacities, rated in terms of *kilobytes* (K, or 1024 bytes) or *megabytes* (MB or M, which is 1,048,576 bytes). Table 7.1 shows the different capacities for each type of floppy disk.

Table 7.1. ***Disk Capacities***

Capacity	Size	Usage
360K	5¼-inch	Standard on IBM PC and PC/XT
1.2MB	5¼-inch	Standard on IBM PC AT
720K	3½-inch	Available for third-party disk drives
1.44MB	3½-inch	Standard on IBM PS/2

Different manufacturers have different ways of labeling the capacity of a disk. Thus, you may see 3½-inch disks labeled as "1.0MB capacity" (or "2HC") or "2.0MB capacity" (or "HD" or "DS HD" for double-sided, high-density). The 1MB disks actually hold 720K of data, and the 2MB disks hold 1.44MB after they are formatted. The reason for the lower capacity after formatting is that PC DOS needs some space for its inner workings, as you will see later. (Another way to tell the capacity of a 3½-inch disk is to check the bottom of the disk—a 2MB disk has two square cutouts at the bottom, while a 1MB disk has only one.)

The 360K 5¼-inch disks may be called "double-sided, double-density" (or DS/DD). The 1.2MB 5¼-inch disks will be labeled "double-sided, quad-density," or simply "quad" or "high capacity." In rare cases, you may find some of the older single-sided disks that have only 180K of storage space. You can consider these to be antiques; they were originally for use with PC DOS 1.X, which Microsoft and IBM no longer support.

Hard-Shell Floppies: A Closer Look

As originally conceived, hard-shell floppy disks were designed to hold up to 720K of storage—twice that of the earliest PC disks. Improving on the original design, IBM incorporated a higher-density version of the 3½-inch disk, which holds 1.4M of storage, into the upper-end models of the PS/2 line. PS/2 Models 50, 60, 70, and 80 now come with at least one 1.44M disk drive as standard equipment.

On this type of disk, a spring-loaded metal cover called a *shutter* (Figure 7.2) prevents dust and fingerprints from coming in contact with the disk surface. This helps protect the disk and the information on it. You will find that it takes quite an effort to bend these disks or physically damage them in any other way without intentionally destroying the shell itself.

If you examine one of these disks, you will see that you can slide this shutter to the side to expose the *read/write hole*, which is also called the "access hole." When your disk drive reads data on the disk or writes new data to it, it slides this metal shutter aside. Normally the shutter remains closed to protect the disk.

If you turn over the disk, you can see a few more details (Figure 7.3). The small center hole is called the *centering hole*. When you put a disk in the disk drive, the drive uses the centering hole to make sure that the disk is in the right place. It also uses what is called the *timing* or *indexing hole* to align the

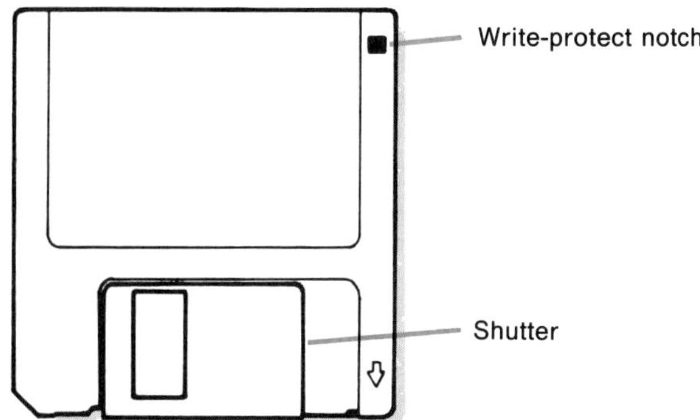

Figure 7.2. ***Top side of a 3½-inch hard-shell floppy disk.***

disk accurately. A spindle on the disk drive inserts itself into these two holes to make sure that the disk is positioned correctly, ready to use.

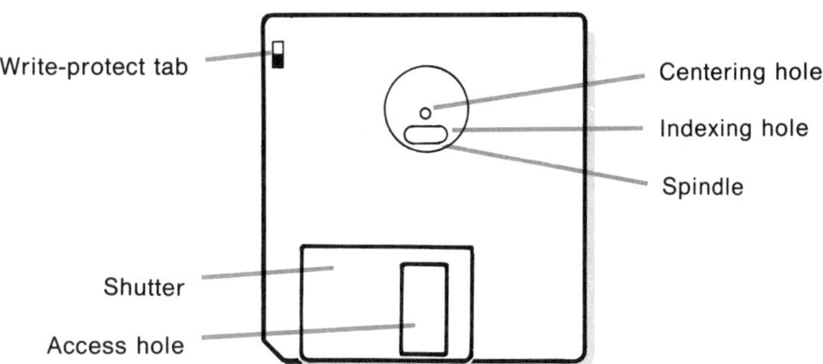

Figure 7.3. ***Bottom side of a hard-shell floppy disk.***

You can also see a small rectangular hole called a *write-protect hole* at the corner of the disk. When this hole is open, PC DOS cannot access the disk to change any information on it, but it can access the disk to read information that is there. You will learn more about write protection later in this chapter when you learn how to copy disks. For now, if you are using 3½-inch disks for the tutorials in this chapter, just make sure that the hole is open. (If it is closed, get another disk, or make sure that the information on that disk is no longer needed and then open the hole.) When you insert a hard-shell floppy disk in the disk drive, be sure that the centering hole is pointed down. You should see only the disk label and the metal shutter as you slide the disk into the drive.

Soft-Shell Floppies: A Closer Look

A soft-shell (5¼-inch) disk contains the same elements as a hard-shell disk, but the two disks are physically a little different. Looking at Figure 7.4—or at one of your own disks—you can see that there is indeed a centering hole, a timing hole, and a write-protect notch. However, the read/write window is exposed. Don't touch it! In fact, don't touch any of the areas that are shaded in Figure 7.4. If you do, you can damage the delicate magnetic coating that covers the disk.

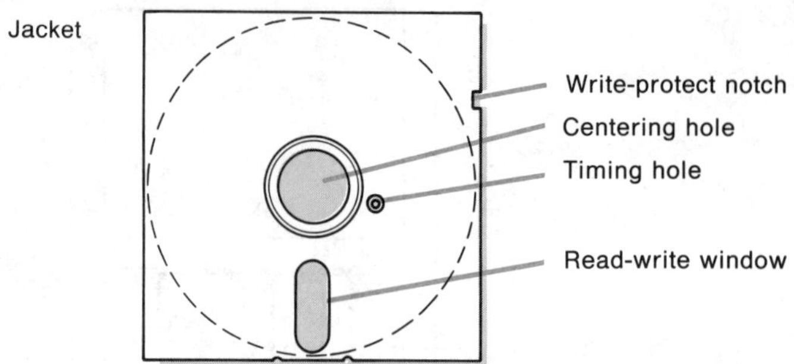

Figure 7.4. ***A soft-shell floppy (5¼-inch) disk.***

When you insert a 5¼-inch disk in the drive, be sure that the "plain" side of the disk—the one without the seams—is facing you. The write-protect notch should be on the left of the disk. If you put a disk in drive A upside down, you'll get the message `Not Ready Error reading drive A:`. Take the disk out, turn it over, and try again.

Disadvantages of Soft-Shell Floppy Disks

As popular as they continue to be, soft-shell floppy disks have two major disadvantages built into them. The first is that a portion of the disk surface is always exposed. This makes the disk highly vulnerable to the dust, smoke, oil, and dirt that is always circulating in the air. Human fingerprints, as well as an occasional spill from a coffee cup or a glop from a jelly doughnut, add to the number of hazards that a floppy disk is exposed to during its useful lifetime.

The second danger to soft-shell floppies is the very fact that they are soft and flexible. The thin plastic jacket that surrounds the actual disk offers some protection from dust and accidental contact, but it cannot prevent a disk from being bent or creased. Once a disk is creased, it is all but doomed to fail when your PC tries to read it. If you have important information stored on that disk, you are out of luck if the drive fails to read it—unless you have made a backup copy of the disk.

Preparing Floppy Disks for Use with PC DOS

As you saw in the Quick Primer, before you can use a disk, PC DOS has to format it into a structure of tracks and sectors and write certain data onto the disk. This chapter assumes that you are familiar with the basic technique of formatting a disk and focuses on a few techniques you can use to refine your skills with this command.

Determining Whether a Disk Needs to Be Formatted

How can you tell whether a disk needs to be formatted? Just get a directory listing of the disk:

```
C:\>dir a:
```

```
General failure reading drive a:
Abort, Retry, Fail?
```

This message indicates that the disk in drive A has not been formatted. Type `a` to abort the command; then format the disk. If you get a message saying that the drive is not ready, you have probably forgotten to shut the drive door or have not closed it all the way.

It is usually a good idea to format several disks at once, especially if you are using an application program that does not have an option for exiting to PC DOS without leaving the program. Otherwise, if you run out of disks, you have to exit from your program, format more disks in PC DOS, and start your program again.

Preventing Accidental Formattings

The FORMAT command wipes out anything that is on a disk. If other users have access to your computer, you might want to rename your FORMAT command so that no one can use your machine to do any disk formatting. To rename FORMAT as "DOFORMAT," for example, you simply type `ren format.com doformat.com` at the PC DOS prompt. After that, you must type `doformat`—or whatever other word you have chosen—to use the FORMAT command.

DOS Shell

Formatting a Disk

To format a disk with the DOS Shell, select "DOS Utilities" from the Main Group on the Start Programs screen. When the pop-up window appears, type whatever options you would ordinarily use on the command line, such as the */f* option for formatting disks to a different capacity.

Formatting Disks in Different Formats

PC DOS knows the type of disk drive you are using and formats the disk accordingly. However, there may be times when you want to format a disk for use in a different type of disk drive.

For instance, you may want to format disks for use in smaller-capacity disk drives if you have a 1.44MB 3½-inch disk drive or a 1.2MB 5¼-inch drive. To format a disk for 720K in a 1.44MB drive (assuming that you have PC DOS 3.3 or later), enter the FORMAT command as `format a: /n:9`. The `/n` switch tells PC DOS to use 9 sectors and 80 tracks. To create a 360K double-sided disk in a high-capacity (1.2M) drive, type the FORMAT command as `format /4`.

Version 4

The /f Option and the Volume Serial Number

PC DOS 4 allows you to use the */f* option to specify the capacity of the disk to be formatted. For example, use `format b: /f:720` to format a 720K disk in drive B, or `format a: /f:360` to format a 360K disk in drive A. The format specified must be suitable for the type of drive used.

PC DOS 4 also generates a volume serial number for the formatted disk. This serial number cannot be changed without reformatting, so it serves to identify the disk uniquely.

Caution

Don't Mix Up Disks
Do not try to format a 1.2MB disk as a 360K disk. The medium will not tolerate it, even though the command may appear to work. Likewise, be careful not to format a 360K disk to a 1.2MB format. Use double-sided, double-density disks only as 360K disks.

Besides preparing disks for use with PC DOS, the FORMAT command allows you to set up a system of disk organization. This will be explained in the next section.

Organizing Your Floppy Disk Filing System

Your floppy disk filing system should reflect the way you prefer to work. For example, you may want to store spreadsheet files separately from word processing documents. You may also decide to store reports on one set of disks and letters on another, or simply store together all the related files for a project. Whichever filing system you choose, PC DOS provides ways for you to name and keep track of your floppy disks.

Tip

Organize for Your Convenience
Disks are relatively inexpensive, so do not try to pack them full of files. The important thing is to keep the information you need readily available so that you do not have to examine complex directory listings to find the files you are searching for. Don't try to organize your floppy disk system in the same way that you would organize a hard disk system. (Chapter 6 contains some very different suggestions for managing your hard disk.)

Naming Disks

The most obvious way to keep track of your disks is to label them clearly and accurately. You can label them in two ways: first, with a gummed label on the outside of the disk so that you know what the disk contains without having to put it in your computer; and second, with a *volume name* that you can see each time you get a directory listing of the disk's contents. These two names should be the same if you expect to remain sane or if you expect others to locate information on your disks. If you physically label a disk as "DEPT BUD" and electronically label it as "EAST SALES," you may have difficulty finding what you are searching for!

Assigning a Name with the FORMAT Command

As you saw in the Quick Primer, when you format a disk, you are prompted for a volume label (with PC DOS versions 3 and later). At this point you can give the disk a volume name. Volume names, which PC DOS also calls "labels," help you identify and group your disks. Many people do not bother with volume names, but they can help you organize your work. They can also identify a disk's owner as well as what the disk contains. This information is useful if you are at a workstation that you share with others.

You have more flexibility when you name disks than when you name files because you can use up to 11 characters and the space character (see the box "Naming Disks"). For example, you could name a disk that holds your spreadsheet budgets for the month of August as AUG BUDGETS. Then, whenever you get a directory listing of that disk, you will see the volume name at the top and you will know which disk you are using:

```
C:\>format a:
Insert new diskette for drive A:
and press ENTER when ready...

... percent of disk formatted

Format complete

Volume label (11 characters, ENTER for none)? aug budgets

562496 bytes total disk space
562496 bytes available on disk

  1024 bytes in each allocation unit
   354 allocation units available on disk

Volume Serial Number is 314D-10F9

Format another (Y/N)? n
C:\>dir a:

Volume in drive A is AUG BUDGETS
Volume Serial Number is 314D-10F9
Directory of A:\
File not found
```

Here you formatted a 360K disk in drive A. After you gave the FORMAT command, inserted the disk in the drive, closed the drive door, and pressed Enter, the disk drive light came on, the disk whirred in the drive, and PC DOS formatted the disk. A message indicated the progress of the formatting process: with PC DOS 4, you see the percentage of the disk that has been formatted; with earlier versions of PC DOS you see the number of the track and side of the disk that is being formatted.

After you saw the `Format complete` message, you were prompted for a volume name. You entered `aug budgets` and pressed Enter. PC DOS then reported the amount of space available on the disk. These numbers are the total amount of usable space, not the amount of space that the disk is rated for. PC DOS lists a different number of bytes from what the disk can actually hold because it is not reporting on the areas that it reserves for its own use. For this 360K disk, the actual capacity is 368,640 bytes (360 × 1024 = 368,640), but PC DOS makes only 362,496 bytes available to you for storage. (The *allocation units* are the sectors on the disk. You do not have to worry about the allocation units now. Later in the chapter you will see why they are important.)

PC DOS then asks you if you want to format another disk. Type `n` and press Enter if you do, and the prompts will start all over again.

If you are using a version of PC DOS that does not prompt you for a volume name, you can use the */v* switch with the FORMAT command to assign a volume name when you format a disk. To do this, enter the FORMAT command as `format a: /v`.

Naming Disks

The rules for naming volumes (disks) are different from those for naming files. You can use the space character and up to 11 of the following characters:

A–Z, a–z, 0–9, $ # & @ ! & ( ) - { } " _ ~

A volume name is the only PC DOS name that can have a space character in it. You cannot use the following characters:

+ = / [ ] : ; , ? * \ < > |

Thus, SALES (MAY) is a valid name, and MAY/SALES is not.

The main difference between volume names and file names is that volume names can have spaces, but they cannot contain periods. If you type a name longer than the allotted 11 characters, PC DOS will use only the first 11 characters. If you use an illegal character, PC DOS will ask you to enter the name again.

Naming a Formatted Disk with the LABEL Command

But what if you want to name a disk that you have already formatted? The FORMAT command wipes out what is already on the disk. However, if you have PC DOS 3 or later, you can go back and label a disk after you have formatted it, or you can change the volume name of a disk that you have already named.

To do this, use the LABEL command. For example, to label a formatted disk in drive A as SEPT SALES, type

```
C:\>label a:sept sales
```

If you do not type a label after the LABEL command, PC DOS prompts you for the label:

```
C:\>label a:
Volume in drive A has no label
Volume Serial Number is 3C4E - 15D7
Volume label (11 characters, ENTER for none)?
```

You can then enter the label that you want to use.

Using LABEL with PC DOS Versions Prior to 3.3

If you are using a version of PC DOS prior to 3.3, do not try to use a space in a volume name that you assign with the LABEL command. PC DOS will interpret the space as a separator between two volume labels, and you will get an `illegal characters in volume label` message.

Changing and Removing Volume Names

A typical floppy disk is good for about 40 hours of usage. Thus, it is likely that you will want to rename a disk from time to time as your use for it changes. For example, you may decide that you will copy important monthly sales reports from several disks onto one disk that you can store as a yearly sales summary. You can copy the reports onto the disk that already has the most reports on it and use the LABEL command to rename the disk to reflect its new contents. For example, to rename the AUG BUDGETS disk to "1990 SALES," enter the LABEL command as `label a:1990 sales`. PC DOS will remove the old label and create the new one.

You can also use the LABEL command to remove a volume name from a disk. To do this, type the LABEL command by itself, with no label. When PC DOS queries you, press Enter. It will respond `Delete current volume label (Y/N)?` and you can type `y` to delete the label or `n` to cancel the command.

Copying Files to Floppies

In your everyday work with your computer, one common task that you perform is copying files from one disk to another. You may need to copy a few files from one disk to another so that you can give the files to a coworker, or you may want to copy some files so that you can reorganize your disk storage system. Since floppy disks can fill up quickly, you may want to copy only your current files onto a blank disk or onto a disk with more storage space. Occasionally, you may also need to make an exact duplicate of a disk, perhaps to use for an archive copy or to give someone else a copy of the disk.

Write Protection

There are times when you want to protect a disk so that neither you nor anyone else can change what is on it. For example, if you copy a program disk that you have purchased, you may want to take the additional step of write-protecting it so that the valuable executable files on it cannot be changed. Likewise, you may want to write-protect disks containing files that you are archiving for long-term storage so that no one can alter the records they contain. If you work with sensitive data, such as salary projections or budgets, you may want to write-protect those disks.

As you saw earlier, floppy disks have either a notch (on 5¼-inch disks) or a tab (on 3½-inch disks) that allows you to protect the data on the disk. If you try to write data onto a disk that is write-protected—by using the COPY command, for example—you will get a `Write protect error reading drive A:` message from PC DOS. If you get this message and you really want to put information on that disk or change it in some way, take the disk out of the drive and remove the *write-protect tab*. These are small gummed stickers, and you will probably find a sheet of them in each box of floppy disks you buy.

To write-protect a hard-shell floppy disk, you simply slide the plastic tab until you can see through it. If you want to be able to change information on the disk or write new information to it, slide the tab back until the hole is covered. If you want to "permanently" write-protect a disk—for example, an applications program that you have purchased—you can pry the plastic tab out of the hole and throw it away. (Later, if you decide that you want to use the disk again for writing, you can simply cover the hole up again with tape.)

The write-protect notch on a soft-shell floppy disk works oppositely from the way it does on hard-shell floppy disks. (In fact, some program disks that you purchase may not have a write-protect notch at all, which means that you cannot change anything on the disk.) To protect the disk from change, you cover the notch with a write-protect tab. Later, if you decide that you want to change the information on the disk, just remove the tab.

Copying Files with the COPY Command

As you saw in the Quick Primer, the COPY command lets you selectively copy files from one floppy disk to another, or from a hard disk to a floppy disk and vice versa.

Caution

Before You Copy a File

When you copy files, there are two important precautions that you should take. First, be careful about the file names you use. The COPY command is not discriminating. For example, if you copy a file on a disk in drive A to a disk in drive B and there is already a file of the same name on drive B, PC DOS will overwrite the file, giving you no warning. Before you copy a file, check the target disk with the DIR command to make sure that there are no duplicate file names. If there is a duplicate, give the copy of the file a different name, as in `copy a:file1 b:file2`.

Second, be careful about specifying the drives. The first drive should contain the files that are to be copied, and the second drive should hold the disk that will become the copy. For example, if you want to copy all the files on the floppy disk in drive A to the current directory on your C drive, give the command as `copy a:*.* c:`, not `copy c:*.* a:`.

Tip

Verifying Your Work

PC DOS has a useful command called VERIFY that checks everything written to a file—each time you make a copy, for example. To turn on automatic verification, just type `verify on` at the PC DOS prompt. When VERIFY is on, however, the speed of your system will decrease somewhat. It is best to turn VERIFY on only when you are making lots of copies or backup disks and then turn it off (by typing `verify off`) when you have finished. VERIFY is normally off. If you turn it on and forget to turn it off again, it will be off the next time you boot PC DOS. You can get the same results by issuing the COPY command with the */v* switch. The /v switch tells PC DOS to check the accuracy of the data that is transferred as it makes the copy. For example, to copy into your current directory on drive C a file named SALESSUM in drive A and to verify the copy, enter `copy a:salessum /v`.

Copying Files from One Floppy to Another with One Floppy Disk Drive

Suppose you want to copy several files from one floppy disk to another, but you have only one floppy drive. It will take a long time to copy the files if you use your single floppy disk drive and give the command as `copy file.txt a: b:` for each file. You will have to swap disks in and out of the drive, and this is time-consuming. Instead, you can use your hard disk to speed up the process.

DOS Shell

Copying Files
Using the DOS Shell, copy files by selecting "File System" from the Main Group on the Start Programs screen. Scroll through the directory list in the left window by using arrow keys or a mouse, and select the directory containing the files to be copied. Next, in the directory listing in the right window, select the files you wish to copy, using arrow keys and the space bar, or a mouse. Finally, select "Copy" from the File menu, type the destination path into the pop-up window, and follow the prompts.

For example, suppose you want to copy only the files named OCT1 through OCT9 from one floppy disk to another. There are many other files on the disk, but they have different names, such as REPORTS and LETTERS.

```
C:\>cd \
C:\>md temp
C:\>copy a:oct? temp

9 File(s) copied

C:\>copy temp\file? a:

2 File(s) copied

C:\>erase temp\*.*

All files in directory will be deleted!
Are you sure? (Y/N) y

C:\>rd \temp
```

You first made a temporary directory on your hard disk and then copied the files to it. Then you removed the floppy disk from drive A and inserted the target disk (the disk that will store the copies) before you issued the second COPY command in the listing. The wildcard character ? told DOS to copy all files beginning with OCT and ending in any character, such as OCT1, OCT2, OCTA, and so forth, and to ignore the other files that were on the original disk.

Tip

PC DOS Prompts with One Floppy Drive
If you have only one disk drive (drive A), PC DOS may sometimes prompt you to insert a disk in drive B. Don't worry; drive B is the same as drive A. PC DOS uses *logical* names for disk drives, which means that it treats the only physical disk drive, drive A, as both drive A and drive B when it needs a second drive. (This is logical? Well, it's computer logic.)

Using XCOPY to Copy Files between Disks

Suppose you want to copy a few files from your hard disk to a floppy disk, and they are in several subdirectories. You could copy the files one at a time from each subdirectory. There is a faster way, however. You can use the XCOPY command. This command also lets you copy only files that were created on or before a certain date or after the last time you made copies. Thus, with XCOPY, you can quickly make copies of only the files you have recently been working with. In addition, the XCOPY command preserves the original directory structure on the copy of the disk so that you will not have to worry about overwriting any files having the same names but located in separate subdirectories.

The XCOPY command is most often used in conjunction with hard disks, so you will find a more extensive discussion of it in Chapter 6, "Managing Your Hard Disk." The following sections focus on techniques for using the XCOPY command with floppy disks.

Copying Files from Subdirectories to a Floppy Disk

If your second computer is a laptop computer or another computer that does not have a hard disk, you will find the XCOPY command handy for copying files from the hard disk on your main computer onto floppies for use with your second computer.

For example, you might want to copy the contents of a directory named REPORTS, and its associated subdirectories, from your hard disk to a floppy in drive A so that you can use it on your laptop. The REPORTS directory on your hard disk contains an AUG subdirectory, and it in turn contains the subdirectories NORTH and SOUTH. These subdirectories contain both .TXT files created with your word processor and various other files not having the .TXT extension. You want to copy the contents of all the .TXT files in these directories onto a floppy disk in drive A:

```
C:\>xcopy c:\reports\*.txt a: /s
Reading source file(s)...

C:REPORTS\FILE1.TXT
C:\REPORTS\AUG\NORTH\FILE1.TXT
C:\REPORTS\AUG\NORTH\FILE2.TXT
C:\REPORTS\AUG\NORTH\FILE3.TXT
C:\REPORTS\AUG\SOUTH\FILE1.TXT
C:\REPORTS\AUG\SOUTH\FILE2.TXT
     6 File(s) copied
```

When you examine the directory of drive A, you will see that the contents of all the subdirectories have been copied. (If a subdirectory is empty, it will not be copied.)

```
C:\>dir a:

Volume in drive A has no label
Volume Serial Number 0E14 - 10F7
Directory of A:\
```

```
FILE1          306  01-02-90  9:24a
AUG       <DIR>     01-05-90  9:51a
     2 File(s) 549184 bytes free

C:\>dir a:\aug

Volume in drive A has no label
Volume Serial Number 0E14 - 10F7
.         <DIR>     01-05-90  9:51a
..        <DIR>     01-05-90  9:51a
NORTH     <DIR>     01-05-90  9:51a
SOUTH     <DIR>     01-05-90  9:51a
     4 File(s) 549814 bytes free

C:\>dir a:\aug\north

Directory of A:\AUG\NORTH
Volume in drive A has no label
Volume Serial Number 0E14 - 10F7

.         <DIR>     01-05-90  9:51a
..        <DIR>     01-05-90  9:51a
FILE1   TXT     306 01-04-90  9:00a
FILE2   TXT     306 01-04-90  9:10a
FILE3   TXT     306 01-04-90  9:11a
     5 File(s)  550208 bytes free
```

You looked first at the contents of the disk in drive A and then at the AUG and NORTH subdirectories. All the .TXT files from the REPORTS directory and its associated subdirectories were copied onto the floppy disk in drive A. The subdirectories REPORTS\AUG\NORTH and REPORTS\AUG \SOUTH were also created, and their .TXT files were copied. (You looked at only the contents of the NORTH subdirectory.) Unlike the COPY command, the XCOPY command automatically creates the required subdirectories on the floppy disk, so your hierarchical filing system is preserved.

Copying Files by Date

Another situation in which you can use the XCOPY command is when you want to copy files created on or before a certain date. For example, you might want to copy just those files created on or after February 16, 1990, so that you can have a copy of only the most recently revised files to work with:

```
C:\>xcopy a:  /d:02-16-90

RFLOP      66773  02-16-90
WRITEPRO    2005  02-17-90
SALESUM     1007  02-18-90
     3 Files copied
```

Using the */d* switch with the XCOPY command copies all the files on the disk in drive A that were created on or before February 16, 1990 into the current directory on drive C.

Caution

When a Single Floppy Isn't Big Enough for All Your Files

The XCOPY command will simply stop when a floppy disk is full. If you need to copy more than your floppy disk will hold (you can check the amount of space available on a disk by using the CHKDSK command, discussed later in this chapter), you have several options. First, you can use the BACKUP command (discussed in Chapter 6, "Managing Your Hard Disk") instead of the XCOPY command. Second, you can issue the XCOPY command with the */p* switch, which tells PC DOS to prompt you before copying each file. Third, you can use the ATTRIB command (discussed in Chapter 6) to turn on the archive attribute for each file that you want to copy. You can then issue the XCOPY command with the */m* switch, which tells PC DOS to copy each file whose archive attribute is on and then reset the attribute to off after the file is copied. When your floppy disk is full, you can insert a blank formatted disk and repeat the XCOPY command with the */b* switch on the same set of files you are copying. Since the only files still having the archive attribute set to on are those that the XCOPY command has not processed yet, this next use of XCOPY will copy only the remaining uncopied files.

Copying Files between Minifloppies and Microfloppies

At times you may want to copy files from a 3½-inch disk to a 5¼-inch disk, or vice versa. If you have both types of disk drives, you will usually have no problem because you can simply use the COPY or XCOPY commands to copy files.

Tip

When a Single File Is Too Big for a Disk

If you copy files from a 3½-inch disk onto a 5¼-inch disk for someone who has only a 5¼-inch disk drive, you can occasionally run into problems because some of the files stored on the larger-capacity disk may be too large to fit on the smaller-capacity disk. Instead, copy the files onto your hard disk first. Then use the BACKUP command to put the copied files onto the 5¼-inch disk. The BACKUP command will break the files into the right sizes for the recipient's smaller-capacity disk. Be sure that your recipient knows to use the RESTORE command. See Chapter 6, "Managing Your Hard Disk," for more details on using the BACKUP command.

But suppose you have only a soft-shell floppy drive and you want to transfer files to another computer that has only a hard-shell floppy disk drive. The obvious solution is to purchase and install a hard-shell floppy drive, but this solution is also expensive (from over $100 to $500). There are alternatives that you may want to consider, especially if you are not planning to do very much file transferring or if you plan to do one large transfer.

If you are transferring files from an older machine, such as from an XT to a PS/2, you can purchase, for about $40, a package from IBM called the IBM

Migration Aid. It lets you transfer files through the parallel ports of both machines (you will need a parallel cable also). The Migration Aid lets you transfer the files either to a hard-shell floppy on the PS/2 or to its hard disk.

The IBM Migration Aid works only one way, however. You can copy files from the laptop or other machine to the PS/2, but not vice versa. A more versatile and an easier to use solution is to buy one of the programs such as Lap Link or Brooklyn Bridge that will send files from one computer to the other over a cable connection, called a null modem, between the serial ports of the two machines. You could also use many other communications programs, but they aren't as fast or as easy to use.

Comparing Copied Files with Originals

Often, you will want to verify that the copies you have made are accurate so that weeks later you do not find yourself with copies of files that you cannot use. You can use the COPY and the XCOPY commands with the */v* switch to instruct PC DOS to verify each copy as it is made. However, you may want to compare copies of files later on to make sure that they match exactly. By using the external command COMP, you can compare files and make sure that they are the same.

For example, assume that you want to compare the copy of \AUG\NORTH\FILE1.TXT that is now in the floppy disk in drive A with its original on drive C:

```
C:\>comp
Enter primary file name
a:\aug\north\file1.txt
Enter 2nd filename or drive id
c:\reports\aug\north\file1.txt

A:\AUG\NORTH\FILE1.TXT and C:\REPORTS\AUG\FILE1.TXT
EOF mark not found
Files compare OK
Compare another (Y/N)? n
```

The `EOF mark not found` message simply indicates that the file does not end with ^Z, which is the case for many files.

What If the Files Do Not Match?

If the files do not match exactly, you will get an error message such as

```
Compare error at offset 37B
File 1 = 64
File 2 = 54
```

This message means that the two files do not match exactly (the bytes are given in hexadecimal notation). You have a questionable copy, so you should copy the file again.

If you try to compare files that are of different sizes, you may get the error message `Files are different sizes`. The COMP command works only on files that are of the same size.

Backups Are Different from Copies

Do not try to compare files with copies you have made by using the BACKUP command (discussed in Chapter 6). They will never match because the BACKUP command places new information at the beginning of each file.

Copying Entire Disks

You will often find it useful to make copies of entire floppy disks to use as backups. For example, you may need to make backup copies of program disks that you have purchased, or you may want to quickly duplicate a disk. If you copy the files one by one, it can take a lot of time. Even if the file names on the disk follow a pattern so that you can use wildcards (such as `copy file? a:`), the copying process is time-consuming and you will have to check to see which file names are on the disk. Instead, DOS provides the external command DISKCOPY to make an exact duplicate of a disk. The Quick Primer showed you how to quickly make a copy of a disk by using the DISKCOPY command.

When to Use COPY *.* and DISKCOPY

There are two ways to copy an entire disk: by using the COPY command as `copy *.*` or by using the DISKCOPY command. What are the differences?

DISKCOPY makes an exact duplicate of the disk that is being copied, track by track. Use it whenever you want to copy a disk that has a lot of files on it, since it is faster than COPY. Also, DISKCOPY formats as it copies. Thus, if your target disk is not formatted, you can save yourself this extra step by using the DISKCOPY command instead of the COPY command. Also, use DISKCOPY if you are copying a system disk (one that you can use to boot your computer).

Use the COPY *.* command when you are copying a disk that you have used for a long period of time. As you work with a disk, its access time may slow down because of the way PC DOS puts files on the disk. The COPY command rearranges files in the most efficient order on the disk. Also, if you are copying to an already formatted disk, use the COPY command. If you are copying files from a hard disk to a floppy disk, you have no choice but to use the COPY command because the DISKCOPY command does not work with hard disks.

Formatting with DISKCOPY

The DISKCOPY command will format a disk automatically as it makes the copy. This is the only PC DOS command that does not require you to use a formatted disk. You do not save any time, though, because formatting with DISKCOPY takes about as long as formatting with FORMAT.

Copying a Floppy Disk with Two Floppy Disk Drives

Assume that you need to copy a floppy disk in drive B that contains all your reports for the month of January to a disk in drive A in order to have a backup copy of that disk:

```
C:\>diskcopy b: a:
Insert SOURCE diskette in drive A:
Insert TARGET diskette in drive B:
Press any key when ready...

Copying 80 tracks
9 Sectors/Track, 2 Side(s)

Formatting while copying

Copy another diskette (Y/N)? n
```

PC DOS prompts you to put the source (original disk) in the first drive you specified and the target (new copy) in the second drive you specify. If you put the disks in the opposite drives, you will overwrite the disk that you are trying to copy.

When PC DOS finishes, the disk in drive A will be an exact duplicate of the disk containing your January reports in drive B. Notice that PC DOS formats the disk in drive A, so you do not have to remember to use the FORMAT command on a disk that you want to copy.

Caution

DISKCOPY Will Overwrite

The DISKCOPY command copies everything that is on the first disk to the second one. If your second disk contains valuable information, that information will be overwritten and lost.

Hitting the Right Target

Unless you specify two disk drives, the current drive is ALWAYS the destination (target) drive. For example, if you issue the DISKCOPY command as `diskcopy b:` while drive A is the current drive, the disk in drive B will be copied onto the disk in drive A. Be careful. Check the prompts that PC DOS presents so that you always get what you want. Look at these combinations, assuming drive A is your current drive:

- If you enter `diskcopy`, the contents of the source disk in drive A are copied to the target disk in drive A.
- If you enter `diskcopy a:`, the contents of the source disk in drive A are copied to the target disk in drive A.
- If you enter `diskcopy b:`, the contents of the source disk in drive B are copied to the target disk in drive A.
- If you enter `diskcopy a: b:`, the contents of the source disk in drive A are copied to the target disk in drive B.
- If you enter `diskcopy b: a:`, the contents of the source disk in drive B are copied to the target disk in drive A.

Making Copies of Disks with Only One Floppy Disk Drive

Suppose you have only one floppy disk drive or you have two floppy disk drives but they are different types. PC DOS can figure out what you want to do if you specify only one drive as both the source and the target:

```
C:\>diskcopy a:
Insert SOURCE diskette in drive A:
Press any key when ready...

Copying 40 tracks
9 Sectors/Track, 2 Side(s)

Insert TARGET diskette in drive A:
Press any key when ready...

Formatting while copying
Copying 40 tracks
9 Sectors/Track, 2 Side(s)

Copy complete
Copy another (Y/N)? n
```

What happened? When PC DOS prompted you to insert the source disk in drive A, you put the disk you wanted to copy in drive A and pressed Enter. PC DOS then read as much as it could from the disk and prompted you to switch disks. You then put a blank, unformatted disk in drive A and pressed Enter. PC DOS formatted that disk and copied what it had read off the first disk onto the second one. It may prompt you to switch disks again, depending on how much is on the source disk—whether it can be read into memory in only one operation.

If PC DOS finds any errors on either disk, it will report the drive, track, and side where the errors are and will then proceed with the copy. You will need to determine whether there are enough errors on either disk to prevent PC DOS from making an accurate copy. In general, having a few bad sectors is all right. However, if you are copying a valuable disk, you may want to get a new, blank disk to use as the target. If the problems are on the source disk, you may need to check the data on that disk or run the CHKDSK command on it, as you will see later.

Copying One Disk to Another Disk

To copy a disk to another disk using DOSSHELL, select "DOS Utilities" from the Main Group on the Start Programs screen. Select "Disk Copy" from the DOS Utilities group, and follow the prompts.

Copying Copy-Protected Disks

You cannot use the DISKCOPY command on some copy-protected disks. You can, however, purchase a special program like COPY II PC, from Central Point Software, that will allow you to make archive copies of your valuable applications programs.

Comparing Disks with the DISKCOMP Command

Once you have made a copy of a disk with the DISKCOPY command, you will probably want to determine that the copy is accurate before you give it to another user or store it for use later. It is much better to check that copy now, when you can immediately use the DISKCOPY command again if necessary, than to find out later that a copy is bad.

You can see if your copy is an exact duplicate by using the DISKCOMP command. Like the DISKCOPY command, it is an external command.

DOS Shell

Comparing Two Disks

To compare two disks using the DOS shell, select "DOS Utilities" from the Main Group on the Start Programs screen. Select "Disk Compare" from the DOS Utilities group, and follow the prompts.

Comparing Disks with One Floppy Drive

Use the DISKCOMP command with either a single floppy drive or two floppy drives. If you have only one floppy drive, PC DOS prompts you when to insert each disk. The following example uses a single floppy drive to verify the copy in drive A that you made from the original disk in the preceding example:

```
C:\>diskcomp a:
Insert FIRST diskette in drive A:
Press any key to continue...

Comparing 40 tracks
9 sectors per track, 2 side(s)

Insert SECOND diskette in drive A:
Press any key to continue...

Diskettes compare OK
Compare another diskette (Y/N)? n
```

First, you entered the command as `diskcomp a:`. When PC DOS prompted you, you inserted the original (first) disk you used in the previous example in drive A and pressed a key. PC DOS then reported the copy operation in terms of tracks, sectors, and sides. When it finished reading the first disk, it prompted you to insert the second disk—the copy of the disk you made previously. PC DOS then compared the data it read from the first disk with the contents of the second disk. If you need to swap disks more than once, you will be prompted to do so.

When you use this command, PC DOS compares disks track by track and reports errors with a message like `Compare error on side x, track y`. If any errors are reported, you should probably DISKCOPY your original disk again.

In addition, you may see the error message: `Unrecoverable read error on drive n, Track x, side y`. If the drive letter is that of the copy, the disk was probably bad to begin with. If the drive letter is that of the original, the problem is on the original disk. Later, you will see how to check that disk by using the CHKDSK command.

Comparing Disks with Two Floppy Disk Drives

If you have two floppy disk drives, you can specify that disks in each drive be compared by entering the command `diskcomp a: b:`. This tells PC DOS to compare the disk in drive A with the disk in drive B.

Needless to say, you cannot use the DISKCOMP command to compare a hard disk and a floppy disk, or to compare two disks with different capacities, such as high-capacity disks and double-sided double-density disks, or disks of different sizes (5¼-inch and 3½-inch disks). You will get the message `Drive or diskette types not compatible` if you try to compare disks of different capacities.

Tip

Comparing Copied Disks

If you copy a disk (with COPY *.* or XCOPY, as you will see later) and then compare the copy to the original with the DISKCOPY command, the two disks will not match. Why? Because the COPY command rearranges the data on the copy, putting related information in contiguous clusters. The DISKCOPY command literally copies (makes an exact duplicate of) the disks.

Using Logical Drives

You have already learned that if you have only a single floppy disk drive, PC DOS sometimes treats it as though it were two drives, A and B. This is an example of PC DOS using *logical* drives. Logical drives are sometimes called *virtual* drives because they are not physically there, although PC DOS acts as if they are.

A logical disk drive can be a nickname for another disk drive, or it can be a second partition of your hard disk, or it can even be a subdirectory, as you will see in the following sections.

Tip

Naming Disk Drives

PC DOS reserves drives A and B for your floppy disk drives. The first hard disk is drive C, and any additional disk drives you add are named drives D and E. If you have more than five disk drives (either physical devices that act like drives, such as tape backup units, or virtual drives, such as RAM disks), you will need to tell PC DOS how many you have by using the LASTDRIVE and DEVICE=DRIVER.SYS commands in your CONFIG.SYS file, as explained in Chapter 11, "Customizing Your System." If you try to use a drive that does not exist on your system or that PC-DOS does not know about, you will get the message `Invalid drive specification`.

PC DOS treats your floppy disk drives as logical drives when you use the JOIN, ASSIGN, and SUBST commands. All of these external commands have one thing in common: they fool PC DOS into thinking that it is using a certain disk drive even though you are actually using a different physical drive. These commands came into PC DOS after version 1. One of their basic purposes, as far as floppy disks are concerned, is to let you use older programs that assume you always have only two floppy disk drives, no hard disk, and no hierarchical directory system.

Changing One Drive to Another with the ASSIGN Command

With the ASSIGN command, you can change one drive to another. For example, suppose you are using a version of WordStar earlier than version 4.0. The early versions of this program expect to find files on drive A and do not recognize drive C. You need to fool WordStar into believing that your drive C is really drive A so that, whenever it looks for something on drive A, PC DOS will instead look at drive C, where your files are stored. You can tell PC DOS to treat drives A and B as though they were drive C:

```
C:\>assign a=c b=c
```

From then on, PC DOS will regard your floppy drives as drive C, even though the program you are running addresses only drives A and B.

Removing an ASSIGNment

Once you have used the ASSIGN command to have PC DOS treat your floppy drives as though they were your hard drive, any commands you give such as `copy a: b:` can cause PC DOS great confusion. Be sure to remove any temporary ASSIGNments you make immediately after using the older program by issuing the command as simply

```
C:\>assign
```

Caution

Remove ASSIGNments, SUBSTitutions, and JOINs
Remove any ASSIGNments, SUBSTitutions, or JOINs before you use some commands. BACKUP, FORMAT, DISKCOPY, DISKCOMP, RESTORE, LABEL, FASTOPEN, JOIN, SUBST, and PRINT do not work (or do not work accurately) with ASSIGN. In addition, JOIN cannot be used on drives created with SUBST. None of these "let's fool PC DOS" commands work with network drives, and they may not work with copy-protected programs.

Creating a Logical Drive Name for a Subdirectory by Using the SUBST Command

The SUBST command can be used to create a logical drive name for a subdirectory. This sounds strange at first, but you may discover that at times you will want to treat one of your subdirectories as if it were a disk drive. As you saw in the previous example, early versions of WordStar, as well as other programs such as Easy Writer 1.10, do not recognize some of PC DOS's later capabilities, like a hierarchical directory structure.

The SUBST command tells PC DOS that a subdirectory is a drive. If your older program does not recognize subdirectories, SUBST is a better choice than ASSIGN because it lets you reroute activity to a subdirectory instead of simply to another disk, as the ASSIGN command does. You provide a temporary alias for the subdirectory that you are using as a disk drive.

For example, you may have an older program such as an early version of WordStar that does not recognize subdirectories. You can use the SUBST command to substitute the name of a disk drive as a temporary alias for a subdirectory. Suppose that on your hard disk drive C you have subdirectories with path names of \WS (where you store the WordStar program files) and

\WS\TXT (where you store the WordStar data files). You can name them drive A and drive B so that you can run WordStar from your hard disk:

```
C:\>subst a: c:\ws
C:\>subst b: c:\ws\txt
```

From then on, PC DOS treats the subdirectory \WS as though it were drive A and the \WS\TXT subdirectory as drive B. The WordStar program can thus locate its executable files on drive A and its data files on drive B, even though they are on the hard disk, drive C. For example, you can type `dir b:` to get a listing of documents in \WS\TXT.

Caution

Using Drive Names with SUBST
Using drive names with the SUBST command has some restrictions. You cannot specify the default drive of the subdirectory; that is, you cannot make C the substitute drive in the previous example. If you type `subst c: c:\ws`, the system will respond with an error message `Path not found`. Also remember that some commands do not work correctly when a substitution is in effect, as stated in the previous Caution.

Once you have used the name of an existing drive as a substitute for a subdirectory name on another drive, the contents of the first drive will no longer be available to you. If your subdirectory is on drive A, for example (A:\INVOICE\NOV), and you substitute drive C for drive A (`subst c: a:\invoice\nov`), the contents of your hard disk will be unavailable. If you get a directory listing of C, you will instead see the contents of A:\INVOICE\NOV.

Using Two Disk Drives as One: The JOIN Command

Assume that you have files located on several disks in different drives and you want to avoid changing the current drive or typing a long path name each time you specify a file. You can use the JOIN command to tell PC DOS to regard two drives as one.

As you saw earlier, if your computer has only one floppy drive, PC DOS treats it as if it were both drive A and drive B. The JOIN command works in just the opposite way. It tells PC DOS to treat an entire disk drive as though it were merely a subdirectory on another drive. It is most often used to join one hard drive to another (and so is discussed in Chapter 6, "Managing Your Hard Disk"), but you can use it to join a floppy drive to a hard drive, or even to join two floppy drives so that you can quickly access files in both drives.

Joining a Floppy Drive and a Hard Drive

With the JOIN command, you can join a floppy drive and a hard drive. For example, you can join drive A to a subdirectory named \TEMP on your drive C.

```
C:\>join a: C:\temp
```

When you issue the JOIN command in the example, PC DOS translates this as "join the whole drive A to the C:\TEMP subdirectory." It automatically creates the C:\TEMP subdirectory if you have not created an empty subdirectory named TEMP. You can then access the files that are physically on drive A just as if they were on drive C. If you get a directory listing of C:\TEMP, you will see a listing of the files that are physically on the disk in drive A.

Joining Two Floppy Drives

Assume that drives A and B on a dual floppy system contain the following files:

```
C:\>dir a:

 Volume in drive A has no label
 Directory of A:\

CLIENT     <DIR>      01-09-90  8:57a
     1 File(s) 539800 bytes free

C:\>dir b:

 Volume in drive B has no label
 Directory of B:\

WORDSTAR   <DIR>      01-09-90  8:57a
DBASE      <DIR>      01-09-90  8:57a
     2 File(s) 559201 bytes free

C:\>join b: a:\client
C:\>dir a:\client

 Volume in drive A has no label
 Directory of A:\CLIENT

WORDSTAR   <DIR>      01-09-90  8:57a
DBASE      <DIR>      01-09-90  8:57a
```

Drive B is now joined to the CLIENT directory on drive A. A directory listing for A:\CLIENT reveals that A:\CLIENT has the subdirectory structure that was formerly on drive B, so you can access the files on drives A and B as if they were on drive A.

Caution

Using JOIN

JOIN can be used only in root directories and in the first level of subdirectories. You will get the message `invalid parameter` if you try to join a deeper subdirectory. Also remember that certain commands cannot be used successfully when a join is in effect, as noted in the earlier Caution.

Removing a Join

To remove a join, you issue the command with the name of the joined drive and the */d* (disconnect) switch. For example, to disconnect the join that was made to drive C in the example, type

```
C:\>join a: /d
```

A Close Look at a Floppy Disk

The following sections will take a look at how your floppy disk drives work and how information is put on a floppy disk so that PC DOS can actually produce the characters that you see on your screen.

How Your Floppy Disk Drive Works

Both types of disks—microfloppies and minifloppies—are coated with a sensitive magnetic coating. Each particle of this coating can change polarity when the magnetic read/write head, also called a *recording head*, of the disk drive passes over it. The recording head creates patterns of *off* and *on* voltages that are equivalent to the binary 1s and 0s that computers use to store information.

When you put a disk in the drive and shut the drive door, a set of clutches grips the disk through the centering hole. They spin the disk itself inside its plastic jacket very rapidly. On a hard-shell floppy disk drive, the metal shutter is pushed aside so that the disk can be read.

A set of arms holds the read/write heads, much like the tone arm on a record player. These heads move back and forth across the spinning disk's surface to access the various areas where information is stored. When the disk is in motion, a light on the front of your computer comes on. You should not try to remove a disk when this light is on.

Because the read/write head of a floppy disk drive actually touches the disk, it is critical that there not be foreign particles on the disk that can cause the read/write heads to crash. A crash can damage both your disk drive and the floppy disk itself.

Physical Details of Floppy Disks

When you format a floppy disk so that PC DOS can use it, PC DOS organizes it into a series of concentric circles called *tracks*, as Figure 7.5 shows. Each track is further subdivided into segments called *sectors*, each of which is 512 bytes. PC DOS uses track and sector numbers much like street addresses to locate data on the disk. The number of tracks and sectors on your floppy disks depends on the type of disk drive you are using as well as the version of PC DOS you have. PC DOS versions 2.0 and later automatically format a disk into 9 sectors. With versions 3.0 and later, PC DOS can format up to 15 sectors on a high-capacity, 5¼-inch disk and up to 18 on a 3½-inch disk. Each disk has either 40 or 80 tracks, numbered from 0 to 39 or from 0 to 79, respectively. The tracks are numbered from the outside in, so track 0 is the outermost track. The first few tracks on a disk contain information that PC DOS uses to locate the data on that disk, as you will see in more detail later. Table 7.2 lists the characteristics of the various types of floppy disks that PC DOS uses.

Table 7.2. ***Characteristics of PC DOS Disks***

Size	Capacity	No. of Sides	Tracks/Side	Sectors/Track
5¼	360K	2	40	8/9
5¼	1.2MB	2	80	15
3½	720K	2	80	9
3½	1.44MB	2	80	18

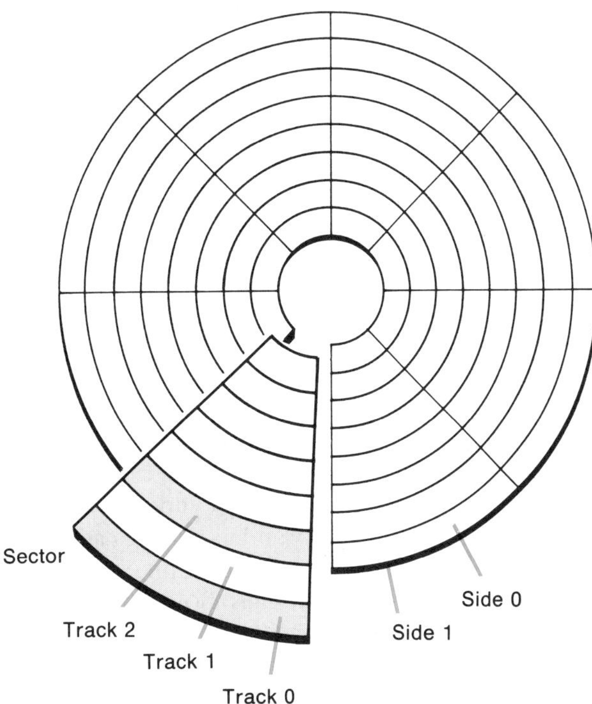

Figure 7.5. ***Tracks and sectors on a floppy disk.***

Now, to make things a little confusing, PC DOS stores data in sectors but reads data in clusters. A *cluster* is a group of sectors. Again, the size of a cluster varies according to the type of disk and the version of PC DOS you are using. On a 1.2MB floppy disk, there is one sector per cluster, but on a typical 360K floppy disk, there are two sectors (1024 bytes) per cluster. You don't really need to know exactly how many sectors there are per cluster in order to use your computer. However, you should look at the following example involving clusters so that you understand how PC DOS accesses and manipulates information on a disk.

Assume that you are using a 360K floppy disk. In this case, a cluster is 1024 bytes. If you want to store a 1500-byte file, PC DOS will need two clusters for it. The first cluster will hold the first 1024 bytes, and the second will hold 476 bytes, with a lot of extra space (called "slack") left over. Each time one of your files gets larger, PC DOS simply allots it more clusters. This may seem a waste of space, but it is actually much faster for PC DOS to perform read and write operations if it can read and write in several sectors at one time. Having each storage segment of equal length allows PC DOS to do this, since data is spaced at equal distances around the disk.

PC DOS fills up a disk with data, sector by sector. When a track gets filled, PC DOS begins to fill the next track on that cylinder. When the cylinder is full, PC DOS moves one cylinder inward and begins to fill it. Thus, data that belongs to very different files may be stored next to each other in adjacent clusters on a disk. PC DOS has a system for figuring out what goes where, though.

Filling Up a Disk
Because of the way PC DOS allocates file space, the smaller your files, the more space wasted. With larger files, space is used more efficiently. This may help explain why some of your disks seem to fill up faster than others.

Who's on First? How a Disk Holds Information

PC DOS keeps track of where everything is on a disk by using a table called the *file allocation table*, or FAT. The FAT is so vital to disk operation that two copies of it are stored on every disk—including your hard disk if you are using one—so that if one copy becomes damaged, the other can be used to locate files. The FAT—both copies of it—is stored in a special area called a *system area* that is reserved on each disk. In fact, the system area comprises the first several sectors of cylinder 0. Remember the discrepancy between a disk's rated capacity and its storage capacity? This is why there is a difference: PC DOS needs a system area on each disk for information it requires.

The system area also holds other information that PC DOS needs to use the disk. First, the *boot record* contains information about the disk itself: the number of bytes per sector that it is using, the number of sectors per cluster, etc. Another part of the system area contains the *directory table*, or root directory, which holds information about each file on the disk.

Putting Humpty Dumpty Together: The FAT

The FAT keeps track of what's in which cluster. It indicates whether a cluster is free (can be used for data), whether it is part of a chain of clusters that makes up a file, whether it is physically bad and cannot be used to hold data, or whether it is the last cluster in a file. So that the FAT can put a file back together like Humpty Dumpty, it uses the disk's directory table.

There is one directory table on each disk. It consists of 32-byte records that contain each file's name and extension, its attributes (such as whether it is read-only or hidden), the time and date it was created or last changed, its starting FAT address, and its size. The file directory also stores the name of each subdirectory, if any, in the same way that it stores information about individual files. Figure 7.6 illustrates how the FAT, the boot record, and the directory table are stored on a typical 5¼-inch, 9-sector-per-track floppy disk.

Instead of storing the address of each file, the directory table simply points to an entry in the FAT. The FAT takes over from there and actually tells PC DOS which sectors on the disk hold the file that is being looked for.

Forgotten, But Not Gone
When you erase files from a disk, the data is still physically present. When PC DOS marks a file that has been deleted, it changes the first byte of its file name to a special hexadecimal character. The actual data is still there, but the FAT views that area as "available." You can recover erased files by purchasing disk utility programs such as the Norton Utilities that will use the FAT to reconstruct an erased file.

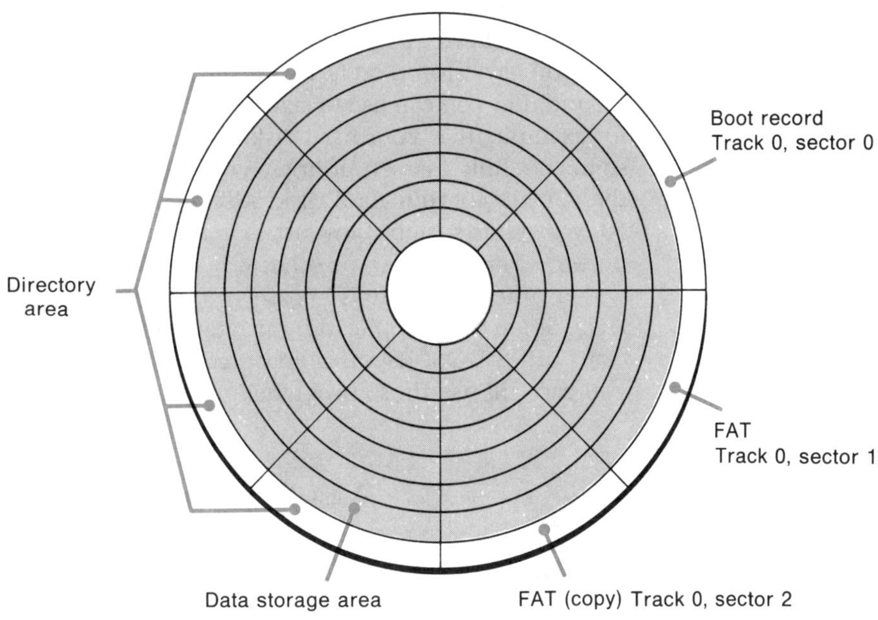

Figure 7.6. ***Location of FAT, boot record, and directory table.***

Making a Better Copy

If you have made heavy use of a disk, don't use it as a source from which to DISKCOPY to another disk. PC DOS stores data on a disk in a random order. As you create and delete files, their data becomes more and more widely scattered across the surface of the disk. This is known as *file fragmentation*. DISKCOPY produces an exact duplicate of a disk, file fragmentation and all. If your source disk has been in use long, use COPY *.* instead of DISKCOPY. This makes a copy of the disk that PC DOS can use more efficiently, since the files on the copy will be in clusters that are closer together.

Creating a System Disk

A disk formatted by using the FORMAT command with no options is good only as a data disk. It doesn't have the special PC DOS system files that are used to start your computer. These special files are named IBMBIO.COM, IBMDOS.COM, and COMMAND.COM. The first two are *hidden* files. This means that you cannot view them, and they are not included in a directory listing, although they occupy disk space. All three of these files are necessary to make a disk bootable because one of PC DOS's first actions when you turn on your computer is to read these files into memory. When you see the A> or C> prompt, you know that PC DOS has read these files and stored their contents in the computer's memory.

If you have a hard disk, PC DOS will automatically boot from the files that you have stored on it. However, it is often handy to have a floppy disk around that you can use to start your computer in an emergency. Suppose, for example, that your hard disk crashes. With a bootable floppy disk and some carefully chosen utilities, you can start your computer and inspect the damage to your hard disk. Also, it is good practice to have a backup copy of your system files just in case the system files on your hard disk become damaged in some other way. Another good reason to keep floppies with a system on them is in case you ever have to use older versions of PC DOS. Some older application programs may not work with the newer versions of PC DOS. If you keep older versions of PC DOS on floppy disks, you can still use those programs.

Making an Emergency Floppy Disk

Be sure to have a floppy disk prepared for hard disk emergencies. If your hard disk fails, then you will be able to start your system from the emergency floppy disk. Often you can "see" the directories and files on the hard disk after you start the system from a floppy disk.

To make an emergency floppy disk, format a floppy disk with the /s option to create a *bootable* hard disk (one that contains a copy of the PC DOS system and COMMAND.COM). Then copy the following PC DOS utilities onto your emergency disk:

ATTRIB.EXE
BACKUP.COM
CHKDSK.COM
COMP.COM
DEBUG.COM
DISKCOPY.COM
EDLIN.COM
FIND.EXE
FORMAT. COM
MORE.COM
RECOVER.COM
RESTORE.COM
SORT.EXE
TREE.EXE
XCOPY.EXE

You might also want to include other helpful utilities in addition to those that come with the PC DOS operating system.

Creating a System Disk with the FORMAT Command

You can use the */s* switch with the FORMAT command to tell PC DOS not only to format a disk but also to set it up as a system disk by putting COMMAND.COM and the hidden files IBMBIO.COM and IBM-DOS.COM on the disk. The system disk can then be used as a start-up disk. The resulting disk will not have any of the external PC DOS commands on it, however.

```
C:\>format a: /s

...percent of disk formatted

Format complete
System transferred
Volume label (11 characters, ENTER for none)?

562496 bytes total disk space
562496 bytes available on disk
  1024 bytes in each allocation unit
   354 allocation units available on disk

Volume Serial Number is 314D-10F9
Format another (Y/N)? n
```

Here, you formatted a blank disk in drive A to become a system disk. As you can see, PC DOS has taken over a certain amount of the disk for its system files. When you see the message `System transferred`, the formatting is complete, and you have created a working start-up disk.

Updating the Version of PC DOS on a Disk

You may have already created several bootable floppy disks that contain older versions of PC DOS. You want to use the newest version of PC DOS with these disks, but if you use the FORMAT command on them to put the newer system files on, your data or programs will be erased. What can you do?

To update the system files on existing system disks to the latest version of PC DOS, you use the SYS command:

```
C:\>sys a:
System transferred
C:\>copy command.com a:
```

First, you put in drive A the disk whose system files you wanted to update. Next, you issued the SYS command (assuming that the new PC DOS system files are on your hard disk and that your PATH command tells PC DOS where to find them). This transferred the system files but did not copy the COMMAND.COM file. You then used the COPY command to copy COMMAND.COM to the floppy disk. (This is unlike the FORMAT command, which transfers all three hidden files at the same time.)

Caution

Room for the System Files

The disk you use with the SYS command should have been previously formatted with space for the system files (use the /s switch in the FORMAT command). If it already contains the system files, you know that it has been formatted this way. If you try to use the SYS command on a disk not previously formatted with the /s switch, you will get the message `No room for system on destination disk`.

Tip

Updating Version 2.0 System Disks to PC DOS 3

With PC DOS versions 3.0 and later, the hidden system files are larger than with earlier versions. If you try to update PC-DOS versions 3.0 or later onto a system disk that now holds PC-DOS 2.0, you will get the message `Incompatible system size`. If you get this message, format a disk with the /s switch and then copy files from your old disk to the new one, making sure that you do not copy the old COMMAND.COM file. In other words, do not type `copy *.*`. The /s switch of the FORMAT command automatically invokes the SYS command to transfer the system files.

Version 4

Using SYS

In PC DOS 4, the SYS command can transfer the system files to any disk having enough capacity for them, provided there are two unused entries in the root directory (which normally means that you have 62 or fewer files there). The disk need not have old system files on it.

Checking Your Disks with the CHKDSK Command

You may have noticed that this chapter has referred to a handy command called CHKDSK. PC DOS provides this external command so that you find out all sorts of things about your disks.

Getting Information about Storage and Memory

Often you will need to know how much space is left on a disk in order to decide whether the disk can hold additional files. You also may need to see how much memory is available for your use, especially if you are running any TSR (terminate and stay resident) programs that can eat up memory. The CHKDSK command reports all this information:

```
C:\>chkdsk a:

Volume Serial Number is 4507 - 1202

562496 bytes total disk space
336896 bytes in 37 user files
 25600 bytes available on disk

  1024 bytes in each allocation unit
   354 total allocation units available on disk
    25 available allocation units on disk

655360 total bytes memory
596944 bytes free
```

Here, you checked a disk in drive A and found that 25,600 bytes were available. In addition, 596,944 bytes of memory were free. If there were hidden files such as the system files on this disk, you would also see a line like

```
70656 bytes in 2 hidden files
```

If you had given the disk a volume name, it would be listed along with its date of creation. As you will see, the CHKDSK command has other uses too. You can use it to optimize the performance of your disks and to repair bad disks.

Version 4

Using MEM

With PC DOS 4, a faster way to find out how much memory is available is to use the MEM command:

```
C:\>mem

   655360 bytes total memory
   654336 bytes available
   122016 largest executable program size

  2097152 bytes total EMS memory
  1769472 bytes free EMS memory

   393216 bytes total extended memory
        0 bytes available extended memory
```

The `largest executable program size` means the total amount of memory available for any program that you wish to run. EMS (expanded memory) and extended memory are shown only if your system has the proper hardware and device drivers installed.

DOS Shell

Getting Disk Usage Information

In the DOS shell, to obtain the disk usage information provided by CHKDSK, select "File System" from the Main Group on the Start Programs screen. Next, select the drive you are interested in, using the control key or a mouse. Finally, select "Show Information" from the Options menu.

Optimizing the Performance of Your Floppy Disks

To see if all your files are stored as efficiently as possible on the disk—in other words, stored in contiguous sectors—give the CHKDSK command as **CHKDSK *.***, or specify the names of the files that you want to check:

```
C:\>chkdsk a:*.*

Volume Serial Number is 4507 - 1202

562496 bytes total disk space
336896 bytes in 37 user files
 25600 bytes available on disk

  1024 bytes in each allocation unit
   354 total allocation units available on disk
```

```
    25 available allocation units on disk

655360 total bytes memory
596944 bytes free

A:\RFLOP contains 7 non-contiguous blocks
```

If you see a large number of noncontiguous blocks, it indicates that there are many fragmented files on the disk. Fragmented files slow down a disk's performance time. There is an easy way to fix them: just COPY the files on that disk onto a blank formatted disk.

Repairing a Disk with the CHKDSK Command

Suppose that you are working with a program that crashes frequently, either because of the software itself or because your computer crashes during a power failure. You can use the CHKDSK command to see if the files on your disk are still usable and to fix any file allocation errors that may have occurred on the disk. To use the command this way, enter it as `chkdsk /f`. (You will be prompted again as to whether you really want CHKDSK to fix the errors.) When CHKDSK operates this way, it converts any lost clusters into ASCII text files with a .CHK extension. These lost clusters are usually caused by a program that began to create a file but stopped because of some error condition, and the lost clusters usually are not complete files. You can TYPE their contents to see what they contain. In most cases, they will not be of much use to you in this format and you are better off just to erase them. You can use your word processor to edit them if there is a file or two that you cannot live without.

CHKDSK Error Messages

When you use CHKDSK, you may see various error messages. Some of them can be of considerable consequence to you. For example, you may see the message `Cannot CHDIR to root`. It means that CHKDSK could not return to your root directory as it checked the files on the disk. If you see this message, try CHKDSK again. If the message persists, your disk is probably damaged. Copy as many files as you can onto another disk. Likewise, if you see `Cannot recover...`, you have another serious problem. Again, copy as many files as you can to another disk. You will find more information on various CHKDSK error messages in Part 3, the Command Reference.

Tip

Use a Recovery Program

PC DOS has a RECOVER command (discussed in Chapter 6, "Managing Your Hard Disk"), but its capabilities are limited. Often you are better off to purchase and use a third-party file-recovery program such as the Norton Utilities if you need to recover lost or damaged files. This set of programs allows you to view and change any area of a disk as well as to restore deleted files and repair damaged disks.

What's Next

To fine-tune the way your computer reads data from disks, turn to Chapter 11, "Customizing Your System." To learn more about files, try Chapter 2, "PC DOS Files"; Chapter 9, "Creating Text Files"; or Chapter 10, "Batch Files." Reading in order? Chapter 8 presents more ways you can use the command line to manage files and directories.

Key Concepts and Words

Before you read further, use the following list to test your understanding of the concepts and words in this chapter.

Disk capacities	Cluster	Logical drives
Minifloppies	Boot record	High density
Microfloppies	System area	Double-sided
File allocation table	Data area	Disk drive
Track	Root directory	Disk format
Sector		

Chapter 8

Besides internal and external commands, PC DOS includes features called redirection *and* piping, *which give you extended control over the programs you use. Use redirection to send the output of a program to a different place—for instance, to the printer instead of the video display. Use pipes to send the output of one program through another program for processing on its way to its final destination. This chapter shows you how to*

- *Use redirection to create quick printouts of output from the COPY, DIR, and TYPE commands*
- *Use pipes and filters to alphabetize directory listings as well as lists in text files*
- *Use redirection to create files that store the output of the DIR, COPY, and TYPE commands*
- *Append one text file to another*
- *Search the contents of a file without opening it*
- *Use files that read other files for instructions instead of waiting for your commands*

Chapter 8

Advanced Use of the Command Line

Don't let the title of this chapter scare you. You will not need a master's degree in computer science to understand the concepts and commands explained here.

Redirection lets you determine where your information comes from (input) and where to send it after you are finished with it (output). This means that you can process the contents of one file and save your work in another file.

Filters are data management tools that you can use to arrange the information in your files. PC DOS provides you with three filters: SORT, MORE, and FIND. The *SORT* filter lets you rearrange lines of text in a file according to certain characteristics. *FIND* lets you locate specific lines of text within a file. And *MORE* slows down the display of a long file so that you can examine it more easily.

Piping lets you link commands and filters together on the command line. This means that you can use the output from one command as the input to another one. One very common use of this command is to create a sorted directory listing. Use the output from the DIR command as the input to the SORT command. You will have a chance to practice this operation and others later in this chapter as you work through the various tutorials.

After you become familiar with redirection, filters, and pipes, you will find yourself using these commands frequently. For a quick review of the various commands and switches covered in this chapter, refer to Table 8.1 at the end of the chapter.

DOS Shell

Obtaining a Command Line

The techniques you will be learning in this chapter must be used on the command line at the PC DOS prompt, or typed into a batch file and run from there. Therefore, if you are using DOSSHELL, you can either exit the shell (by pressing F3 at the Start Programs screen) or press Shift-F9 to obtain a command-line prompt while still running the shell.

Controlling PC DOS's Input and Output with Redirection

Normally, PC DOS receives input from the keyboard and sends output to the display screen. Figure 8.1 illustrates the relationship between input and output devices and PC DOS. PC DOS will always use these devices unless you tell it to use other ones.

You might want to use input devices such as a mouse, a scanner, or a joystick. More exotic devices like digitizers, touch screens, and bar code

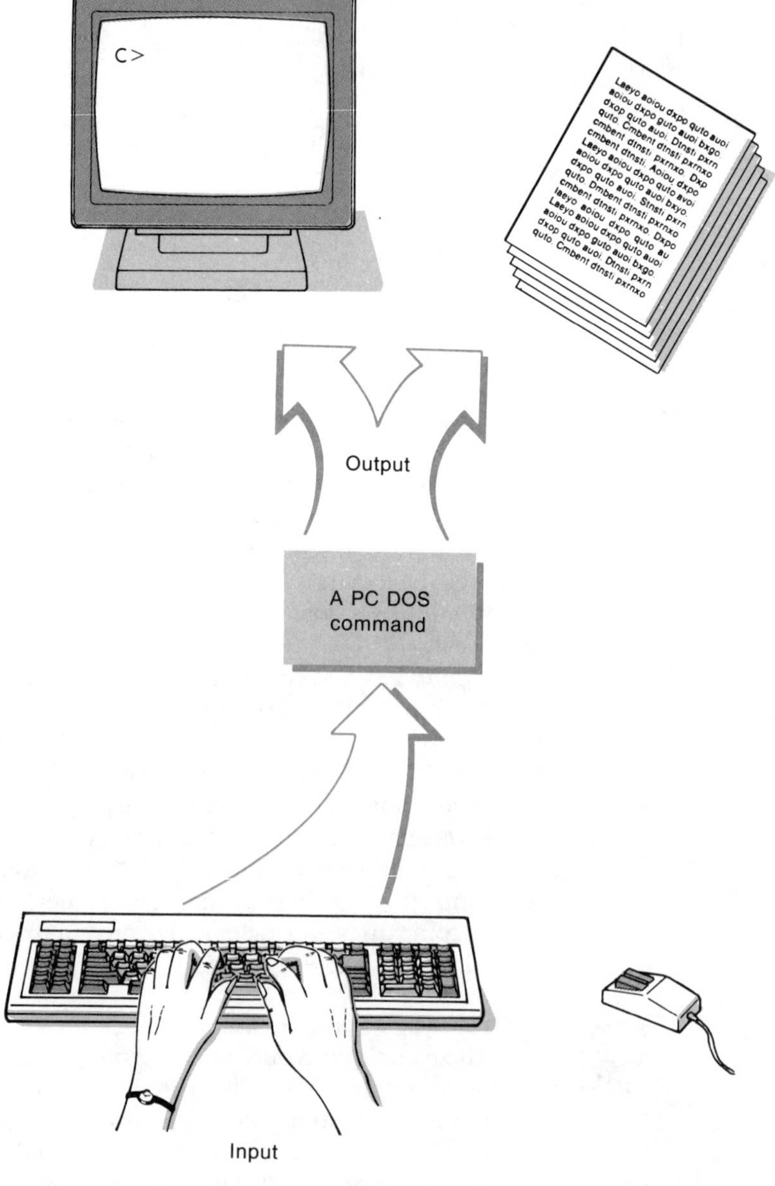

Figure 8.1. ***Input and output devices.***

readers are available. Some engineers are even developing devices that will allow your computer to understand human speech as input.

When you want to look at your input or see the results of your work, you use your screen. The display screen, or monitor, is the most frequently used output device in personal computer systems. Other common output devices are printers, plotters, modems, and FAX boards.

PC DOS will also let you use a file as the source of input. Another file can receive the output. When you designate files as input or output devices, you are *redirecting* PC DOS. This means that you are telling PC DOS to read a file instead of the keyboard, or to send the results of a command to a file instead of to the screen.

Redirecting input or output lets you do a number of convenient things. However, using redirection as input to a command is often problematic. Generally, input controls what a program will do, and if the redirection fails or is inappropriate, the program may fail or act unpredictably.

There are a few simple, very handy examples of redirecting output. For example, you redirect the output of the TYPE command to the printer to make a printed copy of a text file. You can use redirection to save the output of a command as a file. For example, the output from the DIR command can be used to create a directory listing that you can use as the basis for a READ.ME file. After creating the listing, you can use EDLIN to add brief descriptions of the various files on the disk. A file like this can be very helpful when you are trying to locate something on a storage diskette. (See Chapter 9, "Creating Text Files," for more information about EDLIN and READ.ME files.)

Printing Information

Normally, the output generated by a command is displayed on your computer's monitor. However, you may remember the *greater-than* symbol (>) from math classes. In PC DOS, this symbol is used to redirect output. Think of it as a pointer which indicates the file, program, or device to receive the information.

To see how *output redirection* works, try printing a listing of all the files in your directory. Turn on your printer. When it is ready, enter the following command and press Enter:

```
C:\>dir > prn:    ←press Enter
```

The > character before the word `prn:` tells PC DOS to redirect the output of this command to the printer. (Depending on your printer, you may have to press the Form Feed or Line Feed button to advance the printer to the next page. Your printer manual will tell you how to do this.)

Caution

Make Sure the Printer Is Ready

Before redirecting or otherwise sending output to the printer, make sure the printer has been turned on. If the printer has an "on-line" button that makes the connection between printer and computer active, press it also. If you send something to the printer and the printer is not turned on and on-line, your system will probably freeze up and you won't be able to do anything at the keyboard until the printer is ready.

When you execute the command by pressing Enter, the drives will whir and the indicator lights will come on. Despite all this activity, you will not see the directory listing on the screen. This is because you told PC DOS to send the information to your printer rather than to display it. Part A of Figure 8.2 illustrates this process.

Creating a File Redirection is often used to store information in a file. To see how this works, try entering the following command (remember that you must press Enter after typing the command):

```
C:\>dir > testfile
```

The > character before the file name `testfile` tells PC DOS to redirect the output of this command to the file. Again, despite the fact that your computer is obviously working, you will not see the listing on the screen. As you can see in part B of Figure 8.2, PC DOS has sent the information to a file.

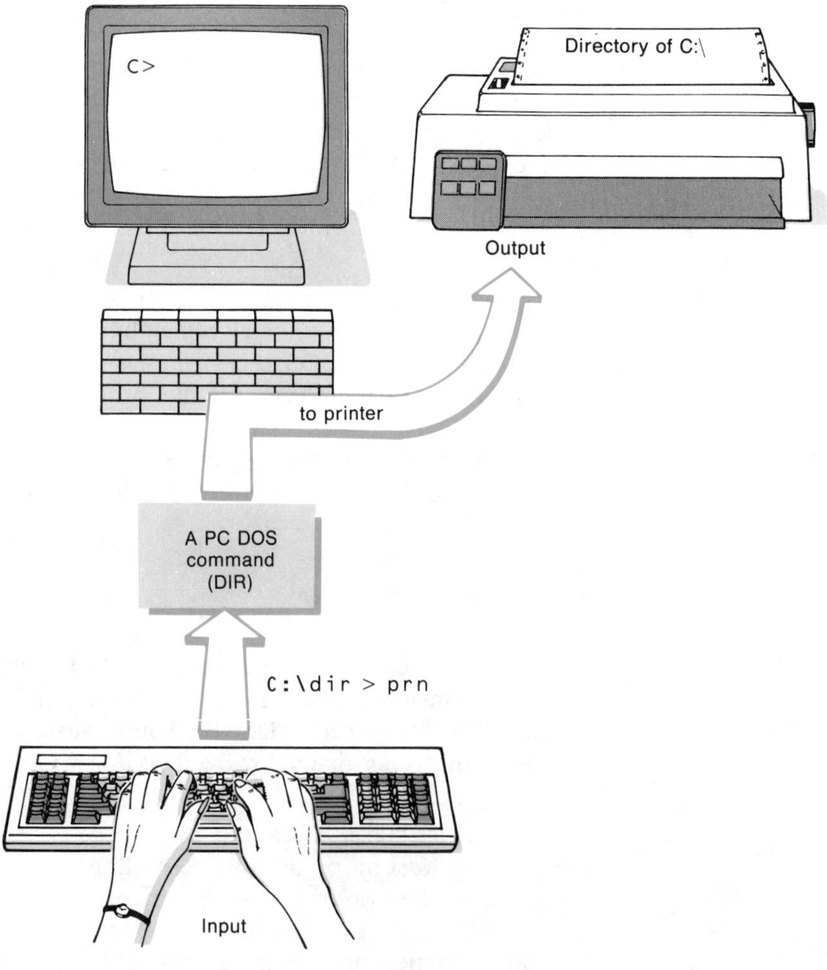

(A) Redirecting output to the printer.

Figure 8.2. ***Redirecting output.***

To find out what happened, you have to look at the file. You can check the new file by using the TYPE command:

```
C:\>type testfile
```

All your file names are listed just as you would expect. However, the listing for TESTFILE shows that it has 0 bytes. That's not possible; you know that TESTFILE contains information because you just used TYPE to view it. Why is it shown as an empty file?

When you redirect output to a file, the first thing PC DOS does is to create the file that will hold the data. Next, PC DOS performs your commands and sends the output to the file. In this example, PC DOS creates a file called TESTFILE. When it reads the directory, TESTFILE is still an empty file. It won't contain any information until *after* PC DOS has sent a copy of the directory listing to this file. Figure 8.3 shows how this process works.

Only one command can be redirected at a time. After the information is copied to the file, the standard output reverts to the display screen. If you

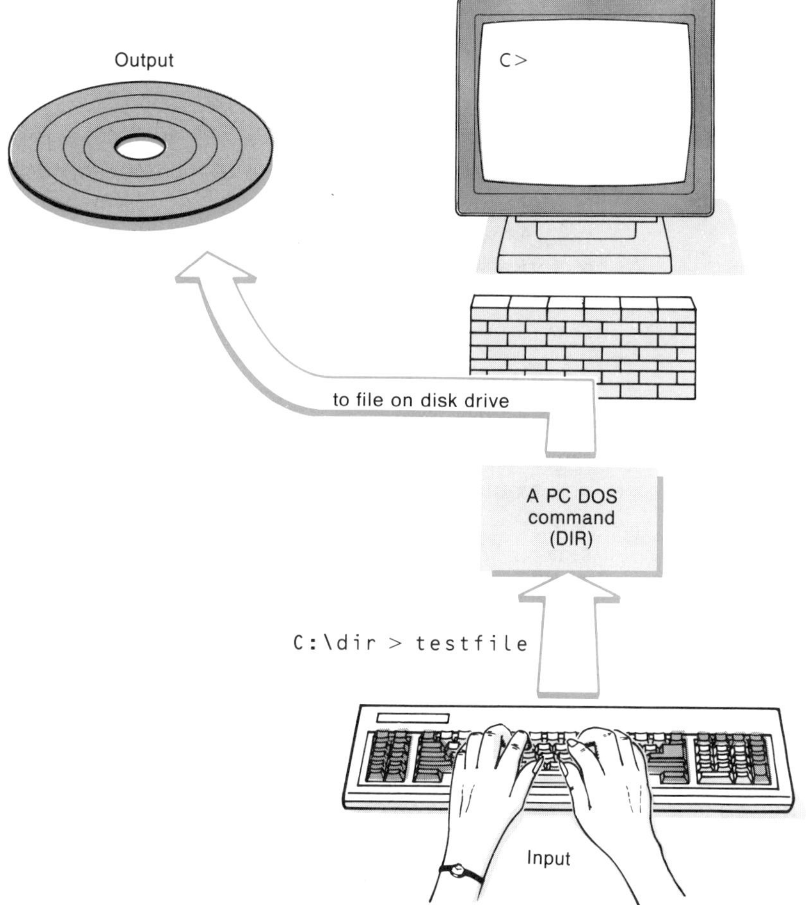

(B) Redirecting output to a disk file.

Figure 8.2. ***(cont.)***

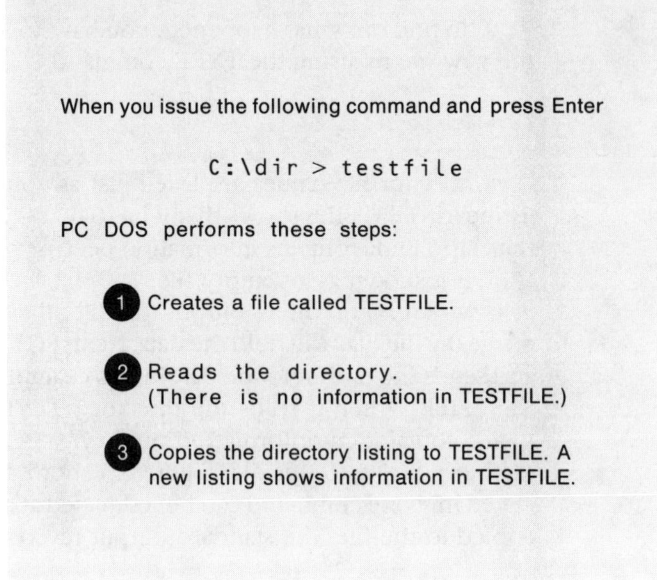

When you issue the following command and press Enter
C:\dir > testfile
PC DOS performs these steps:
1 Creates a file called TESTFILE.
2 Reads the directory. (There is no information in TESTFILE.)
3 Copies the directory listing to TESTFILE. A new listing shows information in TESTFILE.

Figure 8.3. ***Sending output to a new file.***

want to change the destination of the next command, you must include the output redirection character > in the command.

As with other PC DOS commands, you can use directories and subdirectories when you redirect output:

```
C:\>dir \word\letters > lettrdir
```

This command puts the directory listing of the \WORD\LETTERS subdirectory into a file called LETTRDIR. The LETTRDIR file will be in the current subdirectory. If you wanted it in the \WORD\LETTERS subdirectory, you would also have to tell PC DOS where to store the file:

```
C:\>dir \word\letters > \word\letters\lettrdir
```

Check Your File Name
Always check the file name before redirecting output to a file. Be sure that you have given your file a new name. If you redirect output to an existing file, PC DOS writes the new information over the file contents. This will destroy the original data.

Adding to a File

As you know, you cannot use > to add information to an existing file without destroying the original contents of the file. What can you do if you want to save the old information? Fortunately, PC DOS provides a simple solution to this problem. When you want to add new output to the end of an existing file, you include a double pointer (> >) in the command:

```
C:\>dir \word\letters >> lettrdir
```

With this command, the new directory listing is appended to the end of the LETTRDIR file.

Redirection using > > is a handy and safe way of updating any information in a file (e.g., a mailing list). You can also use it to keep updated listings of all your directories in one file. Figure 8.4 illustrates the process of adding new data to an existing file.

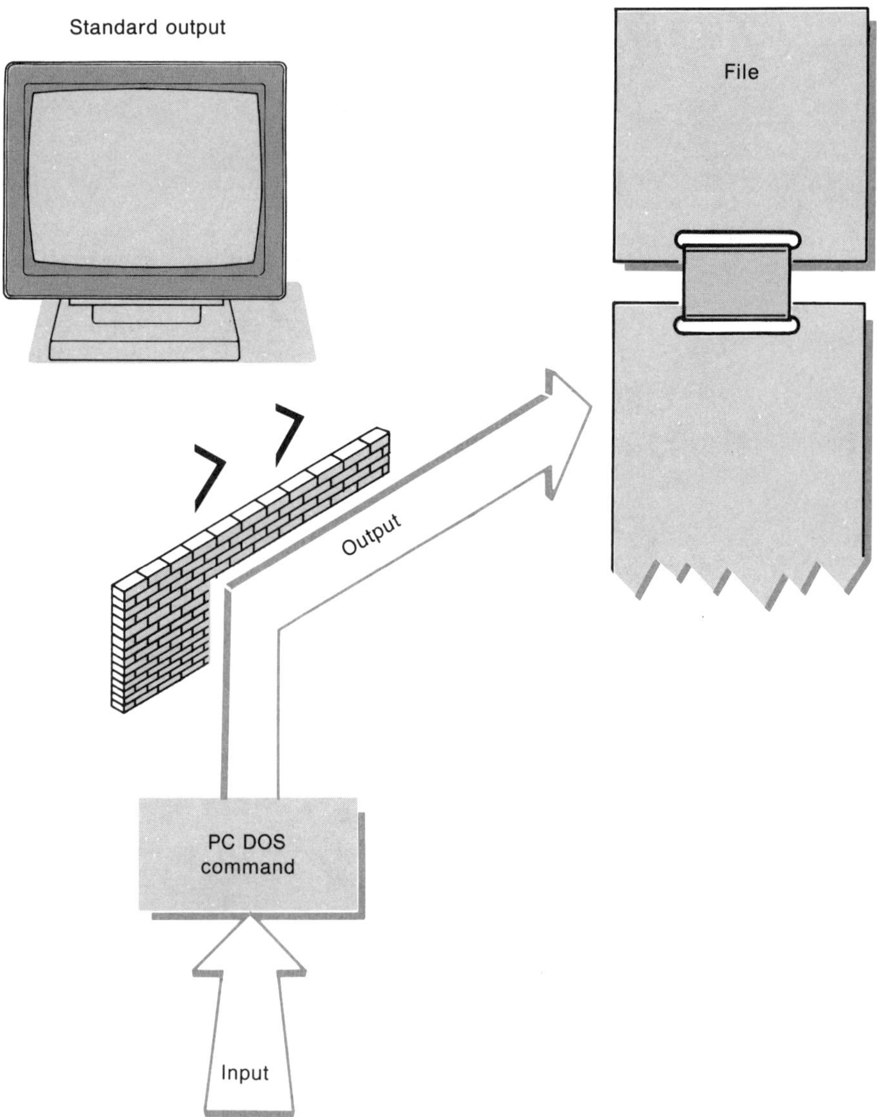

Figure 8.4. ***Appending to a file.***

Reading a File Just as PC DOS can save information to a file, it can also read information from one. *Input redirection* is symbolized by the *less-than* character (<). Think of this symbol as a pointer that tells PC DOS to "take the contents from this file and use it as input." By using this option, you can make a file the standard input device instead of the keyboard.

Input redirection is frequently used in batch files to relieve you of the repetitious entries needed to start up a program. Simply put all the necessary responses in a file. Then redirect the input using this file.

To keep things straight, it is a good idea to name the file after your batch file. For example, if your batch file is called EDITING.BAT, then you will probably want to call your text file EDITING.TXT. This name will help you identify the file later on.

The most frequent use of input redirection is in combination with filters. You will learn about them next.

Using Filters

Filters are special PC DOS commands. They read in data from the designated standard input device, modify the data in some way, and then output the modified data to the designated standard output device. Thus, by their position in the middle of the process (as shown in Figure 8.5), these commands work to filter the data.

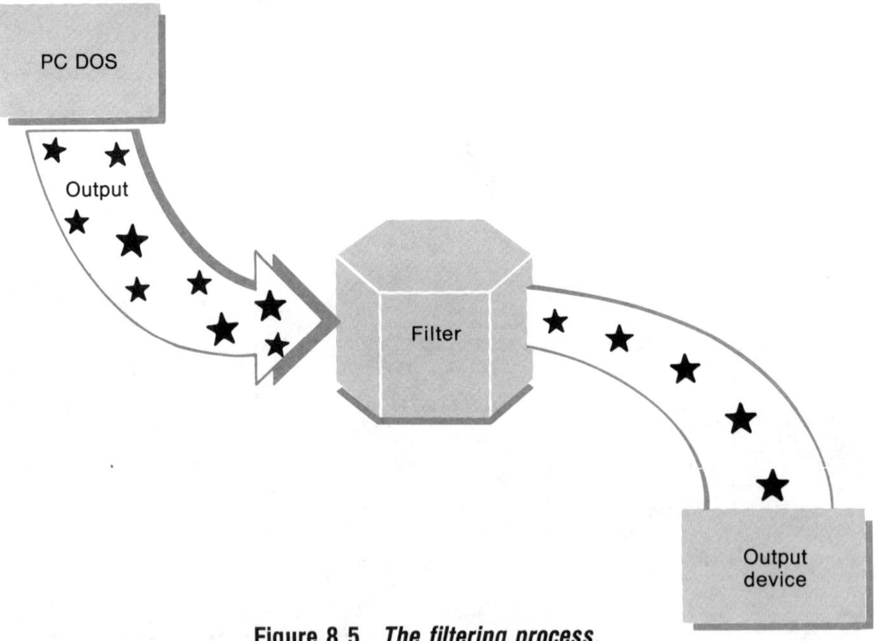

Figure 8.5. ***The filtering process.***

Filters allow you to modify input from a program, command, or file. You may display the output on the screen or save it to a file. Recall that PC DOS contains three filters: SORT, FIND, and MORE.

SORTing a File

The *SORT command* is a filter that rearranges lines of text in a variety of ways. SORT can be executed by itself as a normal command, or it can be piped with other commands.

This filter sorts file contents either alphabetically or by column number. Learning to use SORT is like learning how to drive. You know you existed without it, but it is hard to imagine how. To experience the real pleasure of using SORT, you have to try it on some actual data.

You can use SORT on any ASCII text file. To practice using this command, you will need to create a sample file. The quickest way to create a very short file is to use the COPY CON: command to copy what is typed on the keyboard to the file. COPY CON: tells MS-DOS to copy all the information you are typing on your keyboard (the *console*) and put it directly into a file. (See Chapter 9, "Creating Text Files," for more information about text files and COPY CON:.)

As sales manager for Capital, Inc., one of your jobs is to keep track of the orders your sales people get. Listing 8.1 shows the orders they closed this week. The salespeople's names start in column 1, the names of the companies they sold to start in column 11, and the dollar amount sold starts in column 28. Create the ORDERS.LST file by typing the information shown in Listing 8.1. Since SORT uses columns to rearrange files, be sure to space every entry properly.

Listing 8.1. ***Creating the ORDERS.LST File***

```
C:\>copy con: orders.lst

Joe       Pantheon Corp.  $15,995
George    RAYMOS          $10,992
Mary Lou  Escon           $12,867
Joe       Isentex         $ 9,544
Susan     Sysconix, Inc.  $10,335
George    RAYMOS          $13,255
Mary Lou  Haskell & Co.   $14,758
^Z
```

If you wish, you can use TYPE to look at your file:

```
C:\>type orders.lst
```

SORTing in Alphabetical Order

If you do not enter any special options, SORT will always rearrange your files in standard alphabetical order based on the first character in each line (the first column in the file). Lines beginning with spaces or punctuation will be listed first. Entries beginning with a number will be next. Lines starting with a small letter will be in the third group, and entries beginning with a capital letter will be last. To do this standard SORT, just tell PC DOS to SORT the file.

Caution

SORTing Nonstandard and Foreign Language Characters

SORT is designed to handle letters, numbers, and punctuation. If you try to SORT a file containing graphic characters or characters from the extended character set, you will probably have little success. This is because these characters also have other meanings. They may stand for line breaks, page breaks, or tabs.

If you are using a foreign language character set (see Chapter 13, "International Language Support"), the sorting order will depend on the alphabet for the country involved.

SORT accepts input from another program, command, or file. But you must include the redirection character as part of the statement:

```
C:\>sort < orders.lst
```

With this command you have told PC DOS to sort the contents of the file ORDERS.LST. Since you did not redirect the output to a file, you can watch the screen to see the results of this command, as shown in Listing 8.2.

Listing 8.2. *SORTing ORDERS.LST to the Screen*

```
George     RAYMOS            $10,992
George     RAYMOS            $13,255
Joe        Isentex           $ 9,544
Joe        Pantheon Corp.    $15,995
Mary Lou   Escon             $12,867
Mary Lou   Haskell & Co.     $14,758
Susan      Sysconix, Inc.    $10,335
```

Always keep in mind that SORT rearranges lines by *column*. This means that SORT would interpret 54 as "five followed by four," rather than "fifty-four." For example, if you SORTed the following lines,

```
1
1a
5
5a
10
54
```

you would see these results:

```
1
10
1a
5
54
5a
```

Notice that the list has some out-of-order numbers. You could get around this by redesigning your source file. If the single-digit lines all start with 0, SORT will understand how they should be arranged:

```
01
01a
05
05a
10
54
```

DOS Shell

SORTing Files

DOSSHELL allows you to easily sort your files so that they are displayed by name, extension, date, size, or disk order. For example, to sort files by date, select "File System" from the Start Programs screen and then select "Arrange." Select "System File List"; then select "Options" and "Display Options." You will see a pop-up menu of display options. Select "Sort by:"; then select "Extension." PC DOS will automatically present only one screen of listings at a time. You can scroll the screen to see more. For more information about DOSSHELL, see Chapter 4, "Using DOSSHELL."

Saving Your Results

By using redirection, you can keep the results of a SORT command. Just tell PC DOS to send the output to a file instead of the screen. Try entering the following command:

```
C:\>sort < orders.lst > keepthis.lst
```

Remember, you will not be able to see the results of this sort until you look at the file:

```
C:\>type keepthis.lst
```

SORTing in Reverse Order

SORT will also sort by reverse alphabetical order. To perform a sort so that the end of the alphabet tops the list, you use the */r* option. Enter the following command as shown in Listing 8.3, and PC DOS will respond with your list in reverse order.

Listing 8.3. ***SORTing ORDERS.LIST in Reverse***

```
C:\>sort/r < orders.lst

Susan     Sysconix, Inc.    $10,335
Mary Lou  Haskell & Co.     $14,758
Mary Lou  Escon             $12,867
Joe       Pantheon Corp.    $15,995
Joe       Isentex           $ 9,544
George    RAYMOS            $13,255
George    RAYMOS            $10,992
```

SORTing by Column

The SORT command can do more than just sort in alphabetical and reverse orders. The /+*n* option allows you to sort by any column. Just replace the *n* with the number of the column on which to sort. For example, you could arrange your list by the amount of the purchase, as shown in Listing 8.4.

Listing 8.4. ***SORTing ORDERS.LST by Purchase***

```
C:\>sort/+28 <orders.lst

Joe       Isentex          $ 9,544
Susan     Sysconix, Inc.   $10,335
George    RAYMOS           $10,992
Mary Lou  Escon            $12,867
George    RAYMOS           $13,255
Mary Lou  Haskell & Co.    $14,758
Joe       Pantheon Corp.   $15,995
```

Listing 8.5 shows the previous list alphabetized by customer.

Listing 8.5. ***SORTing ORDERS.LST by Customer***

```
C:\>sort/+11 <orders.lst

Mary Lou  Escon            $12,867
Mary Lou  Haskell & Co.    $14,758
Joe       Isentex          $ 9,544
Joe       Pantheon Corp.   $15,995
George    RAYMOS           $10,992
George    RAYMOS           $13,255
Susan     Sysconix, Inc.   $10,335
```

Finally, you can combine these options. For example, suppose you wanted to know which salesperson made the largest sale. You could enter the command shown in Listing 8.6.

Listing 8.6. ***SORTing ORDERS.LST by Sale***

```
C:\>sort/r/+28 <orders.lst

Joe       Pantheon Corp.   $15,995
Mary Lou  Haskell & Co.    $14,758
George    RAYMOS           $13,255
Mary Lou  Escon            $12,867
George    RAYMOS           $10,992
Susan     Sysconix, Inc.   $10,335
Joe       Isentex          $ 9,544
```

Error Messages

Unless you are working with a very large file, you will probably never see the error messages `Insufficient disk space` and `Insufficient memory`.

`Insufficient disk space` means that there was not enough room on the disk to save the sorted information. To make room on your drive, you can delete any files that you no longer need. Alternatively, you can redirect the output to another drive, like this:

```
C:\>sort <large.fil >a:newfile
```

The message `Insufficient memory` means just what is says. PC DOS sorts a file by loading it into memory, rearranging it, and then sending the rearranged information to the screen or to another file. In a sense, this means that you must have enough memory to load two copies of the file. If you load several RAM-resident programs (like SideKick) and then try to sort a large file, you might get this error message. One way to solve the problem is to remove the RAM-resident programs from memory. You will need to check each program's manual for directions. On the other hand, you may prefer simply to reboot your computer. If so, be sure to perform your SORT before you reload those programs.

FINDing Data

The *FIND command* helps you to locate specific items in a file. It works by finding strings. A *string* is simply a group of characters enclosed in double quotation marks ("). These characters can include upper- and lowercase letters, numbers, and punctuation marks. (Of course, you cannot include double quotes, since FIND will think that they represent the end of the string.)

Caution

FIND Finds Only Exact Matches
Strings within a file will be found only when they *exactly* match the string enclosed in the command. This includes the use of capitals, lowercase letters and all punctuation marks. For instance, if you tell FIND to look for the string "dog", it will *not* identify lines containing either "Dog" or "DOG".

Searching the File

Suppose you want to find out which sales Joe made. Enter the command first, followed by the string. The string must always be enclosed in quotation marks. The name of the file to search is entered last. Every line containing the string will appear on the screen:

```
C:\>find "Joe" orders.lst

Joe       Pantheon Corp.  $15,995
Joe       Isentex         $ 9,544
```

Counting Lines

Now suppose you are not particularly interested in the names of the companies Joe sold to this week. You just want to know how many sales he made. You can use FIND with the */c* switch. The */c* switch tells you how many lines in the file contain the string:

```
C:\>find/c "Joe" orders.lst

---------- orders.lst: 2
```

FIND tells you which file it searched and how many lines contained your string.

Locating Lines

FIND also helps you locate exactly where the string occurs. For every instance of the indicated string, the */n* switch tells FIND to display the line number followed by the line itself:

```
C:\>find/n "Joe" orders.lst

---------- orders.lst

[1]Joe        Pantheon Corp.    $15,995
[4]Joe        Isentex           $ 9,544
```

The line numbers indicate the position of the entries in the original file. For example, there are only two items in the display. Yet Isentex is assigned a line number of 4. The reason it is line 4 is that this sale is the fourth entry in your original ORDERS.LST file.

Locating a string by its line number can be useful in large files. It is a fast and easy way to locate any type of string.

Lines Not Containing the String

Occasionally, you may want to know which lines in a file do *not* contain a particular string. FIND allows you to do this with the */v* option:

```
C:\>find/v "Joe" orders.lst

---------- orders.lst

George    RAYMOS            $10,992
Mary Lou  Escon             $12,867
Susan     Sysconix, Inc.    $10,335
George    RAYMOS            $13,255
Mary Lou  Haskell & Co.     $14,758
```

Combining the /v and /n Options

You can combine the */v* and */n* options. FIND will locate the lines that do not contain the string you named and will display their line number. Try the following command:

```
C:\>find/v/n "Joe" orders.lst

---------- orders.lst

[2]George    RAYMOS            $10,992
[3]Mary Lou  Escon             $12,867
[5]Susan     Sysconix, Inc.    $10,335
[6]George    RAYMOS            $13,255
[7]Mary Lou  Haskell & Co.     $14,758
```

Error Messages

If you accidentally specify an option that does not exist, you will see the following message: `FIND: Invalid parameter P`. (The `P` is replaced by the invalid switch you typed.) Reenter the command, using one of the valid switches.

The two error messages `FIND: Invalid number of parameters` and `FIND: Syntax error` are both alerting you to the same difficulty. They mean that you made a mistake when you typed the string you wanted to find. To correct this problem, make sure that you are using the correct syntax (`find "string" filename`). Remember, you must type a double quote (") before and after the string.

The message `FIND: File not found filename` means that FIND cannot locate the file you specified. The message `FIND: Read error in filename` means that an error occurred when FIND tried to read the file you indicated. In both cases, FIND will tell you which file it looked for. If you made a mistake when you entered the file name, reissue the command correctly. You may want to use DIR to verify the file name. Unfortunately, if you entered the file name correctly and you still get the `FIND: Read error in filename` message, there is something wrong with your file. If you have a backup copy, try using it instead.

MORE Data

Much like the TYPE command, the *MORE command* can be used to display the contents of a file. Its major improvement over TYPE is that MORE will display only one screen of text at a time. When the screen is filled, MORE will wait for you to tell it when to display the next screen of text.

You are probably already familiar with the idea of stopping a text scroll at the bottom of a filled screen. You saw this action when you used the */p* (pause) switch with the DIR command (although in that case the message from PC DOS was `Strike a key when ready...`).

MORE does something very similar. When the screen is full, MORE pauses at the bottom of the screen and displays the message `-- More --` until you press a key to signal MORE to continue. This is how you would use MORE to display your file:

```
C:\>more <orders.lst
```

Since ORDERS.LST contains less than one screen of text, you did not really need to use MORE. Later in this chapter, you will have the opportunity to see how MORE works with a longer file.

Caution

Don't Forget the < Symbol

A common mistake when using MORE is to leave out the < symbol, for example, `more orders.lst`. If you forget the <, the screen will appear to freeze and show nothing. Since you didn't use the redirection symbol, MORE is expecting input from the keyboard. To break out of this situation, type Ctrl-C.

Filters and Redirection

Just as you can use a file as the input for the SORT command, you can also redirect the sorted output to a file. To output the results of a sort to a file, include the output redirection character > and the new file name in the command:

```
C:\>sort/+28 <orders.lst >ranking.lst
```

Of course, you will need to TYPE the file to see its contents, as shown in Listing 8.7.

Listing 8.7. ***Viewing the Contents of RANKING.LST***

```
C:\>type ranking.lst

Joe       Isentex           $ 9,544
Susan     Sysconix, Inc.    $10,335
George    RAYMOS            $10,992
Mary Lou  Escon             $12,867
George    RAYMOS            $13,255
Mary Lou  Haskell & Co.     $14,758
Joe       Pantheon Corp.    $15,995
```

Although it may appear complicated at first, you can understand the command shown in Listing 8.7 by breaking it into steps. You told SORT to receive input from ORDERS.LST, arrange that input starting with column 28, and then send those lines to a new file called RANKING.LST.

Is there a quick way to create a record of Mary Lou's sales? Enter the commands shown in Listing 8.8.

Listing 8.8. ***Creating MARYLOU.LST***

```
C:\>find "Mary Lou" <orders.lst >marylou.lst
C:\>type marylou.lst

Mary Lou  Escon            $12,867
Mary Lou  Haskell & Co.    $14,758
```

In Listing 8.8 you told FIND to search a file called ORDERS.LST, to locate all lines containing the string "Mary Lou", and to send those lines to a file called MARYLOU.LST. Remember, if you want to add information to either of these new files, use the symbol >> to append the new output instead of writing over the existing files.

Piping Commands

Piping is a method of chaining a PC DOS command to other special commands. This is a more sophisticated use of the redirection of input and output. It lets you combine several commands to create exactly the information you want.

For example, this technique is often used to construct personalized directory listings. If you have many files in a subdirectory, you may have trouble locating them. You can speed up your work by using filters. One of the most important benefits of learning the commands and procedures covered in this chapter is the greater ease with which you will be able to organize your files.

Of course, there are no real pipes involved in piping. On the other hand, a pipeline is a useful analogy to help you understand how information flows from input to output devices. A water department's pipeline takes water from reservoirs and pipes it to a purification plant, where it is filtered before it is piped to your home. When you construct a PC DOS pipeline, you do much the same thing.

Your original data either is stored in a source file or will be created by a program. You want to use the output of this program or file as the input to the next file. However, the information does not go directly from the input file to the output file. If it did, you could accomplish the same goal by simply copying the file. Instead, with piping, the data is fed in from the input file, goes through a filtering process where it is modified, and then goes to its destination in the output file.

PC DOS has a special character to link commands and filters. It is the vertical bar (|). (For clarity, this book uses spaces before and after the | character in commands. PC DOS will still be able to follow your instructions if you choose not to use spaces.) To create a piping sequence, separate the various commands, filters, and files with the vertical bar. You can remember this character if you think of it as looking like a piece of pipe, or two pieces of pipe laid end to end. It lets you connect commands, programs, and files together in a long chain. The rest of this chapter will give you practice in using piping.

From time to time, as you use some of the commands in this chapter, you may see strange files like these:

```
%PIPE1.$$$
%PIPE2.$$$
%PIPE3.$$$
.
.
.
```

These files are temporary files. When you use piping, PC DOS creates internal temporary files, like reservoirs, to hold the data as it is being piped. These files are deleted after your commands have been executed.

If you turn off your computer before the commands have been finished, some of these files will be saved to your hard drive. Go ahead and delete them whenever you see them. PC DOS no longer needs them.

SORTing a Directory

You can use filters with almost any PC DOS command. Piping is frequently used with DIR to create a customized directory listing. In the next few pages, you will learn how to combine piping and redirection to copy a listing of your PC DOS subdirectory to a file.

Note: You will be using your PC DOS subdirectory for these examples. Since it contains probably 50 or more files, the example file you create will be very long. This long file will be useful because you will be able to really experiment with the various filters that PC DOS provides. However, since illustrations of that length would be much too long to use in a book, the sample listings printed here will contain only a few files.

SORT not only rearranges your data quickly but, in conjunction with input and output redirection, becomes a powerful file-creation tool as well. You do not have to limit the use of SORT to files. Like all filters, it is really most useful when piped. You can use the output of a command as input into the SORT filter.

You create a piping sequence by chaining the various commands, filters, and files with the vertical bar character. For instance, you can link DIR with SORT to create a sorted directory. Change to the \DOS subdirectory and try the following command shown in Listing 8.9.

Listing 8.9. ***Linking DIR with SORT***

```
C:\>cd\dos
C:\DOS>dir | sort

       10 File(s) 7958528 bytes free

 Directory of  C:\DOS
 Volume in drive C has no label

.            <DIR>        11-07-90  12:24a
..           <DIR>        11-07-90  12:24a
APPEND   EXE     11186     6-17-88  12:00p
BASIC    COM      1065     6-17-88  12:00p
FIND     EXE      5983     6-17-88  12:00p
FORMAT   COM     22923     6-17-88  12:00p
KEYB     COM      9056     6-17-88  12:00p
KEYBOARD SYS     23360     6-17-88  12:00p
PRINTER  SYS     18946     6-17-88  12:00p
READ     ME        599     3-01-90   4:00p
```

The command in Listing 8.9 tells PC DOS to go to the \DOS subdirectory, sort the listing on the first column (because no options are included in the SORT command), and then output the sorted directory to the screen.

There are a few things to remember about piping. First, you must enter the command before you enter the filter. You can test this if you're curious (don't worry, you won't damage any files):

```
C:\DOS>sort | dir
```

Nothing will happen. Each time you press Enter, the cursor simply moves down a few lines on the screen. This is because PC DOS does not understand your instructions. Just press Ctrl-C to end the command. (Remember, Ctrl-C is a handy way to interrupt a command and return to the prompt. See Chapter 9, "Creating Text Files," for more information about special key combinations.)

Second, each command must be completed before you pipe it to the next one. You must enter the command and any switches or options before you add any filters. For example, if you entered **DIR | SORT\DOS**, you would just confuse PC DOS. Again, you would have to press Ctrl-C to end the command.

Of course, you can also redirect the output of a piped command:

```
C:\DOS>dir | sort >listing
```

The directory will not be listed on the screen, but you will hear the drive working and the indicator light will be on. This is PIPE creating the temporary file that holds the output of DIR and the output of SORT. When the sorted directory is completed, it will be redirected to the file named LISTING. If you want to see the sorted display, you can TYPE the file LISTING.

Tip

SORT Leaves the File Contents Unchanged
It is important to remember that when you SORT a file, or when you use any filter to modify it, the contents of the file are not changed. The file remains in the same order as it was before the sort. For example, your \DOS directory listing has not actually been sorted. If you entered DIR, you would get the normal directory listing. This is why it is valuable to redirect the output of a SORT to a file if you want to use the sorted information again.

You can use SORT with any of its options. For example, you can sort by file size as shown in Listing 8.10.

Listing 8.10. ***Sorting by File Size***

```
C:\DOS>dir | sort/+17

MORE     COM      2166   6-17-88  12:00p
READ     ME        599   3-01-90   4:00p
BASIC    COM      1065   6-17-88  12:00p
SYS      COM     11472   6-17-88  12:00p
SHARE    EXE     10301   6-17-88  12:00p
CHKDSK   COM      9850   6-17-88  12:00p
MODE     COM     15487   6-17-88  12:00p
```

For your convenience, Figure 8.6 shows the column numbers in which PC DOS always displays directory information.

Tip

Piped Commands
You can use DIR's switches and wildcards in a piped command. For example, the following sequence will produce a listing of all your COM files sorted by size. Remember to enter a space between DIR and the file name.

```
C:\DOS\>dir \*.com | sort/+17
```

FINDing Files You do not need to limit the use of FIND to a display on the screen or a redirection to a file. You can also use it with commands. For instance, FIND can help you locate files, as shown in Listing 8.11.

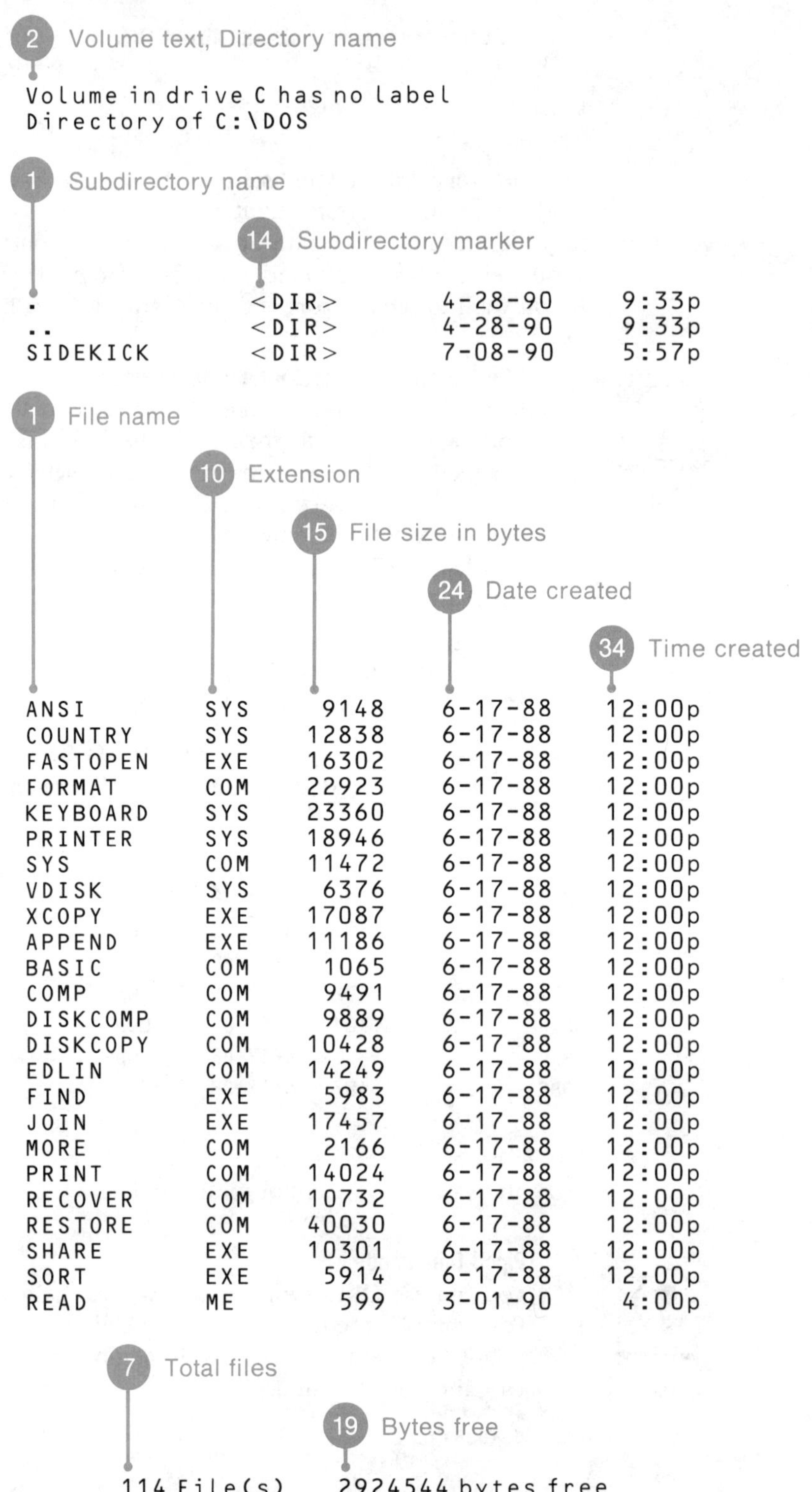

Figure 8.6. ***The column numbers in which directory information is displayed.***

Listing 8.11. ***Using FIND to Locate Files***

```
C:\DOS>dir | find "EXE"

APPEND   EXE    11186   6-17-88  12:00p
FIND     EXE     5983   6-17-88  12:00p
AUTOEXEC BAT      236   9-20-88   9:34a
```

Remember, FIND requires very specific input. If you ask it to find `exe`, it will not find any files. This is because you are searching for a lowercase string, while PC DOS stores file names in capital letters. On the other hand, FIND *will* locate every file in the current (or specified) directory that contains the string `EXE` within its file name, including such files as AUTOEXEC.BAT.

Caution

No Wildcards with FIND
Because FIND looks for *exactly* the string you specify, you cannot use wildcards with FIND. For example, if you try to locate file names containing the string `*.EXE`, you will not find any files.

Of course, only DIR works within a specified directory. Since the command in Listing 8.11 pipes DIR and FIND together, it too can be used only within a specific directory. If you want to search across all your subdirectories for a file, you will need PC DOS 4. If you do not have it, you may wish to obtain a third-party utility that will let you survey your entire hard drive.

DOS Shell

Searching for Files across Directories
DOSSHELL lets you search for files across directories so that you can locate a file anywhere on your drive. To do this, first select "File System" from the Start Programs screen; then select "Arrange." Select "System File List." Then select "Options" and "Display Options." You can now enter the name of the file you want to search for or use wildcards to search for files whose names match a specific pattern. For example, entering `test.*` will search for any files named TEST with any extension, such as TEST.TXT, TEST.WSD, TEST.BAT, and so forth. Unless you specify otherwise, they will be sorted by name, and you will see their size in bytes along with the date and time of creation. For more details on working with DOSSHELL, see Chapter 4, "Using DOSSHELL."

MORE Files The MORE filter might well be the most useful of all. Have you noticed how quickly all those files disappear off the screen? You can combine MORE with any of the previous commands. Try the command shown in Listing 8.12.

Listing 8.12. ***Combining DIR and MORE***

```
C:\DOS>dir | more

 Volume in drive C has no label
 Directory of  C:\DOS
```

```
.             <DIR>     4-28-90   9:33p
..            <DIR>     4-28-90   9:33p
ANSI     SYS     9148   6-17-88  12:00p
DRIVER   SYS     1196   6-17-88  12:00p
FORMAT   COM    22923   6-17-88  12:00p
MODE     COM    15487   6-17-88  12:00p
REPLACE  EXE    11775   6-17-88  12:00p
 -- More --
```

The directory shown in Listing 8.12 contains quite a few files, so it will take PC DOS a few seconds to construct the temporary pipe files. When PC DOS is finished, you will see the contents of your \DOS subdirectory displayed until the screen is filled. The last line reads `-- More --`. To get the remaining listings in the directory, press any key.

When MORE is used as a filter to another command, it automatically causes the output generated by the command to pause whenever the screen has been filled. You will often use it with TYPE when you are trying to read a long file.

Putting It All Together

Of course, you can combine as many filters as you like into one command. This is when you discover the real power of piping. By combining filters, you can do some very interesting things. For example, it would be easier to read a subdirectory listing if the files were arranged alphabetically and the display stopped scrolling automatically when the page was full. This is not difficult at all.

```
C:\DOS>dir | sort | more
```

Another way to redesign the directory is to group together all the same files and then list them with the extensions in alphabetical order. To do this, you need to remember that the extension designation begins in column 10.

```
C:\DOS>dir | sort/+10 | more
```

What if you want to list only certain files? Listing 8.13 shows an example.

Listing 8.13. ***Using SORT and DIR to List Selected Files***

```
C:\DOS>dir | sort/r | find "EXE"

XCOPY    EXE    17087   6-17-88  12:00p
SUBST    EXE     9909   6-17-88  12:00p
SORT     EXE     5914   6-17-88  12:00p
REPLACE  EXE    11775   6-17-88  12:00p
JOIN     EXE    17457   6-17-88  12:00p
```

```
FIND      EXE      5983   6-17-88  12:00p
ATTRIB    EXE      9529   6-17-88  12:00p
AUTOEXEC  BAT       236   9-20-88   9:34a
APPEND    EXE     11186   6-17-88  12:00p
```

The length of the command in Listing 8.13 should not confuse you. Just take it one step at a time. You told PC DOS to select the files in the \DOS subdirectory, sort them in reverse order, and then display only those lines containing the string EXE.

You may combine as many commands as necessary to accomplish the task, as shown in Listing 8.14.

Listing 8.14. *Combining DIR, SORT, FIND, and MORE*

```
C:\DOS>dir | sort/+17 | find "COM" | more

MORE      COM      2166   6-17-88  12:00p
BASIC     COM      1063   6-17-88  12:00p
TREE      COM      3571   6-17-88  12:00p
PRINT     COM     14024   6-17-88  12:00p
CHKDSK    COM      9850   6-17-88  12:00p
 -- More --

FORMAT    COM     22923   6-17-88  12:00p
MODE      COM     15487   6-17-88  12:00p
BASICA    COM     36403   6-17-88  12:00p
FDISK     COM     48216   6-17-88  12:00p
```

SORTing a Directory by Date

By combining commands, you can achieve results that are unobtainable any other way. For instance, you may have noticed that you cannot combine SORT and DIR to create a directory sorted by date. This is because PC DOS lists file dates by month, date, and year, like this: MM-DD-YY. However, SORT arranges data by columns of information. Imagine that you wanted to sort the following three files:

```
MORE      COM      2166   6-17-88  12:00p
READ      ME        512   1-08-90   4:55a
CLEAR     EXE      1005  10-02-85   1:29p
```

If you told PC DOS to SORT these files on column 24, you would get the following results:

```
READ      ME        512   1-08-90   4:55a
MORE      COM      2166   6-17-88  12:00p
CLEAR     EXE      1005  10-02-85   1:29p
```

While the months are in the proper order, the years are still scrambled.

This is the real advantage of combining commands by using pipes, filters, and redirection. Without too much effort, you can create a directory listing sorted by date. Use FIND to isolate the files for each year and use SORT listing sorted by date. Use FIND to isolate the files for each year and use SORT to arrange that year's files by date. Then append the sorted information to a new file. Try this sequence of commands:

```
C:\DOS>dir | sort/+24 | find "-80 " > datesort.lst
C:\DOS>dir | sort/+24 | find "-81 " >> datesort.lst
C:\DOS>dir | sort/+24 | find "-82 " >> datesort.lst
C:\DOS>dir | sort/+24 | find "-83 " >> datesort.lst
C:\DOS>dir | sort/+24 | find "-84 " >> datesort.lst
C:\DOS>dir | sort/+24 | find "-85 " >> datesort.lst
C:\DOS>dir | sort/+24 | find "-86 " >> datesort.lst
C:\DOS>dir | sort/+24 | find "-87 " >> datesort.lst
C:\DOS>dir | sort/+24 | find "-88 " >> datesort.lst
C:\DOS>type datesort.lst | more
```

Putting Pipe Commands in Batch Files

As you have probably noticed, some pipe commands can get pretty complicated. If you have a favorite that you want to use frequently, put it in a batch file. Chapter 10, "Batch Files," has examples, as does Part 3, the Command Reference, in the entry for SORT.

Redirecting Piped Output to the Printer

By redirecting the output of a piped command to your printer, you can make printed records that contain exactly the information you need in the format you prefer. For example, you could create an alphabetized list of your EXE files. Turn on your printer. When it is ready, enter the following command:

```
C:\DOS>dir | sort | find "EXE" > prn:
```

The word `prn:` tells PC DOS to redirect the output of this command to the printer. (Depending on your printer, you may have to press the Form Feed or Line Feed button to eject the final page of this listing. Your printer manual will tell you how to do this.)

Table 8.1 summarizes the commands and switches used in this chapter.

What's Next

Chapter 9, "Creating Text Files," shows how to use the function keys to control the command line template and presents a thorough examination of text files and how to manipulate them. Chapter 10, "Batch Files," shows how to use redirection, pipes, and filters in batch files. Chapter 6, "Managing Your Hard Disk," is a complete tutorial for learning to use PC DOS commands to organize and manage information on your hard disk. Chapter 5, "PC DOS Files," explains the nature of PC DOS files.

Table 8.1. ***Special Characters, Filters, and Switches***

Character	Format	Description
<	*command* < *file name*	Accept input to a command from a file or other device.
>	*command* > *file name*	Send output from a command to a file or other device.
>>	*command* >> *file name*	Add output from a command to the end of a file.
|	*command* | *filter*	Link two or more commands and filters on one line.
		Filters and Switches
SORT	SORT < *file name*	Rearrange lines of data within a file.
/r	SORT/r *file name*	Rearrange lines in reverse order.
/+n	SORT/+*n file name*	Rearrange lines starting with the information in column *n*. (You replace *n* with the column number.)
FIND	FIND *"string" file name*	Locate lines containing a particular *"string"* within a file.
/c	FIND/c	Count the number of lines that contain the string.
/n	FIND/*n "string" file name*	Identify by line number the lines containing the string.
/v	FIND/v *"string" file name*	Locate all lines that do *not* contain the string.
MORE	MORE < *file name*	Display one screen of information at a time; wait until a key is pressed and then display the next screen.

Note: Words printed in italics indicate parameters that you must supply. For example, SORT < *file name* means that you must enter the name of the file to be sorted.

Key Concepts and Words

Before you read further, use the following list to test your understanding of the concepts and words in this chapter.

Redirection	Text columns	Sort file contents
Data management commands	Find text strings	Directory listing organization
Devices	Command line	Filters
Standard input and output	Files	Command and filter linking
Strings	Input and output redirection	Pipes

Chapter 9

The PC DOS operating system relies on text strings and text files for many of its controls. Typing from the keyboard produces text; the names of files, directories, and commands are text; directory listings, batch files, and the CONFIG.SYS file are text files. A PC DOS system provides many editing features to let you create text and manipulate text files. When you enter a command, PC DOS stores that command as the "template." Many of the function keys are designed to manipulate the template and redisplay it on the screen. PC DOS includes a text editing program named EDLIN.COM. This chapter prepares you to

- *Display the template, or parts of the template, with the function keys*
- *Use your keyboard's text-specific keys: the Ins, Del, Esc, Backspace, and cursor keys*
- *Create and edit text files with the EDLIN line editor*
- *Generate graphics characters to create boxes and borders in your files*

Before you begin: Review the concepts covered in Chapter 5, "PC DOS Files."

Chapter 9
Creating Text Files

Typing `dir` to get a directory listing is one thing; typing 16 separate commands each morning to set up your computer as you want it is quite another. Text files simplify and expedite long tasks. Properly written, text files can even transfer information from one program to another!

The first file you will work with is the *command line*. Although you may not have thought about the command line in this way before, it is really a one-line text file. Rather than being written to your hard drive, it is stored in RAM. When you press the Enter key, you essentially close the file and send it to PC DOS to read. You will learn how to use the function keys (F1 through F6) to edit the command line. These keys can also be used to edit a line of text in a regular file.

Next, you will learn how to create a file and store it. In the Quick Primer, you learned about a convention called COPY CON:, which lets you create very short files quickly and easily. When you need to work with longer files, you may want to use EDLIN. This small editing utility is included free with PC DOS. It lets you create and modify text files on a line-by-line basis. This chapter will show you how to use EDLIN commands.

ASCII Text

ASCII (American Standard Code for Information Interchange) is a specific code scheme used by PC DOS to recognize the letters, numbers, and punctuation marks that make up a text file. ASCII files contain their text information in exactly the same format as you enter it. When displayed, ASCII files make perfect sense.

You will probably use your word processor to create letters, reports, and other long text files. Word processors provide a wealth of formatting capabilities that are important for creating attractive documents. However, in order to do this, word-processed files contain special codes (for example, codes for margin settings or for bold type) that tell the printer how to format your text.

Unfortunately, PC DOS has trouble interpreting text that contains these special formatting codes, and this can be a problem when you want to create text that PC DOS can read. For example, if you use the PC DOS TYPE command to display a word-processed file, it will jump and scroll oddly; it may even be completely illegible. (Many word processors do have commands that you can use to create ASCII text files.)

Tip

Word Processor Terminology for ASCII Files

Word processors use different terminology to describe ASCII text files. WordStar calls ASCII files "non-document mode," while WordPerfect allows you to save a file as "DOS Text." Many memory-resident utility programs such as SideKick have "notepads" that create ASCII text files.

The ASCII code for representing text is the most commonly used method of text manipulation in today's computers. Using ASCII thus provides the highest degree of flexibility when you are transferring text files to many different types of computers.

Another advantage of entering data in ASCII code is that ASCII files can be used by many types of programs. This increases the flexibility of your data files. For example, you could create a proposal in your spreadsheet program, send the figures to an ASCII file, and then use your word processor to include those figures in a memo. Like many editors, EDLIN enters and stores files in ASCII code.

In addition to the letters, numbers, and punctuation marks you enter, ASCII code includes three characters to define the file structure. When you press Enter at the end of a line, two characters (the carriage return and the line feed) are inserted. These characters carry the message "stop this line and move down to the next line." You will not see them when you display or print ASCII text files.

The *Ctrl-Z* character is used to indicate the end of a file. When you use the TYPE command to display the contents of a file, you will see this character. It is shown with a caret (^) to indicate the control key, like this: ^Z. You will not see this character when you print the file.

ASCII text files are used in three main areas of data entry: text files, batch-processing files (see Chapter 10, "Batch Files"), and source code (a list of instructions that your computer either runs directly or compiles into a working program). You can use EDLIN to edit any of these files.

Uses for ASCII Text

ASCII files have many uses. You can create ASCII text files that contain instructions controlling your computer. The Quick Primer introduced CONFIG.SYS and AUTOEXEC.BAT, two special files that your system responds to at startup. (See Chapter 11, "Customizing Your System," for a more detailed explanation of the CONFIG.SYS and AUTOEXEC.BAT files.)

You can also use ASCII to write your own *batch files* for automating a complicated sequence of commands. All batch files, including the

AUTOEXEC.BAT file, are ASCII text files. (See Chapter 10 for more information about the ways you can use batch files to simplify the work you do with your computer.)

Another type of short ASCII file you might work with is a *READ.ME file*. Many programs include a file called READ.ME, README.TXT, README.1ST, or some other variation on that theme. This file often contains information about updates to the software, special operating tricks, and other notes that may not be in the manual.

You may want to create your own READ.ME files. For example, when you give diskettes to other people, it is a nice idea to add a brief READ.ME file so that they will know what to look for. It is also wise to put a READ.ME file on storage diskettes. Months later, it will help you to identify the files on the diskette and remember why you created them.

In general, ASCII files are a lingua franca of the computer world. Because most word processors can accept ASCII files as well as their own special formats, people who use different word processors can easily share ASCII files.

ASCII files are also the standard format for communicating between different computer systems. With the appropriate hardware and software, you can transfer ASCII files between your PC and a bulletin board, or send them over a public network or LAN as electronic mail.

All of the ASCII files just mentioned can be edited by using the programs and commands that you will learn about in this chapter.

Using the Special Keys

Table 9.1 contains a brief review of certain keys, unique to computing, that are used when entering text. For a further explanation of these keys, see the Quick Primer.

Table 9.1. ***Special Keys for Entering Text***

Key	Ctrl Combination	Purpose
Enter		Indicates the end of a line or an entry; tells PC DOS to execute the commands you have typed.
Esc	^[	If used before Enter has been pressed, puts a backslash (\) on your command line to indicate that the text you typed is canceled and moves the cursor down one line so that you can enter a new command.
Caps Lock		A toggle key that allows you to change the mode in which letters are entered. When you first turn on your computer, letters are entered in lowercase; if you press the Caps Lock key, they are entered in uppercase. Caps Lock mode stays in effect until you press the key again. Note that when Caps Lock is on, you must press Shift to enter punctuation symbols and letters in lowercase.
Ctrl	^	Used in combination with other keys to control your computer; see "Using the Control Key."

Table 9.1. *(cont.)*

Key	Ctrl Combination	Purpose
Backspace	^H	Moves the cursor back to the left along a line, erasing characters as it moves.
←		The Left Arrow key (number "4" on the numeric keypad). Backspaces along a line but does not erase characters.
Shift-PrtSc		Sends a copy of the entire screen to the printer (called "dumping the screen").
Ctrl-PrtSc	^PrtSc	Causes each line on the screen to be printed as it is entered (called "echoing the screen") until you turn off the echoing by pressing Ctrl-PrtSc again.
Ctrl-P	^P	Echoes the display to the printer, line by line.
Ctrl-N	^N	Turns off the echo function.
Num Lock		Switches the numeric keypad between *cursor control mode* and *number input mode.*
Ctrl-S	^S	Freezes the screen display so you can read a long list of file names or text; pressing any key allows the display to move.
Del		Removes the character at the cursor.
Ins		Switches from *typeover mode* (the typed character replaces an existing character) to *insert mode* (text is inserted between existing characters).
F6	^Z	Ends a file.
Ctrl-Alt-Del	^Alt-Del	Reboots your computer.

Besides the special keys listed in Table 9.1, there are other special keys such as Scroll Lock, Alt, and Break. However, these keys are generally not used for entering ASCII text. See the Quick Primer for information about these keys.

Using the Control Key

Standard PC computer keyboards use specific keys (like PrtSc or Num Lock) to perform certain actions. Some machines (such as laptop computers) may not have these special keys.

If your machine does not have these special keys, you can often use the Ctrl key in conjunction with another key to perform these actions. For example, you can press Ctrl-Z (^Z) instead of F6 to mark the end of a file, or Ctrl-H (^H) instead of the Del key to delete a character. Ctrl-P (^P) is the same as Ctrl-PrtSc, and Ctrl-[(^[) is the same as Esc.

If you want to, you can use the Ctrl combinations even if you do have these special keys. They are built into PC DOS. Many of them operate in a wide variety of other programs, as well as in PC DOS.

The Function Keys

The function keys are keys F1 through F8. They can be used to perform several editing operations with one keystroke. Figure 9.1 shows the location of the function keys on two different keyboards. On older keyboards there are ten function keys located in two columns on the left side of the keyboard. The new "enhanced" keyboards have twelve function keys in a single row across the top of the keyboard. Some laptop computers have a special key that is used in combination with a number key to perform the service of a dedicated function key.

(A) Older keyboard with 10 function keys.

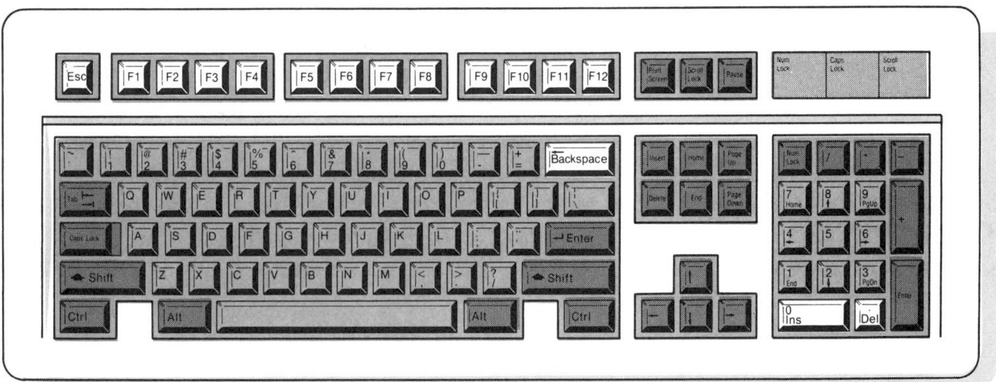

(B) Newer, enhanced keyboard with 12 function keys.

Figure 9.1. ***The function keys and the special editing keys.***

Table 9.2 lists the most frequently used key for each operation. If you find that one of the keys does not work as expected, check your user's guide to see how your computer uses the function keys. If your function keys are different from the ones listed here, write down the keys you use in the blank, first column of Table 9.2, opposite the appropriate purpose. This section contains a tutorial that gives you an opportunity to practice using the function keys.

As you work with PC DOS, you will occasionally find yourself issuing several consecutive commands that are only slight variations of each other. For example, when you execute the PC DOS command `md \dirname\` to make

Table 9.2. ***Function Key Operations***

Your Key	Key	Ctrl Combination	Purpose
	F3		Copies the entire template.
	F1 or Right Arrow →		Copies one character.
	← (Backspace)		Backs up and removes one character. *Note*: The Backspace key is not the same as the Left Arrow key.
	F2		Copies up to a specified character (character will not be included).
	F4		Skips up to the specified character (character will be included).
	Del		Removes one character.
	Ins		Allows you to enter new characters.
	F5		Stores current text as new template; does not issue command to PC DOS.
	Esc	^[	Cancels the last command line entry without storing the current text to the template.
	F6	^Z	Ends a file.

a subdirectory, you will usually follow that with the command `cd \`*`dirname`*`\` to change to that directory. Typing the same thing over and over can become tedious. The function keys can simplify the process by helping you reuse parts of the same command without having to retype the whole command.

Reusing the Command Line: The Template

When you type a line into the computer and press Enter, it is stored in a special place in the computer's memory called the *keyboard buffer*. The line that you typed is the *template*. With just a few keystrokes, you can often reuse the template as a pattern for your next command. A diagram of this sequence is shown in Figure 9.2.

What can you do with a template? Well, most of the information you enter into PC DOS consists of short lines of text. By using the function keys F1 through F6 and some of the special keys (like Esc, Ins, and Del), you can retrieve all or part of the previously entered command and enter it again or edit it and turn it into a new command. PC DOS editing keys are designed to make this process easier and faster.

Recalling the Template with the F3 Key

When you enter a command or line of text into your computer (in other words, when you press Enter after typing the command), it becomes the template in your input buffer. If you wish, you can use the template as the basis for your next command.

To see how this works, try making a new subdirectory and then making it the current directory. Type the command `md \waite\` and press Enter. Now change to your new subdirectory. This is where the template can save you some work. Since the command you want to issue is `cd \waite\`, type the letter `c`. Then use the F3 Copy All function to recall the remainder of the line from the template. Press F3 (Copy All), and PC DOS returns the template. The

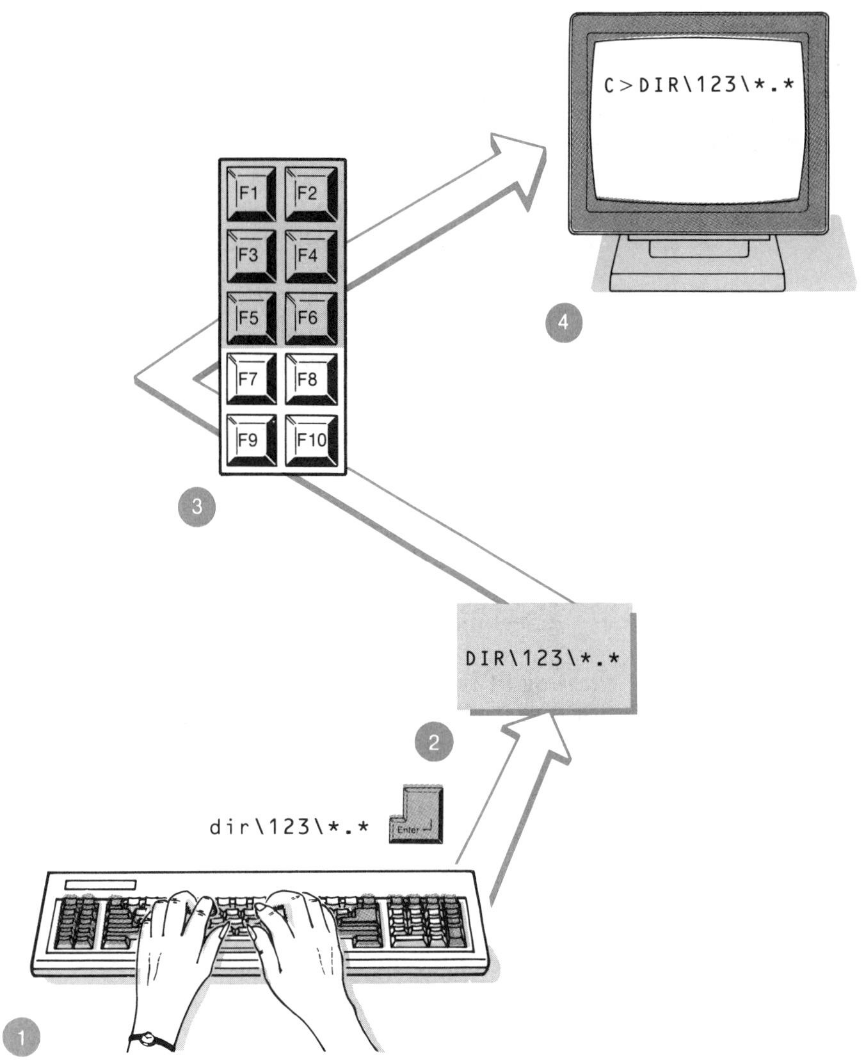

1. Type a line at the keyboard and press Enter.
2. The line is automatically stored in the template.
3. Use the function keys F1–F6 to retrieve and modify whatever is in the template.
4. The template appears on the screen.

Figure 9.2. ***How a template works.***

last step is to press Enter. You should see the following results on your screen, and \WAITE\ should be your current subdirectory.

```
C:\>md \waite\
C:\>cd \waite\
C:\WAITE\>
```

Notice that when you pressed F3, the template started from your location on the command line. PC DOS did not repeat the whole template from the beginning. Instead, the text you typed was placed over the existing text.

Copying One Character with the F1 Key

Sometimes you need only part of the template. One way to copy part of the template is to press F3 and then backspace until you reach the part you want. However, it is often easier to copy the template one character at a time until you get to the part to be edited.

Press F1 once. You will see the letter `c`. Press F1 four more times. Now PC DOS displays `cd \w`. Press and hold F1 to display the entire command.

Tip

Using the Arrow Keys to Move Around in the Template
You can also use the Left and Right Arrow keys (either the ones on the separate cursor pad for extended keyboards, or the 4 and 6 keys on the number keypad—make sure that Num Lock is off!) to move around in the template. Try this: Press the → key once to copy one character; press and hold it to copy to the end of the line. Now press the ← key once to backspace one character, or press and hold it to return all the way to the command prompt. You can do this as many times as you like in either direction; it will not affect the template.

Copying up to a Character with the F2 Key

Pressing F1 is one way to copy part of the template. There is a quicker way, however. You can use F2 to retrieve all of the template up to the first occurrence of a particular character. Notice that the character you specify will *not* be included in the new template.

To see how this works, press F2 and then type `i`. You will see the following characters on your screen:

```
C:\WAITE\>cd \wa
```

The characters in the template are copied up to the first occurrence of `I` in `WAITE`. To copy up to the letter `E`, press F2 and then type `e`.

Removing One Character with the Del Key

You can use the Del key to remove a character from the template. To see how this works, press F2 and type `i` to copy up to the letter `I`. Press Del to remove it from the template. Now press F3 to display the rest of the template. You will see the following results:

```
C:\WAITE>cd \wate\
Invalid directory

C:\WAITE\>
```

If for some reason you actually *do* have a subdirectory called `\WATE`, the next step in this tutorial will show you an easy way to change back to your \WAITE subdirectory.

Inserting a New Character with the Ins Key

You can insert new information into the template with the Ins key. Again, press F2 and then type `t` to copy up to the letter `T`. Press Ins to temporarily put PC DOS into *insert mode* and type `i`. Now press F3 to complete the command. Your results should look like this:

```
C:\WAITE>cd \waite\
C:\WAITE\>
```

Skipping up to a Character with the F4 Key

Just as you can copy up to a character, you can also *skip up* to a character. To do this, press F4 and then indicate the character you want to skip up to. The specified character will become the first character in the new template.

For example, if you press F4 and then type `w`, the characters `cd \` will be skipped over. If you press F3 to display the template, you will get the following result:

```
C:\WAITE>waite\
Bad command or filename

C:\WAITE\>
```

Of course, PC DOS has no idea what you are doing.

Returning to the Old Template with the Esc Key

You already know that you can press Esc to cancel whatever you have just typed. Pressing Esc puts a backslash (\) on your command line to indicate that the text you typed is canceled, and the cursor moves down to the next line so that you can enter a new command.

When you press Esc, any changes you may have made to the template are not saved. The last line entered with the Enter key will still be the current template.

To see how this works, type `This is a test` and press Esc. On the next line, type `of the Escape key.` and press Esc again. Finally, press Ins, type `cd \`, press F3 to copy the original template, and then press Enter. You will see these lines on your screen:

```
C:\WAITE> This is a test\
         of the Escape key.\
         cd \waite\

C:\WAITE\>
```

Creating a New Template with the F5 Key

Sometimes you will want to store a line in the template without sending it to the computer. You can use F5 to do this.

When you press F5, PC DOS places the symbol @ at the end of the line to show you that it has been entered into memory as the current template, and the display scrolls down one line to let you enter the new command. Just as with Esc, you will not see a new command prompt. As far as PC DOS is concerned, you are still using the original command line.

To see how this works, press F3 to copy the template. Type `12345` and press F5. Press F3 again to retrieve the new template. Notice that the numbers you typed have been added to it. Now type `abcde` and press Esc. Press F3, and you will see that the letters you typed were not added. Press Esc again; press F2 and type `1` to copy up to the numbers you added, and then press Enter. Your display will look like the following:

```
C:\WAITE\>cd \waite\12345@
        cd \waite\12345abcde \
        cd \waite\12345\
        cd \waite\

C:\WAITE\>
```

If you are unsure of the difference between F5 and Esc, take a few minutes now to experiment with F5 and Esc until you feel comfortable using the two functions. Table 9.2, shown earlier, is a helpful summary of these and the other function keys.

Editing keys and function keys may be new to you. They might even seem confusing at first. However, as you become more familiar with them, you will find them very helpful when you are entering duplicate or repetitive commands or when you want to correct mistakes without typing in the entire line again. Practice using the editing and function keys until you're proficient at them. Your payoff will be increased efficiency and productivity at the keyboard.

Word Processor Special Keys
Remember that your word processor probably assigns meanings to many of your special keys. These meanings are usually different from the ones that PC DOS uses when you are typing at the command line. Many word processors such as WordPerfect use the function keys, sometimes in combination with the Ctrl, Shift, and Alt keys, to execute menu commands. Keys such as Ins and Del will probably work the same, however.

A Brief Reminder: Creating a File with *COPY CON:*

As you learned in the Quick Primer, the fastest way to create a short text file is to use the COPY command to copy what you type on the keyboard to a file. To do this, use the CON: device name as the source file for your copy. This method is usually the easiest way to create files that contain only a few lines.

CON: is a reserved device name that PC DOS uses to recognize the keyboard and display of the computer system. (See Chapter 5, "PC DOS Files," and Chapter 11, "Customizing Your System," for more information about device names and reserved words.) Originally, CON: referred to the operator's console on a mainframe computer. On a PC, CON: refers to your keyboard and display. Therefore, the command COPY CON: tells PC DOS to copy all the information you are typing at your keyboard and to put it directly into a file.

To create a file, just type `copy con:` and the file name. When you press Enter, PC DOS advances one line and waits for you to type the contents of the next line. You must press Enter at the end of each line.

The only real disadvantage of using COPY CON: is that you cannot go back and edit a line after pressing Enter. You will need to use EDLIN or some other line editor to do that. If you are making changes to a very short file, you may want to use COPY CON: to retype it from scratch. If you use the same destination file name, the previous file will be replaced automatically.

When you are finished, press Ctrl-Z. You will see `^Z` on your screen. This is the *end-of-file marker*. It tells PC DOS to store the file. (If you press F6, PC DOS will insert this character for you and store the file automatically.) PC DOS responds by telling you `1 File(s) copied`. This message means that the file has been stored. To see what the file looks like, use the PC DOS TYPE command. Try using COPY CON: to enter the file shown in Listing 9.1.

Listing 9.1. *The COPY CON:* Command

```
C:\WAITE>copy con: notes
This is a note file containing some text
that I entered to review the use of COPY CON:.
^Z

        1 File(s) copied
C:\WAITE>type notes
This is a note file containing some text
that I entered to review the use of COPY CON:.

C:\WAITE>
```

Editing Text Files

When you want to create a new file or add, delete, or modify text in existing files, you use an *editor*. An editor lets you move text around inside a file or even transfer information from one file to another. There are several different types of editors: word processors, text processors, and line editors.

PC DOS comes with a special editing program called *EDLIN*. EDLIN is a *line-oriented* text editor. Its sole purpose is to let you create and edit ASCII files on a line-by-line basis. (The ASCII text format is discussed at the beginning of this chapter.) EDLIN is most convenient to use when you are editing files that are too long to be easily rewritten using COPY CON: but are too short to justify using your word processor. In practice, this means that you will normally use EDLIN to work with files that are between five and twenty lines long.

Word Processors

Word processors are technically known as *full-screen editors*. This is because they use the entire screen to display text. Each full screen is like a window displaying a specific section of your entire file.

For the purposes of this chapter, the most important feature of word processors is that they are more concerned with the printout than the file. Word processors insert special characters in the file that tell the printer how to format the text. They can specify margins, page numbers, boldface or underlined text, and many other attractive options.

However, if you use PC DOS's TYPE command to read a file containing these characters, the results will be strange. There will be all sorts of odd characters displayed on the screen, and the text will probably jump and scroll in bizarre ways. It may even be impossible to read. And, of course, if you create a batch file in one of these formats, PC DOS will not be able to understand it.

If your word processor has a text or nondocument mode, you can use that to create a plain ASCII text file. However, the command structure usually varies widely from program to program. Even though you know how to use one word processor, you may not be able to use another one easily. One of EDLIN's main advantages is that it is found on almost every PC DOS computer. If you are using your friend's system to work on a text file, and she does not have your favorite word processor, you can still get your work done if you know how to use EDLIN.

Text Processors

Text processors are a cross between word processors and line editors. They are full-screen editors that create ASCII files. Many compilers (such as BASIC, C, or Pascal) provide a text processor for entering program source code. Another very common text processor is the "notepad" type of editor that comes with programs such as SideKick. Like word processors, text processors generally have a wide variety of editing commands. Unfortunately, the command structure varies widely between programs. Again, if you need to create a text file, you can always use EDLIN.

Line Editors

Unlike word processors and text processors, EDLIN is a *line editor*. In fact, its name is short for "EDit LINes." Line editors are more limited than full-screen editors and a little more difficult to use. Each line of text is identified by a *line number*. You use these line numbers to specify a "window," or portion of the file, to work on.

EDLIN's most confusing feature is that it does not automatically display your file. If you want to edit a line, you must enter that line number. EDLIN will then display only that line. If you want to see a group of text lines, you must specifically tell EDLIN to display them. In general, before you can do anything, you must first tell EDLIN exactly where you want it done.

Actually, since EDLIN has a limited set of commands, it is not very complicated to use. Although the extra steps involved in using EDLIN can slow you down and can even be a little frustrating until you are familiar with the commands, EDLIN can be extremely useful when you are creating generic files (like READ.ME) or batch files.

The Basics of Using EDLIN

This section introduces the basic features of EDLIN and explains how to use EDLIN. The next section, "Additional EDLIN Commands," covers further uses for the basic commands and shows you the remaining EDLIN commands. Table 9.5, located at the end of this chapter, summarizes all the EDLIN commands.

Loading a File

It is very easy to load a file into EDLIN. At PC DOS's command prompt, just type `edlin` and the file name. For practice, you can use the NOTES file that you created earlier with the COPY CON: command.

EDLIN will respond with the message `End of input file`. This means that EDLIN has loaded a copy of your file into memory and positioned itself at the end of the file. An asterisk (*) is the prompt; it shows that EDLIN is waiting for your instructions.

```
C:\WAITE>edlin notes
End of input file
*
```

Ready and Waiting

The EDLIN prompt is a single asterisk (*) appearing at the left of the screen. Like other text editors, the editor can either be in command mode or entry mode. *Command mode* (with the asterisk prompt appearing at the far left of the screen) means that EDLIN is waiting for a command. *Entry mode* means that the letters you type are added to the file as text, rather than being treated as commands.

EDLIN receives its instructions from you in the form of one-letter commands. The format of these commands is simple. Enter the number of the line you wish to modify and the letter of the command. Like PC DOS commands, EDLIN commands can be entered in either upper- or lowercase letters. (For the sake of clarity, the examples in this book use uppercase letters only.) To indicate a range of lines, enter the first line number, a comma, the last line number, and the command. You will have plenty of opportunity to practice this as you work with the various EDLIN commands in the following exercises.

You cannot enter text when you are in command mode. You will need to shift to entry mode. The entry prompt is the number of the line on which you are working, followed by an asterisk. EDLIN indicates that you are in entry mode by indenting this prompt five spaces. Again, you will have several opportunities throughout this chapter to practice shifting between command mode and entry mode, and to practice using entry mode. Figure 9.3 illustrates the difference between these two prompts and their modes.

Line Numbers

EDLIN identifies each line of text in your file with a *line number*. These numbers are sequential from the beginning of the file. In other words, the first line is always line 1, the second line is line 2, and so on to the end of the file. In the next section of this chapter, you will see these numbers when you learn how to use the L (List) command to display your file.

You do *not* enter these line numbers as you enter text. They are only reference points within EDLIN. They are not part of the text in your file. When you exit EDLIN, the line numbers are no longer necessary, so they will not be saved. You will not see any line numbers if you use PC DOS's TYPE command to look at the file.

Every time you make a change to the file, EDLIN renumbers it automatically. However, the new numbers are not displayed until you ask to see them. This is one of the most important reasons why you should form the habit of frequently using the L command to look at your file.

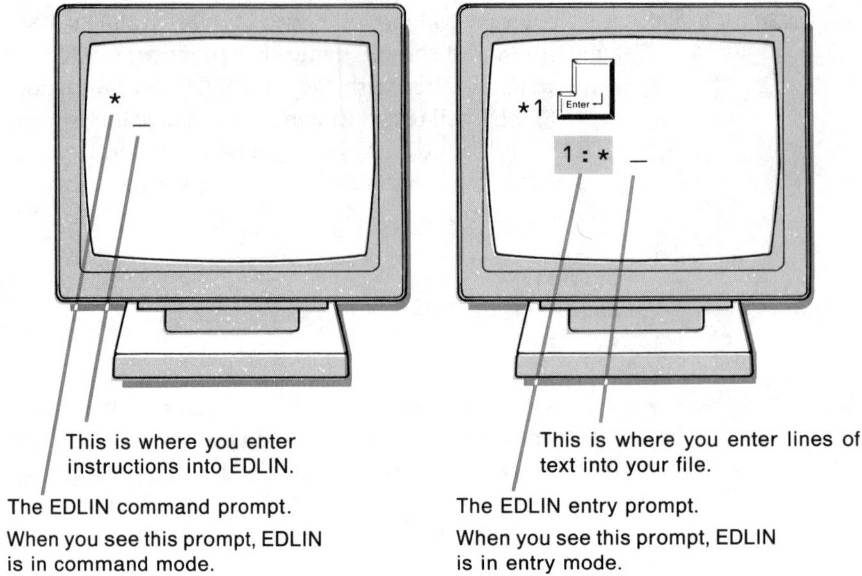
*
*1 Enter
1 : *
This is where you enter instructions into EDLIN.
The EDLIN command prompt.
When you see this prompt, EDLIN is in command mode.
This is where you enter lines of text into your file.
The EDLIN entry prompt.
When you see this prompt, EDLIN is in entry mode.

Figure 9.3. ***The EDLIN prompts.***

Displaying Your Work with the L Command

You should always start an EDLIN session by looking at your file. This lets you verify the contents of your file and the number of the line you want to work with. You will also need to look at your file after every major operation (such as deleting or moving lines) to see how the line numbers have changed. Use the L (List) command to list the contents of an EDLIN file.

The easiest way to use this command is to simply enter `L` at the command prompt, as shown in Listing 9.2. If your file is less than 23 lines long, EDLIN will display the entire file. (You will learn other ways to use this command later in this chapter.) Try doing that now.

Listing 9.2. ***Listing the COPY CON*: File**

```
*L
        1:*This is a note file containing some text
        2: that I entered to review the use of COPY CON:.
*
```

The Current Line

When you used the L command, did you notice that the first line was marked by an asterisk? This is because it is the *current line*. When you load a file into EDLIN, the first line starts out as the current line. If you shift into entry mode, the line of text you are currently working on becomes the current line. In command mode, the current line refers to the last line of text you modified, whether by typing text into it in entry mode or by issuing a command that affected it.

Getting the Right Line by Using Line Numbers

To edit a specific line within an EDLIN file, just enter its line number at the command prompt. EDLIN immediately moves you to the entry prompt, where you can make changes to the line. Once you are at the entry prompt, if you decide not to edit the line after all, press Enter or Ctrl-C to return to the command prompt.

To see how this works, try editing the first line of your NOTES file. Type `1` and press Enter. EDLIN displays the current contents of line 1, followed by the entry prompt. Type in a new phrase: `This is a completely new line of text`; press Enter to return to the command prompt. Remember to use the L command to look at your file. Your complete listing should look like the one in Listing 9.3.

Listing 9.3. ***Editing the First Line***

```
*1
        1:*This is a note file containing some text
        1:*This is a completely new line
*L
        1:*This is a completely new line
        2: that I entered to review the use of COPY CON:.
*
```

Notice the asterisk following line 1. This reminds you that line 1 is the current line.

Keyboard Shortcuts

Earlier in this chapter, you learned how to use the function keys in PC DOS to help you edit the template. You can use the same keys in EDLIN to edit the current line. The following example uses most of the function keys to illustrate this principle.

Type `1` and press Enter to get the entry prompt for line 1. Press F2 and then type `c` to copy up to the first letter of `completely`. Press F4 and then type `n` to skip up to `new`. Press F1 three times to display `new`. Press Ins and type `, improved text`. Press F3 to copy the remainder of the line, and Enter to return to the command prompt. When you use the L command to look at your file, your listing will look like the one in Listing 9.4.

Listing 9.4. ***Keyboard Shortcuts in EDLIN***

```
*1
        1:*This is a completely new line
        1:*This is a new, improved text line
*L
        1:*This is a new, improved text line
        2: that I entered to review the use of COPY CON:.
*
```

Saving Your Work with the E Command

The E (Exit) command tells EDLIN that you want to end the editing session. To save all edited text to the file stored on disk, type `E` at the command prompt. (You do not need to specify a line number.) After copying your work to the hard drive, EDLIN returns you to the PC DOS prompt.

Use PC DOS's DIR command to verify that the file was indeed saved correctly. You will also see a file called NOTES.BAK. That is a *backup file*.

EDLIN creates it as a safety measure. You will find out more about backup files later in this chapter.

When you return to PC DOS, you can use the TYPE command to display the contents of the file you have been working on, as shown in Listing 9.5. You will see your file, exactly as you entered it. Of course, there are no line numbers. Remember that line numbers are not part of the data in EDLIN files. They are simply reference points EDLIN uses when editing or creating files, and they are not saved with the file. Also, note that the lines are not neatly formatted with flush margins as you would expect with a full-fledged word processor. Since the file is intended merely to be the equivalent of a brief "sticky note," this is no problem.

Listing 9.5. ***Exit and Display***

```
C:\WAITE>dir *.*

 Volume in Drive C: has no label
 Directory of C:\WAITE

.          <DIR>
..         <DIR>
NOTES   .
NOTES   .BAK

C:\WAITE>type notes
This is a new, improved text line
that I entered to review the use of COPY CON:.

C:\WAITE>
```

Additional EDLIN Commands

In this section you will learn about the many time-saving commands EDLIN contains for your convenience. You will also learn some further uses for the commands already mentioned. If you take the time to master these commands, you will find that EDLIN may even be easier to use than your word processor when you are editing a short ASCII file.

Loading EDLIN You already know that loading EDLIN is as simple as typing `edlin`, followed by the name of the file you wish to load. If EDLIN finds a file with the name you specify, it will respond with the message `End of input file`. This tells you that EDLIN has loaded a copy of your file into memory and positioned itself at the end of the file, ready to begin editing.

Besides the message `End of input file`, there are two other possible responses to your command. The first involves the creation of a new file. If you are using EDLIN to create a file, and the file name you specify does not yet exist, EDLIN will tell you that this is a `New file`, and will provide you with a command prompt so that you can begin creating the file.

The other possible response is "no response." If you are loading an extremely large file, you may get no message at all. When EDLIN simply displays an asterisk without telling you anything else, it means that your file was too large to be completely loaded. EDLIN has loaded as much of the file as possible into memory and is ready for commands. Refer to "Managing a Large File" at the end of this chapter for information about some special commands you can use in this situation. Table 9.3 summarizes the three possible opening responses from EDLIN.

Table 9.3. *EDLIN's Opening Messages*

Message	Meaning
`New file`	You are creating a file that did not exist before.
`End of input file`	You have successfully loaded an existing file and are ready to begin editing.
(No message)	You have loaded a portion of your file. The file is too large to fit into the available memory. When you have finished editing this portion, you will need to use the W (Write) and A (Append) commands to load the next portion of this file.

Now you can practice using EDLIN to create a new file. You already know that it is a good idea to put a READ.ME file on your storage diskettes so that you can identify the files on them. It is also a good habit to keep a similar READ.ME file in each subdirectory.

At the PC DOS prompt, enter `edlin read.me` to create this file. EDLIN tells you that this is a new file and presents you with a command prompt. You are now ready to begin editing.

```
C:\WAITE>edlin read.me
New file
*
```

Entering Information with the I Command

The I (Insert) command tells EDLIN to add a new line to the file. Specify where you want to add a line and type `I`. Any text you type will be inserted into the file.

When you start a new file, you must type `I` to tell EDLIN to begin entering text. Since a new file has no lines yet, you do not need to specify a line number. EDLIN will respond with the entry mode prompt.

Start typing the text shown in Listing 9.6 into your READ.ME file. At the end of a line, press Enter, and EDLIN will automatically supply a new entry prompt for the next line. When you have entered all the text you want, press Enter to advance to a blank line, and F6 to return to command mode.

Tip

Changing from Entry to Command Mode

EDLIN makes it easy to return from entry mode to command mode. You may press either Ctrl-C, Ctrl-Z, or F6 (to issue the Ctrl-Z character). IBM PC users may even use the Ctrl-Break key combination. If you use one of the Ctrl combinations, remember to hold down the Ctrl key while you press the letter key and then release both keys together.

Listing 9.6. ***Using EDLIN to Create a File***

```
New file
*I
        1:*The \WAITE subdirectory holds
        2:*the sample files that I created
        3:*using the techniques I learned in
        4:*the chapter on Creating Text Files.
        5:*^Z
```

Special Ways to Specify a Line

Recall that, when using EDLIN, you need to specify a line or lines before you issue a command. EDLIN includes some shortcuts to help you move around from line to line more easily.

You already know that you can select a line for editing by entering its line number at the command prompt. Do this now by typing 1 and pressing Enter at the command prompt. Press Enter without typing any text to accept the current version of the line and return to the command prompt.

When you want to make modifications to your current line, you do not need to know the current line number. You can take a shortcut—just enter a period. To see how this works, enter . at the command prompt. EDLIN will display an entry prompt for line 1, accept it, and return to the command prompt.

Some commands can even be used without a line number. Earlier you saw that entering L at the command prompt caused EDLIN to display a range of lines centered around the current line.

With many of EDLIN's commands, you can use the pound sign (#) instead of a specific line number to indicate the end of the file. Using # with an editing command tells EDLIN that you want to "do this operation at the end of the current file in memory." You will experiment with this shortcut later in this chapter.

Finally, you can use the current line as a shortcut to get to a new location. A plus sign (+) tells EDLIN to advance a specified number of lines. A minus sign (−) tells EDLIN to go back the specified number of lines.

For example, type +1 and EDLIN will respond with an entry prompt for line 2. The current line was line 1; adding one gives you line 2. Return to the command prompt and type +2 to get an entry prompt for line 4 (line 2 + two gives you four). Return to the command prompt again. Type -3 to get back to line 1.

Now type +4. EDLIN responds with a new command prompt. Apparently, nothing happened. Actually, you have made line 5 the current line. Since there were only four lines of text in your file, there was no line for EDLIN to display. (You could have used this trick to add a line to your file by combining +4 with the I command.) To verify that this is what happened, type -3 at the command prompt. As you would expect, EDLIN will respond with an entry prompt for line 2. Return to the command prompt for the next exercise. Your display will look like Listing 9.7.

Listing 9.7. ***Specifying a Line***

```
*1
        1:*The \WAITE subdirectory holds
        1:*
*.
        1:*The \WAITE subdirectory holds
        1:*
*+1
        2:*the sample files that I created
        2:*
*+2
        4:*the chapter on Creating Text Files.
        4:*
*-3
        1:*The \WAITE subdirectory holds
        1:*
*+4
*-3
        2:*the sample files that I created
        2:*
```

Inserting Lines with the I Command

You can use the I command to add more lines to an existing file. However, you must first tell EDLIN where to insert the lines. As with other commands, you do this by entering the line number before you enter the command.

To see how this works, try inserting a line. First, enter the L command to look at your file before inserting the new lines. Type **3I** at the command prompt. EDLIN gives you an entry prompt for line 3 and waits for you to enter text. Press Enter when you have finished typing the following line: **(I used COPY CON: to create NOTES)**. EDLIN now advances you to line 4. Use F6 to return to command mode and then use the L command to display your new file, as shown in Listing 9.8.

Listing 9.8. ***Inserting Lines***

```
*3I
        3:*(I used COPY CON: to create NOTES)
        4:*^Z
*L
        1: The \WAITE subdirectory holds
        2: the sample files that I created
        3:*(I used COPY CON: to create NOTES)
        4: using the techniques I learned in
        5: the chapter on Creating Text Files.
*
```

The asterisk in front of line 3 indicates that line 3 is now the current line.

Note that when lines are inserted or deleted, EDLIN renumbers the file automatically. However, it does not display the new numbers until you ask to see the file again. This is another reason why you should form the habit of regularly using the L command to check your file.

Copying Lines with the C Command

Use the C (Copy) command to copy a line or a range of lines to any part of the file. This command requires three line numbers: the first line of the block to be copied, the last line of the block (even if that block is only one line), and the line number before which the copied lines should appear. The numbers are separated by commas.

If you want to copy several lines of text into the middle of a file, EDLIN will make room for these lines automatically. You can see how this works by copying lines 1 and 2 to line 4. Type `1,2,4C` and press Enter. Type `L` to look at the results. EDLIN has inserted the new lines and renumbered the file. (You will have an opportunity to rearrange the text later.)

Now you can try copying line 3 to the end of the file. An easy way to do this is to use the # character mentioned previously. To do this, type `3,3,#C` at the command prompt. This tells EDLIN to copy everything from the beginning of line 3 to the end of line 3 into a new line at the end of the file. Use the L command to display the file, as shown in Listing 9.9.

Listing 9.9. ***Copying Lines***

```
*1,2,4C
*L
         1: The \WAITE subdirectory holds
         2: the sample files that I created
         3: (I used COPY CON: to create NOTES)
         4: The \WAITE subdirectory holds
         5: the sample files that I created
         6: using the techniques I learned in
         7: the chapter on Creating Text Files.
*3,3,#C
*L
         1: The \WAITE subdirectory holds
         2: the sample files that I created
         3: (I used COPY CON: to create NOTES)
         4:*The \WAITE subdirectory holds
         5: the sample files that I created
         6: using the techniques I learned in
         7: the chapter on Creating Text Files.
         8:*(I used COPY CON: to create NOTES)
*
```

Displaying Your Work with the L Command

You already know that you can use the L command to list the contents of a file. EDLIN offers you several different ways to do this.

If your file is less than 23 lines long, EDLIN will display the entire file when you type `L` without any line numbers. When you are working with a longer file, EDLIN lists 23 lines of text centered on the current line. (Remember that the current line is the last line to which you made changes.)

You can also tell EDLIN exactly which lines to list by entering a range of numbers. To do this, enter the number of the first line, a comma, the last line number, and the L command. (If you are working with a long file, you must limit the size of the range to 23 because this is the maximum number of text lines that EDLIN can display at one time.) Type **2,5L** at the command prompt and press Enter to display lines 2 through 5.

As a convenience, EDLIN can also figure out the range for you. Just indicate where you want to begin, and EDLIN will show a 23-line block starting with that line number. For example, if your file was long enough, **43L** would tell EDLIN to display lines 43 through 65. Try typing **4L** and pressing Enter again to see how this works, as shown in Listing 9.10.

Listing 9.10. ***Various Ways to Use the L Command***

```
*2,5L
         2: the sample files that I created
         3: (I used COPY CON: to create NOTES)
         4: The \WAITE subdirectory holds
         5: the sample files that I created
*4L
         4: The \WAITE subdirectory holds
         5: the sample files that I created
         6: using the techniques I learned in
         7: the chapter on Creating Text Files.
         8:*(I used COPY CON: to create NOTES)
*
```

Removing Material with the D Command

EDLIN lets you delete the current line, a specified line, or a range of lines. To do this, enter the number of the line, or lines, you want to remove, followed by the D (Delete) command. If you need to delete a range, enter the first line number, a comma, the last line number and the D command.

Caution

Think Twice before Deleting a Line

Once you delete a line, there is no automatic way to restore it. If you change your mind, you will need to retype the line. Therefore, *always* double-check the line numbers of the items you want to delete before issuing this command! If you enter the wrong line number, you will lose your line. In fact, if you enter the D command without any line number, EDLIN will delete the *current line*.

Try deleting the current line. Return to command mode and issue the L command to check the file. Since line 8 is the current line, you can type **.D** at the command prompt and press Enter. EDLIN will remove line 8 from the file and give you a new command prompt. When you use the L command to list the file again, you will see that line 8 really is gone, and EDLIN has renumbered the remaining lines.

To delete a range, type **4,5D** and use the L command to display the results of your work, as shown in Listing 9.11.

Listing 9.11. ***Removing Lines***

```
*L
          1: The \WAITE subdirectory holds
          2: the sample files that I created
          3: (I used COPY CON: to create NOTES)
          4: The \WAITE subdirectory holds
          5: the sample files that I created
          6: using the techniques I learned in
          7: the chapter on Creating Text Files.
          8:*(I used COPY CON: to create NOTES)
*.D
*L
          1: The \WAITE subdirectory holds
          2: the sample files that I created
          3: (I used COPY CON: to create NOTES)
          4: The \WAITE subdirectory holds
          5: the sample files that I created
          6: using the techniques I learned in
          7:*the chapter on Creating Text Files.
*4,5D
*L
          1: The \WAITE subdirectory holds
          2: the sample files that I created
          3: (I used COPY CON: to create NOTES)
          4:*using the techniques I learned in
          5: the chapter on Creating Text Files.
*
```

Notice that line 4 has become the current line.

Moving Lines with the M Command

Use the M (Move) command to move a block of information within an EDLIN file. In a sense, this command combines the C command and the D command because it lets you remove a block of text from its original location and copy it into a new one.

Like the C command, the M command requires three line numbers: the beginning and ending line numbers to define the block to be moved and the line number before which you want the items to appear. (Always list your file to be sure that you are using the correct line numbers.)

To see how this works, use the L command to display your file. Type **4,5,3M** at the command prompt to move lines 4 through 5 to line 3. Type **L** to see your results, as shown in Listing 9.12.

Listing 9.12. ***Moving Lines***

```
*L
          1: The \WAITE subdirectory holds
          2: the sample files that I created
          3: (I used COPY CON: to create NOTES)
          4:*using the techniques I learned in
```

```
        5: the chapter on Creating Text Files.
*4,5,3M
*L
        1: The \WAITE subdirectory holds
        2: the sample files that I created
        3:*using the techniques I learned in
        4: the chapter on Creating Text Files.
        5: (I used COPY CON: to create NOTES)
*
```

Searching for Strings with the S Command

Suppose that you want to edit part of a file containing the phrase "New Year's Day," or suppose that you want to verify a change from "Mulcahey and Sons" to "Mulcahey and Associates" in a letter. An easy way to do this is to search through your file for a *string*.

In computerese, a string is a group of ASCII characters (they need not make up an English word or sentence). The characters may include letters, numbers, spaces, and punctuation marks. One way to find a specific place in a file is to use the S (Search) command to search for a word or character pattern. You do this by entering the S command, followed by the string you would like to find. If the string of text is found, the first line on which it occurs becomes the current line. If the string is not found, EDLIN informs you of that fact.

The S command can be used in a variety of ways. If you enter it without specifying a line number, EDLIN will begin searching in the line after the current line. Try searching for the word "the" by typing **Sthe** at the command prompt, as shown in Listing 9.13. Notice that you do not need to use spaces, commas, or any other character to separate the search string ("the" in this example) from the S command. Since the current line was line 3, EDLIN displays a copy of line 4 and returns you to the command prompt.

You may precede the S command with a single line number if you want to search a specific line. If you want to search every line from the beginning of the file, you can specify line 1. For example, type **1She** to search for the word "he"; EDLIN will respond with a copy of line 1. Once EDLIN has found the string, you can repeat the same search by typing **S** at the command prompt. You do not need to retype the string. Try this now to display a copy of line 2.

Using the S Command

When you use the S command to locate a string, EDLIN displays a copy of the line but remains in command mode. The line now displayed is the current line; you can edit it by typing the line number or a period.

If you wish, you can enter the S command with a range of numbers to search a block of lines, or you can enter the **#** character to search from the current line to the end of the file.

There is one catch to all this: the S command can find only exact matches to your string. It looks at all punctuation, including spaces, and it can even tell the difference between uppercase and lowercase letters. You can demonstrate this by typing **1S The**, leaving one blank space between **S**and **The**. EDLIN tells you that your string is "Not found." Your string wasn't found because there is no space before the word "The" in the first line, and, in the remainder of the file, the word is not capitalized.

Listing 9.13. *Searching for Strings*

```
*L
         1: The \WAITE subdirectory holds
         2: the sample files that I created
         3:*using the techniques I learned in
         4: the chapter on Creating Text Files.
         5: (I used COPY CON: to create NOTES)
*Sthe
         4:*the chapter on Creating Text Files.
*1She
         1:*The \WAITE subdirectory holds
*S
         2:*the sample files that I created
*1S The
Not found
*
```

Making a Global Search with the ? Command

You can continue searching after each occurrence of the string without reentering the S command. To perform a *global search*, precede the S command with a question mark.

Type `1?Sthe` at the command prompt, as shown in Listing 9.14. At each occurrence of the string, EDLIN asks you if the line displayed is the one you want. When EDLIN displays a copy of line 2, answer `n`; EDLIN will continue to look for the string. Answer `n` again when you see the copy of line 3. When you answer `y` to line 4, you are telling EDLIN that this is the line you wanted to find. The search ends, and you are returned to the command prompt.

Listing 9.14. *A Global Search*

```
*1?Sthe
         2:*the sample files that I created
O.K.? n
         3: using the techniques I learned in
O.K.? n
         4: the chapter on Creating Text Files.
O.K.? y
*
```

Replacing Text with the R Command

Like the S command, the R (Replace) command searches the file looking for the specified pattern. However, it goes a step further by replacing every instance of the string with a new string. Figure 9.4 compares the R and S commands.

The format of the R command is similar to that of the S command. However, you use `^Z` to separate the search string from the replacement string. You can experiment with this command by replacing every instance

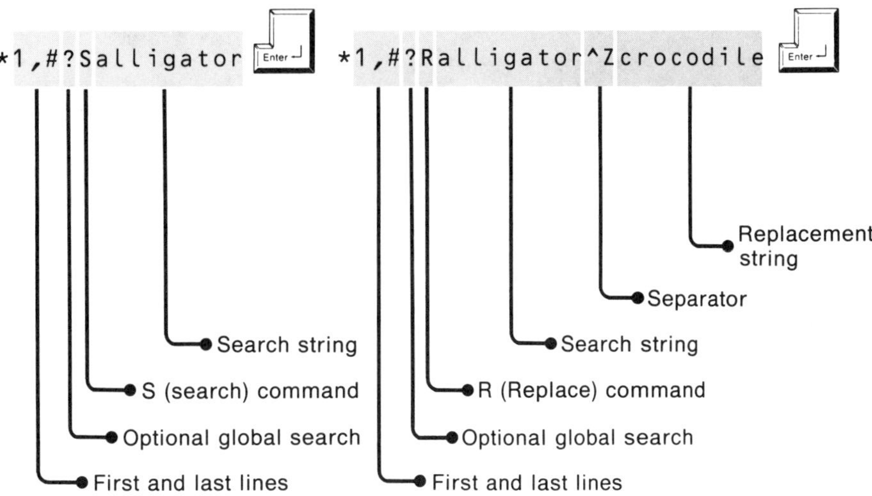

Figure 9.4. ***Comparing the S and R commands.***

of the word "the" in your file with the word "alligator." Type **1,#Rthe^Zalligator** at the command prompt and press Enter, as shown in Listing 9.15. (Remember to use F6 to issue the ^Z character.) EDLIN displays only the changed lines. Use the L command to display the entire file. As you can see by the asterisk, line 4 is now the current line.

Listing 9.15. ***Replacing a String***

```
*1,#Rthe^Zalligator
        2: alligator sample files that I created
        3: using alligator techniques I learned in
        4: alligator chapter on Creating Text Files.
*L
        1: The \WAITE subdirectory holds
        2: alligator sample files that I created
        3: using alligator techniques I learned in
        4:*alligator chapter on Creating Text Files.
        5: (I used COPY CON: to create NOTES)
```

Making Selective Replacements with the ? and R Commands

If you are not sure whether you want to replace every occurrence of the string, you can use a question mark (?) with the R command. When you type ?R, EDLIN searches for the original string, displays the line with the new string inserted, and prompts you to confirm the replacement.

To see how this works, switch the word "alligator" back to "the" by typing **1,#?Ralligator^Zthe**, as shown in Listing 9.16. Type y at each line to confirm the correction. (If you answer n to this query, no replacement will be performed in this line. In either case, the search will continue to the last line.) Since line 4 is the last line you change, it will be the current line when you list the file.

Listing 9.16. ***A Global Replace***

```
*1,#Ralligator^Zthe
        2: the sample files that I created
O.K.? y
        3: using the techniques I learned in
O.K.? y
        4: the chapter on Creating Text Files.
O.K.? y
*L
        1: The \WAITE subdirectory holds
        2: the sample files that I created
        3: using the techniques I learned in
        4:*the chapter on Creating Text Files.
        5: (I used COPY CON: to create NOTES)
```

Transferring Lines between Files with the T Command

Occasionally you may want to add lines from one file to another. You can use the T (Transfer) command to do this. Just tell EDLIN at which line to insert the transferred text, enter the T command, and type the name of the file to be transferred.

As a demonstration, you can place the text of the NOTES file at the end of your READ.ME file by typing the command `#Tnotes`, as shown in Listing 9.17. When you use the L command to display your new file, you will see that the first line of the inserted text is now the current line.

Listing 9.17. ***Transferring Lines***

```
*#Tnotes
L
        1: The \WAITE subdirectory holds
        2: the sample files that I created
        3: using the techniques I learned in
        4: the chapter on Creating Text Files.
        5: (I used COPY CON: to create NOTES)
        6:*This is a new, improved text line
        7: that I entered to review the use of COPY CON:.
*
```

Creating a Frame with the Extended Characters

As a final touch, you might like to dress up your ASCII file with a double-ruled frame. You can do this with the *extended character set*. Although there are no keys for these characters, you can enter them by pressing and holding the Alt key while you type in the three-digit number on the number keypad. The character will appear on your screen when you release the Alt key. Table 9.4 shows the ASCII extended characters and the keys you press to create them.

At the command prompt, type `6,7D` to remove lines 6 and 7 from your file, as shown in Listing 9.18. Type `1I` to insert a new line at the top of the file. Press Alt-`205`and repeat 34 times to draw a line. Press Enter and F6 to return to command mode. Type `1,1,#C` to copy this line to the end of the file. Use the L command to display your efforts.

Listing 9.18. ***Extended Characters***

```
*6,7D
*1I
        1:*----------------------------------
        2:*^Z
*1,1,#C
*L
        1: ----------------------------------
        2: The \WAITE subdirectory holds
        3: the sample files that I created
        4: using the techniques I learned in
        5: the chapter on Creating Text Files.
        6: (I used COPY CON: to create NOTES)
        7:*----------------------------------
*
```

Caution

Printing the Extended ASCII Characters
Some printers will not print the extended ASCII characters. Other printers need to be in an "IBM emulation mode" in order to do so. If you have problems printing such characters, see your printer documentation.

Quitting EDLIN without Saving Your Work by Using the Q Command

You already know that the E (Exit) command tells EDLIN to save all edited text to the file stored on disk, end the editing session, and return you to the PC DOS prompt. Sometimes, however, you will find that you want to leave EDLIN without saving your work. You might want to stop a session because you decide that you do not really want to make any changes. On the other hand, you might realize that you have changed your mind so many times that it would be easier to start over. Fortunately, the Q (Quit) command lets you abandon the edited version of a file without saving the new file or altering the original file on the disk.

Caution

Think Twice before Using the Q Command
The Q command does not save your file to the diskette! It simply cancels the current editing session.

Type `Q` at the command prompt now. As a safeguard, EDLIN prompts you to confirm the Q command. This is your last chance. Type `n` to continue with the edit. A `y` response would destroy the information entered in this editing session and return you to the PC DOS prompt.

```
*Q
Abort edit [Y/N]? n
*
```

Making Use of .BAK Files

You may remember that when you use the E (Exit) command to end the editing session, it creates files having the original file name and the extension .BAK.

Table 9.4. ***The ASCII Extended Character Codes***

Dec	ASCII	Dec	ASCII	Dec	ASCII	Dec	ASCII
128	Ç	160	á	192	└	224	α
129	ü	161	í	193	┴	225	β
130	é	162	ó	194	┬	226	Γ
131	â	163	ú	195	├	227	π
132	ä	164	ñ	196	─	228	Σ
133	à	165	Ñ	197	┼	229	σ
134	å	166	ª	198	╞	230	μ
135	ç	167	º	199	╟	231	τ
136	ê	168	¿	200	╚	232	Φ
137	ë	169	⌐	201	╔	233	Θ
138	è	170	¬	202	╩	234	Ω
139	ï	171	½	203	╦	235	δ
140	î	172	¼	204	╠	236	∞
141	ì	173	¡	205	═	237	φ
142	Ä	174	«	206	╬	238	ε
143	Å	175	»	207	╧	239	∩
144	É	176	░	208	╨	240	≡
145	æ	177	▒	209	╤	241	±
146	Æ	178	▓	210	╥	242	≥
147	ô	179	│	211	╙	243	≤
148	ö	180	┤	212	╘	244	⌠
149	ò	181	╡	213	╒	245	⌡
150	û	182	╢	214	╓	246	÷
151	ù	183	╖	215	╫	247	≈
152	ÿ	184	╕	216	╪	248	°
153	Ö	185	╣	217	┘	249	•
154	Ü	186	║	218	┌	250	·
155	¢	187	╗	219	█	251	√
156	£	188	╝	220	▄	252	η
157	¥	189	╜	221	▌	253	^{2}
158	Pt	190	╛	222	▐	254	■
159	ƒ	191	┐	223	▀	255	(blank)

Type **e** at the command prompt to exit from EDLIN, as shown in Listing 9.19. At PC DOS's prompt, use the DIR command to display the two .BAK files in your \WAITE subdirectory.

As a precaution, EDLIN automatically creates a backup file whenever it loads a text file. This backup has the same name and contents as your original text file. However, it always has the three-letter extension *.BAK*, no matter what extension the original file had.

Backup files can be a blessing. Should the computer lose power or malfunction while a file is being edited, only the work during the current editing session will be lost. The backup file, which contains a duplicate version of the original file's text, will remain intact.

You should never edit a file with a .BAK extension. After all, if you alter the backup file, you will not have an unedited copy when you need it. You can use PC DOS's COPY command (discussed in the Quick Primer) to copy the contents of a .BAK file to a new file. For example, type **copy read.bak readme.new**. Now you can begin the editing process all over again.

This concludes your EDLIN tutorial. Since it is good housekeeping to get rid of unnecessary files, you may use the PC DOS DEL and RD commands (discussed in the Quick Primer) to erase these files and remove the \WAITE subdirectory from your hard drive.

Listing 9.19. ***Concluding the EDLIN Tutorial***

```
*E

C:\WAITE>dir *.*
 Volume in drive C has no name
 Directory of  C:\WAITE

.           <DIR>
..          <DIR>
NOTES
NOTES    BAK
READ     ME
READ     BAK
        4 File(s)

C:\WAITE>copy read.bak readme.new
        1 File(s) copied

C:\WAITE>del *.*
Are you sure [Y/N]? y
C:\WAITE>cd\
C:\>rd \waite
```

Tip

Creating a READ.ME File

One way to create a READ.ME file is to change to a subdirectory in which you keep data files. Using the principle of redirection (explained in Chapter 8, "Advanced Use of the Command Line"), type **dir *.* > read.me**. This will create a copy of your current directory listing and store it in a file called READ.ME. Now you can use EDLIN to add explanatory comments after each file name in the list.

Managing a Large File

As you know, the only time you would not receive a message from EDLIN after entering a file name is when the file you want to load is too large to fit completely into memory. EDLIN will read in as much of the file as will fit, reserving 25 percent of the memory. (EDLIN operates with this 25-percent safety reserve at all times.) Your original file is still safe on the disk.

When you have a very long file to edit, it is usually more practical to use your word processor in text mode. Therefore, you probably will never use the EDLIN commands. However, when you have no other options, it is nice to know they exist.

Clearing Memory: Writing to a File with the W Command

When EDLIN displays the command prompt without first displaying the `end of input file` message, it means that only the first part of your file has been loaded into memory. To access the part of your file not yet loaded, you must make room in memory.

You can do this by using the W (Write) command to write some of the lines in your file back to the disk. For example, if you type **2100W**, EDLIN will write the first 2100 lines of your file back to the disk.

If you are not sure how many lines should be stored, you can enter the W command without any line numbers. Starting with the first line, EDLIN will write back as many lines as necessary until memory is only 25 percent full. You will then have 75 percent of the available memory space to use.

Loading into Memory: Appending to a File with the A Command

Now that you have made room for your file in memory, you must use the A (Append) command to load the next part of your file. Enter the number of lines you want to load and type **A**. For example, type **2100A** to load the next 2100 lines.

As a precaution, EDLIN automatically loads the next lines in sequence. For example, you cannot skip over the middle 2100 lines if you want to append the last 2100. This is because there is still a section of your file in memory. If you were able to load two sections of your file that did not belong together, you would destroy your original file when you saved your work.

If you do not specify any line numbers, EDLIN simply copies new lines until 75 percent of memory has been filled.

Summary of EDLIN Commands

Table 9.5 summarizes the EDLIN commands. As you continue to use your computer, you will find that these keys and commands can be very helpful in creating and editing text files.

Table 9.5. ***EDLIN Commands and Shortcuts***

Command/ Symbol	Usage	Function	Example	Description
.	.	Indicates the current line.	.L	List the current line.
#	#	Indicates the last line.	#D	Delete the last line.
+	+*n*	Selects a line that is	+5	Advance 5 lines.

Table 9.5. *(cont.)*

Command/ Symbol	Usage	Function	Example	Description
		n lines ahead of the current line.		
–	– *n*	Selects a line that is *n* lines back from the current line.	`-5`	Back up 5 lines.
,	*x,y*	Separates the beginning (*x*) and end (*y*) of a range.	`5,15`	Indicate a range of lines from 5 through 15.
L	L	Lists the file.	`L`	List the entire file.
			`5,15L`	List lines 5 through 15.
I	I	Inserts a line.	`5I`	Insert a new line before line 5.
C	*x,y,z*C	Copies a range of lines from *x* through *y* to a new location *z*.	`,,5C`	Copy current line to line 5.
			`1,5,15C`	Copy lines 1 through 5 to line 15.
M	*x,y,z*M	Moves a line or range of lines to a new location; delete original line.	`,,5M`	Move current line to line 5.
			`1,5,15M`	Move lines 1 through 5 to line 15.
D	D	Deletes a line or range of lines.	`D`	Delete the current line.
			`5D`	Delete line 5.
			`5,15D`	Delete lines 5 through 15.
S	*x,y*S*t*	Searches a range of lines to locate a string (*t*).	`5,15St`	Search lines 5 through 15 for the string `t`; stop at first occurrence.
			`S`	Repeat identical search.
?S	*x,y*?S*t*	Performs a global search.	`5,15?S`	Search lines 5 through 15 without repeating command.
R	R*t*^Z*u*	Replaces first string (*t*) with second (*u*).	`Rt^Zu`	From current line to end of file, replace `t` with `u`.
			`5,15Rt^Zu`	Make replacement only within lines 5 through 15.
?R	?R*t*^Z*u*	Performs a selective replacement.	`?Rt^Zu`	Verify each instance before replacing `t` with `u`.
			`5,15?Rt^Zu`	Perform replacement only within lines 5 through 15.
T	T*file*	Transfers the contents of another file (*file*) to the current file.	`Tlist`	Copy the contents of the file `list` to the current line.
	*x*T*file*	Transfers the contents of another file into line *x*.	`5Tlist`	Copy the contents of `list` to line 5.

Table 9.5. *(cont.)*

Command/ Symbol	Usage	Function	Example	Description
W	W	Writes lines of a file from memory to a file on disk.	W	Save lines from the current file to disk until memory is only 25% full.
			2222W	Save 2222 lines from memory to disk.
A	A	Appends from a file on disk to a file in memory.	A	Load from disk into memory until memory is 75% full.
			2222A	Load 2222 lines (if possible) from disk to memory.
E	E	Exits; saves your work.	E	Save and exit.
Q	Q	Quits; does not save.	Q	Exit without saving edited version of file.

What's Next

Chapter 5, "PC DOS Files," discusses files in general, what they are, different types of files, and how to organize and manipulate them. Chapter 10, "Batch Files," presents a complete tutorial on *batch files*, which are text files that contain sequences of command lines. Chapter 8, "Advanced Use of the Command Line," teaches how to use the redirection and piping features with filtering programs to send text files to the printer, append one text file to another, sort the contents of a text file, and find text strings within a file. Chapter 11, "Customizing Your System," shows you how to use text strings and text files to fine-tune PC DOS and accommodate various programs and devices.

Key Concepts and Words

Before you read further, use the following list to test your understanding of the concepts and words in this chapter.

ASCII
Keyboard buffer
Text strings
Search and replace
Extended character codes
.BAK files
Control key
Function keys
Command-line template
Full-screen editors
Line editors
EDLIN
Current line
Text file editing
Extended character set
Backup files
Large files
File loading
Appending files

Chapter 10

Use batch files when you want to run a "batch" of commands one after another. Storing commands in batch files lets you automate repetitive and hard-to-remember routines. With over 40 listings, this chapter presents many examples of PC DOS features and commands, and teaches you to

- *Create or modify batch files and store them in their proper subdirectories*
- *Use the special PC DOS "batch subcommands," such as ECHO, IF, FOR, and others*
- *Create simple, useful batch files with ordinary PC DOS internal and external commands*

Chapter 10
Batch Files

As you become familiar with PC DOS, tasks that you find difficult at first become routine. You become increasingly aware of using certain sequences of commands in the same pattern, over and over again.

PC DOS lets you store one or more commands in a batch file. Later, instead of having to remember and retype the command sequence, you simply type the name of the batch file and PC DOS will execute all of the commands in the batch file.

Learning to make batch files is easy and can be fun. Your batch files are your own creations. You can string together any commands you want and save them as a batch file. To run your batch file, type its name on the command line and PC DOS will execute the commands. And batch files make a terrific playground for learning to use PC DOS commands.

What Is a Batch File?

A *batch file* is a text file containing one or more command lines. Any command line that works will also work in a batch file. As a simple example, you can create a batch file containing only a single command. For instance, your batch file might be simply `dir`.

Since a batch file is a text file, it contains only *ASCII text characters*, that is, the characters produced by any standard typewriter. A batch file does not contain control characters such as Ctrl-C or Ctrl-S. You create a batch file just as you would create any other text file—by using a text editor or by using the COPY CON: convention (see Chapter 9, "Creating Text Files"). The only restriction is that each line must have fewer than 127 characters.

Naming Your Batch File

You can give your batch file any legal name that you wish, but you must use the .BAT extension. You cannot give your batch file the name of any of the PC DOS internal commands. Generally, you should not give your batch file the same name as any of the PC DOS external commands or devices or any other executable program. Some examples of batch file names are TODO.BAT, OPENUP.BAT, and MOVEFILE.BAT.

There is one batch file name that is special: *AUTOEXEC.BAT*. If a file named AUTOEXEC.BAT is located in the root directory, PC DOS as part of the loading process will run the AUTOEXEC.BAT file automatically, before presenting the system prompt for the first time. Further discussion of the AUTOEXEC.BAT file is presented later in Chapter 11, "Customizing Your System," and Chapter 12, "Installing a PC DOS System."

Running Your Batch Files on Other PC DOS Computers

There are some differences between versions of PC DOS. Generally, higher-numbered versions of PC DOS let you create batch files with greater capabilities. But if you create a batch file that depends on features found only in later versions of PC DOS, the batch file won't work if you try to use it on a system running an earlier version. Of course, batch files that run on early versions of PC DOS will work on all later versions.

Steps for Developing Your Batch File

It is a good idea to store most of your batch files in their own special directory. Also, you should establish a directory that is safe for testing your creations. After you create a batch file, always check it with the TYPE command and then run it.

Setting Up Your Directory Structure

The examples throughout this chapter assume that you have set up your directories according to the suggestions in the Quick Primer. Listing 10.1 shows that directory structure.

To this you will add a new directory, \BATS, and its subdirectories, \BATS\TEST and \BATS\BAKS.

Listing 10.1. ***Your Directory Structure***

```
C:\>dir
 Volume in drive C is CAROL
 Directory of  C:\
AUTOEXEC BAT            10-10-90   11:00a
CONFIG   SYS            10-10-90   11:05a
DOS           <DIR>     10-10-90   11:15a
SYS           <DIR>     10-10-90   11:16a
PROGS         <DIR>     10-10-90   11:17a
UTILS         <DIR>     10-10-90   11:18a
ACCOUNTS      <DIR>     10-10-90   11:19a
CLIENTS       <DIR>     10-10-90   11:20a
```

```
SUPPLIER     <DIR>       10-10-90   11:21a
INVNTORY     <DIR>       10-10-90   11:22a
PLANS        <DIR>       10-10-90   11:23a
        11 File(s)  26009600 bytes free
C:\>
```

In the preceding directory, the AUTOEXEC.BAT file is an ordinary batch file. Its name, **AUTOEXEC**, is part of the design of the PC DOS operating system. As part of the loading process, PC DOS searches for the AUTOEXEC.BAT file name in the root directory. If an AUTOEXEC.BAT file exists, PC DOS will execute the commands in that file before it displays the system prompt.

Caution

AUTOEXEC.BAT—Handle with Care!
The contents of the AUTOEXEC.BAT file may be critical to your system's performance. Don't change the contents of AUTOEXEC.BAT unless you understand them. Refer to Chapters 11 and 12 for more information about AUTOEXEC.BAT.

The CONFIG.SYS file contains information controlling the process that loads PC DOS when you turn on your computer power switch or reset the computer. The \DOS directory contains the PC DOS utilities (the external commands such as DISKCOPY.COM, FORMAT.COM, and so on). The \SYS directory contains device drivers and other files with the .SYS extension (such as ANSI.SYS, KEYBOARD.SYS, and PRINTER.SYS). The \PROGS directory contains programs that you use most often. The \UTILS directory contains various utility programs that are not part of PC DOS.

The remaining directory names, \ACCOUNTS, \CLIENTS, \SUPPLIER, \INVNTORY, and \PLANS, represent other directories on your system.

For the directory structure presented in Listing 10.1, your PATH statement might include C:\;C:\DOS; C:\SYS;C:\PROGS;C:\UTILS.

Making the \BATS Directory

Most of your general-purpose batch files belong in a general batch file directory. Use the MD command to make a directory called \BATS. The \BATS directory will be the home for most of your batch files.

Making \BATS\TEST and \BATS\BAKS

In developing your batch files, you may sometimes make mistakes. That is why you should have a separate directory for developing and testing your batch files. Use the CD command to make \BATS the current directory; then use the MD command to make a subdirectory called \TEST. The \BATS\TEST directory will be the safe area in which you try out your batch files to be sure they work the way you want them to. Make another subdirectory named \BAKS to store your backup files. Some of the examples in this chapter assume that you are using these subdirectory names.

Listing 10.2 shows how to create the \BATS, \BATS\TEST, and \BATS\BAKS directories.

Listing 10.2. *Making Directories for Batch Files*

```
C:\>md bats
C:\>cd bats
C:\BATS>md test
C:\BATS>md baks
C:\BATS>dir

 Volume in drive C is CAROL
 Directory of  C:\BATS

.            <DIR>      10-19-90   4:05p
..           <DIR>      10-19-90   4:05p
TEST         <DIR>      10:19-90   4:21p
BAKS         <DIR>      10-19-90   4:22p
        4 File(s)  26009600 bytes free

C:\BATS>
```

When you have made the \BATS directory and its two subdirectories, use the CD command to make the \BATS\TEST directory the current directory.

You will create and test your batch files in the \BATS\TEST directory. After you test them, store the finished batch files in the \BATS directory.

Creating a Batch File

You can create a batch file by using the COPY CON: convention or by using a text editor.

If you are using a word processing program, be sure that it is in the text editing mode (see Chapter 9, "Creating Text Files"). If you are not sure how to use your word processor to create a pure ASCII text file, find out or use a bona fide text editor. Many people like the convenience of a "pop-up" text editor that is loaded as a terminate and stay resident (TSR) program.

Also, be sure that your text editing program is stored in a directory specified by the PATH statement and that it can edit and store files in the \BATS\TEST directory, which should be the current directory when you are creating batch files.

The PC DOS operating system includes a text editor called EDLIN (EDit LINe). The EDLIN text editor is a *line-oriented* editing program rather than a *full-screen* editing program, but it does create pure text files. (See Chapter 9 for a tutorial on how to use EDLIN.)

Many experienced users think poorly of EDLIN. In fact, for many writing jobs EDLIN is much clumsier to use than a full-screen word processor. But for writing batch files, EDLIN works just as well as any word processor. The reason is that most batch files are short, often just a few lines long. The argument in favor of learning EDLIN is that it is part of the PC DOS operating system, available on any PC DOS machine—it's free and it suits the purpose.

If you use the COPY command to create your batch file, when you are done, enter Ctrl-Z (hold down the Ctrl key and type **z**). PC DOS will close the file, saving its new contents.

Ctrl-Z: The PC DOS End-of-File Marker

PC DOS recognizes a special character sequence—Ctrl-Z followed by a carriage return (the Enter key)—as a signal to close a file. The Ctrl-Z is referred to as the *end-of-file* (EOF) marker.

The Ctrl-Z and Enter sequence is stored in the file as an instruction to PC DOS (like other control sequences such as Ctrl-C) identifying the end of the file. When the TYPE program encounters the Ctrl-Z end-of-file marker, it quits without displaying the Ctrl-Z itself.

Check Your Text Editor

Check your text editor to make sure that it closes its files correctly. First use your text editor to create a very short batch file; then quit the editor and try to run the batch file. If the batch file works, your text editor is fine. If the batch file doesn't work, your text editor may not be closing the file properly.

Your First Batch File

Some of the most useful batch files are quite short, containing as few as one, two, or three lines in all. The first example batch file in this chapter, CL.BAT, simply issues the CLS command to clear the screen. This batch file would be more trouble than it's worth except that its simplicity makes it a good first stepping stone, leading quickly to truly useful small batch files.

Because the first listings are short, the examples assume you will use the COPY CON: convention. If you use a text editor, you should have no trouble following along. Listing 10.3 shows how to create CL.BAT.

Listing 10.3. ***Creating the CL.BAT Batch File***

```
C:\BATS\TEST>copy con: cl.bat
cls
^Z
        1 file(s) copied

C:\BATS\TEST>
```

Type the commands as shown in Listing 10.3. When you enter Ctrl-Z and press Enter, PC DOS will display the message `1 File(s) copied` and then present the system prompt.

Checking Your Work

Always check to see that your batch file exists as you expect. Instead of using the DIR command, use the TYPE command. You will verify that the file exists in the current directory, and you will read its contents as well. Listing 10.4 shows how the TYPE command responds.

Listing 10.4. *TYPE the CL.BAT File*

```
C:\BATS\TEST>type cl.bat
cls
C:\BATS\TEST>
```

The results of the TYPE command should be identical to the lines you typed when you created the file, except that the Ctrl-Z will be missing. Remember that Ctrl-Z is an instruction that identifies the end of the file; it is not part of the file itself. Check to be sure that the current directory (shown in the prompt) is correct and that each line in the file is exactly as it should be. If so, try running your batch file.

Running Your Batch File

To run CL.BAT, type `cl` on the command line. You don't have to type the .BAT extension. PC DOS will find CL.BAT and execute the CLS command to clear the screen. Listing 10.5 shows the effect of running the CL.BAT batch file.

Listing 10.5. *Running CL.BAT*

```
C:\BATS\TEST>cl

C:\BATS\TEST>cls
```

(The screen is blank)

```
C:\BATS\TEST>
C:\BATS\TEST>
```

Stopping Your Batch File with Ctrl-C

You can stop your batch file in the middle of execution by typing Ctrl-C (or Ctrl-Break). PC DOS will query you `Terminate Batch File? (y/n)` and halt any execution until you respond with `y` to quit or `n` to continue.

Caution

When in Doubt, Ctrl-C Out

When your batch file isn't working the way you expect, use Ctrl-C as an emergency stop. After your file has stopped, you can continue execution if you wish, or you can discontinue execution and return to the normal PC DOS prompt.

Avoiding the Double Prompt

Notice that the CL.BAT batch file produces not one, but two, final prompts. This is because the Ctrl-Z is on a separate line rather than at the end of the last command line in the file. Every line in your batch file is terminated by a carriage return. Thus, after PC DOS executes the command on a line, it displays the prompt in response to the carriage return. In other words, the carriage return at the end of a line triggers the prompt.

In Listing 10.5, the carriage return following the CLS command forced PC DOS to display the prompt. And the carriage return following the Ctrl-Z on the next line forced PC DOS to display another prompt.

Caution

Ctrl-Z on a New Line

Even though the double prompt is awkward, there are reasons for entering the Ctrl-Z on a separate, final line. If you print the contents of more than one batch file (for instance, `copy 1.bat prn: copy 2.bat prn:`), the result may be that the last line of the first file also includes the first line of the second.

To avoid confusion, you can advance the page in the printer, either manually or by sending one or more blank lines. Alternatively, you can place the Ctrl-Z on a separate line in the batch file and live with the double prompt.

The double prompt phenomenon may seem novel when you first encounter it, but you may soon find it annoying. The next batch file shows how to avoid the double prompt by placing Ctrl-Z at the end of the last command line.

Follow along in Listing 10.6 to create, check, and run the D?.BAT batch file. The question mark illustrates the use of an unusual text character as part of a file name.

D?.BAT contains only the DIR command. This file, too, by itself is more trouble than it is worth, but later you will use the COPY command with the + option to merge CL.BAT and D?.BAT. This is a powerful trick for combining small batch files.

Listing 10.6. ***Creating the D?.BAT Batch File***

```
C:\BATS\TEST>copy con: d?.bat
dir^Z
        1 file(s) copied

C:\BATS\TEST> type d?.bat
dir

C:\BATS\TEST>d?

C:\BATS\TEST>dir

 Volume in drive C is CAROL
 Directory of  C:\BATS\TEST

.            <DIR>       10-19-90   4:05p
..           <DIR>       10-19-90   4:05p
CL       BAT         7   10-19-90   1:05p
D?       BAT         5   10-20-90   1:10p
        4 File(s)  26009600 bytes free

C:\BATS\TEST>
```

In Listing 10.6, use the COPY command to create D?.BAT. Be sure to enter the terminating Ctrl-Z at the end of the same line as the DIR command.

Use the TYPE command to verify that the file is correct, and run D?.BAT by typing d? on the command line. PC DOS will present the prompt and run the DIR program, displaying the directory, then present a single prompt when done.

Notice that the directory listing shows that CL.BAT contains 7 bytes and D?.BAT contains 5 bytes. The difference reflects the different ways you entered Ctrl-Z in the file. By entering Ctrl-Z on its own line, you typed more characters (the extra carriage return, which includes the line-feed character) than you did by entering the Ctrl-Z at the end of the last command.

Combining Batch Files

While neither CL.BAT nor D?.BAT is practical in its own right, combining them creates a batch file that clears the screen and presents a directory listing free from leftover screen clutter.

Combine the two files by using the COPY command with the + symbol. Do not use space characters to separate the + symbol from the two file names. *Note*: If you do not specify a destination file name, the COPY command will append the contents of the second file to those of the first. If you specify a destination file name, PC DOS will create, or overwrite, that file to contain the combined contents.

Tip

PC DOS Tricks with TYPE and COPY

You can add lines to an existing text file by using the TYPE command and the double redirection symbols (> >) or by using the COPY command and the plus sign (+).

Using double redirection for the output of the TYPE command appends the text of the TYPEd file to another file, expanding the size of the second file.

You can use the COPY command with the plus symbol to copy the contents of one file plus the contents of a second file into a new file that includes text of the original two (for instance, `copy this.bat+that.bat both.bat`).

Listing 10.7 shows the steps for combining CL.BAT with D?.BAT as a new destination batch file, CLD.BAT.

Listing 10.7. ***Creating the CLD.BAT Batch File***

```
C:\BATS\TEST>copy cl.bat+d?.bat cld.bat
CL.BAT
D?.BAT
        2 file(s) copied

C:\BATS\TEST>type cld.bat
cls
dir
C:\BATS\TEST>cld
C:\BATS\TEST>cls
```

(The screen is blank)

```
C:\BATS\TEST>dir

 Volume in drive C is CAROL
 Directory of  C:\BATS\TEST

.            <DIR>       10-19-90   4:05p
..           <DIR>       10-19-90   4:05p
CL       BAT         7   10-19-90   1:05p
D?       BAT         5   10-20-90   1:10p
CLD      BAT         9   10-20-90   1:17p
        5 File(s)  26009600 bytes free

C:\BATS\TEST>copy cld.bat \bats
```

The PC DOS Batch Command Facility

The *batch command facility* is part of the design of the COMMAND.COM command interpreter program (the program responsible for displaying the prompt and interpreting what you type on the command line). Normally, when you type a command, PC DOS loads whichever program you name and lets the program take control of the entire system. When the program is done, PC DOS automatically reloads COMMAND.COM.

The .BAT extension tells PC DOS to use its batch command facility to interpret this as a batch file. PC DOS stores the entire file into memory and then starts to execute the first line. To begin, PC DOS displays the command prompt, just as it does when it is ready to accept your command. Then it executes the first command line in your batch file.

After executing the first command line, PC DOS again displays the prompt and executes the second line in the batch file. This process continues until PC DOS has executed the entire batch file, at which point it displays the prompt to signal its readiness to accept your next command.

The Structure of the Command Line

PC DOS always interprets the first character string on the command line as a command or as the name of a program to be run. This first character string is called the *head* of the command line. The PC DOS command line uses the space character as a *delimiter* (a delimiter is a character used to separate text strings on the same line). All text that follows the first space character on the command line is called the *tail*.

The PC DOS PATH Search Order

When you want to run a program, you type its name on the command line. To load that program, PC DOS searches for a program having a name that matches the character string you typed at the head of the command line. PC DOS always follows a particular search order.

First, PC DOS tries to match the head of the command line with the names of the internal commands.

Second, PC DOS looks in the current directory and tries to match the head with the names of programs having the .COM extension, then with names of programs having the .EXE extension, and finally with names of programs having the .BAT extension.

Third, if it does not find a match in the current directory, PC DOS begins to search in the other directories specified by the PATH command, inspecting the contents of each directory in the order specified by the PATH statement. PC DOS looks first for .COM programs, then for .EXE programs, and finally for .BAT files in each directory. It continues inspecting directories in the order they occur in the PATH specification, searching each for .COM, then .EXE, and lastly .BAT files.

PC DOS quits the search when it finds a match or when it has failed to find a match after searching all directories specified by the PATH command.

Caution

Complete File Spec Disallows Other PATH Searches
Entering the path specification of a program will subvert the PATH search. For example, if you enter \BATS\TEST\XCOPY, PC DOS will search the \BATS\TEST directory for the XCOPY command and, if it doesn't find XCOPY, it will abandon further search.

Putting Batch Files in Other Directories

You may want some batch files to belong to particular directories. These are batch files that you want to run only when the particular directory is the current directory.

This strategy lets you keep a short boot-up PATH statement in your AUTOEXEC.BAT file rather than a long one that includes many directories. A batch file local to a particular subdirectory can include an alternative PATH statement along with a sequence of commands that loads a program, lets you use that program, and then restores the original boot-up PATH statement after you are done.

Caution

.BAT Files versus .COM and .EXE Files
Do not put a batch file in a directory that contains an .EXE or a .COM file having the same name. PC DOS will find the .EXE or .COM file first, and the batch file will not be executed—even if you type the .BAT extension. For example, suppose you create a batch file named DIR.BAT. Even if you type `dir.bat` on the command line, PC DOS will execute the internal command, DIR. Similarly, if CHKDSK.COM is specified by the same directory as your batch file, CHKDSK.BAT, PC DOS will always execute CHKDSK.COM, even if you enter `chkdsk.bat`.

Simple Batch Files

You can create simple batch files combining common PC DOS commands. These batch files can perform a variety of chores for you, such as customizing the prompt, changing the PATH specification, and executing programs not specified by the PATH statement.

As an example, the MODE command lets you adjust the settings that govern the way PC DOS interfaces with various devices such as printers and modems. But to use the MODE command, you have to look up the correct settings for the device. To save yourself time, you can record the appropriate MODE command in a batch file and then reuse it as necessary.

Listing 10.8 shows how SETCND.BAT and SETNORM.BAT use the MODE command to set a standard dot-matrix printer to print condensed type and normal type.

Listing 10.8. ***Adjusting LPT1: with the MODE Command***

```
C:\BATS\TEST>copy con: setcnd.bat
mode lpt1: 132, 6, p^Z
        1 File(s) copied

C:\BATS\TEST>copy con: setnorm.bat
mode lpt1: 80, 6, p^Z
        1 File(s) copied
```

A Batch File Can Include Any Program

You can enter anything you wish in your batch file, as long as each line is a valid command. For example, your batch file could include a command to load and run a word processor or spreadsheet or any other program you like. When PC DOS loads the program, the batch command facility stores any remaining lines in your batch file, no matter how many hours you use your program. When you quit your program, PC DOS executes the rest of the lines in the batch file.

Batch Files Using Redirection, Pipes, and Filters

As you become comfortable using PC DOS, you will probably find that its filtering, redirection, and piping capabilities are increasingly helpful to you. But the command lines that invoke these stunts can quickly become long—a perfect application for batch files.

For a handy, one-line batch file, enter the command `dir | sort` to see the contents of a large directory listing displayed in alphabetical order. You can save this alphabetized listing as a file. As another example, entering the command `dir | sort > dirlist` pipes the output of the DIR command as input to the SORT program, whose output is redirected into a file named DIRLIST. The following list provides examples of command lines you might include in a one-line batch file:

`dir	sort`	Displays an alphabetized directory listing
`dir	sort	more`	Displays a similar listing one screen-full at a time
`dir	sort > dirlist`	Creates a file, DIRLIST, that contains an alphabetized directory listing
`chkdsk /v > \bats\test`	Displays a list of all files in \BATS\TEST with information on bad clusters on the disk drive

Greeting and Logging-In

If more than one person uses the same machine, you can use batch files to customize the machine for each person. Create a batch file for each person and give each batch file the name of the person for whom it is written. Each user can type his or her own name, and PC DOS will run that person's custom batch file.

DOS Shell

The Program Start Commands
DOSSHELL has a facility called Program Start Commands. This facility allows you to create a special batch file to be inserted into the shell's menu program. You can use these batch files as commands to get information from the user and to specify start-up options for the program. All of the regular batch file commands can be used.

Listing 10.9 shows how to make a simple greeting batch file for "Hunter" by using the PROMPT command to customize the prompt.

Listing 10.9. ***Custom Batch Files for User's Name***

```
C:\BATS\TEST>copy con: hunter.bat
prompt $p$  Hunter $g $
cd \bats\test
dir ^Z
        1 file(s) copied

C:\BATS\TEST>
```

Use the TYPE command to make sure that HUNTER.BAT is correct. Then run HUNTER.BAT to see how it works.

Tip

Adding a Space at the End of the Prompt
You can add a space at the end of the prompt to separate the prompt from the first word you type on the command line. Type the command **$g $** on the prompt command line (see Listing 10.9). This command string produces the greater-than (>) symbol followed by the space character. Notice that all of the prompts from here on in this chapter have a space after the prompt.

When Hunter types his name, PC DOS will execute the batch file named HUNTER.BAT, changing the prompt and displaying a listing of the current directory. Listing 10.10 shows the results.

Listing 10.10. ***Hunter Logs in***

```
C:\> hunter
C:\> prompt $p$  Hunter  $g $
C:\  Hunter  > cd \BATS\TEST
C:\BATS\TEST  Hunter  > dir

 Volume in drive C is CAROL
 Directory of  C:\BATS\TEST
```

```
.            <DIR>       10-19-90   4:05p
..           <DIR>       10-19-90   4:05p
CL       BAT         7   10-19-90   1:05p
D?       BAT         5   10-20-90   1:10p
CLD      BAT         9   10-20-90   1:17p
HUNTER   BAT        44   10-21-90   9:30a
        6 File(s)  26009600 bytes free
 Volume in drive C is CAROL
```

Changing the Prompt

You can change the prompt to suit yourself. Look up the entry for PROMPT in the Command Reference to get ideas. Here are some examples of prompt commands and their result:

`prompt $p$g $`	Displays the current path followed by a greater-than symbol and a space
`prompt $t $g $`	Shows the time followed by a greater-than symbol and a space
`prompt $d $t $g $`	Gives the date and time followed by a greater-than symbol and a space
`prompt $a`	Does not display a prompt—the prompt is blank

Changing the Current Directory and Path

You can use the CD command in your batch files to change the current directory. For example, you can use the CD command to create a batch file called GOTEST.BAT that contains the single line `cd \bats\test`. This batch file will change the current directory to \BATS\TEST.

As you will soon see, you can even use the PATH command to change the PC DOS path specification for your system. However, before you do so, make sure that you can restore the old path. In other words, don't make a new path specification without having a way to restore the original.

Batch files make convenient tools for quickly changing over to programs that use alternative directories. One benefit is that you can have shorter path specifications, so the time it takes PC DOS to search the whole path is shorter.

The PATH Statement in the AUTOEXEC.BAT File

Most AUTOEXEC.BAT files include a PATH statement. The *PATH statement* is the text string `path` followed by an equal sign (=), followed by a text string naming all the directories in which PC DOS is to search for commands and executable programs.

Every time you turn on or reboot your system, PC DOS automatically executes the PATH command and records the statement as part of the environment.

Creating PATHCHGN.BAT and PATHBACK.BAT

To run the batch files in your \BATS directory, you will have to modify the path specification in the environment to include the \BATS directory.

Caution

Be Careful with Your AUTOEXEC.BAT File
If you are unfamiliar with your system's AUTOEXEC.BAT file and its contents, do not try to alter your AUTOEXEC.BAT file. The contents of the AUTOEXEC.BAT file control many of the features of your system. Any changes may alter the performance of your system.

Listings 10.11 and 10.12 show two batch files that will solve your problem: PATHCHNG.BAT will create a new path specification, and PATHBACK.BAT will restore the original path specification.

Caution

Why You Should Save the Current Path before You Change It
PATHCHNG.BAT in Listing 10.11 is a full-fledged batch file. If you type `pathchng` on the command line, PC DOS will execute the command, changing the path specification on your system. If you haven't created a batch file to restore the original path specification, you will have to reboot your system. Use the Ctrl-Alt-Del key combination, or press the reset button, or turn the power off for ten seconds and switch it back on.

Listing 10.11. ***Changing the PATH Command with PATHCHNG.BAT***

```
C:\BATS\TEST> copy con: pathchng.bat
PATH=C:\;C:\BATS;C:\BATS\TEST;C:\DOS;C:\SYS;\C:PROGS^Z
        1 file copied

C:\BATS\TEST> type pathchng.bat
```

The path specification in PATHCHNG.BAT now begins with the root directory (C:\), followed by C:\BATS and C:\BATS\TEST, and then by the other directories. The reason for placing the batch file directories first is so that PC DOS will search them first.

Listing 10.12. ***Saving the Original Path with PATHBACK.BAT***

```
C:\BATS\TEST> path > pathback.bat
PATH=C:\;C:\DOS;C:\SYS;C:\UTILS;C:\PROGS

C:\BATS\TEST> type pathback.bat
```

The PATH command generates a message—the path specification. Normally PC DOS sends the message to the video display for you to read. The redirection symbol (>) forces PC DOS to store the message as a new file named PATHBACK.BAT (see Chapter 8, "Advanced Use of the Command Line").

As usual, use the TYPE command to verify that there really is a file named PATHBACK.BAT and that it contains the original path specification (use the PATH command again to compare).

Protecting Destructive PC DOS Commands

Some programs create destructive results. A few PC DOS external commands can destroy the directory structures on your disks. The FORMAT command will eradicate the entire directory structure on a floppy diskette or hard disk. The DISKCOPY command has a similar effect. The FDISK command creates and deletes partitions on the hard disk. Deleting a partition will effectively destroy any data that may have previously existed on the partition. You may have other utility programs that have similar effects.

Batch files can help you protect your system from misuse of destructive programs. Make a separate directory for the programs you feel are destructive. For instance, you can make a subdirectory directory called \DOS\PROT to specify the dangerous programs, as shown in Listing 10.13. Do not specify the \DOS\PROT directory in the PATH statement.

Listing 10.13. ***Contents of the \DOS \PROT Directory***

```
C:\DOS\PROT> dir
FORMAT   COM           3-21-90   4:44
DISKCOPY COM           3-21-90   4:44
FDISK    COM           3-21-90   4:44
        4 File(s)  26009600 bytes free
```

To execute programs in the \DOS\PROT directory, create batch files that contain the full specification for the commands. Listing 10.14 shows a batch file that formats the A drive.

Listing 10.14. ***Executing Protected Programs***

```
C:\BATS\TEST> copy con: formata.bat
\dos\prot\format a:^Z
        1 file copied

C:\BATS\TEST> type formata.bat
```

You can use FORMATA.BAT instead of the FORMAT command to format a floppy diskette in the A drive. The format program will operate normally, and, when you are done, PC DOS will return C:\BATS\TEST as the current directory.

Tip

Renaming the PC DOS Destructive Commands

You can rename the PC DOS commands. For example, rename the FORMAT.COM command to FORMAS.COM (and remember to change `format` to `formas` in FORMATA.BAT). The advantage is that neither you nor anyone using your system will type `format` and perhaps inadvertently format a disk containing important information.

You can create other batch files similar to FORMATA.BAT by including various parameters, such as the name of the B drive or the */s* option switch (which directs the FORMAT command to copy the PC DOS operating system onto the disk). Your batch files can include other commands also, such as CHKDSK. In Listing 10.15, the FORMAT and CHKDSK commands are combined in the batch file FBCK.BAT.

Listing 10.15. ***Combining the FORMAT and CHKDSK Commands in FBCK.BAT***

```
C:\BATS\TEST> type fbck.bat
\dos\prot\format b:
chkdsk b:
```

Replaceable Parameters: Flexible Batch File Input

Once PC DOS begins to execute a batch file, it continues automatically until the batch file has been completed. Unfortunately, the PC DOS batch file facility does not let you alter or respond to commands once execution has begun (other than to terminate with Ctrl-C). To avoid this problem, you need to create a batch file that lets you choose the files on which to operate.

The batch file facility has a feature that allows you to include *replaceable parameters* in your batch files. With a little analysis, this term will soon make sense.

Passing Parameters to Your Batch File

The term *parameter* refers to any of the elements that may occur in the tail of the command line. For instance, if you type `copy *.bak \bats\baks`, the head is `copy` (the name of a program), and the tail is the parameters `*.bak` and `\bats\baks`, which (in programming parlance) you "pass" to the COPY command program.

Understanding Input

Every program has input and output, whether it is a PC DOS internal command, external command, a word processor or database managing program, or a batch file. For example, the COPY program, like most of the PC DOS commands, is designed to accept the tail of the command line as its *input*. Its *output* is the act of copying the specified files.

Similarly, your batch file can accept input specified in the tail of the command line. The term for that input is *parameter*. The tail of the command line can contain one or more parameters. Each parameter consists of a text string separated by a space character.

For every parameter that occurs on the command line, there are one or more matching replaceable parameters in the batch file. The parameters you enter as input to your batch file become input to the commands in your batch file.

Batch Files Using a Replaceable Parameter

Listing 10.16 shows T.BAT—a batch file that uses a single replaceable parameter with the TYPE command.

Listing 10.16. ***Contents of the T.BAT File***

```
C:\BATS\TEST> type t.bat
type %1
C:\BATS\TEST> t cld.bat
cls
dir

C:\BATS\TEST>
```

The T.BAT file uses the TYPE command with a strange new addition, `%1`, which is a replaceable parameter. To use this batch file, type its name, `t`, on the command line along with a parameter—the name of the file whose contents you wish displayed (here, `cld.bat`).

The PC DOS batch file facility stores the tail. And as PC DOS executes the batch file, it replaces any occurrence of `%1` with the first parameter specified in the tail.

If you type `t Harry`, PC DOS will store the text string `Harry`. Then, as PC DOS executes the batch file, it will substitute `Harry` for `%1`. When the TYPE program begins execution, it will receive as its input the text string `Harry`. The TYPE program will try to find a file named HARRY and type its contents. Table 10.1 gives some handy batch file commands that use a single replaceable parameter.

Table 10.1. ***One-Parameter Command Lines***

Command	Meaning
`cd %1`	Changes any directory to the current directory
`copy %1 prn:`	Copies any file to the printer
`copy %1 \bats\baks`	Copies any file to \BATS\BAKS
`copy %1.bak \bats\baks`	Copies files with .BAK extensions to \BATS\BAKS
`dir %1`	Provides a directory listing for whatever you name
`dir %1.bat`	Provides a directory listing for files with .BAT
`dir	find "%1"	sort`	Finds a text string in a directory listing
`more < %1`	Displays whatever you specify, page by page
`more < %1 > prn:`	Prints whatever you name, a page at a time
`sort %1`	Sorts whatever you specify
`type %1`	Types any file you name
`type %1 > prn:`	Types a file, redirected to the printer
`type %1.bat`	Types a file with a .BAT extension

Listing 10.17 shows how to create PRT_CND.BAT. This file sets the printer typeface to condensed mode, prints the file you name, and then restores the printer to normal mode.

Listing 10.17. ***Printing in Condensed and Normal Modes with PRT_CND.BAT***

```
C:\BATS\TEST> copy con: prt_cnd.bat
mode lpt1: 132, 6, p
copy %1 lpt1:
mode lpt1: 80, 6, p^Z
        1 File(s) copied

C:\BATS\TEST> type t_cnd.bat
```

Parameters from %1 to %9

You are probably wondering why the designers of PC DOS chose the combination of a percent sign and an integer to signify a replaceable parameter. Actually, there is a reasonable explanation for their choice. PC DOS needs to identify a unique text string. Compared with most other keyboard characters, the percent sign is rarely used, so it was chosen to indicate a replaceable parameter.

The integer corresponds to the parameter position in the command-line tail. The first text string in the tail corresponds to %1, the second to %2, the third to %3, and so on. PC DOS allows replaceable parameters from %1 to %9. Thus, you can pass a maximum of nine parameters to your batch file. Listing 10.18 shows how T_ALOT.BAT uses many replaceable parameters.

Listing 10.18. ***TYPEing Many Files with T_ALOT.BAT***

```
C:\BATS\TEST> copy con: t_alot.bat
type %1
type %2
type %3
type %4
^Z
        1 File(s) copied

C:\BATS\TEST>
```

To use T_ALOT.BAT, type `t_alot` on the command line, followed by a space and the names of from one to four files. If you enter one file name, the PC DOS batch file facility will substitute that file name for the replaceable parameter on the first line (`type %1`) and nothing for the replaceable parameters on the subsequent lines. Then T_ALOT.BAT will type the file. The remaining lines will simply execute "empty" TYPE commands, generating the error message `Invalid number of parameters.`

If you follow T_ALOT with two file names, PC DOS will substitute the first file name for %1, the second for %2, and nothing for the others. Then T_ALOT.BAT will type each file, one after the other. You can include up to nine TYPE commands within T_ALOT.

In Listing 10.19, the batch file CP.BAT uses two replaceable parameters and makes a new copy of the CL.BAT file, named CL.BAK.

Listing 10.19. ***Copying Anything to Anything with CP.BAT***

```
C:\BATS\TEST> type cp.bat
copy %1 %2
C:\BATS\TEST> cp cl.bat cl.bak
CL.BAT
        1 File(s) copied

C:\BATS\TEST>
```

In Listing 10.19, PC DOS analyzes the command line, accepting the text string `cp` as the name of an executable file (your batch file, CP.BAT) and storing `cl.bat` as the first parameter and `cl.bak` as the second parameter. When PC DOS runs CP.BAT, it replaces `%1` with `cl.bat` and `%2` with `cl.bak`.

If you enter only one parameter on the command line, for example, `cp cl.bat`, PC DOS will replace `%1` with `cl.bat` and `%2` with nothing. The COPY program will make its attempt and then display the message `File cannot be copied onto itself`.

Listing 10.20 uses CP.BAT to create another batch file, MOVIT.BAT, which you may find extremely useful.

Listing 10.20. ***Using CP.BAT to Create MOVIT.BAT***

```
C:\BATS\TEST> cp con: movit.bat
C:\BATS\TEST> copy con: movit.bat
copy %1 %2
erase %1^Z
        1 file(s) copied

C:\BATS\TEST> type movit.bat
copy %1 %2
erase %1
C:\BATS\TEST>
```

The CP.BAT file consists of `copy %1 %2`, so PC DOS makes the parameter replacement as `copy con: movit.bat`. PC DOS then displays the prompt and the first line in the batch file, which shows that the parameters have been replaced, as you can see from the listing.

This is the standard use of the COPY CON: convention, so you must type in the text for the MOVIT.BAT file, shown as two lines, `copy %1 %2` and `erase %1^Z`. The Ctrl-Z finishes the COPY CON: process, and PC DOS copies the text into the new file, MOVIT.BAT. To see how MOVIT.BAT works, use the COPY command to create a copy of CL.BAT named CL.BAK (`copy cl.bat cl.bak`).

Listing 10.21 shows the directory listing for \BATS\TEST, the current directory. Listing 10.22 shows how to use MOVIT.BAT.

Listing 10.21. ***The \BATS\TEST Directory Listing***

```
C:\BATS\TEST> dir

 Volume in drive C is CAROL
 Directory of C:\BATS\TEST

.            <DIR>       10-19-90    4:05p
..           <DIR>       10-19-90    4:05p
CL        BAT          7 10-19-90    1:05p
D?        BAT          5 10-20-90    1:10p
CLD       BAT          9 10-20-90    1:17p
HUNTER    BAT         44 10-21-90    9:30a
PATHCHNG  BAT         54 10-21-90   10:45a
PATHBACK  BAT         40 10-21-90   10:48a
FORMATA   BAT         21 10-21-90    2:22p
FBCK      BAT         22 10-21-90    2:28p
T         BAT          9 10-21-90    2:31p
PRT_CND   BAT         54 10-21-90    2:38p
T_ALOT    BAT         30 10-21-90    2:46p
CP        BAT         12 10-21-90    2:56p
MOVIT     BAT         22 10-21-90    3:02p
CL        BAK          7 10-19-90    1:05p
        16 File(s)  26009600 bytes free
```

In MOVIT.BAT, you use one command, MOVIT, to do the work of two, COPY and ERASE. MOVIT.BAT accomplishes a common task—the transfer of a file from one file spec area (a directory or even a disk drive) to another and the cleanup of the first file spec area. Listing 10.22 shows how to use MOVIT.BAT to transfer files having the .BAK extension to the \BATS\BAKS directory.

Listing 10.22. ***Moving .BAK files to \BAKS with MOVIT.BAT***

```
C:\BATS\TEST> movit *.bak \bats\baks
C:\BATS\TEST> copy *.bak \bats\baks
CL.BAK
        1 File(s) copied

C:\BATS\TEST> erase *.bak
C:\BATS\TEST> dir \bats\baks
```

Type `movit *.bak \bats\baks` on the command line. PC DOS replaces all occurrences of `%1` with the text string `*.bak` and all occurrences of `%2` with the text string `\bats\baks`.

PC DOS then executes the first line, as shown (`copy *.bak \bats\baks`), and makes a copy of CL.BAK (the only file in the current directory having the .BAK extension) in the \BATS\BAKS directory.

Finally, PC DOS executes the last line, **erase *.baks**, and erases CL.BAK from the current directory, \BATS\TEST. Listing 10.23 shows a few sample MOVIT command lines.

Listing 10.23. ***Examples of MOVIT Command Lines***

```
C:\BATS\TEST> movit *.* a:
C:\BATS\TEST> movit \bats\baks\*.* a:\bats\baks
C:\BATS\TEST> movit a:*.* b:
```

Earlier in the chapter, Listing 10.7 showed you how to use the COPY command to combine two batch files. Listing 10.24 shows how to extend that technique with replaceable parameters.

Listing 10.24. ***Adding Lines to Any Batch File with ADDMORE.BAT***

```
C:\BATS\TEST> copy con: addmore.bat
copy %1+con: %2^Z

        1 File(s) copied
C:\BATS\TEST> type addmore.bat
```

To run ADDMORE.BAT, type **addmore** followed by two parameters. You could create CPD.BAT, an improved CP.BAT file, by adding the DIR command to CP.BAT. Type **addmore cp.bat cpd.bat** on the command line. PC DOS will display **CP.BAT** followed by **CON:** and accept your input until you press Ctrl-Z. Then PC DOS will display **1 File(s) copied** and return the prompt. Use the TYPE command to type out CPD.BAT, and you will see the contents of CP.BAT followed by whatever you have input.

Using the Percent Sign in Batch Files

Because the percent sign indicates a replaceable parameter to PC DOS, using it as part of a legitimate name presents a problem. For example, you may encounter a file name such as JUNE%21.RPT. PC DOS will interpret the %2 in that string as a replaceable parameter. To get around this, the PC DOS designers chose to use double percent signs to signify a single occurrence of %. Thus, in your batch file, you would type JUNE%%21.RPT to refer to JUNE%21.RPT.

Use double percent signs to refer to the replaceable parameters themselves. For instance, %%1 refers to the %1 replaceable parameter.

Listing 10.25 shows how to pipe the output of the TYPE command to the FIND filter and then use redirection to record the output of the FIND program as a new file.

Listing 10.25. ***FINDME.BAT Uses Three Replaceable Parameters***

```
C:\BATS\TEST> copy con: findme.bat
type %1 | find "%2" > %3^Z
        1 File(s) copied

C:\BATS\TEST> type findme.bat
```

As an exercise, use FINDME.BAT to capture the `%1` in MOVIT.BAT and record the `%1` in a new file, MOVIT.?1. Type `findme movit.bat %%1 movit.?1` at the system prompt.

PC DOS will execute the contents of FINDME.BAT. The output of the TYPE program will type the contents of MOVIT.BAT, and PC DOS will pipe that as input to the FIND program. Because PC DOS eliminates the first percent sign, the FIND program will look for the text string `"%2"` in MOVIT.BAT. The redirection symbol will direct the output of the FIND program to a new file named MOVIT.?1.

The %0 Replaceable Parameter

The replaceable parameters from %1 to %9 refer to the elements of the command-line tail, in the order in which they occur. It makes sense, therefore, that %0 refers to the command-line head. If you use %0 in your batch file, PC DOS will replace it with the name of your batch file. For example, in the command `+ cld.bat`, `+` corresponds to %0 and `cld.bat` to %1.

Expanding Parameters with the Shift Command

The replaceable parameters limit the number of command-line parameters that you can enter to nine. However, at times you may want to operate a batch file with more than nine parameters.

For instance, you might want to use the TYPE command to display the contents of all the batch files in \BATS\TEST. You can't use a wildcard with the TYPE command (as in `type *.bat`), but you can solve the problem with the SHIFT command.

The SHIFT command has the effect of rotating the parameters on the command line one place to the left, so that the first parameter drops out, the second becomes the first, the third becomes second, and so on. Listing 10.26 shows a simple batch file that uses the SHIFT command to ECHO eleven parameters.

Listing 10.26. ***ECHOing beyond %9 Parameters***

```
C:\BATS\TEST> type 9plus.bat
@echo off
cls
rem 9plus.BAT displays all 10 integers plus one more
echo %1
```

```
shift
echo %1
shift
echo %1
shift
echo %1
shift
echo %1
shift
echo %1
shift
echo %1
shift
echo %1
shift
echo %1
shift
echo %1
shift
echo %1
C:\BATS\TEST> 9plus 1 2 3 4 5 6 7 8 9 0 Joker
```

You can add as many more ECHO/SHIFT combinations as you wish, although there is a limit to how many parameters you can enter on the command line. The command line accepts a total of 127 characters, including the head and the tail.

PC DOS Batch File Subcommands

The IBM documentation for PC DOS refers to *batch file subcommands.* These are simply internal commands that are especially useful in batch files. There is no restriction on using them outside of batch files as commands on the command line. As you will see, some of these batch-file internal commands are especially handy for managing your batch file displays.

Caution

Making Your Batch Files Portable

One of the advantages of batch files is being able to use them on other PC DOS (and MS-DOS) systems. Unfortunately, however, batch files are not universally portable between systems. Even between the versions of PC DOS, there are differences in the features of the batch command facility. To make truly universal batch files, you must confine yourself to using features that exist in all versions, from 2.0 to the current version.

With the exception of the @ character and the CALL command, which were introduced in version 3.3, the batch file subcommands listed in Table 10.2 work in all versions of PC DOS, although with slight differences in the way the ECHO command generates a blank line.

Table 10.2. *Batch File Subcommands for All PC DOS Versions*

Command	Function
@	Placed first on a line, suppresses display of the line
= =	Works with IF; tests to see if text strings on either side match, as in `if %1 == cl.bak copy %1 \bats\baks`
%%*X*	Works with FOR; represents an element within a set
%0–%9	Replaceable parameters for elements of command-line tail
CALL	Executes another batch file and then continues with next line
DO	Works with FOR; indicates the start of a second command
ECHO	Displays the following text on the display screen
EXIST	Works with IF; refers to existence of a file, as in `if exist cl.bak copy cl.bak \bats\baks`
FOR	Used with %%X, in, (set), do; allows multiple command execution, as in `for %%a in (\bats\test\*.bak) do copy %%a \bats\baks`
GOTO	Forces PC DOS to execute the command on a labeled line
IF	Used with EXIST, = =, NOT; the condition determines command execution
IN	Works with FOR; associates %%*X* with elements of a set
NOT	Works with IF; negates (inverts) EXIST or = = condition, as in `if not exist cl.bak echo cl.bak does not exist in current directory`
PAUSE	Halts the scrolling of the display until the user hits a key
REM	Directs PC DOS to ignore the balance of text on the line
(set)	Works with FOR; specifies elements on which to operate, as in `for %%z in (cl.bat c?.bat cd.bat) do type %%z`
SHIFT	Rotates replaceable parameter correspondence

Presentation on Screen: Batch File Output

The output of your batch file consists of the output of each of the programs, one after the other. In many cases, the rapid succession of batch file commands goes too fast to be useful and presents information on the screen that becomes dazzlingly complex. Controlling the way your batch file commands display their messages on the screen is a large part of the art of making batch files.

Using the CLS Command for Neatness

To clear the screen of extraneous display, you may wish to enter the CLS command as the first line in your batch file. The CLS command clears the screen, making it easy to identify your batch file's messages. Before you use CLS as your first command, however, be sure to read the following caution.

Caution

Use CLS with Care

If the CLS command is the first command in your batch file, the entire screen will be erased, and the prompt will appear on the top line. Watch out! You may want to refer to the contents of the screen after your batch file executes. Think carefully before using CLS as your first command.

Using the ECHO Command to Display Text

In writing batch files, you will discover many different reasons for displaying a line of text. For example, you may want to tell the user what to expect as your batch file executes. But, you can't simply enter a line of text in a batch file. PC DOS will interpret it as a command, treating the first word as the head and looking for a program to match. For instance, a line beginning `This batch file...` will direct PC DOS to execute a program named `This`, passing it the parameters `batch file...`. As another example, certainly you would not want blindly to execute `Format a spare floppy`.

The ECHO command is the batch-facility internal command that solves the problem. ECHO directs PC DOS to display whatever text follows on the same line. As an example, when PC DOS encounters the line `echo Hi, there!`, it passes the string `Hi, there!` to the ECHO command for execution.

ECHO ON and ECHO OFF

The ECHO command by itself returns one of two messages—ON or OFF. You can enter `echo on` or `echo off` to change the state. The default state is ECHO set to ON.

When you set ECHO to OFF, you direct PC DOS to suppress ECHOing the batch file commands to the screen. Listing 10.27 shows this effect.

Listing 10.27. ***Turning ECHO ON and Turning ECHO OFF with EKO.BAT***

```
C:\BATS\TEST> type eko.bat
cls
echo on
echo Echo is now ON
echo Grace
echo off
echo Echo is now OFF
echo under
echo on
echo Echo is now ON
echo pressure
C:\BATS\TEST> eko
```

(The screen is blank)

```
C:\BATS\TEST> echo on
C:\BATS\TEST> echo ECHO is now ON
Echo is now ON
C:\BATS\TEST> echo Grace
Grace
C:\BATS\TEST> echo off
Echo is now OFF
under
C:\BATS\TEST> echo Echo is now ON
Echo is now ON
C:\BATS\TEST> echo pressure
pressure

C:\BATS\TEST>
```

When you type eko, PC DOS runs EKO.BAT. The CLS command clears the screen. Line 1 contains echo on to be sure that the ECHO setting really is on. PC DOS then returns the prompt and displays line 2, echo Echo is now ON. After executing it, PC DOS displays the next line, Echo is now ON.

When PC DOS gets to the line containing echo off, it executes the command, turning the state of ECHO to OFF afterward. PC DOS no longer displays the prompt or repeats the command lines in the batch file, although it executes them, as you can see from the line Echo is now OFF.

When PC DOS encounters the line echo on, it again displays subsequent command lines in the batch file. Usually, you should include an echo off statement as the first line in your batch file.

Making Blank Lines

You may find that your screen is often cluttered with old messages that you don't want to erase. But as your batch file generates its messages, the new text may be easy to miss unless it is set off between blank lines. The importance of this formatting consideration is easy to discount until you have developed a few batch files. To generate a blank line on the screen, you must use the ECHO command.

The features of the ECHO command work differently between PC DOS versions 3.x (versions 3.0, 3.1, 3.2, and 3.3) and versions 2.x (versions 2.0 and 2.1).

To generate a blank line using PC DOS versions 3.0 and higher, use the ECHO command immediately followed by a period. Do not insert a space character between the ECHO command and the period. In PC DOS versions 2.0 and 2.1, use the ECHO command followed by two spaces. Listing 10.28 shows how to use the ECHO command with PC DOS versions 3.0 and higher to display blank lines.

Tip

How to Generate a Blank Line in All Versions of PC DOS

For a truly universal way to generate a blank line, follow the ECHO command with a space and Ctrl-H. The Ctrl-H corresponds to ASCII code 008, which is the traditional code for the Backspace key. Your text editor may or may not allow you to input Ctrl-H directly. If not, enter ASCII code 008 in your batch file by holding down the Alt key, typing 008 on the numeric keypad (not the number keys above the standard keyboard), and then releasing the Alt key.

Listing 10.28. ***Displaying Blank Lines***

```
C:\BATS\TEST> type ekoblank.bat
echo off
echo.
echo.
echo Blank lines help
echo.
echo.
echo.
C:\BATS\TEST> ekoblank
echo off
```

```
Blank lines help

C:\BATS\TEST>
```

Listing 10.28 works as shown if you are using PC DOS versions 3.0 and higher. For PC DOS versions 2.0 and 2.1, follow the ECHO command with two spaces rather than a period.

Tip

Using Redirection with ECHO

You can use the ECHO command with redirection to create a one-line text file. If you type `ECHO whatever >whatfile`, PC DOS will create a new file called WHATFILE that contains the text `whatever`. Use double redirection to append additional lines to an existing file. For example, `echo whatever more >> whatfile` will add a new line `whatever more` to WHATFILE.

Suppressing a Command-Line Display with @

PC DOS version 3.3 includes a feature that lets you suppress the display of a command. If you begin a line with the @ character as the first character on the line, PC DOS will not display the prompt or the command. Using the @ character acts as an immediate ECHO OFF command that affects only the current line. PC DOS versions 3.2 and earlier do not include this feature.

Using the PAUSE Command to Present One Screen at a Time

Use the PAUSE command to suspend execution of your batch file. The PAUSE command halts execution at the point where it is inserted, generates a blank line, and prints the message `Strike any key when ready.`

The PAUSE command lets you break your batch file execution into screen-sized portions so that they are more readable. It also gives you the opportunity to terminate the batch file at that point, before the next commands execute. Listing 10.29 shows how to combine the PAUSE command with ECHO to present a portion of a batch file and give the user the option to continue or terminate.

Listing 10.29. ***Using PAUSE for Readability and Control***

```
C:\BATS\TEST> copy con: fmta_p.bat
@echo off
echo.
echo.
echo Do you want to FORMAT A: or terminate FMTA_P.BAT?
echo.
echo Press Ctrl-C to terminate FMTA_P.BAT or
pause
format a:^Z
        1 File(s) copied

C:\BATS\TEST> FMTA_P

Do you want to FORMAT A: or terminate FMTA_P.BAT?
```

```
Press Ctrl-C to terminate FMTA_P.BAT or

Strike any key when ready...
```

Listing 10.29 shows the contents of FMTA_P.BAT followed by the output on the screen up to the PAUSE line. If the user enters Ctrl-C, the PC DOS batch command facility will display the message `Terminate batch job? (Y/N)`.

If the user types `y`, PC DOS will return the prompt. If the user types `n`, PC DOS will continue running the batch file. Notice that Listing 10.29 uses the @ character to suppress the first line, `echo off`.

Adding Graphics Characters

You can put graphics characters in your batch files to add impact to your messages. There is a trade-off, however, between the value of the added impact and the time it takes to create the extra graphics characters. To enter a graphics character, hold down the Alt key and use the numeric keypad to enter three integers. Then release the Alt key. Listing 10.30 shows how to create a message within a box.

Listing 10.30. ***Creating a Boxed Message with Graphics Characters***

```
C:\BATS\TEST> type gf_char.bat
@echo off
echo.
echo.
echo.
echo   In the next screen, GF_CHAR.BAT will present
echo        the DOUBLE-BAR BOX characters
echo      and their ALT-integer equivalents
echo.
pause
echo.
echo.
echo  ╔══════════════════════════════════════╗
echo  ║                                      ║
echo  ║    ALT 201 ╔ (upper left corner)     ║
echo  ║                                      ║
echo  ║    ALT 205 ═ (horizontal dbl bar)    ║
echo  ║                                      ║
echo  ║    ALT 187 ╗ (upper right corner)    ║
echo  ║                                      ║
echo  ║    ALT 186 ║ (vertical dbl bar)      ║
echo  ║                                      ║
echo  ║    ALT 200 ╚ (lower left corner)     ║
echo  ║                                      ║
echo  ║    ALT 188 ╝ (lower right corner)    ║
echo  ║                                      ║
echo  ╚══════════════════════════════════════╝
echo.
```

```
echo.
echo   end of GF_CHAR.BAT
C:\BATS\TEST>
```

To create the top line of the box, type **echo**, followed by three spaces, Alt-201, then a few dozen Alt-205 characters, then Alt-187, and finally Enter. To create the first blank line within the box, type **echo**, followed by three spaces, Alt-186, then a few dozen spaces, then Alt-186, and finally Enter. Continue this procedure, typing text amongst the spaces to create your message. Finish the box with Alt-200, a set of Alt-205 characters, and Alt-188.

Listing 10.31 shows how to make BEEP.BAT, a batch file that beeps. If this seems trivial, you will be surprised at its utility once you use it.

Listing 10.31. ***BEEP.BAT Rings Your Bell***

```
C:\BATS\TEST> copy con: beep.bat
@echo off
echo ^G
echo ^G^Z
        1 File(s) copied

C:\BATS\TEST> type beep.bat
```

You can enter Ctrl-G in one of two ways, depending on the design of your text editor. Either hold down the Alt key and type **007**, or hold down the Ctrl key and type **g** (Ctrl-G). You can experiment with other graphics characters for other effects. (See Chapter 9, "Creating a Text File.")

Using the REM Command to Describe a Batch File

The REM command directs PC DOS to skip over the REM line. Use the REM command to enter comments that explain the purpose of your batch file.

If your batch files are short and the instructions obvious, you will be tempted to skip the step of using the REM command for documentation. Watch out. This is a bad habit. What is obvious to you may not be obvious to someone else.

If you cultivate the habit of documenting your batch files, using REM will be second nature. If your habit is to skip the documentation step, the job will seem like a chore and you will tend to forget it. Later on, even you may be mystified by the contents of a batch file that once seemed crystal clear.

The IF Command Sets a Condition

Because batch files work automatically, you need some protection from runaway commands. For instance, MOVIT.BAT will blindly copy whatever is first specified on the command line to whatever is specified second, and then blindly erase the first. If you make a mistake, MOVIT will obey your command. The IF command lets you build some protection into your batch files.

To use the IF command, combine it with other text to form an **IF state-**

ment. Put the IF statement at the beginning of a line, followed by another command.

The IF statement acts as a filter or guard to enable conditionally a command that follows on the same line. If the condition of the IF statement is met, then PC DOS will run the command that follows. If the IF statement is not met, then PC DOS will ignore the balance of the line and proceed to execute the next line.

An IF statement consists of the IF command followed by an expression that uses one of three types of operators: the word EXIST, the symbol ==, and the word ERRORLEVEL. Each of these IF operators works differently.

IF a File EXISTs, Then the Command Operates

You may want the operation of a batch file command to be dependent on whether a certain file exists. For instance, MOVIT.BAT will copy whatever you specify as the first parameter to whatever you specify as the second parameter, and then blindly erase the first. If a file with the same name as the second parameter exists, you may not want the COPY command to overwrite it. You can use the IF EXIST expression to make the operation of a command dependent on the existence of a particular file.

The EXIST operator works with the IF command and a file name. When PC DOS encounters an IF statement such as `if exist cl.bat type cl.bat`, it looks for the specified file, CL.BAT. If PC DOS finds CL.BAT, it will execute the TYPE command that follows on the same line.

Make sure that you spell out the entire file specification. PC DOS will search only the current directory or whatever directory path you include as part of the filespec. Listing 10.32 shows a simple use of an IF EXIST statement.

Listing 10.32. *WHAT_IF.BAT, a Simple IF EXIST Demo*

```
C:\BATS\TEST> type whatif.bat
@echo off
rem  This is WHATIF.BAT (IF EXIST statement with one variable)
cls
echo.
if exist %1 echo %1 exists!
C:\BATS\TEST> whatif whatif.bat
```

WHATIF.BAT turns ECHO OFF and includes a REM statement. It clears the screen, generates a blank line, and then presents an IF EXIST statement that uses replaceable parameters. If you type `whatif whatif`, PC DOS will interpret the IF EXIST statement to mean "IF there EXISTs a file specified as `whatif.bat`, then ECHO `whatif.bat exists!`" Listing 10.33 shows how to use an IF EXIST statement to improve the MOVIT.BAT file.

Listing 10.33. *Enhancing MOVIT.BAT with IF EXIST*

```
C:\BATS\TEST> type movit.bat
copy %1 %2
erase %1
C:\BATS\TEST> copy con: move.bat
```

```
@echo off
rem MOVE.BAT checks to see if a file named %2 exists.
rem If so, MOVE.BAT provides a warning and an option to terminate
if exist %2 echo A file named %2 exists.
if exist %2 echo Do you want to overwrite %2?
if exist %2 echo Press Ctrl-C to abort or
if exist %2 pause
copy %1 %2
erase %1^Z
        1 File(s) copied

C:\BATS\TEST> type move.bat
```

The first part of Listing 10.33 shows the contents of MOVIT.BAT, which copies a file specified by the first parameter to whatever is specified by the second parameter. If the second parameter specifies a file that exists, MOVIT.BAT will overwrite it with the contents of the first file.

In MOVE.BAT, an IF EXIST statement will prevent a blind overwrite, letting you choose to overwrite it or not.

The first IF statement in MOVE.BAT is `if exist %2 echo A file named %2 exists`. PC DOS executes this line by examining the IF statement `if exist %2` and searching for a file specification that matches the second parameter on the command line (`%2`).

If PC DOS does not find a file specified by `%2`, it will ignore the ECHO statement and begin to execute the next line, `if exist %2 echo Do you want to overwrite %2?`. Similarly, if PC DOS cannot find a match for the second parameter, it will also ignore the balance of that line and move on.

The effect is that if the second parameter specifies an existing file, MOVE.BAT will execute the commands on all lines that begin with `if exist %2` and ECHO the warning, letting the user choose to abort the operation with Ctrl-C or continue. If there is no existing file specification that matches `%2`, PC DOS will ignore all lines that begin `if exist %2` and will execute the last two lines, `copy %1 %2` and `erase %1`.

Notice that MOVE.BAT does not include a CLS command. The reason is that you may want to use MOVE.BAT as you refer to an existing screen display.

Tip

Testing for Hidden Files with IF EXIST

You can use the IF EXIST statement to test for hidden files. For example, type `if exist ibmsys.com ...` to see if the PC DOS operating system is on a disk.

IF a Text String Matches, Then a Command Operates

You may want to match a text string with one of the command-line parameters, letting a match enable a command. To do this, create an IF expression using the IF command with two equal signs typed together (==).

As an example, the statement `IF %1 == Dave PROMPT $p$ Dave $g $` will try to match the first parameter with the text string `Dave`. If the match is successful, PC DOS will carry out the PROMPT command; if not, PC DOS will move to the next line.

The match must be exact. If Dave types `dave` or `DAVE`, PC DOS will reject the match. You may have to enter several lines that contain alternative spellings.

Caution

Omitting Parameters May Halt a Batch File
Sometimes, the user may not enter any parameters at all. If the PC DOS command requires parameters to operate, it will not be able to interpret the line and will generate an error message, halting your batch file.

If you have a reason to identify a missing or nonexistent parameter, you must create an IF statement that will accept a successful match. But matching a nonexistent parameter to a nonexistent text string requires some trickery. Remember that PC DOS treats a parameter as a text string, substituting it wherever it finds the replaceable parameter in your batch file.

Tip

Detecting a Nonexistent Parameter
Type a valid text character followed by the replaceable parameter. Then type `==` and type the same text character on the other side of the `==` to test the match. For example, type `!%1 == !` (the `!` is a valid text character).

If the user has included a parameter, PC DOS will substitute it, and the expression will not match. Only if the user types in nothing will both sides of the == signs match, and voila: you have detected nothing. Very useful.

Listing 10.34 shows how to create an IF == statement that lets you enable a command if the user has not entered a parameter on the command line.

Listing 10.34. ***Detecting a Missing Parameter***

```
C:\BATS\TEST> type catch0.bat
@echo off
rem CATCHO.BAT detects a missing parameter
echo.
if !%1 == ! echo No parameter entered
echo.
if %1! == ! echo No parameter entered
echo.
echo CATCHO.BAT is done
C:\BATS\TEST>
```

The two significant lines in CATCH0.BAT begin with `if !%1 == !` and `if %1! == !`. Both lines work in the same way. If the user enters no parameter, PC DOS will substitute nothing for `%1`, in which case `! == !` is a match and PC DOS will execute the ECHO command.

If the user enters a parameter, then neither IF statement will match. PC DOS will skip the lines without executing either of the ECHO commands and will finish by executing the last two lines. Listing 10.35 shows how to use an IF == statement to change the prompt for `Janice`.

Listing 10.35. *Changing the Prompt for Janice*

```
C:\BATS\TEST> type janice.bat
@echo off
rem JANICE.BAT requires one parameter.
rem If the command line parameter is any spelling of janice,
rem JANICE.BAT will set the prompt to reflect the current PATH
rem followed by Janice  >  and a space character.
if %1 == janice prompt $p$  Janice  $g $
if %1 == Janice prompt $p$  Janice  $g $
if %1 == JANICE prompt $p$  Janice  $g $
if !%1 == ! echo Please enter your name.
C:\BATS\TEST> janice janice
```

The first line turns the ECHO setting to OFF. The next three lines compare `%1` to each of the three likely spellings—`janice`, `Janice`, and `JANICE`. The prompt command is the same for all three lines. If Janice enters her name, PC DOS will alter the prompt.

If the user enters anything else, the first tests for Janice will not match. If the user enters no parameter, then the last line will match `!%1 == !` and enable the ECHO command `Please enter your name.`

If the parameter is anything else, no line will match, and the batch file will complete without executing any commands.

Check Completion with IF ERRORLEVEL

The IF ERRORLEVEL expression will make a command operation depend on a special value stored in memory known as *ERRORLEVEL*. Some programs are designed to record their success or failure by entering a number into the ERRORLEVEL memory location.

The ERRORLEVEL value is 1 byte in size, and it can reflect a value from 0 to 255. Generally, a 0 value indicates success, and any other value indicates failure. There are a variety of reasons why a program might not successfully complete its mission. The range of ERRORLEVEL values from 1 to 255 lets a program reflect the reason for failure, or at least provide a clue.

Not all programs set the ERRORLEVEL value. Of those that do, each does so according to its own design. Table 10.3 shows which PC DOS external commands set the ERRORLEVEL value and why.

An IF ERRORLEVEL statement specifies a number from 0 to 255. If the ERRORLEVEL value equals or exceeds the number specified in the IF ERRORLEVEL statement, PC DOS will enable the command. If the ERRORLEVEL value is less than the number specified in the IF ERRORLEVEL statement, PC DOS will move to the next line.

For example, when PC DOS encounters the statement `if errorlevel 1 echo Help!`, it will check the ERRORLEVEL value and display `Help!` if the ERRORLEVEL value is 1 or greater. In other words, only if the ERRORLEVEL value is 0 will PC DOS ignore the `echo Help!` command.

Some "third party" programs (from manufacturers other than IBM) set the ERRORLEVEL value to provide a clue to various failure conditions. Look in the software documentation or call the manufacturer's support service to find the meanings of the ERRORLEVEL values.

Table 10.3. ***PC DOS Commands and ERRORLEVEL Settings***

Command (PC DOS Version)	ERRORLEVEL Settings	
BACKUP	0	Normal
(2.0 to 4)	1	No files match specifications
	2	File sharing contention
	3	Ctrl-Break or Ctrl-C termination
	4	Unknown error caused termination
FORMAT	0	Normal
(3.2 to 4)	3	Ctrl-Break or Ctrl-C termination
	4	Unknown error caused termination
	5	Fixed disk N termination
GRAFTABL	0	Normal code page installation
(3.3 to 4)	1	Previous code page installed
	2	No previous code page installed
	3	Invalid parameter
	4	PC DOS version does not match
KEYB	0	Normal
(3.3 to 4)	1	Invalid code number, page, specification
	2	Invalid definition file
	3	Driver not loaded
	4	CON: device not found
	5	Specified code page not prepared
	6	Invalid translation table
REPLACE	0	Normal
(3.2 to 4)	1	Ctrl-Break or Ctrl-C termination
	2	No files match specification
	3	Invalid PATH specification
	5	Denied access to file
	8	Insufficient memory
	11	Invalid command line
	15	Invalid drive specification
	22	PC DOS version does not match
RESTORE	0	Normal
(2.0 to 4)	1	No files match specifications
	2	File sharing contention
	3	Ctrl-Break or Ctrl-C termination
	4	Unknown error caused termination
XCOPY	0	Normal
(3.2)	1	No files match specification
	3	Ctrl-Break or Ctrl-C termination
	4	Unknown error caused termination

EXIT CODE is a term sometimes used to refer to the ERRORLEVEL value that a program records; the meanings are identical.

To use an IF ERRORLEVEL statement properly, you have to know what the various ERRORLEVEL values signify and then create your IF ERRORLEVEL statement to enable a command that is appropriate.

Also, you should remember that the IF ERRORLEVEL statement will be satisfied if the value in memory is equal to or greater than the value specified in the IF ERRORLEVEL statement. In other words, when PC DOS encounters the statement `if errorlevel 1 dir`, it will run the DIR command if the ERRORLEVEL value is 1 or higher. Listing 10.36 shows how to enter several IF ERRORLEVEL statements in a batch file.

Listing 10.36. ***Using a Hierarchy of ERRORLEVELs***

```
C:\BATS\TEST> copy con: xcheck.bat
@echo off
@rem XCHECK.BAT runs the XCOPY command and checks ERRORLEVEL
xcopy %1 %2
if ERRORLEVEL 4 echo Something is wrong, please fix
if ERRORLEVEL 3 echo Ctrl-C termination: try again?
if ERRORLEVEL 1 echo File(s) not found
if ERRORLEVEL 0 echo Success!^Z
        1 File(s) copied

C:\BATS\TEST> type xcheck.bat
```

The first command in XCHECK.BAT is to run `xcopy %1 %2`. After the XCOPY program is done, PC DOS checks the ERRORLEVEL value. If it is 4 or greater, PC DOS enacts `echo Something is wrong, please fix`. If the ERRORLEVEL value is less than 4, PC DOS skips the balance of that line.

In either case, PC DOS goes to the next line. If the ERRORLEVEL value is 3 or greater, PC DOS will enact `echo Ctrl-C termination: try again?`

Notice that if the ERRORLEVEL value is 4 or greater, it is also greater than 3, 1, or 0. So if the ERRORLEVEL value is 4, PC DOS will run all lines in the batch file. This is a clumsy situation that can be remedied with an IF NOT statement. If the ERRORLEVEL is 3, PC DOS will not enact the command for ERRORLEVEL 4.

IF NOT You may want to enable a command only if a file does not exist, or if two text strings don't match, or if the ERRORLEVEL value is not greater than a particular number. In that case, begin the line with an IF NOT statement.

To create an IF NOT statement, use the NOT command immediately after IF and before the balance of the statement. For example, `if not exist %2 copy %1 %2` enables the COPY command only if a file specified by `%2` does not exist. Listing 10.37 shows how to use an IF NOT statement to enhance MOVE.BAT as MOV12.BAT.

Listing 10.37. ***Protecting against File Overwrite with IF NOT***

```
C:\BATS\TEST> copy con: mov12.bat
@echo off
if %1! == ! echo Please specify a file.
if not exist %1 echo %1 not found, please check
if exist %2 echo.
if exist %2 echo %2 exists! Do you want to overwrite %2?
```

```
if exist %2 echo To abort MOV12.BAT, enter Ctrl-C
if exist %2 echo.
if exist %2 echo If you wish to overwrite %2
if exist %2 pause
copy %1 %2
if exist %2 erase %1
rem MOV12.BAT checks that there is at least one parameter and
rem that the first parameter specifies an existing file,
rem and checks for an existing file that matches %2,
rem giving the user the option to overwrite or terminate^Z
        1 File(s) copied

C:\BATS\TEST> type mov12.bat
```

If the user forgets to specify any parameters at all in MOV12.BAT, the first line will match `%1! == !` and PC DOS will echo a reminder. If there are no parameters, PC DOS will skip the balance of the IF statements—no files have been specified—and the COPY command will display the message `invalid parameters`.

If there is no file name that matches `%1`, PC DOS will echo `%1 not found, please check` and move to the next line.

If there is an existing file with a name that matches `%2`, PC DOS will echo the fact, letting the user abort or continue. Otherwise, PC DOS will skip to the COPY and ERASE commands. Notice that the REM statements are grouped at the end of the file.

The Truth about IF and IF NOT

Table 10.4 compares the results of the two commands `move12 cl.bat` and `move12` for an IF statement and a comparable IF NOT statement. In the first case, `move12 cl.bat` substitutes `cl.bat` for the %1 replaceable parameter. In the second place, `move12` substitutes nothing for the %1 replaceable parameter.

The condition in the IF statement `if !cl.bat == !` is false, but its counterpart, `if ! == !`, is true. The condition in the IF NOT statement is reversed, so that `if not !cl.bat == !` is true, and its counterpart, `if not ! == !`, is false. In other words, inserting NOT in an IF condition reverses its effect: if the condition `! == !` is true, the condition `not ! == !` is false.

Table 10.5 shows how the NOT command affects IF ERRORLEVEL statements. It compares IF NOT ERRORLEVEL statements with their IF ERRORLEVEL equivalents.

Adding Choices with the GOTO Command

PC DOS generally operates on your batch files by attempting to execute each line in order, beginning with the first line, then the second line, then the third, and so on throughout the batch file.

The GOTO command lets you design batch files so that PC DOS can skip over groups of lines and even return to reexecute a line or a group of lines several times, depending on your design.

Table 10.4. ***Comparing IF and IF NOT Statements***

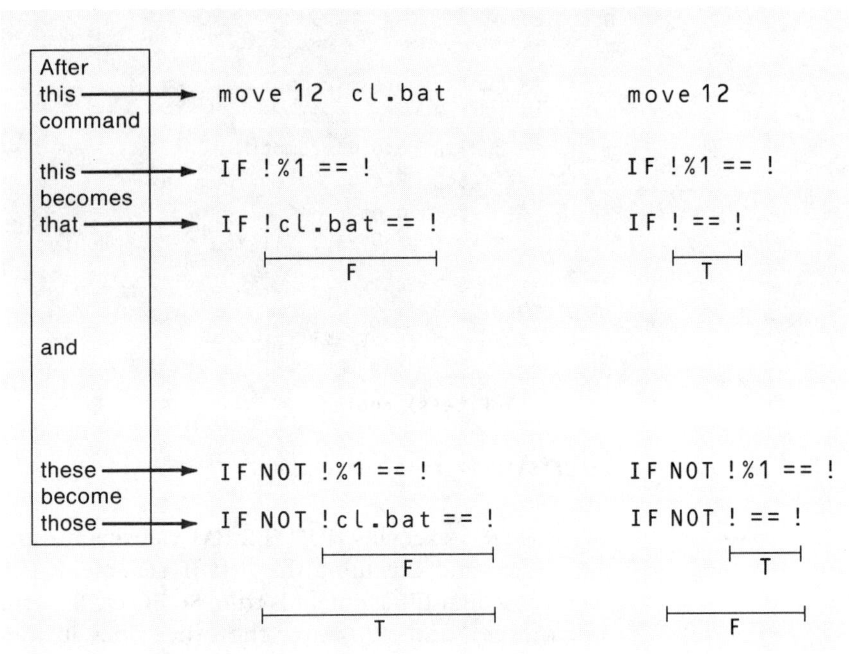

Table 10.5. ***IF and IF NOT ERRORLEVEL Equivalences***

IF NOT ERRORLEVEL	Equivalent IF ERRORLEVEL
IF NOT ERRORLEVEL = 255 *xxx*	IF ERROR LEVEL= 0 to 254
IF NOT ERRORLEVEL = 5 *xxx*	IF ERRORLEVEL = 0 to 4
IF NOT ERRORLEVEL = 1 *xxx*	IF ERRORLEVEL = 0
IF NOT ERRORLEVEL = 0 *xxx*	IF ERRORLEVEL = 1 to 255

GOTO Uses Labels

To use the GOTO command to jump to another line, you must identify that line with a label. When you use the GOTO command with that label, you direct PC DOS to jump to and execute that line and the following lines.

A *label* is a text string that begins with a colon and is located at the head of a line. You can choose any valid text string for a label. PC DOS will recognize only the first eight characters. If you wish, you can create a label with more than eight characters. If you have more than one label in your batch file, be sure that the first eight letters of each label make up a unique name.

You can use the GOTO command to jump to a label that is located either before or after the line containing the GOTO command. Listing 10.37 shows how to use the GOTO command to skip other statements.

Listing 10.37. *Hunter Gets a Prompt*

```
C:\BATS\TEST> copy con: password.bat
@echo off
cls
if %1 == hunter goto mkprompt
if %1 == Hunter goto mkprompt
if %1 == HUNTER goto mkprompt
if !%1 == ! echo Please enter your name.
if !%1 == ! goto done
if not !%1 == ! echo Hey, %1! You're not Hunter!
goto done
:mkprompt
prompt $p$  Hunter  $g $
:done^Z
        1 File(s) copied

C:\BATS\TEST> type hunter.bat
```

PC DOS executes HUNTER.BAT as usual, turning ECHO OFF, clearing the screen, and executing the first IF statement. If Hunter types `password hunter`, the first IF statement is true. So PC DOS executes the rest of the line, `goto mkprmpt`, and skips over the other lines in the batch file to the line containing `:mkprmpt`.

If Hunter types `password Hunter` or `password HUNTER`, PC DOS will test the IF statements and ultimately jump to the `:mkprmpt` line.

If someone types `password` with no parameters, PC DOS will try out each line, finally test `if !%1 == !` as true, and execute the ECHO command `Please enter your name.` PC DOS will execute the next line, `if !%1 == !`, which will also test true, enabling the command `goto done`. PC DOS will skip all other lines and GOTO the line labeled `:done` and finish.

If someone uses any other name with PASSWORD.BAT, PC DOS will try each IF == statement until it reaches `if not !%1 == !` and then ECHO `Hey, %1! You're not Hunter!` The next line, `goto done`, will direct PC DOS to skip over the rest of the batch file to the last line.

Caution

Line Order Can Be Important
The order in which the lines occur in batch files is sometimes critical. You cannot move the line `if not !%1 == !` to the beginning of the file because it will enable the command `echo Hey, %1! You're not Hunter!` for every parameter, including variations of Hunter. However, you can move up either of the two lines that begin `if !%1 == ! ....`

Speeding Over REM Lines

You can use the GOTO command to skip over REM lines. This prevents PC DOS from taking the time to read each REM line. PC DOS takes a finite amount of time to read a line in a batch file. The longer the line, the more time it takes PC DOS to read it (and REM lines are usually long). Listing 10.38 uses the GOTO command to jump over REM lines and to restrict the output to the appropriate ERRORLEVEL.

Listing 10.38. *XCHECK.BAT Skips REMS with a GOTO Command*

```
C:\BATS\TEST> copy con: xcheck.bat
@echo off
goto xcp
rem The new improved XCHECK.BAT uses the GOTO command
rem to skip over REM lines and skip false ERRORLEVEL tests.
:xcp
xcopy %1 %2
if ERRORLEVEL 4 echo Something is wrong, please fix
if ERRORLEVEL 4 goto done
if ERRORLEVEL 3 echo Ctrl-C termination: try again?
if ERRORLEVEL 3 goto done
if ERRORLEVEL 1 echo File(s) not found
if ERRORLEVEL 1 goto done
if ERRORLEVEL 0 echo Success!
:done^Z
        1 File(s) copied

C:BATS\TEST> type xcheck.bat
```

An ERRORLEVEL of 4 will enable the first ECHO message and the first `goto done` line, directing PC DOS to skip the other lines and finish. An ERRORLEVEL of 3 will force PC DOS to skip over the ERRORLEVEL 4 lines, enable the ERRORLEVEL 3 lines, and skip to done. The result is that an ERRORLEVEL value will generate a single appropriate message.

Understanding Loops

The term *loop* refers to the process of recycling the same commands. As you will soon see, you can use the GOTO command to create a loop by jumping back to a label. Such loops can be very handy, for instance, to copy or print many files or to automate repetitive tasks. The upcoming listings offer you several useful batch file loops.

Not all loops are useful ones, however, and not all are created deliberately. Because batch files allow a great deal of automation, you can create loops sometimes without realizing it. One such loop is an endless loop, the topic of the next discussion.

Endless Loops

A loop that repeats itself forever is called an *endless loop*. Endless loops are sometimes useful, but often they are a nuisance. Listing 10.39 shows two examples of tiny endless loops that recycle forever until you interrupt them with Ctrl-C.

Listing 10.39. *REPEAT.BAT and REPEETER.BAT—Endless Loops*

```
C:\BATS\TEST> copy con: repeat.bat
repeat^Z
        1 File(s) copied

C:\BATS\TEST> copy con: repeeter.bat
```

```
:repeeter
goto repeeter
^Z
        1 File(s) copied

C:\BATS\TEST> type repeeter.bat
```

REPEAT.BAT contains a single line, **repeat**. When PC DOS executes this line, it calls REPEAT.BAT and executes itself over and over.

REPEETER uses the GOTO command to direct PC DOS to jump to the line labeled **:repeeter** and then reexecute the GOTO command over and over.

As displayed, REPEAT.BAT doesn't work and REPEETER.BAT works too well. The placement of the Ctrl-Z is important. In REPEAT.BAT, the Ctrl-Z immediately follows the command, placing an end-of-file marker between the **repeat** and the carriage return (press Enter) that directs PC DOS to accept the command line. REPEETER.BAT won't accept Ctrl-C or Ctrl-Break, so the only way to break the loop is to press Ctrl-Alt-Del or push the hardware reset button. Listing 10.40 in the following discussion shows how to create a loop to print files.

Useful Batch File Loops

The key to using a loop is to control it. One way to break a loop when a task is complete is to embed IF statements to test for conditions such as the existence of files or parameters. Let the IF statements control GOTO commands that force PC DOS to jump out of the loop sequence.

Suppose that you include the statement **if !%1 == ! goto done** followed by a SHIFT command within a loop. When the parameters have shifted out, the IF statement will force a jump to the line labeled **done**. Listing 10.40, QPRN.BAT, shows how to make an automatic print command and how to use multiple parameters with the TYPE command. Listing 10.41, CPA.BAT, copies files to the A drive, recording any invalid parameters specified on the command line.

Listing 10.40. ***QPRN.BAT Quick Printer and TYPEM.BAT***

```
C:\BATS\TEST> type qprn.bat
@echo off
:repeat
echo. > prn:
echo  The name of this file is %1 > prn:
echo. > prn:
copy %1 prn:
echo. > prn:
echo. > prn:
shift
if %1K == K goto done
goto repeat
:done
```

```
C:\BATS\TEST> qprn move12.bat move.bat movit.bat
C:\BATS\TEST> type typem.bat
@echo off
goto start
rem TYPEM.BAT allows you to use multiple parameters on the
rem command line. Enter TYPEM FILE1 FILE2 FILE3 and so on.
rem TYPEM.BAT will shift through all parameters until the
rem IF statement detects no more parameters and executes
rem the GOTO DONE command, thus breaking the loop.
:start
type %1
shift
if %1x == x goto done
goto start
:done
C:\BATS\TEST> typem qprn.bat typem.bat
```

In Listing 10.40, QPRN.BAT uses redirection to echo blank lines and the name of each file to the printer. It then uses the COPY command to print the file and issues two more blank lines to the printer. The SHIFT command rotates the parameters on the command line. The IF statement directs PC DOS that if no parameters remain to skip over the `goto repeat` statement and jump to the `done` label. If a parameter remains, the IF statement fails, and PC DOS executes the next line, `goto repeat`. Then PC DOS jumps up to the `:repeat` label and recycles through the commands until no parameters remain.

TYPEM.BAT uses a loop to recycle from the `start` label to the `goto start` statement. The SHIFT command rotates multiple parameters. As long as a parameter fills the `%1` spot, the IF statement fails. When all parameters are shifted, the IF statement tests true, and executes the `goto done` line.

Listing 10.41. ***Copying Files to the A Drive with CPA.BAT***

```
C:\BATS\TEST> type cpa.bat
@echo off
echo CPA.BAT will copy all specified files to the A: drive
:start
if !%1 == ! goto done
if not exist %1 goto no1
:DOIT
copy %1 A:
shift
goto start
:no1
echo The file %1 does not exist
if not exist badspec echo. > badspec
echo The file %1 does not exist >> badspec
echo. >> badspec
echo. >> badspec
goto start
```

```
REM  This REM line will never be displayed.
:done
if exist badspec echo Check BADSPEC!
echo  No more filenames. CPA.BAT is done.
C:\BATS\TEST> cpa cl.bat d?.bat cld.bat cp.bat
```

CPA.BAT, as shown in Listing 10.41, makes a copy on the A drive of all files specified as command-line parameters (the last line shows an example). The listing shows how to use multiple labels with GOTO commands to respond to varying conditions as the batch file loops through its commands.

As long as valid parameters remain, CPA.BAT will cycle through the main body of the loop, from `:start` to the first occurrence of `goto start`. An invalid parameter will cause a jump to `:no1`, where the block of instructions will record the invalid parameter in a file named BADSPEC and then jump back to `:start`. When the SHIFT command has rotated through all parameters, the `if !%1 == ! goto done` statement will jump to `:done`.

Notice that the label `:DOIT` is not used, and does no harm other than adding a tiny time delay. Also notice that because the REM line occurs right after `goto start` and before `:done`, PC DOS will jump around it without ever executing it. Good thing it isn't an important instruction! Be careful how and where you place labels.

Creating a Timer

It takes PC DOS a finite amount of time to execute a command. Depending on the speed of your machine, it may take a tenth of a second or more for PC DOS to read a line containing the ECHO command followed by 60 characters. A batch file that contains many such lines multiplies the time it takes PC DOS to complete the batch file.

Other commands take longer. Redirecting the output of an ECHO command to a new file may take from one to three or four seconds. Erasing a file may also take up to a few seconds. Listing 10.42 shows how to combine such commands within a loop to create a rough timer.

Listing 10.42. ***EGG.BAT—A Variable Timer***

```
C:\BATS\TEST> type egg.bat
if exist %1 goto abort1
if exist %2 goto abort2
if exist %3 goto abort3
if !%1 == ! goto done
copy con: %1
:more
type %1 > %1.%1
dir *.* > nul:
if !%2 == ! goto onedown
:two
type %1 > %1.%2
type %1.%1 >> %1.%2
type %1 > %2
```

```
type %1.%1 >> %2
type %1.%2 >> %2
type %2 > %2.%1
type %2 >> %2.%2
type %2.%1 >> %2.%2
dir *.* > nul:
if !%3 == ! goto twodown
:three
type %1 > %1.%3
type %1.%1 >> %1.%3
type %1.%2 >> %1.%3
type %1.%3 >> %2
REM and so on
dir *.* > nul:
:threedown
dir *.* > nul:
erase %1.%3
dir *.* > nul:
:twodown
dir *.* > nul:
erase %2.%2
dir *.* > nul:
erase %2.%1
dir *.* > nul:
erase %2
dir *.* > nul:
erase %1.%2
dir *.* > nul:
:onedown
dir *.* > nul:
erase %1.%1
dir *.* > nul:
erase %1
dir *.* > nul:
if %1 == s shift
if %1 == s goto more
if %1 == t shift
if %1 == t goto more
if %1 == u shift
if %1 == u goto more
goto done
:abort1
echo  %1 exists! EGG.BAT will not overwrite %1!
:abort2
echo  %2 exists! EGG.BAT will not overwrite %2!
:abort3
echo  %3 exists! EGG.BAT will not overwrite %3!
:done
echo  Time's up!
C:\BATS\TEST> egg s 1 2 3
```

You can continue to add statements and loops to EGG.BAT. Notice that the SHIFT statements multiply the time it takes EGG.BAT to complete, until the number of parameters is fewer than three. Listing 10.43 shows how to make an endless loop that is a surprisingly attractive "screen-saver" and that can repeat a reminder message.

Listing 10.43. ***ORION.BAT—A Screen-Saver and Reminder***

```
C:\BATS\TEST> type orion.bat
@ECHO OFF
CLS
REM   This is ORION.BAT
REM      It demonstrates a simple loop with many uses.
REM      You can run ORION.BAT as an attractive endless
REM      loop that acts as a "screen-saver" and contains
REM      a reminder message of your choice.
ECHO.
REM      It can be used as a quick and easy note pad by
REM      creating a little bat that will call up EDLIN
REM      or any other editor and automatically load the
REM      current ORION.BAT from the BATS directory.
ECHO.
REM      (Send the backup file, ORION.BAK, that the
REM      editor creates to a "lists" directory for safe-
REM      keeping.)
ECHO.
REM      Since the speed of the scrolling is determined by
REM      the spacing of the dots, it is continuously variable.
REM      This mimics the operation of a timer. By including
REM      an IF comparison with an "erase if not zero," a loop
REM      can be made to cycle as many times as needed by
REM      deleting a number of "dummy files." When the
REM      directory is empty, ORION can then sound an alarm
REM      or move on to some other DOS or BAT duty.
ECHO.
REM      ALL NOTES MUST BE ENTERED BELOW THE :REPEAT LABEL
:REPEAT     .
ECHO                              .
ECHO                                                                 .
ECHO      .
ECHO                    .
ECHO                                .
ECHO.
ECHO                                                      .
ECHO.
ECHO                                                                 .
ECHO                                                        .
ECHO                           .
ECHO                                                               .
```

```
ECHO.
ECHO.
ECHO              .
ECHO.
ECHO      .
ECHO.
ECHO          .
ECHO                                        .
ECHO.
ECHO.
ECHO                                           .
ECHO                                  .
ECHO                                        .
ECHO                                                                  .
ECHO                                                           .
ECHO                                                     .
ECHO                                                             .
ECHO.
ECHO.
ECHO            .
ECHO.
ECHO     .
ECHO                               .
ECHO                    .
ECHO.
ECHO                                                     .
ECHO    .
ECHO        .
ECHO                                     .
ECHO.
ECHO           ET PHONE HOME
ECHO                                                    .
GOTO REPEAT
:END
C:\BATS\TEST>
```

Use a text editor to arrange the dots as you like, and add occasional other graphics characters if you wish. Include whatever message you want. When you run ORION.BAT, the lines will scroll over and over in an endless loop, creating the effect of stars. Your message will appear once in every loop. Record how long it takes your message to scroll around to the same position on the screen, and you can use ORION.BAT as the basis for a timer.

A Simple Name and Number Database

Listing 10.44 shows a batch file that creates a simple name and address database.

Listing 10.44. ***ADDADD.BAT Adds a Name and Address to ADDLIST***

```
C:\BATS\TEST> type addadd.bat
@ECHO OFF
CLS
IF EXIST C:\BATS\TEST\%1 GOTO OOPS
REM if not exist C:\bats\test\%1 goto add

:ADD
ECHO  At the prompt, enter the name and address the way that
ECHO  it should appear on an address label. You MUST start
ECHO  and end with a blank line.
ECHO.
ECHO  EXAMPLE
ECHO        (return)     (This is an empty line)
ECHO        FIRSTNAME LASTNAME (return)
ECHO        STREET ADDRESS (return)
ECHO        CITY STATE ZIP (return)
ECHO        (return)     (This is an empty line)
ECHO        (Ctrl-Z)
ECHO.
ECHO  After you enter the name and address,
ECHO  ADDADD.BAT will display the file.
ECHO  Be SURE to check your typing.
ECHO.
COPY CON: %1
TYPE %1
ECHO  Is this correct? If not, press Ctrl-C. If so,
PAUSE
COPY %1 C:\BATS\TEST
TYPE %1 >> C:\BATS\TEST\ADDLIST
ERASE %1

:OOPS
ECHO                              OOPS!
ECHO             ADDADD notes that a file specified as %1
ECHO             already exists.
ECHO.
ECHO             You must add a specifier to the file name.
ECHO.
REM goto dir

:DIR
ECHO Here is the directory listing(s) of %1
DIR C:\BATS\TEST\%1
:END
C:\BATS\TEST>
```

ADDADD.BAT stores names and addresses in a file named ADDLIST. It creates a file and then uses the TYPE >>command to append the contents of that file to the end of ADDLIST, a master list of names and addresses. Finally, ADD.ADD.BAT erases the first file.

You can use the FIND command to search ADDLIST for a name and address. The COPY or TYPE command can send the contents of ADDLIST to the printer to make labels. With a similar batch file, you can create a name and telephone number list.

Expanding Choices with the FOR Command

If you want to display each batch file in your \BATS\TEST directory, you can get a directory listing and then use the TYPE command for each file. However, that is repetitious, since you cannot use the TYPE command with multiple parameters. As an alternative, you could create a batch file that combined the TYPE command with a replaceable parameter and the SHIFT command, but you would still have to enter the names of all the files on the command line.

A FOR statement can automate the whole task. A valid FOR statement combines the FOR command with several other new elements, IN, (*set*), and DO. The essence of a FOR statement is: FOR every item IN a set (or group), DO perform a command on that item.

If you apply a FOR statement to the preceding problem of how to display all the batch files in the \BATS\TEST directory, the result is: FOR every file IN the \BATS\TEST directory, DO use the TYPE command to TYPE each file.

The FOR Statement Syntax

A FOR statement takes the following general form:

```
FOR %%a in (set) do command %%a
```

You can divide the FOR statement into three parts: `FOR %%a`, `in (set)`, and `do command %%a`.

The odd-looking `%%a` character is called the *dummy parameter*. You can use any letter from the alphabet—%%b, %%t, %%s, %%p will do as well. The dummy parameter represents each of the members of the set. The phrase `FOR %%a` means *for each individual member . . . (of the following set).*

The key part is `in (set)`. The `set` is usually two or more items of a similar type (nearly always files). You can identify the files in \BATS\TEST as a set, also all files specified as \BATS\BAKS*.BAK, or the three file groups specified as \BATS\TEST*.BATS, \BATS\TRIAL*.BATS, and \BATS\BAKS*.BAK.

The last part of the FOR statement is `do command %%a`. The meaning is to perform the command on each member of the set.

The following FOR statement will display each batch file in the \BATS\TEST directory:

```
for %%a in (\bats\test\*.bat) do type %%a
```

PC DOS will run the TYPE command to type the contents of every batch file in the \BATS\TEST directory. In Listing 10.45, TYPM.BAT types multiple files in the \BATS\TEST directory. In Listing 10.46, a FOR statement is used to first copy and then erase .BAK files.

Listing 10.45. ***Typing Multiple Files with TYPM.BAT***

```
C:\BATS\TEST> type typm.bat
@ECHO OFF
CLS
IF .%1==. GOTO EMPTY
FOR %%x IN (%1 %2 %3 %4 %5) DO TYPE %%x
GOTO END
:EMPTY
ECHO TYPM.BAT DEMO REQUIRES AT LEAST ONE PARAMETER
:END
```

Listing 10.46. ***Copying and Erasing .BAK Files with MOVFOR.BAT***

```
C:\BATS\TEST> type movfor.bat
@ECHO OFF
CLS
ECHO.
FOR %%x IN (\BATS\TEST\*.BAK) DO COPY %%x \BATS\BAKS
ECHO.
FOR %%x IN (\BATS\TEST\*.BAK) DO ERASE %%x
ECHO.
:END
C:\BATS\TEST>
```

Tip

Using a FOR Statement Outside of a Batch File
You can enter the FOR command at the system prompt, but don't use double percent signs as the dummy parameter. For example, `for %i in (\BATS\BAKS\*.bat) do type %i`.

Using Wildcards in a Set

Here are examples of FOR statements using wildcards:

```
for %%a in (\bats\test\*.bat \bats\baks\*.*) do type %%a

for %%b in (\bats\test\*.bat \bats\baks\*.*) do comp %%b

for %cc in (\bats\test\*.bat \bats\baks\*.*) do dir %%c

for %%d in (\bats\test\*.bat) do if exist \bats\baks\%%d erase %%d

for %%a in (*.*) do if exist B:%%a echo %%a is on this disk too.

for %%b in (%1 %2 %3 %4) do type %%b

for %%c in (*.*) do if exist C:%%c copy C:%%c A: /v

for %%g in (*.*) do if not exist \bats\baks\%%g copy %%g
\bats\baks
```

Caution

Don't Use GOTO, Redirection, or CALL Commands in FOR Statements
Don't use redirection with FOR statements. PC DOS will interpret the dummy parameter as the explicit name of a file rather than operate on the members of the set. Also, don't end a FOR statement with a GOTO or CALL command. The statement will execute one time, then pop to the label or .BAT file, never to return.

Using the CALL Command

You may want to "call" another batch file into operation. If you simply include the name of that batch file as a command, it will call the other batch file, but when that batch file completes, control will return to the PC DOS prompt. That means you have to make the call to another batch file as the last command, as shown in Listing 10.47.

Listing 10.47. ***Calling a Second Batch File***

```
C:\BATS\TEST> type caller
@echo This is CALLER.BAT
@cld
C:\BATS\TEST>
```

If you are writing a batch file for PC DOS 3.3 or 4, you can use the CALL command in your batch files to call another batch file. When the second batch file has executed, control will turn to the first batch file, continuing instructions where it left off, as shown in Listing 10.48.

Listing 10.48. ***Using the CALL Command***

```
C:\BATS\TEST> type callcall.bat
@echo This is CALLCALL.BAT
call cld
@echo Here is CALLCALL.BAT, again
C:\BATS\TEST>
```

Be careful when you call one batch file from another. Including the proper parameters for the "called" batch file may be a problem. There is also the danger that your first batch file can call a second batch file, which inadvertently calls the first batch file, and off they go in an endless loop.

What's Next

Now that you can write batch files, learn more techniques to make your system responsive by reading Chapter 11, "Customizing Your System." Chapter 9, "Creating a Text File," explains the nature of text files and how to create them. Chapter 8, "Advanced Use of the Command Line" teaches how to use redirection, pipes, and filters. Chapter 5, "PC DOS Files," explains types of PC DOS files and how to use them. Chapter 6, "Managing Your Hard Disk," teaches how to use many PC DOS commands to manipulate files and directories.

Key Concepts and Words

Before you read further, use the following list to test your understanding of the concepts and words in this chapter.

- Text files
- Text editor
- Text string
- Delimiter
- Batch file facility
- .BAT
- AUTOEXEC.BAT
- Devices
- EDLIN
- Parameter
- Variable
- Destructive commands
- How programs work
- Reserved device names
- Organizing directories
- Commands
- Command line
- Labels

Chapter 11

Your PC DOS system allows a tremendous amount of flexibility. Not only can you choose from among many video display types, disk drives, printers, memory schemes, and other devices, you also have the largest available number of software application programs of any computer system in history. But the price you pay for this flexibility is that you often have to customize PC DOS especially for each device or software program. With the tricks in this chapter, you can tailor your computer's operations to the needs of your application programs and any special devices. You will learn

- *What to add to your CONFIG.SYS and AUTOEXEC.BAT files to enhance your system performance*
- *How to create fast "virtual disk drives" in memory*
- *About programs that stay in memory while you're running other programs (TSRs)*
- *How to make use of computer memory above the normal 640K limit (EMS)*
- *How to use DEBUG to check or edit programs and create short utilities*
- *How to take a "snapshot" of the contents of your computer's memory*

Chapter 11
Customizing Your System

To customize your system, you must learn about the tools available and how and when to use them. The customization tools can be found in three "toolboxes": your CONFIG.SYS file, your AUTOEXEC.BAT file, and the set of options and features provided with your specific application.

Tools for Tuning Your System

On start-up, PC DOS automatically reads first the CONFIG.SYS file and then the AUTOEXEC.BAT file. In general, these files specify the operation of PC DOS itself. However, they also affect your applications indirectly, since applications call upon PC DOS when they use system resources (such as writing a file to disk). You install optional PC DOS features in your system by adding appropriate statements to these files, using any editor that can handle ordinary text files. (If you don't know how to add statements to a file, see Chapter 7, "Creating Text Files.")

The third set of tools comes with your application, and affects only that application. These tools can involve settings that you put on the command line, in the PC DOS environment, or into a special file that the application reads when starting up.

The best way to become familiar with the CONFIG.SYS and AUTOEXEC.BAT files is to look at an example of each, taken from a working PC DOS system. Your goal will not be to learn all the details about how each statement works, but to familiarize yourself with the kinds of things that you can control by using these files.

The CONFIG.SYS File

The *CONFIG.SYS* (CONFIGure SYStem) file is primarily a list of directives that tells PC DOS whether you want certain features or not, and how much memory to allocate to a given feature. The features you select, with a few exceptions, remain in effect until you next start the system.

PC DOS automatically reads the CONFIG.SYS file each time you start your system. Here is an example of a CONFIG.SYS file:

```
device=c:\dos\xma2ems.sys frame=d000 p254=c000 p255=c400 /x:64
device=c:\sys\dasddrvr.sys
device=c:\sys\ibmcache.sys /e:256
device=c:\mouse1\mouse.sys
device=c:\dos\ansi.sys
lastdrive=e
break=on
buffers=3
files=20
shell=c:\dos\command.com /p /e:256
install=c:\dos\fastopen.exe c:=(50,25)
```

For now, ignore the details and consider the kinds of things that the CONFIG.SYS statements accomplish.

Device Drivers

The statements that begin `device=` are used to load into memory special control programs called *device drivers*. Device drivers make it possible for PC DOS commands and your applications to use the devices connected to your system—such as expanded memory boards, external disk drives, and mice. You can recognize device drivers because their file names end with *.SYS*. When a device driver is loaded into memory, it is hooked into PC DOS. When programs call upon standard PC DOS services to do such tasks as open a file, write data to disk, or read the current mouse position, the device driver intercepts these requests and turns them into specific instructions for the device. In turn, the driver provides information to PC DOS or your application about the current status of the device.

PC DOS has built-in device drivers to handle some standard devices, such as the system clock, the serial and parallel connectors (ports), and the internal disk drives.

As you probably know, PC DOS systems have expansion slots to which you can add expansion cards to control additional disk drives, more memory, printers, modems, and other hardware. PC DOS, like the inside of your computer, has its own "expansion slots" within memory. The DEVICE statement tells PC DOS to load the specified device control program from disk, install it in the next highest available piece of memory, and hook it up so that it can be called on whenever the device is needed. Figure 11.1 shows how this works.

In the sample CONFIG.SYS file shown earlier, the DEVICE statements load a variety of device drivers. In the order they appear in the file, the drivers provide control for the expanded memory board, add a program that fixes a problem with the PS/2 BIOS, install a disk cache (which works somewhat like the disk buffers mentioned earlier), provide a control program allowing some applications to use the mouse, and load the enhanced PC DOS display and keyboard program, ANSI.SYS. Device driver programs are needed only to control specific devices. If you don't have a mouse (or have one but never use

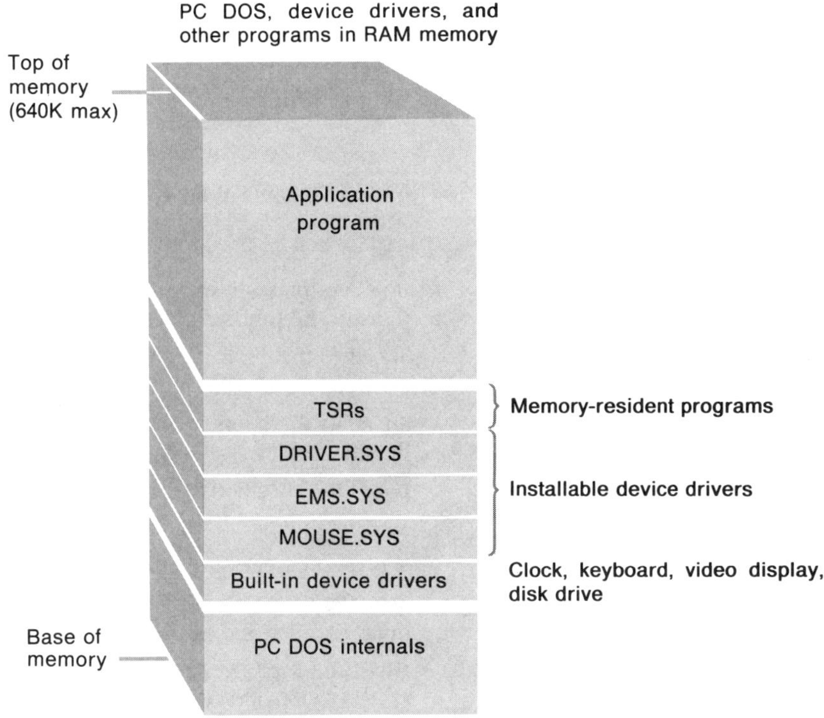

Figure 11.1. ***Installable device drivers in PC DOS.***

it), there is no reason to have a `device=mouse.sys` statement in your CONFIG.SYS file. Although most drivers are quite small as programs go, each one uses some memory that would otherwise be available for your application. ANSI.SYS, for example, uses about 4.5K.

In the sample CONFIG.SYS file, the DEVICE statements have all been put together at the beginning of the list to make it easier to find them. PC DOS loads device drivers in the order that it finds them in the CONFIG.SYS file. A few DEVICE statements depend on some other driver being loaded first, and you should watch for references to this in the documentation. Otherwise, statements in your CONFIG.SYS file can be in any order.

Settings in CONFIG.SYS

With the exception of the INSTALL statement at the end of the file (which will be discussed later), the remaining statements in the CONFIG.SYS file are PC DOS settings. The following box summarizes them. Each setting customizes PC DOS by changing its default behavior (what it will do if you don't provide that setting) or by adding a capability to the basic system. Each setting allocates (reserves) a certain amount of memory to store some information. In the case of the LASTDRIVE and FILES statements, blocks of memory are set aside to hold information about the characteristics of disk drives and files, respectively. The BUFFERS statement specifies the number of buffers that will hold data recently read from disk. The SHELL statement tells PC DOS where to find the COMMAND.COM program needed to interpret and run commands. It also specifies that 256 bytes of memory be set aside to hold the list of labels and information (the environment) mentioned earlier. (In this group of statements, only the BREAK statement is a little different in that it doesn't allocate memory but simply tells PC DOS to check as often as possible to see whether the user has decided to stop a program by pressing Ctrl-Break.)

Elements of the CONFIG.SYS File

The following settings can be used to customize PC DOS:

BREAK	If set on, makes it easier to stop a program by pressing Ctrl-C. Can also be run as a command.
BUFFERS	Specifies the number of memory blocks used to hold data sectors read from disk.
COUNTRY	Specifies the country whose time, date, and numeric formats will be used by PC DOS.
DEVICE	Loads the specified device driver.
FCBS	Sets the number of file control blocks available.
FILES	Sets the number of file handles available.
LASTDRIVE	Specifies the highest drive letter that can be used (thus, the maximum number of disk drives of all types).
SHELL	Gives the location of the command processor (usually COMMAND.COM) and the size of the environment.
STACKS	Sets the number and size of stack frames (used to process interrupts, or signals, from devices).
INSTALL	Loads PC DOS memory-resident commands (FASTOPEN, KEYB, NLSFUNC, and SHARE are supported).
SWITCHES	Treats an enhanced keyboard like a conventional keyboard, for compatibility with older applications.

Version 4

The INSTALL Statement

The final statement, beginning with `install=`, is new with PC DOS 4. It runs one of four PC DOS commands: FASTOPEN, KEYB, NLSFUNC, and SHARE. FASTOPEN allows PC DOS to store information used to locate files (and sectors within files) in memory for fast access. (See Chapter 6, "Managing Your Hard Disk." KEYB and NLSFUNC are discussed in Chapter 13, "International Language Support.") SHARE is loaded automatically by PC DOS 4 if you have established a single disk partition larger than 32MB. It is also used with networks, which are not covered in this book. Any of these four commands can also be run simply by putting the command on a line in the AUTOEXEC.BAT file or on the PC DOS command line, for example:

```
fastopen c:=(50,25)
```

Loading these commands with an INSTALL statement in your CONFIG.SYS file is the preferred method because it allows PC DOS to store the information used by the commands more efficiently in memory, in the same way that it "plugs in" drivers specified in DEVICE statements.

Version 4

The CONFIG.SYS File

If you have installed PC DOS 4, the SELECT program created a CONFIG.SYS file for you, with settings that reflect choices you made during the installation process. For example, the INSTALL statement for the FASTOPEN command is included only if you told SELECT that you want either a "balanced" or a "maximum" workspace for PC DOS. You can see what is in your CONFIG.SYS file by giving the command `type \config.sys`.

If you have followed the instructions in Chapter 12, "Installing a PC DOS System," for installing PC DOS versions earlier than 4, you will have a much shorter CONFIG.SYS file. When you are done with this chapter, you will have added the statements you need to customize your system performance.

The AUTOEXEC.BAT File

The *AUTOEXEC.BAT* (AUTOmatic EXECution, BATch) file is a list of programs that you want to run when you start the system. Here is an example:

```
path c:\dos;c:\mks\bin;c:\wp50;c:\utils;c:\tc
append c:\dos;c:\wp50
set comspec=c:\dos\command.com
set glob=c:\mks\bin\glob.exe
set memo_dir=c:\twg\upcdos\memo
verify off
prompt $p$g
graphics
mode con: delay=1 rate=32
print /d:lpt1:
\memo\memo r
\utils\skn
```

Many of the programs listed in this AUTOEXEC.BAT file are PC DOS commands. The next box lists the commands most commonly used in AUTOEXEC.BAT.

PATH and APPEND (see Chapter 6, "Managing Your Hard Disk") set up lists of directories to be searched automatically for programs or data files, respectively. The next three statements add items, called *variables*, to the environment list by using the SET command. (*Variable* simply means a label that has information associated with it—information that can be changed as desired.)

COMSPEC is a special variable telling PC DOS where to find the COMMAND.COM file. To provide more memory for your application, PC DOS removes most of its own instructions before loading and running a program. After the program has ended, PC DOS reloads the missing instructions from the COMMAND.COM file. PC DOS expects to find COMMAND.COM in the root (highest-level) directory of the disk from which the system was started. If you wish to move COMMAND.COM to another directory, say the \DOS directory, you need a statement such as

```
comspec=c:\dos\command.com
```

GLOB and MEMO are examples of user-defined variables. They don't have any meaning to PC DOS, but they hold paths that are used by applications. The MKS Toolkit, a set of UNIX-like utility programs for PC DOS systems, uses GLOB to hold the path of a utility program that it uses every time you run an MKS command. Memory Mate (a memory-resident, "pop-up" personal database) uses the MEMO variable to tell it where to find its database files. You will learn how to add your own variables to the environment later.

VERIFY is a command that can be turned on or off. When it is on, it tells PC DOS to check all data immediately after storing the data on the disk.

The PROMPT command specifies that the PC DOS prompt will show the current directory as well as the current drive (for example, `C:\DOS>`).

The GRAPHICS command loads a program into memory that can be triggered by pressing the PrtSc key, allowing you to print any graphics image on the screen.

The MODE command has many variations. In the preceding example AUTOEXEC.BAT file, it affects the CON: device (the keyboard part) and controls how soon—and how quickly—a key will repeat once you start to hold it down. This feature is new with PC DOS 4.

The PRINT command loads another program into memory to keep track of one or more files that you want printed, and sends the data to the printer while you run another program.

Elements of the AUTOEXEC.BAT File

The following commands are frequently run from the AUTOEXEC.BAT file:

APPEND	Specifies directories containing data files.
ASSIGN	Has requests for one drive to go to another.
COMSPEC	Specifies the location of COMMAND.COM.
DOSSHELL	Runs the menu-driven user interface for PC DOS 4.
GRAPHICS	Enables printing of graphics from the screen.
JOIN	Accesses a drive through a directory on another drive.
MODE	Controls the screen, keyboard, printer, serial port, or other device.
PATH	Specifies the directories containing programs.
PRINT	Allows you to print data while running your application.
PROMPT	Sets the format for the command prompt.
SET	Sets an environmental variable (such as COMSPEC).
SUBST	Uses a drive letter as shorthand for a path.
VERIFY	Checks each sector written to disk for accuracy.

Note that any other command or program can be run by using its name in the AUTOEXEC.BAT file.

Running Programs

The last two statements in the example AUTOEXEC.BAT file aren't PC DOS commands. They run utility programs, namely Memory Mate and SideKick. You can run any program from your AUTOEXEC.BAT file simply by giving its name and path if it isn't in the starting directory. Be aware, though, that if you put a regular program like dBASE IV in your AUTOEXEC.BAT file, it will take control of the computer as usual, and any commands remaining in AUTOEXEC.BAT won't be run until you leave the program. Thus, any application you want to run at the beginning of *every* session should be placed last in AUTOEXEC.BAT. Memory Mate and SideKick are not regular programs, however. They are TSR, or terminate and stay resident, programs, like the PRINT command. They reserve an area of memory and store their program instructions there, taking up residence in memory. After this happens, they return control to PC DOS, and any following statements in AUTOEXEC.BAT will be executed. When AUTOEXEC.BAT is finished, you can run a regular applications program. Other aspects of TSR programs will be discussed later.

Version 4

The AUTOEXEC.BAT File

If you have installed PC DOS 4, the SELECT program created an AUTOEXEC.BAT file for you, with settings that reflect choices you made during the installation process. For example, the GRAPHICS command is included only if you told SELECT that you want either a "balanced" or a "maximum" workspace for PC DOS. You can see what is in your AUTOEXEC.BAT file by using the command `type \autoexec.bat`.

Compare the AUTOEXEC.BAT file on your system with the example shown. You should be able to recognize most of the settings used. Of course, your AUTOEXEC.BAT may not have programs like Memory Mate or SideKick in it.

If you have followed the instructions in Chapter 12, "Installing a PC DOS System," for installing PC DOS versions earlier than 4, you will have a much shorter AUTOEXEC.BAT file. When you are done with this chapter, you will have added the statements you need to customize your system performance.

Where Do You Go from Here?

As you have seen, there are many ways to specify additional features to be used by your system and to control its performance. The variety of possible entries in CONFIG.SYS and AUTOEXEC.BAT may seem a bit daunting, but most of the possibilities fit into one of the following categories:

- Determining how PC DOS will interact with you (PROMPT, BREAK)
- Adding a capability to PC DOS (PRINT, GRAPHICS, drivers installed with DEVICE, and MODE)
- Making room for internal housekeeping information (FILES, LASTDRIVE, and SHELL)
- Helping to find files and run applications (PATH, APPEND, some variables established with SET, and commands that run applications from AUTOEXEC.BAT)
- Speeding up disk I/O operations (BUFFERS, FASTOPEN)

Some commands, such as MODE, serve more than one purpose. Thinking about the purpose of a particular command will help you figure out what it affects and when you are likely to want to use it. When you customize your system, concentrate first on the things that have the biggest impact on performance, that give you the most bang for the buck. If you have a hard disk, it is strongly recommended that you read the sections in Chapter 6, "Managing Your Hard Disk," that deal with BUFFERS, FASTOPEN, the disk cache, and file optimization. For many users, disk operations are the single area where the most improvement in performance is available at little or no cost.

Programs and Memory Use

Besides the disk buffers and cache already mentioned, there are other ways you can set aside memory to provide added performance or convenient features. This section looks at some PC DOS features such as the virtual disk and the PRINT command, and at memory-resident utility programs. While reading about these features, keep in mind that they all use memory. You will have to decide if the benefit they provide is worth the loss of available memory to your application program. Most users today have their memory divided among several features and programs in addition to their main application. By trying out different settings for these features and observing how your main program runs, you may be able to achieve a satisfactory balance among the competitors for your system's memory.

Creating a Virtual Disk

One way to speed up access to files is to improve access to the physical disk drive. There is also another way. You can reserve an area of memory and use a device driver program that allows PC DOS to treat that portion of memory as though it were a disk drive. This portion of memory is termed a *virtual disk*. Since the memory area looks just like a disk drive to PC DOS, you can use the COPY or XCOPY command to copy to the memory area whichever programs and other files you are going to use. (In fact, you can use *most* commands that are designed to work with physical disk drives. You can't use FORMAT on a memory drive, however.) When your application program is running, it thinks that it is reading and writing data in disk sectors. Actually, however, all of the data is stored in RAM. And, as you have seen, data can be moved to and from RAM much faster than it can be by using a physical disk controller and drive. PC DOS versions 3 and later provide the VDISK.SYS driver as a tool to create such a virtual disk (often called a RAM disk).

Caution

Save RAM Disk Files before Turning Off the Power
Remember that a virtual disk resides in RAM, and that anything stored in RAM vanishes when you turn off the power or restart the system with Ctrl-Alt-Del. Before doing either of these things, you must use the PC DOS COPY or XCOPY command or some other means to copy back to the physical disk any files on which you have worked.

A typical VDISK setting in the CONFIG.SYS file looks like this (assuming that the file VDISK.SYS is in the DOS directory on drive C):

```
device=c:\dos\vdisk.sys 128 512
```

The first number specifies 128K as the size for the virtual disk, and the second number, 512, specifies a sector size of 512 bytes (the same as that used on most physical disks). If you are going to be working with many tiny files having fewer than 256 characters in them, you can save space on the virtual disk by specifying 256-byte (or perhaps 128-byte) sectors. Otherwise, you should stick with 512-byte sectors, since the fewer sectors that have to be transferred per file, the faster the virtual disk will run.

When you restart your system and the CONFIG.SYS file is processed, you will briefly see a message like this:

```
VDISK version 3.40 virtual disk D:
   Buffer size: 128 KB
   Sector size: 512
   Directory entries: 64
```

(Your version number may be different, and the numbers shown will of course reflect the values you set.) Notice that PC DOS assigned drive letter D to the virtual disk. If the system didn't have a hard disk, it would have assigned the letter C. PC DOS follows the same rules that it uses for installing external drives (see Chapter 11, "Installing a PC DOS System"). You should make a note of the letter that appears so you know how to refer to your drive.

Tip

Installing More Virtual Disks

You can install more than one virtual disk by putting additional `device=vdisk.sys` statements in your CONFIG.SYS file. If the total of "real" and virtual drives is greater than five, however, you will have to use the LASTDRIVE setting to specify a higher maximum number of drives. For example, if you had four real drives and three virtual ones, you would need to specify `lastdrive=g`, since G is the seventh letter in the alphabet.

PC DOS actually allows you to specify a third number: the total number of entries for the root directory of the virtual disk. Since the default, 64, is suitable for just about any application, you shouldn't need to specify this value.

Caution

Using Extended and Expanded Memory for the Virtual Disk

PC DOS 4 allows you to add the */e* option to specify that extended memory be used for the virtual disk. As explained in the discussion of IBMCACHE in Chapter 6, "Managing Your Hard Disk," PS/2 Model 50 and higher systems have at least 384K of extended memory available. If you want to use all of your extended memory for the virtual disk, you can specify

```
device=c:\dos\vdisk.sys 384 512 /e
```

Alternatively, you can use *expanded*, instead of regular or extended, memory by specifying the */x* option:

```
device=c:\dos\vdisk.sys 384 512 /x
```

This creates the same size of virtual disk, but in expanded memory. Which should you use? Generally, if you have both extended and expanded memory, use extended memory for the virtual disk and/or disk cache, and save expanded memory for use with your applications. Many applications today know how to use expanded memory, but few use extended memory.

Figure 11.2 shows how a virtual disk can reside in extended or expanded memory on an AT or PS/2 system.

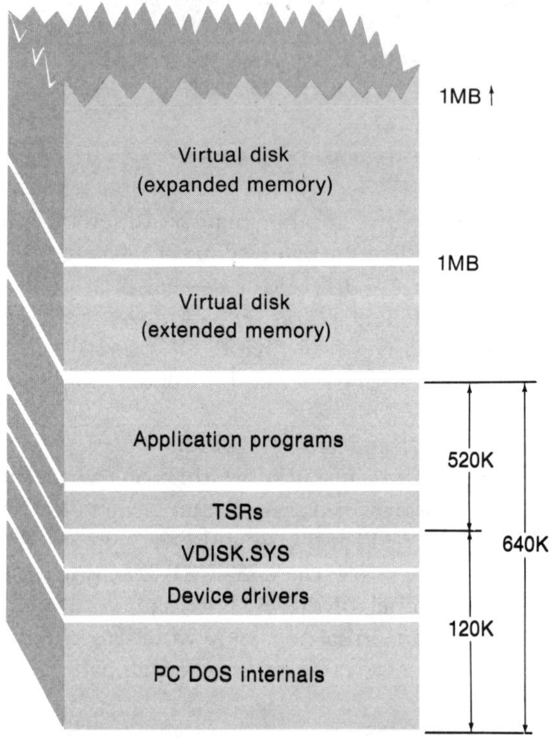

Figure 11.2. *Virtual disk in extended or expanded memory for a sample AT or PS/2 configuration.*

Virtual Disks and Communications Software

If you use extended memory for a virtual disk, you may experience problems with some communications software. While data is being transferred to or from a virtual disk in extended memory, servicing of *interrupts*—signals sent by devices to the CPU—is suspended. The communications software uses interrupts to control the flow of data to your system over the modem. If interrupts are being generated rapidly (to handle blocks of data being transferred on the modem at high speeds, for example), some of these interrupts can be lost because VDISK.SYS has temporarily disabled interrupt service. The result can be a loss of data and the receipt of an error message from your software (such as "data overflow").

If you receive an error message, you can have VDISK.SYS handle fewer disk sectors when transferring data. This reduces the time that interrupts are disabled, and may restore proper data transmission with your communications software. To reduce the number of disk sectors, specify a number after the /e option, for example:

```
device=c:\dos\vdisk.sys 384 64 /e:1
```

The `1` tells VDISK to transfer only one sector at a time. The default (when there is no number after the /e) is 8— this is also the maximum. If your communications problems disappear, you can start adding 1 to the number until the problems reappear. If you then subtract 1, you should have the number that allows VDISK.SYS to move data as efficiently as possible without causing interrupt problems. If the problem doesn't disappear even with specifying `/e:1`, try another communications program, since not all have problems with VDISK.

When Should You Use a Virtual Disk?

A virtual disk might be useful if you run a program or group of programs that can't use expanded memory. By setting up a virtual disk in extended or expanded memory and by copying the programs to it, the programs can be run, and can reload themselves, from RAM rather than disk. This can also help with games, which frequently are limited to standard memory. Remember to copy any data files that are created or changed back to the real disk. Better yet, having created a virtual disk, you can use batch files to copy files to and from the virtual disk. For example, you could run the older version of WordStar (which can't use expanded memory) like this. First, create a batch file (see Chapter 10 for a tutorial on batch files) to load WordStar to the virtual disk (assumed to be drive D here):

```
C:\>copy con: loadws.bat
copy c:\ws\ws*.* d:
^Z
   1 file(s) copied
```

Next, create a batch file to automatically copy any text files you have created or changed on the virtual disk back to real drive C:

```
C:\>copy con: savews.bat
copy *.doc c:\work
^Z
   1 file(s) copied
```

This example assumes that you keep your text files in the WORK directory of drive C and that you use the extension .DOC for your text files. If you use more than one extension, you can include one COPY command for each, or you could use `copy *.* c:\work`. This last command has a minor disadvantage in that it will copy your WordStar program files back to your data directory along with your text files.

If you have a fast hard disk, the improvement using this strategy may not be very great. But if you are using a system with no hard disk, such as some laptops, it can be very useful, since floppy drives are so slow. Further, on such systems you can load the programs from the floppy in drive A. That allows you to use drive A (which ordinarily holds the applications program) as an additional data drive, and you avoid having to swap the application disk in and out. Of course, if you have no extended or expanded memory (and systems without hard disks usually don't), you will be able to do this with small applications programs that don't need much memory for operation.

Caution

Putting COMMAND.COM on Your Virtual Disk

If you have a floppy-only system, put the following command in your AUTOEXEC.BAT file (assuming that your virtual disk is drive C):

```
copy a:command.com c:
set comspec=c:\command.com
```

A copy of COMMAND.COM is now on your virtual disk, and because you have specified its location (`c:\command.com`) in the special PC DOS variable COMSPEC, PC DOS will be able to reload COMMAND.COM from the virtual disk whenever it is finished running a program. This means you will no longer have to periodically find your PC DOS start-up disk and insert it in drive A.

Your Application and Its Competitors

As a user, a speedup in disk operations using buffers, a cache, or a virtual disk is very noticeable to you. You are conscious of the time spent waiting for the disk drive to finish whirring or chittering so that you can get on with the next task. But with any program, most of the time is spent not with the disk but with the CPU, moving data around in memory, performing calculations, and sending data in the form of text or images to the screen. You experience system sluggishness here not in waiting perhaps ten seconds for something to be written to disk, but in many individual seconds or fractions of a second. The cursor that hesitates before it moves to the next line, the elaborate word processor that can't keep up with a fast typist, or the spreadsheet that takes longer and longer to recalculate as it gets bigger are common examples. To understand how your system can slow down, it is helpful to look briefly at how programs see PC DOS.

To you the user, PC DOS is a set of commands that you can use to manage your files and run your programs. To an application program such as a word processor, however, PC DOS provides a set of *system calls*—program routines that can be called on to perform actions such as getting the text you've just typed at the keyboard and storing it in the program's memory area. Consider what happens when you are typing in a word processing screen. The word processing program receives the characters you type from a *buffer* (memory area) managed by PC DOS. To examine your input, format it, and put it on the screen, the word processor must deal with this keyboard buffer.

When the PC was first introduced, people could use only one program at a time—the main application. Nothing competed with the application program for memory or for access to system services (such as reading the keyboard buffer). Thus, the speed of the application depended mainly on its own efficiency and the inherent speed of the CPU and hardware. For many users today, the situation is different. Even though only one program at a time can be run by PC DOS, several memory-resident programs can take turns running and using system resources.

Running Programs That Multitask

If you are running a program such as Microsoft Windows or Desqview, that program is really just another PC DOS program—albeit a sophisticated one. Programs like Windows take over management of your PC resources, providing an interface between you and PC DOS. They divide memory between various programs and give each active program a chance to run for a fraction of a second, and then go on to the next program. This gives the appearance that several programs are running at once. Programs such as Windows usually provide their own expanded or extended memory management, disk cache, and background printing facility. You should follow the suggestions given in the program documentation. Some of the features discussed in this chapter (such as the virtual disk and background printing) duplicate functions already provided by Windows and similar programs.

TSR Programs and Application Speed

Today, many people regularly use one or more memory-resident programs together with their application. You have probably been introduced to the idea of a *terminate and stay resident* (TSR) program. Except when a special environment such as Microsoft Windows is built "on top of PC DOS" to manage multiple programs, only one program can be active at a time in a PC DOS system—usually your main application program. When most memory-resident programs are installed in memory, however, they normally include an instruction that is activated briefly each time you press a key. Any time you press a key, the keyboard generates an interrupt to signal the arrival of new data. PC DOS reads the code generated by the key you press and puts the appropriate character in the keyboard buffer. Because of the instruction inserted by the memory-resident program, however, the incoming character is also examined by the TSR program. If it is the special character that the program uses as its "trigger," or *hot key*, the memory-resident program takes over and the application program is suspended. This is why, for example, when SideKick is loaded, you can press Ctrl-Alt and type n and the SideKick Notepad will pop up over your WordPerfect screen. This is a very useful capability, since it allows you to interrupt your work to write a note, do a calculation, check your date book, dial a phone number, cut and paste data to the screen of your interrupted application, and other useful things.

Unfortunately, there is a price to pay for the convenience of TSR programs. First, of course, they use memory. In order to be able to spring instantly into action when wanted, they must have at least the core of their instructions already in memory. Reducing total memory by adding TSR programs can slow down the main application if the application is forced to use the disk to store some of the data it is working with. The other potential slowdown comes from the monitoring of the keyboard interrupt by several TSR programs, for example, SideKick, a pop-up reference guide, and a keyboard macro program that allows you to redefine your keyboard, and so on.

Each TSR must in turn examine each key-press, so this can slow down data input. You experience the slowdown when the characters you type on the screen lag behind your typing. In many cases, this slowdown is hardly noticeable, however. Because of competition and evolution in the area of desktop utility programs, each new version of these programs brings new features—but this means that they tie up more memory.

There are also PC DOS commands that work similarly to TSR programs. Any device driver that involves the keyboard or screen can slow data entry a little, for example, ANSI.SYS. Table 11.1 at the end of this chapter lists how much memory various PC DOS commands use.

Background Processing: The PRINT Command

A related example of "competition" with your application is the PRINT command. Unlike a TSR that just checks your keystrokes but otherwise doesn't do anything, PRINT is designed to grab the CPU whenever your application program isn't running, and use the time to send files to the printer. The effect seems to be that files are being printed while you do other work, but actually control is being swapped back and forth rapidly. Your program does a little work, then PRINT does a little work, and so on. If your word processor is reasonably responsive, it can keep up with your typing even while printing is going on.

To use PRINT to print files while you do other work, you must be at the PC DOS prompt. (Many applications have commands that give you a PC DOS prompt and let you return to the application when you are done with PC DOS.) Make sure your printer is turned on, and type `print` followed by the name of the file to print. You can use the special wildcard characters to print more than one file at a time. Here's an example:

```
C:\>print report?
Name of list device [PRN]:    ←press Enter to accept

  C:\ACCTS\REPORT1 is currently being printed
  C:\ACCTS\REPORT2 is in queue
  C:\ACCTS\REPORT3 is in queue
```

The file REPORT1 is now being printed. The other two files, REPORT2 and REPORT3, are in the *queue*—they are waiting in line to be printed.

Once you are printing files, you can add more files to the queue:

```
C:\>print /p report4 letter

  C:\ACCT\REPORT4 is currently being printed
  C:\ACCT\LETTER is in queue
```

The response indicates that PC DOS has caught up with printing the first three files. Of the two files you added, REPORT4 is being printed, and LETTER is in the queue to await its turn. If a file has been queued but not yet printed, you can remove it from the queue—in other words, cancel its printing:

```
C:\>print letter3 /c
```

This command cancels the printing of `letter3`, provided it hasn't been printed yet.

Finally, you can type just `print` to get a list of the files waiting to be printed, or type `print /t` to cancel printing of the rest of the files in the queue.

Tip

Printing Word Processor Files

Some word processors have the built-in capability to print files while you are editing other files. You do not need the PRINT command in that case. The PRINT command by itself doesn't know anything about formatting text. If you want to use PRINT to print text files created by a word processor, you should first set your word processor to "print to a disk file" and then use PRINT to print the disk file.

As an alternative to PRINT, you can use your printer's own memory buffer if it has one (most laser printers have large buffers). If you tell the word processor to print the file as usual, all or most of the file will end up in the printer's buffer. Once all of the file can be sent to the buffer, your PC no longer needs to deal with the printer, and control returns to your application program.

The *first* time you run PRINT, you can specify a variety of settings. By default, the PRINT command uses a 512-byte buffer to hold data waiting to be printed. If your printer is fast, this may not be enough. To set up PRINT to use a larger buffer, type `print` followed by `/b:` and the buffer size in bytes. For example, `print /b:2048` sets aside 2048 bytes (2K) for the printer buffer. You can specify up to 16,384 bytes (16K). You should choose the lowest value that keeps your printer running steadily so that you don't waste memory.

If you will have more than 10 files waiting in line to be printed, use the */q* (queuesize) option. For example, the command `print /q:20` allows up to 20 files to be queued at once. You can specify any number from 4 to 32.

Finally, if you are *not* going to use a printer connected to the first parallel port (LPT1: or PRN:), you need to specify the */d* (device) option. For example `print /d:com2` says to use the printer connected to the COM2: serial port.

Note that all of these options must be used in the first PRINT command of the session. Therefore, if you are using more than one option, you must combine them in the same command. If you will be using PRINT every session, it makes sense to put the appropriate PRINT setup command in your AUTOEXEC.BAT file.

The Command Reference discusses other options that you can use to tune the PRINT command so that it does as much work as possible without slowing your main application unacceptably.

Tuning Your Use of Memory

One way to minimize the impact of memory-resident programs on overall performance is to use expanded memory as much as possible. Some of the newer TSR programs use only a small amount of main memory and install the bulk of their instructions in expanded memory. Alternatively, if your application itself can use expanded memory, it may need less of main memory, freeing main memory for use by memory-resident programs. Finally, your choice of software can make a difference. When choosing TSR utility programs, ask yourself:

- Can this program use expanded memory?
- Does this program have many features that I'm not likely to use? If so, can I control which features are installed, and thus how much memory will be tied up?
- Can I run a program for my main application that includes the desired utility features? (Integrated programs may include features like notebooks, calculators, and cut-and-paste capability in addition to a main function such as word processing or spreadsheets. The TSR program may no longer be needed.)
- Would I be better off with an integrated environment such as Microsoft Windows, where utilities and application programs can be run at the same time, with the environment managing memory use (including expanded memory)?

In general, the trade-off is that with TSRs you can do your own integration, choosing the features you want to use together with your application program. An integrated program avoids potential conflict over memory resources and usually has a more seamless integration than stand-alone utilities. But the integrated program may not have all the features you need, and you usually can't add other programs to it. With an environment such as Windows, you can also get a fairly seamless integration, and you can add new applications as your needs change—but some of your existing applications may not run well in the environment.

Customizing Your Applications

The next arena in which you can improve the performance (and perhaps the ease of use) of your PC is your main application itself. Many users learn just enough about their applications to get some work done using the *default*, or built-in, settings and features provided. A small investment of time spent in reading documentation can pay big dividends, though. This section will give you tips on where to look for useful features.

There are three main ways that you can customize your applications (other than selecting certain features from menus while the program is running). You can use: command-line options, information placed in the environment, and information read from a start-up or initialization file.

Customizing the Command Line

By now you've probably used a variety of PC DOS commands. You know that many of them use *option switches* on the command line. Option switches are used to specify certain features that you want the command to use. For example, the following DIR command tells PC DOS to print a wide listing in several columns rather than the default single-column listing:

```
C:\>dir /w
```

Any PC DOS program that wishes to can read the options on its command line, however. The options that the program will accept are given in its documentation. For example, you can start WordPerfect 5.0 like this:

```
C:\>wp /r
```

WordPerfect will use expanded memory for about 300K of help messages and other files that it would otherwise have to read from disk each time they are needed. If you were using extended memory and had set up a virtual disk (discussed earlier in this chapter), you might specify:

```
C:\>wp /d-d:
```

WordPerfect would store its temporary files on the virtual disk D.

If you don't want to type a complicated string of options, all you have to do is create a batch file:

```
C:\BATCH>copy con: wpr.bat
wp /r /d-d:
^Z
        1 file(s) copied.
```

Customizing through the Environment

Earlier you read the phrase "the PC DOS environment." This concept isn't as mysterious as it sounds. PC DOS provides an area of memory that serves as a kind of master bulletin board on which information can be written. When PC DOS loads a program to be run, it copies the contents of the bulletin board to the program's memory area. The program can use the information for whatever it wishes.

Examining the Environment

The PC DOS SET command can be used to read what is on this bulletin board as well as to post new items or change existing ones. Type `set` and press Enter:

```
C:\>set
PATH=C:\DOS;C:\MKS\BIN;C:\WP50;C:\UTILS;C:\TC
APPEND=C:\WP50;C\TC
PROMPT=$P$G
COMSPEC=C:\DOS\COMMAND.COM
GLOB=C:\MKS\BIN\GLOB.EXE
MEMO_DIR=C:\MEMO
```

You should recognize a few of the names listed. Each name (such as `PATH`) is called an *environmental variable*. A variable is something that can be changed. The text following the equals sign is the information associated with that name, or its *value*. The first three variables here were actually specified by various PC DOS commands:

`PATH`	Directories to be searched for programs
`APPEND`	Directories to be searched for other files used by programs (see the following tip on APPEND)
`PROMPT`	Format for PC DOS prompt

Each of these commands places the information you gave it in the environment by creating a variable, which can be accessed by any program. In fact, when PC DOS runs each program, it places a copy of the environment in the program's data area.

By the way, PC DOS always lists variables and their values in uppercase, but you can type them in lowercase.

Tip

Putting Your APPEND List in the Environment

For the APPEND command, the default is to place the APPEND path list in an area of memory belonging to the APPEND command itself. If you type

```
append /e
```

and then type `append` again with a path list, the path list will be placed in the environment. Since many programs examine the environment, the information is more likely to be useful there. (See Chapter 6, "Managing Your Hard Disk," for more information on using the APPEND command.)

COMSPEC, as you saw earlier, is a special variable that PC DOS uses to find the COMMAND.COM file. Since all sorts of information can be put in the environment, new versions of PC DOS can define and use other standard system variables.

Chapter 10, "Batch Files," explains how batch files can use the information in environmental variables and can in turn create new variables or change existing ones. The following discussion explains the use of the environment with your applications programs.

Setting Environmental Variables

The variables `GLOB` and `MEMO_DIR` in the previous listing were not created by PC DOS commands. They were specified by using commands such as these:

```
set glob=c:\mks\bin\glob.exe
set memo_dir=c:\memo
```

To set a variable, simply enter a SET command at the command prompt or, more usually, in your AUTOEXEC.BAT file. Be careful not to put any spaces before or after the equals sign. If you put a space before the equals sign, the space is considered part of the variable name. If you put a space after the equals sign, it is considered part of the variable's information, or value.

To remove the value of an existing variable, type the name and an equals sign. For example, the following command removes the variable `GLOB` from the environment:

```
C:\>set glob=
```

Why would you want to set these variables? Well, variables are one of the ways that you can customize some application programs. In this case, the MKS Toolkit (a powerful set of utilities for PC DOS systems, derived from the UNIX operating system) needs to let all of its utility programs know where they can find the program **GLOB.EXE**. The utilities use **GLOB.EXE** to process their command line. By setting this variable, you ensure that any MKS program can find the path C:\MKS\BIN\GLOB.EXE in the environment. The **MEMO_DIR** variable is similar: it tells the program Memory Mate where to find the directory containing its database. For WordPerfect, you can set a variety of features by using a command like this:

```
C:\>set wp=/r/b-15/m-corres
```

As the WordPerfect manual explains, WordPerfect when it runs will find the **wp** variable in the environment. The information given there tells it to use expanded memory for much of its program instructions (**/r**), make a backup copy of the current document automatically every 15 minutes (**/b-15**), and load the macro (custom command combinations) file called **corres** whenever it starts up (**/m-corres**). (As you can see, WordPerfect allows you to use either the command line or the environment to control its optional features.)

Initialization Files

Some applications receive their start-up options through an initialization file. With some applications, this file is not intended to be edited by the user, and it is maintained by the application as the user makes various menu choices. For other applications, you can edit the file by using any word processor or text editor that handles plain ASCII text.

Important Features for Customization

Once you've determined the ways your application can be customized (menu, command-line options, the environment, or an initialization file), it's time to look for the most important features or options you can select. Not everything discussed here will be available in every application, but the following areas are the most important ones to check.

Expanded Memory

Probably the most important information you can learn from your manual is whether your application supports expanded memory, and what setting to use if it does. There are two main advantages to expanded memory: first, the application will probably be able to load more data into memory and have to keep fewer (or no) temporary files on disk. Second, applications using expanded memory are likely to need less—perhaps far less—of your standard memory below 640K. This may mean that you can load more memory-resident programs there. (Not all memory resident programs can use expanded memory, though an increasing number can put most of their instructions in expanded memory, using only a few K of standard memory.

Safety Features

If you are working with very important data, look for an option that makes timed backups. Programs such as WordPerfect allow you to specify that the current file will be copied to disk automatically after a specified interval. With a hard disk, you will scarcely notice the occasional interruption, and if the power fails, you will lose only work done since the last backup.

Many programs (especially word processors) automatically rename the "old" copy of a file with an extension such as .BAK or .BK!, allowing you to in effect work with a new copy. Others allow you to select this as an option. This gives you some protection against inadvertently deleting your only copy of a file. You will eventually want to delete those .BAK files, but since that is probably a unique extension, you can use a global command such as `del *.bak` when your session or project is over.

For many people security is an important aspect of safety. Some programs support the use of passwords for program or file access, or have the ability to encrypt a file. Chapter 6, "Managing Your Hard Disk," discusses security features in more detail.

Video Display Options

Some programs automatically sense what kind of video display is available and set their default number of lines accordingly. Other applications are less smart but do allow you to specify that you have an EGA or a VGA. Doing so may get you more colors as well as more text per screen.

If you are using a compatible non-IBM adapter (such as an EGA), you may discover that the display doesn't work right—the screen is distorted, or perhaps it blanks out entirely. The reason may be that your adapter is compatible with the display services provided by the PC's BIOS (Basic Input/Output System) for use by programs, but your application program bypasses the BIOS and manipulates the hardware's special memory locations (*registers*) directly. This means that the application's designer has decided that speed is more important than compatibility. The speed comes from avoiding the overhead involved in using the BIOS program routines. The incompatibility arises from relying too closely on the hardware being identical. If the application includes an option for "BIOS display output" or if it supports the ANSI.SYS driver (or mentions the display compatibility problem), set the option as instructed.

Some older displays produce an annoying flicker when direct methods of video output are used by a program. In such cases, look for a "no flicker" option. This will probably slow the screen scrolling, but that may be preferable to the flicker. Only you can judge.

Customizing with DEBUG

Suppose your program has an annoying quirk, or is missing an important feature. Often, you simply have to wait and see if the vendor releases a new version that solves the problem. However, you can sometimes fix the problem with the help of a tool called *DEBUG*.

DEBUG is a PC DOS utility program designed for programmers. It allows you to examine and change the contents of bytes anywhere in your PC's memory or at any position in a disk file. It also allows programmers who use assembly language, the most detailed kind of programming, to examine and test programs in an attempt to find the cause of errors or "bugs"—thus the name *debug*.

The use of DEBUG by programmers is beyond the scope of this book. IBM no longer provides documentation for DEBUG in the regular PC DOS reference manuals, though you can buy the *PC DOS Technical Reference*

Manual to obtain the documentation. Better, if you are interested in taking programs apart to see how they work, you can consult books such as *The Waite Group's MS-DOS Bible* or *The Waite Group's Tricks of the MS-DOS Masters*, both published by Howard Sams.

The focus of this discussion is limited to some ways that you can use DEBUG to customize your system and your applications. Many PC books and magazines provide fixes for bugs or problems with popular applications programs. These may be things that the vendor doesn't think are important enough to require a revision of the program. In other cases, it isn't so much a bug but a feature that many people would work differently. (A classic example with WordStar is redefining the delete key so that it actually deletes the character under the cursor.) Possibly, if it's an older program, the vendor may be out of business. Enterprising hobbyists and other programmers can come to the rescue and offer instructions for modifying your copy of the program and fixing the problem or adding a neat enhancement. Also, many books and magazines have short utility programs that you can type in. How do you get all the program instructions into a file that can be executed by PC DOS? How do you take your application program's .COM or .EXE file and make the changes that are needed? Both are easy to do with DEBUG.

You can't use an ordinary text editor to edit program files because the text editor would see the bytes of program instructions and data as an apparently random collection of all 255 ASCII characters. To demonstrate, try this command:

```
C:\>type \dos\more.com
```

You will see a jumble of characters including a few happy-face characters and hear a beep. The happy faces are representations of two otherwise unprintable control characters. The beep is produced by the character with ASCII value 7. You can imagine your word processor choking if you tried to edit the MORE.COM program with it.

What is needed is a way to see and change the actual numeric values of the individual bytes. Here's a look at that same MORE.COM program file using DEBUG:

```
C:\>debug \dos\more.com
-d
9350:0100  EB 1C 90 01 00 02 00 80-02 43 50 20 20 20 20 20   .........CP
9350:0110  20 01 00 02 00 80 00 02-02 00 43 50 00 00 E8 3D   ..........CP...=
9350:0120  02 73 07 E8 1C 03 B4 4C-CD 21 B8 0C 44 BB 02 00   .s.....L.!..D...
9350:0130  B9 7F 03 8D 16 68 02 CD-21 72 10 8D 3E 68 02 80   .....h..!r..>h..
9350:0140  7D 06 01 75 06 8B 45 10-A2 64 02 B4 0F CD 10 88   }..u..E..d......
9350:0150  26 65 02 33 DB B4 45 CD-21 8B E8 B4 3E CD 21 BB   &e.3..E.!...>.!.
9350:0160  02 00 B4 45 CD 21 B8 03-33 CD 21 72 22 80 FA 00   ...E.!..3.!r"...
9350:0170  74 1D B8 02 57 8B DD BE-03 01 B9 0D 00 BF 11 01   t...W...........
-
```

You give DEBUG the name of the file to be examined. It responds with a hyphen (-) prompt. Typing `d` (for "dump") displays the contents of the COMMAND.COM file. (By default, DEBUG always starts at location 100h when examining a .COM file, skipping over header information that normally isn't changed.)

In the display, each line begins with an address. For the first line, the address is 9350:0100. For the simple kinds of patching you will be doing, you need pay attention only to the second part of the address—0100 in this case. That is the relative position in the file. Following the address are sixteen 2-digit hexadecimal numbers: thus each line displays the contents of 16 bytes. Again, you don't care what the numbers mean. You just have to identify what needs to be changed.

To exit DEBUG, type q for "quit."

Patching a Program

Now that you've taken a look at the world from DEBUG's point of view, some practical examples will be discussed. The first one uses WordStar version 3.3. WordStar has a feature allowing you to begin a line with a period. You follow that period with formatting commands or comments that you don't want to be printed. WordStar will show a line like this on the screen but won't print it:

```
.this is a comment
```

Suppose, though, that you do want to print such lines. Perhaps you have a computer language that has words that begin with a period, like ".asm" or ".print" or ".put." You don't want every line beginning with one of these words to disappear from the printout. WordStar doesn't have a menu item that you can select to change the "nonprinting line character" from a period to something else. Fortunately, some enterprising soul, writing in one of the PC magazines, discovered that there is a particular byte in the WS.COM file that WordStar checks to find out what character to use to begin a non-printing command line. The byte holds the ASCII value of that character. Right now, it's hexadecimal value 2E, the ASCII code for a period. You want to change it to something else. You could use hex value 40, which is the *at* sign (@). (You don't need to worry about what these hexadecimal values are in the more familiar decimal system.) Here's how it's done.

First, copy your WS.COM file to another name, such as TEST.COM. (You want to keep the .COM extension so that you can run it as a program after you've modified it.) Now type:

```
C:\WS>copy ws.com temp.com
C:\WS>debug temp.com
-
```

Caution

Don't Use DEBUG on Your Original Program

Never use DEBUG on your *original* copy of a program file. The wrong changes in a program can make it unusable. Always make a working copy for use with DEBUG, test it, and then rename it to replace your regular working copy. Your original distribution copy should remain untouched.

Next, since the magazine told you that the location of the byte that you need to change is hex position 395 in the WS.COM file (here TEMP.COM), you type the DEBUG command e (for "enter"):

```
-e 395
3065:0395  2E.40
```

This command says, "I want to enter data starting at location hex 395." DEBUG responds by repeating the address (location) and showing the value that is currently there, 2E hex. This is the correct value, so you've got the right place. Typing `40` replaces 2E with 40.

The last step is to tell DEBUG to write the file back to disk by typing the write command `w`, and then typing `q` to quit DEBUG and return to the PC DOS prompt:

```
-w
Writing 5380 bytes
-q
C:\WS>
```

Now, you can run the patched version of WordStar:

```
C:\WS>test
```

It should run just like the regular WS.COM, except that it will now use the @ character for its "command start character." Once you're satisfied with it, you can copy TEST.COM back to WS.COM. (Remember: you are replacing your *working* copy, not the original distribution copy, which you should never use with DEBUG.)

There is a minor variation on this procedure. In the previous example, the contents of a byte were being changed, but the total length of the file was not changed. Suppose, however, that you are instructed to add a few bytes to the end of a file. DEBUG keeps track of the original length of the file in the *CX register*, one of several special storage locations in the CPU that can be manipulated by assembly language programmers. Suppose you loaded a file that had 8 bytes in it and you added 3 more by using the DEBUG Enter command (`e`) discussed previously. If you just type `w` to write out the file, only 8 bytes will be written out because that's the original length that DEBUG knows about. To get DEBUG to write out 11 bytes, do this:

```
-rcx
CX 0008
:b
-w
Writing 000E bytes
```

The `rcx` command displays the contents of the CX register and then a colon on the next line. You can now type in the new file length to be put in the CX register. Since you are working in hexadecimal, which uses sixteen rather than ten digits, you can't type 11. Instead you type the letter `b`. (Either upper- or lowercase is fine. The letter `a` is 10 in decimal, `b` is 11, `c` is 12, `d` is 13, `e` is 14, and `f` is 15.) Now when you type `w`, DEBUG responds that it is writing `000E` (in other words, 11 bytes), and the file is saved with your additions.

Making a New Program with DEBUG

There are two ways to create a .COM program with DEBUG. (The somewhat more complex .EXE programs won't be discussed here. Most utility programs provided in books and magazines are .COM programs, anyway.) The first way involves using the DEBUG Enter command (e) to put in the file the individual bytes making up the program's machine-level instructions:

```
C:\>debug
-n beep.com
-e 100 b2 07 b4 02 cd 21 cd 20
-rcx
CX 0000
:8
-w
Writing 0008 bytes
-q
```

The n command tells DEBUG to create a new file, using the name beep.com. The e command here is followed by 100h, the address where instructions start in a .COM program. The hexadecimal numbers b2, 07, b4, 02, cd, 21, cd, and 20 correspond to machine instructions and data needed by the program. The rcx command displays the contents of the CX register. This is a new file, and DEBUG doesn't know its length yet, so the register has 0 in it. Typing 8 puts the correct length in CX, and the w command reports that it wrote out 8 bytes. (In counting the length, you count the number of values listed after the e command, *except* the starting address, 100).

You can probably guess what this program does. If you type the following command, the BEEP.COM program you just created will run, and the speaker will beep:

```
C:\>beep
```

Typing an Assembly Language Program

An alternative way to give short programs in a magazine is to write them in *assembly language*. This is a series of short program commands that a program called an *assembler* turns into a series of bytes with the appropriate machine instructions in them. (If you want to learn more about assembly language, you can consult a good primer such as *The Waite Group's Assembly Language Primer for the IBM PC/XT*.)

The following program turns off the Num Lock key. You may recall that this key sets the numeric keypad so that it enters numbers rather than controls the cursor. Because the new IBM enhanced keyboard provides a separate cursor control pad, IBM has set up the PS/2 so that Num Lock is automatically on when the system is started. If you are accustomed to using the "old" cursor control keys on the numeric keypad, this can be annoying. Once you've created NUMOFF.COM, however, you can put it in your AUTOEXEC.BAT file and have it turn off the Num Lock key automatically at the start of each session.

To create the NUMOFF.COM program, type a (for "assemble") in DEBUG:

```
C:\>debug
-n numoff.com
-a
94C3:0100 mov dx,0040
94C3:0103 mov ds,dx
94C3:0105 mov al,[0017]
94C3:0108 and al,df
94C3:010A mov [0017],al
94C3:010D int 20
94C3:010F    ←press Enter here
-rcx
CX 0000
:f
-w
Writing 000F bytes
-q
```

Once you have typed `a`, you type in the program instructions from the printed listing one at a time, pressing Enter after each. DEBUG shows the new current address at each line. Press Enter on a line when you are finished assembling. Next, use the `rcx` command and enter the file length, `F`. (Remember that `F` is hexadecimal for 15.) You get the length by noticing that the first line you entered started at `100h`, and the new address after the last line was `10Fh`. Since you start at `100`, the subtraction is easy, even in hexadecimal.

Test NUMOFF.COM by pressing the Num Lock key. If your keyboard has a Num Lock light, it should come on. In any case, you can try the arrow keys on the numeric keypad and observe that they produce numbers. Now type

```
C:\>numoff
```

The light (if any) will go out, and the arrow keys will work.

Using DEBUG Scripts

One problem with DEBUG is that it's hard to correct mistakes. If you put the wrong number somewhere, you have to use an `e` command with the correct address and value for changing it. Fortunately, you can put all of the instructions that DEBUG needs to make (or patch) a program into a plain text file with a text editor or word processor (in ASCII text mode). For example, the instructions for creating BEEP.COM can be put in a file that looks like this:

```
n beep.com
e 100 b2 07 b4 02 cd 21 cd 20
rcx
8
w
q
```

Now you use redirection to have DEBUG take its input from the file (called here BEEP.SCR, for "script"):

```
C:\>debug < beep.scr
-n beep.com
-e 100 b2 07 b4 02 cd 21 cd 20
-rcx
CX 0000
:8
-w
Writing 0008 bytes
-q
```

What happens looks just as though you had typed it in yourself. DEBUG displays its prompt but gets its lines of input from the file BEEP.SCR. (For more on the power of redirection, see Chapter 8, "Advanced Use of the Command Line.")

The script file for the NUMOFF program would look like this:

```
n numoff.com
a
mov dx,0040
mov ds,dx
mov al,[0017]
and al,df
mov [0017],al
int 20

rcx
f
w
q
```

Note that there has to be a blank line after the last program instruction (`int 20` in this case). This tells DEBUG to stop assembling and start accepting commands again.

DEBUG isn't to everyone's taste, but it does give you yet another way to customize your system—and learn more about it at the same time.

Conserving Memory

Whether it's disk buffers, a cache, a virtual disk, a device driver, or memory-resident utility programs, you're likely to start running out of memory as you seek to extend your system's capabilities. If your application starts to slow down or you get the message `insufficient memory`, it's time to take inventory of your system configuration. Over the course of months, you may find that you've installed device drivers for two different mice. Now you have changed mice, but you've forgotten to take out the old driver. Or you find that you have created a virtual disk in expanded memory. You did that so you could copy the files for a program to the virtual disk, but now you've replaced the program with one that knows how to use expanded memory directly. Wouldn't it be better to free the expanded memory used in that virtual disk so that your new application can take advantage of it?

Taking Inventory

The first step is to print out your CONFIG.SYS and AUTOEXEC.BAT files. The easiest way to do this is to turn on your printer and type the following commands. (This example assumes that your printer is connected to the first parallel port, which is also called LPT1:.)

```
C:\>copy config.sys prn:
C:\>copy autoexec.bat prn:
```

The general procedure is to review the purpose of each setting, command, or program that you have established in these files. Ask yourself whether you still need that feature. The following topics are ones that you should consider.

PC DOS Settings

Settings such as BUFFERS and FASTOPEN can provide significant performance improvement. However, you should review your current set of application programs. Also review the discussion of these settings given earlier in the chapter to see if your programs are the kind that benefit greatly from having the number of data buffers and FASTOPEN directory buffers that you do. Perhaps the programs you now use don't use the disk as often, or use random access (minimizing the usefulness of buffers), or use fewer files (reducing the number of FASTOPEN buffers needed). Don't be afraid to retune.

In the case of FILES, FCBS, and BUFFERS, however, note that your application's documentation may state the required or recommended values. (The FCBS setting is used to provide space for file control blocks, which aren't used by most modern programs. If you've replaced an older program, you can probably drop your FCBS setting.)

Code-Page Switching

As explained in Chapter 13, "International Language Support," PC DOS provides a number of commands that allow you to use foreign language characters and formats for other countries. Unless you are using your PC in, or for, a country other than the United States, you don't need the KEYB, NLSFUNC, GRAFTABL, or CHCP commands. Nor do you need the COUNTRY setting, the DISPLAY.SYS or PRINTER.SYS device driver, or any of the MODE commands dealing with code pages. (If you delete any of these, though, delete *all* of them, or you'll get error messages.)

Device Drivers: The DEVICE Statement

Most devices are controlled by PC DOS through a device driver that you install with a `device=` statement in your CONFIG.SYS file. Look at each DEVICE statement. Does it control a device you no longer have, or one that you have but never use? If you use a device such as a scanner only rarely, you might want to put the word `rem` (for remark) in front of any DEVICE statement or other statement referring to that device in either the CONFIG.SYS or the AUTOEXEC.BAT file. This tells PC DOS to ignore the setting or command on that line. Since the command or setting is still there, however, you can reactivate it simply by removing the word `rem` and restarting the PC.

Also note that some mice, clock boards, and other devices sold in earlier years were controlled by a .COM program run from the AUTOEXEC.BAT file. This program installed the device driver in memory, rather than having PC DOS install it with a DEVICE statement.

Version 4

Use REM in PC DOS 4 CONFIG.SYS

All versions of PC DOS will accept the `rem` keyword in the AUTOEXEC.BAT file. PC DOS 4 also accepts it without complaint in the CONFIG.SYS file. Earlier versions of PC DOS will issue an ignorable error message when they find `rem` in a CONFIG.SYS statement. (See Chapter 10, "Batch Files," for more on using the REM command.)

If your settings or commands use one of the piping or redirection characters (|, >, or <), enclose the character in quotes. For example, the following command prevents the DATE command from actually being run and its output from being put in the LOG file:

```
rem date ">" log
```

Memory-Resident Utility Programs

If you need a utility program only occasionally, consider running it from the command line rather than having it loaded into memory at the start of each session. (For example, Memory Mate can be run either as a memory-resident program or from the command line as an ordinary program.) Although it is convenient to have a TSR program ready to pop up whenever you need it, such pop-up programs reduce the amount of memory available for your other applications.

How Much Memory Does It Use?

As you examine each feature to decide whether it should be kept unchanged, adjusted, or discarded, the actual amount of memory it uses is an important factor. A feature of marginal usefulness that requires only 4K is more likely to be kept than if it required 30K.

For settings and programs supplied by PC DOS, approximate memory use in kilobytes is given in Table 11.1. For items such as file handles or stack frames that use only a small amount of memory each, the number of each that you can get for aproximately 0.5K is given.

For programs that you've added yourself (such as IBMCACHE, another disk cache, a mouse driver, SideKick, and so on), first use the CHKDSK command (PC DOS 4 users can use the faster MEM command instead) and note the total memory available. (MEM calls this "maximum executable program size.") Next, disable the statement or statements in your AUTOEXEC.BAT and/or CONFIG.SYS file that involve this program, by placing a `rem` keyword before them. Restart the computer, and run CHKDSK or MEM again. The difference between the two memory totals is the amount of memory saved by not using the program in question. You can also use this procedure with settings such as FASTOPEN whose memory use varies according to several different specifications.

Table 11.1. *Memory Usage for PC DOS Commands and Features*

Feature	Memory Used (in K)
APPEND	7.5
ASSIGN	1.5
BUFFERS	0.5 per buffer
FASTOPEN	8.5 for `fastopen c:=(20,20)`
	0.5 per 10 additional directory buffers
	0.5 per 32 additional cluster list buffers
FCBS	0.5 for about 18 file control blocks
FILES	0.5 for 8 file handles
GRAFTABL	1.0
GRAPHICS	5.5
KEYB	6.0
LASTDRIVE	0.5 for 6 drives (`lastdrive=f`)
MODE	0.5 (when resident for device control)
NLSFUNC	3.0
PRINT	6.0 (default; add 0.5 per 3 files to queue after the first 10)
SHARE	5.5 (default; add 0.5 per 32 file locks)
STACKS	0.5 for ten 32-byte stack frames
VDISK.SYS	1.0 (plus size of virtual disk)
XMA2EMS.SYS	20 (varies somewhat)

The next section discusses the MEM command, new with PC DOS 4. If you have an earlier PC DOS version, the discussion is still worthwhile. Even though you can't run the MEM command on your own system, you can use the listings to learn what the memory allocation in a typical system looks like.

Getting a Memory Snapshot with the MEM Command

PC DOS 4 offers another tool to help you sort out the programs that have been loaded in your system and the amount of memory they use. In its simplest form, the MEM command tells you how much of each kind of memory (regular, expanded, or extended) your system has and how much of each is currently unused and available for your programs. Here is an example:

```
C:\>mem
    655360 bytes total memory
    654336 bytes available
     73936 largest executable program size

   2097152 bytes total EMS memory
   1769472 bytes free EMS memory

    393216 bytes total extended memory
         0 bytes available extended memory
```

In this system, some of the expanded memory is being used by WordPerfect, and all of the extended memory is devoted to the disk cache (IBMCACHE).

Tip

MEM versus CHKDSK for a Fast Report
If you only want to know how much memory is available, MEM is faster than CHKDSK because MEM doesn't perform any disk access.

MEM can produce two other reports. If you use the */program* option, you can get a list of all of the programs (including device drivers) in your system. The */debug* option gives the most complete report, listing all of the built-in devices and features as well as all programs and device drivers. This report is the final topic of this chapter.

First, some background. The example system is an IBM PS/2 Model 50 with 640K of standard memory, 384K of extended memory, and 2MB of expanded memory. The user has just invoked the "go temporarily to DOS" feature of WordPerfect to suspend WordPerfect and get a PC DOS command prompt.

```
C:\>mem /debug > snapshot
```

Since the report is long and scrolls off the screen, redirection was used to save the output in the SNAPSHOT file. (Redirection is discussed in Chapter 8, "Advanced Use of the Command Line.") The report will be shown a little at a time, with pauses for discussion. It starts out like this:

```
Address     Name        Size      Type
-------     --------    ------    ------
000000                  000400    Interrupt Vector
000400                  000100    ROM Communication Area
000500                  000200    DOS Communication Area
```

The addresses are the hexadecimal numbers, running from lowest to highest, that are used to refer to all memory locations in the PC. (To avoid confusion, such "hex" numbers are often written with an *h* after them. For example, 100h means 100 hexadecimal, or 256 decimal.) The report goes from the bottom of memory to the top. Some calculators, including the SideKick calculator feature, have hex and decimal keys that you can use to convert numbers between formats.)

The `Name` column is blank so far, but many things that have names will be coming along. The `Size` and `Type` columns will be your main concern. The `Size` column gives the size of the item (area, driver, program, and so on).

The `Type` column describes the general function of the program or feature in this part of memory. The `Interrupt Vector` is used to specify the location of the program routines that will respond when an interrupt occurs—such as the signal indicating that a key has been pressed. In fact, most TSR programs work by putting their own starting address in place of the regular system keyboard routine. This is what allows the TSR to take over for a moment, examine the key-press, and then return control to the system routines. The `DOS Communication Area` stores data that was copied from the read-only memory (ROM) when PC DOS started up. Since you can't change data stored in ROM, PC DOS needs to copy it to RAM, where it can update it during processing.

The next part of the listing shows the following information:

```
000700       IBMBIO      002470     System Program
                 CON:                 System Device Driver
                 AUX:                 System Device Driver
                 PRN:                 System Device Driver
                 CLOCK$               System Device Driver
                 A: - C:              System Device Driver
                 COM1:                System Device Driver
                 LPT1:                System Device Driver
                 LPT2:                System Device Driver
                 LPT3:                System Device Driver
                 COM2:                System Device Driver
                 COM3:                System Device Driver
                 COM4:                System Device Driver
```

Do you recognize these names? You are now starting to look at the memory that belongs to the internal PC DOS services, which were loaded from the file IBMBIO.COM when PC DOS started. `CON:` is the built-in device driver for the console (keyboard and display). You probably recognize most of the names for the parallel and serial ports that are used in PC DOS commands. Notice that all recognized disk drives and the system clock (`CLOCK$`) are also included.

As the tour of memory continues in the next part of the listing, you see more recognizable names. While the built-in devices can't be changed or removed to save memory, you are now looking at the installable device drivers and the settings such as FILES, FCBS, and BUFFERS. The devices shown here are `IBMCACHE`, the PS/2 disk cache program; `EMM`, an expanded memory manager; `DASDDRVR`, a PS/2 BIOS supplement; and `MOUSE`, a mouse driver. By looking at the `Size` field (column 3), you can see exactly how much memory each of the drivers and other features take. You can review the purpose of each driver and setting, and decide whether you need it.

```
002B70       IBMDOS      0088A0     System Program

00B410       IBMBIO      00AB50     System Data
               IBMCACHE  003F60      DEVICE=
               EMM       0029C0      DEVICE=
               DASDDRVR  0001E0      DEVICE=
               MOUSE     002660      DEVICE=
                         000380      FILES=
                         000100      FCBS=
                         000650      BUFFERS=
                         0001C0      LASTDRIVE=
                         000CD0      STACKS=
```

You may remember that MEM was run from WordPerfect—and this next part of the listing shows where WordPerfect (`WP`) lives in memory in this system. Notice that the `Type` field (the last column) specifies `Program`, `Environment`, or occasionally `Data`. `Program` refers to the area of memory containing actual program code. `Environment` is that copy of the system environment provided to each program. `Data` is a segment of memory used by programs to store other information.

```
015F70      WP          0000A0    Environment
016020      IBMDOS      000010    -- Free --
016040      FASTOPEN    002720    Program
018770      COMMAND     001640    Program
019DC0      COMMAND     000100    Environment
019ED0      APPEND      001E20    Program
01BD00      SKN         0000A0    Environment
01BDB0      SKN         00E420    Program
02A1E0      IBMDOS      000040    -- Free --
02A230      SHELLB      000E80    Program
02B0C0      WP          061190    Program
08C260      COMMAND     0000D0    Data
08C340      COMMAND     001640    Program
08D990      COMMAND     0000B0    Environment
08DA50      MEM         0000C0    Environment
08DB20      MEM         0120D0    Program
```

Do you recognize other names in the preceding listing? **FASTOPEN** and **APPEND** are PC DOS commands that reside in memory. The **MEM** program is of course what you're running to generate this report. There are two sets of COMMAND names (i.e., COMMAND.COM). One is the original from which WordPerfect was run; the other is the second copy that was run from WordPerfect in order to run the MEM command. This is a bit wasteful, but when you return to WordPerfect, that second copy of COMMAND.COM will be removed from memory. SideKick (**SKN**) has also taken up residence, and a few pieces of memory are marked "free." They are owned by IBMDOS (part of the PC DOS internal program) until a program requests a memory allocation.

Finally, the report ends with total memory statistics and a list of expanded memory handles. These handles are used by PC DOS and applications to allocate and access chunks of expanded memory in much the same way that programs use file handles to refer to files.

```
    655360 bytes total memory
    654336 bytes available
     73936 largest executable program size

Handle      EMS Name     Size
-------     --------     ------
     0                   000000
     1                   004000
     2                   04C000

  2097152 bytes total EMS memory
  1769472 bytes free EMS memory
   393216 bytes total extended memory
        0 bytes available extended memory
```

What's Next

Chapter 12, "Installing a PC DOS System," teaches techniques for adding hardware to your system and even installing a PC DOS system from scratch. Chapter 10, "Batch Files," presents a complete tutorial on how to create a batch file. Chapter 6, "Managing Your Hard Disk," contains material on formatting and partitioning hard disks.

Key Concepts and Words

Before you read further, use the following list to test your understanding of the concepts and words in this chapter.

- Application programs
- Memory resident
- Environment
- Device drivers
- Virtual or RAM disks
- CONFIG.SYS
- AUTOEXEC.BAT
- DEBUG
- Memory usage
- Memory inventory
- Terminate and Stay Resident programs (TSRs)
- Enhanced Memory Specification (EMS)

Chapter 12

Ready to upgrade to the latest version of PC DOS? Thinking of adding memory, a printer, hard drive, mouse, or display to your system? Read this chapter to prepare for these and all other installation situations. You'll learn to

- *Install a basic PC DOS system from scratch*
- *Upgrade to PC DOS 4 (or earlier) on either a hard-disk or a floppy-disk system*
- *Add expansion hardware or more memory on your computer*
- *Set up AUTOEXEC.BAT and CONFIG.SYS files to install device drivers and set PC DOS parameters*

Chapter 12
Installing a PC DOS System

Your PC, each piece of expansion hardware, and PC DOS itself all come with an instruction manual. Such manuals have a narrow focus and therefore can go into great detail. You should follow their instructions and observe any warnings or other advice they give. Unfortunately, most of these documents don't tell you enough about how to connect one device to another or how to include the settings or commands that PC DOS needs to use the device properly, and what to do if there are problems.

While all PC DOS systems have a great deal in common, there are incompatibilities, differences between models, and other potential problems. For example, the new 3½-inch 720K disk drives won't work with versions of PC DOS prior to 3.2 without special driver programs that enable earlier versions of PC DOS to recognize them. A standard RGB color monitor that works fine with the low-resolution CGA adapter won't work at all with one of the new high-resolution VGA boards. This chapter points out these potential problems and helps you make sure you're on the right track.

Out of the Box: Setting Up Your PC Hardware

You are probably eager to begin learning how PC DOS works and how to make it work for you, but first you have to unpack the boxes, hook the thing up, and get PC DOS onto the floppy or hard disk. While it never hurts to see if someone can help you, there's nothing particularly difficult about hooking up a PC—many home stereo systems sold these days are much more complicated to connect!

Planning Your Installation

Before you start plugging things in, take some time to think about where and how you will want to use your PC. For the easiest installation, you will want to allow for the following:

- A sturdy desk with enough space on it for the PC, keyboard, and possibly a mouse, and with room left to spread out your papers, reference manuals, and so on. Don't forget room for the printer!
- Space between the rear of the desk and the wall so that the PC's fan can circulate air. Don't put the PC near a heating vent.
- A position for the desk so that direct sunlight doesn't shine either in your eyes or on the PC screen.
- A sufficient number of grounded power outlets. If the number of outlets is limited—or even if it isn't—consider buying a power strip with a surge suppressor. A surge suppressor is inexpensive insurance against dangerous voltage spikes. If your area is subject to frequent power interruptions or "brownouts," consider getting a UPS (Uninterruptible Power Supply). Although these units are expensive ($800 or more), they give you time to save your work when the power goes out. Some also offer "power conditioning," which continuously filters the line current and prevents voltage variation and other harmful conditions. (Most laptops, by the way, switch to the battery automatically if the power goes out, providing some of the benefit of a UPS.)
- A nearby phone outlet for hooking up a modem later.

What You Need

You should have a base unit that houses the CPU, memory chips (RAM), the hard disk drive, and one or more floppy disk drives. If possible, buy a PC that already has 640K of RAM installed—the maximum PC DOS can directly use. While a few users can get along with 512K or even 256K, many major application programs today require 512K, and benefit from having more. PC DOS itself, and possibly additional utility programs, will need some of your memory. This book assumes that the typical user today will be using a hard disk. Instructions are provided for floppy-based systems, however.

You should also have a keyboard, a video display monitor (and the expansion card that contains the *video adapter*, or control circuit), and an additional expansion card containing at least one serial connector and one parallel connector for connecting printers, modems, and other peripheral devices. Some systems, notably the IBM PS/2 series, have the full amount of standard PC DOS memory, video circuitry, and serial and parallel connectors built into the base unit rather than using expansion cards. If you're not sure whether your system includes all of these essentials, ask your dealer. If possible, have the dealer install all the necessary equipment and any options you wish. If you do need to install memory chips or expansion cards yourself, see the sections titled "Expanding Your Memory" and "Installing Expansion Hardware" for details.

When you are setting up your system, it is best to start with just the basic components already mentioned. Later discussion will describe a number of options that you might want to add, but it is always safer to make sure the basic components are working correctly before installing add-ons.

Connectors and Cables

A variety of cables and connectors are used with PCs. They connect the monitor, printer, or other device to the connectors on the back of the system unit (either built-in or on the rear edges of expansion cards). Figure 12.1 shows the most common kinds of connectors used (aside from power cables, which are the standard three-pronged variety used in many appliances). Figure 12.2 shows where the corresponding connections are found in the three typical systems: the PC or XT, the AT, and the PS/2 Model 50. Of course, you should look at your particular system and its documentation to identify the purpose of each connection provided.

Power cables are always provided for the base unit and monitor. Keyboards almost always come with the cable attached. The other end goes into a circular connector in the back of the system unit (for PC, XT, or AT) or a small square connector (PS/2). The monitor also needs a video cable with a connector that matches the connector in the base unit—which is either attached to a video adapter card (on PC, XT, or AT) or built into the back of the base unit (on PS/2). Video connectors tend to differ from one model of PC to the next, and you may have to get a cable with different connectors on both ends in order to use a particular monitor with your PC. A printer requires an appropriate serial or parallel cable, depending on the connection (or interface) found in the printer. The other end plugs into the matching connector on an expansion card or is built into the system unit (the PS/2 provided the first serial and parallel connectors as built-ins). A modem requires a special serial cable (which is not the same as a serial printer cable). Printer and modem cables used on PCs are highly standardized, though you do need to check to see if the printer end of a parallel printer cable uses the "Centronics-type" connector shown in Figure 12.1. If it does, you need a special cable that has the Centronics interface on the printer end and a regular parallel connector on the computer end.

In all connectors, a group of pins is inserted into a group of holes or sockets. The connector with the pins is called the *male*; the one with the sockets is called *female*. If you end up with both the connector end and the connection socket being of the same "gender," you can buy a connector called a *gender converter*, or *gender mender*, as shown in Figure 12.2. Buy the one that has the opposite gender to your cable and connection. It is best to make sure that the dealer from whom you buy the system includes all of the correct cables.

Checking Out the System

You're now ready to test the system. Plug in the keyboard, monitor, and base unit. If you are using PC DOS 4, find the diskette labeled "Install." For earlier PC DOS versions, find the system disk; it may be labeled something like "Startup/Operating."

Insert the diskette in your floppy drive. If you have more than one floppy drive, the start-up disk always goes in the left drive (if the drives are side by side) or the top drive (if they are arranged vertically). This drive is called *drive A*. (Chapter 1 in the Quick Primer gives more information about disks and how to insert them.) Turn on the monitor and base unit.

At first you will just hear the fan whirring and see a very short blinking line (the cursor). If everything is all right, you will soon see a message indicat-

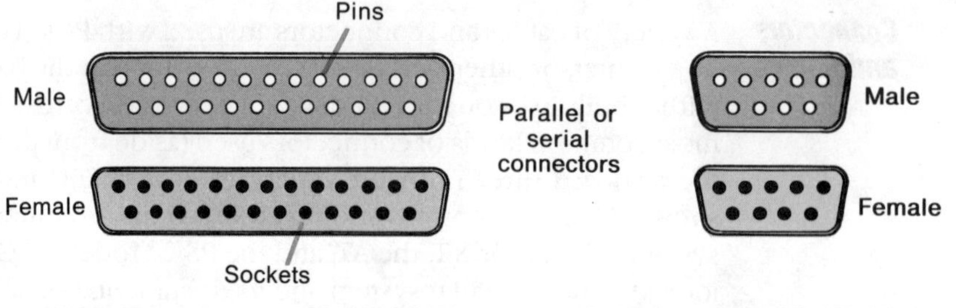

(A) DB-25 (used on most PC, XT, PS/2).

(B) DB-9 (used for PC, XT, AT video, AT serial).

(C) DIN-6 (used for PS/2 mouse and keyboard).

(D) DB-15 (used for PS-2 video).

(E) 36-pin Centronics-type parallel printer connector (used at printer end; other end is usually DB-25).

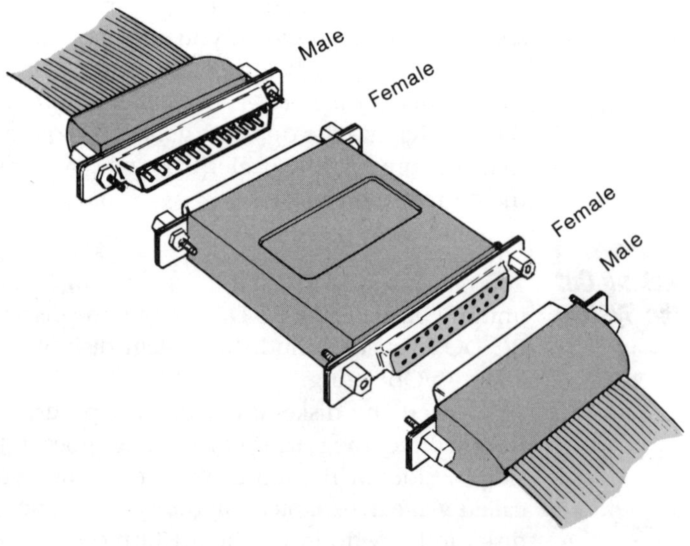

(F) Gender converter (known as a "gender mender").

Figure 12.1. ***Typical connectors.***

ing that memory is being tested, in the form of a running total. For example, if you have 640K of RAM, you should see something like this:

```
0640 KB OK
```

Depending on the amount of memory installed, the memory test can take up to a minute or so. (*Note*: some early PC and XT models don't show a total; the cursor simply continues to blink while the memory is being tested.)

Following the memory test, the light on your floppy drive will come on. The drive will whir briefly and then stop a moment, and the system will beep once. The drive will start up again. The system is now loading the PC DOS system files from the disk. (If you didn't put a disk in the floppy drive, the

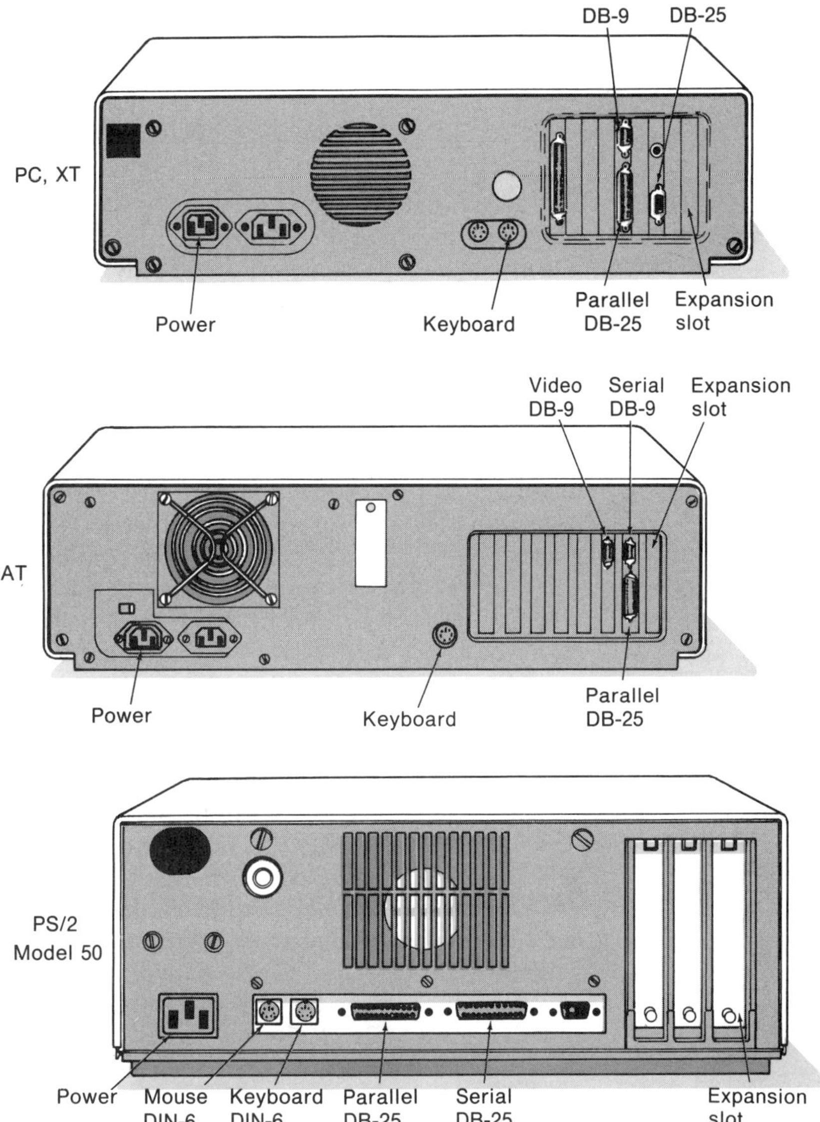

Figure 12.2. *Typical PC connections.*

system would then try to load PC DOS from the hard drive. Unless you or someone else had transferred the PC DOS files to the hard disk, however, this would result in a `drive not ready` error. You will learn how to set up the hard disk for PC DOS later.)

Version 4

You're Ready to Install PC DOS 4

Once PC DOS is loaded, if you used the PC DOS 4 INSTALL disk, you will see the first screen of the SELECT program.

If you have used the system disk for an earlier version of PC DOS, you will now be asked for the date and time. Chapter 2 in the Quick Primer explains more about these prompts and how to deal with them and eventually eliminate them. For now, you can either type in the date and time or just press Enter for each prompt, and not set them. You will then see a prompt like this:

```
A>_
```

You can now skip ahead to the sections on installing PC DOS.

Suppose Something Went Wrong?

Instead of the SELECT screen or a PC DOS prompt, you may hear some beeps and see a number on the screen indicating an error. It is possible that you did not install an expansion board correctly or did not properly connect the cables between the base unit and your peripheral devices. You may even have a bad memory chip on the main board. How do you find out what is wrong? PC DOS has a built-in POST (Power-On Self Test) that can give you some important diagnostic information. POST runs as soon as the power is turned on, testing memory and a variety of connections and internal devices.

One way the POST communicates is by sound. As mentioned before, the single short beep that you hear just after the floppy drive is accessed is normal. If you hear no beep (or another sound), the PC may not be getting power. Check your system unit's power connection and the power outlet. If you hear a continuous beep or a series of short beeps, your power connection may be loose, or there may be something wrong with the power supply. A long beep followed by two short ones may indicate a problem somewhere on your system board, while a long beep followed by one short beep points to a problem with your video display adapter.

Thus, even if severe problems prevent the PC from displaying anything on the screen, you've learned a bit. If the problem doesn't affect the screen display, however, the POST can be much more specific. It displays on the screen a diagnostic code consisting of a three- or four-digit number. Table 12.1 lists the diagnostic codes and the corresponding problem area. In the table, the important digits are shown followed by *X*s indicating less important digits that can vary. Of course, you should write down any diagnostic codes you receive in case you need to have repairs made by a technician.

On a PS/2, when POST is run with the Reference Diskette in the drive and an error occurs, POST will retrieve a more descriptive error message from the disk and display it on the screen. Write down the error message for later reference. Error 165 probably means that you physically installed an adapter board but did not update the stored system information accordingly.

Error codes consisting of a string of numbers ending in 201 indicate a problem with memory—perhaps a loose chip. See the later sections "Overview for Expansion Cards" and "Dealing with Memory Problems" for more information to help you pinpoint the problem.

Table 12.1. ***Diagnostic Codes for Pinpointing Problems***

Error Code	What to Check
1*XX*	Problem on system board (did you install chips there?)
161	Battery (PS/2)
162	Device configuration error (PS/2)
163	Date/time error (bad clock?)
164, 165	System options not properly set (PS/2; check device documentation; may need to run "change configuration" on Reference diskette)
2*XX*	RAM (bad or loose memory chip)
3*XX*	Keyboard (did you connect the cable properly?)
305	Bad fuse on system board (PS/2)
4*XX*	Monochrome display (did you install the expansion board securely?)
5*XX*	Color display (ditto)
6*XX*	Diskette drive
7*XX*	Math coprocessor (8087, 80287, etc.)
9*XX*	Printer adapter
11*XX*	Asynchronous communications (serial connector)
12*XX*	Alternate (second or later) serial adapter
13*XX*	Game (joystick) adapter
14*XX*	Graphics printer
15*XX*	SDLC (communications converter) adapter
17*XX*	Hard disk
18*XX*	Other expansion unit (bus extender)
20*XX*	Binary synchronous communications adapter
21*XX*	Alternate binary synchronous communications adapter

Overview of PC DOS Installation

You have now tested your PC hardware and verified that your system operates correctly. (If you want to test your printer or modem, see the sections titled "Installing a Printer" and "Installing a Modem," respectively.) You are now ready to install a working copy of PC DOS in your system. The general steps involved are

1. Prepare the hard disk (assuming you have one) so that you can install PC DOS on it.
2. Copy the hidden system files (IBMBIO.COM and IBMDOS.COM) and the command interpreter (COMMAND.COM) to your new PC DOS start-up disk.

3. Copy the rest of the PC DOS utility programs, device drivers, and so on to the PC DOS start-up disk.
4. Prepare AUTOEXEC.BAT and CONFIG.SYS files that will control various features of your system and run programs automatically at start-up.

These general steps apply to every PC DOS installation. However, if you have PC DOS 4, you will be using a menu-driven program called SELECT that will automate most of the process of installing and configuring PC DOS. If you are using an earlier PC DOS version, you will have to do more of the steps by hand. Since PC DOS 4 is the current version at the time of writing, and an increasing number of people will be using it, the discussion of PC DOS 4 installation with the SELECT program will come first, before the installation procedure for earlier versions of PC DOS. Also installation of PC DOS on a hard disk is different from installation on a floppy. In this chapter, as elsewhere in this book, it is assumed that you will be using a hard disk. Differences for floppy-only users will be noted, however.

Preparing Your Hard Disk

There are three steps involved in preparing a hard disk for use with PC DOS: low-level formatting, partitioning, and high-level formatting. For convenience, the low-level formatting is often done at the factory, and you may want your dealer to do the rest of the work for you. What do these steps involve?

Low-level formatting puts magnetic marks on the disk that enable the drive controller to find the physical sectors. *Partitioning* divides the disk into one or more areas that will be recognized by PC DOS using letters such as *C:*, *D:*, and so on. As far as PC DOS is concerned, each letter represents a separate disk drive. *High-level formatting* takes a partition and creates the FAT (file allocation table) and a directory that PC DOS uses to find out where data is stored on the disk.

Is PC DOS Already There?

To see what (if anything) has already been done with your hard disk, try to get a directory by typing the following command at the PC DOS prompt:

```
A>dir c:
```

(If you are looking at the SELECT screen, press Esc and then F3 to get a PC DOS prompt. You can run SELECT again by pressing Ctrl-Alt-Del.) Your directory may look like this:

```
 Volume in drive C is PCDOSDISK
 Volume Serial Number is 1454-3E20
 Directory of  C:\

SYS          <DIR>      09-10-88  11:03a
CONFIG   SYS        647 12-31-88   4:43a
AUTOEXEC BAT        553 12-31-88   4:42a
COMMAND  COM      37637 06-17-88  12:00p
```

```
DOS          <DIR>      05-17-88  11:15a
       5 File(s)    20482176 bytes free
```

If your directory looks like the one here, you're probably home free: you already have a working PC DOS disk and you can skip the section on installing PC DOS. (This is true even if the special start-up files CONFIG.SYS and AUTOEXEC.BAT files aren't there. That just means you have some more setup work to do, as discussed at the end of this chapter.) Alternatively, you may see a directory that starts out like this:

```
 Volume in drive C is PCDOSDISK
 Volume Serial Number is 1454-3E20
 Directory of  C:\

COMMAND  COM     37637 06-17-88  12:00p
FORMAT   COM     22923 06-17-88  12:00p
MORE     COM      2166 06-17-88  12:00p
GRAPHICS COM     16733 06-17-88  12:00p
XCOPY    EXE     17087 06-17-88  12:00p
CHKDSK   COM     17771 06-17-88  12:00p
BACKUP   COM     33754 06-17-88  12:00p
```

This means that the PC DOS utility files were installed in the root directory of the disk rather than in a directory called \DOS. Later you will learn how to move them if you wish.

Another possibility is that you will get a directory having only a few PC DOS files in it—perhaps only COMMAND.COM, the program that PC DOS uses to process your commands. (As Chapter 5, "PC DOS Files," explains, there are also two hidden PC DOS files called IBMDOS.COM and IBMBIO.COM, which aren't shown in the directory listing.) PC DOS is a separate purchase, and it isn't legal for a dealer to put a copy of it on your disk without paying IBM for it. But some dealers, particularly "gray market" ones, do this. Putting on just the minimum files is a compromise. Nevertheless, if this has been done, it means your hard disk has been prepared, and you can skip the rest of this section and move on to installing PC DOS.

Caution

Has Your Dealer Already Set Up Your Hard Disk?
Some dealers do complete preparation of your hard disk, including installing any application programs you purchase with your system. If this has been done, **do not** perform any of the steps discussed later for preparing your hard disk, such as running FDISK or FORMAT. PC DOS has probably already been installed with your other programs.

If you're not sure whether you really have PC DOS installed on your hard disk, you can verify it by removing the disk from your floppy drive and pressing Ctrl-Alt-Del to restart the system. If you get a PC DOS prompt (preceded by the time and date prompts if you do not have an AUTOEXEC.BAT file yet), then type `ver` at the prompt to find out which version of PC DOS was installed.

How Much Has Already Been Done?

You may not be lucky enough to have PC DOS already installed. The next best thing is to have a disk that has been given a low-level format and has been partitioned, but doesn't have PC DOS on it. If the directory you received looks like the following, it means that your disk is properly formatted but has nothing on it:

```
 Volume in drive C is 890-881-04
 Directory of  C:\

File not found
```

Consult Chapter 6, "Preparing Your Hard Disk," and skip over the section on low-level formatting. Read enough of the discussion on partitioning and FDISK to determine whether you might need to change the partition(s) you were given—you probably won't have to.

Finally, you might get the following message instead of a directory listing:

```
Drive not ready
```

This message probably means that your drive is not partitioned and/or hasn't received a high-level format. See Chapter 6 to determine what needs to be done. When you have finished the necessary steps there, you can return here to install PC DOS.

Installing PC DOS 4

PC DOS 4 is sold in 5¼-inch and 3½-inch disk versions. Make sure that you have the version matching the disk size used by your drive A because you cannot copy one format to the other even if you have a file transfer program like Lap Link. The 3½-inch version has two 720K disks labeled "Install" and "Operating." The 5¼-inch version has five 360K disks labeled "Install," "Select," "Operating1," "Operating2," and "Operating3." SELECT will ask you to insert these disks as needed to copy PC DOS files to your hard disk or to floppies.

Caution

If Your Existing PC DOS Isn't from IBM

The PC DOS 4 SELECT program will refuse to install PC DOS 4 on a hard disk that has any version of MS-DOS (as opposed to PC DOS) on it. SELECT checks for an "IBM" signature in the boot sector. If you are expert with the DEBUG utility, you could use it to change the signature to "IBM." The safest thing to do, however, is to run PC DOS 4 from a floppy and use its SYS command (by typing `sys c:`) to copy the PC DOS 4 system files to your hard disk. If you now restart with the Install diskette, SELECT should work. If all else fails, you can use BACKUP to make backups (preferably two) of your hard disk, then run PC DOS 4 from a floppy, and use its FORMAT command to erase the hard disk. After you have run

SELECT, you will have to use RESTORE to put your data back on your hard disk.

The SELECT program can be run only by starting the system with the PC DOS 4 INSTALL diskette in drive A. It cannot be run from the command line.

Follow this procedure to install PC DOS 4. Put the PC DOS 4 INSTALL diskette in drive A and press Ctrl-Alt-Del to restart the system. You will see the screen shown in Figure 12.3.

IBM
DOS SELECT
DOS 4.0_
(C) Copyright IBM Corp. 1988.
All rights reserved.
Press Enter (↵) to continue or Esc to Cancel

Figure 12.3. ***SELECT title screen.***

Press Enter to continue. You will see a screen that describes what blank disks you will need. These disks need not be formatted ahead of time. If they already contain data, the data will be erased, however.

If you are installing the entire PC DOS system on your hard disk, you need only one blank floppy disk (360K 5¼-inch or 720K or 1.44MB 3½-inch). Label this disk "SELECT COPY." When the installation is over, it will be your working copy of the Select program (for possible reinstallation in the future).

Most users with hard disks will want to put all of PC DOS on the hard disk. If, however, you already have another operating system such as OS/2 or XENIX on your hard disk, the area of the hard disk used for system start-up already belongs to the other operating system. You will be doing a hybrid installation with the key system files (IBMDOS.COM, IBMBIO.COM) going on a floppy, while the rest of PC DOS will reside on your hard disk. You should label your disks as follows: for 1.44MB disks, a single disk called "Start-up"; for 720K disks, a "Start-up" and a "Shell" disk; for 360K disks, four disks labeled "Start-up," "Shell," "Working1," and "Working2."

If you are installing to floppies only, and are using 1.44MB 3½-inch disks, you also need only one floppy to hold the entire PC DOS system. If you have 720K 3½-inch disks, you need two floppies, which you should label "Start-up" and "Shell." If you have a 5¼-inch drive (either 360K or 1.2MB format), you need four 360K 5¼-inch disks, which you should label "Start-up," "Shell," "Working1," and "Working2." Note that while you can use a 1.2MB drive, you must still use 360K disks in it when installing PC DOS.

Now that your disks are ready, press Enter. The next screen lists the keys that you will be using while running the SELECT program:

```
                        Introduction


As you view the SELECT displays, you will be asked to make a
choice or type an entry. If you are uncertain about what to
choose or type, you can accept the predefined choice or press the
F1 help key for more information about an item.

You will be using these keys in the SELECT program:

    Enter              To proceed to the next step.
    Esc                To cancel the current display.
    Tab                To move to the next entry field.
    PgUp/PgDn          To scroll information one page at a time.
    Up/Down Arrow      To move the highlight bar to the next item.
    F1                 To view the help information.
    F3                 To exit SELECT.
    F9                 To view key assignments while viewing help.
    Left/Right Arrow   To scroll data fields horizontally
                         to the left or right.

You can press Enter, Esc, and F1 keys when they appear on the display.
```

These key selections are rather intuitive. For example, the Tab key moves you to the next item going across, the Up and Down Arrows move you up and down among selections, Enter confirms a selection or moves you to the next screen if you're done with the current one, and Esc backs you out of what you are doing and returns you to the preceding screen. At any time until SELECT actually starts copying your files, you can back up all the way to the beginning screen by continuing to press Esc. At the beginning screen you can press F3 to exit to the PC DOS prompt. Note that if the Enter, Esc, or F1 key is a valid selection at a given moment, its name will appear at the bottom of the screen (the names have been omitted from the listings here). You don't have to worry about memorizing these keys. As you'll see in a moment, you can display a list of them at almost any time.

Now press Enter. The next screen looks like this:

```
                 Specify Function and Workspace

SELECT sets up your computer to run DOS and your programs most
efficiently based on the option you choose.

Note:  You can review the results of your choice later in this
```

```
program.

Choose an option:

     1. Minimum DOS function; maximum program workspace

     2. Balance DOS function with program workspace

     3. Maximum DOS function; minimum program workspace
```

This screen is the key to your whole installation. Unlike earlier versions, PC DOS 4 will build quite detailed AUTOEXEC.BAT and CONFIG.SYS files for you, based on this choice and on any changes you make later in the installation process. Settings and commands in these two start-up files will set your directory search path and the PC DOS prompt. They will also provide a number of features that enhance performance of the disk drive, speeding up your application programs in many cases.

Your choice here determines how much memory you will trade for faster processing of PC DOS commands and your applications. Option 2, "Balance DOS function with program workspace," is highlighted. This means that it is the default that will be selected if you simply press Enter. To select an alternative item, use the Up and Down Arrow keys, and the highlight bar will move to that item. Press Enter when you want to select the current item and move to the next screen.

This is also a good time to press F1 to try the on-line help to see what additional information is available. The help will pertain to the currently highlighted item.

You can scroll (move the text) in a help window by moving text one line at a time with the Up or Down Arrows. If there is more than one "page" of help text (that is, it says something like "1 of 3,") press the PgUp and PgDn keys to move to the next or preceding page of text.

Notice that whenever you are looking at a help box you can press F1 again to get an explanation of the Help facility itself (which you probably don't need). Additionally—and more useful—you can press F9 to get a list of the various special keys mentioned earlier.

DOS Memory versus Program Memory

IBM recommends that you select Option 1 (minimum DOS) if you have only 256K of memory, Option 2 (balanced) if you have 512K, and Option 3 if you have more (up to the 640K that PC DOS uses). In fact, the three configurations will leave you with about 560K, 550K, and 535K, respectively, for your applications. You are most likely to need the "minimum" or "balanced" configurations if you run applications that require 512K and you still want to sneak in a memory-resident program such as SideKick.

Country and Keyboard

The next screen deals with the fact that different countries have different keyboard layouts to accommodate the various special characters used in their national languages. There are also differences in the formats used for date and time (as when PC DOS shows you a file directory listing) and differences in currency symbols. For a further explanation of these national formats, see Chapter 13, "International Language Support."

The default choice here is Option 1, "Accept Predefined country and keyboard." If you bought your PC in the United States, the American format and keyboard are predefined. Unless you want to use a format for a different country, press Enter. Use Option 2 if you need to set a different country and/or keyboard. You will then be prompted for your choice on additional screens.

Location for PC DOS Files

The next screen displays the available drives on your system. If you are installing to a hard disk, you would normally select "C," which will be highlighted. For floppy installation, select "A."

Use the next screen to specify the directory in which you want the PC DOS utilities (external command files) to be placed:

```
                    Specify DOS Location

You can accept the DOS directory name shown or type a new
directory name.

DOS Directory . . . .C:\[DOS                            ]

To select option 1 below, press Enter.  To change your option,
press the tab key, highlight your choice and then press Enter.

    1. Update all DOS files on fixed disk

    2. Copy non-system files to directory specified
```

The default shown, C:\DOS, is a good choice because it keeps your root directory from being cluttered. (However, if you wish to keep an earlier version of PC DOS on your hard disk for compatibility reasons, you can change the directory to, for example, C:\DOS4.

Options 1 and 2 at the bottom of the screen are very important. Option 1, the default, tells SELECT to replace *all* the PC DOS files on your hard disk, including the hidden system files. This is necessary if you want to be able to start PC DOS 4 from the hard disk when you turn on your computer. Usually you will want to do this. If, however, you have another operating system on your hard disk—OS/2, for example—you should select Option 2, which copies only the nonsystem files to the specified directory, as discussed earlier. *Note*: If you want Option 1, just press Enter at the PC DOS directory prompt; if you want Option 2, press Tab instead, and then use the Down Arrow key and Enter to select Option 2.

Printer Selection

The next three screens deal with printers. The first one asks how many printers you have (in other words, how many you wish to connect). The next screen allows you to specify each printer. Most of the printers listed are IBM. If you have a non-IBM printer that emulates an IBM one, choose the corresponding IBM printer. The IBM 5152 Graphics Printer Model 2 seems to be a good choice for owners of many parallel Epson, Star, and similar dot matrix printers. Owners of laser printers (which usually are serial) can try IBM 4201 Proprinter or one of the other Proprinter models. If nothing else works, the "plain vanilla" parallel or serial printer selections should work, though you probably won't be able to print graphics. Your printer documentation should describe the emulations available. Check there also for printer switch settings that you may need to make your printer IBM-compatible.

The last printer screen allows you to specify the port (connection) for any serial printer(s) you chose earlier. Select the port to which your printer will be connected. If the system comes with a built-in serial port, the port is designated COM1:. Additional serial ports on an expansion card would be COM2:, COM3:, etc. If you have printing problems later, make sure that your printer is connected to the port you specified. Also make sure that any switches on printer cards have been set to designate the correct port—see your printer card documentation.

Reviewing Your Selections

The next screen allows you either to accept all of the choices you have made or to review them before continuing. It is recommended that you review them by selecting Option 2. (If you wish to install expanded memory, you **must** review your selections and set expanded memory to On because SELECT never sets it automatically.)

You will see this screen:

```
                    Review Selections

SELECT made these selections for you.  You can accept these
selections or change any of them.  If you change an item from No
to Yes, it will increase the amount of memory DOS uses.

To change a selection, use the up and down arrow keys to
highlight your choice, then press the spacebar.  To accept all
the selections, press the Enter key.
                                              Choice:
Code Page Switching                             No
Expanded Memory support                         No
Extended display support (ANSI.SYS)             Yes
File performance enhancements (FASTOPEN)        Yes
GRAFTABL display support                        No
GRAPHICS PrtSc support                          Yes
DOS SHARE support                               No
DOS SHELL                                       Yes
Virtual Disk support (VDISK.SYS)                No
```

Note that these items will be set according to the hardware that SELECT found in your system and the amount of PC DOS workspace you chose earlier (minimum, balanced, or maximum). For example, if you choose only minimum PC DOS memory, the extended display support (ANSI) and the file performance enhancements (FASTOPEN) will be set to No. They are set to Yes if you choose a balanced or maximum PC DOS workspace.

Although SELECT does a good job of setting a reasonable configuration based on your choices, you will probably want to change some settings eventually. While viewing this screen, you can toggle any item from Yes to No (or vice versa) by moving the highlight bar to the item with the Up or Down Arrow keys and then pressing the space bar.

A brief summary of the settings and suggested changes follows. If you change your mind after running SELECT, you can always run SELECT again and make different choices. Remember, however, that all of these items actually represent statements that will be created in your CONFIG.SYS or AUTOEXEC.BAT files. This means that you can fine-tune them by editing the appropriate file (this is also much faster than rerunning SELECT). To do so, read Chapter 11, "Customizing Your System," for more discussion of the trade-offs involved. If you need to learn how to edit the CONFIG.SYS and AUTOEXEC.BAT files, read Chapter 9, "Creating Text Files." For the most detailed information, turn to the Command Reference and read the appropriate entry from the list given at the end of the following summaries.

Code-Page Switching This selection allows you to use the alternative character sets needed for certain countries. If you selected the default United States setting earlier, `Code Page Switching` will be set to No. If you set up the system for another country on the Country Selection screen, and that country is one of those (such as French Canada) requiring code page support, this selection will be set to Yes. See Chapter 13, "International Language Support," for more details. (Command Reference: CHCP, DISPLAY.SYS, KEYB, MODE (Code page preparation), PRINTER.SYS)

Expanded Memory Support SELECT never sets this option to Yes automatically. If you want to use expanded memory (memory over 640K) and have an IBM memory expansion board, set this to Yes. If you have a non-IBM memory expansion board, you will have to install the driver that comes with it separately; see the later section in this chapter "Expanding Your Memory." (Command Reference: XMAEM.SYS, XMA2EMS.SYS)

Extended Display Support This selection is set to Yes in the balanced and maximum workspace configurations. Regardless of configuration, set ANSI to Yes if you will be using applications or batch files that require ANSI.SYS. If you will not be using ANSI, set this item to No to save about 4K of memory. (Command Reference: ANSI.SYS)

File Performance Enhancements This option is set to Yes in the balanced and maximum configurations when you are installing to a hard disk. It installs the FASTOPEN program, which speeds up disk access by storing information about recently accessed files in memory. Unless you really need more memory, leave this option as Yes. See Chapter 11, "Customizing Your System," for more information on fine-tuning this setting to suit your applications. *Note*: do not set this to Yes in floppy-only installation; FASTOPEN works only with hard disks. (Command Reference: FASTOPEN)

GRAFTABL Display Support This option is set to Yes only if SELECT detects that you have a CGA display *and* you have selected a country that needs code-page support. You should leave this setting where SELECT has put it.

GRAPHICS PrtSc Support This selection installs the GRAPHICS program, a driver that allows you to print screen graphics on a suitable printer. SELECT sets it to Yes if you have selected a balanced or maximum workspace *and* have selected a suitable printer. If you will never print screen graphics, you can set this to No and save about 5K of memory. (You can always run GRAPHICS from the command line when you need it.) (Command Reference: GRAPHICS)

DOS SHARE Support This selection provides network file-sharing support. It is also necessary for supporting disk partitions larger than 32MB. If you are using such a partition, SELECT sets this to Yes. You should also set it to Yes if you will be using a network (check your network documentation). (Command Reference: SHARE)

DOS SHELL SELECT always sets this option to Yes so that the menu-driven DOSSHELL user interface will run automatically when you start the system. Leave this option set to Yes at least until you've read Chapter 4, "Using DOSSHELL," and tried the shell's many features. However, you can set it to No if you don't want the shell to run automatically at start-up. (Command Reference: DOSSHELL)

Virtual Disk Support This selection installs the VDISK.SYS driver, which sets up an area of memory to be used like a very fast disk drive. It is never set automatically to Yes. Set it to Yes only if you will be using a virtual disk (RAM disk).

Review Screens

The next screens allow you to change or add to the values that SELECT has set for you. The first of these screens is the DOS Parameters Screen:

```
                        DOS Parameters

SELECT has set these values for you (if any).  Press Enter to
accept these values or type in new values.

DOS PATH . . . . . . [C:\DOS                                >

APPEND PARAMETERS  . [/E                                    ]
APPEND PATH  . . . . [C:\DOS                                >

PROMPT . . . . . . . [$P$G                                  >
```

The PATH setting, introduced in the Quick Primer, lists the directories that PC DOS will search for commands or application programs. If you know that you will be creating directories for your applications, you can insert them here. Separate each path with a semicolon.

The APPEND setting is needed only for programs that load special data or program overlay files (check your application's documentation). For such programs, add the directory containing the overlays to the APPEND PATH list.

If you are installing a hard disk, the PROMPT is set so that it shows the current drive and directory. This is the format used in this book, and it is recommended.

The review screens that you see next depend on which settings SELECT has made for you. For example, if you selected a minimum workspace and didn't change File Performance Enchancements to Yes, you will not be presented with the FASTOPEN parameters to set.

Unless you set Shell to No, you will definitely see the following screen:

```
                    DOS SHELL Parameters


SELECT has set these values for you (if any).  Press Enter to
accept these values or type in new values.


SHELL parameters . .        [/MOS:PCIBMDRV.MOS/TRAN/COLOR/DOS>
```

These DOSSHELL options are discussed in detail at the end of Chapter 4, "Using DOSSHELL." The only one you should check now is /MOS. It specifies the *mouse driver*—the program that gives PC DOS information about where the mouse is and whether a button has been pressed. On a PS/2, SELECT will specify /MOS:PCIBMDRV.MOS, which loads the IBM PS/2 mouse driver. This will also work with the version of the Microsoft mouse that plugs into the PS/2 mouse connector. Drivers for two other mice are included with PC DOS: PCMSPDRV.MOS specifies the Microsoft parallel interface mouse, and PCMSDRV.MOS specifies the Microsoft serial interface mouse. Change to the one appropriate for your mouse. If you have a non-Microsoft mouse, check the documentation for compatibility. If your mouse isn't one of the above kinds, it comes with its own driver. Delete /MOS:PCIBMDRV.MOS from the parameters and install your mouse driver according to its documentation. DOSSHELL will then use that driver instead of any of its own. Note also that the PC DOS mouse driver works only with DOSSHELL. If you are using other applications with your mouse, you should install its own driver and remove the /MOS specification as above.

If you have selected GRAPHICS, its review screen will come up. You will probably need to add parameters to specify the way graphics images will be printed, and you will need to supply information about your printer. Press F1 and read the help information for a useful summary. For more information, look up GRAPHICS in the Command Reference.

If you have selected Expanded Memory support, SELECT will attempt to set the memory page numbers appropriately. You should leave the settings as is, unless your memory expansion card's documentation suggests other settings. If you have trouble, read about expanded memory boards later in this chapter and read the Command Reference entries for XMAEM.SYS and XMA2EMS.SYS.

If you have selected a virtual disk (VDISK), the review screen that pops up will have no parameters listed. This represents a default 64K virtual disk in standard memory, which is not very useful. Decide how large a virtual disk you want, and decide whether it should be in extended or expanded memory (hardly anyone will have room for it in the standard 640K memory). Specify the size in bytes (for example, 360) and then either */e* for extended memory or */x* for expanded memory. *Note*: If you have a PS/2 Model 50 or higher, you have 384K of extended memory available (the space between 640K and 1 MB). After you have decided how much (if any) of this memory you want to use for the IBMCACHE program (see Chapter 11, "Customizing Your System"), you can use the rest for a virtual disk if you wish. It is better to save the much more widely used expanded memory for applications and other PC DOS functions.

For the remaining review screens, you should not need to make any changes. If you wish, however, you can stop and read Chapter 11, "Customizing Your System," and then decide on new settings, and enter them on the appropriate screen. Remember that you can always edit these settings directly in your CONFIG.SYS or AUTOEXEC.BAT files. Similarly, you will be presented with the following screen with more settings that you can change:

```
            Configuration Parameters

SELECT has set these values for you.  Press Enter
to accept the values shown or type in new values.

BREAK. . . . . . [ON ]     (ON/OFF)
BUFFERS  . . . . [25,8  ]  (1-99,1-8)
FCBS . . . . . . [20,8  ]  (1-255,0-255)
FILES  . . . . . [8  ]     (8-255)
LASTDRIVE  . . . [E]       (A-Z)
STACKS . . . . . [      ]  (8-64,32-512)
VERIFY . . . . . [OFF]     (ON/OFF)
```

Again, your settings will vary with your hardware and the workspace configuration you have chosen.

Once you are past this screen, SELECT will start copying files from its floppy disks. You will be prompted for disks as necessary. The installation will take only a few minutes.

Merging Your AUTOEXEC.BAT and CONFIG.SYS Files

SELECT creates two files named AUTOEXEC.400 and CONFIG.400 by using the commands and settings you specified while running SELECT (or by using commands and settings that it decided you needed based on your hardware). If you have no old AUTOEXEC.BAT or CONFIG.SYS file, you can simply type the following at the PC DOS prompt before starting the system:

```
C:\>ren autoexec.400 autoexec.bat
C:\>ren config.400 config.sys
```

If you have old AUTOEXEC.BAT or CONFIG.SYS files with settings that you may want to keep (for example, if you upgraded to PC DOS 4 from an earlier version), use a text editor, word processor (in ASCII text mode), or the PC DOS EDLIN editor to merge the files. For instructions on how to use EDLIN and other help in working with text files, see Chapter 9, "Creating Text Files." Chapter 11, "Customizing Your System," looks at the AUTOEXEC.BAT and CONFIG.SYS files in greater depth.

Running PC DOS

If you did a complete installation to hard disk, simply restart the machine and you will be running from the hard disk; DOSSHELL will start up. If you haven't finished reading the Quick Primer, press F3 to exit the shell and continue working in the Quick Primer at the PC DOS prompt. If you wish to explore DOSSHELL, turn to Chapter 4.

Tip

Be Comfortable
Your productivity depends, to a great extent, on your comfort. If you will be sitting at your PC for many hours each day, take the time to adjust the monitor position, brightness, and contrast to suit your eyes. Many software packages allow you to adjust colors for the various kinds of text and background. Many people find black text on white background to be better than the reverse.

Also check your chair height and keyboard placement, especially if your hands or back hurt after several hours of work.

If you installed to floppies (or did an installation with the system files on floppies and the other files on the hard disk), SELECT copied the appropriate files to your labeled disks. How many disks you have depends on your format. If you have one 1.44MB disk, it is your start-up disk as well as your working disk. If you have 720K disks, use the Startup diskette to start with the hybrid floppy/hard installation, or to start an all-floppy installation without DOSSHELL. To start an all-floppy installation with DOSSHELL, insert the Startup disk, then swap it for the Shell disk, and type `dosshell`. In some floppy configurations you will have to swap in "working" disks to access the less commonly used PC DOS commands. Use the DIR command to learn which disk has the command you need.

Installing PC DOS 3.3 and Earlier Versions

Versions of PC DOS prior to 4 do not have the extensive menu-driven installation program described in the previous sections. You have to copy the PC DOS files to your hard disk yourself, and set up AUTOEXEC.BAT and CONFIG.SYS files with appropriate commands and settings for controlling and configuring your system. This is easy, as you will soon see.

Most of these versions of PC DOS come with a single floppy disk containing the key system files (IBMBIO.COM, IBMDOS.COM, and COMMAND.COM), 40 or so programs that run the external PC DOS commands (such as CHKDSK and XCOPY), files that let you use the BASIC language, and an assortment of device drivers such as ANSI.SYS and DRIVER.SYS. Sometimes there is a second disk with the less frequently used programs on it. Starting with PC DOS 3.2, both 3½-inch and 5¼-inch disk versions are available (some packages have both sizes of disks).

Backing Up Your PC DOS Distribution Disks

Regardless of whether you are installing to your hard disk or will be using floppies only, the first step is to back up your PC DOS distribution disk(s). Obtain one blank disk (or one with unneeded data) for each copy. These disks do not have to be already formatted, since DISKCOPY will format them for you if necessary. Put the disk marked "System" or "Startup" in your drive A, and start the system. When you see the PC DOS prompt, type the following if you have only one floppy drive:

```
A>diskcopy a:
```

You will be prompted to exchange the PC DOS disk and your blank disk until the copy is complete. When asked if you want to make another copy, you can reply y to make an extra copy of your master disk, or to copy any other disks in your PC DOS package.

If you have two floppy drives of the same size (that is, both 5¼-inch or both 3½-inch), you can put the disk that will receive the copy in drive B and type this instead:

```
A>diskcopy a: b:
```

The copy will proceed without your having to swap disks. Again, you will be asked if you want to make more copies.

If you have a floppy-only system, you can skip ahead to the section titled "AUTOEXEC.BAT and CONFIG.SYS Starters." You will use one of the copies of your distribution disk to start the system for each session. You will then normally want to swap the disk in drive A for one containing your application program. With some applications, you can erase all of the files containing PC DOS commands that you don't use often, and then copy your application program to the disk. This may allow you to run your application without swapping disks.

Putting PC DOS on Your Hard Disk

Most of you have hard disks, however, so you have some more work to do. To install PC DOS prior to version 4 on a hard disk, make sure that the hard disk has received a low-level format, has been partitioned with FDISK, and has been given a high-level format and the system files with the FORMAT /s command. If you're not sure, see the earlier section titled "Preparing Your Hard Disk" and see Chapter 6.

Caution

To Install PC DOS 4

If you are installing PC DOS 4, you should not use the procedure given here. Read the earlier section, "Installing PC DOS 4," which walks you through the menu-driven SELECT installation program.

When you used the `format c: /s` command, part of PC DOS was put on your hard disk—enough for you to start the system from it. If you do start your system, however, you won't be able to do much because all of the files that PC DOS uses to run external commands aren't on the hard disk yet, nor is there an AUTOEXEC.BAT or a CONFIG.SYS file for configuring your system. The next step is to copy the rest of the PC DOS files to the hard disk. The best way to do this is to create a subdirectory called DOS to hold these files. Having a subdirectory for your PC DOS files (and one for each application and its files) makes it easier for both you and PC DOS to find what you need. With your PC DOS distribution disk in drive A, type the following:

```
A>md c:\dos
A>copy *.* c:\dos
```

These commands create the DOS directory on drive C and copy all of the PC

DOS files to it. After reading Chapters 6 and 11, "Managing Your Hard Disk" and "Customizing Your System," you can refine this organization further, but this is fine for now.

If your distribution package for PC DOS has more than one disk, simply put the next disk in drive A and repeat the COPY command with a new blank floppy.

Upgrading Your PC DOS Version

If you have an earlier version of PC DOS (before 4), you should seriously consider upgrading. If you have one of the new types of floppy drives (3½-inch 720K or 1.44MB), you may *have* to upgrade in order to use them, since they are not supported by versions of PC DOS prior to 3.2. If you have an older version such as PC DOS 2.1, you are being deprived of many useful new commands and features. If you have a hard disk larger than 32MB, you may want to upgrade to PC DOS 4 so that you can define your disk as a single partition, regardless of size. This means that you need only one letter (such as C:) to refer to the whole disk, rather than having to pretend that you have several hard disks. If you want to introduce new users to PC DOS, the menu-driven DOSSHELL interface provided by PC DOS 4 can be very useful.

Generally, if you are upgrading, you should upgrade to the latest version (PC DOS 4 at the time of writing) to get the latest features. The SELECT program discussed earlier will step you through the entire process. Note, however, that every new version of PC DOS creates a few incompatibilities with existing software, especially programs that work intimately with the PC DOS internals and the disk structure. Before upgrading, you might want to check to see if such utility programs will still work, or if upgraded software is available.

If you are upgrading to a version earlier than PC DOS 4, you should follow this procedure. Back up all the data on your hard disk to be safe (see Chapter 6, "Managing Your Hard Disk," for information on how to use the BACKUP command). Use DISKCOPY to make working copies of your new PC DOS distribution disks. Then, with a copy of your master disk in drive A, type

```
A>sys c:
```

Next, copy all of the files on your distribution disk(s) to the DOS directory on your hard disk (assuming you've made one, as suggested earlier). The new versions of the PC DOS files will replace the earlier ones. Everything should now work, and you should be able to start the system from the hard disk with the new PC DOS version.

AUTOEXEC.BAT and CONFIG.SYS Starters

PC DOS 4 automatically creates extensive AUTOEXEC.BAT and CONFIG.SYS files with most of the commands and settings you will need. With earlier PC DOS versions, however, you must create your own versions of these important files before you can take full advantage of your PC. The most important settings and commands will be discussed here, while Chapter 11 explores further options, refinements, and trade-offs.

As you may know, the AUTOEXEC.BAT and CONFIG.SYS files are ordinary text files. They must always be in the root, or top-level, directory on the disk. On the hard disk, this directory is referred to in commands as C:\. You can create these files with any text editor, such as the handy pop-up notepad that comes with SideKick or similar desktop utility programs. You can also use a full-blown word processor such as WordPerfect, but in this case you must be sure to save the file as a generic PC DOS text file (most word processors refer to these as ASCII text or DOS text files). If you don't have a text editor or word processor handy, refer to Chapter 9, "Creating Text Files," to learn how to create a text file directly from the PC DOS prompt. You can also learn there how to use EDLIN, a simple line editor that comes with PC DOS. In this chapter it will be assumed that you have chosen one of these text entry methods, and the mechanics of entering the text will not be considered.

Since the agenda here is to get your system running, the many nuances of each command or setting will not be discussed. Remember that every command (such as PATH) or setting (such as FILES) has its own extensive entry in the Command Reference at the back of this book. Some of these commands or settings are introduced in the Quick Primer. Those commands and settings affecting the performance and memory allocation of the system are further discussed in Chapter 9, "Customizing Your System." The PATH and APPEND commands and other commands affecting the use of the hard disk are also discussed in Chapter 6, "Managing Your Hard Disk."

AUTOEXEC.BAT Commands

The AUTOEXEC.BAT file will contain PC DOS commands and, optionally, utility and application programs that you will run automatically each time you start the system. Its presence will also prevent you from being prompted for the date and time each time you start the system. Any command or program that can be run from the PC DOS prompt can also be run from AUTOEXEC.BAT.

Searching with PATH and APPEND

The PATH command lists the directories that PC DOS will search for commands or program names that you type at the prompt. The command consists of a list of directory locations (paths) separated by semicolons. Normally you should list the directory containing your PC DOS command files first and then the directories containing your application programs, in order of how frequently you use them. Here is an example:

```
PATH=C:\DOS;C:\WP;C:\123;C:\UTILS
```

(All of these settings and commands can be entered in lowercase, by the way. PC DOS always converts them to uppercase when listing them for you.) This path specifies the following search order: the DOS directory, the WordPerfect directory, the Lotus 1-2-3 directory, and a directory containing miscellaneous utility programs.

Use the APPEND command if you have programs that need to find other programs (sometimes called *overlays*) or data files while running your application. This fact will usually be mentioned in your application's documentation. The format for APPEND is the same as that for PATH:

```
APPEND=C:\123;C:\UTILS
```

Here, only Lotus 1-2-3 and some programs in the UTILS directory need to find programs or data files, so these are the two directories given in the APPEND statement.

Setting the Prompt

The default PC DOS prompt shows only which disk drive is currently active:

```
C>
```

It is very useful, however, to know which directory you are currently working in. Therefore, the following statement in your AUTOEXEC.BAT file will create a prompt that shows both the drive and the current directory:

```
prompt $p$g
```

Now, if you are currently in the WordPerfect directory, the PC DOS prompt will appear as:

```
C:\WP>
```

Other AUTOEXEC.BAT Entries

A number of other commands and settings can be included in your AUTOEXEC.BAT file, as you will discover when you work through this book. Here are a few possibilities:

```
mode lpt1:=com1:
\dos\fastopen c:=100
\dos\graphics
\utils\sk
```

The MODE command would be included if you had a printer connected to a serial port. MODE redirects printer output that would ordinarily be sent out the parallel port (of course, MODE has many other uses). The FASTOPEN command here (available starting with PC DOS 3.3 and enhanced with PC DOS 4) reserves memory to hold 100 names of directory paths to help PC DOS reopen frequently used files more quickly. The GRAPHICS command allows you to print your screen on an IBM-compatible graphics printer. SK is the SideKick program, which installs itself in memory when first run.

Settings in the CONFIG.SYS File

The CONFIG.SYS file is used for two main purposes: to install special driver programs needed by some devices (such as external disk drives and mice) and to establish certain settings that affect your system performance.

FILES and BUFFERS

The FILES setting determines how many files (up to 255) can be open at one time. Since memory must be reserved to hold information for each file, you want to be able to open as many files as your applications need, but without an excess. Check your application to see if it recommends a FILES setting.

The BUFFERS setting determines how many blocks of memory (buffers) will be used to hold data being read from the disk. When your application requests data from a disk sector, the whole sector can be placed in a buffer, reducing the need for repeated disk reads. The optimum value varies with the kind of applications you use. A good general-purpose value is given in the following setting, but see Chapter 11 for further considerations:

```
files=20
buffers=25
```

The DEVICE Driver Statement

If you want to use the enhanced ANSI screen-control commands, a mouse, a disk cache for speedier disk access, an external disk drive, or one of many other devices, you will need to insert a DEVICE statement in your CONFIG.SYS file for each device. The appropriate DEVICE statement is usually given in the documentation accompanying a program that uses ANSI graphics or a device that requires a driver. Here are some examples:

```
device=c:\dos\ansi.sys
device=c:\dos\ibmcache /e:256
device=c:\mouse\mouse.sys
device=c:\dos\driver.sys /d:1 /f:0 /t:40
```

These DEVICE statements install the following: the ANSI.SYS driver for enhanced screen and keyboard capabilities, the IBMCACHE disk cache for PS/2 machines, a mouse driver, and a driver enabling a PS/2 to use a second external 360K disk drive. Note that IBMCACHE is not supplied with PC DOS; it comes with the PS/2, and you should follow IBM's instructions for its installation. Mouse drivers are usually included when you buy a mouse. Several other drivers are supplied with PC DOS, and have extensive descriptions in the Command Reference. The appropriate DEVICE statements are also discussed in the remaining sections of this chapter, which deal with add-on hardware.

Moving COMMAND.COM: The SHELL Setting

One more common addition to CONFIG.SYS is the SHELL statement. This specifies the name and location of the program that will interpret your PC DOS commands. In standard PC DOS, this program is called COMMAND.COM. At present, if you followed the installation instructions given earlier, you have two copies of COMMAND.COM: one in your root directory (C:\) and one in the C:\DOS directory. PC DOS expects to find COMMAND.COM in the start-up directory (the root) unless told otherwise. As mentioned before, however, it is good practice to leave only the hidden system files—IBMDOS.COM and IBMBIO.COM—and the AUTOEXEC.BAT and CONFIG.SYS files in the root directory. Anything else can be moved, including COMMAND.COM. The following statement tells PC DOS to find COMMAND.COM in your \DOS directory:

```
shell=c:\dos\command.com /p
```

You can now remove COMMAND.COM from the root directory:

```
C:\>del c:\command.com
```

Other uses for the SHELL statement are discussed in Chapter 11 and in the SHELL entry for the Command Reference.

Up and Running

By now you should have installed either PC DOS 4 or an earlier version, have PC DOS on your hard disk (assuming you have one), and have functional AUTOEXEC.BAT and CONFIG.SYS files so that your system starts properly. You may wish to read (or reread) the Quick Primer before continuing. After you have become more familiar with PC DOS and your applications, you will find it useful to read Chapter 11 to learn how to fine-tune your system's performance using PC DOS commands and settings.

Installing Expansion Hardware

The rest of this chapter deals with common items of add-on hardware used by many PC users. One feature that almost all of these devices have in common is that they are connected to your system through, and controlled by, a plug-in card in an expansion slot. In addition to the physical connection, most devices also need a *logical connection*. This connection is provided by a device driver program, which PC DOS installs in memory automatically at start-up, usually by using a DEVICE statement in your CONFIG.SYS. This program translates requests made by PC DOS or your application program to commands that control the device. It also interprets the signals sent by the device, such as "I'm ready for more data." You provide the specifications needed for the driver in a DEVICE statement placed in your CONFIG.SYS file.

The general procedure for installing expansion cards will be introduced first. This will be followed by brief sections explaining the main kinds of devices you can add to your PC, with tips for installation of each device and including, where appropriate, a typical DEVICE statement for your CONFIG.SYS file.

Overview of Expansion Cards

Each rectangular expansion card contains circuitry for a particular purpose, which can include additional RAM memory for your system, interface circuits and connectors for serial and/or parallel devices, a controller for floppy or hard disk drives, and so on. The card has an *edge connector* along part of the bottom that carries electrical signals between the circuits on the card and the rest of the PC, via a pathway called a *bus*.

The compatibility of an expansion card with a particular model of PC depends on which bus is provided by the system. The PC and XT provide an 8-bit bus; the AT has a 16-bit bus (but also accepts 8-bit cards). The terms *8-bit, 16-bit*, and *32-bit* refer to how much data can be sent along the bus at a time. The more that can be sent, the faster data can be transferred, and thus performance improved.

The PS/2 Models 25 and 30 use the same bus as the PC/XT. The PS/2 Model 30/286 uses the AT bus. The other PS/2 models (50, 60, 70, and 80), however, use a completely different bus, called the *Micro Channel Architecture* (MCA), which provides a much more sophisticated 16- or 32-bit connection. The point to remember is that MCA cards cannot be used in non-MCA machines, and vice versa. For example, a memory expansion card designed for the AT will work in a PS/2 Model 30 (which uses the "standard" bus) but not in a PS/2 Model 50 (which uses the MCA bus). Figure 12.4 shows an 8-bit PC expansion card, a 16-bit AT expansion card, and a 16-bit MCA expansion card.

You can often get your dealer (either local or mail order) to install all the necessary expansion boards for you at the time you purchase your system. If so, you may want to skip the next sections devoted to installing expansion cards and read them later if and when you have to add a card yourself.

Instructions for installing a particular card are usually provided with the card, although sometimes they may be more cryptic than you would like. The basic owner's manual for the system usually also has a section on installing expansion cards. The procedure is simple and requires only that you exercise reasonable care. The only tool you might need is a screwdriver.

Before doing anything else, make sure the base unit and monitor are off. You might even want to unplug them from the electric outlet to be doubly sure. Although it is unlikely that you will get a serious electric shock from working with a live PC, it is easy to inadvertently make a short circuit that can cause a big repair bill. If you are in an area that has static electricity, it is a good idea to touch a grounded object to discharge any static buildup.

The next step is to remove the cover from the base unit by removing the screws from the back of the base unit. Use a screwdriver for the PC/XT/AT or just turn the knobs on the PS/2. If you're not sure which screws you need to remove, consult your system documentation. Make sure you put the screws in a safe place where you can find them later. Now lift the top up at a shallow angle, and then pull it forward.

You will see a set of expansion slots (from 3 to 8, depending on the PC model). Where each slot meets the side of the PC's case, there is a small metal cover that must also be removed by unscrewing it.

Before inserting the card, check its documentation to see if the card has one or more DIP switches. These are small boxes with (usually 4 or 8) little sliding switches built into them (see Figure 12.5). The switch positions are usually labeled "1" for On and "0" for Off. These switches control aspects of the card's functioning, such as configuring a serial connector card to be COM2: rather than COM1:. (Most Micro Channel cards don't use DIP switches. Instead, you run a program on your system's Reference Diskette that configures the card. This will be described in your card's documenta-

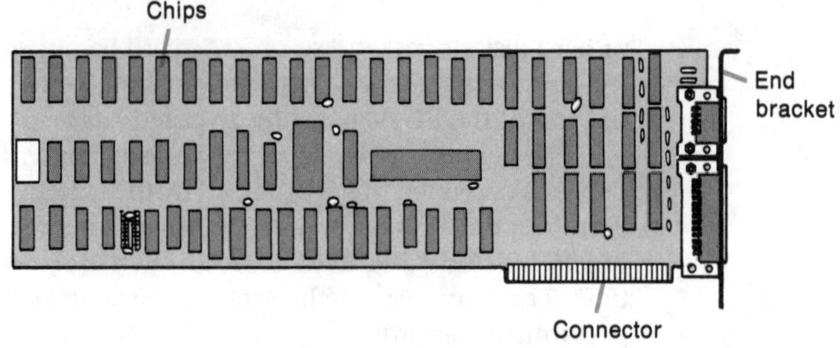

(A) PC, XT, AT (8 bits).

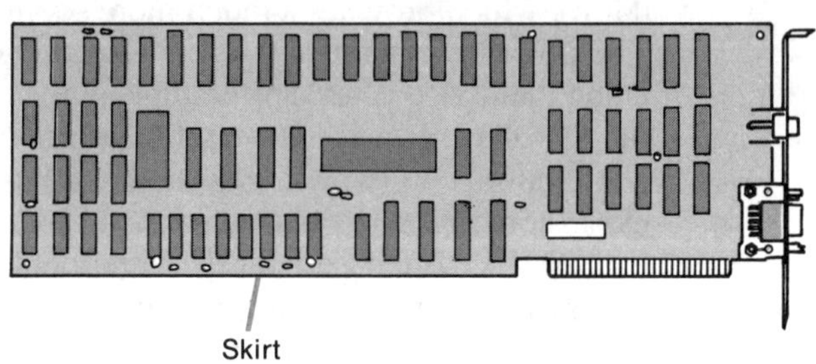

(B) PC, XT (8 bits).

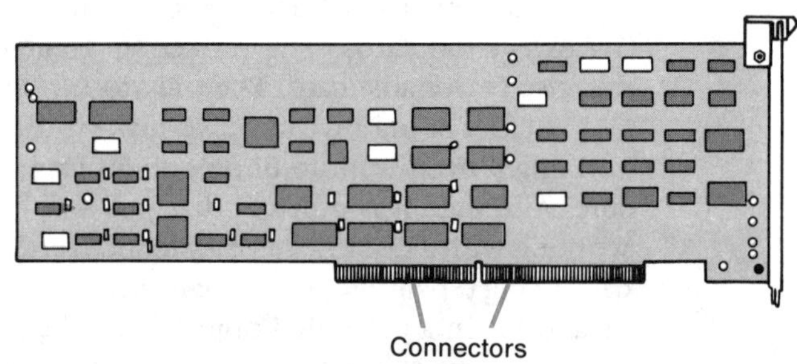

(C) PC, AT (16 bits).

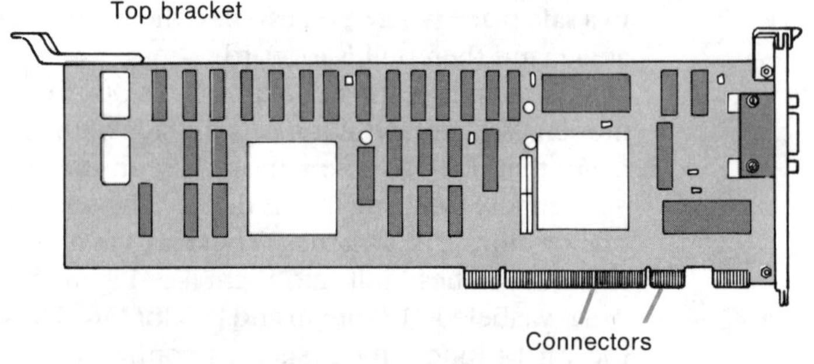

(D) PS/2 Model 50, etc., Micro Channel (16 or 32 bits).

Figure 12.4. *Types of expansion cards.*

tion.) After determining the switch settings you need, you can use a pencil or very small screwdriver to slide the switches into the appropriate positions. Also check your card's documentation (and if necessary your system documentation) to see if there are DIP switches on the system board itself that have to be set. In the PC, XT, and AT, for example, you may have to set a switch that specifies how much RAM you will be using. Another switch determines which video card will be active when the system is started (assuming you have more than one installed).

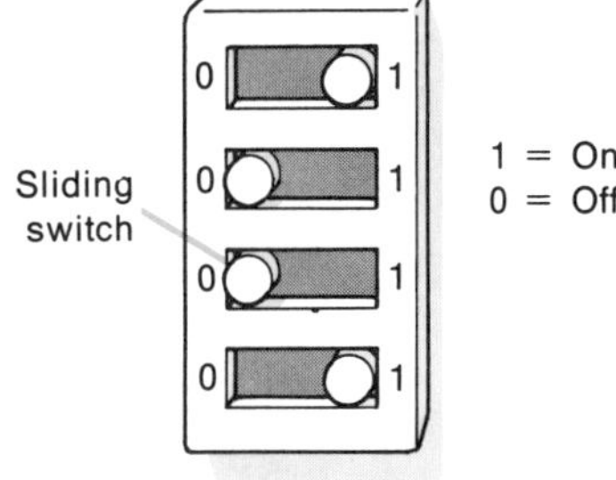

Figure 12.5. ***DIP switches.***

Write Down the Original Switch Positions

Before changing any DIP switch settings, write down the current switch positions. That way, if you get confused or make a mistake, you can restore the original settings.

The next question is "Which slot should this card go in?" The documentation for the card should specify whether it can be used only in a certain slot. Generally, you can use any slot in the PC and XT. In the AT, however, slots 1 and 7 are the 8-bit PC/XT type, while slots 2 through 6 and slot 8 are 16-bit slots with two rather than one connector. In other words, they look like two slots in line with each other, corresponding to the two connectors on a 16-bit card. An adapter designed for 16-bit operation must be put in slots 2 through 6 or 8.

An 8-bit PC/XT card can also be used in an AT, but there are two potential problems, one physical and one electronic. Some PC/XT cards have their bottom extending into a *skirt* that is as long as the edge connector (see Figure 12.4). Since the 16-bit AT slots have two connectors, the skirt bumps into one of the connectors, and such cards must be put in one of the 8-bit slots (1 or 7).

Even if an 8-bit card fits into an AT slot, you may get reduced performance. A memory board designed to transfer 8 bits at a time will slow down the performance of an AT whose CPU is designed to move data in 16-bit chunks. Such considerations will be touched on later whem memory expansion is discussed in detail.

Now that you've decided where the card is to go, grasp it and approach the slot, holding the card parallel to the slot and the wide end (which replaces the slot cover) facing toward the rear of the system unit. (*Note*: Expansion cards are connected differently in the PS/2 Models 25 and 30; see your system documentation.)

Now you're ready to put in the card. Push the card steadily into the slot until it is firmly in place. You may find it helpful to rock the card gently forward and backward to seat it. The card must be fully seated to have a proper electrical connection. Note that some cards (including MCA cards) have a guide into which you should insert the top of the card while you are pushing the bottom into the slot. Figure 12.6 shows an expansion card seated in its slot (this happens to be a 16-bit AT card).

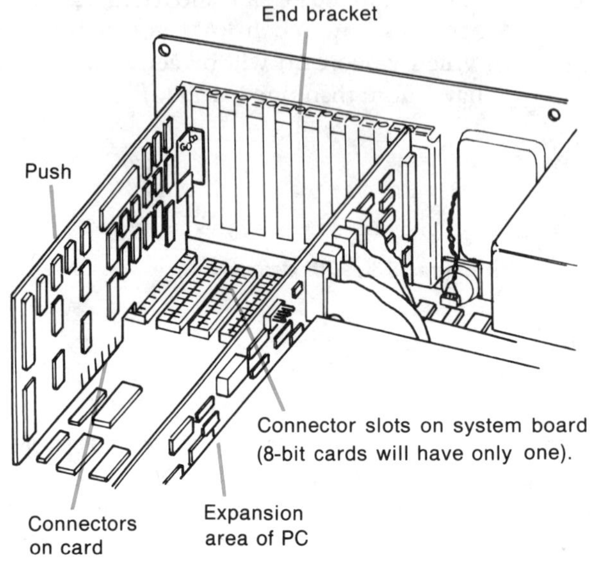

Figure 12.6. ***Expansion card seated in a slot.***

When you've installed the expansion card(s), slide the cover back on the system unit (again, on the PS/2 Models 25 and 30, it works a bit differently, so check your documentation). Insert and tighten the screws in the back of the base unit. Any ports (device connectors) provided with the card will be sticking out the opening in the base unit at the end of the card. You can now connect the appropriate cable to the port and, on the other end, to the device. (See the earlier discussion "Connectors and Cables.")

Expanding Your Memory

Many applications now support expanded memory beyond the 640K traditionally used by PC DOS (if you're not sure, check your application's manual). Expanded memory allows applications such as WordPerfect to handle large amounts of text or data much more quickly, and it allows working environments such as Microsoft Windows to keep more programs active at a time. Starting with PC DOS 4, PC DOS itself can use expanded memory to speed up file access. Finally, expanded memory can reduce the amount of the primary memory (the first 640K) needed by applications or by PC DOS. This allows more memory for programs that can't run in expanded memory, such as many memory-resident programs.

You should choose a card compatible with the expanded memory standard (EMS) 4.0. You should also be aware that while any EMS 4.0 card should allow applications to run under PC DOS 3.X or 4, PC DOS 4 commands themselves can use expanded memory only if the drivers that come with PC DOS 4 are installed. Unfortunately, these drivers appear to work only with genuine IBM memory expansion boards.

The system board is designed to hold up to a certain amount of memory. Early PCs and XTs use four rows of 64K chips, for a total of 256K "on board." The AT uses various combinations of 64K or 256 chips (depending on the model; early models used two piggybacked 64K chips in each socket) for a total capacity of 512K. PS/2 Models 25 and 30 come with 640K of memory installed, and Models 50 and above come with at least 1MB installed. Many PC-compatible systems are sold with at least 512K installed, some with 640K or even 1MB. It is easiest to specify the amount of memory you want at the time of purchase, and 640K is recommended for most users. If your system has less than 640K, it is not taking advantage of the maximum memory directly usable by PC DOS, and chances are that your applications aren't running as well as they could (some may not run at all!).

Buying and Installing System Memory

The first step is to expand your system board to its full capacity. You can have your dealer do this for you, or buy the chips and do it yourself. Remember to buy only the chips you need to reach the maximum capacity of your system board. For example, an AT system board holds up to 512K of memory. If you bought it with 256K, you can buy 18 128K chips to expand it to 512K.

Chips usually come in little plastic tubes containing nine chips, or one row's worth. You need to specify the correct size. Generally 64K is used for the system board, but 256K and even 1MB chips are increasingly being used on large-capacity expansion cards. Check your card's documentation. You should also check with the dealer to make sure the chips operate at a fast enough rate to keep up with your CPU. The speed of chips is measured in nanoseconds (ns), or billionths of a second. While 200-ns or even 250-ns chips may be fast enough for older PCs and XTs, most PCs sold today, especially those with 80286 or 80386 chips, run much faster and require faster memory chips.

If you install your own chips, make sure your system is turned off before opening up the system unit. Be careful to avoid static electricity—touch a grounded object if possible. When inserting the chips into the sockets, be careful not to bend the little legs. If you have to bend a leg to fit it in the corresponding socket hole, do it gently. Make sure each chip is firmly seated with all legs in the corresponding holes. When you are done, restart the system.

Dealing with Memory Problems

If everything goes well, the start-up memory test will run as usual, except that it will report a new total memory that includes the amount you have added. Your installation is complete, and you can skip the rest of this section.

Your PC has a built-in way of checking whether data has been stored correctly in memory. All PCs use an extra bit in each memory byte to hold a *parity* value. This value is generated by counting the number of ones in the other 8 bits, and setting the parity value to one or zero depending on whether the number of ones is even or odd. (*Odd parity* means that the bit is set to one when the number of other ones is odd; *even parity* means that it is set to one when there are an even number of other one bits.)

The POST tests memory by writing a bit pattern into each byte of memory, noting the parity value, reading the pattern back, and verifying that the parity value is correct. This test is also automatically performed by the hardware while you are running your applications. Whenever the parity doesn't match, it means that one or more bits are wrong, and the memory chip involved may be defective. The system is halted, and a code is displayed on the screen. The format can be

```
<bank> <position> 201
```

or

```
<bank> XXXX <position> 201
```

where `bank` is a single digit describing which bank (row) contains the bad chip, `XXXX` refers to digits that are irrelevant to the purpose here, `position` refers to the position of the chip in the bank, and `201` is the code that means a RAM error.

The four banks on the system board are numbered 0 through 3. Memory banks included on a memory expansion card are numbered starting with 4. The chip position is given by a two-digit value: 00 is the leftmost chip (the chip containing the parity value); the other chips in the row are indicated by the values 01, 02, 04, 08, 10, 20, 40, and 80 (from left to right). If you see the values AA or FF, it means that you set the memory configuration DIP switch wrong. Check your documentation to ensure that the switch setting matches the amount of memory you have installed.

For example, either one of the codes 020 201 and 0534220 201 means that there is a bad chip in bank 0 (the first bank on the system board) at position 20 (the seventh chip from the left). Note that in the first number of the longer code you look at only the first and last two digits.

When you have found out which chip has caused the error, you should turn the system off. If the chip is on an expansion card, you may have to remove the card to get at the chip. Check to see if the chip is pushed in all the way. Every leg of the chip must be seated in the corresponding socket. If a leg is bent, remove the chip. (You can do this by hand, but an inexpensive plastic chip pulling tool will come in handy.) *Gently* straighten out the bent leg, and reseat the chip. If the chip is on an expansion card, reinsert the card. Turn on the system and observe the POST results again. If you still get errors, you will probably have to replace the chip in question.

Expanding Memory to 640K and Beyond

To increase your total memory to 640K, you need a memory expansion card that fits one of your expansion slots. For example, a PC with a maximum of 256K on the system board needs a 384K expansion card to reach 640K. You can buy this card either *populated* (already containing the memory chips) or *0K*. In the latter case, you must buy the chips and install them in the sockets on the board (using the same procedure as that given earlier for installing chips on the system board). Note that if you are installing a memory expansion card in an AT, it should be a 16-bit card designed for that purpose and must be installed in one of the 16-bit slots (slots 2 through 6 or slot 8).

Before buying a memory expansion card, consider whether you might want to add expanded memory beyond 640K. Expanded memory is being used by an increasing number of applications and by PC DOS itself, starting with version 4. The best thing to do is to buy a memory card that is fully configurable. This means that it can include both the necessary memory to bring your system up to the 640K maximum of standard PC DOS memory *and* up to several megabytes of additional (expanded) memory. For example, if you are upgrading a 512K AT and buy a configurable card with 2MB of memory, you can, using the DIP switches and following the instructions that come with the card, designate 128K of the memory to backfill your system memory to 640K, and designate the rest as expanded memory. If you don't buy a configurable card, you have to buy a 128K expansion card to expand to 640K and then buy a separate card for expanded memory—this wastes a slot. Also, if you buy a fully configurable card with a high capacity (2MB or 4MB), you can install as much memory on it as you can afford now, and add more later.

(Most Micro Channel cards are inherently configurable, and instruct you to use options on your Reference Diskette to configure them. Since PS/2s all come with at least 640K, you don't have to worry about backfilling system memory. An additional advantage of the Micro Channel approach is that you can change your configuration simply by rerunning the Reference Diskette, without having to open up your system and change DIP switches.

Completing the Installation

If you are adding expanded memory beyond 640K, you must also install a device driver to enable applications to use it. If you are using one of the following IBM memory expansion boards or another board that fully emulates one of these, and you are using PC DOS 4, the driver XMA2EMS.SYS is provided with PC DOS 4:

IBM 2MB Expanded Memory Adapter

IBM PS/2 82086 Expanded Memory Adapter/A

IBM PS/2 80286 Memory Expansion Option

See the XMA2EMS.SYS entry in the Command Reference for a discussion of how to specify the DEVICE statement for your CONFIG.SYS and how to set memory addresses and frame sizes if necessary. An example statement for an AT would be:

```
device=c:\dos\xma2ems.sys
```

For an 80386 machine such as the IBM PS/2 Model 80, a special driver, XMAEM.SYS, is used to emulate the IBM memory expansion adapter. The XMA2EMS.SYS driver interacts in turn with this driver. The two drivers must be installed in the order shown:

```
device=c:\dos\xmaem.sys
device=c:\dos\xma2ems.sys
```

If you are using a non-IBM memory card, or a version of PC DOS prior to 4, you must use the device driver provided with the card. The card's documentation should give you the appropriate DEVICE statement for your CONFIG.SYS. If the driver is not specified as meeting the EMS 4.0 specification but instead mentions an earlier specification (such as EMS 3.2), check with the vendor to see if an upgraded driver is available. Older versions may not work with the newest application programs.

Adding Device Connections (Ports)

Many expansion cards include connectors for printers, modems, and other devices. As far as PC DOS is concerned, each device connection (port) lives in a particular address in memory. To communicate with the device, PC DOS or an application uses a machine instruction that copies data to that address, or reads the value stored at that address by the device. PC DOS provides some standard port addresses. These addresses are what you refer to when you use LPT1:, LPT2:, or LPT3: for parallel ports, or COM1:, COM2:, or COM3: for serial ports.

If you need to add ports to your system, it is best to buy cards that provide two or more ports, or that combine ports with another function such as added memory—this will save on expansion slots. When installing the card, make sure you set the DIP switches as specified in the documentation. If, for example, you already have one parallel and one serial port, you'll want to set a parallel/serial port card so that its parallel port is LPT2: and its serial port is COM2:. If you set two cards so that they use the same port, one or both will not work properly.

Accelerator Cards and Coprocessors

You can also buy a plug-in card that replaces your CPU with a newer, faster, more capable model. As mentioned earlier, the various models of PCs are designed to use different kinds of buses allowing data to be moved in 8-, 16-, or 32-bit chunks. The other factor that determines how quickly data can be moved (or, essentially, how fast your computer "computes") is the central processor, or CPU chip. The 8086 and 8088 CPUs used in PCs and the older XTs can move data only 8 bits at a time, while the 80286 can move data 16 bits at a time, and the 80386 can move data 32 bits at a time. (To take full advantage of the data capacity of the newer chips requires revision of the software, however.) Neither PC DOS nor many applications have been revised to get the most out of an 80386. Also, while the newer processors can deal directly with large amounts of RAM, PC DOS can run only in what is called *real mode*, allowing it a maximum of 640K of direct-access memory.

For a given processor, the faster its internal clock runs, the more instructions it can execute per second. Clock speed is measured in megahertz (MHz). For example, the 80286 in a PS/2 Model 50 runs at 10MHz, and various manufacturers offer 80286 machines that run at 16MHz or 20MHz. Some 80386 machines on the market can run at more than 30MHz.

Before buying any accelerator card, check with the manufacturer or dealer to make sure that your memory chips are fast enough to keep up with it. Their rating in nanoseconds—*ns*—should be stamped on them. The card you buy should be configurable from the keyboard because some applications won't run properly at the high "turbo" speed. Describe your system and be alert for any possible incompatibilities.

Accelerator cards can give you a performance improvement that is modest or better. Note, though, if you have an XT with an 8-bit bus, a 16-bit processor isn't going to run at full effectiveness. You can replace the whole system board (sometimes called a *mother board*) with one having a 16-bit or a 32-bit bus, but this is a major operation best left to a technician. It may be better to simply buy a new machine.

One improvement that is definitely recommended for applications involving intensive calculation (such as spreadsheets, statistics programs, some drafting programs, and so on) is to buy a *numeric coprocessor chip*. This is a chip that your system can use to help it perform arithmetic faster. The 8087 coprocessor is used with the 8088 or 8086, the 80287 is used with the 80286, and the 80387 with the 80386. Most systems have an empty socket into which you plug the coprocessor chip. Check your applications documentation to find out if it uses the coprocessor and if you need to select certain options to enable it.

Adding Floppy or Hard Drives

It is often desirable to add one or more disk drives. You may want to add a first hard disk to an older PC that came only with floppies. You may want to replace an older 10MB or 20MB hard drive with a larger 60MB one, or add a second hard drive that can be used to hold an exact copy (*mirror image backup*) of the data on your main hard disk. If you have only one floppy drive, adding a second one makes it easier to copy floppies. If you have an AT with only one floppy drive that uses the 1.2MB format, you've probably learned that your drive can read, but not reliably write, the 360K format. Adding a 360K floppy drive will solve that problem. You can also exchange data more readily with your colleagues if you add a 3½-inch disk drive to a PC, XT, or AT or add a 5¼-inch drive to your new PS/2. Prices for both hard and floppy drives have fallen dramatically.

Options and Alternatives

Depending on your PC model and the devices you have already installed, there are several ways you can add floppy or hard drives to your system. To add a drive you need two things: a disk controller card (and appropriate cable) and the drive itself. Floppy drives can be *internal*, fitting in one of the drive compartments (*bays*) in the system unit, or *external*, in a stand-alone case. Hard drives can also be internal or external. You can also get a hard drive complete with controller on a single expansion card.

First decide what kind of drive(s) you want to add. For floppy drives, this is simply a matter of determining the format: 360K, 1.2MB, 720K, or 1.44MB. Remember, however, that the 1.2MB drive cannot reliably write

360K disks. On the other hand, the 1.44MB 3½-inch drive *can* write the 720K 3½-inch format. For hard disks, both capacity and access speed are important. The smallest readily available hard drives have a capacity of 20MB, but 30MB costs very little more, and 60MB is increasingly popular. As for speed, the slower (and somewhat cheaper drives) use stepper motors. Drivers with voice coil motors are faster and more reliable, usually have higher capacity, and are somewhat more expensive. The average access rate (time to find a track) can range from about 20 milliseconds (ms) up to about 85 ms. Faster is better, though you reach a point of diminishing returns. Forty to 50 ms is reasonable for most uses, but a machine that is acting as a network server should have a faster hard disk. Use of a disk cache program or certain PC DOS settings can speed up the actual (effective) access time, as well; this is discussed in Chapter 11, "Customizing Your System."

Physical Considerations

If you have an older system such as the original IBM PC or COMPAQ portable, the power supply has a capacity of only 63.5 watts. There may not be power to spare for an add-on hard drive, since hard drives use more power than floppies. You should check with the dealer. If there is a power problem, you can buy a higher-capacity power supply (such as 150 or 200 watts), though if you are not handy with electronics you probably should have a dealer install it. Another alternative (in the case of add-on hard disks) is to buy one of the "disks on a card" that has a low power rating.

Next, assuming you aren't buying an all-in-one disk on a card, check your system documentation to see if you can use your existing controller. The controller on most PC, XT, and AT models can support several internal and external drives. If your controller has an available connector, you need only make sure that the add-on drive has the appropriate cable. If your controller has no room for connecting the desired drive, you will have to buy an additional controller and install it in a free expansion slot (or buy a disk-on-a-card). As with other kinds of cards, remember that Micro Channel PS/2s use controllers that are different from the older PC standard.

The next thing to check is whether there is room for an internal drive in your PC. Older PCs were designed for two full-height drives, but the more compact half-height drives are increasingly common. (You can buy a bracket assembly that allows you to put half-height drives in the full-height bay of an older PC.) If there is no room left in the system unit, you can either get an external drive with its own case or (in the case of hard disks) buy a drive-on-a-card.

All drives come with installation instructions—some more readable than others. The installation varies somewhat with the PC model. If you have to disconnect and remove existing components to install the drive, make a careful note of what went where, and what each set of screws belongs to. Note the instructions for connecting cables. In addition to the connection to the drive controller, some drives take their power directly from the PC bus, while others use a *Y connector* that allows them to share the power supply with the system board. If the job looks uncomfortably complicated, have a technician at a local dealer do the job. Paying for half an hour of his or her time is probably worth the peace of mind. An advantage of the drive-on-a-card is that, though it is more expensive than regular drives, installation simply involves plugging in the drive card like any other expansion card.

Before you close up your system unit, check the system documentation to see if a DIP switch setting on the system board must be changed to allow access to the new drive. Whether a setting is needed and which switches have to be set depend on the PC model. If you are installing the drive on a PS/2 Micro Channel model, there are no switches to set. Instead, you run the "Install an Option" selection on your Reference Diskette to change the system's internal configuration information to include the new device.

Telling PC DOS about Your New Hard Drive

Most drives sold today already have a low-level format. See the earlier section "Preparing Your Hard Disk" for the procedure to check the current status of your disk. If you need to perform a low-level format, see Chapter 6. This chapter also gives instructions for running FDISK to partition your disk, and FORMAT to do the high-level format. If your new disk is the only hard drive in the machine, see the earlier sections on installing PC DOS for the procedure to put PC DOS on the disk and make it the start-up disk.

Caution

Custom Drivers for Large Hard Disks
Before PC DOS supported disk partitions greater than 32MB, some system and drive vendors provided driver programs that modified PC DOS to allow huge partitions. Although most of these programs work well under ordinary circumstances, they usually do not work with special utility programs (such as Norton or Mace utilities) that work directly with the hard disk file structure. Also, if someone unknowingly starts the system from a floppy drive that doesn't have the special driver and tries to access the hard disk, directories and data can be destroyed or jumbled. It is safer to obtain an upgraded version of PC DOS.

If this is a second (or later) hard drive, run FDISK as described in Chapter 6, "Managing Your Hard Disk." You will see the additional menu item "Next fixed disk." Select it to turn FDISK's attention to your own disk, and then create your partition as discussed earlier. FDISK will automatically assign the drive letter that you will be using to refer to the disk in PC DOS commands. The first hard drive is always drive C. The second one is given a letter that depends on the number of floppy drives already present. For example, if you have three floppy drives and two hard drives, the drives would be A: (floppy), B: (floppy), C: (hard), D: (floppy), and E: (hard). (If you are using PC DOS 4, it is easiest to define one partition per hard drive; for earlier versions, you must break large drives into partitions of 32MB or less.)

Tip

Specifying the Total Number of Drives
If you have more than five drives total (hard and floppy), you will have to add the statement `lastdrive=`*`letter`* to your CONFIG.SYS, where *`letter`* corresponds to the total number of drives. For example, `lastdrive=g` allows for a total of seven drives (A, B, C, D, E, F, and G). The default, `lastdrive=e`, provides for five drives. (LASTDRIVE is available starting with PC DOS 3.0.) If you have defined additional logical drives (see the Command Reference entries for FDISK and DRIVER.SYS), these must also be counted in the total. If LASTDRIVE is not set correctly, you will receive the

`Invalid Drive Specification` error message when you try to refer to the excess drives.

Telling PC DOS about Your New Floppy Drive

If you have installed a 3½-inch drive, you may have to upgrade your PC DOS version. The 720K 3½-inch format is not supported until PC DOS 3.2, and the 1.44MB format requires PC DOS 3.3. If you need to upgrade, you might as well upgrade to PC DOS 4 (see the earlier section "Upgrading Your PC DOS Version" for more information).

Now that your drive is installed, you may need to make some changes to your CONFIG.SYS file before PC DOS will recognize it. The ROM BIOS of each PC includes information about the standard drive configuration of the machine. This normally takes care of the internal disk drives provided by the design of the machine. For example, most PS/2s come with a single internal floppy drive and an internal hard drive. If you add an external 360K floppy drive to a PS/2, the BIOS will not recognize it. Fortunately, PC DOS provides a device driver called DRIVER.SYS, which adds the necessary information for the new disk drive to the table of drive information that was originally loaded into memory from the BIOS. If you are not sure whether you need DRIVER.SYS, simply try to access your new drive using its drive letter. (The first two floppy drives are A and B; the first hard drive is C. After that, drives are assigned letters in the order of installation.) If the following happens, you need a DRIVER.SYS statement to tell PC DOS about this drive. (You may also need a LASTDRIVE setting; see the last Tip.)

```
C:\>dir e:
General Failure Error
```

Similarly, the following message indicates that you need a DRIVER.SYS statement:

```
C:\>dir e:
Invalid Drive Specification
```

The general format for the DRIVER.SYS statement in your CONFIG.SYS file is as follows for PC DOS 4:

```
device=driver.sys /d:drive number /f:form factor
```

The `drive number` describes the order of installation of physical drives. The first drive is number 0 and always refers to an internal drive. The second drive (either internal or external) is number 1, and the third drive (which must be external) is drive 2. Numbers 3 through 127 refer to additional drives. Note that hard drives are *not* counted for this purpose, and DRIVER.SYS should not be used with hard drives (FDISK takes care of them).

The `form factor` describes the drive capacity. Zero is 360K 5¼-inch, 1 is 1.2MB 5¼-inch, 2 is 720K 3½-inch, and 3 is 1.44MB 3½-inch. If you omit the `/f:` specification, 2 (the 720K drive) is assumed. Thus, if you are installing a second (external, 360K) floppy drive in a PS/2 (which comes with one internal floppy drive), the statement in your CONFIG.SYS would be

```
device=c\dos\driver.sys /d:1 /f:0 /c
```

(This assumes that you have put the DRIVER.SYS file in the DOS directory on drive C. Note that the `1` following `/d:` specifies the *second* drive; the first drive is `0`. The `/c` is used for those drives that can sense when the drive door has been left open, allowing PC DOS to inform the user of this fact. This feature is supported by all drives on PS/2s and most drives (excepting some 360K drives) on ATs and the XT-286 machine.

In an AT that already has a 1.2MB 5¼-inch drive and a 360K drive, a third, external 720K 3½-inch drive would be specified using:

```
device=c:\dos\driver.sys /d:2 /c
```

The `/f:` option is not needed, since the 720K drive is the default.

For PC DOS 3.2 and 3.3, the DRIVER.SYS statement is similar, except that the form factor (*/f:*) option is not available. You must instead specify the number of tracks (*/t:*), sectors (*/s:*), and heads (*/h:*) on the drive. Each of these has a default, so some specifications can be omitted. The heads specification can be omitted for all but old 160/180K single-sided drives, which have only one head. Here is what you need for each of the four currently used drive formats:

Format	Track, Sector, Head Specification
360K	/t:40
720K	None needed
1.2M	/s:15
1.44M	/s:18

Thus, the two examples given earlier (the 360K drive for the PS/2 and the 720K drive for the AT) would look like this for PC DOS 3.2 or 3.3:

```
device=c:\dos\driver.sys /t:40
device=c:\dos\driver.sys
```

Finally, you can have more than one DRIVER.SYS setting in your CONFIG.SYS, either if you have more than one add-on drive or if you are creating alternative drive letters (logical drives). The Command Reference entry for DRIVER.SYS explains when and how this is useful.

Upgrading Your Screen Display

Unless you will be running only simple text-based applications, you will need a video display with graphics capability. Many of the newest word processors require video graphics to display different fonts and special characters on the screen. Desktop publishing virtually requires graphics, with higher resolution allowing you to see more text at a time and giving greater accuracy of representation. Most spreadsheet and database programs offer graphing functions (pie charts, line graphs, and so on), which also require a graphics display. For these applications you should get an EGA (Enhanced Graphics Adapter) and a compatible color monitor, or the newer higher-resolution VGA (Video Graphics Array) and the special *analog* or *multisynch* type of monitor that it requires. Before you buy any monitor, find out if it is compatible with your video display adapter.

If you have an older system that has a monochrome text-only display adapter (MDA) or a low-resolution CGA (Color Graphics Adapter) display, you can upgrade to one of the two most common current standards: EGA (Enhanced Graphics Adapter) or VGA (Video Graphics Array) display with high resolution and the ability to display many colors. The EGA provides 640x350 screen points (pixels) in 16 colors; the VGA provides 640x480 pixels in 16 colors, or 320x200 pixels in 256 colors. Such displays are particularly suited to high-end word processing, desktop publishing, graphing, drawing, and design applications. (If you have a PS/2, these superior graphics capabilities are already built-in.)

The EGA or VGA display capability actually involves two components: the video graphics adapter card that is plugged into an expansion slot and the use of a suitable monitor. In selecting a display card, if you are not buying an IBM card (which costs more than the competition and usually has fewer features), you must consider the issue of compatibility. It is best to read the periodic surveys of graphics adapters (and monitors, for that matter) in the trade publications. Your card should be described as *register compatible*. This means that programs that write directly to special memory locations (*registers*) will work in the same way as with the IBM cards. Cards described as only *BIOS compatible* may not work with some applications. Some cards come with a printer port, which will save you an expansion slot.

The color quality and sharpness of a monitor's image is partly subjective. It is always a good idea to view the monitor you are interested in using while you run a favorite application. The type of electronics used by the monitor must also be considered. There are three common types today: RGB, analog, and multiscan. Without going into the technicalities, note that you need an RGB or multiscan monitor for EGA, and an analog or multiscan monitor for VGA. However, not all multiscan monitors work satisfactorily with VGA, which needs a high scan rate, so you need to check. If you have EGA and want to upgrade to the more expensive VGA eventually, choose a suitable multiscan monitor and you won't have to replace it later. Finally, you will need a suitable cable to connect your adapter card and monitor.

Installation involves plugging in the adapter card, setting any DIP switches on the card and/or your system board according to the directions provided, and connecting the monitor to your adapter card.

In most cases you will not need to make changes to your CONFIG.SYS or AUTOEXEC.BAT files to use your new video display. If you are using national language character sets, however, you should see Chapter 13, "International Language Support," for instructions involving the DISPLAY.SYS driver and the MODE statement. Also, you may need to change the options you use with the GRAPHICS command to allow it to print higher-resolution screen displays (see the Command Reference entry for GRAPHICS). Many new applications allow you to specify the display resolution you want to use, and will optionally display 50 lines or more of text on a single screen using EGA or VGA; consult your documentation.

Using the MODE Command to Set or Restore Your Video Display

The MODE command includes several options involving the video display. One common use of MODE is to reset your video display after leaving a program that didn't properly restore it. (These tend to be older, less sophisticated programs or games.) By typing the following command, you can restore a standard 80-column display on the EGA or VGA:

```
C:\>mode co80
```

To restore an 80-column monochrome display, type

```
C:\>mode bw80
```

Note that bw stands for "black and white," though many monitors use green, amber, or some other single color for the mono display. See the Command Reference for additional features of MODE that affect the video display.

Using High-Resolution Displays with Applications

Some applications programs automatically detect the fact that you have an EGA or VGA display, and provide you with more colors and possibly more text lines on the screen. Other applications default to a standard mono display but allow you to specify an EGA or VGA. See your application documentation for details.

To Specify the Number of Lines Displayed

With PC DOS 4, you can also specify the number of lines that will be displayed. You can specify 43 lines for an EGA, or 50 for VGA. If you have an EGA installed and put the following statement in your AUTOEXEC.BAT file, PC DOS will come up with 43 lines available for directory listings and other PC DOS operations.

```
mode co80,lines=43
```

If you add the following command to your CONFIG.SYS file (assuming that the ANSI.SYS driver is in your DOS directory), ANSI.SYS will also try to force your applications to use the number of lines that you have set in the MODE command. This may not work properly with some programs. In that case, remove this statement.

```
device=c:\dos\ansi.sys /l
```

Installing a Printer

The decision of what kind of printer to get is beyond the scope of this book. The market changes too rapidly for timely recommendations. Many major PC magazines run survey articles and reviews comparing printer features.

The first step in installing a printer is to determine whether it uses a serial or parallel connection. Some offer both; see the printer manual. Dot-matrix printers tend to have parallel connections, while most laser or daisy wheel printers use serial connections. If the printer doesn't come with the appropriate cable, note the type of connector on the printer side and the type of connector on the computer's serial or parallel port. Some printers (usually older dot-matrix parallel printers) use a Centronics-type connector on the printer end, but a regular DB-25 connector on the computer end. For a serial printer used with an AT, you may have to get a special connector with a DB-9 on the computer end and a DB-25 on the printer end. If your computer doesn't have a free port of the appropriate type, you can obtain and install an expansion card that provides the port. For more on connectors, see the earlier discussion "Connectors and Cables."

You can test your printer by typing:

```
C:\>copy con: lpt1:
```

Substitute another port name for `lpt1:` if the printer is connected elsewhere, for example `lpt2:` for a second parallel port, or `com1:` for the first serial port.

Type a line of text and press Enter. The text should be printed correctly on the printer. If it is garbled, check to see that the printer's DIP switches are set correctly. For a serial printer, check the documentation for the speed (baud rate), parity, and number of data and stop bits needed, and the corresponding DIP switch settings. You may also need to use a MODE command to set the computer's serial port properly. See the Command Reference entry for MODE (serial port control) for a complete discussion of options for the serial port. If nothing comes through, check the physical connection to make sure the connectors are pushed in all the way. Also make sure you specified the correct port in your COPY CON: command.

Assuming it is working, each line you type will be echoed at the printer. Press Ctrl-Z to end the COPY command. You have now tested the basic operation of your printer. (Many printers also have built-in "self-tests" that you can run; see your printer manual.)

Version 4

Installing a Printer with SELECT

If you have bought a new printer, you may wish to rerun the SELECT program and select that printer on the printer screen. This will install the proper options for graphics printing (the GRAPHICS command) and for code-page switching (if you have selected a country other than the United States).

If the printer is an IBM model, standard PC DOS features should work automatically with it, though you will have to select certain options. If you wish to print screen graphics, see the Command Reference entry for GRAPHICS. If you wish to use characters for a national language other than United States English, see Chapter 13, "International Language Support."

If the printer is not from IBM, it probably has an "IBM compatible mode" or "emulation" in which it uses the standard IBM character set and responds to commands used by a popular printer such as the Epson dot-matrix printers or the HP Laserjet. The mode is usually set by setting one or more DIP switches in the printer; again, see your printer manual.

Finally, when you install an applications program such as a word processor or desktop publishing program, the program will ask you what printer you have. If your model is not among those listed, set it to an emulation mode and specify the printer it emulates.

Installing a Modem

As you probably know, a *modem* (modulator/demodulator) is a device that allows data to be transmitted over telephone lines. You would use a modem with appropriate communications software to dial an information service or bulletin board, to send files to another user, or to connect your home computer with a larger computer at work.

Modems come in two types: external and internal. An *external* modem has its own case, and is connected to one of your system's serial ports with a modem cable. An *internal* modem is built into an expansion card that goes into an available expansion slot. It doesn't require a separate serial port. Internal modems are a bit cheaper, but they tie up an expansion slot. Also, if you buy an internal modem for an AT you can't use it in a Micro Channel PS/2, or vice versa. With either type of modem, a standard phone cord also connects the modem to a telephone jack.

The modems most commonly used by PC users transmit data at 1200 *baud*, or about 120 characters a second, though 2400-baud modems are increasingly common. Most modems use a standard command set invented by the Hayes Corporation, and you should buy a Hayes-compatible modem to ensure that it will work with communciations programs.

Check your modem documentation for DIP switch settings. Then check the documentation for the communications program that you will be using, and see what modem settings are required. If a serial port is being used by another device (such as a serial printer), set your modem to use the next available port name (e.g., COM2: or COM3:).

Once you've installed your modem, you can perform a basic test from the PC DOS command line. Obtain the phone number of a computer that you want to dial (or use a voice phone number in your office, but warn the person whose phone you are using!). Now try to dial the number from the modem as follows:

```
C:\>echo atdt1234567 > com1:
```

Use your number in place of **1234567** of course, and change the **COM1:** to another serial port if necessary. The **atdt** is a Hayes command meaning "attention, dial with tone dialing." If your modem is connected properly, the phone should dial the number. If you get an answer, type:

```
C:\>ath0
```

This command hangs up the modem. Without communications software, you can't carry on much of a conversation with the computer at the other end. You can now read the instructions that came with your communications software.

Should There Be a Mouse in Your House?

Many applications benefit from the use of a pointing device, the most popular of which is the mouse. A mouse allows you to point to, select, and move screen objects. The two main purposes are to allow easy selection of menu items, files, directories, and so on, and to make it easy to draw designs and pictures. The Microsoft Windows environment and the new PC DOS 4 DOSSHELL interface both work best with mice.

Before buying a mouse, decide where to connect it. There are versions of mice that can be connected to a serial port, a special mouse port (on PS/2s), or an expansion card (this is called a *bus mouse*). Microsoft, for example, makes all three types. Which you choose (other than for PS/2s) depends on whether you have more serial ports or more expansion slots. All things being equal, the serial mouse is cheaper, since it doesn't need an expansion card. Most mice work by mechanical means—a rolling ball in the base of the mouse. However, *optical mice* are also available. These mice scan grid lines on a special mouse pad. The optical mouse has the advantage of fewer moving parts, but it must be used with the mouse pad.

The mouse will come with a driver program that must be installed via a DEVICE statement in your CONFIG.SYS (or, occasionally, run as a program from your AUTOEXEC.BAT file). If you buy a mouse from someone other than Microsoft or IBM, you should make sure that the driver is compatible with them. Remember that a mouse works only with applications that are designed to take advantage of it. Check your application documentation for references to mice.

Version 4

Installing a Mouse Driver with SELECT

If you are using PC DOS 4, see the earlier discussion "Review Screen" for DOSSHELL parameters used with SELECT. The discussion will help you determine which mouse driver to install.

Other Devices

There are many other devices that you can connect to your PC. Printers, of course, can be connected to parallel or serial ports. There are alternative input devices such as joysticks, trackballs, or graphics tablets. There are scanners for reading printed text or graphics. For communication, there are modems and FAX boards. For mass storage, there are CD ROMS, WORM (write once, read many times) drives, tape drives, and removable cartridge drives. There are network connectors to link your PCs to others.

Before buying any of these items, consider the following:

- What other items are needed before the device can actually be used?
- With what software is this device compatible?
- What are the limitations of the device?
- Does this device have special hardware requirements, for example, an 80286 or 80386 processor or a math coprocessor chip?
- If you are considering adding this device to a PS/2, is the device compatible with the Micro Channel? (Remember that standard PC expansion cards will not work with a PS/2 Model 50 or higher.)

Before installing any of these devices, read the provided documentation carefully. Check especially for the following:

- Card installation instructions, including DIP switch settings (for standard PCs) or instructions for using the Reference Diskette (for PS/2s)
- Instructions for installing the device driver (this normally specifies a DEVICE statement for your CONFIG.SYS file)
- Cautions and tips for best performance and for preserving your data (for mass storage devices)

What's Next

Chapter 11, "Customizing Your System," continues the themes this chapter begins, expanding on techniques for developing your CONFIG.SYS and AUTOEXEC.BAT files to add PC DOS device drivers and set parameters. Chapter 6, "Managing Your Hard Disk," presents related material concerning installing, formatting, and partitioning hard disks. Chapter 10, "Batch Files," teaches all about creating and using batch files.

Key Concepts and Words

Before you read further, use the following list to test your understanding of the concepts and words in this chapter.

RAM	Ports	Error diagnosis
Floppy disk drive	Accelerator cards	Format
Hard disk drive	Coprocessors	Expanded and extended memory
Keyboard	MDA	Device connections
Video display monitor	CGA	System speedup
Expansion cards	EGA	Devices
Printer	VGA	Device drivers
Modem	RGB	
Mouse	Power On Self Test (POST)	
Connectors		
Cables		

Chapter 13

PC DOS machines are used all over the world, partly because its code-page feature lets you type and print characters from alphabets used in other countries. In this chapter, you'll learn

- *How the PC's character sets for the keyboard, display, and printer use "code pages" to let users type and print character sets for different languages*
- *How to select a country format and a keyboard layout*

Chapter 13
International Language Support

If you've received a letter from a European country, you may have noticed that some of the alphabetical letters have accent marks that aren't ordinarily used in English. You may also have noticed that the month and day appeared in a different order from American usage. A letter from Great Britain may be dated 8 December 1990, for example. If your company receives invoices in foreign currencies, you may have noticed differences in the numeric and currency formats—the use of a period instead of a comma in numbers, for example.

If you have bought a standard PC for use in the United States, you don't have to worry about any of these differences, unless you need to prepare text for foreign use. All of the appropriate characters and formats for American usage are built into the hardware. Should you wish to tailor PC DOS operation to the needs of another country, however, you need to set up your keyboard, video display, and printer so that you can use the special characters and format conventions for that country.

National Differences

IBM has made an effort to allow users in each country to tailor the text capabilities of their PCs to their own national standards for

- Keyboard layout
- Diacritical (accent) marks
- Date and time formats
- Numeric format

- Currency format
- Sorting order

Keyboard Layout

Overall, most national PC keyboards follow the typewriter layout that has been standard for almost a hundred years. A few letters are found in different positions, reflecting frequency of use in different languages. Figures 13.1 and 13.2 show French and German keyboards for the AT and the enhanced keyboards. Notice that on the French and German keyboards the letters *q* and *z* (among others) appear in positions different from those on American keyboards. The other change in the keyboard layout is the addition of diacritical marks such as the German umlaut and French cedilla. (Diacritical marks are accents and other marks that modify how a letter is pronounced.) Note that the PC DOS 3.3 manual has a complete set of keyboard layouts for supported languages. Starting with PC DOS version 4, they are found in a separate publication called *IBM Keyboard Layouts for Your PC and PS/2*.

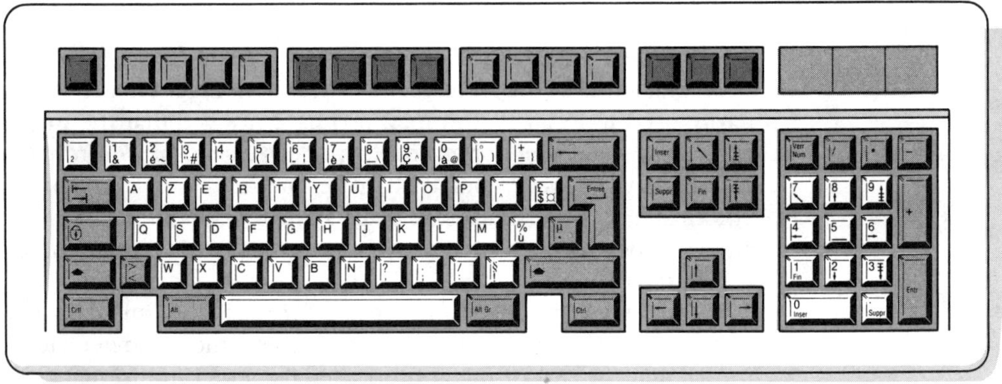

(A) French Enhanced PC.

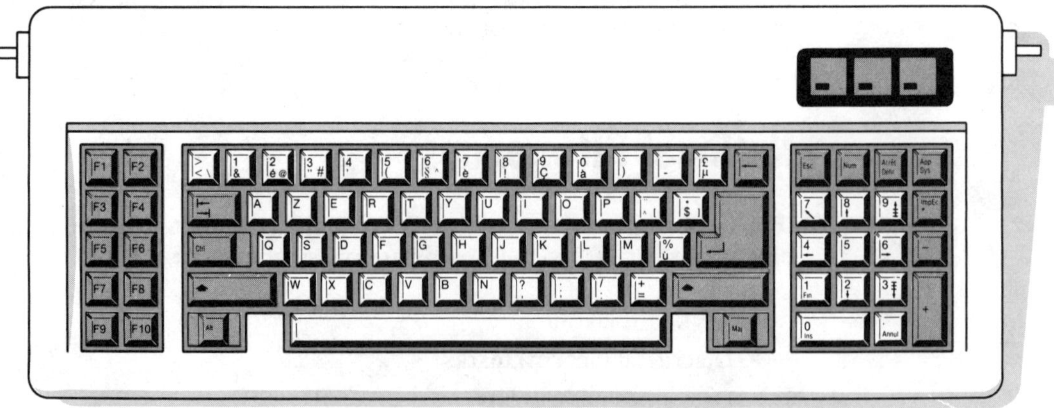

(B) French AT.

Figure 13.1. *French keyboards.*

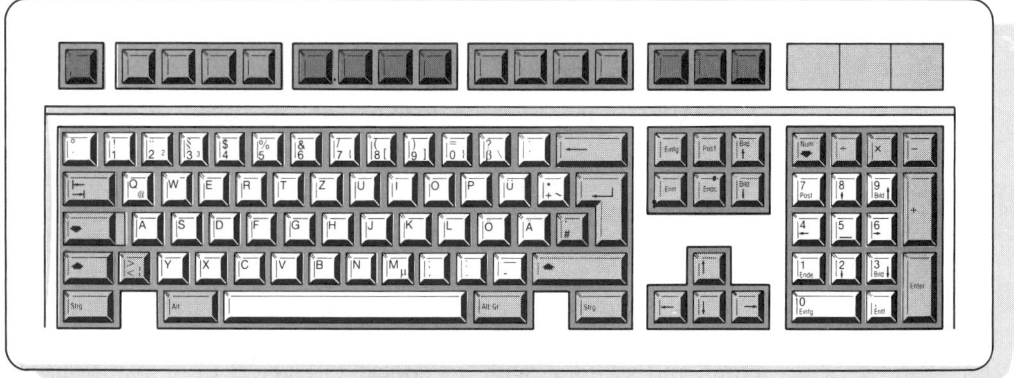

(A) German Enchanced PC.

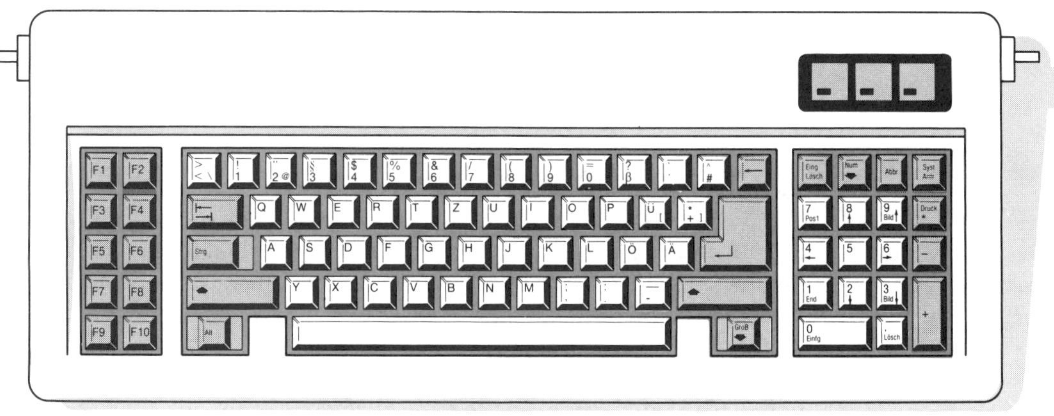

(B) German AT.

Figure 13.2. ***German keyboards.***

Tip

Users of PC DOS Versions 3.2 and Earlier

Starting with PC DOS version 3.0, you can select a national keyboard layout and specify the COUNTRY setting for date, time, and other formats, but features involving the use of national language character sets (code pages) are available only with PC DOS versions 3.3 and later. If you want to use multiple character sets and print them on your printer, you will have to upgrade your PC DOS.

Date, Time, and Other Formats

The date and time formats determine how PC DOS will show the date and time for files in directory listings, and how the DATE and TIME commands will accept input when you want to set the date or time. The discussion of these commands elsewhere in this book assumes the American formats, which are the default. However, if you have installed support for a different country, the DATE and TIME commands will accept and display dates in that country's format.

The numeric format describes how groups of digits will be separated and how the decimal point will be shown. For example, the amount *1,000,000.00* in American format appears in some European formats as *1.000.000,00*.

The currency format specifies the symbol that will be used (dollar sign, pound sign, or an abbreviation for the currency name) and whether the symbol appears before or after the number, with or without a space following the symbol if it precedes the number. It also specifies how many decimal places will be shown (two for dollars and most other currencies).

The sorting order specified for a given country affects how the SORT command will deal with the special characters used in various languages.

It is important to realize that installing support for a language other than English affects only the particular PC DOS features just discussed. The names of PC DOS commands and the text of messages displayed by PC DOS do not change. (However, you may be able to get a special version of PC DOS in which commands and messages have been translated to a different language.)

What Are Code Pages?

Supporting a national language other than United States English on your PC involves installing *code pages*, or alternative character sets. A character set provides the capability to key in, display, and print all of the symbols needed for normal writing: upper- and lowercase letters of the alphabet, numerals, punctuation marks, and a variety of other characters that serve special purposes. If all languages used the same characters, only one character set would be needed. Since there are differences between the characters needed for English, French, and German, for example, PC DOS needs a way to use more than one set of characters and a way to allow the user to choose which one(s) to use. This idea is similar to the typewriters that have snap-in balls for changing the character set.

The ASCII Character Set

To see how PC DOS provides alternative character sets, you need to understand how characters are stored and used inside the PC. As you may know, computers don't really store characters; they store only numbers. A particular byte in memory may have the number 65 stored in it. If a program is using this piece of memory to store a number that it is using in a spreadsheet, it will interpret the 65 as a number (or perhaps as part of a larger number). However, if your word processor is using that memory to store something you've written, it will see the 65 and display the letter *A*. Why? Because it is treating this piece of data as a character. The whole set of characters used in PCs is called *ASCII*, for American Standards Committee for Information Interchange. The ASCII code assigns a number between 0 and 255 to each possible character that might be used. Character number 65 happens to be the uppercase letter *A*. The first 128 characters are shared in common with nearly every kind of PC made, and involve control characters (such as Ctrl-C), the upper- and lowercase alphabets, the numerals, and the most commonly used English puncutation marks. The second 128 codes, sometimes called the *extended character set* or *graphics character set*, include less frequently used symbols, some letters of the Greek alphabet, and characters useful for drawing lines and simple graphics. Figure 13.3 shows a table of the characters used in the United States. Each code corresponds to a two-digit hexadecimal number. The letter *A*, for example, is 41 in the hexadecimal system, or 65 in the decimal system. Don't worry if you aren't familiar with hexadecimal numbers; the table is shown just so that you can see what characters are available.

Hex Digits 1st → 2nd ←	0-	1-	2-	3-	4-	5-	6-	7-		8-	9-	A-	B-	C-	D-	E-	F-
-0		►		0	@	P	`	p		Ç	É	á	░	└	╨	α	≡
-1	☺	◄	!	1	A	Q	a	q		ü	æ	í	▒	┴	╤	β	±
-2	☻	↕	"	2	B	R	b	r		é	Æ	ó	▓	┬	╥	Γ	≥
-3	♥	‼	#	3	C	S	c	s		â	ô	ú	|	├	╙	π	≤
-4	♦	¶	$	4	D	T	d	t		ä	ö	ñ	┤	─	╘	Σ	⌠
-5	♣	§	%	5	E	U	e	u		à	ò	Ñ	╡	┼	╒	σ	⌡
-6	♠	▬	&	6	F	V	f	v		å	û	ª	╢	╞	╓	µ	÷
-7	•	↨	'	7	G	W	g	w		ç	ù	º	╖	╟	╫	τ	≈
-8	◘	↑	(	8	H	X	h	x		ê	ÿ	¿	╕	╚	╪	Φ	°
-9	○	↓	)	9	I	Y	i	y		ë	Ö	⌐	╣	╔	┘	Θ	·
-A	◙	→	*	:	J	Z	j	z		è	Ü	¬	║	╩	┌	Ω	•
-B	♂	←	+	;	K	[	k	{		ï	¢	½	╗	╦	█	δ	√
-C	♀	∟	,	<	L	\	l	|		î	£	¼	╝	╠	▄	∞	η
-D	♪	↔	-	=	M	]	m	}		ì	¥	¡	╜	═	▌	φ	^{2}
-E	♫	▲	.	>	N	^	n	~		Ä	₧	«	╛	╬	▐	ε	■
-F	☼	▼	/	?	O	_	o	⌂		Å	ƒ	»	┐	╧	▀	∩	

Figure 13.3. ***United States character set (code page).***

Now consider what happens when you press, say, the *z* key on your keyboard. The circuitry on the keyboard sends a signal called a *scan code* that is unique to each key or key combination. When PC DOS started up, it loaded a table of ASCII character values from ROM. The table assigned an ASCII character to each key code, and thus the table is called a *code page*. The key code for the key marked *z* is, not surprisingly, assigned the ASCII value for the character *z* (which happens to be 122 in decimal, or 7A in hexadecimal).

This character table enables PC DOS to translate the code generated by your key-press into the appropriate character from the table. A similar built-in table for the video display is used to display the *z* you typed on your screen. If you send the *z* character as part of a file to the printer, the printer uses its own character table in ROM (or in a font in RAM for more sophisticated printers) to control the hammer, print head, or laser beam to print the character.

Redefining the Keyboard

Now suppose you want to use a different keyboard layout—for example, the one for Germany. In order to do so, you must replace the table that translates key-presses with one that translates the keys to the appropriate German characters. In other words, this table redefines the keyboard as though you had physically rearranged the keys. When this new code page is loaded, the keypress for the character marked *z* on a standard keyboard no longer has the ASCII value for the *z* character. It has the ASCII value for *y*. Therefore, pressing the key marked *z* actually generates the character *y*, which is in that position on the German keyboard, as shown in Figure 13.1.

The character table (code page) for the video display must also be replaced so that the correct characters will appear on the screen. And, if you wish to print the text, the table for the printer must also be changed. Figure 13.4 shows schematically how this process works, and it lists the PC DOS device drivers and commands that are used in each part of the process. These will be discussed individually later.

Installing Code Pages

Here is an overview of what you must do to set up code pages for a national language, assuming that you have PC DOS 3.3 or later:

- Select the country format (COUNTRY setting in CONFIG.SYS).
- Select an appropriate keyboard layout for that country (KEYB command in AUTOEXEC.BAT).
- Load information that PC DOS needs for displaying extended characters and switching among code pages (NLSFUNC command in AUTOEXEC.BAT (or load with INSTALL in CONFIG.SYS for PC DOS 4).
- Install support for code pages in the video display (DISPLAY.SYS driver in CONFIG.SYS and, if using CGA graphics, GRAFTABL in AUTOEXEC.BAT).
- Install support for code pages in the printer (PRINTER.SYS driver in CONFIG.SYS).
- Load code pages for the console screen and keyboard (MODE CON: CP PREP command in AUTOEXEC.BAT).
- Load code pages for the printer (MODE LPTx: CP PREP command in AUTOEXEC.BAT).

Once you have prepared the code pages, you can

- Select or change the current code page for all devices (CHCP command).
- Select or change the code page for a particular device (MODE CON: CP SELECT or MODE LPT: CP SELECT command).

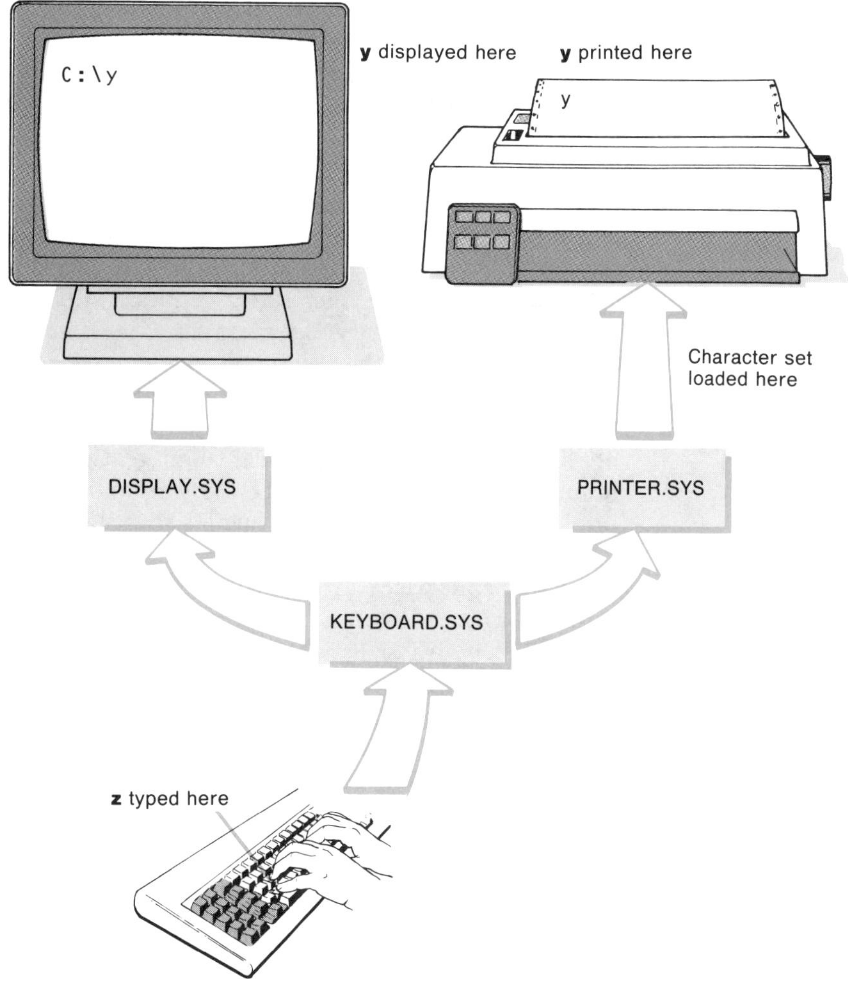

Figure 13.4. ***Character set translation.***

- Check the status of your code pages (MODE device CP /STA or MODE /STA command).

Let PC DOS 4 Do the Work

Setting up a code page probably looks like a lot of work to you, but there is good news. If you are installing PC DOS 4, you can have PC DOS set up for you all of the CONFIG.SYS and AUTOEXEC.BAT statements that support and prepare code pages. You can skip all the way to the later section "Loading and Using Code Pages."

If you are using a version of PC DOS earlier than 4, the SELECT command will do part (but not all) of the work. Finally, even if you have to put all of the necessary statements into your AUTOEXEC.BAT and CONFIG.SYS files yourself, once it is done you don't need to do it again (unless, of course, you move to another country).

Using PC DOS 4 SELECT to Select Format, Keyboard, and Code Pages

At the same time you install PC DOS 4 using the SELECT program, you can effortlessly install code page support. Start the SELECT program, following the instructions in Chapter 12, "Installing a PC DOS System." The second screen after the introductory screens is entitled "Select Country and Keyboard." The default (if you press Enter) is to accept the predefined country and keyboard, which is normally "United States." To select a different country and keyboard, move the highlight to item 2 (using the Down Arrow key) and press Enter. On the next screen, entitled "Country Selection," move the highlight to the country you want to use. If the country you want is not listed, choose a country on the list that has similar language and conventions. Press Enter, which moves you to the Keyboard Selection screen. Choose the keyboard layout for the language you will be using. If the language you want is not listed, choose the most similar language. Continue with PC DOS installation as described in Chapter 12. Be sure to select the correct printer and printer port on the appropriate menus so that code-page support will be installed for them. (If you do not have an IBM printer, you probably won't be able to use code pages on your printer. See the later section on PRINTER.SYS for further discussion.)

When your installation is complete, examine the AUTOEXEC.BAT and CONFIG.SYS files (AUTOEXEC.400 and CONFIG.400) that SELECT has created. You will find that the appropriate COUNTRY, KEYB, and MODE statements have been put in AUTOEXEC.400 and that the DEVICE=DISPLAY.SYS and DEVICE=PRINTER.SYS statements have been put in CONFIG.400. When you have renamed these files to AUTOEXEC.BAT and CONFIG.SYS (or merged them with any existing AUTOEXEC.BAT and CONFIG.SYS files), you can simply restart the system or press Ctrl-Alt-Del, and you will be ready to use the code page for your country. You can now skip to the section "Loading and Using Code Pages."

Using Earlier Versions of SELECT

The SELECT installation program is also available in PC DOS versions 3.0 through 3.3. Unlike PC DOS 4 SELECT, these earlier programs are used by typing options at the command line. They don't provide menus or on-line help.

SELECT for PC DOS 3.0 and 3.1 works only on floppy disks, so if you are running PC DOS from a hard disk, you should skip to the section "Installing Code-Page Support by Hand." To create a floppy disk from which you can start PC DOS and load code-page support, put a copy of your PC DOS system disk in drive A and type a command in this form:

```
A:\>select country-code keyboard-layout
```

Caution

Making the Start-up Disk for PC DOS 3.3 and Earlier
Versions 3.0 and 3.1 of SELECT use DISKCOPY to copy all the files from your PC DOS system disk to the new disk, while versions 3.2 and 3.3 use FORMAT to put the system files on the disk. In both cases, *any existing data on the target disk will be lost*, including any existing AUTOEXEC.BAT or CONFIG.SYS file.

> Even though SELECT for PC DOS 3.2 and 3.3 will work on hard disks, remember that running it will format the disk and remove any existing data. It is therefore recommended that you follow the later instructions on installing code-page support by hand rather than using SELECT on a hard disk. (SELECT for PC DOS 4 *can* be used to put PC DOS on a hard disk that has existing data; see Chapter 12 for details.)

In your SELECT command, use the appropriate country code and keyboard layout as given in Table 13.1. To use Table 13.1, first choose the country you want. If it is not listed, choose the most similar country. If the country has an asterisk (*) following the code pages, the first (national) code page requires supplementary software available from IBM dealers in that country. The second code (850) is available "out of the box." If the country has two asterisks (**) following the code pages, the first (national) code page is available only in a special Asian version of PC DOS 4.

The 850 code, available as an alternative code page for most countries, is the *multilingual character set*, which is designed for exchanging data between most countries and with IBM mainframe computers.

If no keyboard layouts or keyboard IDs are given for a particular country, the country does not have its own. Choose the keyboard layout and keyboard IDs from a country that uses a similar language and/or code page. In the case of languages that use non-Roman alphabets (e.g., Arabic, Chinese, Japanese), you will have to use codes for a country with a language using the Roman alphabet (such as English or French). Local IBM dealers may be able to provide help and further information.

The following examples show you how to create a PC DOS start-up disk that supports the German formats. With your PC DOS system disk in drive A, make drive A your current drive and type

```
A:\>select 049 gr
```

As you can see from Table 13.1, **049** is the country code for Germany, and **gr** is the keyboard layout. (Remember that "keyboard layout" is not the same as "keyboard IDs," which are used to distinguish different keyboards. The keyboard IDs are available only starting with PC DOS 4 and only for AT and enhanced keyboards.) Depending on the version of SELECT, the DISKCOPY and DISKCOMP, or FORMAT and XCOPY, commands will also be run. You will be prompted when it is time to insert the disk that will receive your new working copy of PC DOS. (The system disk is called either the *source disk* or the *first disk*. The disk being copied to is called either the *target disk* or the *second disk*, depending on your version.) The new disk will end up with all of the files needed to use PC DOS and most PC DOS commands and with the country format and keyboard layout that you have specified.

If you have two floppy drives, you can speed up SELECT by specifying the drives as follows:

```
a:\>select a: b: 049 gr
```

This command tells SELECT to use the system files in drive A and make the new start-up disk in drive B.

Table 13.1. ***Country, Code Page, and Keyboard Information***

Country	ID	Code Pages	Keyboard Layout	Keyboard IDs
Arabic-speaking	785	864, 850*		
Australia	061	437, 850		
Belgium	032	850, 437	BE	120
Canada (French-speaking)	002	863, 850	CF	058
Denmark	045	850, 865	DK	159
Finland	358	850, 437	SU	153
France	033	437, 850	FR	120, 189
Germany	049	437, 850	GR	129
Hebrew-speaking	972	862, 850*		
Italy	039	437, 850	IT	141, 142
Japan	081	932, 437**		
Korea	082	934, 437**		
Latin America	003	437, 850	LA	171
Netherlands	031	437, 850	NL	143
Norway	047	850, 865	NO	155
Peoples Republic of China (simplified Chinese)	086	936, 437**		
Portugal	351	850, 860	PO	163
Spain	034	437, 850	SP	172
Sweden	046	437, 850	SV	153
Switzerland (French-speaking)	041	850, 437	SF	150
Switzerland (German-speaking)	041	850, 437	SG	000
Taiwan (traditional Chinese)	088	938, 437**		
United Kingdom	044	437, 850	UK	168, 166
United States	001	437, 850	US	103

Notes:
German-speaking Switzerland is assigned the keyboard ID 000 to distinguish it from French-speaking Switzerland. Its actual keyboard layout is the same as the latter (150).
Keyboard IDs are valid only for the new "enhanced" keyboards such as those found on PS/2s.

*Country is new to PC DOS 4. The first (national) code page requires supplementary software available from IBM dealers in that country. The second code is available "out of the box."
**Country is new to PC DOS 4. The first (national) code page is available only in a special Asian version of PC DOS 4.

You will also find that an AUTOEXEC.BAT file and a CONFIG.SYS file have been placed on your new start-up disk. The AUTOEXEC.BAT file for the German example will look like this:

```
country = 049,437,a:\country.sys
```

The first number is the country ID, and the second number is the default code page (the first one listed for that country in Table 13.1). The path name gives the location of the file COUNTRY.SYS on the disk.

Remember that statements in the AUTOEXEC.BAT and CONFIG.SYS files take effect automatically when the system is started or restarted. To see the effect of this statement, you can restart your system and issue the DIR command for your DOS directory:

```
C:\>dir c:\dos

 Volume in drive C is PCDOSDISK
 Volume Serial Number is 1454-3E20
 Directory of  C:\DOS

.            <DIR>      17.05.88   11.15
..           <DIR>      17.05.88   11.15
COMMAND  COM      37637 17.06.88   12.00
FORMAT   COM      22923 17.06.88   12.00
MORE     COM       2166 17.06.88   12.00
GRAPHICS COM      16733 17.06.88   12.00
XCOPY    EXE      17087 17.06.88   12.00
```

(Only the first part of the directory is shown.) Notice that the dates and times for the files in the directory are now given in the German format: day.month.year for the date, and hour.minute for the time.

The COUNTRY.SYS file is provided with PC DOS starting with version 3.3 and is used to load the country-specific information needed for the national format. Since versions of SELECT prior to PC DOS 4 are recommended primarily for floppy disks, the examples here have paths on drive A. In general, it is a good idea to use the complete path name with the COUNTRY setting and other code-page related commands. PC DOS will usually look in the current directory (the start-up directory in this case), but by giving the path name you don't have to worry about the current directory.

For versions of PC DOS prior to PC DOS 3.3, separate keyboard driver programs were provided for the major countries. Thus, for Germany the statement provided will look like this:

```
keybgr
```

(You can look at your system disk with the command `dir a: keyb*` to find out which keyboard programs are included.)

For PC DOS 3.3, the AUTOEXEC.BAT file will contain the following statement, using the values for the default keyboard layout code and code page as given in Table 13.1:

```
keyb gr,437,a:\keyboard.sys
```

The KEYB command specifies the layout and code page that will be used for the keyboard. The file KEYBOARD.SYS (provided starting with PC DOS 3.3) contains the keyboard information that is loaded into memory. Once this has been done, your keyboard has been redefined to that layout. In this example, if you now press the key marked *z*, you'll see a *y* on the screen.

Depending on the version of SELECT used, there will be other useful statements in the AUTOEXEC.BAT file, including PATH to which you will want to add the relevant directories. See Chapter 12, "Installing a PC DOS System," for more information about setting up basic AUTOEXEC.BAT and CONFIG.SYS files.

Installing Code-Page Support by Hand

As mentioned earlier, you can use the national keyboards and the COUNTRY setting with PC DOS 3.0, but there is little else you can do with code pages until PC DOS 3.3. Therefore, the rest of this chapter assumes that you are using PC DOS versions 3.3 or later.

If you have used SELECT, the KEYB command and the COUNTRY setting have been established for you. If you have not used SELECT, begin by inserting a KEYB command in your AUTOEXEC.BAT file and a COUNTRY setting in your CONFIG.SYS, using the formats discussed earlier with the appropriate country code and keyboard layout.

Installing General Support for Code-Page Switching

The NLSFUNC command enables PC DOS to load information about the characters that are specific to the country chosen in the COUNTRY setting. It also enables PC DOS to load instructions into memory that allow use of the CHCP command for changing code pages (this is discussed later). PC DOS 3.3 users will normally run this command from their AUTOEXEC.BAT file:

```
nlsfunc
```

The NLSFUNC command needs to access the COUNTRY.SYS file. It will look for it using the path you used in your COUNTRY setting. If you did not specify a path there, you can specify it in the NLSFUNC command, for example:

```
nlsfunc c:\dos\country.sys
```

Version 4

An Alternative to NLSFUNC

For PC DOS 4, a recommended alternative to the NLSFUNC command is to use the INSTALL statement in your CONFIG.SYS file (instead of AUTOEXEC.BAT):

```
install=c:\dos\nlsfunc.exe
```

With the INSTALL command, you must always use the complete path name *and* the .EXE extension.

Adding Display Support for Code Pages: DISPLAY.SYS and GRAFTABL

For versions of PC DOS prior to 3.3, no separate display support was provided for code pages. Starting with PC DOS 3.3, the DISPLAY.SYS driver is used for this purpose. If you have used PC DOS 4 SELECT, the appropriate DEVICE statement should already be in your CONFIG.SYS, and you need not add anything to it.

The format for the DISPLAY.SYS statement is

```
device = path:display.sys con: = (display-type,
hardware code page, number of additional code pages,
number of subfonts per code page)
```

The *display types* supported are

Mono	Monochrome adapter, PC DOS 3.3 only
CGA	Color Graphics Adapter, PC DOS 3.3 only
EGA	Enhanced Graphics Adapter
LCD	Liquid-crystal display for IBM convertible (portable) computer

Version 4

Mono and CGA Adapters

Even though mono and CGA adapters aren't supported for use with alternative code pages in PC DOS 4, they can still be used with the default code page. You won't be able to switch them to an alternative code page, however. Users with MCGA or VGA adapters (such as those found on the various PS/2 models) should use EGA.

The *hardware code page* is the default one provided in ROM. For PCs sold in the United States (and many sold elsewhere), it is 437. PCs sold in other countries may be set up so that their national code page is in the hardware. If you're not sure, put a comma in place of this number or try 437. If you have problems, consult your system documentation or dealer.

The *number of additional code pages* specifies how many other code pages will be accommodated in memory. The default is 1, and it can be up to 12. No country currently has more than 2 code pages, so you normally should specify 1 (i.e., one code page in addition to the hardware code page) if 437 is one of the code pages used with your country. Otherwise, specify 2 so that you can use both of your country's code pages. You can specify other code pages if you need them, but do not specify more than you need, since each one ties up some memory.

The final number is the number of *subfonts*, or variant groups of characters. The default is 1. The maximum values are 2 for EGA and PS/2 Models 25 and 30 (MCGA), 3 for VGA (PS/2 Models 50 and higher), 3 for the high-resolution IBM 8514/A adapter, and only 1 for the IBM PC Convertible LCD display. Unless your application calls for them, you probably don't have to specify subfonts.

Here are two complete DISPLAY.SYS settings. The first one is for a PC AT with an EGA display:

```
device=c:\dos\display.sys con:=(ega,437,2)
```

This setting assumes a hard disk with DISPLAY.SYS in the C:\DOS directory. It specifies hardware code page 437 and two additional code pages, with no subfonts. This setting would be for someone whose country doesn't use code page 437, which is in ROM.

The following setting is correct for a German user who has a PS/2 Model 50 (with a VGA adapter) and wants to use subfonts:

```
device=c:\dos\display.sys con:=(ega,437,(1,2))
```

Notice the extra parentheses around the numbers for additional code pages and subfonts. Since 437 is one of the code pages for Germany, and it is in hardware on this system, only one additional code page will be needed.

Many users no longer use the CGA adapter because of its poor resolution. If you wish to use the CGA in its 320x200 graphics mode for displaying text, you will find that the extended characters (those with ASCII values over 128) are not legible as a result of the low resolution. You need these extended characters for some applications that use them to draw simple graphics such as boxes. You also need them if you are using code pages, since many of the special characters used in national languages are found in this part of the character set. PC DOS versions 3.1 and later provide the GRAFTABL command to solve the problem. It loads a redefined character set for the extended characters, providing a more legible display. To use it, put a statement like this in your AUTOEXEC.BAT file:

```
graftabl 865
```

In the preceding command, GRAFTABL will load code page 865, for Norway or Denmark. The other code pages that can be used with GRAFTABL are 437 (United States—the default); 850 (multilingual, available only in PC DOS 4); 860 (Portugal); and 863 (French-speaking Canada). Only one code page can be used at a time, so you will have to use another GRAFTABL command if you want to change code pages. You can of course use GRAFTABL at the command line if you wish. Remember that GRAFTABL is needed only if you are using the CGA in graphics mode. In particular, PS/2 owners never need it.

To see which code page is currently being used by GRAFTABL, type

```
C:\>graftabl /status
Active code page: 865
```

(You can abbreviate `/status` as `/sta`.)

Version 4

Getting a List of Supported Code Pages

In PC DOS 4 you can type `graftabl ?` to get the list of supported code pages.

Adding Printer Support for Code Pages: PRINTER.SYS

IBM-compatible printers have the United States character set built-in (usually including the extended or graphics characters). If you wish to print text created using any other code pages, you must use the PRINTER.SYS driver to enable the printer to use other code pages. Unfortunately, this support is generally available only for certain printers made by IBM. Many other printers have the IBM US character set, but they don't have the code pages in ROM. You may wish to check the documentation for non-IBM printers, however. Like DISPLAY.SYS, PRINTER.SYS is available starting with PC DOS 3.3.

To install PRINTER.SYS, use a statement in your CONFIG.SYS having this form:

```
device=path:\printer.sys port = (printer-type, hardware code
pages, additional code pages)
```

The *printer type* must be one of the following:

4201	IBM 4201 Proprinter series IBM 4202 Proprinter XL
4208	IBM 4207 Proprinter X24 (PC DOS 4 only) IBM 4208 Proprinter XL24 (PC DOS 4 only)
5202	IBM 5202 Quietwriter III

The device specified (the *port*) is a parallel printer port, and can be LPT1:, LPT2:, LPT3:, or PRN: (PRN: is normally the same as LPT1:). The *hardware code page* is the one that is actually built into the printer's ROM. It will be one of the following: 437, 850, 860, 863, or 865. For the IBM Quietwriter III, either one or two hardware code pages can be specified. The last number is the number of *additional code pages* that can be stored in memory. The maximum number is 12. If you have specified two hardware code pages, however, no additional code pages can be loaded, and 0 must be specified for the last number.

Here is a specification for the IBM 4201 Proprinter:

```
device=c:\dos\printer.sys lpt1:=(4201,437,1)
```

This specification assumes that the PRINTER.SYS file is in the DOS directory on drive C. The hardware code page is 437, and one additional code page can be loaded into memory.

The next specification might be used with the Quietwriter III:

```
device=c:\dos\printer.sys lpt1:=(5202,(437,850),0)
```

This specification is more complicated because the Quietwriter III can have two hardware code pages, which are stored in a cartridge. (Be sure that you have put in the correct cartridge for the code pages you specify—PC DOS has no way to check this.) In this case, the hardware code pages are 437 and 850. Notice that when two hardware code pages are used, they must be enclosed in a separate set of parentheses and preceded by a comma. The 0 following the hardware code pages must also be specified. (If you wish, you can specify only one hardware code page with the Quietwriter; in that case, you can use additional code pages.)

Finally, if you have more than one printer, you can repeat the whole specification starting with the device, all in the same statement:

```
device=c:\dos\printer.sys lpt1:=(4201,437,2) lpt2:=(4208,850,1)
```

Loading and Using Code Pages

The settings and commands discussed so far enable code-page support. In other words, they specify global information that PC DOS needs for a given country (the COUNTRY setting), they load a keyboard layout (the KEYB command), and they reserve space in memory for the code pages needed by the display (DISPLAY.SYS) and printer (PRINTER.SYS). Before you can use code pages, however, you must load the actual character information for each code page. The MODE command, a multipurpose device controller, provides several statements dealing with code pages.

Using MODE to Prepare Code Pages

To load one or more code pages into memory, use a command in this form:

```
mode device cp prep=(code page(s)) information-file
```

To load code pages for the console (keyboard and video display), specify `con:` for the device. To load code pages for the printer, use the name of the port to which the printer is connected, which must be `lpt1:`, `lpt2:`, `lpt3:`, or `prn:` (`prn:` is the same as `lpt1:` in most configurations).

The phrase `cp prep` stands for `codepage prepare`, and you can use the full form if you wish. Follow it with an equal sign, an opening parenthesis, and the number of the code page. If you specify more than one code page, put a comma between code-page numbers. A closing parenthesis follows the last code page. Finally, give the path and name for the code-page information file for the specified device. The files available are:

4201.CPI	IBM Proprinter 4201
4208.CPI	IBM Proprinter X24 and XL24 (PC DOS 4 only)
5202.CPI	IBM Quietwriter III
EGA.CPI	EGA, VGA, MCGA, and compatible displays
LCD.CPI	Liquid-crystal display (for IBM convertible laptop)

Assuming you are a German user with an EGA display, you could load the code pages for your console as follows:

```
mode con: cp prep=(437,850) c:\sys\ega.cpi
```

This statement loads code pages 437 and 850 for the console, reading information from the file EGA.CPI in the SYS directory on drive C.

In the next example, the user loads the code pages needed for an IBM Proprinter 4201:

```
mode lpt1: cp prep=(437,850) c:\sys\4201.cpi
```

(This specification assumes the printer is connected to the first parallel printer port, LPT1:.) Note that if you will be using the code pages only in a cartridge installed in your IBM Quietwriter, this statement is not necessary.

You can load one or more code pages if you need to. Remember, however, that the number of code pages you can load (other than those built into the display or printer hardware) cannot be more than the number of additional code pages you specified for that device in the DISPLAY.SYS or PRINTER.SYS statement in your CONFIG.SYS file.

If you have correctly specified it, the message `Mode prepare code page function completed` will be displayed briefly while your CONFIG.SYS file is being processed at start-up. If you see the message `Code page operation not supported on this device`, you probably gave the wrong device name (only CON:, LPT1:, LPT2:, LPT3:, or PRN: may be used). The message `Failure to access code page font file` means that you should check the path and file name that you gave for the code page information (.CPI) file in your MODE command. If you see the message `Failure to access device` followed by a port name (such as `lpt1:`), make sure that you have put the correct PRINTER.SYS or DISPLAY.SYS device statement in your CONFIG.SYS file.

Normally you will use these MODE commands in your AUTOEXEC.BAT file, so the code pages you need will be loaded automatically at the start of each session. You can issue a new MODE command at the command prompt, however. The code pages specified in the new command will replace the old ones. If you wish to replace only some of the code pages, put a comma in place of any that you wish to keep. For example, the following command would keep code page 437 but substitute 863 for 850:

```
mode lpt1: cp prep=(,,863) c:\sys\4201.cpi
```

Selecting a Code Page

The MODE code-page-prepare commands load the code pages for the specified devices into memory. The final step in using code pages is to select the code page you will actually be using for each device.

The easiest way to select a code page is to use the CHCP command, which was introduced with PC DOS 3.3. This command selects a code page to be used by *all* devices—the keyboard, screen, and printer. Here is an example:

```
C:\>chcp 850
Active code page: 850
```

This command selects code page 850 (the multilingual character set). Before you use this command, you should have run the NLSFUNC command (the easiest way is to put it in your AUTOEXEC.BAT file) and you should have put the MODE CP PREP CON: and MODE CP PREP LPT1: (or other printer port) statements in your AUTOEXEC.BAT file. If the correct mode command hasn't been run for a device such as the printer, you will see the message `Code page XXX not prepared for all devices`, where `XXX` is the code-page number. The code page is set for all prepared devices, but not for whatever devices weren't prepared. Check your MODE statements again. The message `Code page XXX not prepared for system` means that *no* device with prepared code pages was found, and the CHCP command had no effect.

Checking the Code Page for a Device

Usually the CHCP command is all that you need to change code pages. Occasionally, however, you may want to use a different code page for one device while keeping another code page for the rest of the system. For example, suppose you have sent a document to the printer using the PRINT command. You have been using code page 850, but while the document is being printed, you want to create another document using code page 437. If you use the command `chcp 437`, the code page for all devices, including the printer, will be changed to 437. This is not good because the printer will not be able to correctly print the document that used code page 850. A solution is to change just the console to code page 437, leaving the printer set to code page 850. You can do this with the command:

```
C:\>mode con: cp sel=437
```

In the preceding command, `con:` is the device. If you were using this command with a printer, you would use LPT1: or another printer port. The phrase `cp sel` stands for `codepage select`, and you can use the longer form if you wish.

Restoring a Damaged Code Page

Remember that code pages for the printer and console are kept in memory (except for those built into the hardware). If you shut off the printer and turn it on again later, any code page stored in the printer's RAM is lost. To reload (*refresh*) the code page for your printer, you can use this command:

```
C:\>mode lpt1: cp ref
```

This command assumes that your printer is connected to LPT1:. Note that you don't give a code-page number with this command; PC DOS uses the last one given for that device. You can type the longer phrase `codepage refresh` if you wish.

You can also use this command to restore the code page for the video display by specifying `con:` as the device. This action is normally not needed, however. The code page for the display is in system RAM and is seldom lost, unless a badly behaved program corrupts that part of memory, in which case you probably have other troubles as well. If you restart the system, of course, the AUTOEXEC.BAT and CONFIG.SYS files are processed again, and all code-page setup specified there is done again.

Checking Code-Page Status

The last command needed for code pages gives you the current status of the code pages for one or all devices. For example, you can find out the current code page for the printer as follows:

```
C:\>mode lpt1: cp /sta
Active code page for device CON is 437
Hardware code pages:
  code page 437
Prepared code pages:
  code page 850

MODE status code page function completed
```

Here you asked for information about the printer (connected to LPT1:). The phrase `cp /sta` is an abbreviation for `codepage /status`, and you can use the longer form if you wish. If you see the message `No codepage has been SELECTED`, check to make sure that you have the proper device driver statement and the MODE CP PREP statement for that device.

If you leave out the name of the device in the MODE code-page-status command, the code-page status for *all* devices is given:

```
C:\>mode /sta

Status for device LPT1:
-----------------------
LPT1: not rerouted
RETRY=NONE

Active code page for device LPT1 is 437
Hardware code pages:
  code page 437
Prepared code pages:
  code page 850

MODE status code page function completed

Status for device LPT2:
-----------------------
LPT2: not rerouted

Status for device LPT3:
-----------------------
LPT3: not rerouted

Status for device CON:
----------------------

Active code page for device CON is 437
Hardware code pages:
  code page 437
Prepared code pages:
  code page 850

MODE status code page function completed

Status for device COM1:
-----------------------
RETRY=NONE
```

The preceding command is actually a general status command that includes other functions of MODE having nothing to do with code pages. Here you are concerned only with the code-page statuses, and the only devices having code pages here are CON: and LPT1:. You can ignore the other information. (For a complete survey of everything you can do with the MODE command, see the Command Reference.)

You now know how to prepare and select code pages for the keyboard, video display, and printer. Once you have completed your settings in the AUTOEXEC.BAT and CONFIG.SYS file, you need only use the CHCP and occasionally the MODE CP SEL or MODE device /STA commands in your daily work. You have also mastered one of PC DOS's more arcane features!

What's Next

Chapter 11, "Customizing Your System," and Chapter 12, "Installing a PC DOS System," both discuss issues relating to setting up your system for various uses.

Key Concepts and Words

Before you read further, use the following list to test your understanding of the concepts and words in this chapter.

ASCII	Code-page preparation
Byte	Code-page selection
Alternative character sets	Damaged code-page restoration
Code pages	Code-page status
Code-page printer support	

Part 3
Command Reference

The comprehensive Command Reference presents individual entries for all PC DOS commands, reserved words, and other features, including details for all options.

Each entry provides succinct rules for use as well as background descriptions and numerous examples. In addition, comments, notes, warnings, and special tricks help you explore the nuances of each PC DOS feature. Each entry also refers to related PC DOS commands and other features and to chapters that present related concepts.

Explanations describe how to use each command, offering full descriptions of every option for all versions of PC DOS, with discussions of error messages. Numerous examples illustrate typical uses, with tips and techniques for users.

Command Reference

The following pages present a reference guide to every command, setting, device driver, and configuration file used by PC DOS, in alphabetical order. The discussion for each entry is suitable for intermediate and advanced users and includes a definitive explanation, example of syntax, explanations of changes and improvements through the various PC DOS versions, and one or more examples of use with tips for users.

The special Compatibility Box shows the availability of each feature in PC DOS versions 2 to 4, and indicates whether the entry has a corresponding function in the DOS Shell windowing interface and even whether it exists in the new OS/2 operating system.

Types of Entries

Although all entries are in one alphabetical sequence for ease of referral, four different types of PC DOS features are discussed. Each entry is identified as a user command, batch file subcommand, configuration setting, or system resource.

Commands There are two types of user commands: internal and external. Internal commands are part of the PC DOS COMMAND.COM interface program, for example, DIR and COPY. Running internal commands is fast, because no disk access is required. Many of the most powerful PC DOS commands are external, however; they are provided as separate utility programs on disk. Examples of external commands include FORMAT and PRINT. Both internal and external commands can be used on the command line and in batch files.

Batch Commands Batch commands are used to control the operation of batch files, which allows your PC to perform tedious, repetitive tasks automatically. (See Chapter

10, "Batch Files.") These commands include IF, FOR, and SET. Although some of these commands can be used on the command line, they are most commonly found in batch files and are thus grouped into this category to remind you of that function.

Settings Settings are special commands that you put in your CONFIG.SYS file to control the general operation of your system and its use of resources. For example, the FILES setting controls the number of open files that is accommodated by the system, and the BUFFERS setting determines how much memory is used to store file information for fast retrieval from memory.

Resources Resources are other files and programs that are provided with PC DOS. Many of them, with file names ending in the .SYS extension, are device drivers. Device drivers are special programs that allow other PC DOS commands and application programs to control the screen, keyboard, printer, mouse, and even RAM disks and expanded memory boards. (See Chapter 11, "Customizing Your System," and Chapter 12, "Installing a PC DOS System," for an introduction to device drivers.) Examples of device drivers include ANSI.SYS, PRINTER.SYS, and VDISK.SYS.

Format for Reference Entries

Understanding the purpose of the various parts of each reference entry will help you use the Command Reference more efficiently. Each reference entry can have as many of the following parts as are appropriate. First, the name of the command and its identifier appears.

SAMPLE **External Command**

The Compatibility section indicates how the feature has evolved through succeeding revisions of PC DOS. A triangle (▲) under a version number indicates that the feature is available in that version of PC DOS. **If the version number is printed in boldface type, the feature was enhanced in some way, starting with that version.** If nothing appears under a version number, the feature is not available in that version.

Compatibility	2.0	2.1	3.0	**3.1**	3.2	3.3	4.0	OS/2 (DOS mode)	OS/2 (prot.)
	▲	▲	▲	▲	▲	▲	▲		▲

Because versions of PC DOS prior to 2.0 are obsolete, they are not covered. The most significant revisions are the whole-numbered ones: 2.0, 3.0, and 4.0.

The final two versions indicated are for the convenience of people who use (or are considering using) both PC DOS and OS/2. OS/2 (DOS mode) means the OS/2 "compatibility box," which provides most PC DOS 3.3 features under OS/2. OS/2 (prot.) refers to the OS/2 "protected" mode, whose features differ from those of PC DOS in many important ways.

Thus, in the example above, the command is available starting at least with PC DOS 2.0 and was enhanced with version 3.1. The command is not available in the OS/2 PC DOS compatibility box, but is available in OS/2 protected mode.

Comments and notes in the reference entry give details of the new capabilities added to a feature in succeeding versions of PC DOS. Also, examples that work only under certain versions of PC DOS are so identified.

The icons used throughout this book to identify caution, tip, shell, and version 4.0 text are also used in the Command Reference.

Following the name of the command or other feature are one or two sentences briefly summarizing the purpose of the command. For example

External Command **SAMPLE**

This text gives a succinct definition of the command. It may also describe the command's most common use.

Parts of the Command Reference

Each reference entry is divided into two main parts: a Quick Reference and a Detailed Reference.

The Quick Reference gives you the essential rules as clearly and succinctly as possible for using a particular feature. This is where you can refresh your memory as to the syntax, rules for usage, and available options for the command or other feature. The Quick Reference consists of all the material immediately after the command's summary paragraph and contains, as appropriate, the following entries.

Format This gives you the form in which you should construct the command or setting in order for it to be properly understood and executed by PC DOS. For example, the format for the DIR command is

```
dir drive, directory, or file name options
```

Words in monospace listing font are to be typed exactly as given: for example, every DIR command begins with the word `dir`. Words or phrases in italics, on the other hand, describe the kind of information you should provide. In this case, you follow `dir` with the name of the disk drive, directory, or individual file name for which you want a listing. Similarly, the word `options` indicates that you can use one or more options, as given in the Options section.

Options Many commands have options that control their behavior. The first time they are mentioned, options are shown in italics , followed by a brief description, for example:

/w allows user to swap disks.

However, some options must be followed by additional information. The kind of information needed is also described in italics. For example:

/b:*buffer-size* specifies buffer size in bytes and means to type `/b:` (including the colon), followed by the number of bytes to be reserved for the buffer. The kind of information needed is always described in more detail in the Procedure section.

Sample Use This provides an example showing correct syntax and usage. More detailed examples are given in the Detailed Reference section.

Procedure This explains step by step what you need to do to use the command. For example: Following `dir`, type the name of the drive, directory, or file that you want listed. (If you want to list the current directory, you can leave out the name.) See Chapter 6, "Managing Your Hard Disk," for a detailed discussion of directories, subdirectories, and path names. You can also use wildcards to specify a group of related files.

Related Commands More than 80 different commands and other features are provided by PC DOS. It is thus sometimes hard to remember which one you need for a given purpose. To help you find the right features to solve a given problem, the names and brief descriptions of related commands or other features are given here. For example, the entry for DIR gives the following related commands:

CD changes the current directory.

MD (or MKDIR) makes a new directory.

RD (or RMDIR) removes an empty directory.

CHKDSK obtains a summary of disk and memory usage.

Detailed Reference As shown in the following example, the Detailed Reference part of the entry is introduced by a color bar and begins with an explanation of concepts useful for understanding the feature.

DETAILED REFERENCE

Explanation For example, the discussion of DEVICE reminds you briefly what a device driver is, why it is needed, and about the possible uses (and pitfalls) of the command or feature.

Comments The Comments section points out the most efficient use of the feature, circumstances under which you should not use it, and useful tricks and traps or pitfalls.

Error Messages Any error messages that you might receive while using the feature are summarized. Where the wording of messages differs, the message as given by PC DOS 4 is used.

Return Codes Some commands return a value that can be tested by the IF ERRORLEVEL statement. These values are summarized here.

Examples At least one example, and usually several, are given here. The examples are used to show a variety of typical uses for the feature and generally start with the simplest and graduate to the most complex.

Related Chapters The chapters from Parts 1 and 2 that introduce the feature or discuss relevant concepts are listed.

The alphabetical listing of PC DOS commands, settings, and resources begins on page 504.

ANSI.SYS

Resource

Compatibility	2.0	2.1	3.0	3.1	3.2	3.3	**4.0**	OS/2 (DOS mode)	OS/2 (prot.)
	▲	▲	▲	▲	▲	▲	▲	▲	▲

Use the ANSI.SYS driver and ANSI control sequences to set the screen display mode and to provide extended display and keyboard functions. Programs can use the ANSI functions to change the screen resolution and colors, move the cursor, delete characters, set character attributes, and redefine keys (make "keyboard macros").

Note: ANSI.SYS contains technical material. It is atypical of the entries in the Command Reference. Be assured that other entries will be more easily grasped but just as useful.

Format

`device=ansi.sys` enables the ANSI driver in the CONFIG.SYS file.

Esc [*parameter;... command* issues ANSI commands from a program.

Options

Version 4

Options Added to ANSI.SYS in PC DOS Version 4

/x allows extended keys (keys such as Alt key combinations and function keys) to be redefined. (See the fourth reference table at the end of this section.)

/l tries to keep the same number of lines on the screen as specified in a previous MODE command, even if an application attempts to change it.

/k does not allow ANSI.SYS to use extended functions of the new "enhanced" keyboard (not the same as "extended keys," many of which are found on all keyboards). This option is useful for applications that do not support the enhanced keyboard functions of the new 101- or 102-character keyboards.

See the tables at the end of this entry for the ANSI commands and parameters.

Sample Use

`prompt $e[2J` is a batch file statement that clears the screen and homes the cursor.

Procedure

As a user, if your software specifies ANSI support, put the statement DEVICE=ANSI.SYS in your CONFIG.SYS file. Some programs require this command. If the file ANSI.SYS is not in the root directory of your startup drive, give the full path name.

To use ANSI commands from the command line or in a batch file, use the PROMPT command with *$e* to send the Esc character to the ANSI.SYS driver. Follow this with the appropriate string of characters as described in the tables at the end of this entry (Example 2).

Related Commands

DEVICE installs the ANSI.SYS device driver. CONFIG.SYS is the file for the DEVICE=ANSI.SYS statement.

PROMPT sends an Escape character to "trigger" ANSI.SYS.

DETAILED REFERENCE

Explanation The ANSI.SYS device driver must be enabled before programs can use ANSI control sequences. This is done automatically at startup by placing the statement DEVICE=ANSI.SYS in your CONFIG.SYS file.

Once it is installed in memory, the ANSI.SYS driver watches the characters a program is sending to the display. When an Escape character is detected, the ANSI driver checks to see whether a [(left bracket) character immediately follows it. If so, the character sequence up to the first blank or invalid character is interpreted as an ANSI control sequence instead of being displayed.

The reference tables at the end of this entry break the ANSI functions down into five major categories.

- cursor and screen control
- character rendition (attributes)
- screen mode (setting resolution)
- key assignments (macros)
- enhanced keyboard key codes

Each table gives a list of escape sequences and parameter values, and explains their purpose and meaning.

Comments For performance reasons, many programs by default write directly to the PC hardware (particularly true of programs that make heavy use of graphics), which usually requires that the hardware be "100 percent PC compatible." Some programs offer an "ANSI" option that uses the ANSI commands to control the display, allowing the program to run on less compatible machines, albeit more slowly. Therefore, you should only use the ANSI driver if your software requires it or supports it and does not otherwise run on your hardware.

Many things that you can set using ANSI.SYS, such as the screen mode and key definitions, may be redefined by one of your application programs, causing you to lose your "custom" setup after running the application. One way to handle this is to run the program from a batch file; in the batch file, after the line that runs the program, you can reissue the appropriate ANSI commands to restore your preferred setup.

The keyboard macro facility of ANSI works, but it is not nearly as easy to use as one of the many memory-resident keyboard redefinition and macro utilities, such as SuperKey.

Examples **Example 1**: In the CONFIG.SYS file, enable the ANSI.SYS device driver and allow extended keys to be redefined (in PC DOS only).

```
device=c:\drivers\ansi.sys /x
```

Here all the device drivers (including ANSI.SYS) are in the directory C:\DRIVERS; thus this path name was used. The */x* option allows extended key combinations to be redefined.

Be sure that you use a DEVICE command to enable ANSI.SYS (and reboot if necessary for it to take effect) before trying the following examples.

Example 2: From a batch file, issue an ANSI command that creates a "paper-like," black-on-white display.

```
C:\>copy con: paper.bat
prompt $e[30;47m
prompt $p$g
^Z
     1 file(s) copied
```

As mentioned earlier, each ANSI command must be preceded by an Escape character to tell the ANSI driver that the sequence is a command. The problem is that if you merely press the Esc key, PC DOS interprets this keystroke as a request to cancel the current line of input instead of storing the Esc character. You can get around this problem by using the PROMPT command; with this command, $e specifies sending an Esc character. The rest of the command follows the format shown in the second reference table at the end of this entry. The [identifies what follows as an ANSI command rather than just an Esc character. The 30 specifies a black foreground (so characters are displayed in black). The semicolon is used to separate multiple commands. The 47 specifies a white background. The final *m* tells ANSI.SYS that the command being given involves screen control.

The second line of the batch file restores the standard prompt for this book, showing the current drive and directory. Restore whatever prompt you are using immediately. Because the prompt specified in the latest PROMPT statement is issued after every PC DOS command line is processed, failure to reestablish the prompt results in the ANSI command being reissued and the screen being cleared and reset after every command.

To restore the default screen, use the MODE CO80 command (assuming a color system).

Example 3: Set a high-resolution VGA screen in a batch file.

Version 4

VGA Settings Available in Version 4

```
C:\>copy con: hires.bat
prompt $e[=17h
prompt $p$g
^Z
     1 file(s) copied
```

This command's format is that used in the third reference at the end of this entry. The result is a 640-by-480 color VGA mode with 50 lines (the equivalent of entering `mode co80 lines=50`). This is supported only in PC DOS 4, and you must have the appropriate VGA hardware, of course. (The resulting display unfortunately scrolls quite slowly.)

Example 4: Use ANSI.SYS to assign a command to one of your function keys.

```
C:\>prompt $e[0;63;"cls";13p
```

When dealing with an extended key such as a function key, the keycode 0 is always specified first. The 63 represents the F5 key. (See the fifth reference table at the end of this entry.) The string cls is output, followed by character 13 (a carriage return). As a result, typing F5 gives the same result as typing the CLS command followed by a carriage return.

If you use several key assignments regularly, you might want to install them automatically by putting them in your AUTOEXEC.BAT file or in another batch file (perhaps called KEYS.BAT) that you can invoke from AUTOEXEC.BAT using the CALL command.

Reference Tables

In the tables, Esc represents the Escape character, which you can enter using `prompt $e` or by an appropriate display statement in a program. The variable # refers to a number: The allowable range of numbers depends on the command sequence involved. When more than one number is used, numbers are separated by semicolons. An ellipsis (...) indicates that you can use as many numbers as you want. Note that the command letter at the end of the string is case-sensitive.

Some options are available only with PC DOS 4; these are noted where appropriate.

Table R.1 lists the ANSI assignments for controlling the cursor and screen.

Table R.1. ***ANSI Cursor and Screen Control***

Code	Description
Move Cursor Esc[#;#H	The first number is the destination line; the second is the column. The default values for line and column are 1, so if no numbers are given, the cursor is moved to the "home" position. Note that the sequence Esc[#;#f can be used for the same function; the only difference is the command letter f. (IBM calls this latter command "Horizontal and Vertical Position.")
Cursor Up Esc[#A	Move the cursor up # lines. The default is 1. The column position is not changed. This command is ignored if the cursor is already at the top line.
Cursor Down Esc[#B	Move the cursor down # lines. The default is 1. The column position is not changed. This command is ignored if the cursor is already at the bottom line.
Cursor Forward Esc[#C	Move the cursor forward # columns. The default is 1. The line position is not changed. This command is ignored if the cursor is already in the rightmost column.
Cursor Back Esc[#D	Move the cursor backward # columns. The default is 1. The line position is not changed. This command is ignored if the cursor is already in the leftmost column.
Get Cursor Position Esc[6n	Get the current cursor line and column position. ANSI returns the current position in the form of the sequence Esc[#;#R, where the first number is the line and the second number is the column. This sequence is returned to the current STDIN (standard input device). This is usually the keyboard, but it can be redirected. Note: Do not use this command as part of a PROMPT statement.
Save Cursor Position Esc[s	Save the current cursor position for future reference. This can be used, for example, to allow you to return to the beginning of an input field following an error. Use the next command (Restore Position) to move the cursor back to its original position.

Table R.1. *(cont.)*

Code	Description
Restore Cursor Position Esc[u	Returns the cursor to the position it had when the Save Position command was last issued.
Clear Screen Esc[2Jn	Clear the screen and move the cursor to the home position (line 1, column 1).
Erase to End of Line Esc[K	Erase from the cursor position to end of line.

An example of a cursor control command is Esc[10;20H, which moves the cursor to line 10, column 20.

ANSI command sequences also can be used to control the color and other characteristics of characters displayed on the screen. The format for a set attribute sequence is Esc[*#*;...m, which sets the character attributes according to numbers from Table R.2. More than one attribute number can be used; the numbers are separated by semicolons. A lowercase m must follow the last number.

Table R.2. *Set Graphics Rendition (Character Colors and Display Characteristics)*

Number	Attribute
0	All attributes off (normal text)
1	Bold (high intensity)
4	Underscore (each character is underlined)
5	Blink (characters flash on and off)
7	Reverse video (for example, black on white)
8	Invisible characters (same color as background)
30	Black foreground
31	Red foreground
32	Green foreground
33	Yellow foreground
34	Blue foreground
35	Magenta foreground
36	Cyan foreground
37	White foreground
40	Black background
41	Red background
42	Green background
43	Yellow background
44	Blue background
45	Magenta background
46	Cyan background
47	White background

An example of an attribute command is Esc[5;31;42m, which sets blinking characters, red foreground, and green background.

Additionally, ANSI control sequences can be used to set the screen width, resolution, and other behavior. The format is Esc[=#h, which sets the screen mode #, as given in Table R.3.

Table R.3. ***Set Mode (Display Resolution)***

Number	Mode
0	40 x 25, monochrome
1	40 x 25, color
2	80 x 25, monochrome
3	80 x 25, color
4	320 x 200, color
5	320 x 200, monochrome
6	640 x 200, monochrome
7	Wrap at end of line (input typed past the end of a line results in a new line.)
Modes 14 through 19 are available only with PC DOS 4. (EGA modes can display 43 lines of text; VGA modes can display 50 lines of text.)	
14	640 x 200, color
15	640 x 350, mono (EGA)
16	640 x 350, color (EGA)
17	640 x 480, color (VGA)
18	640 x 480, color (VGA)
19	320 x 200, color

Version 4

An example of the screen mode command is Esc[=3, which sets an 80-column-by-25-line color screen display.

The reset screen mode has the format Esc[=#l and resets the screen mode to mode # as given in Table R.3. (The only real use of this command is that when mode 7 for wrap is on, it can be turned off by Esc[=7l. Note that the last command character is a lowercase l.)

ANSI control sequences can be used to reassign keyboard keys, as shown in Table R.4. That is, a keyboard key can be set so that ANSI converts it to a different key or even a whole string of characters. This allows the creation of "keyboard macros" that can make it easier for users to give commands to your program.

An example of a key assignment command is Esc[64;27p, which sets the @ (at sign) key to output an Escape character rather than an @. Another example is Esc[64;"dir"p, which sets the @ key to automatically type the string dir.

You can also reassign function keys and key combinations using the Ctrl,

Shift, Alt, and function keys. To do so, you must specify an "extended ASCII code" consisting of a 0 and then one of the codes shown in Table R.5.

Table R.4. ***Reassigning Keys with ANSI***

Code	Description
Reassign Key	Give the decimal ASCII code Esc[#;#...p for the key you want to reassign. Then give one or more ASCII codes (separated by semicolons) for the characters you want output when the key is pressed, with a lowercase p following the last ASCII code number.
Esc[#;c...p	For this format, give the decimal ASCII number for the key to be reassigned. Then give a string of characters (actual characters, not code numbers), in double quotes, that you want output when the key is pressed. Follow the closing quote with a lowercase p.

Table R.5. ***Extended Function Key Codes***

Key	Codes											
First Key	F1	F2	F3	F4	F5	F6	F7	F8	F9	F10	F11	F12
None	59	60	61	62	63	64	65	66	67	68	133	134
Shift	84	85	86	87	88	89	90	91	92	93	135	136
Ctrl	94	95	96	97	98	99	100	101	102	103	137	138
Alt	04	105	106	107	108	109	110	111	112	113	139	140

For example, the extended key code for Alt F1 is 0 followed by 104. You could define this key to output the string type by using the ANSI command sequence Esc[0;104;"type"p

ANSI commands are provided for controlling extended key values (those generated by the enhanced 101- and 102-key keyboards), such as those found on newer ATs and all PS/2s. The codes are shown in Table R.6

Table R.6. ***Enhanced Keyboard Key Codes***

Code	Description
Esc[0q	Disable the extended key value reassignments on enhanced keyboards.
Esc[1q	Enable extended key value reassignments on enhanced keyboards. Equivalent to using the /x option.

Related Chapters Chapter 10–Batch Files
Chapter 11–Customizing Your System

External Command

APPEND

Compatibility	2.0	2.1	3.0	3.1	3.2	3.3	4.0	OS/2 (DOS mode)	OS/2 (prot.)
						▲	▲	▲	

Use the APPEND command to run an application (regardless of the directory in which you are currently working) by specifying the directories that contain files the application needs. Also, use it as a setting in the CONFIG.SYS file.

Format

`append` *`options`* loads the APPEND utility.

`append` *`directory;...`* specifies directories to be searched.

`append ;` erases the list of appended directories.

`append` lists the currently appended directories.

Options

/e puts a list of the appended directories into the DOS environment (as a variable named APPEND).

/x allows programs to use the DOS services "search first," "find first," and "exec." (This option has a different meaning in PC DOS 4; see following.)

Version 4

APPEND Has New Options in Version 4

PC DOS 4 adds some new options to APPEND and redefines the meaning of the /x option.

/x:on or /x allows APPEND to search for executable (program) files; that is, files with the extensions .EXE, .COM, or .BAT. This includes the functionality of the PATH command within APPEND.

/x:off does not allow APPEND to search for executable (program) files. This is the default.

/path:on allows APPEND to search for a file elsewhere even if a specific path name was used. This is the default.

/path:off allows APPEND to search for a file only if a file name alone (not a path) was used.

Sample Use

`append c:\bin`

Procedure

Your first APPEND command should normally be append /e (or possibly append /e /x in PC DOS 3.3); this establishes the APPEND variable in the environment and a small memory-resident program that allows for future changes to the APPEND list.

Version 4

Use /x to Find Executable Program Files in Version 4

If you want PC DOS 4 to search for executable program files, add the /x:on option to your first APPEND command.

Next, use APPEND followed by the list of directories you want searched for files, using the same format as that used by PATH (see Example 1). During the rest of the session, you can issue an APPEND command with a different list of directories at any time necessary; the new list replaces the previously stored one.

To see the current list of appended directories, type `append` with no parameters (see Example 2). Type `append ;` to erase the current list of appended directories (see Example 3). In most cases, you should place your initial append command(s) in your AUTO-EXEC.BAT file so they run automatically at the start of the session.

Related Commands PATH specifies directories to be searched for executable programs as opposed to data files.

SET shows the APPEND list when it is in the DOS environment.

JOIN appends a whole drive to a specified directory.

ASSIGN applies a different drive to a particular drive letter

SUBST uses a drive letter to stand for another drive or path

AUTOEXEC.BAT runs APPEND commands automatically at startup time.

DETAILED REFERENCE

Explanation The APPEND command in effect supplements the PATH environmental variable. PATH specifies the directories where frequently used programs are stored so that the DOS command processor is able to find and run the program regardless of the current directory. Many applications programs, however, have data files that they need to access while running, such as overlays, configuration files, and help message files. By using APPEND with a list of directories similar to that used with PATH, you can tell DOS where to search for these needed data files.

For example, if you have a word processor, such as the older version of WordStar in the \WS directory, you can put that directory in your path, and the PC DOS command processor will find it even if the current directory is, for example, C:\LOTUS. The program will not run properly, however, because it will try to load its overlay files from C:\LOTUS rather than C:\WS. If you put the command `append c:\ws` in your AUTOEXEC.BAT file (a good place is just following your PATH statement) then WordStar will run properly because PC DOS will help WordStar find its overlay files in the C:\WS directory.

Comments The /e option puts the list of appended directories into the DOS environment. In other words, it creates an environmental variable called append containing the list (see Example 4). The advantage of this option is that many programs, particularly programming tools, such as assemblers and compilers, check the DOS environment and use the append list to find needed files. Note that if you choose to use the /e option, you must make your first APPEND command of the session append /e, with no directory list. (Follow it with an APPEND command with a directory list.)

Note also that if you use the /e option, and then use the COMMAND command to start another DOS command processor, the APPEND information is placed in the new processor's environment. However, any changes in the APPEND list that you make while running this new processor are not updated in the original processor's environment. If you want a common APPEND list to be maintained for all environments, avoid the /e option, and a single copy of the APPEND information will be kept within the APPEND program itself, thus always reflecting the latest changes regardless of the environment or command processor in use.

You can specify network drives as well as local ones with the APPEND command.

Caution

Your Program Reads and Writes to the Current Directory

Although APPEND can be quite useful, it has a few problems. Some programs will read a file from an appended directory, but will write the updated version in the current directory. Thus, the next time the application loads the file, it displays the one that has not been updated.

If you have specified /x:on to allow searching for executable files, be aware that APPEND finds the *first* such file with the requested name, regardless of extension. This means that if you want STARTUP.EXE in the third directory in your APPEND list, and a file called STARTUP.BAT is in the first directory, the latter file is the one found by APPEND.

In general, some applications may become "confused" because APPEND causes them to load the wrong files. Try deactivating APPEND by typing `append;` and run your application again to see whether the problem clears up. If so, try removing the affected directories from your APPEND command, removing any /x:on option, or both.

If you are using the IBM PC Network program or the IBM PC LAN program, use the PC DOS version of APPEND, not the one that comes with the network program. For other network software, consult your documentation.

If you are using TopView or wish to use an ASSIGN command, make sure your first APPEND command is executed before loading TopView or executing the ASSIGN command.

If you specify an incorrect path name in an APPEND command, you do not get the `Invalid path` message until an actual attempt to search the directory is made.

Examples Example 1: Set up an APPEND list.

```
C:\>append c:\bin;c:\ws;
```

Application programs in the \BIN and \WS directories are now able to find their data files.

Example 2: Examine the current APPEND list.

```
C:\>append
APPEND=C:\BIN;C:\WS;
```

Example 3: Erase the APPEND list.

```
C:\>append ;
C:\>append
No append.
```

Example 4: Set up APPEND to use the PC DOS environment and then use the SET command to examine the environment.

```
C:\>append /e
C:\>append c:\wp50;c:\lotus;
C:\>set
COMSPEC=C:\COMMAND.COM
PATH=C:\;C:\BIN;C:\WS;C:\C5;
PROMPT=$p$g
APPEND=C:\WP50;C:\LOTUS;
```

The SET command, when given without a parameter, displays the current variables in the PC DOS environment, including the variable *append*, which contains the list of directories used in the preceding APPEND command. Observe the identical syntax for the PATH and APPEND lists. Usually the APPEND list is a subset of the PATH list and contains those directories that have applications which need to access special data files.

Related Chapters
Chapter 5–PC DOS Files
Chapter 6–Managing Your Hard Disk
Chapter 11–Customizing Your System

ASSIGN

External Command

Compatibility	2.0	2.1	3.0	3.1	3.2	3.3	4.0	OS/2 (DOS mode)	OS/2 (prot.)
	▲	▲	▲	▲	▲	▲	▲	▲	

Use the ASSIGN command to send requests involving files on a particular drive to another drive. This command is used mainly with older programs that "expect" to be run from drive A or B.

Format

`assign` *`old drive=new drive...`* assigns drives.

`assign` removes all assignments.

Sample Use

`assign a=c`

Procedure

To set up drive assignments, type `assign` followed by the letter of the drive to be assigned, an equal sign, and the letter of the drive to be used in place of the assigned drive (Example 1). (Do not put colons after the drive letters.) If you need to assign more than one drive, use additional pairs of drive letters (Example 2). To remove all drive assignments, type `assign` without any parameters (Example 3).

Related Commands

JOIN refers to a drive as though it were a directory on another drive.

SUBST refers to a directory using just a drive letter.

TRUENAME reveals the path to the true location of the file.

DETAILED REFERENCE

Explanation Although most programs written these days allow files to be read from or written to whatever disk drives are available, some older programs are written to use specific drives, such as drive A or B. Many systems now have hard disks or RAM disks with designations such as drive C, D, or E. You can use the ASSIGN command to redirect disk accesses to drives that would not otherwise be recognized by the program. For example, you can put a program that recognizes only drive A on your hard disk C, and use the ASSIGN command to convert all requests for files on drive A to requests for the same files on drive C.

Comments ASSIGN is useful when you need it, but you shouldn't need it often. Use it to "fool" those few application programs that insist on using a specific drive. If you are writing a program, don't refer to specific drives.

ASSIGN usually does not work with programs (mostly games) that have copy protection schemes which require that a certain drive be used.

Caution

ASSIGN and other PC DOS Commands
Don't use ASSIGN while doing "housekeeping" with other PC DOS commands. At best, you will be confused about what drive or directory you are really looking at, as illustrated in Example 1. Some PC DOS mode commands, such as FORMAT, DISKCOPY, and DISKCOMP, ignore drive reassignments; others, such as BACKUP, RESTORE, LABEL, PRINT, SUBST, and JOIN, fail or cause undesirable results when used with reassigned drives, because they do not receive the correct information about the physical drives.

Examples Example 1: On a system that has a floppy drive A and a hard drive C, assign all requests to drive B so that they are directed to drive C.

```
C:\>assign b=c
C:\>dir b:
  Volume in drive B has no label
  Directory of  B:\CORRES
 .            <DIR>        1-04-88   3:28p
 ..           <DIR>        1-04-88   3:28p
 JS1228           1082  12-28-87   2:45p
 MW0111B          5081   1-11-88   7:09p
 EX1             17450   1-20-88   5:22a
         5 File(s)   6742016 bytes free
```

Drive B was assigned to drive C and the command dir b: shows the current directory on drive C (C:\CORRES). Although the DIR command "thinks" that it is dealing with drive B (as shown by its referring to the drive as B in the listing), the megabytes of free disk space shown reveal that the actual directory request went to drive C, the hard disk.

Example 2: Assign both drives A and B to drive C.

```
C:\>assign a=c b=c
```

Note that several drives can be assigned to the same drive letter or to different drive letters. Here, requests to either drive A or drive B are directed to drive C.

Example 3: Remove all drive assignments.

```
C:\>assign
```

Related Chapters Chapter 6–Managing Your Hard Disk
Chapter 7–All About Floppy Disks
Chapter 11–Customizing Your System

ATTRIB

External Command

Compatibility	2.0	2.1	3.0	3.1	**3.2**	3.3	4.0	OS/2 (DOS mode)	OS/2 (prot.)
				▲	▲	▲	▲	▲	▲

Use the ATTRIB command to protect files from being removed or changed, giving them "read only" status, and to "mark" files for backup.

Format `attrib` *`attribute settings file or directory option`*

Options */s* applies attributes to files in all subdirectories of specified directory.

Sample Use `attrib +r letter.txt`

Procedure After typing `attrib`, specify one or both of the following attribute settings.

+*r* sets read-only status.

–*r* removes read-only status.

+*a* sets "to be archived (backed up)" status.

–*a* removes "to be archived (backed up)" status.

You can include settings for one or both of the read-only and archive attributes (Example 1).

Note: The ability to change the archive bit was added starting with PC DOS 3.2. Next, specify the files whose attributes you want to set. You can use a file name, file name with wildcards, or a directory name with wildcards (Example 2).

DOS Shell

Change File Attributes from within the DOS Shell
From the Start Programs screen, select File System in the Main Group. From the File System window, select the file(s) whose attribute(s) you wish to change. From the File menu, select Change Attribute. You can now choose the attribute you wish to change: Archive, Hidden, or Read Only.

Related Commands BACKUP backs up files with the archive attribute set.

RESTORE restores files whose archive attribute was subsequently set.

XCOPY copies files with the archive attribute set.

DETAILED REFERENCE

Explanation The ATTRIB command allows you to turn the read-only and archive attributes of a file on or off. If the read-only attribute of a file is on, the file cannot be modified or deleted, but it still can be read. Using this attribute can protect important files from accidental deletion.

The archive attribute is used to determine which files will be backed up by the BACKUP command. PC DOS automatically turns on the archive attribute of a file when a new file is created or an existing file is modified. By using the command backup /m (see the BACKUP entry), you can back up only those files that have been created or changed since the last backup. This is called an *incremental backup*, and it allows you to keep your backup up to date without doing a complete, time- and disk-consuming backup each time. You can use the ATTRIB command to turn on the archive attribute for an unchanged file if you want to include it in such a backup for convenience. You can also turn off the archive attribute so that a new or changed file won't be included in a backup. (In addition to the BACKUP command, copies made with the command xcopy /a, xcopy /m, or restore /m are also affected by the setting of the archive attribute.)

The ATTRIB command can be used with a single file, a group of files specified by wildcard, or a directory and all of its subdirectories (using the /s option). By combining the ATTRIB and BACKUP or XCOPY commands in a batch file, you can create automatic backup programs for maintaining backups for particular projects.

Comments It should be clear that making files read-only with the ATTRIB command protects against accidental damage to your data, but does not protect against malicious damage, because someone can always use ATTRIB to remove read-only status from a file and then delete or change it.

Examples Example 1: Protect the file CONTRACT.90 from being deleted or changed.

```
C:\>attrib +r contract.90
```

The specification +r sets the read-only attribute. Any attempt to change or delete this file will now result in the `access denied` message.

Example 2: Protect all C programs in the directory SRC from being deleted or changed and mark them for future backup.

```
C:\>attrib +r +a src\*.c
```

The attributes +r +a set the read-only and archive attributes. This protects the affected files from change and ensures that they will be included in the next backup. Because C programs traditionally have an extension of .C, this extension is specified with a wildcard to process all C program source files.

Example 3: Protect all files on the disk in drive A from being deleted or changed.

```
C:\>attrib +r a:\*.* /s
```

Note that you can't get away with using just the drive name to process all files on drive A; the wildcards are needed. The /s specifies that all subdirectories and their files (or subdirectories) will be processed. Thus, every file on the disk will be affected.

Related Chapters

Chapter 5–PC DOS Files
Chapter 6–Managing Your Hard Disk

AUTOEXEC.BAT

Resource

Compatibility	2.0	2.1	3.0	3.1	3.2	3.3	4.0	OS/2 (DOS mode)	OS/2 (prot.)
	▲	▲	▲	▲	▲	▲	▲	▲	

Use the AUTOEXEC.BAT file to execute several PC DOS commands automatically every time you start your system. For example, you can set system variables, such as the search path, and you can specify programs that you want to run automatically at the start of the session. The AUTOEXEC.BAT file is also frequently used to install memory-resident programs.

Format

The AUTOEXEC.BAT file is an ordinary ASCII text file, containing a series of commands that are run just as if they were typed on the command line. This file must be placed in the root directory of the startup drive.

Sample Use

Here is a simple example of an AUTOEXEC.BAT file:

```
@echo off
verify on
path c:\;c:\dos;c:\51;c:\wp;
append c:\wp;
set include=c:\c51\include
set lib=c:\c51\lib

\utils\skn
```

This example is explained in the Detailed Reference section.

Procedure

You can create a simple AUTOEXEC.BAT by typing `copy con: autoexec.bat` (assuming the current directory is the startup directory and then typing the commands one line at a time. Press the F6 key or the Ctrl-Z key combination to save the file to disk. An easier alternative is to use any text editor or word processor that works in plain ASCII text mode to add to or revise this file. (For information on creating such files, see Chapter 9, "Creating Text Files.")

Related Commands

COMMAND starts a secondary command processor and optionally runs AUTOEXEC.BAT.

PATH lists the current path, frequently set in the AUTOEXEC.BAT file.

APPEND allows you to run the AUTOEXEC.BAT file from your current directory.

Version 4

New Ways to Start Programs in Version 4

CONFIG.SYS, which, in PC DOS 4, can also be used to start programs.

INSTALL, which, in PC DOS 4, can be used to start programs in the CONFIG.SYS file.

DETAILED REFERENCE

Explanation AUTOEXEC.BAT follows the same rules as other batch files (see Chapter 10, "Batch Files," for details). The commands in the AUTOEXEC.BAT file are run automatically only at startup, although you could rerun them later by typing

```
autoexec
```

at the PC DOS prompt. This might be useful if you wanted to restore your original search path, for example. You can also start a new PC DOS command processor and run AUTOEXEC.BAT again by using the command `command /p`. (See the COMMAND entry.)

Comments You will want at least a minimal AUTOEXEC.BAT file in order to set your system search path (see PATH entry) and to prevent the system from asking you for the time and date at startup. (This behavior is a vestige of the early days when PCs did not come with built-in clocks.) PC DOS users also frequently use an AUTOEXEC.BAT file to install memory-resident programs, such as SideKick.

Example Example 1: Examine a more or less typical AUTOEXEC.BAT file.

```
@echo off
verify on
path c:\;c:\dos;c:\51;c:\wp;
append c:\wp;
\utils\skn
set include=c:\c51\include
set lib=c:\c51\lib
```

This is the file shown in the Sample Use section. The @ECHO OFF statement suppresses display of the batch file lines as they are executed. (The @ prevents even the ECHO OFF line from being displayed; this feature is available starting with PC DOS 3.3. The VERIFY ON command ensures that all disk writes will be checked for accuracy, at some cost in system speed.

The PATH command sets the search path so that the root directory of drive C, the DOS directory, the C51 (C compiler) directory, and the WP directory will be searched for commands or executable programs. The APPEND command specifies that the WP directories will also be searched for overlay files needed by the word processor. (See the entries for PATH and APPEND for details.) SET commands are used to set environmental variables to tell the compiler where to find its "include" files and libraries. Finally, the SideKick program in the UTILS directory will be run. (Because it is a stay-resident program, it will remain in memory, ready to be triggered as needed.)

Version 4

Conserve Memory with Install in Version 4
In PC DOS 4, you can run four PC DOS commands that have memory-resident portions, FASTOPEN, KEYB, NLSFUNC, and SHARE, by specifying them with an INSTALL statement in your CONFIG.SYS file. PC DOS uses memory more efficiently when the commands are installed in this way instead of being run from AUTOEXEC.BAT. Other memory-resident programs can also be installed with INSTALL, but the benefits of doing so are uncertain.

Related Chapters
Chapter 6–Managing Your Hard Disk
Chapter 11–Customizing Your System
Chapter 12–Installing a PC DOS System

BACKUP

External Command

Compatibility	2.0	2.1	3.0	3.1	3.2	3.3	4.0	OS/2 (DOS mode)	OS/2 (prot.)
	▲	▲	▲	▲	▲	▲	▲	▲	▲

Use the BACKUP command to back up all or part of the contents of one disk to another. The most common use of BACKUP is to back up the contents of a hard disk to several floppies.

Format `backup` *`source disk or directory destination disk options`*

Options

/s backs up all subdirectories of the specified directory and their subdirectories, etc. This is the most commonly used option because it is needed for backing up the entire contents of a hard disk (see Example 1).

Note: The remaining options check only the specified directory (or the root directory of the specified drive) for files that meet the specified criteria for BACKUP, unless the /s option is also specified.

/l:file name makes a log file containing the name of each file backed up and the sequential number of the disk to which it has been backed up (see Example 1). If you do not specify a file name, the file BACKUP.LOG is created and placed in the root directory of the source disk. This option is recommended because it enables you to restore a specific file that has been damaged or accidentally deleted by looking up its disk number in the log file, inserting that disk, and using RESTORE. For extra security, copy the log file to a floppy disk for use if the hard disk is damaged.

/d:MM-DD-YY backs up only those files that were created or last modified on or after the specified date. This option is useful for doing incremental backups; for example, doing a complete backup on the first day of each month and then doing a backup at the end of each week, backing up only those files that have been created or changed since the last backup. Incremental backups reduce the amount of time spent doing backups while keeping the backup disks up to date.

/t:HH:MM:SS backs up only those files that were created or modified after the time specified. You can combine this option with /d to specify both date and time.

/m backs up only those files that have been created or changed since the last backup. This provides a simpler way to do incremental backups, although the backups would not be organized by date or time.

/a adds the files to be backed up to the backup disk without erasing any files that are already there. This option can save disk space when you are doing incremental backups to large-capacity floppy disks. Note: This option cannot be used with backup disks created under DOS version 3.2 or earlier.

/f formats each backup disk before using it. You can use this option to make a backup using a new box of floppy disks and not have to format them separately first.

Note: This option works only if the disks used have a capacity equal to the maximum capacity of the backup drive, such as 1.2MB for AT floppy drives and 1.44MB for IBM PS/2 floppy drives.

Version 4

BACKUP Formats Disks Automatically in Version 4

The /f option is not used with BACKUP in PC DOS 4, because if the destination disk is not already formatted, it is automatically formatted before the files are backed up. This does not apply when backing up to a hard disk, which must be already formatted.

DOS Shell

Use of BACKUP Feature of the DOS Shell

From the Start Programs screen, select DOS Utilities in the Main Group. From the utility options given, select Backup Fixed Disk (assuming you wish to back up a hard disk). The BACKUP command operates in the same way as the command-line examples shown in the Examples section of this entry.

Sample Use

```
backup c:\*.* a:
```

Procedure

Type BACKUP followed by the name of the disk or directory you wish to back up. Next, type the name of the disk drive to be used for the backup (usually A). Follow this with any options you wish to use, in any order (see Options).

Related Commands

RESTORE makes backed up files available for use.

COPY makes immediately usable copies of files.

XCOPY uses options similar to those provided by BACKUP, but makes immediately usable copies.

DISKCOPY makes an exact sector-by-sector copy of a disk on another disk.

DETAILED REFERENCE

Explanation

The BACKUP command copies files from the source disk (usually the hard disk, drive C) to the destination disk (usually a floppy disk in drive A). The operation of BACKUP is different from that performed by commands such as COPY or XCOPY, however. Starting with PC DOS 3.3, BACKUP has improved efficiency; in order to reduce the number of disks needed, BACKUP packs the files it copies together on the backup disk, with a separate "control" file giving the location to which each file should be restored when using the backup disk (see RESTORE). Because of this packing or "archiving" operation, files on the backup disk cannot be read or used directly; they must first be restored using the RESTORE command.

The BACKUP command displays the path name of each file as it is backed up. When the backup disk is filled to capacity, you are prompted to insert the next disk. BACKUP numbers the backup disks starting with 01. It is a good idea to put the corresponding numbers on the disk labels so that disks will be inserted in the correct order when restoring from the backup. Note that any existing files on the backup disk are destroyed unless the /a option is used (see Options).

Comments You can back up just a few files by specifying file names with wildcards, or back up a floppy disk rather than the hard disk, but there is little advantage in doing so. COPY is easier to use for copying a few files, and XCOPY is a versatile tool for copying one or a few directories. BACKUP is most useful for copying when the backed up files will not fit on a single floppy disk, which is normally the case when backing up the contents of a hard disk.

Tip

Back Up One Hard Disk with a Second

Starting with PC DOS 3.0, BACKUP can back up files to a hard disk. Because hard disks are much cheaper than they used to be, some users find it convenient to have two hard disks of the same capacity and to back up files from the working disk to the backup disk every day.

Because BACKUP is a rather complicated command with many options, you may wish to save your most commonly used BACKUP commands in batch files for repeated use.

Caution

Watch Out for BACKUP Idiosyncrasies

When backing up data to floppies, you should use only disks that have the same capacity as the drive being used. For drive A on a typical AT system, this means 1.2MB disks; for drive A on a typical PS/2 system, this means 1.44MB disks.

You cannot use BACKUP to back up from write-protected disks, because the archive bit of the source files must be changed to indicate that they have been backed up. (For obvious reasons, you can't back up to a write-protected disk, either!)

The BACKUP command does not back up the system files (IBMBIO.COM or IBMDOS.COM) or COMMAND.COM. You should use DISKCOPY to make a backup copy of your PC DOS distribution disk containing these files.

Remember that if you want to back up all subdirectories on a disk (and any directories at lower levels), you must specify the /s option. Also, if you want to add files to an existing backup, you must include the /a option. Failure to do so will lead to all existing data on the backup disk being erased; however, you will receive a warning message and have an opportunity to abort the backup.

In a network environment, you may not be able to back up every file that you want to. Any files that you don't have access to (because the device on which they are stored is not on the network or the file is being used by someone else) will not be backed up. The path name of the file and the message `Not able to backup file` will be displayed on the screen. You may wish to redirect the output of backup to an error file to catch such messages for later perusal (Example 3).

It is best to physically label and number your set of backup floppies before you start the backup. It is easy to get confused and put the wrong disk in the drive.

In PC DOS 3.1, BACKUP has a bug that prevents it from copying a read-only file onto multiple disks, because it marks the destination file as read-only after creating the first part of it and thus is unable to write to it to continue the copy.

Note: See the Caution on page 190 regarding BACKUP.

Exit Codes The BACKUP command returns one of the following exit codes:

- 0 backup ran normally
- 1 no files were found to back up
- 2 some files were not backed up due to file-sharing conflicts (file in use by another user on the network)
- 3 user terminated backup with Ctrl-Break
- 4 backup terminated due to some error (check for error messages)

Examples Example 1: Back up the entire contents of hard disk drive C to multiple floppy disks and make a backup log file.

```
C:\>backup c:\*.* a: /s /l
```

The wildcard is needed to specify "all files," and the /s option specifies that all directories and subdirectories on drive C are to be processed. The /l option causes a log file to be created with the path names of all files that were backed up; because no file name is specified, the default file BACKUP.LOG is placed in the root directory of drive C. The first message shown is

```
Insert backup diskette 01 in drive A:
Warning!  Files in the target drive
a:\ root directory will be erased
Press any key to continue
```

As the backup proceeds, path names of the files being backed up are listed. When the disk is filled, you are prompted to insert the next disk.

```
\DOS\COMMAND.COM
\DOS\SYS.COM
\DOS\FORMAT.COM
\DOS\MORE.COM
\DOS\CHKDSK.COM
```

```
\DOS\DISKCOPY.COM
Insert backup diskette 02 in drive A:
Warning!  Files in the target drive
a:\ root directory will be erased
Press any key to continue
```

Example 2: Back up every file in the ACCOUNTS directory of hard disk drive C that has been created or changed since 5:00 PM, May 31, 1990.

```
C:\>backup c:\accounts\*.* a: /d:05-31-90
/t:17:00:00
```

Here the wildcard specifies that all files in the ACCOUNTS directory will be checked for possible backup. Because /s is not used, any subdirectories in the ACCOUNTS directory will not be examined. The use of the /d and /t options specifies the earliest date and time for which files will be backed up.

Example 3: Back up every file on hard disk drive C that has been created or modified since the last backup, adding the backups to the existing contents of the backup disk in drive A. Capture any error messages in a file for later inspection.

```
C:\>backup c:\*.* a: /m /a /s > error
```

The /a option specifies that backup files should be added to existing files on the backup disks in drive A. By default, any files existing on the backup disks are deleted.

Related Chapters

Chapter 6–Managing Your Hard Disk
Chapter 7–All About Floppy Disks
Chapter 10–Batch Files

BREAK

Internal Command, Setting

Compatibility	2.0	2.1	3.0	3.1	3.2	3.3	4.0	OS/2 (DOS mode)	OS/2 (prot.)
	▲	▲	▲	▲	▲	▲	▲	▲	▲

Use the BREAK command or the BREAK setting in your CONFIG.SYS file to determine how much of the time the user will be able to interrupt a program by pressing Ctrl-Break (or Ctrl-C). You can determine whether PC DOS will check for this keystroke any time a program has called for PC DOS operations or only during screen, keyboard, or print operations.

Format

`break` shows current status of BREAK setting.

`break` *`setting`* sets break status interactively.

`break=`*`setting`* sets break status in the CONFIG.SYS file.

Settings

on turns on extended checking for Ctrl-Break keystrokes.

off turns off extended checking for Ctrl-Break keystrokes.

Sample Use `break on` is used in a command line, AUTOEXEC.BAT, or other batch file. `break=on` is used in a CONFIG.SYS file.

Procedure You can control the setting for BREAK in three ways: by using the BREAK command on the command line, putting it in a batch file (usually AUTOEXEC.BAT), or by setting the value of BREAK in the CONFIG.SYS file. To find out the current setting of BREAK, type `break` with no setting (Example 1). To set BREAK, type `break` followed by `on` or `off` as appropriate (Example 2). To set BREAK in the CONFIG.SYS file, type `break=` followed by `on` or `off` as appropriate (Example 4).

Related Commands AUTOEXEC.BAT is a resource file for setting BREAK at startup.
CONFIG.SYS is an alternate resource file for setting BREAK at startup.

DETAILED REFERENCE

Explanation A command convention in the PC world allows the user to "bail out" of a program by pressing the Ctrl-Break or Ctrl-C keys. How rapidly a program responds to this key combination depends on whether BREAK is on or off. When it is off (the default), the system responds to Ctrl-Break only while an operation involving the keyboard, screen, printer, or auxiliary device is being performed. This means that a program cannot be interrupted by Ctrl-Break while it is, for example, performing calculations or doing disk I/O.

When BREAK is on, the check for Ctrl-Break is done whenever any system call is being performed, including disk access. This means that when BREAK is on, you can interrupt the running program at almost any time, unless the program has made other provisions for handling user breaks.

Comments When using most sophisticated programs, it is probably best to leave BREAK off, which is the default. Most such programs provide their own handling for Ctrl-Break anyway, to prevent a disruptive exit. For programs that do not override your setting for BREAK, leaving BREAK on slows down intensive operations, such as disk access, because of the constant checking. Interrupting a program with Ctrl-Break can have undesirable consequences, such as data not being written to disk completely or the screen being left in a video mode that is no longer wanted. Having BREAK on might be useful when testing programs such as public domain utilities, where the ability to "pull the plug" quickly might prevent damage to data or make you wait to regain control of the machine.

Examples **Example 1**: Find out the current setting for BREAK.

```
C:\>break
BREAK is off
```

Example 2: Set BREAK on.

```
C:\>break on
C:\>break
BREAK is on
```

First, `break on` was typed; then just `break` was typed, which gave a message saying that `break is on`.

Example 3: Show how a batch file can be interrupted when BREAK is on.

When you run a batch file (a file with the .BAT extension), and BREAK is on, you get a message prompt asking whether you want to terminate the batch job. Here is an example batch file.

```
c:\>copy con: test.bat
@echo off
echo this is line 1
echo this is line 2
echo this is line 3
echo this is line 4
echo end of test.bat
^Z
     1 file(s) copied.
```

The lines that will be echoed have been numbered so that you can see where you are in the batch file when you interrupt it with Ctrl-Break.

```
c:\>test
this is line 1
this is line 2
^C                              ←Interrupted by ^C
Terminate batch job (Y/N)? n    ←Said "no" to prompt
this is line 4                  ←Batch file resumes
end of test.bat
```

Example 4: Set BREAK on in the CONFIG.SYS file.

```
break=on
```

Related Chapters Chapter 10–Batch Files
Chapter 11–Customizing Your System
Chapter 12–Installing a PC DOS System

BUFFERS

Setting

Compatibility	2.0	2.1	3.0	3.1	3.2	3.3	4.0	OS/2 (DOS mode)	OS/2 (prot.)
	▲	▲	▲	▲	▲	▲	▲	▲	▲

Use the BUFFERS setting in your CONFIG.SYS file to set the amount of memory to be used for disk buffers, which increases the speed of access to frequently used data.

Format `buffers=`*`number of buffers`* in PC DOS 3.3 and earlier.

Options

Version 4

BUFFERS Syntax Varies in Version 4
`buffers=number of buffers,read-ahead sectors` in PC DOS 4.
/x puts buffers in expanded memory. Increases maximum buffers to 10,000 (PC DOS 4).

Sample Use

`buffers=8` is a statement used in the CONFIG.SYS file, PC DOS 3.3 or earlier.

`buffers=30,8` is a statement used in the CONFIG.SYS file, PC DOS 4.

Procedure

By default, PC DOS allocates 10 buffers on a system with 256K memory and 15 for a system with 512K or more of memory. Each buffer uses 532 bytes of memory, so the default is a bit over 15K of buffer memory. To change this setting in your CONFIG.SYS file, specify `buffers=` followed by a number between 1 and 99 (in other words, 512 bytes for about 50K of buffer memory.)

Version 4

SELECT Automatically Sets BUFFERS = 20 in Version 4
With PC DOS 4, the SELECT program sets buffers=20 in your CONFIG.SYS file if you accept the "Balance PC DOS function with program workspace" option. To change this setting, edit your CONFIG.SYS file so that buffers= is followed by the number of buffers (1–99).

Optionally, follow this number with a comma and the number of buffers the system should read ahead (1–8). If you wish to use expanded memory for your buffers, add the /x option (but see the later discussion of the use of expanded memory in Example 2). If you use the /x option, you can specify total buffers up to 10,000, depending, of course, on the amount of expanded memory available.

Related Commands

DISKCACHE sets up disk cache for IBM PS/2 machines.

VDISK.SYS is a driver that sets up virtual (RAM) disks.

CONFIG.SYS is a file containing the BUFFERS setting.

DETAILED REFERENCE

Explanation

Using disk buffers speeds up data access by reading a whole 512-byte sector into memory the first time a program accesses a record (such as 128 bytes) from it. Because many programs read data sequentially, the program is likely to ask for the next 128 bytes. Because the whole sector is now in memory, the data is read from memory, a very fast process, instead of being read again from the disk, which, because it is a mechanical device, is considerably slower. The data from the least recently accessed sectors is replaced as necessary by that from newly accessed sectors, thus keeping the most frequently used data in memory.

Version 4

Control Reading of Sectors in Version 4
PC DOS 4 makes the use of buffers even more efficient by allowing you to specify that from 1 to 8 sectors be "read ahead." That is, when a new sector needs to be read, a number of following sectors

are read at the same time. Because the overhead involved in reading several sectors is not much more than for reading only one, this can be efficient when used with programs that read data sequentially. Examples of such programs are word processors loading text files, most spreadsheet programs, and database programs that read the whole database into memory. On the other hand, having read-ahead sectors can be less efficient if you use applications that read sectors from arbitrary (random) disk locations. This is typical of database programs that do not keep the database in memory. For such applications, you should experiment with a high (30 or more) total number of buffers, but few (or no) read-ahead buffers.

Comments You should be careful about setting BUFFERS to a high value (more than 50). Using buffers is trading some memory for increased performance. Many PC DOS users find memory to be a scarce resource, although this can be somewhat alleviated by using expanded memory (under DOS 4). There is also overhead involved in searching a large number of buffers, so for best performance you should observe whether data access starts to slow down at high BUFFERS settings. The only way to find out is to start at buffers=20, increase the value in steps of 5 or 10, and try to observe how often your commonly used applications read from the disk. PC DOS 4 users can similarly "tune" the number of read-ahead buffers.

Note: If you are using the IBMCACHE disk cache, set buffers=3.

BUFFERS May Be Unnecessary
The system disk cache has a much greater impact on performance than does the buffers setting, and the cache uses a more efficient method for managing the disk. Experiment with eliminating the BUFFERS setting if you are using a cache.

Expanded Memory and PC DOS 4
When using expanded memory for buffers under PC DOS, you must have an appropriate expanded memory driver installed, such as XMAEM.SYS and/or XMA2EMS.SYS. These drivers appear to work only with IBM hardware, so owners of third-party memory boards may have to check with the manufacturer to obtain a PC DOS 4 compatible driver.

PC DOS uses expanded memory page 255. Any application that uses this page to map to the disk input/output area will interfere with the operation of BUFFERS.

Examples **Example 1**: In the CONFIG.SYS file, allocate about 20K (40 532-byte blocks) for disk buffers.

```
buffers=40
```

Example 2: With PC DOS 4, specify 120 total buffers and 8 read-ahead buffers, using expanded memory.

Version 4

Use the /x Option with EMS Memory in Version 4

```
buffers=120,8 /x
```

The /x option does two things: It allows a total number of buffers over 99, and it places the buffers in expanded memory. A very high setting like this would be suitable for an application that reads large amounts of data sequentially from disk. The use of expanded memory conserves scarce base memory.

Related Chapters Chapter 11–Customizing Your System
Chapter 12–Installing a PC DOS System

Batch Command — CALL

Compatibility	2.0	2.1	3.0	3.1	3.2	3.3	4.0	OS/2 (DOS mode)	OS/2 (prot.)
						▲	▲	▲	▲

Use the CALL command as a statement in a batch file to transfer control to another batch file. When the second batch file ends execution, control returns to the original batch file at the statement following the CALL.

Format `call batchfile options ...`

Options No fixed options, but accepts options to be passed to the called batch file.

Sample Use `call wom.bat` is a statement used in a batch file.

Procedure The CALL command is always used as a statement in a batch file. Follow CALL with the name of the batch file to be called, followed by any parameters you wish to send to the called batch file.

Note: If you do not need a return of control to the original batch file, the CALL statement is not needed; simply name the second batch file and it is executed.

Related Command COMMAND is a "pre-DOS 3.3" way to call another batch file.

DETAILED REFERENCE

Explanation Some tasks, such as setting up custom system configurations or installing software, often involve writing lengthy batch files. Batch files, like other kinds of programs, are easier to write, debug, and maintain if they are broken down into a number of small units that each perform one particular function. You can write a short main batch file that uses the CALL command to run other batch files as needed.

The CALL command is also convenient because it allows you to follow the name of the batch file to be called with additional information to pass to that batch file. For example, in the statement

```
call printdir c:\backup
```

the PRINTDIR batch file is given the name of the directory to be printed, C:\BACKUP. More than one item (separated by spaces) can be given. These items are accessed by the called batch file just as though they had been typed on a command line calling that batch file. Thus, the parameters are accessed in the called batch file by using %1 to represent the first parameter, %2 the second, and so on. (See Example 2 and Chapter 10, "Batch Files" for further details.)

Comments You don't have to use the batch file's file name extension in the CALL statement; an extension of .BAT is assumed. The batch file specified must be in the current directory, a directory listed on your current path, or in the directory used in a path name given for the batch file. (See PATH entry.)

Any changes made to the environment by the called batch file remain after control returns. A called batch file can, in turn, call another batch file. Control always returns to the last calling file, then the previous caller, and so on. A batch file can even call itself, but make sure that it checks for a condition that will eventually terminate it. For earlier PC DOS versions: If you are using a version of PC DOS prior to 3.3, you can still call a batch file from the current batch file and return. To do so, use the statement `command /c batfile` where batfile is the name of the batch file you wish to call. This statement loads a secondary command processor for executing the called file and thus uses some extra memory.

Example Example 1: Show the flow of control when one batch file calls another.

Create a main batch file and save it as FIRST.BAT.

```
C:\>copy con: first.bat
@echo off
echo This is the first batch file
echo calling the second batch file
call second
echo now back in the first batch file
```

Create a second batch file and save it as SECOND.BAT.

```
C:\>copy con: second.cmd
echo This is the second batch file
```

Execute the first batch file and observe the results.

```
C:\>first
This is the first batch file
calling the second batch file
This is the second batch file
now back in the first batch file
```

Related Chapter Chapter 10–Batch Files

Internal Command

CD (CHDIR)

Compatibility	2.0	2.1	3.0	3.1	3.2	3.3	4.0	OS/2 (DOS mode)	OS/2 (prot.)
	▲	▲	▲	▲	▲	▲	▲	▲	▲

Use the CD (or CHDIR) command to change to a new current directory.

Format `cd` *`drive:directory`* changes the current directory.

`cd` displays the path name of the current directory.

Note: CHDIR is the "official" name of this command, but a synonym, CD, is provided and is easier to type—it will be used here.

Sample Use `cd c:\wp\corres`

Procedure To change to another directory on the current drive, type `cd` followed by the path name to that directory (Examples 1 and 2). Typing `cd \` changes to the root directory of the current drive; `cd ..` changes to the parent of the current directory. (See Chapter 6 "Managing Your Hard Disk" for more information about constructing path names.)

To change the current directory on a drive other than the current drive, start the path name with the drive letter followed by a colon (Example 3).

To display the path name of the current directory on the current drive, type just `cd`. (As an alternative, you can have the the current directory displayed as part of the prompt by giving the command `prompt $p$g`; this has been adopted as a practice in this book; see PROMPT for details.) You can also use CD with just a drive designation (such as A:) to find out what the current directory on a particular drive is.

DOS Shell

SELECT a Directory to Make It the Current Directory Using the DOS Shell
When you are using the DOS Shell File System, you can change directories simply by scrolling through the file window using the keyboard or the mouse and selecting the name of a directory. To change the current disk drive, press Ctrl followed by the drive letter.

Related Commands APPEND directs programs to find special files in other directories.

DIR lists the contents of a directory.

MD (MKDIR) creates a new directory.

PATH finds programs without changing the directory or using a path name.

RD (RMDIR) removes a directory.

DETAILED REFERENCE

Explanation PC DOS maintains a current directory for each disk drive. Files (including programs) in the current directory on the current drive can be accessed simply by using the file name. Programs in directories listed in the PATH command can also be found by file name without changing directories. You can access files (not specified in PATH or APPEND commands) outside the current directory, but you must either use a path name or first change to the directory containing the file and then give the file name.

Comments Note that changing the directory on a drive other than the current one does not change the current drive. To change the current drive, type the desired drive's letter and a colon (Example 4). Also, note that previous ASSIGN, JOIN, and SUBST commands can change the directory actually accessed from the current directory.

Examples Example 1: Change the directory on the current drive, using a complete path name.

```
C:\>cd \acct\data
```

Example 2: Change the directory by using a relative path name.

```
C:\>cd ..\corres
```

Here the change is from the DATA subdirectory of the ACCT directory to the CORRES subdirectory, which is at the same level. The special name `..` means "the parent directory of the current directory," so this path name is the same as \ACCT\CORRES.

Example 3: Change the directory on a different drive.

```
C:>cd a:\startup
```

The path name begins with A:\ to indicate that you want to change the current directory on drive A. Notice that the current directory shown in the prompt does not change, because the current drive is still drive C.

Example 4: Change the current drive.

```
C:\>a:
A:\STARTUP>
```

Typing `a:` makes drive A the current drive, as shown by the change in the prompt. The current directory for that drive (set in the previous example), is STARTUP.

Related Chapters Chapter 7–All About Floppy Disks
Chapter 4–Using DOSSHELL
Chapter 6–Managing Your Hard Disk

Internal Command

CHCP

Compatibility	2.0	2.1	3.0	3.1	3.2	3.3	4.0	OS/2 (DOS mode)	OS/2 (prot.)
	▲	▲	▲	▲	▲	▲	▲	▲	▲

Use the CHCP command to change the code page (defined character set) used for the video display, keyboard, and printer. This allows you to use and display characters used by a variety of national languages.

Format

`chcp` shows code number of active code page.

`chcp` ***code page number*** sets a new code page.

Sample Use

`chcp 850`

Procedure

To find out which code page is currently in use, type just CHCP. (Code pages are listed in Chapter 13 "International Language Support.") To set a new code page, type `chcp` followed by the number of the code page to be used.

Preparing to Use Code Pages: In order to use code page switching, you must run the NLSFUNC command to install extended character information, you must select the appropriate keyboard support with the KEYB command, and you must load the appropriate code pages with the MODE command. In addition, you must install the DISPLAY.SYS driver with the appropriate options. If you wish to use code-page switching with a printer, you must install PRINTER.SYS (which only works with various models of the IBM Proprinter and Quietwriter). The reference entries for the commands and drivers mentioned have detailed information; in addition, Chapter 13 walks you through the installation of code page support.

Related Commands

COUNTRY specifies the country and code page in the CONFIG.SYS file (not needed if the desired country is the United States, with code page 437).

DEVICE specifies devices involved in code page switching.

GRAFTABLE allows display of extended national language characters using graphics mode.

NLSFUNC enables use of extended country information in code pages (required).

MODE specifies code pages for the screen and printers (required).

KEYB specifies keyboard layout (required).

SELECT installs PC DOS with specified country and keyboard settings.

CONFIG.SYS is used for DEVICE statements.

AUTOEXEC.BAT is used for running code page setup commands automatically.

DETAILED REFERENCE

Description

Because of the widespread international use of personal computers, a number of code pages (character sets) are provided to accommodate the needs of different languages. Chapter 13 shows these character sets and the associated keyboard layouts.

For systems sold in the United States, code page 437 is the default code page. As an alternative, IBM has provided a multilingual code page (850) that is a common standard used on IBM minicomputers and mainframes throughout the world, so it is useful for exchanging data with these systems. The CHCP command allows you to change between the currently active code page for a given country and an alternate code page that has been "prepared" (loaded from an information file into memory). For example, a system using the U.S. country information can switch between code pages 437 and 850.

Comments Code pages are not really needed by most U.S. domestic users. If you are such a user, you need code pages only if you wish to exchange data with systems that use the multilingual character set (code page 850) or if you want to use alternate character sets on one of the supported IBM printers.

The SELECT command allows you to create a new DOS disk that, on startup, installs specified country information and a default code page.

Note: At the time you issue the CHCP command, the appropriate code page information files (which have the extension .CPI) must be present at the location that was given when the code pages were prepared with COUNTRY, DEVICE, or MODE commands. It is easiest to leave these files in the root directory of your startup disk (such as hard disk drive C) or in a directory reserved for device drivers.

Examples **Example 1**: Find out which code pages are currently available.

```
c>chcp
Active code page:  437
```

Because a code page has not yet been prepared, the active code page is 437, the default for U.S. PCs.

Example 2: After preparing code pages (as described in Chapter 13), change the code page to the multilingual character set, code page 850.

```
c>chcp 850
c>chcp
Active code page:  850
```

After setting the new code page, the CHCP command was typed by itself to verify that the new page had been set.

Related Chapters Chapter 12–Installing a PC DOS System
Chapter 13–International Language Support

External Command

CHKDSK

Compatibility	2.0	2.1	3.0	3.1	3.2	3.3	4.0	OS/2 (DOS mode)	OS/2 (prot.)
	▲	▲	▲	▲	▲	▲	▲	▲	▲

Use CHKDSK to find out how many directories and files are on the specified disk or directory, how much space remains on the disk, the total amount of RAM available, and the amount of RAM that is currently free. CHKDSK also checks the disk's FAT (file allocation table), reports fragmentation and inconsistencies, and offers the opportunity to recover some kinds of "lost" files.

Format `chkdsk` *`drive:file name options...`*

Options */f* fixes disk problems, such as lost clusters, subject to your approving the operation by typing `y` and pressing the Enter key at the prompt. If this option is not specified, CHKDSK reports how much space would be saved by fixing problems, but doesn't fix anything.

/v displays path names of all files on specified drive (see Example 4).

Sample Use `chkdsk c: /v`

Procedure To obtain a disk and memory report, type `chkdsk` followed by the drive letter and a colon (unless you are examining the current drive).

To obtain a report on file fragmentation, follow `chkdsk` with a file name or a wildcard name such as `*.*` to examine all files.

To have CHKDSK fix errors such as lost clusters, use the /f option. (See the detailed description for an explanation of common disk problems.)

Note: CHKDSK does not wait for you to insert a disk in a floppy drive. Insert the disk you wish to check before running CHKDSK. (If you have only one disk drive, and the CHKDSK program isn't on the disk to be checked, put the disk with CHKDSK on it in the drive, and type `chkdsk b:`. You will be prompted to put the disk you want to check in drive B; on a one-drive system, however, drive B is really drive A, so you put the disk to be checked into the drive in place of the disk containing CHKDSK.)

Version 4

Use the MEM Command to Report Available Memory in Version 4
With PC DOS 4, if you just need to know how much memory is available for running a program, it is faster to use the MEM command, which does not have to read the disk.

DOS Shell

Getting Disk and File Information with the DOS Shell
You do not need to run CHKDSK to obtain statistics about your files, directories, and disks while running DOSSHELL. While in the File System, you can select Show Information from the Options menu. This shows detailed information about the currently selected file, its directory, and the disk on which it resides.

Related Commands RECOVER restores as much as possible of a file with bad sectors.

BACKUP and RESTORE reorganize fragmented files.

DETAILED REFERENCE

Explanation CHKDSK is a multipurpose utility command. Its functions can be put in three categories: 1) disk storage information, 2) memory usage information, and 3) file analysis and recovery. Each of these will be discussed in turn.

Disk Usage: CHKDSK always reports the following information about the specified disk. (The disk in the current drive is the default if no drive is specified.)

- The volume name and the date the volume was created
- The disk's total storage capacity in bytes
- The number of hidden (system) files and the total number of bytes used by them
- The number of directories and the total number of bytes used for the directories themselves (not their files)
- The total number of user (nonhidden) files on the disk and the total number of bytes they use
- The number of bytes that belong to bad sectors. (These are sectors that have bad or unreliable media. They are discovered and "locked out" at the time the disk is formatted; see FORMAT entry.) These sectors are not available for storing data.
- The total number of free (available) bytes of storage on the disk.

Version 4

Allocation Units Vary among Disk Types in Version 4

In PC DOS 4, CHKDSK also reports the number of bytes in each allocation unit. This is the smallest amount of disk space that is allocated for a file, and it varies with the kind of media used. The total number of allocation units and the number of them that are still available (free) is also given.

Memory Usage: In addition, for DOS mode only, CHKDSK reports the total available DOS memory and the amount of memory currently free. Note that only the 640K maximum memory usable by DOS is normally reported, not any extended or expanded memory that is available on the system.

File Analysis: Each file on the disk is actually stored as a chain of clusters. The file allocation table (FAT) is essentially a list of all the clusters on the disk with the number of the file (if any) to which the cluster belongs. (See Chapter 6, "Managing Your Hard Disk," and Chapter 7, "All About Floppy Disks," for more details.)

Program problems, power interruptions, or hardware problems can occasionally lead to a set of clusters being "broken off" from a file. The CHKDSK command compares the cluster entries in the FAT with the files in the directories and reports on the number of "lost" clusters and chains it finds—clusters that have a number indicating that they are in use, but which do not belong to a valid file. CHKDSK also indicates the number of bytes of disk storage tied up in lost clusters.

Because lost clusters are marked as "used" by DOS, they are not available for use for storing new files. You can type the command `chkdsk /f` to tell CHKDSK to turn these chains of lost clusters into files. Each chain is given an arbitrary file name of the form `FILEnnnn.CHK`, where nnnn represents a four-digit sequential number beginning with 0000.

Occasionally, CHKDSK is not able to recover all of the lost clusters in one pass. Therefore, it's a good idea to rerun CHKDSK if you still get a message that refers to lost clusters, repeat the chkdsk /f command, and so on.

You can examine these files, work with any usable data, or delete the files to return their storage space to the pool of free space on the disk. Example 2 shows how to deal with lost clusters that are found by CHKDSK.

If you specify a file name (or a name using wildcards), CHKDSK also reports on any matching files that have chains of clusters not stored contiguously (that is, one after another) but instead scattered on different parts of the disk. Disk access slows down when files are fragmented, because the disk head has to be repositioned frequently, and the system must wait for the next cluster to come under the disk head. The CHKDSK command does not rearrange fragmented files, but you can reorganize them either by doing a BACKUP followed by a RESTORE or through the use of one of the many available disk optimization programs. (The ease of use provided by such programs as Norton Utilities or Ultra Utilities is often worth the modest expense.) Example 3 shows a disk fragmentation report.

CHKDSK may also report on several other disk problems:

Invalid Directories: Sometimes CHKDSK displays a directory name followed by the message `Convert directory to file?`. This means that the directory format is badly garbled, and CHKDSK is unable to use the directory to obtain information about files. If you respond `y` to this message, you can then examine the file (by using TYPE or MORE or a word processor) to find out as much as possible about what files were in the directory.

Cross-Linked Files: A cross-linked file is an error that causes the FAT to indicate that a particular cluster belongs to two different files. The CHKDSK command reports the situation, but takes no action. You can often recover these files by copying them to another disk, where they are linked into a new directory and FAT.

Caution

Use COPY, Not DISKCOPY for Disk Problems

If you are dealing with a disk that has cross-linked files or one that is poorly optimized (has many noncontiguous sectors as reported by CHKDSK), you can use COPY (or XCOPY) to copy the files to a new disk. When the files are copied, they are placed in contiguous sectors. Do not use DISKCOPY. DISKCOPY copies disks not file by file, but sector but sector. Therefore, it copies the files to the new disk at the same fragmented locations.

Invalid Cluster Numbers: Sometimes the FAT ends up with an invalid first cluster number for a file. This often results in a nonexistent "file" tying up huge amounts of disk space. Running CHKDSK with the /f parameter causes this file to be truncated to zero length, freeing the incorrectly allocated space. You can then delete the file to remove the directory entry.

Caution

CHKDSK with Networks, JOIN, SUBST, and ASSIGN

CHKDSK does not work on a drive that is connected to a network. On a network, you must generally run CHKDSK from the machine that actually has the drive in question. You may have to suspend network operations before you run CHKDSK; see your network documentation.

CHKDSK does not process a directory that has been joined to the directory under inspection through the use of the JOIN command. Therefore, the statistics for this directory are not reflected in the totals displayed for the disk.

CHKDSK does not work with "disks" created by using the ASSIGN command to assign a drive letter to a directory. To run CHKDSK to analyze files in such a directory, either remove the assignment or specify the actual path name of the directory in the CHKDSK command line.

Examples Example 1: Get a disk and memory usage report.

```
C:\>chkdsk
Volume PCDOSDISK   created 10-20-1990 11:11a
Volume Serial Number is 1454-3E20

  21170176 bytes total disk space
     71680 bytes in 3 hidden files
    169984 bytes in 75 directories
  16142336 bytes in 949 user files
     71680 bytes in bad sectors
   4714496 bytes available on disk
      2048 bytes in each allocation unit
     10337 total allocation units on disk
      2302 available allocation units on disk

    655360 total bytes memory
    464928 bytes free
```

Because no drive was specified, the current drive (C) was used. The report on allocation units does not appear with versions of PC DOS prior to 4.

Example 2: Find and fix lost clusters.

```
C:\>chkdsk a:
Volume PCBOOK created -- 1-10-1990  4:25pm
Errors found.  F parameter not specified.
Corrections will not be written to disk.
1 lost clusters found in 1 chains.
Convert lost chains to files (Y/N)?
2048 bytes disk space would be freed.
```

Because the /f parameter was not specified, no actual corrections are actually made to the disk, even if `y` is typed in response to the prompt. The corrections can be made by rerunning the command as `chkdsk a: /f` and responding `y` to the question.

Example 3: Get a report on disk fragmentation in a directory on drive A.

```
C:\>chkdsk a:
Volume LAPLINK created --  8-9-1990  2:28pm
   730112 bytes total disk space.
    47104 bytes in 3 hidden files.
     2048 bytes in 1 directories.
   218112 bytes in 18 user files.
   462848 bytes available on disk.
   654304 bytes total storage
   308512 bytes free
A:\logfile
    contains 2 non-contiguous blocks.
```

The report indicates that the file LOGFILE is slightly fragmented. It could be optimized by being copied to another disk or to another directory on the same disk.

Example 4: Save a list of files from the disk to a file.

```
C:\>chkdsk a:\*.* /v > alist
```

The wildcard means that CHKDSK will process all files in the root directory of the disk in drive A. Note that the search does not extend down through any subdirectories in drive A. The > (greater than) symbol redirects the output (the file list) to the file ALIST.

This file can now be examined.

```
C:\>type alist
Directory A:\
A:\IBMBIO.COM
A:\IBMDOS.COM
A:\COMMAND.COM
A:\AUTOEXEC.BAT
A:\CONFIG.BAK
A:\AUTOEXEC.BAK
A:\CONFIG.SYS
730112 bytes total disk space.
 53248 bytes in 2 hidden files.
 29696 bytes in 5 user files.
5647168 bytes available on disk.
```

Related Chapters

Chapter 5–PC DOS Files
Chapter 6–Managing Your Hard Disk
Chapter 7–All About Floppy Disks

CLS

Internal Command

Compatibility	2.0	2.1	3.0	3.1	3.2	3.3	4.0	OS/2 (DOS mode)	OS/2 (prot.)
	▲	▲	▲	▲	▲	▲	▲	▲	▲

Use the CLS command to clear the display screen.

Format `cls`

Sample Use `cls`

Procedure Type `cls` to clear the display screen.

Related Command ANSI can be used for extensive screen and cursor control.

DETAILED REFERENCE

Explanation This command clears the screen and displays a new command prompt in the upper left corner of the screen. It is sometimes useful to issue this command at the start of a batch file to provide a clean screen before displaying a menu or other information. Use the CLS command by itself, without any arguments or parameters.

Related Chapter Chapter 10–Batch Files

COMMAND

External Command

Compatibility	2.0	2.1	3.0	3.1	3.2	3.3	4.0	OS/2 (DOS mode)	OS/2 (prot.)
	▲	▲	▲	▲	▲	▲	▲	▲	

Use COMMAND as part of a SHELL statement to install a command processor with modified characteristics (such as a larger environment) at startup. You can also use COMMAND in a batch file to execute another batch file or program in a separate command processor without affecting the original environment.

Format `command` *`options`*

Version 4

Syntax Varies in Version 4

`command` *`drive:path options`*

Options */c string* executes commands specified in a string and then returns to the main processor. The original environment is not changed.

/p keeps the new command processor loaded until the system is restarted.

/e:size, starting with PC DOS 3.2, specifies an environment of *size* (between 160 and 32,768) bytes. In PC DOS 3.1, specifies the number of 16-byte "paragraphs" to be used for the environment. Note: If you use both the /e and /c options, the /e option must come first.

Version 4

The /*MSG* Option Speeds Error Reports

/MSG loads the text used by COMMAND.COM for displaying error messages involved with command interpretation (parsing), files, device, and memory operations into RAM. This is recommended for speeding operation of floppy-based systems, because the messages won't need to be read from disk repeatedly.

The /p option must also be specified if you wish to use the /MSG option.

Sample Use

```
command /e:256 /c cd \temp
```

Procedure

Normally, you will not type COMMAND from the command line, although this will work, creating a secondary command processor. If you want to modify the way COMMAND.COM runs (for example, to provide it with a larger environment for PC DOS variables), put a `shell=command.com` statement in your CONFIG.SYS file, following command.com with the appropriate options as given above. (See the SHELL entry for more discussion and examples of this usage.)

If you do wish to start a new command processor interactively, type `command` from the PC DOS prompt. Use the /e option if you need to increase the environment size for the new processor. Type `exit` when you are ready to return to the original command processor. (See Example 1.)

To start a new command processor that will remain in memory until you restart the system, use the /p option. Note that if an AUTOEXEC.BAT file exists, it will be executed as the new processor is loaded.

To start a new command processor that executes a specified command and then returns, use the /c option (see Example 2). (If /p and /c are used together, /p is ignored.)

Version 4

Version 4 Adds New Features to the COMMAND Command

With PC DOS 4, speed up operation on floppy-based systems by specifying the /p and /MSG options. Also, with PC DOS 4, you can specify a drive and directory following the word *command*. PC DOS will find COMMAND.COM in this directory and set the COMSPEC variable to hold this path for subsequent reloading of the command processor (Example 4).

Related Commands

CALL executes a batch file from another batch file.

COMSPEC is a setting used by COMMAND.COM for reloading.

SHELL is a setting used with COMMAND to install a command processor at startup.

CONFIG.SYS is used for the SHELL=COMMAND statement.

DETAILED REFERENCE

Explanation

The program COMMAND.COM is the PC DOS command processor—the program that interprets your commands and prepares programs for execution. The COMMAND command simply executes this program, loading and running a new command processor "on top of" the old one. The new processor is considered to be "secondary," because it is run from the original processor, which is suspended until the new one is terminated.

(If COMMAND is specified in a SHELL statement in the CONFIG.SYS file, however, this starts the *original* command processor, not a secondary one.)

Comments As is shown in Example 3, when a new command processor is started with COMMAND, it "inherits" its environment from the original processor. Any changes that the new processor makes to its environment do not affect the environment of the original processor.

Use COMMAND in a Batch File
In earlier versions of PC DOS, one common use of COMMAND was to allow a batch file to run another batch file (using, for example, a batch file statement such as command /c newbat) and then return to the original batch file. Starting with PC DOS 3.3, you can use the CALL command to execute another batch file and return, without tying up additional memory by loading a secondary command processor.

When PC DOS Can't Find COMMAND.COM
PC DOS needs to reload most of COMMAND.COM after running a program. If PC DOS can't find the COMMAND.COM program, it checks the directory listed in your COMSPEC environmental variable. At startup, this variable contains the path where COMMAND.COM was originally found, unless you specify a different location. On floppy-based systems, PC DOS may find that you have removed the disk containing COMMAND.COM. In this case, you will be asked to insert the disk with COMMAND.COM into the drive that had contained it.

Examples Example 1: Start a new PC DOS command processor with a size of 2048 bytes. Use the MEM command to demonstrate how memory is used and released by the new command processor.

Note: If you are using a version of PC DOS prior to 4, you can use the CHKDSK command to obtain the amount of memory available—it just takes a little longer.

```
C:\>mem

    655360 bytes total memory
    654336 bytes available
    464928 largest executable program size
   2097152 bytes total EMS memory
   2097152 bytes free EMS memory

    393216 bytes total extended memory
    262144 bytes available extended memory

C:\>command /e:2048
```

```
IBM DOS Version 4.00
          (C)Copyright International Business Machines Corp 1981, 1988
          (C)Copyright Microsoft Corp 1981-1986

C:\TWG\UPCDOS\REF>mem

    655360 bytes total memory

    654336 bytes available
    456992 largest executable program size
   2097152 bytes total EMS memory
   2097152 bytes free EMS memory
    393216 bytes total extended memory
    262144 bytes available extended memory
C:\TWG\UPCDOS\REF>exit

C:\>mem

    655360 bytes total memory
    654336 bytes available
    464928 largest executable program size

   2097152 bytes total EMS memory
   2097152 bytes free EMS memory

    393216 bytes total extended memory
    262144 bytes available extended memory
```

First, MEM was used to see how much memory was available. The important number here is "largest executable program size," which reflects the amount of base RAM available: 464,298 bytes in this case. Next, COMMAND was run, specifying an environment size of 2048 bytes. When MEM was run again from the new command processor, available memory had shrunk by about 7K to 456,992 bytes. This represents the 2048-byte environment for the new processor, plus about 5K of overhead.

(The amount will vary slightly with the version of PC DOS used.)

After using EXIT to leave the new command processor, MEM was used again to show that total memory had returned to the original amount.

Example 2: Start a new PC DOS command processor, execute a command, and return automatically.

```
C:\>command /c dir /w c:\utils

 Volume in drive C is MAINDISK
 Volume Serial Number is 1454-3E20
 Directory of  C:\UTILS

.               ..              ARC     EXE     UNSQ     COM    PKXARC   COM
ARCE      COM   BACKALL   BAT   INCBACK BAT     STARSET  COM    F720     BAT
```

```
STRIP    COM    SYS33    BAT    WSCONV   EXE    WSASCII COM    SKN      COM
SYS33    CMD    RECV35   COM    BOOT     COM    BOOT    DOC    SNGLSPC  COM

 SNGLSPC DOC    SSPC     BAT
       22 File(s)    5915200 bytes free
```

Example 3: Start a new PC DOS command processor. Make some changes in the environment and then return to the original processor.

```
C:\>command
IBM DOS Version 4.00
          (C)Copyright International Business Machines Corp 1981, 1988
          (C)Copyright Microsoft Corp 1981-1986
C>prompt DOS>
DOS>set newvar=1
DOS>set
COMSPEC=C:\COMMAND.COM
PATH=C:\;C:\DOS;C:\WSWORK;C:\MKS\BIN;C:\C5;
PROMPT=DOS $p$g
NEWVAR=1
DOS>exit
C:\>set
COMSPEC=C:\COMMAND.COM
PATH=C:\;C:\DOS;C:\WSWORK;C:\MKS\BIN;C:\C5;
```

A new command processor was started, and then the prompt was changed to DOS>. SET was then used to create the variable *newvar*, and then used again to show the new prompt setting and the new variable. Finally, the EXIT command terminated the new command processor, and SET again was used to show the original environment. You can see that the variable PROMPT that we set while running the secondary command processor has disappeared, the original prompt is displayed, and the variable NEWVAR that was defined in the secondary command processor isn't listed in the original environment.

Example 4: Start a secondary command processor and set COMSPEC for it.

```
A:\>command c:\dos
```

Here, the new command processor looks in the C:\DOS directory on the hard disk, rather than at the floppy disk A, when it comes time to reload.

Related Chapters Chapter 10–Batch Files
Chapter 11–Customizing Your System

External Command

COMP

Compatibility	2.0	2.1	3.0	3.1	3.2	3.3	4.0	OS/2 (DOS mode)	OS/2 (prot.)
	▲	▲	▲	▲	▲	▲	▲	▲	▲

Use COMP to compare two files or sets of files, displaying any differences.

Format COMP prompts for file names (for interactive use) `comp` ***`filespec filespec`***

Sample Use `comp chap1 chap1.bak`

Procedure If you type just COMP, you will be prompted for the names of the two files to be compared. Instead, you can type COMP followed by the specifications of the two files to be compared.

File specifications can be complete paths or simple file names (if you are comparing files in the current directory). To compare two groups of related files, use wildcards. To compare the files in one directory with the corresponding files in another, use the directory names rather than file names (Example 5).

Related Command DISKCOMP (to compare contents of two disks)

DETAILED REFERENCE

Explanation COMP compares two files byte for byte. If the files match exactly, COMP reports `Files compare OK` (Example 2). If the files do not match (that is, if there is at least one byte position where the files differ), COMP displays each position where there is a difference, as a hexadecimal offset (with the first byte being offset 0), and gives the value of the data byte each file has at that position, also in hexadecimal (Example 3). COMP stops the comparison if more than ten differences are found.

If one of the files being compared is shorter than the other, COMP points this out and does not compare the files (Example 4).

COMP will continue to prompt for further pairs of files to compare until you answer `n` to the prompt.

This interactive behavior (continual prompting for (Y/N)?) can be annoying if you want to use COMP in a batch file. Example 6 shows how to get around this problem. This batch file compares two files, displays the results, and exits without your input being required.

If you keep a backup copy of a directory, you can use COMP to check whether your backup is up to date, as shown in Example 5. Because differences between files are displayed in hexadecimal rather than ASCII format, COMP is not useful for seeing precisely how two text files differ.

Comments Most PC DOS files use a Ctrl-Z character to mark the end of file. Some programs, however, save files with a size rounded up to the nearest 128 bytes, even though the actual data may have ended sooner. Because COMP compares according to the file size as shown in the directory, this can cause COMP to report mismatches near the end of the file. COMP alerts you to this situation with the message `EOF mark not found`.

Examples The first three examples use four files.

File	Contents
fox	The quick brown fox
quick	The quick brown fox
cat	The quiet brown cat
fox2	The quick brown fox jumped

Example 1: Compare files interactively.

```
C:\>comp
 Enter primary file name
fox

Enter 2nd file name or drive id
geese

C:FOX and C:GEESE

C:GEESE - File not found

Compare more files (Y/N)? n
```

Here, a nonexistent file (GEESE) was specified, which resulted in an error message. PC DOS then asked if the user wanted to compare more files.

Example 2: Compare two files, specifying file names in the command.

```
C>comp fox quick

C:FOX and C:QUICK

Files compare OK

Compare more files? (Y/N)n
```

Example 3: A comparison where the files are different.

```
C:\>comp fox cat

C:FOX and C:CAT

Compare error at OFFSET 7
File 1 = 63

File 2 = 65
```

```
Compare error at OFFSET 8
File 1 = 6B

File 2 = 74

Compare error at OFFSET 10
File 1 = 66

File 2 = 63

Compare error at OFFSET 11
File 1 = 6F

File 2 = 61

Compare error at OFFSET 12
File 1 = 78

File 2 = 74

Compare more files? (Y/N)n
```

The contents of the files diverge, starting at the eighth character, which is reported as offset 7, because the first character is considered to be offset 0. Notice that characters 10 through 16 (hexadecimal offsets 9 through F) again match, so these positions aren't reported. The next mismatch is at character 17 (hex offset 10).

Example 4: A comparison where one file is longer than the other.

```
C:\>comp fox fox2

C:FOX and C:FOX2

Files are different sizes

Compare more files (Y/N)? n
```

Example 5: Compare contents of two directories.

```
C:\>comp c:\animals a:\animals

C:\ANIMALS\FOX and A:\ANIMALS\FOX

Files compare ok

C:\ANIMALS\QUICK and A:\ANIMALS\QUICK

Files are different sizes

C:\ANIMALS\CAT and A:\ANIMALS\CAT
```

```
A:\ANIMALS\CAT - File not found

C:\ANIMALS\FOX2 and A:\ANIMALS\FOX2

Files compare ok
Compare more files (Y/N)? n
```

Naming directories rather than single file names causes COMP to compare corresponding files in the two directories. Mismatching files and files that don't exist in both directories are pointed out.

Example 6: Write a batch file that compares two files without requiring further user input.

```
C:\BATS>type cmp.bat
echo n n | comp %1 %2
C:\BATS>_
```

The previous batch file is handy for comparing two files (no wildcards) without further fuss. The ECHO command sends the two n characters to the standard input for the COMP program via a pipe. This provides "no" answers for both questions that COMP might ask. Because this is a single line batch file, you can type it in on the command line—be sure to specify file names rather than replaceable parameters.

Related Chapters

Chapter 5–PC DOS Files
Chapter 6–Managing Your Hard Disk

COMSPEC

Setting

Compatibility	2.0	2.1	3.0	3.1	3.2	3.3	4.0	OS/2 (DOS mode)	OS/2 (prot.)
	▲	▲	▲	▲	▲	▲	▲	▲	

Use the COMSPEC statement in your CONFIG.SYS file to specify the location of the PC DOS command processor COMMAND.COM so that it can be reloaded after running a program.

Sample Use

```
comspec=a:\command.com
```

Procedure

In your CONFIG.SYS file, begin a statement with `set comspec=` followed by a complete path name that specifies the location of the command processor COMMAND.COM.

Related Commands

SHELL customizes the command processor.

COMMAND runs a secondary command processor.

SET sets COMSPEC or other environmental variables.

DETAILED REFERENCE

Explanation When PC DOS runs a program, it makes a large portion of the memory containing COMMAND.COM's code available to the application program. This maximizes the amount of usable memory for applications. When the program terminates, PC DOS must reload the overlaid portions of its code from the file COMMAND.COM on disk. During startup, PC DOS creates the environmental variable COMSPEC and stores in it the path from which COMMAND.COM was loaded. Thus, on a typical system, if you type `set` to view environmental variables, one of the variables listed will be comspec=c:\command.com (or perhaps c:\dos\command.com, if you have well-organized directories). On a hard disk system, there is seldom any need to change this setting. On a floppy system, however, you may run applications that require that the program disk be swapped into drive A in place of the DOS startup disk (see Example 1).

Example Example 1: Specify a different location for the command processor.

```
A:\>type run.bat
set comspec=b:\command.com
dbms
set comspec=a:\command.com
^Z
     1 file(s) copied
```

Here you have a system with two floppy disk drives. You want to run a database program, and while doing so, you want to use a function of that program that allows you to run a PC DOS command processor to perform housekeeping duties. To run the database program, however, you must remove the PC DOS startup disk from drive A and put in the program disk. If you try to "shell to DOS" from the program, an error will occur, because PC DOS will want to load COMMAND.COM from its starting location A:\COMMAND.COM. The problem is that you don't happen to have room on the disk in drive A to store a copy of COMMAND.COM. Therefore, you create this batch file and put it on your DBMS program disk. You also put a copy of COMMAND.COM on the data disk that will be kept in drive B. The batch file starts by resetting COMSPEC to B:\COMMAND.COM; then the program DBMS is run. Now, PC DOS will be able to find a copy of COMMAND.COM whenever it needs one. After the DBMS program exits, the batch file resets COMSPEC to its original location, A:\COMMAND.COM

Related Chapter Chapter 11–Customizing Your System

CONFIG.SYS

Resource

Compatibility	2.0	2.1	3.0	3.1	3.2	3.3	4.0	OS/2 (DOS mode)	OS/2 (prot.)
		▲	▲	▲	▲	▲	▲	▲	▲

Use the CONFIG.SYS file to configure your system and to provide device support.

Format The CONFIG.SYS file is a regular ASCII text file. It should be placed in the root directory of the startup drive.

Sample Use The following CONFIG.SYS file is more or less typical.

```
break=on
buffers=20
files=8
lastdrive=E
shell=c:\dos\command.com /p /e:256
device=c:\sys\xma2ems.sys frame=D000 p255=C000
device=c:\dos\display.sys con:=(ega,437,1)
device=c:\dos\printer.sys lpt1:=(4201,437,1)
device=c:\mouse1\mouse.sys
device=c:\dos\ansi.sys
INSTALL=C:\DOS\FASTOPEN.EXE C:=(50,25)
install=c:\dos\keyb.com us,437,c:\dos\keyboard.sys
install=c:\dos\nlsfunc.exe c:\dos\country.sys
```

These settings will be described in general terms in Example 1.

Note: PC DOS creates these files with the statements in all capital letters, but you can type your CONFIG.SYS statements in lowercase, which is easier, and PC DOS will interpret them as capital letters.

Procedure You can create a CONFIG.SYS file by typing `copy con: c:\config.sys`. Then, type one statement per line. Press F6 (or Ctrl-Z) to save the file to disk. However, most systems already have a fairly extensive CONFIG.SYS file, resulting either from automatic PC DOS installation (especially with version 4) or subsequent customization. You can add to an existing CONFIG.SYS file by typing `copy c:\config.sys+con:`, typing your additional statements, and then pressing F6 or Ctrl-Z to save the file. The easiest way to deal with CONFIG.SYS, however, is to use any editor (such as EDLIN on the PC DOS disk) or word processor that can handle ASCII text files.

Whichever way you do it, use a command such as `copy config.sys config.bak` to save the current version in case you get into trouble. See Chapter 9, "Creating Text Files" for more information.

Related Commands AUTOEXEC.BAT is a batch file used to run commands or programs automatically.

DEVICE installs a device driver via CONFIG.SYS.

In addition to the previous commands, see the individual reference entries for the various configuration settings (such as BUFFERS) and for the various device drivers that can be installed via the DEVICE statement (such as VDISK.SYS).

DETAILED REFERENCE

Explanation When the system is started, PC DOS uses a file called CONFIG.SYS (if present) in the root directory of the startup drive to set system characteristics, install device drivers, and provide support for other facilities. Each statement that can be used in the CONFIG.SYS file has its own reference entry with detailed explanations. This section provides an overview and quick reference.

The sections that follow list the statements that can be used in the CONFIG.SYS file, giving a brief description of each, and indicating its default (if any). The default values are used by PC DOS if there is no CONFIG.SYS file, there is no applicable statement in the file, or the applicable statement has a syntax error.

Comments Many CONFIG.SYS settings can be optimized based on your experience with the kinds of applications you run. For example, one user might find that increasing the size of the disk cache (such as IBMCACHE) speeds up an application that makes frequent disk accesses (such as a database program). A user running a calculation-intensive program (such as CAD) might find it better to have a small cache and devote more memory for the use of the program's internal data. Other applications might benefit from installation of a RAM disk (VDISK). Reading this entry and the entries for the specific settings will help you determine your optimum system configuration. Also see Chapter 11, "Customizing Your System."

System Configuration Settings BREAK determines whether the system will check for the Ctrl-Break keystroke whenever a program requests a PC DOS system service. Under the default break=off, the system checks for a "user interrupt" (Ctrl-Break) only while a DOS program is performing screen and keyboard I/O, printing, or "auxiliary" operations. Setting break=on allows you to interrupt DOS programs that spend little time performing screen I/O or that perform mainly disk I/O, such as compilers.

BUFFERS sets the number of 512-byte memory buffers (between 1 and 99) that will be used to hold disk sectors that have been partially read. This considerably speeds access to data, because a given sector will only need to be read once from the disk, with reading of subsequent portions from memory. See the BUFFERS entry for considerations involved in using buffers with a disk cache. Default: buffers=15 on systems with at least 512K of memory; many applications recommend a value of about 20.

Version 4

Specify Read-Ahead Sectors with the BUFFERS Command in Version 4
PC DOS 4 allows a second number to be specified, telling PC DOS to read 1 to 8 additional disk sectors ahead, improving buffer efficiency for applications that read data sequentially. A new option, */x*, tells PC DOS to use expanded memory for the disk buffers and allows a total of up to 10,000 buffers (memory permitting).

COUNTRY identifies the country whose format will be used for time, date, decimal numbers, sort collating sequence, and so on. Default: country=001 (U.S.)

DEVICE is used to specify device drivers, which are programs installed by PC DOS to provide device access and control for applications. The statement DEVICE= is followed by the name of the driver to be used; there are usually several such statements in CONFIG.SYS. The following device drivers are provided with PC DOS:

ANSI.SYS provides extended cursor control and keyboard macros.

COUNTRY.SYS supplies information needed for country-specific display formats.

DISPLAY.SYS allows code-page switching on EGA and LCD displays. (PC DOS 4 adds MCGA, VGA, and IBM 8514/A displays.)

DRIVER.SYS assigns logical drive letters to disk drives and specifies disk format.

IBMCACHE.SYS is a disk cache to improve hard disk access; provided for IBM PS/2 only, on PS/2 Reference disk.

KEYBOARD.SYS supports alternative keyboard configurations and character sets.

PRINTER.SYS allows printing of alternate code pages (character sets) on certain IBM printers.

VDISK.SYS installs a virtual (RAM) disk.

Version 4

Specify EMS in Your CONFIG.SYS File in Version 4

PC DOS 4 adds two new drivers that implement LIM 4.0 expanded memory support for a number of PC DOS commands (such as BUFFERS and FASTOPEN).

XMA2EMS.SYS provides support for EMS for an IBM 2MB Expanded Memory Adapter or IBM PS/2 80286 Expanded Memory Adapter/A or Memory Expansion Option.

XMAEM.SYS emulates the IBM PS/2 80286 Expanded Memory Adapter /A on 80386 systems such as the IBM PS/2 Model 80. This allows these systems to use the XMA2EMS.SYS driver to provide expanded memory support.

FASTOPEN is available starting with PC DOS 3.3. It specifies a number of buffers that can be used to hold the directory information for recently opened files, speeding up repeated accesses to these files.

Version 4

Specify Use of BUFFERS in EMS Memory in Version 4

PC DOS 4 adds a second option that specifies a number of buffers to hold information from the disk's file sector list in memory, further speeding up file access. Also, an */x* option allows use of expanded memory for the buffers.

FCBS determines the number of files that can be opened through the use of file control blocks (FCBs) and the number of blocks that will be protected from being closed automatically to make room for new files. This is an obsolete method found mainly in older (pre-version 2.0) PC DOS programs, so this setting may not be needed. The default is fcbs=4,0.

FILES specifies the maximum number of file handles that can be open at any one time. File handles are the more modern alternative to file control blocks (FCBS) and are used by most contemporary applications. The default is files=8.

LASTDRIVE specifies the last drive letter that can be assigned and thus the total number of drive names that may be used. The default is lastdrive=e.

SHELL selects an alternate command processor. It can pass optional parameters to the command processor. The main reason to change this setting is to set a larger environment for PC DOS variables via the */e* parameter. (See the entry under COMMAND.) Custom shells can also be installed. Default is shell=c:command.com /p.

STACKS specifies the number and size in bytes of stack frames used to handle hardware interrupts. The default is stacks=0,0 for the IBM PC, XT, and Portable PC, and stacks=9,128 for the IBM AT and PS/2. This may need to be changed for the use of certain devices (such as the new enhanced keyboard) that can generate numerous interrupts under certain circumstances. (See the STACK entry for more details.)

Example Example 1: Examine the example CONFIG.SYS file given earlier.

```
break=on
buffers=20
files=8
lastdrive=E
shell=c:\dos\command.com /p /e:256
device=c:\sys\xma2ems.sys frame=D000 p255=C000
device=c:\dos\display.sys con:=(ega,437,1)
device=c:\dos\printer.sys lpt1:=(4201,437,1)
device=c:\mouse1\mouse.sys
device=c:\dos\ansi.sys
INSTALL=C:\DOS\FASTOPEN.EXE C:=(50,25)
install=c:\dos\keyb.com us,437,c:\dos\keyboard.sys
install=c:\dos\nlsfunc.exe c:\dos\country.sys
```

In this CONFIG.SYS file, the BREAK=ON setting makes it easier for the user to interrupt programs by typing Ctrl-Break. The BUFFERS setting provides 20 512-byte buffers to hold recently accessed data from disk sectors. The FILES setting allows up to 8 file handles to be open at one time (for many applications, you'll need more—try 20). The LASTDRIVE setting says that the letters A through E will be legal names for drives.

The SHELL setting is used to specify an environment of 512 bytes to allow for more system variables.

The DEVICE statements load device drivers for expanded memory (PC DOS 4 only), the display and printer (required only for code page support), the mouse, and the ANSI screen control functions.

Finally, the INSTALL settings (PC DOS 4 only) install PC DOS commands that become memory-resident: the FASTOPEN command for faster disk file access and the KEYB and NLSFUNC commands (used only for code page support).

Remember that every item that has been mentioned has its own reference entry. These settings are also discussed in appropriate chapters.

Related Chapters Chapter 9–Creating Text Files
Chapter 11–Customizing Your System
Chapter 12–Installing a PC DOS System
Chapter 13–International Language Support

COPY

Internal Command

Compatibility	2.0	2.1	3.0	3.1	3.2	3.3	4.0	OS/2 (DOS mode)	**OS/2 (prot.)**
	▲	▲	▲	▲	▲	▲	▲	▲	▲

Use the COPY command to copy one or more files, to combine files, and to transfer files between certain devices such as the keyboard (console) and the printer.

Format `copy` *`source options destination options`* where source and destination are file names or complete path names.

Options */a* applies to preceding file name and all following file names until another /a or a /b is encountered. Treats source files as text files, copying them up to (but not including) the first end-of-file character (Ctrl-Z, ASCII 26 or 1AH) encountered. If used with a destination file, puts an end-of-file character at the end. This is the default if files are being combined. It is also the default for copying to and from devices such as the keyboard, serial port, or parallel port.

/b applies to preceding file name and all following file names until another /b or an /a is encountered. Treats source files as binary, copying all characters including end-of-file characters. Does not add an end-of-file character to destination files. This is the default if files are not being combined.

/v verifies that the file(s) were copied correctly. If the VERIFY ON command has been issued, this option is not needed. Verification involves rereading data and thus slows down disk operations somewhat. See VERIFY entry for further details.

Sample Use

```
copy letter letter.bak
```

Procedure To copy files, type `copy` followed by the source file name and then the destination file name (Example 1). Any valid path names can be used; additionally, standard wildcards (* and ?) can be used to specify a group of files to be copied or to indicate the name to be used for destination files (see Examples 2 and 3 and Chapter 5, "PC DOS Files," and "Chapter 6, "Managing Your Hard Disk").

To copy keyboard input to a file, use con: (meaning console) as your source file, followed by the desired destination; see Example 4. You can also print a file by using the name of the printer device (typically PRN: or LPT1: for parallel printers, or COM1: or COM2: for serial printers or modems) as the destination.

To combine files, separate the source file names with a + (Example 5) or use a wildcard file name followed by a + (Example 6). To combine binary files, include the */b* option to ensure that the complete files are combined (Example 7).

DOS Shell

Use the COPY Feature of the DOS Shell
To copy files while running DOSSHELL, select File System from the Start Programs screen. From the file tree window, select the directory containing the file(s) that you want to copy. Then, from the file list window, select the files. Select Copy from the File menu. You will be prompted to type the destination directory for the copies.

Related Commands REN renames a file but does not move or copy it.

BACKUP copies files to backup device (combines files on destination).

XCOPY copies selected files and directory trees.

DISKCOPY copies an entire disk, sector by sector.

VERIFY (when set to ON) verifies all copies.

DETAILED REFERENCE

Explanation COPY is a versatile command; although in essence, it only does one thing, copy files, the ramifications of this behavior can be surprising. For example, because devices (such as the console and printer port) are considered to be a special kind of file in PC DOS, files can be copied directly from keyboard input to a disk file or printed by copying them to the appropriate device. The following examples show the wide range of capabilities offered by the COPY command.

Comments COPY cannot be used by itself to transfer a file between two computers using serial ports, because it doesn't provide the necessary "handshaking" to synchronize the ports. Some "bridge" utilities, however, allow drives on other machines to be accessed by COPY and other PC DOS commands. COPY can be used to test a modem by sending modem commands to (for example) COM1:, but actual online communications requires additional software.

Tip

Using the Right Copying Tool
Of the four copying commands, COPY, XCOPY, DISKCOPY, and BACKUP, COPY is generally best for copying one file, a group of files in the same directory, or an entire directory. Remember that COPY does not copy subdirectories of the source directory.

You should normally use DISKCOPY rather than COPY to make an exact copy of a disk. While copy *.* to a destination will copy all files at the current directory level to the destination drive or directory, using DISKCOPY when there are many files is somewhat faster. This is because DISKCOPY, like XCOPY and BACKUP, reads as much data from the source as will fit in RAM and then writes it to the destination, which minimizes disk access time. Also, COPY does not copy hidden system files, so you can't make a bootable copy using it alone.

If you wish to unfragment files for faster disk access (rearrange them so that each file occupies consecutive disk sectors), use COPY or XCOPY, not DISKCOPY, however. DISKCOPY copies an entire disk sector by sector, preserving the fragmentation on the target disk.

XCOPY is the most versatile copying tool. Its many features slow it down somewhat, but it allows you to copy whole "trees" of directories and subdirectories with a single command. It also allows you to select files for copying according to date, time, and archive status. Because it prereads as many files as will fit in memory, XCOPY may be faster than COPY for copying a large number of files, regardless of source.

Use BACKUP to back up large amounts of data (such as on a hard disk) to a series of destination disks. Remember that files copied by BACKUP are not usable until RESTORE has been applied to them.

It is recommended that you read the reference entries for all of the commands discussed here and become familiar with the special features of each.

Examples Example 1: Make a backup copy of the CONFIG.SYS file.

```
C:\>copy config.sys config.bak
        1 File(s) copied.
```

The current drive and directory is the default destination. For example, if you are currently in the root directory of drive A, you could copy AUTOEXEC.BAT from drive C to drive A by typing `copy c:\autoexec.bat`.

COPY always reports the number of files copied. It also reports if a specified file could not be found. If you wish to copy a file to the same directory, you must give the copy (destination) a name different from the original; COPY refuses to copy a file to itself.

Example 2: Copy files using a wildcard in the source file name.

```
C:\>md c:\dos\sys
C:\>copy c:\dos\*.sys c:\dos\sys
C:\DOS\ANSI.SYS
C:\DOS\EGA.SYS
C:\DOS\DRIVER.SYS
C:\DOS\VDISK.SYS
C:\DOS\MOUSE.SYS
        5 File(s) copied.
```

First, a subdirectory called SYS was created in the DOS directory on drive C. The * wildcard was then used to copy all files ending in .SYS (i.e., device drivers) to the new directory. You could then delete the originals and change the relevant paths in CONFIG.SYS, ending up with a better-organized main DOS directory.

Caution

A COPY Pitfall

There's a trap to look out for when copying multiple files to a destination directory. Consider the following listing.

```
C:\>copy *.bak a:examples
EX2.BAK
EX7.BAK
EX4.BAK
EX1.BAK
EX5.BAK
LOG.BAK
        1 File(s) copied.
```

Perhaps what you thought you did was copy all of the files with the .BAK extension to a directory called EXAMPLES on drive A, but notice that COPY only reported one file copied! COPY actually counts, not the number of files it copied, but the number of files it made. The problem here was that there was actually no directory called EXAMPLES on the destination disk, so COPY copied the source files one at a time onto a destination file called EXAMPLES, each copy overwriting the preceding one. The final result is that the destination file EXAMPLES contains only the contents of LOG.BAK. If you don't notice this, and you delete the original files, you will have lost the data in the other files. It is always a good idea to use DIR to verify the status of the destination files before deleting any originals.

Example 3: Copy files using wildcards for both source and destination.

```
C:\>copy ex? a:\ex?.bak
EX2
EX7
EX4
EX1
EX5
        5 File(s) copied.
C>dir a:\*.bak
 Volume in drive A is WORK2
 Directory of  A:\
EX2      BAK      210   5-06-88   5:24p
EX7      BAK      716   5-06-88   5:47p
EX4      BAK      128   5-06-88   5:32p
EX1      BAK       58   5-07-88  10:18a
EX5      BAK      151   5-06-88   5:33p
        5 File(s)   269824 bytes free
```

The wildcard in the source selects all files with ex followed by a single character. The wildcard in the destination creates a kind of template for naming the destination the same as the source, but with the addition of the extension .BAK.

After the copy, DIR was used to verify that all files reached the destination.

Example 4: Create a batch file by copying keyboard input to a disk file.

```
C:\>copy con: show.bat
@echo off
dir %1
type %1
^Z
        1 File(s) copied.
C:\>show show.bat
 Volume in drive C is PCDOSDISK
 Volume Serial Number is 1454-3E20
 Directory of  C:\DOS\UTILS
SHOW     BAT        17   5-07-88  12:01p
       1 File(s)    8202240 bytes free
dir %1
type %1
```

This technique is useful for creating short batch files or test data files when there is no text editor available. The source file name here is CON:, which is a reserved name referring to the console (keyboard). When this is specified as the source file for a copy, COPY copies whatever you type to the specified destination (SHOW.BAT in this case), until you type a Ctrl-Z indicating end-of-file. The batch file that was created shows a directory listing for the specified file name, followed by a listing of the file's contents.

Tip

Simulating a Typewriter

Here's another quick and dirty trick that can save time. Assuming you have a printer connected, you can print a file (for example, your AUTOEXEC.BAT file) by typing `copy autoexec.bat lpt1:`. This copies the file to the printer port, and the printer prints it. Of course, there will be no pagination or other special formatting, so it works best for short notes. For a no-frills word processor, try `copy con: lpt1:`. This prints each line of text on the printer as you type it at the keyboard, until you type a Ctrl-Z.

In preparing this book, one of the authors needed to print large files on an HP LaserJet II in another room. Rather than moving either the printer or the desktop system, the file was first printed to disk by WordPerfect, properly formatted for the printer. The disk was then inserted into a laptop connected to the printer, and the command copy prntfile lpt1: loaded into the printer's buffer, from which it was printed without further ado. There was no need to tie up the laptop by running WordPerfect on it.

Example 5: Copy the contents of two files into a third file.

```
C:\>type file1
line one
line two
C:\>type file2
```

```
line three
line four
C:\>copy file1+file2 file3
FILE1
FILE2
        1 File(s) copied.
C:\>type file3
line one
line two
line three
line four
```

The TYPE command is used here to show the contents of FILE1 and FILE2, and then COPY was used to combine them. Notice the + indicating that the two source files are to be combined in creating the destination file.

Example 6: Add several files to a specified file, using wildcards.

```
C:\>copy log+*.add
LOG
LOG1.ADD
LOG2.ADD
LOG3.ADD
        1 File(s) copied.
C:\>type log
line one
line two
line three
added line one
added line two
added line three
```

Here you have a file LOG consisting of three lines, and three files with the extension .ADD, each with one line. Notice that the source files consist of LOG plus all files matching the wildcard *.add. Because no destination is specified, the destination file has the same name as the source file. (In other words, a file cannot be *copied* to itself, but it can be *combined* with itself.)

Example 7: Copy binary files.

```
:\C>copy egrep.exe+ngrep.exe tgrep.exe
EGREP.EXE
NGREP.EXE
        1 File(s) copied.
C:\>dir *.exe
 Volume in drive C is PCDOSDISK
 Volume Serial Number is 1454-3E20
 Directory of  C:\
EGREP    EXE    15008   6-10-87  11:11a
NGREP    EXE    15008   6-10-87  11:11a
```

```
TGREP    EXE     1133   5-06-88   5:43p
        3 File(s)   8220672 bytes free
```

Here the combining of binary files is illustrated. Although you probably would never want to combine program (.EXE) files, they will be used here to show what can happen when you attempt to combine other binary files, perhaps some kinds of data files. Notice that the source files EGREP.EXE and NGREP.EXE were combined into the destination file TGREP.EXE, but that the directory listing reveals that all's not well: The destination file is only 1133 bytes long, not the 30,016 bytes you were expecting. The problem is that the default for combining files is to treat them as text files; thus, the source files were copied only up to the first occurrence of a Ctrl-Z, which, in binary files, is just another hexadecimal value that can turn up anywhere. Here's how to get a complete, accurate copy.

```
C:\>copy /b egrep.exe + ngrep.exe tgrep.exe
EGREP.EXE
NGREP.EXE
        1 File(s) copied.
C:\>dir *.exe
 Volume in drive C is PCDOSDISK
 Volume Serial Number is 1454-3E20
 Directory of  C:\
EGREP    EXE    15008   6-10-87  11:11a
NGREP    EXE    15008   6-10-87  11:11a
TGREP    EXE    30016   5-06-88   5:45p
        3 File(s)   8192000 bytes free
```

Here the /b option was used to tell COPY to treat all files as binary files; the size of the destination file is now correct.

Related Chapters

Chapter 5–PC DOS Files
Chapter 6–Managing Your Hard Disk
Chapter 7–All About Floppy Disks
Chapter 9–Creating Text Files

COUNTRY

Setting

Compatibility	2.0	2.1	3.0	3.1	3.2	3.3	4.0	OS/2 (DOS mode)	OS/2 (prot.)
			▲	▲	▲	▲	▲	▲	▲

Use the COUNTRY setting in CONFIG.SYS to specify the country (nation) whose date, time, currency, and other formats will be used by PC DOS.

Format

`country=`*`country-code,code-page,path name`* (PC DOS 3.3 and later)

`country=`*`country-code`* (PC DOS 3.0, 3.1, and 3.2)

Sample Use

`country=001,437` is used in a CONFIG.SYS file.

Procedure When you need to specify that PC DOS use the formats for a country other than the default (United States), follow country= with the three-digit country code (see Chapter 13, "International Language Support"). For PC DOS 3.3 and later, if you wish to specify a code page other than the default one for the country specified, type a comma followed by that code page number. (The code page must be one of the two supported for that country.) If the country information file is other than the file COUNTRY.SYS in the root directory of the startup drive, specify the complete path name to be used. If you specify a country and a path name but no code page, you must use two commas between the country and the path name (Example 2).

The default if no COUNTRY statement is given in CONFIG.SYS is country code 00 (United States), code page 437, and the code page information file is COUNTRY.SYS in the startup directory.

Note: If you are installing PC DOS on a disk that is being formatted, you can use the SELECT command to place automatically a COUNTRY statement with the appropriate code in your CONFIG.SYS file.

Version 4

Use SELECT to Specify a Country in Version 4
In PC DOS 4, the SELECT program gives you the option of specifying a country other than the default United States and an appropriate keyboard layout.

Related Commands NLSFUNC must be run to load code page support.

SELECT installs PC DOS on a new disk and places a COUNTRY statement in CONFIG.SYS.

CHCP changes between prepared code pages.

TIME, DATE, and DIR are commands whose display formats are affected by the COUNTRY setting.

SORT is a command whose operation is affected by the COUNTRY setting.

DETAILED REFERENCE

Explanation Different countries have different formats for displaying dates, times, and decimal numbers. They also may have different collating sequences (order of characters) used for sorting data. The COUNTRY setting, together with MODE and NLSFUNC, allows PC DOS to accommodate international needs by allowing for country-specific formats and code pages. See Chapter 13, "International Language Support," for a description of the steps involved in preparing and using code pages.

Comments By default, domestic copies of PC DOS come set for the United States, and a COUNTRY statement is not needed for switching between the United States and multilingual code pages. A COUNTRY statement with the appropriate country code is needed for using date, time, decimal, and sort collation formats for another country, or if you want to switch code pages between those defined for another country. The ability to specify a path name other than the default C:\COUNTRY.SYS (starting with PC DOS 3.3) allows flexibilty in organizing the root directory, as well as providing for new formats to be added by developers.

Examples Example 1: Set up PC DOS to use the format for Germany (country code 049) by editing the CONFIG.SYS file to contain the following statement.

```
country=049
```

After restarting the system, use the DIR command to show the new date and time formats.

```
 Volume in drive C is PCDOSDISK
 Volume Serial Number is 1454-3E20
 Directory of C:\KERMIT

.            <DIR>      13.11.87  17.13
..           <DIR>      13.11.87  17.13
MSKERMIT INI       381  21.04.88   0.15
MSKERMIT EXE     84776  28.07.85  23.42
UUADDR              51  22.11.87   9.33
        5 File(s)   5706304 bytes free
```

Note that the date format is now dd.mm.yy rather than mm-dd-yy, and that the time format uses a 24-hour format with periods to separate hours and minutes rather than a 12 hour AM/PM format with colons as separators.

Example 2: Specify the United States country code but with the multilingual code page as the default and with a country information file in the SYS directory.

```
country=001,850,c:\sys\country.sys
```

The code 001 specifies the United States country code; 850 specifies the multilingual code page, which provides a common format for exchanging data between most countries that use PC-compatible systems. The path name is necessary so that the COUNTRY.SYS file will be found in the SYS directory of drive C rather than the root (startup) directory. Note that if you wish to omit the code page, you must replace it with a comma: country=001,,c:\sys \country.sys.

Related Chapters Chapter 12–Installing a PC DOS System
Chapter 13–International Language Support

Internal Command

CTTY

Compatibility	2.0	2.1	3.0	3.1	3.2	3.3	4.0	OS/2 (DOS mode)	OS/2 (prot.)
	▲	▲	▲	▲	▲	▲	▲	▲	

Use the CTTY (change terminal) command to connect an external console to your system via a serial port or custom device. The external console (which can be a terminal or another micro) becomes the standard input and output.

Format

`ctty` ***`device-name`*** switches I/O to an external terminal.

`ctty con:` resets I/O to main system.

Sample Use

`ctty com:1`

Procedure

To use an external terminal or computer as your console for keyboard input and screen display, type `ctty` followed by the name of the port to which the terminal device is connected. Normally, this is a serial port: AUX:, COM1:, COM2:, COM3:, or COM4:. To use a custom device driver, specify the path name of the driver rather than the port name. To return keyboard and screen I/O to the main system, type `ctty con:`.

Related Commands

ANSI.SYS is a device driver for enhanced keyboard and screen functions.

DEVICE installs device drivers in CONFIG.SYS.

DRIVER.SYS assigns disk drive letters.

MODE sets operation modes for serial ports and other devices.

SHARE loads support for network file sharing.

DETAILED REFERENCE

Explanation

The CTTY command is used to allow you to control your system from an external terminal. Although not one of the more commonly used PC DOS commands, it can be used in situations where you need or would like remote access to your system, for example, by dial-up on a modem line. If you have a system with a built-in monitor that stops working, you can connect another computer or terminal to the system, use CTTY, and be able to work with data on the system's hard disk.

Comments

A device used as an external terminal must be capable of both input and output operations—a printer would not work, for example, because you couldn't get data into the system from it. By itself, the connection established by CTTY moves characters back and forth but doesn't provide any other terminal functions (such as an addressable cursor). Some devices may come with custom device drivers. To use such a device, specify `ctty` ***`devname`*** where devname is the actual path and name of the device driver. The device driver then serves as a mediator between the terminal connection at the port and the main system.

CTTY is only effective with programs that are "well-behaved," that is, those that do device I/O only through the appropriate PC DOS system calls instead of accessing devices directly. This means that it doesn't work with standard IBM BASIC, for example.

Examples Example 1: Use a device connected to COM2: as a remote terminal.

```
C:\>ctty com2:
```

Example 2: Use a device with a custom driver connected to COM1:.

```
C:\>ctty c:\sys\specdev
```

This assumes that this device has been installed so that it is known to PC DOS as a character device.

Related Chapter Chapter 11–Customizing Your System

DATE

Internal Command

Compatibility	2.0	2.1	3.0	3.1	3.2	3.3	4.0	OS/2 (DOS mode)	OS/2 (prot.)
	▲	▲	▲	▲	▲	▲	▲	▲	▲

Use the DATE command to set or display the system date.

Format `date` has interactive use and prompts for date.

`date` *`mm-dd-yy`* sets the date.

Sample Use `date 07-22-90`

Procedure If you want to find out the date, type `date`. The date is displayed, and you are prompted to enter a new date; press Enter to terminate the command without changing the date (Example 1). To change the date, you can either type `date` and respond to the prompt with a date (Example 2) or type `date` immediately followed by a date (Example 3). On systems configured for the U.S., dates are entered in the form mm-dd-yy, where mm is a month number from 1–12 inclusive, dd is a day number from 1–31 inclusive, and yy is a two-digit year number from 00–99 inclusive. For the year, the numbers 80–99 are interpreted as the years 1980–1999, and the numbers 00–79 are interpreted as the years 2000–2079. (See comments below for alternate formats.)

DOS Shell

Use SELECT to Show the Date on the DOS Shell Screen
The DOS Shell utility shows the date in the upper left corner of the screen if the startup option /date was specified. This option is installed by SELECT as a default.

Related Commands TIME sets or displays system time.

COUNTRY determines date format.

DIR displays dates of file creation and access.

DETAILED REFERENCE

Explanation In PC DOS, the system date is normally maintained automatically by reading the onboard battery-powered clock found in most systems. PC DOS does not ask you for the date on startup unless there is no AUTOEXEC.BAT file. (AUTOEXEC.BAT does not actually have to have the DATE command in it, however, unless you want the date displayed on startup.) Because the PC DOS date algorithm keeps track of the variable lengths of months and even the occurrence of leap year, you should not have to set the date under normal circumstances, except after changing clock batteries.

Tip

Setting the Clock

If you use the DATE command, but the date shown in subsequent sessions is incorrect, it means that you must use a special program to change the actual clock setting. This is generally true when you have an add-on clock board (found mainly on older PCs) rather than a built-in system clock. In this case, you must run a utility supplied with the board.

If you have a built-in clock, but have to change batteries, you will probably have to run your system's clock utility. This usually comes on a System or Diagnostics disk—for the IBM PS/2, this is called the Reference Diskette.

Comments The format used for the date is controlled by the COUNTRY setting in CONFIG.SYS and defaults to U.S. format, mm-dd-yy. Dates can also be entered in the formats mm/dd/yy or mm.dd.yy; they will be converted to mm-dd-yy format if the United States format is in effect. Leading zeroes need not be entered, and the century digits (19 or 20) can be entered if you wish.

Examples Example 1: Find out today's date.

```
C:\>date
Current date is Sun 5-08-1990
Enter new date (mm-dd-yy):   ←Press Enter
```

Because all that was wanted was the date, Enter was pressed in response to the prompt.

Example 2: Set the date interactively.

```
C:\>date
Current date is Sun 5-08-1990
Enter new date (mm-dd-yy): 7-4-90
```

You also could have entered the date as 07-04-90, 7/4/1990, or 7.4.90.

Example 3: Set the date directly.

```
C:\>date 12-31-90
C:\>date
Current date is Fri 12-31-1990
```

Related Chapters Chapter 11–Customizing Your System
Chapter 12–Installing a PC DOS System

DEL (syn. ERASE)

Internal Command

Compatibility 2.0 2.1 3.0 3.1 3.2 3.3 4.0 OS/2 (DOS mode) OS/2 (prot.)

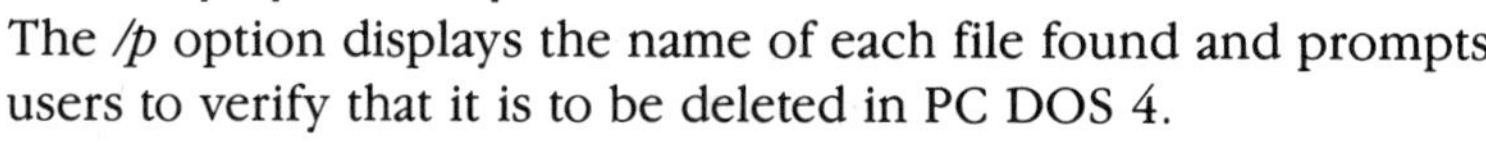

Use the DEL command to delete (remove) a file or group of files from the disk.

Format `del file or directory name` Note: ERASE can be used as a synonym for DEL. Neither DELETE nor ERA are valid, however.

Options

Version 4

Use the /p Option to Report Files Deleted in Version 4
The /p option displays the name of each file found and prompts users to verify that it is to be deleted in PC DOS 4.

Sample Use `del address.dat`

Procedure To delete a file, give the file name, or path name if the file is not in the current directory (Example 1). To delete a group of similar files, you can use wildcards (Example 2). To delete all the files in a directory, use the name of the directory (Example 3). If you wish the user to be prompted before deleting each file, add the /p option (PC DOS 4 only). (Example 4).

DOS Shell

The DOS Shell Utility Lets You Delete Unrelated Files
In DOSSHELL, delete a file or group of files by selecting File System from the Main Group on the Start Programs screen. Next, in the Directory Tree window, select the directory containing the file or files to be deleted. (If you have been working with files previously, make sure they aren't still selected, or they will be deleted. You can use Show Information from the Options Menu to see whether any files are listed as Selected. If so, use Deselect All from the File menu to remove their selection status.) Then, in the file list window, select the file(s) to be deleted. Note that unlike the case of the command-line version of DEL, you can select multiple unrelated file names. Finally, select Delete from the File menu. You will be prompted to confirm each deletion, unless the option "Confirm on delete" has been turned off.

Related Commands FORMAT erases all files from the disk.

RD deletes an empty directory

DETAILED REFERENCE

Explanation

The DEL command does not actually remove the contents of deleted files from the disk. Rather, it marks the file as deleted on the disk's directory and marks its sectors as available for subsequent use. The actual data belonging to the file is still on the disk, but it will be lost when its sectors are used to hold newly created (or extended) files. Therefore, if you accidentally delete a file or files, do not issue any commands or run any programs that write to disk if you wish to recover the deleted file. You can then use any of many commercially available utilities (such as Norton, Mace, or Ultra Utilities) to recover the file, as long as its sectors have not been overwritten.

Caution

Don't Delete Directories by Mistake!

If you issue a command to delete what you think is a file and receive a message like this:

```
C:\>del temp
All files in directory will be deleted!
Are you sure (Y/N)?n    ←Type n or press Enter to abort
```

this means that you are in fact dealing with a directory. Type `n` or press the Enter key to abort the deletion unless you really want to delete all of the files in the directory, in which case you should type `y` followed by Enter. Note that deleting all the files in a directory does not delete the directory itself; use RD to remove the directory. It is best not to use DEL with disks or directories that are involved with a current ASSIGN, JOIN, or SUBST command. This is because these commands substitute one disk letter or path for another and thus can easily confuse you about which directory or file is actually involved.

Examples

Example 1: Delete a file that is not in the current directory.

```
C:\>del a:\progs\oldprog.exe
```

If you are going to delete a number of different files in a particular directory, you can save typing by changing (CD) to that directory; that way, you can use simple file names rather than path names to specify files.

Example 2: Delete a group of files using wildcards.

```
C:\>del dict*.ov?
```

This deletes all files in the current directory whose names start with DICT and whose extensions start with .OV.

Example 3: Delete all the files in a directory.

```
C:\>del include
All files in directory will be deleted!
Are you sure (Y/N)?y    ←Type y to confirm
```

As a safety precaution, you are asked whether you really want to delete all the files in the directory. You must type `y` and press Enter to confirm the deletion; typing anything else aborts the process. Note that using `include` is equivalent to specifying include*.*.

Example 4: Write a batch file that deletes all the files in a directory after prompting the user to verify each deletion.

```
C:\>copy con: delall.bat
@echo off
del %1 /p
^Z
     1 file(s) copied
C:\>delall c:\temp
C:\TEMP\CPDEVS.OUT,     Delete (Y/N)?y
C:\TEMP\CPPREP.OUT,     Delete (Y/N)?n   ←This one wasn't deleted
C:\TEMP\CLOCK.OUT,      Delete (Y/N)?y
```

Under PC DOS 4, you can add the /p option to prompt the user for each deletion. You can use this to go through a directory and choose what to keep and what to throw out. You can also use it in a batch file, such as DELALL.BAT here, to help protect less experienced users against mistakes.

Related Chapters

Chapter 4–Using DOSSHELL
Chapter 5–PC DOS Files
Chapter 6–Managing Your Hard Disk
Chapter 7–All About Floppy Disks

DEVICE

Setting

Compatibility	2.0	2.1	3.0	3.1	3.2	3.3	4.0	OS/2 (DOS mode)	OS/2 (prot.)
	▲	▲	▲	▲	▲	▲	▲	▲	▲

Use the DEVICE setting in your CONFIG.SYS file to load device drivers automatically at startup. Device drivers provide support for hardware, such as the keyboard, video display, disk drives, serial and parallel ports, and mice.

Format `device=`*`device driver name parameters`*

Options Options vary with the device driver used.

Sample Use `device=vdisk.sys 720 256 32`

Procedure

Use a separate statement in CONFIG.SYS for each driver you wish installed at system startup. In each statement, type `device=` followed by the driver program's name. (Drivers normally have the extension .SYS and usually reside in the root directory of the startup drive, although users who like things tidy often create the directory \SYS or \DOS\SYS for housing them. If the driver is not in the root directory, give the complete path name.) Follow the driver name with any parameters needed by that particular driver.

Note: see Chapter 11, "Customizing Your System," for a general discussion of device drivers and see the CONFIG.SYS entry for an overview of device drivers that are supplied with PC DOS. See the entries for particular drivers (for example, PRINTER.SYS) for a detailed discussion of each driver or set of drivers.

Related Commands

CONFIG.SYS is a file containing DEVICE statements.

ANSI.SYS is an extended screen-keyboard driver.

DISPLAY.SYS contains support for code page switching for video display.

DRIVER.SYS allows access to disk drives and assigns drive letters.

PRINTER.SYS supports code page switching for certain printers.

VDISK.SYS is a virtual disk driver (RAM disk).

XMAEM.SYS is an expanded memory driver for 80386 systems (PC DOS 4).

XMA2EMS.SYS is a LIM 4.0 expanded memory driver (PC DOS 4).

DETAILED REFERENCE

Explanation

The CONFIG.SYS file contains settings that take effect during system startup. One of its important functions is to install device drivers that allow application programs to communicate with the various hardware devices. Hardware vendors often provide custom drivers for use with their products; these are usually installed using DEVICE statements in the CONFIG.SYS file, though some are installed by setup programs in the AUTOEXEC.BAT file. (See the product's documentation.)

Comments

PC DOS installs an internal clock drive automatically at startup. Do not specify CLOCK.SYS in a DEVICE statement. Also, do not specify COUNTRY.SYS in a DEVICE statement; this driver is installed by the COUNTRY setting.

Examples

Example 1: Put a statement in CONFIG.SYS to install the ANSI.SYS device driver.

```
device=ansi.sys
```

Example 2: Supply a CONFIG.SYS statement to install a (hypothetical) CD-ROM driver, from a directory other than the root directory of the startup drive.

```
device=c:\refbase\cdrom.sys
```

Related Chapters

Chapter 11–Customizing Your System
Chapter 12–Installing a PC DOS System

DIR

Internal Command

Compatibility	2.0	2.1	3.0	3.1	3.2	3.3	4.0	OS/2 (DOS mode)	OS/2 (prot.)
	▲	▲	▲	▲	▲	▲	▲	▲	▲

Use the DIR command to display information about specified directories or files. The resulting list includes the name of each file as well as its size and the date and time the file was created or last modified.

Format `dir` *drive, directory or file name options*

Options */w* lists in wide format just file and subdirectory names.

/p pauses a listing after each screenful is displayed.

Sample Use `dir c:\dos /p`

Procedure Following DIR, type the name of the drive, directory, or file that you want listed. (If you want to list only the current directory, you can leave out the name.) See Chapter 6, "Managing Your Hard Disk," for further discussion of path names and their use. You can also use wildcards to specify a group of related files.

Related Commands CD changes the current directory.

MD creates a new directory.

RD removes an empty directory.

CHKDSK obtains a summary of disk and memory usage.

DETAILED REFERENCE

Explanation Every PC DOS disk, whether hard or floppy, contains a directory that lists the names of all files on the disk and information such as the size of each file in bytes and the date the file was created or last modified. Starting with PC DOS 2.0, files can be arranged in a hierarchy where a directory can contain subdirectories as well as files, and each subdirectory in turn can contain more files and subdirectories. (The PC DOS file system is discussed in more detail in Chapter 5, "PC DOS Files," Chapter 6, "Managing Your Hard Disk," and Chapter 7, "All About Floppy Disks.")

The DIR command reads this information for the files (and any subdirectories) of the current directory of the specified drive (or of the current drive if none is specified) (Example 1). If a directory is specified, a listing of the files and any subdirectories in that directory is displayed (Example 2). If a file or path name with wildcards is used, information about the matching files is displayed (Example 3).

DOS Shell

The DOS Shell Utility Shows the Current Directory
While you are working in the File System screen under DOS-SHELL, the window on the left side of the screen, entitled Direc-

tory Tree, lists the entire structure of directories and subdirectories on the currently logged disk. By selecting any directory in this list you can obtain a display in the right (file list) window that is similar to that given by the DIR command. Use Show Information in the Options menu to obtain the total number of files and the total space used by the current directory and on the current disk.

Examples Example 1: List the contents of the current directory.

```
C:\>dir c:

 Volume in drive C is PCDOSDISK
 Volume Serial Number is 1454-3E20
 Directory of C:\KERMIT

.            <DIR>      11-13-87   5:13p
..           <DIR>      11-13-87   5:13p
MACROS       <DIR>       1-22-88   2:34p
MSKERMIT INI       381   4-21-88  12:15a
MSKERMIT EXE     84776   7-28-85  11:42p
PCJS0901          1728   9-01-88   1:21a
UUADDR              51  11-22-87   9:33a
        7 File(s)   5725312 bytes free
```

Because you did not specify a directory, the current directory on drive C, which happens to be KERMIT, is displayed. The label of the disk (if any) is given first, followed by the disk serial number (PC DOS 4 only). For each file, the name (including any extension), size, and date and time of creation (or last modification) is listed. Subdirectories are identified with the word <DIR> in place of the size. The first two entries, the special subdirectories . and .. are always present. They allow shorthand reference to this directory and its parent (next higher) directory, respectively. Finally, the total number of files (including subdirectories) and the number of free (available) bytes on the disk is given.

Example 2: List a directory using a path name.

```
C:\>dir a:\ref
Volume in drive A has no label.
Directory of A:\REF
REFINTRO         7040  1-12-88  4:18p
QUEST1           1618  1-12-88  4:43p
     4 file(s)   717824 bytes free
```

Here, the path name A:\REF was used to specify a different drive and directory. When a specific path is used, the special . and .. subdirectories are not listed.

Example 3: List the root directory of drive C on one screen by using the /w option.

```
C:\>dir c:\ /w
 Volume in drive C is PCDOSISK
 Volume Serial Number is 1454-3E20
 Directory of C:\

LOGFILE     DATSCIENCE    REFERENCE     BASIC       SMALTALK
DOS         AUTOEXEC      BATTEMP       C51         COM
TMP         CONFIG        SYSWP50       REPORTS     CPROGS
TURBOC      WINDOWS       GAMING        ML          KERMIT
UTILS       MOUSE1        PROLOG        DOSUTIL     PERSONAL
TWG         MKS           BOOKS         ACCT        WRITING
USENET      SPOOL
       32 File(s)    5803136 bytes free
```

Only the names of the entries are shown. Thus, you can't tell, for example, whether a given entry represents a file or a directory. The /w option does, however, allow PC DOS to fit more directory entries on one screen. An alternative way to look at large directories is to use the /p option; this lists the complete information for each file, but one screen at a time.

Press any key to view the next portion of the directory.

Example 4: List selected files by using a wildcard.

```
C:\>dir c:\dos\drivers\*.sys
 Volume in drive C is MAINDISK
 Volume Serial Number is 1454-3E20
 Volume Directory of C:\DOS\DRIVERS
ANSI     SYS      1678   3-17-87  12:00p
COUNTRY  SYS     11285   3-17-87  12:00p
DISPLAY  SYS     11290   3-17-87  12:00p
DRIVER   SYS      1196   3-17-87  12:00p
KEYBOARD SYS     19766   3-17-87  12:00p
PRINTER  SYS     13590   3-17-87  12:00p
VDISK    SYS      3455   3-17-87  12:00p
CONFIG   SYS       109   8-29-88   1:50p
IBMCACHE SYS      8032   8-17-88  11:40a
        9 File(s)     5803136 bytes free
```

By using the * wildcard in the name *.sys, a listing of all the device drivers in the C:\DOS\DRIVERS directory was obtained.

Related Chapters

Chapter 4–Using DOSSHELL
Chapter 5–PC DOS Files
Chapter 6–Managing Your Hard Disk
Chapter 7–All About Floppy Disks

External Command

DISKCOMP

Compatibility	2.0	2.1	3.0	3.1	3.2	3.3	4.0	OS/2 (DOS mode)	OS/2 (prot.)
	▲	▲	▲	▲	▲	▲	▲	▲	▲

Use the DISKCOMP command to compare the contents of two floppy disks.

Format `diskcomp` *`drive drive2 options`*

Options */1* compares only the first side of the disks, even if they are double-sided.

/8 compares only 8 sectors per track, even if the first disk has 9 or 15 sectors per track.

Sample Use `diskcomp a: b:`

Procedure To compare two disks using the same floppy drive (such as drive A), type `diskcomp` followed twice by the same drive letter (Example 1). If you are using the default (current) drive, you can type `diskcomp` (Example 2). You will be prompted to swap disks as necessary. To compare disks in two different drives, specify the drive letters of the two disks to be compared (Example 3). You can also use the /1 and /8 options to limit the extent of the comparison (Example 4).

DOS Shell

The DOS Shell Lets You Compare Two Disks
To compare two disks while running DOSSHELL, select DOS Utilities from the Main Group on the Start Programs screen. Next, select Disk Compare. You will be prompted for the letters of the drives containing the disks to be compared.

Related Commands COMP compares specific files.

DISKCOPY copies entire disks.

DETAILED REFERENCE

Explanation The DISKCOMP command compares two disks track by track. It reports the track number and side (0 or 1) of each mismatch (if any). A mismatch is simply a file position where the two data bytes differ. If there are many mismatches (perhaps you put in the wrong disk?), press Ctrl-C to abort the comparison. After the comparison is completed, you are prompted to compare another pair of disks.

Comments Generally speaking, the size and physical format of the two disks to be compared must be the same. For example, you cannot compare a 360K 5.25-inch disk with a 720K 3.5-inch disk, nor can you compare a 360K 5.25-inch disk with a 1.2MB 5.25-inch disk. However 160K and 180K 5.25-inch disks can be compared with each other, as can 320K and 360K 5.25-inch ones. An error message is given for invalid combinations of formats.

DISKCOMP Idiosyncrasies

When comparing disks using the same drive, it doesn't matter which disk you insert first. However, you must make sure you are consistent about swapping the disks.

DISKCOMP cannot be used with hard disks or with virtual disks. You should not attempt to use DISKCOMP with drives affected by the SUBST or JOIN commands, or with drives that are being used by a network.

If you copied all the files from one disk to another using the COPY or XCOPY commands, DISKCOMP will probably not consider the two disks to be the same. This is because DISKCOMP compares the actual sectors, and COPY and XCOPY do not necessarily put the files in the same sectors on the target disk. DISKCOMP can, however, be used to verify a copy made with DISKCOPY.

DISKCOMP ignores the volume serial number, so otherwise identical disks with different serial numbers (PC DOS 4) will be reported as identical.

Examples Example 1: Compare the contents of two disks in drive A.

```
A:\>diskcomp a: a:
Insert FIRST diskette in drive A:
Press any key when ready . . .
                                          ←Press a key
Comparing 80 tracks
9 sectors per track, 2 side(s).
Insert SECOND diskette in drive A:
```

The number of tracks and of sectors per track depends on the physical disk format being used. This example uses 720K 3.5-inch disks.

The side and track location of each mismatch is reported. For example

```
Compare error on side 1, track 5
```

As the comparison continues, you will be prompted to swap disks as necessary. You are prompted to swap disks until the disks have been compared completely. If there are no mismatches at all, the following message is displayed:

```
Compare OK
```

When the comparison has been completed, you are asked whether you want to compare more disks.

```
Compare another diskette (Y/N)?
```

Example 2: Compare two disks using the default drive.

```
A:\>diskcomp
```

Because the current drive is A and you have not specified drives, DISKCOMP assumes that you wish to compare two disks using drive A. Note that this form of the command will not work from the C> prompt, because you cannot use a hard disk for comparison.

Example 3: Compare disks on two different drives.

```
C:\>diskcomp a: b:
```

Both drive letters must be specified. No disk swapping will be needed.

Drives A and B must contain disks with the same physical format, with the minor exceptions noted previously.

Example 4: Compare an old single-sided, 8-sector disk to a double-sided 360K disk.

```
C:\>diskcomp a: b: /1 /8
```

The /1 option tells DISKCOMP to compare only the first side of the disks, even if the first disk has two sides. The /8 option specifies that only 8 sectors per track will be compared. These options are rarely needed but can be used to compare old DOS 1.0 disks to current format 360K disks.

Related Chapter Chapter 7–All About Floppy Disks

External Command

DISKCOPY

Compatibility	2.0	2.1	3.0	3.1	3.2	3.3	4.0	OS/2 (DOS mode)	OS/2 (prot.)
	▲	▲	▲	▲	▲	▲	▲	▲	▲

Use the DISKCOPY command to make a copy of an entire disk, track by track.

Format diskcopy *source-drive destination-drive*

Options */1* copies only the first side of the disk. Use only to copy from a single-sided 5.25-inch disk.

Sample Use diskcopy a: b:

Procedure If you want to use a single drive to make the copy, use the drive's letter for both source and destination (Example 1). If you do not specify drives, a single-drive copy is made using the default drive (Example 2). You will be prompted to swap disks as necessary. To use two drives, specify the letters of the drives containing the source and destination disks (Example 3). If you need to copy an old single-sided disk, add the /1 option. After the copy is completed, you will be asked whether you want to copy more disks.

DOS Shell

The DOS Shell Utility Lets You Copy Disks

To make a copy of an entire disk using DOSSHELL, select DOS Utilities from the Main Group on the Start Programs screen. Next, select Disk Copy. You will be prompted for the source and destination drive letters.

Related Commands COPY copies selected files between disks or directories.

XCOPY copies contents of specific directories and subdirectories.

BACKUP copies contents of hard disk to multiple floppies.

DISKCOMP compares contents of two disks.

DETAILED REFERENCE

Explanation The DISKCOPY command copies the entire contents of the disk in the source drive to the disk in the destination drive. The same drive can be used for both source and destination; you are prompted to swap disks as needed. Any existing contents of the destination disk are overwritten. If the destination disk is not already formatted, it is formatted before the copy is made. The resulting disk is identical track for track and sector for sector with the original.

The source and destination disks must generally have the same physical format; for example, you cannot copy a 360K 5.25-inch disk to a 720K 3.5-inch disk (use COPY or XCOPY to copy the files instead). An exception is that 160K and 180K 5.25-inch disks can be copied interchangeably, as can 320K and 360K 5.25-inch disks. An error message is given for invalid combinations of formats. However, if the destination disk is either unformatted or formatted to a higher capacity than the source disk, DISKCOPY will format the destination disk to the same capacity as the source disk and attempt to make the copy. The copy may not be reliable, and this usage is not recommended.

The /1 option is normally used only to copy old single-sided disks.

Tip

Use the Right Tool!
DISKCOPY copies all tracks and sectors of the disk, not just those that are used by existing files. It is usually much faster to use COPY or XCOPY to copy one or a few files, or the contents of a directory.

DISKCOPY does not unfragment files; use COPY or XCOPY to copy badly fragmented files to a new disk or directory. DISKCOPY is most useful when you want to copy an entire disk without having to deal with its directory structure, or to make multiple copies of a disk.

To copy your hard disk to a set of floppy disks (in other words, to make a complete backup), use the BACKUP command.

Caution

Be Careful When Copying Two Disks on a Single Drive
When making single-drive copies, be sure to label the disks and keep track of which is the source and which is the destination.

Drive reassignments made with the ASSIGN or SUBST commands are not recognized by DISKCOPY. DISKCOPY should not be used with drives logically connected with the JOIN command. DISKCOPY cannot be used with hard disks, virtual disks, or network disks.

Examples Example 1: Make an exact copy of a disk in drive A.

```
A:\>diskcopy a: a:
Insert SOURCE diskette in drive A:
Press any key when ready . . .
Copying 80 tracks
9 sectors per track, 2 side(s).
Insert TARGET diskette in drive A:
Press any key when ready . . .
```

You will be prompted to swap the source and destination disks as necessary. When the copy is completed, the following message is displayed:

```
Copy another diskette (Y/N)?
```

Example 2: Make a default single-drive copy.

```
A:\>diskcopy
```

Because no drives are specified, a single-drive copy is made on the current default drive (A in this case).

Example 3: Copy the disk in drive A to a disk in drive B.

```
A:\>diskcopy a: b:
Insert SOURCE diskette in drive A:
Press any key when ready . . .
Copying 80 tracks
9 sectors per track, 2 side(s).
Insert TARGET diskette in drive B:
Press any key when ready . . .
```

The copy now proceeds as in Example 1, but without disk swapping.

Related Chapter Chapter 7–All About Floppy Disks

Resource DISPLAY.SYS

Compatibility	2.0	2.1	3.0	3.1	3.2	3.3	4.0	OS/2 (DOS mode)	OS/2 (prot.)
						▲	▲		

Use the DISPLAY.SYS device driver to enable code page switching with the EGA, PS/2, and other display adapters.

Note: Code page switching is not needed by most users in the United States, although it may be useful for multinational applications. See Chapter 13, "International Language Support," for a full discussion of code page switching and step by step instructions for installation.

Don't Worry about DISPLAY.SYS in Version 4

In PC DOS 4, you probably will not need to worry about DISPLAY.SYS at all. During the installation process, PC DOS will determine what display hardware you have and make the appropriate settings.

Note: The IBM monochrome and CGA adapters are not supported for code page switching in DOS 4, although they can be used with the default character set.

Format

device=display.sys con:=(*display-type,hardware-page,code-pages, sub-fonts*)

Options The display device specified must be one of the following:

mono controls monochrome adapter (PC DOS 3.3 only).

cga controls Color Graphics Adapter (PC DOS 3.3 only).

ega controls Enhanced Graphics Adapter or PS/2 graphics adapter.

lcd controls IBM convertible (laptop) LCD adapter.

The hardware code page is normally 437 for United States users. If you have problems, try omitting this number.

The number of additional prepared code pages must be from 0 through 12, with a default of 1, which is normal for U.S. users.

Note that prepared code pages are not supported for the monochrome or CGA displays, so a value of 0 should be used with these.

The maximum number of subfonts depends on the adapter used: 2 for EGA and PS/2 Models 25 and 30; 3 for PS/2 Models 50 and above, and the high resolution 8514/A adapter, and 1 for the IBM Convertible LCD.

This number is also the default in each case, so you normally don't need to enter it.

If you specify subfonts, the numbers of code pages and subfonts are enclosed in their own parentheses.

Sample Use

```
device=display.sys con:=(ega, 437, 1)
```

Procedure First, determine if you are using or should be using code page switching. (See Chapter 13, "International Language Support".) If you will be using code page switching, determine the type of display adapter you are using. (If you have a PS/2 or other machine with the VGA adapter, use the EGA option.)

In your CONFIG.SYS file, begin a statement with `device=display.sys con:=`, followed by numbers in parentheses for the device type, the hardware code page number, the number of additional code pages to be prepared, and the number of subfonts on the adapter.

If you put your device drivers in a directory other than the root directory of the startup drive, give the complete path to the DISPLAY.SYS file; for example, `device=c:\sys\device.sys con:=(ega, 437, 1)`(see Example 1).

Related Commands ANSI.SYS is a device driver for extended screen and keyboard functions.

CHCP specifies or changes code page.

CONFIG.SYS is a file for installing DRIVER.SYS.

COUNTRY supplies country information for code page switching.

CTTY enables remote terminal operation.

DEVICE is a statement for installing device drivers.

GRAFTABL allows display of extended graphics characters.

MODE sets display mode and characteristics for other devices.

NLSFUNC supports extended country information.

SELECT installs DOS on a new disk; includes code page specification.

DETAILED REFERENCE

Explanation Basically, a code page is a character set (or group of related character sets) that provides the characters and other symbols used for various national languages. The DISPLAY.SYS driver takes care of preparing the hardware adapter for displaying the specified code page(s).

Comments Although the setting used is EGA, the support for code page switching on the IBM PS/2 is not functionally equivalent to EGA support. For those applications that require you to specify the graphics adapter, use MCGA (for PS/2 Models 25 and 30) and VGA for other PS/2 models. If these settings are not available, try EGA.

Example Example 1: Prepare a system with EGA for code page switching.

```
device=c:\sys\display.sys con:=(ega, 437, 1)
```

The path is given so that PC DOS can find the DISPLAY.SYS file in the SYS directory. The parentheses specify that an EGA adapter will be used, the hardware code page will be 437 (United States), and that one additional code page should be prepared.

Related Chapter Chapter 13–International Language Support

External Command — DOSSHELL

Compatibility	2.0	2.1	3.0	3.1	3.2	3.3	4.0	OS/2 (DOS mode)	OS/2 (prot.)
							▲		

Version 4

Use the DOSSHELL command with PC DOS 4 to provide easy to use, menu-driven access to your programs and files. Note: See Chapter 4, "Using DOSSHELL," for a complete guide to using the many functions provided by DOSSHELL and a discussion of customizing shell features through startup options.

Format `dosshell`

Sample Use `dosshell`

DOSSHELL

Procedure Before you use DOSSHELL, you should have run the PC DOS 4 SELECT command. See Chapter 12, "Installing a PC DOS System," for a guide to using SELECT. Among other things, this program prepares the batch file DOSSHELL.BAT, which will include options appropriate to your hardware. A typical DOSSHELL.BAT file looks like this:

```
@C:
@CD C:\DOS
@SHELLB DOSSHELL
@IF ERRORLEVEL 255 GOTO END
:COMMON
@BREAK=OFF
@SHELLC
/TEXT/MOS:PCIBMDRV.MOS/TRAN/COLOR/DOS/MENU/MUL/SND/MEU
:SHELL.MEU/CLR:SHELL.CLR/PROMPT/MAINT/EXIT/SWAP/DATE
:END
@BREAK=ON
```

As shown in the batch file, the options follow the name SHELLC, which is the main shell program. To add or change any of these options, edit the DOSSHELL.BAT file with any ASCII text editor. (Before doing so, it is a good idea to use the command `copy dosshell.bat dosshell.bak` to save a copy of your original settings.) The tutorial on DOSSHELL groups the startup options by functional category and gives a brief description of each one.

Caution

Use the EXIT Command to Avoid Loading DOSSHELL Twice
If you want the shell to run automatically at startup, put the command DOSSHELL in your AUTOEXEC.BAT file. If you prefer to use COMMAND.COM and the regular command line most of the time, you can run the shell by typing `dosshell` at any PC DOS command prompt.

If, when you are using DOSSHELL, you select Command Prompt or pres Shift-F9 to work at the regular PC DOS prompt, type `exit` to return to DOSSHELL. If you type `dosshell` rather than `exit`, the shell will run, but you will have loaded an additional copy of the resident part of COMMAND.COM and tied up valuable memory.

Related Commands AUTOEXEC.BAT is a file for running DOSSHELL automatically at startup.

COMMAND runs the PC DOS command processor.

COMSPEC specifies the command processor location.

EXIT exits a secondary command processor; should be used to return to DOSSHELL.

INSTALL loads memory-resident programs at startup.

SELECT installs PC DOS and customizes options.

SHELL specifies an alternate command processor.

DETAILED REFERENCE

Explanation DOSSHELL is a batch file that runs a series of programs (SHELLB.EXE and SHELLC.EXE) that provide menu-driven access to PC DOS functions as well as a facility for selecting and running your application programs.

When the batch file runs the SHELLC.EXE program, it passes it a series of options separated by slashes (see Example 1). These options control the shell's display mode and resolution, what components of the shell will be active on startup, how the shell will use the disk and expanded memory, and other features of the shell's operation.

DOS Shell

Bugs and Problems

Early versions of PC DOS 4 may have a bug that causes DOSSHELL, when run in resident mode (by removing the /TRAN startup option), to tie up all but about 64K of memory, making it impossible to run most applications. IBM dealers should have "fix" update disks available to fix this and other bugs.

Remember that even without bugs, running the shell in resident mode, although convenient for floppy-based systems, may not leave enough memory for your applications. Transient mode is recommended in any case for hard disk systems, and SELECT installs it by default.

Example Example 1: Take the DOSSHELL.BAT file given in the preceding Procedure section and make the following changes:

- change the shell so that it runs in graphics rather than text mode
- have the shell remain memory-resident
- prevent user access to the command prompt from the shell

To make these changes, the line in DOSSHELL.BAT that follows SHELLC is edited so that it reads as follows:

```
@SHELLC
/MOS:PCIBMDRV.MOS/COLOR/DOS/MENU/MUL/SND/MEU:SHELL.MEU
/CLR:SHELL.CLR/MAINT/EXIT/SWAP/DATE
```

Compare this with the previous listing. First, the */TEXT* option was removed; this makes the shell run in graphics mode if a graphics adapter is available. The */TRAN* (transient) option was also removed; this means the shell remains in memory rather than being reloaded after each program is run. Finally, the */PROMPT* option was removed; this means that the user cannot access the PC DOS command prompt from within the shell. Such tailoring of the shell's operation can be combined with its menu facilities to create custom working environments for less experienced users.

Related Chapters Chapter 4–Using DOSSHELL
Chapter 9–Creating Text Files
Chapter 12–Installing a PC DOS System

DRIVER.SYS

Resource

Compatibility	2.0	2.1	3.0	3.1	3.2	3.3	4.0	OS/2 (DOS mode)	OS/2 (prot.)
					▲		▲	▲	

Use the DRIVER.SYS device driver to enable PC DOS to recognize add-on disk drives. You can also use it to allow single-drive copying with disk swapping (see Example 3).

Format `device=driver.sys /d:` *`drive-number`* `/t:`*`tracks`* `/s:`*`sectors per track`* `/h:`*`heads`* `/c /f:`*`device form factor`*

Note: All but the drive number are optional. The possible values and defaults are given in the Options section. A separate DRIVER.SYS statement must be included in the CONFIG.SYS file for each add-on drive.

Options */d:* is a physical drive number, starting with 0 for the first internal floppy drive, 1 for the second, and so on. Do not use 1 for add-on drives, as this is reserved for a standard second internal drive (even if you don't have one). Hard drives are numbered starting with 128, the second is 129, and so on. This option is required; there is no default.

/t: is the number of tracks per disk side. The default is 80, so this need not be specified for 1.2MB 5.25-inch disks and 720K and 1.44MB 3.5-inch disks.

/s: is the number of sectors per track. The default is 9, so this need not be specified for 360K 5.25-inch disks or 720K 3.5-inch drives.

/h: is the number of disk heads. The default, 2, applies to nearly all commonly available drives.

/c: is used for disk drives that can detect when the drive door is open, such as internal floppy drives on PS/2s and many AT-type machines.

/n: specifies a nonremovable block device, i.e., a hard disk drive. This option is available in PC DOS 3.2 and 3.3, but is not used in PC DOS 4.

/f: specifies device type or "form factor." This is basically the total capacity. The default is 2, so it need not be specified for 720K 3.5-inch drives.

Sample Use

```
device=driver.sys /d:1
```

Procedure Place a statement in your CONFIG.SYS file beginning with device= driver.sys. (If you have placed the file DRIVER.SYS somewhere other than in the root directory of the startup drive, give the complete path name, such as device=c:\sys\driver.sys.) Next specify /d:, followed by the physical drive number, where 0 is the first internal drive; 1, the second drive; 2, the third drive (which must be external), and so on. (Start add-on drives with drive number 2, not 1.) If your drives do not use the defaults for tracks, sectors per track, and heads (see following text and table), specify these values with the /t:, /s:, and /h: options respectively. Add /c if you are using drives that can detect when the drive door is open. Finally, specify the device form factor (device format) with the /f: option (not needed if the drive is 720K).

Related Commands ASSIGN assigns an existing drive letter to a different drive.

CONFIG.SYS is a file for installing DRIVER.SYS.

DEVICE is a statement for installing device drivers.

FASTOPEN assigns directory buffers for disk drives.

FDISK creates and manages disk partitions.

FORMAT prepares a blank disk for use.

LASTDRIVE specifies the last drive letter.

SELECT installs PC DOS on a new disk.

SUBST assigns a drive letter to a path.

SYS copies PC DOS system files to a disk.

VDISK.SYS is a device driver for RAM (virtual) disks.

DETAILED REFERENCE

Explanation PC DOS automatically recognizes a certain standard configuration of disk drives, depending on the class of machine involved. For example, AT-type machines normally have a single internal 1.2MB floppy plus a hard disk, whereas PS/2-type machines usually come with an internal 1.44MB floppy plus a hard disk. If you have such a configuration and your drives are properly recognized by PC DOS, you do not need a DRIVER.SYS statement.

Many users, however, wish to install additional drives. For example, owners of older AT-type machines may find it convenient to install a 720K or 1.44MB 3.5-inch floppy drive so that they can read and write this increasingly popular format. The DRIVER.SYS device driver allows these add-on disk drives to be recognized by PC DOS and assigns them drive letters on startup. For example, if you have an AT-type machine with an internal 1.2MB floppy (known to PC DOS as drive A) and an internal hard disk (known as drive C), you can install an additional 1.44MB 3.5-inch floppy drive and have it referred to as drive D (drive B is always reserved as an alternate designation for drive A, to allow single-drive copying).

Comments PC DOS uses certain rules to assign a drive letter to an add-on drive. In all cases, A and B are reserved for the first internal floppy drive, and C is reserved for the first internal hard drive. Additional drives (floppy or hard) are assigned the letters D and E as they are encountered.

Tip

Check Your Changes to the CONFIG.SYS File
After changing your CONFIG.SYS and rebooting, use the DIR command (such as dir d:) to verify the drive letter assignments and the physical drives to which they correspond. Also, make sure that the directory shows the correct total disk capacity. If it shows the wrong number, you may have specified one of the disk characteristics incorrectly in your DRIVER.SYS statement.

Notes: If you have many internal and external drives, you may have to assign a new "highest drive letter" to accommodate all of them. See the LASTDRIVE entry for details.

To aid in the use of DRIVER.SYS (and the FORMAT command), Table R.7

shows the appropriate values for the most commonly available floppy drives. For hard drives, consult the manufacturer's documentation.

Table R.7. *Characteristics of Common Disk Drives*

Form Factor	Size	Capacity	Tracks/Side	Sectors/Track
0	5.25"	360K	40	9
1	5.25"	1.2MB	80	15
2	3.5"	720K	80	9
3	3.5"	1.44MB	80	18

Examples

Example 1: Install an add-on 720K 3.5-inch floppy drive on an AT-type machine.

```
device=c:\sys\driver.sys /d:2
```

Because all of the device drivers on this particular system are stored in the root directory's SYS subdirectory, the complete path must be given. This machine has a single internal 1.2MB floppy drive (drive number 0), and the number 1 is reserved, so drive number 2 is specified for the new second drive. Because this type of drive has the default number of tracks and sectors and the default device type (form factor), none of these options need be specified.

Example 2: Install an add-on 360K floppy drive on a PS/2-type machine.

```
device=c:\sys\driver.sys /d:2 /t:40 /f:0
```

Here a bit more information is required, because the 360K floppy drive has 40 rather than the default 80 tracks/sector, and has device type (form factor) number 0.

Example 3: Use a DRIVER.SYS statement to allow an add-on 1.44MB drive to be used in single-drive copying.

```
device=c:\sys\driver.sys /d:3 /s:18 /f:7
device=c:\sys\driver.sys /d:3 /s:18 /f:7
```

On this system, there are already two floppy drives (perhaps one 1.2MB and one 360K). The first DEVICE statement installs a third floppy drive of 1.44MB capacity, physical number 3 (the existing drives are numbers 0 and 2, with 1 reserved), with 18 sectors/track and device type 7. Assuming the system also has a hard drive, this new floppy drive will be assigned drive letter D. The second DEVICE statement is an exact copy of the first. It assigns drive letter E to the same drive. (As you can see, the same drive can be referred to using several drive letters.) This means you can now copy one 1.44MB disk to another, even though you have only one 1.44MB drive, by typing `diskcopy d: e:`; PC DOS will prompt you to swap disks as necessary. Remember that the single-drive copy capability is available automatically; if you have a single floppy drive, you can say `diskcopy a: b:` without needing a DRIVER.SYS statement.

Related Chapters Chapter 7–All About Floppy Disks
Chapter 11–Customizing Your System

Batch Command — ECHO

Compatibility	2.0	2.1	3.0	3.1	3.2	3.3	4.0	OS/2 (DOS mode)	OS/2 (prot.)
	▲	▲	▲	▲	▲	▲	▲	▲	▲

Use ECHO in a batch file to display a message and to specify whether lines in a batch file are displayed as they are executed.

The ECHO command has two different uses. When used with the settings on and off, it determines whether each line in a batch file is displayed on the screen as it is run. When followed by a line of text, ECHO displays the text.

Format `echo [on or off]` turns display of batch file lines on or off.

`echo text` displays text

`echo` shows current status of echo display.

Sample Use `echo FILE NOT FOUND!`

Procedure To have each line in a batch file displayed as it is run, type the line `echo on` in the batch file. To suppress the display of batch file lines, type `echo off` (Example 2). The default is echo on. To have a batch file display a message, put an ECHO command in the batch file, followed by the desired message text (Example 3). To determine the current status of batch file echoing, type `echo` (Example 4).

Related Commands REM puts an explanatory (remark) line in a batch file.

PAUSE pauses execution of a batch file until a key is pressed.

TYPE displays the contents of a file.

DETAILED REFERENCE

Explanation The ECHO command is useful for allowing your batch files to communicate with the user without cluttering the screen with extraneous information. If you start your batch file with echo off and then use ECHO commands to display messages to the user, the user will see only your messages and the output of PC DOS commands rather than the lines of the batch file itself. To see the difference this makes, compare Examples 1 and 2. You can also use ECHO commands to help you debug a batch file (Example 3).

Comments The ECHO can also be typed interactively (at the PC DOS prompt), but this isn't very useful. Note that you can display a blank line by using the command ECHO. (There must be no space before the period.) For a "cleaner" display from your batch file, you might want to follow echo off with a CLS (clear screen command). You can also use ECHO to help debug a batch file. For example, echo %1 will display the first parameter typed on the batch file's command line, and echo %name% displays the value of the environmental variable *name*. (See Chapter 10, "Batch Files," for more information.)

Note that starting with PC DOS 3.3, you can suppress the echoing of any batch file command by typing @ as the first character of the command. Thus @echo off not only turns off subsequent echoing, it also prevents the display of the echo off statement itself.

It is a good idea to type the command `echo on` at the end of your batch file, to restore the default echo behavior.

Examples Example 1: Show how a batch file runs when ECHO is on.

Here's a batch file that displays the specified directory sorted in alphabetical order. It simply takes the output of the regular DIR command and sends it to the SORT command via a pipe (|).

```
C:\>copy con: sortdir.bat
rem print a sorted directory
echo Sorted directory of %1
dir %1 | sort
^Z
 1 file(s) copied
```

This is what this commane file looks like when it is run:

```
C:\>sortdir c:\pcdosbib\ref

C:\>rem print a sorted directory
C:\>echo Sorted directory of c:\pcdosbib\ref
Sorted directory of c:\pcdosbib\ref

C:\>dir c:\pcdosbib\ref    | sort

     20 File(s)    5820416 bytes free.
 Directory of C:\PCDOSBIB\REF
 The volume label in drive C is MAINDISK.
.            <DIR>        1-17-90  11:36a
..           <DIR>        1-17-90  11:36a
ADDPATH  BAT        18    6-25-90  12:4.1p
BIBHEAD            128    5-01-90   1:17p
DIR      REF      7168    2-17-90   4:49p
DISKSWAP            67    6-23-90   1:08p
ERRMSG              96    6-23-90   1:01p.
EX1                186    6-25-90   1:43p
EX2                 40    6-25-90  12:41p
EX3                205    6-23-90   1:10p
MEMMAN   NOT       512    5-04-90  10:24a
REFAC            96384    5-03-90   5:02p.
REFCD            95360    5-10-90   1:35p
```

```
REFDE           17384   6-25-90    1:38p
REFINTRO         7040   1-12-90    4:18p
REFLIST          7424   1-19-90    3:22p
REFNOTES         1119   2-24-90    4:54p
SORTDIR  BAT       74   6-25-90    1:42p.
STRIP    COM       76   2-26-90    4:49a
TEMP              981   6-25-90   12:51p
```

This display is confusing because lines from the batch file, including the REM (remark) line, are displayed along with the results of the PC DOS commands.

Example 2: Show the same batch file when it is run with ECHO off. Here the SORTDIR.BAT file is modified to turn echo off, clear the screen, and display just the directory contents. Note that ECHO is turned back on when the batch file is done, to be consistent and restore default settings.

```
C:\>copy con: sortdir2.bat
@echo off
cl,s
rem print a sorted directory
echo Sorted directory of %1
dri %1 | sort
echo on
^Z
 1 file(s) copied
```

Running this version of the command file produces the following:

```
C:\>sortdir2 c:\pcdosbib\ref
Sorted directory of c:\pcdosbib\ref


      23 File(s)   5791744 bytes free
 Directory of C:\PCDOSBIB\REF
 The volume label in drive C is MAINDISK.
.            <DIR>      1-17-90   11:36a
..           <DIR>      1-17-90   11:36a
ADDPATH  BAT       18   6-25-90   12:41p
BIBHEAD           128   5-01-90    1:17p
DIR      REF     7168   2-17-90    4:49p
DISKSWAP           67   6-23-90    1:08p
ERRMSG             96   6-23-90    1:01sp
EX1              1119   6-25-90    1:43p
EX2                67   6-25-90    3:02p
EX3               205   6-23-90    1:10p
MEMMAN   NOT      512   5-04-90   10:24a
REFAC           96384   5-03-90    5:02p
REFCD           95360   5-10-90    1:35p
REFDE           19971   6-25-90    1:59p
REFDE    BK!    17384   6-25-90    1:38p
REFINTRO         7040   1-12-90    4:18p
REFLIST          7424   1-19-90    3:22p
```

```
REFNOTES          1119   2-24-90   4:54p
SORTDIR  BAT        74   6-25-90   1:42p
SORTDIR2 BAT        98   6-25-90   3:01p
SORTDIR3 BAT        84   6-25-90   1:44p
STRIP    COM        76   2-26-90   4:49a
TEMP               981   6-25-90  12:51p
```

Example 3: Use ECHO to debug a batch file. Here, the batch file PARAMS.BAT prints its command-line parameters (options).

```
C:\>copy con: params.b.t
@echo off
cls
echo First param: %1
echo Second param: %2
echo Third param: %3
echo on
^Z
 1 file(s) copied
```

Here's what happens when you run PARAMS.BAT:

```
C:\>params one two three
First param: one
Second param: two
Third param: three
C:\>
```

Example 4: Show the current echo status.

```
C:\>echo
ECHO is on.
```

Related Chapter Chapter 10–Batch Files

EXIT

Internal Command

Compatibility	2.0	2.1	3.0	3.1	3.2	3.3	4.0	OS/2 (DOS mode)	OS/2 (prot.)
	▲	▲	▲	▲	▲	▲	▲	▲	▲

Use EXIT to terminate a secondary command processor.

Format `exit`

Sample Use `exit`

Procedure Type `exit` at the PC DOS prompt to exit the current command processor (normally, a copy of COMMAND.COM). You will receive a prompt from the command processor that has started the current one. If the current command processor is the original (highest level) one, EXIT has no effect.

Related Commands COMMAND starts a new PC DOS command processor.

INSTALL installs a memory-resident PC DOS command at startup.

PROMPT specifies the PC DOS command prompt.

DETAILED REFERENCE

Explanation The command processor is the program that interprets commands you type at the PC DOS prompt. This processor is normally the program COMMAND.COM. (Even in DOS 4, when you use the menu-driven DOSSHELL interface, the actual underlying command processor is COMMAND.COM.)

You can start a new copy of COMMAND.COM at the PC DOS prompt by typing `command`. The new processor that is started, and which is now giving you the PC DOS prompt, is called a "secondary processor" (or sometimes a "child" processor). Typing `exit` at the secondary processor's prompt returns you to the parent processor. You can, in fact, have several layers of such "nested" processors, although it is hard to think of a use for such an arrangement.

If an application program is running and a secondary processor is started, the application program regains control after EXIT is typed. Many application programs allow users to start a secondary processor (sometimes called the "DOS shell" function) in order to accomplish housekeeping tasks not otherwise provided for by the program's own commands. After you have exited the secondary processor, you are returned to the precise place where you left the program, so you can continue editing the file, working with spreadsheet cells, or whatever. The application program often sets up the secondary processor with a prompt that reminds the user to type `exit` to return to the application.

Comments See the COMMAND entry for further explanation of the use of child command processors and the relationship between the environments of child and parent processors.

Examples See the COMMAND entry for examples showing the creation of secondary command processors and the return to the original processor via the EXIT command.

Related Chapters Chapter 8–Advanced Use of the Command Line
Chapter 10–Batch Files

FASTOPEN

External Command

Compatibility	2.0	2.1	3.0	3.1	3.2	3.3	4.0	OS/2 (DOS mode)	OS/2 (prot.)
						▲	▲		

Use FASTOPEN to speed access to hard disks by storing in RAM the directory information for recently accessed files.

Format `fastopen` *`drive: =buffered-entries`* (PC DOS 3.3)

Options

Version 4

Version 4 Uses Variation of Syntax

`fastopen` *`drive:=(buffered-entries,sector list entries) options`*
(PC DOS 4)
/x places all buffers in expanded memory.

Sample Use `fastopen c:=50` (PC DOS 3.3)

`fastopen c:=(100,200)` (PC DOS 4)

Procedure For DOS 3.3, specify FASTOPEN followed by the letter of the drive to be buffered, an equal sign, and the number of directory entries to be accommodated by the buffer. This number must be between 10 and 999 (Example 1). Multiple drive and entry numbers can be specified, as long as the total of buffered entries does not exceed 999 (Example 2).

Normally, this statement should be put in your AUTOEXEC.BAT file so that the buffers will be set up automatically at the start of each session.

Version 4

Version 4 Lets You Specify Buffers and Sectors in Version 4

For DOS 4, specify FASTOPEN followed by the letter of the drive to be buffered, an equal sign, and two numbers in parentheses and separated by a comma. The first number is the number of directory entries to be accommodated by the buffer, between 10 and 999. The second number is the number of entries for storing file sector lists from the directory, and must be between 1 and 999 (Example 3).

This statement can be put in your AUTOEXEC.BAT file, or it can be installed using the INSTALL setting in your CONFIG.SYS file (Example 4).

Related Commands BUFFERS sets the number of buffers to hold recently accessed data from disk.

FCBS specifies the number of file control blocks to be provided to applications.

FILES specifies the maximum number of open files.

INSTALL installs FASTOPEN via CONFIG.SYS (PC DOS 4 only).

STACKS specifies the number of stack frames (PC DOS 3.3 and later).

DETAILED REFERENCE

Explanation The FASTOPEN statement provides faster access to files needed by your applications. It does this by storing the directory paths and other control information for recently accessed files in RAM. This allows files to be accessed again by retrieving the directory information from memory rather than by rereading the directory on disk.

Version 4

Specifying Sectors Can Speed Response in Version 4
Under DOS 4, FASTOPEN also stores the lists of file data sectors for recently accessed files in memory. This speeds up the actual retrieval of data from the file by avoiding additional reading of the directory.

Comments If you specify only a drive letter without any numbers, space for 34 directory entry buffers and 34 sector list buffers (DOS 4) is provided by default.

FASTOPEN can only be used with hard disks. It cannot be used with drives that have been specified in a JOIN, SUBST, or ASSIGN command, nor may it be used with network drives.

Version 4

Specify Zero Buffers, But Keep the Comma in Version 4
If you omit *one* of the buffer numbers, no buffers of that type are allocated. The comma must still be included (see Example 5).

The total number of directory entry buffers for all drives specified cannot exceed 999. Similarly, the total number of sector list buffers for all drives cannot exceed 999.

Note on Directory Entry Buffers (first number): If you specify a low number of entry buffers (such as the minimum of 10 or even the default of 34) and use a considerable number of files, you will not take best advantage of buffering, because all of your directory entries won't be in RAM. On the other hand, if you specify too large a number (such as the maximum of 999), it may take more time to search through memory than it would to read the directory from disk. We recommend specifying about 200 for the first number, possibly more if you use many files. Each buffer uses 35 bytes; consider using expanded memory (/x) if available.

Note on Sector List Buffers (second number): This number (PC DOS 4 only) specifies the number of buffers to be used for holding data sector lists for files. If the files on your disk are scattered or fragmented, more numbers must be kept in the sector list, and thus a larger value for this number is needed. Setting the number too small means that lists must be continuously reread from disk, reducing performance. Consider 300 or 400 for this number; each buffer uses 16 bytes. Use expanded memory if available (/x option).

Version 4

Using Expanded Memory in Version 4
The /x option allows FASTOPEN to take advantage of expanded memory, leaving more of the 640K PC DOS base memory available for your application. You must have an expanded memory driver installed using a DEVICE statement that precedes the

FASTOPEN statement to use this option. (See the entries for XMAEM.SYS and XMA2EMS.SYS and Chapter 12, "Installing a PC DOS System.") A maximum of one EMS page of 16K is available for all buffers. Because directory entry buffers are 35 bytes each, and sector list buffers are 16 bytes each, you can still fit, for example, 200 of each type of buffer in expanded memory.

Also, expanded memory page 254 must be active. If you use XMA2EMS.SYS without specifying pages, this page is active by default. If you specify pages, however, you must specify page 254 as well (see the entry for XMA2EMS.SYS for further discussion).

Examples

Example 1: Under DOS 3.3, specify number of directory entry buffers.

```
fastopen c:=150
```

This statement in the AUTOEXEC.BAT file specifies that enough buffers for 150 directory or file entries will be reserved in memory.

Example 2: Under DOS 3.3, specify directory entry buffers for multiple hard drives.

```
fastopen c:=100 d:=200
```

Example 3: Under DOS 4, specify both directory entry buffers and sector list buffers, in expanded memory.

```
fastopen c:=(200,100) /x
```

This specifies 200 directory entry buffers and 100 sector list buffers. The /x option specifies that expanded memory be used.

Example 4: Under DOS 4, use an INSTALL statement in CONFIG.SYS to activate FASTOPEN.

```
install=c:\dos\fastopen.exe c:=(250, 250)
```

The previous examples used commands that would normally be put in the AUTOEXEC.BAT file, although you could type them at the command prompt as well. Here, the CONFIG.SYS file is used instead, with the INSTALL statement. This takes advantage of new program code in PC DOS 4 that provides for more efficient allocation of memory. Note that you must specify the exact path to the FASTOPEN program on disk. See the entry for INSTALL for further information.

Example 5: Under DOS 4, specify the number of directory entry buffers but omit the number of sector list buffers.

```
fastopen d:=(200,)
```

Here, only the number of directory entry buffers is specified. You must include the comma, however.

Example 6: Under DOS 4, set default buffer values.

```
fastopen c:
```

Because only the drive letter was specified, this is equivalent to typing `fastopen (34,34)`.

Related Chapters Chapter 6–Managing Your Hard Disk
Chapter 11–Customizing Your System

Setting **FCBS**

Compatibility	2.0	2.1	3.0	3.1	3.2	3.3	4.0	OS/2 (DOS mode)	OS/2 (prot.)
			▲	▲	▲	▲	▲	▲	

Use the FCBS setting in your CONFIG.SYS file to specify the number of file control blocks (FCBs) that can be in use at one time while file sharing is loaded.

Format `fcbs=total-blocks,total-reserved`

Sample Use `fcbs=20,5`

Procedure Type `fcbs=` followed by the total number of file control blocks you want to be open at once, a comma, and then the number of these blocks to be protected from being closed when no longer in use.

Related Commands BUFFERS specifies the total number of disk file buffers.

FILES specifies the number of files that can be opened through the use of file handles.

SHARE shares files in a network and sometimes requires that FCBS be set.

DETAILED REFERENCE

Description The older style of PC DOS programming uses file control blocks (FCBs) to hold information needed for managing open files. If you are running older programs that open many files, such as databases, you may need to supply the FCBS setting to ensure that enough space will be reserved for file control information. Programs written for versions of PC DOS starting with 2.0 normally use file handles rather than FCBs to refer to file control information, and therefore, most users will not need an FCBS setting. Note: FCBS only has an effect when file sharing is loaded—usually a network situation. See the SHARE entry.

Comments If you receive error messages referring to lack of file control blocks, try setting the first value after fcbs= to the number specified for files= in your CONFIG.SYS, and the second number to about 1/4 of the first. (If you don't have a FILES setting, it defaults to 8.) The second number in the FCBS specification refers to the number of file control blocks that, once opened, will be "reserved" and kept open even when PC DOS needs to remove some FCBS to make room for newly opened files.

Examples Example 1: Provide for a maximum of 15 file control blocks, of which 4 will be reserved and protected from removal.

```
fcbs=15,4
```

Related Chapters Chapter 5–PC DOS Files
Chapter 6–Managing Your Hard Disk
Chapter 11–Customizing Your System

FDISK

External Command

Compatibility	2.0	2.1	3.0	3.1	3.2	3.3	4.0	OS/2 (DOS mode)	OS/2 (prot.)
	▲	▲	▲	▲	▲	▲	▲	▲	▲

Use the FDISK command to create and manage partitions on a hard disk.

Note: See Chapter 6, "Managing Your Hard Disk," for a step by step approach to creating and managing your disk partitions. This entry presents concise reference information.

Version 4

Partition Your Hard Disk When You Install PC DOS Version 4
When you install DOS 4 on a system whose fixed disk is not yet partitioned, the SELECT program (see Chapter 12, "Installing a PC DOS System") will take you through the steps of partitioning your disk, so in most cases you will not need to run FDISK directly. However, you may need to run FDISK if you do not wish to accept the decisions made by SELECT, or if you want to change existing partitions or logical drive assignments.

Note: If you have installed a previous version of PC DOS and now wish to use partitions larger than 32MB, you must back up your hard disk (see BACKUP), create the new partitions (see Chapter 6, "Managing Your Hard Disk"), and then run SELECT to install DOS 4.

Format `fdisk` starts the menu-driven FDISK program.

Sample Use `fdisk`

Procedure Type `fdisk` to display the menu of operations. The main menu is as follows:

```
                    IBM DOS Version 4.00
                  Fixed Disk Setup Program
              (C)Copyright IBM Corp. 1983, 1988

                       FDISK Options

Current fixed disk drive: 1
```

```
Choose one of the following:

1. Create DOS Partition or Logical DOS Drive
2. Set active partition
3. Delete DOS Partition or Logical DOS Drive
4. Display partition information
5. Select next fixed disk drive
 Enter choice: [1]
```

Option 1 is used to create a new partition or to assign logical drives (areas of disk referred to by a letter such as C or D) for accessing all or part of an existing (or newly created) partition. Option 2 selects the one partition that will be active (the one that will be used to start the system). Option 3 deletes a partition. It will warn you that you will lose access to any data in the deleted partition. It also allows you to remove a logical drive assignment. Option 4 gives you a summary of information about your partitions. Option 5 is displayed only if you have more than one hard disk.

Version 4

Specify Size in Terms of Megabytes or Percentages in Version 4
In DOS 4, partition sizes are displayed in terms of megabytes and percentage of total disk space used. They can be entered in either megabytes or percentages (by following the number with a percent sign). This is much easier than referring to the 35K cylinders.

Related Commands

ASSIGN assigns a drive letter to a different drive, until the end of the session or until the drive is reassigned.

DRIVER.SYS is a driver to assign logical drive letters to floppy drives.

FORMAT prepares a disk or partition for use.

SELECT installs DOS 4 on a hard disk and partitions the disk if it does not contain any PC DOS partitions.

SUBST assigns a drive letter to an existing drive or path, until the end of the session or until the drive is reassigned.

DETAILED REFERENCE

Description

PC DOS considers each hard disk to be made up of one or more *partitions*. A partition consists of a number of cylinders (about 35K each) of disk space. There can be up to 4 partitions on the same hard disk. For example, if you want to run more than one operating system (such as PC DOS and a version of UNIX) from the same hard disk, you will need at least one partition for PC DOS and one for UNIX. Only one partition in the system can be the "active" partition: that is, the one that is used to start the system from the hard disk. Another use for multiple partitions is with the large (40MB, 60MB, or even more) hard disks now available.

Extended Partitions: DOS 3.3 allows you to set up "extended partitions" that are larger than 32MB. You still must have a primary partition, which is restricted to 32MB, so for example, a 40MB hard disk might be divided into a 32MB primary partition and an 8MB extended partition, although a

20MB–20MB division would probably be easier to use. You assign "logical drives" for accessing this space, and PC DOS assigns the familiar drive letters C, D, etc., to them. Each of these logical drives is limited to accessing 32MB. For example, on a 60MB hard disk, you could have a 30MB primary partition referred to as C, a 30MB secondary partition with a logical drive D (20MB), and a logical drive E (10MB).

Version 4

The 32MB Limit in Version 4

If you are running a version of PC DOS prior to 4, the maximum space you can assign to a logical drive is 32MB. PC DOS 4 removes this 32MB limit, although it may still be convenient to have several logical drives for the use of different departments, projects, etc.

Many systems "come out of the box" with a standard DOS partition already installed and formatted on the hard disk.

Note: To reorganize your existing partitions, you must first delete them. This destroys all data in the affected areas, so always make sure you have a current backup first (see BACKUP entry).

Other Operating Systems: OS/2 uses the same partitions as PC DOS. An OS/2 partition can be accessed by DOS, and vice versa. Note, however, that OS/2 1.0 does not recognize logical drives larger than 32MB. For operating systems such as XENIX or UNIX, consult the operating system documentation for instructions on setting up partitions.

Extended Partitions: Extended partitions allow versions of PC DOS starting with 3.3 to use areas of the hard disk beyond 32MB. If your hard disk has more than 32MB, create one or more extended partitions. (This is optional for DOS 4.)

Logical Drives: Each extended partition is referred to in PC DOS commands (and applications programs) by one or more logical drives, which are given letters, such as D or E. These letters are used in the same way as those referring to floppy drives or hard disks that have only one partition. Option 1 of FDISK has a submenu that allows you to assign or change these logical drives. Note that logical drives are also created by installing the DRIVER.SYS driver, but these logical drives are normally used to provide single-drive copying on floppy drives.

Active Partition: The *active* partition is the primary partition from which the system will be booted when it is turned on. If you create a single partition on the disk that uses all available space, it is automatically active. If you decide to create more than one partition, choose option 2 of FDISK and select the partition you wish to make active.

Deleting Partitions: You cannot directly change the size of a partition once it has been allocated. You can, however, select option 3 of FDISK and delete one or more partitions, and then reallocate them as needed. However, *you must back up the data on the affected partitions first*! (See BACKUP entry.) Deleting a partition makes any data on it inaccessible.

Displaying Partition Data: To review the current setup of the current hard disk, select option 4 of FDISK. A list of partitions on the disk will be shown. For each partition the following information is listed:

```
                    Display Partition Information

Current fixed disk drive: 1

Partition Status   Type    Size in Mbytes   Percentage of Disk Used
 C: 1        A    PRI DOS         20        100%

 Total disk space is   20 Mbytes (1 Mbyte = 1048576 bytes)
```

From left to right, the line of information for each partition lists the drive letter (there can be more than one for a given partition, listed on separate lines), partition number, status (A means active), type (PRI DOS means primary PC DOS partition), size in MB, and percentage of total disk space used.

The above format is used by PC DOS 4; earlier versions of FDISK show partitions in terms of the starting and ending cylinders and require sizes to be entered in cylinders.

Select next fixed-disk drive: If you have more than one hard disk drive, you can select this option of FDISK to work with partitions on the next hard drive.

Comments All partitions must be formatted before they can actually be used. See FORMAT. The usual sequence in setting up a new system with PC DOS is to run FDISK to establish the primary PC DOS and any other partitions, and then run FORMAT to prepare the partitions for use. As noted earlier, SELECT can be used under PC DOS 4 to allocate and format default partitions automatically. FDISK will not work properly with substitute drive letters.

Examples Because FDISK is menu-driven, no listing of examples is given.

Related Chapters Chapter 6–Managing Your Hard Disk
Chapter 12–Installing a PC DOS System

Setting

FILES

Compatibility	2.0	2.1	3.0	3.1	3.2	3.3	4.0	OS/2 (DOS mode)	OS/2 (prot.)
	▲	▲	▲	▲	▲	▲	▲		

Use the FILES setting in your CONFIG.SYS file to specify the total number of files that can be open at one time.

Format `files=max-number`

Sample Use `files=12`

Procedure In your CONFIG.SYS file, type a statement beginning with `files=`. Follow it with the maximum number of files to be open at one time. This number must be between 8 and 255. The default value, if there is no FILES setting (or if you accept the default in the SELECT program), is 8.

Related Commands BUFFERS sets up buffers for file information.

FASTOPEN stores directory information in memory.

FCBS sets the maximum number of file control blocks.

SHARE supports file sharing on a network.

DETAILED REFERENCE

Explanation Most modern PC DOS programs access files through data structures called file handles. (Some older programs require direct access to FCBs or file control blocks. The FILES setting has no effect on these file operations. See the FCBS entry to learn how to increase the number of such files that can be accommodated.)

The system preassigns five file handles (standard input, the keyboard; standard output, the video display; standard error; standard printer; and standard auxiliary serial device). With the default of 8 file handles, this allows only 3 more files to be opened simultaneously by all programs currently active. (Though PC DOS is not a multitasking system, you can have a "background" program, such as a print spooler, or another memory-resident program, such as SideKick, opening additional files. Especially if the main application opens several files at once (as do many database programs, for example), you will get a `Too many open files` error. You can fix this by using a FILES setting with a larger number of files.)

Comments Each file handle for which space is reserved uses an additional 64 bytes of memory. If memory is tight, experiment to find the smallest number that allows your applications to run. If memory is not very tight, files=20 is recommended.

Note: In addition to the limit on total files open for all programs, there is also a limit of 20 open files per program (65,534 if "extended file handles" are used). Thus, the lower of the numbers specified by FILES and 20 (or 65,534) is the maximum number of files any one program can use.

Example Example 1: Allow up to 40 files to be open at one time.

```
files=40
```

The maximum number of files that can be used by any one program is now 20 (unless extended FCBs are used), but the maximum for all programs, including memory-resident programs, is 40.

Related Chapters Chapter 5—PC DOS Files
Chapter 11–Customizing Your System

External Command

FIND

Compatibility	2.0	2.1	3.0	3.1	3.2	3.3	4.0	OS/2 (DOS mode)	OS/2 (prot.)
	▲	▲	▲	▲	▲	▲	▲	▲	▲

Use the FIND command to display lines in a file that contain a specified string.

Format `find options "string" file name(s)`

Options */c* displays the count (total) of lines that contain the specified string, or if the */v* is also used, displays the count of lines that do not contain the string.

/n displays each matching line preceded by a number indicating its position in the file, with the first line being line 1. If used with */v*, lines not containing the specified string are displayed instead, preceded by their line numbers.

/v specifies that only lines not containing the specified string are considered to be matches and displayed.

Sample Use

```
find /c "San Francisco"
c:\personl\address
```

Procedure After typing `find` and the appropriate options, type the string (in double quotes) that you wish to search for. Finally, type one or more names of files that you want to search for the string. Wildcards (* and ?) may not be used (but see Example 7). If the file is not in the current directory, supply the complete path name. (See Chapter 6, "Managing Your Hard Disk," for a discussion of path names.)

Related Commands TYPE displays all lines in a file.

COMP compares files and shows differences.

DISKCOMP compares the contents of two disks.

DETAILED REFERENCE

Explanation The FIND command is useful for searching one or more files for a specific string of data. Remember to surround the string with double quotes; use two double quotes to represent a single double quote in the string; that is, """hello""" specifies the string "hello". The string can contain spaces, but it will not be matched if it is split between two lines in the file. FIND is case-sensitive; that is, the command `find "mary" address` will not find Mary. FIND has no concept of "words"; that is, a search for `program` will also find programming and programmer.

By using the /n option, you can also see the relative line number of each matching line. This can be handy because you can load the file into an editor or word processor and tell it to move the cursor to the specified line.

FIND can be combined with other PC DOS commands to create useful batch files, some examples of which follow. The main weakness of FIND is that it cannot be used to search recursively (searching through all the files in a directory, then through the files in the subdirectories, and so on), nor does it show the context (nearby lines) of lines that contain the specified string. However FIND could be used for very simple database chores involving lists of names, addresses, and phone numbers, as long as all the information about each person can be put on one line.

Examples These examples use the following two files:

```
C:\>type phones1
James Johnson 415 976-9189
Betty Lou          202 433-1567
Richard Smith 415 929-1877
Mark Morrison 408 546-1496
Mary Davis        707 911-2135
Agnes McCarthy 415 533-9658

C:\>type phones2
Lazarus Short   212 577-1910
Mabel Pleasance 415 411-7656
Nifty Computers 415 678-1134
Fernando Juarez 408 367-1345
James Carpenter 415 466-7891
```

Example 1: Find Betty Lou in the PHONES1 file.

```
C:\>find "Betty Lou" c:\personal\phones1
---------- C:\PERSONAL\PHONES1
Betty Lou        202 433-1567
```

Because the file being searched wasn't in the current directory, a path name was given. Notice that FIND prints the name of the file searched.

Example 2: Count the number of lines in a file.

```
C:\PERSONAL>find /c " " phones1

---------- PHONES1: 6
```

This example searches for all lines containing a space and uses the /c option to count them. The assumption is that every line contains at least one space. This could be used to provide a rough line count for normal text files (but not binary files or files with only one word per line).

Example 3: Find people in PHONES2 whose phone numbers are not in the 415 Area Code.

```
C:\PERSONAL>find /v "415 " phones2

---------- PHONES2
Lazarus Short212 577-1910
Fernando Juarez 408 367-1345
```

Here the /v option is used to find all lines that do not contain the string "415 ". The space after the 415 ensures that only area codes, rather than the prefixes or numbers themselves, will be matched.

Example 4: List all the people named James in both PHONES1 and PHONES2.

```
C:\PERSONAL>find "James" phones1 phones2

---------- PHONES1
James Johnson 415 976-9189

---------- PHONES2
James Carpenter 415 466-7891
```

When you search for multiple files, each file is searched separately. (Thus, for example, the /c option gives separate counts for each file.)

Example 5: List all the directories (and only the directories) in the root directory of drive C, in sorted order.

```
C:\>dir c:\ | find "<DIR>" | sort

AGT          <DIR>       6-07-90   2:24a
BINDEXE      <DIR>       5-19-90   2:22p
COM          <DIR>       5-16-90  10:26p
DOS          <DIR>       5-17-90  11:15a
DOSEXE       <DIR>       5-19-90   2:23p
MKS          <DIR>       2-03-90  10:55a
OS2          <DIR>      11-26-90  11:33a
OS2BIB       <DIR>       1-04-90   3:25p
OS2PROGS     <DIR>       5-08-90   3:39p
OS2TOOL      <DIR>       2-05-90  11:14p
PERSONAL     <DIR>       2-18-90  10:25a
PROTEXE      <DIR>       5-19-90   2:22p
SPOOL        <DIR>       1-01-90   5:42p
STARTUP      <DIR>      11-13-90   5:13p
TMP          <DIR>       1-05-90  10:54p
UTILS        <DIR>      11-13-90   5:13p
WINDOWS      <DIR>       5-14-90   8:01p
WP50         <DIR>       1-04-90  12:20p
```

The DIR command is used to generate a directory listing of the root directory of drive C. The pipe (|) directs this output to the FIND command, which searches it for the string "<DIR>", which indicates a directory. The output of FIND (the matching lines) is in turn sent to the SORT command, which sorts them into alphabetical order.

Example 6: Write a batch file that numbers the lines in a file and saves the numbered file to disk.

```
C:\>copy con: numlines.bat
find /n " " %1 > %1.num
^Z
 1 file(s) copied.
C:\>numlines c:\personal\phones1      ←Invoke batch file
C:\>type c:\personal\phones1.num      ←Display results

---------- PHONES1
[1]James Johnson  415 976-9189
[2]Betty Lou      202 433-1567
[3]Richard Smith  415 929-1877
[4]Mark Morrison  408 546-1496
[5]Mary Davis     707 911-2135
[6]Agnes McCarthy 415 533-9658
```

The batch commands search (as in Example 2) for all lines with a blank, but this time the /n option is used to prefix each line with a line number. (The %1 represents the file name typed on the command line when the batch file is run.) The > operator directs the output of the FIND command to a disk file, which is given the same name as that of the file searched, with the .NUM extension added.

Example 7: Write a batch file that allows you to search multiple files and to use wildcards.

```
C:\>copy con: multfind.bat
@echo off
rem finds string in multiple files
rem usage: find "string" files
for %%f in (%2 %3 %4 %5 %6 %7 %8 %9) do find %1 %%f
echo on
^Z
 1 file(s) copied.
C:\>multfind "James" c:\personal\phones?

---------- PHONES1
James Johnson 415 976-9189

---------- PHONES2
James Carpenter 415 466-7891
```

The FIND command by itself does not accept wildcards (? or *) that would allow you to search a group of similar files. You can fix this with a bit of batch programming. The batch file BATFIND.BAT uses a FOR loop to search up to eight different files whose names are given on the command line. The syntax of the FOR loop automatically expands any names with wildcards into a list of matching names (see FOR entry for more details). The parameter %1 takes the first item given on the command line (after the name multfind) and uses it for the string to be matched in the FIND command; each file given, including files matching any wildcards, is searched separately. Note that multfind won't work with options (such as /v), but you could write "custom" versions in which the appropriate option is included in the FIND command.

Related Chapters Chapter 5–PC DOS Files
Chapter 8–Advanced Use of the Command Line
Chapter 10–Batch Files

Internal Command, Batch Command — FOR

Compatibility	2.0	2.1	3.0	3.1	3.2	3.3	4.0	OS/2 (DOS mode)	OS/2 (prot.)
	▲	▲	▲	▲	▲	▲	▲	▲	▲

Use the FOR command interactively or in a batch file to repeat execution of one or more commands.

Format To use interactively, `for %variable in (set) do command`

To use in batch file, `for %%variable in (set) do command`

Sample Use `for %f in (note1 note2) do type %f` (interactive)

`for %%f in (note1 note2) do type %%f` (batch)

Procedure Follow `for` with a variable consisting of a single character preceded by one percent sign (if the command is being typed at the command line) or two percent signs (if the command is part of a batch file). Follow this with the word `in`, and then, in parentheses, the names of files(s) or command-line parameters (such as %1) that you want to be processed. File names can be complete path names and can include wildcards. Next, type the word `do` followed by the command you want to be performed. When you want to refer in the command to the file or parameter that is currently being processed, use the same variable you used following FOR.

Related Commands GOTO transfers control to another line in a batch file.

IF tests a condition in a batch file.

DETAILED REFERENCE

Explanation The FOR command is normally used in batch files, although it can be typed at the command prompt. The FOR command executes the specified command once for each item given in the set in parentheses, substituting the item in the list wherever it appears in the command (Example 1).

In general, FOR is used to apply the same PC DOS command to a series of files or to a group of files matched by a wildcard. When used with a set of command-line parameters (such as %1 %2 %3 %4), it can process multiple files whose names are given on the command line.

Comments Although %%f (for "file") is traditionally used as the variable, any single character will do. You must be consistent about case, however; if you start with %%f, you will not get a correct result if you use %%F in the command part of the statement.

Caution

The FOR Command Has Some Restrictions
There are some limitations to the FOR command. You can only have one command line in the "do" part of the statement. You cannot "nest" one FOR command inside another one. You cannot use the piping (|) or redirection (> or <) operators in a command used with FOR. In a batch file, if you attempt to use a command following a FOR to jump to a label via a GOTO, control will not return to the FOR statement automatically; if you attempt to use another GOTO to get back to the FOR statement, the FOR will start over again with the first matching item, which is not very useful. Nevertheless, FOR is useful for simple repetition of a single command.

Examples **Example 1**: Use an interactive FOR command to display several files.

```
C:\>for %f in (list1 list2 *.txt) do type %f
```

Many PC DOS commands, such as TYPE, accept only one file name on the command line or don't accept wildcards (or have both limitations). You can get around this by using a FOR command to repeat another PC DOS command for each file named, including each file that matches wildcards. In this example, this is equivalent to executing the following separate commands:

```
type list1
type list2
type *.txt    ←This is actually illegal on the command line
```

Because the last item used a wildcard, the FOR command automatically "expands" *.txt and passes the matching files one at a time to the TYPE command, via the variable %f.

Example 2: Use a FOR statement in a batch file to delete several files. The DEL command doesn't accept multiple file names, but you can do it this way:

```
C:\>copy con: wipe.bat
for %%f in (%1 %2 %3 %4 %5 %6 %7 %8 %9) do del %%f
^Z
 1 file(s) copied.
```

Here, the set of values in parentheses represents command-line parameters typed when the batch file is invoked (see Chapter 10, "Batch Files," for an explanation of command-line parameters). The syntax is similar to Example 1, except that here the FOR statement steps through the files typed on the command line, with %1 representing the first name typed, %2 the second, and so on. If any of the names typed include wildcards, all matching names are stepped through automatically. Now, you can type `wipe *.bak letter1 letter3 memo?` and have all of the files (and matching sets of files) deleted; you can use up to nine different names. You can use this technique with other commands such as TYPE, as noted previously.

Related Chapters Chapter 8–Advanced Use of the Command Line
Chapter 10–Batch Files

External Command — FORMAT

Compatibility	2.0	2.1	3.0	3.1	**3.2**	**3.3**	**4.0**	OS/2 (DOS mode)	OS/2 (prot.)
	▲	▲	▲	▲	▲	▲	▲	▲	▲

Use the FORMAT command to prepare a disk or hard disk for use.

Format

```
format drive: options
```

Options

/1 formats a disk for single-sided use (5.25-inch drives only).

/4 formats a 360K disk in a 1.2MB drive. Warning: resulting disk may not be readable in a 360K drive.

/8 formats a 360K disk for 8 sectors/track (actually gives 320K capacity, used with PC DOS versions before 2.0).

/s copies operating system files to the disk: the hidden files IBMBIO.COM and IBMDOS.COM, and COMMAND.COM.

/b formats a disk with the default number of sectors per track of the drive used (9 or 15), reserving space for the system files, but does not copy them to the disk. Designed to allow any PC DOS version of SYS to place the appropriate system files on the disk.

/t:tracks formats disk to hold specified number of tracks. Default is 80, which fits standard 720K and 1.44MB disks, so this isn't usually needed

/n:sectors formats 3.5-inch disk to hold specified number of sectors. Default depends on type of drive in use: 9 for 720K drive, 18 for 1.44MB drive. Normally used to format a disk to less than full capacity.

Note: In DOS 4, if you specify either /n or /t, you must specify both. These options are not allowed for hard disks.

Version 4

Version 4 Lets You Specify Media Capacity

/f:capacity formats a floppy disk to specified capacity. Possible values: 160, 180, 320, 360, 720, 1200, or 1.2, 1440 or 1.44. You can follow the number with K, KB, or M as appropriate, but this is optional. Drive must be capable of handling specified capacity. DOS 4 only.

/v:label specifies volume label to be used for disk. If this option is not used, you are prompted for a label after formatting. In DOS 4, in addition to the label, a volume serial number is automatically generated.

Sample Use

```
format a: /s:9 /v:backup1
```

Procedure Type `format` followed by the letter for the drive in which the disk to be formatted is. Don't specify a hard disk drive unless you actually want to remove all the data on it! Note that you will be warned if you attempt to format a hard disk and will be asked to type its volume label to indicate that you really want to format the disk. Also note that FORMAT ignores drive reassignments. If the disk to be formatted is of the default format for the drive in use (for example, the first floppy drive on an IBM PS/2 Model 50 or higher is a 1.44MB high density drive), you do not need to specify track or sector parameters. To format a disk for a capacity less than the default for the drive in use, specify the number of tracks and sectors as necessary. (See Example 1 and following description section.) To specify a volume label for the disk, use the /v parameter. If this parameter is not specified, you will be prompted for a volume name after formatting is completed.

DOS Shell

The DOS Shell Utility Lets You Format a Disk
While running DOSSHELL, you can format a disk by selecting DOS Utilities under the Main Group on the Start Programs screen. Select the Format option. Note that you will still have to provide the appropriate command-line options if the disk is to be formatted to a capacity different from the maximum drive capacity.

Related Commands LABEL labels (or changes the label) on a formatted disk.

SYS copies system files to a formatted disk.

VOL displays the label of a disk.

FDISK creates or manages hard disk partitions.

DETAILED REFERENCE

Explanation The FORMAT command marks off the appropriate number of tracks and sectors on the physical disk or hard disk platter. It also constructs a FAT (file allocation table) and a file directory. The effect of doing this is to render any existing data on the disk inaccessible by "normal" means; however, if you accidentally format a disk, many commercial, public domain, and shareware products can help you recover the data. If you intend to attempt recovery, however, *do not write any new files to the disk*!

Caution

Use Care When You Use the FORMAT Command on Your Hard Disk
Be sure that a hard disk has a PC DOS partition before you run FORMAT on it. (If in doubt, use FDISK to examine and if necessary, create the partition(s).) If there is no PC DOS partititon, FORMAT will move on to the next hard disk (if present), which can destroy your data.

Drive and Disk Compatibility: To format a disk, you need to know two things: the default capacity of the drive you are using and the designed capacity of the disk itself. See entry for DRIVER.SYS for the relevant figures for capacity, sectors, and tracks for the four common kinds of PC disks.

Make sure you have a disk that is physically able to receive the desired format.

Do not format a 360K disk to 1.2MB or a 720K (usually marked 1MB) disk to 1.44MB. 1.2MB disks are usually marked as "double-sided, quadruple density" and 1.44MB disks are usually marked "DS HD" or "double-sided, high density" or "2MB."

Most AT-type systems have a 1.2MB 5.25-inch floppy drive as drive A. This means that on such a system, you can format a 1.2MB disk with just `format a:`. If you want to format a 360K disk in this drive, you can type `format a: /n:9` (the /t value is 80 by default). You could also use `format a: /4`.

Caution

Some 1.2MB Drives May Not Work Properly with a 360K Disk
Some 1.2MB drives cannot reliably write 360K disks that can be read on 360K drives. Check with the manufacturer or experiment with non-critical data.

PS/2-type systems have a 1.44MB 3.5-inch floppy drive as drive A. On such a system, you can format a 1.44MB disk by typing `format a:`. You can format a 720K capacity disk in the 1.44MB drive by typing `format a: /n:9`. Do not format 1.44MB capacity disks to 720K.

Version 4

Easier Disk Formatting in Version 4
DOS 4 adds the /f option to make it easy to format a variety of disks without having to remember anything about tracks and sectors. Specify /f: followed by the number representing the capacity to which the disk is to be formatted, assuming the drive and media are compatible with the capacity desired. In general, DOS 4 is much "smarter" than earlier versions about recognizing the default capacity of drives and disk. See Example 2.

Making a System Disk: The /s option tells FORMAT to copy the files needed to make the newly formatted disk a bootable PC DOS disk. When you use this option, the system files IBMBIO.COM and IBMDOS.COM should be on the current drive. If they are not, you will be prompted to insert in the current drive a disk with the system files. The file COMMAND.COM should be in the root directory of the current drive or in a location specified by the environmental variable COMSPEC (normally defined by a SET COMSPEC= statement in the CONFIG.SYS file.

Formatting and New Hard Drives: Many hard drives are sold "out of the box" already partitioned and formatted for PC DOS. If this is not the case with your hard drive, you must first run FDISK to set up the desired PC DOS partitions (see FDISK entry and Chapter 6, "Managing Your Hard Disk") and then run FORMAT before you can install PC DOS on the disk.

Tip

Use the LABEL Command to Change a Volume Label
You can change the label given with the FORMAT command without reformatting the disk; use the LABEL command. You may wish to make batch files for the most common combinations of format combinations and give them names such as f720.cmd (for "format a 720K disk"). That way you don't have to worry about typing the wrong options. (In DOS 4, you can use the /f option instead.)

Starting with PC DOS 3.0, the FORMAT command requires that

the Enter key rather than "any key" be pressed. Therefore, for compatibility in batch files, include the Enter (in other words, a Carriage Return or ASCII character 13) rather than a random key in any file used with the FORMAT command.

Exit Codes The FORMAT command sets one of the error codes shown in Table R.8 on exit. These can be tested in a batch file to ensure that the format ran correctly.

Table R.8. ***FORMAT Command Exit Codes***

Value	Meaning
0	Most recent format ran successfully
1-2	Not defined
3	User terminated format by pressing Ctrl-Break
4	Most recent format terminated due to error (see error message displayed)
5	User specified a hard disk and then typed n to abort the format

Examples Example 1: Format a 720K disk in a 1.44MB drive (pre-PC DOS 4).

```
C:\>format a: /n:9
Insert a new diskette in drive A:
and press Enter when ready.
Head 1     Cylinder: 20
```

Note that the /n:9 option was included so that PC DOS would format a 720K disk rather than the default for the drive, 1.44MB. Because both sizes of 3.5-inch formats use 80 tracks, and 80 is the default for /t:, this option did not have to be specified.

After you press Enter, the formatting begins, the numbers for Head: and Cylinder: changing to reflect progress. When formatting has been completed, you receive a message similar to this:

```
730112 bytes total disk space
730112 bytes available on disk
```

Occasionally, bad physical sectors are detected. In this case, you will be told how many bytes were in bad sectors and how many bytes are actually available on the disk. Given today's lower disk prices, it is probably best not to use disks with bad sectors, even though the bad sectors have been "locked out" by PC DOS.

If you did not specify a label with the /v option, you are prompted for a label.

```
Formatting has been completed.
Enter up to 11 characters for the volume label,
or press Enter for no Volume label
                                   ←type label and press Enter or press Enter
Format another diskette (Y/N)?
```

Example 2: Format a 720K 3.5-inch disk under PC DOS 4.

```
C:\>format a: /f:720
Insert new diskette for drive A: and press ENTER
when ready...
                                   ←press Enter
     xx percent of disk formatted.
Format complete

Volume label (11 characters, ENTER for none)?
                                   ←press Enter for no label
    730112 bytes total disk space
    730112 bytes available on disk

         1024 bytes in each allocation unit
       713 allocation units available on disk

Volume Serial Number is 0B06-17C8
```

Note that you could, if you want, specify 720K or 720KB rather than just 720. In any case, you don't have to know anything about tracks or sectors. In DOS 4, the running display shows the percent of the disk that has been formatted, rather than the track and sector currently being formatted. (The percentage here is represented as "xx".) After the formatting is completed, DOS 4 adds some additional information: the size of an "allocation unit" and the number of allocation units available on the disk. An allocation unit (here, 1024 bytes) is the smallest amount of disk space that will be used for a file or an addition to a file. Finally, the system-generated volume serial number (new with DOS 4) is displayed.

Example 3: Make a system disk in drive A.

```
format a: /s /v:dosboot
```

Here the default (high) capacity is being used, so the disk can hold the system files and a complete set of the PC DOS commands and utilities (which will be copied to it later). Formatting proceeds as in Example 1, except that you are also informed that the system has been transferred. The disk summary after formatting also shows the amount of space used by the system files.

Related Chapters

Chapter 6–Managing Your Hard Disk
Chapter 7–All About Floppy Disks

GOTO

Batch Command

Compatibility	2.0	2.1	3.0	3.1	3.2	3.3	4.0	OS/2 (DOS mode)	OS/2 (prot.)
	▲	▲	▲	▲	▲	▲	▲	▲	▲

Use the GOTO command in a batch file to transfer control to the line following the specified label.

Format `goto` *`label`*

Sample Use `goto diskerr`

Procedure This command is used only in batch files. To use GOTO, put a label of up to 8 characters, preceded by a colon, on a line by itself. (See the discussion of labels later in this entry.) Follow the label with lines containing batch commands that you want executed under some specified condition. Elsewhere in the batch file, when you want these commands to be executed, use GOTO followed by the label name (without the colon). Normally you would test the condition with an IF, so that the GOTO is executed only if the test is true. For more information, see the IF entry and the following examples.

Related Commands IF tests conditions in a batch file.

CALL calls another batch file from a batch file.

DETAILED REFERENCE

Description GOTO is a concept familiar to people who have programmed in traditional versions of languages such as BASIC or FORTRAN. When combined with IF, it tests a particular condition and, if the condition is true, jumps to a labeled section of the batch file and executes the commands there.

Labels When the GOTO command is executed, control jumps to the line in the batch file following the label specified in the GOTO command. Although labels longer than 8 characters are allowed, only 8 characters are considered significant. The characters in the label name as used in the GOTO command must match in case those in the label itself; :end and :End are considered to be different. Because a colon is used to begin a label, a label cannot contain an embedded colon. It also cannot contain a period; additionally, versions of PC DOS differ somewhat in what nonalphanumeric characters may be used in labels. For maximum compatibility, always start the label with a letter, make it no longer than 8 characters, and use letters and numbers only.

Comments Modern programming languages have largely dispensed with GOTO in favor of more readable and controllable structures, but it is still necessary and useful for batch files. However, PC DOS starting with version 3.3 also provides the CALL statement, which you can use to perform commands conditionally without jumping around in the batch file (see Example 4).

Examples Example 1: Create an "endless" loop with a GOTO command.

```
C:\>copy con: loop.bat
@echo off
:loop
echo Caught in a loop!
goto loop
^Z
   1 file(s) copied.
C:\>loop
Caught in a loop!
Caught in a loop!
Caught in a loop!    ←Press Ctrl-C to stop
```

This is a classic loop: when the GOTO statement executes, control jumps back to the line following the label `loop`. The GOTO is again executed, sending control back to the label `:loop`, and so on. To "break out" of the loop, press Ctrl-C (or Ctrl-Break). This also shows that the GOTO command isn't very useful without an IF test somewhere.

Example 2: Test a condition with IF and GOTO

```
C:\>copy con: backit.bat
@echo off
if exist %1.bak goto end
copy %1 %1.bak
:end
^Z
 1 file(s) copied.
```

The IF statement checks to see that the file named on the command line exists with an extension of *.BAK. (See the IF entry for a discussion of conditions that can be tested.) If it does, control goes to the label `:end` and the batch file terminates. If the file does not exist, however, the COPY command is executed. Although this illustrates a use of GOTO with a test, you don't really need the GOTO with simple tests. This batch file could be rewritten as

```
@echo off
if not exist %1.bak copy %1 %1.bak
```

You generally need to use GOTO with IF only when there are more than two alternative procedures to follow (here, the procedures are just "copy" or "don't copy") or when several commands are to be executed consecutively if the condition is true.

Example 3: Three choices with IF and GOTO. Here's a better example of the use of GOTO:

```
C:\>copy con: back.bat
@echo off
rem back up data or indexes
if %1==data goto :data
if %1==index goto :index
```

```
rem error
echo usage: back data or back index
goto :end

:data
echo insert data disk in A:
pause
copy *.dat a:
echo data files copied!
goto :end

:index
echo insert index disk in A:
pause
copy *.inx a:
echo index files copied!

:end
^Z
 1 file(s) copied
```

In "real world" batch files, you want to handle errors, such as the user not typing a valid option. Here, the valid ways to call the batch file are BACK DATA to copy the data files to drive A, and BACK INDEX to copy the index files there. The name given by the user on the command line, represented by %1 is checked; if it is "data" or "index," a GOTO sends control to the appropriate label. If neither valid name was specified, control continues into the "error" section, the user is shown the correct format for the command, and then GOTO END sends control to label :END, which is the exit point for the batch file. Notice that this GOTO is absolutely necessary; try removing it, and you will see that control simply continues through the "error" section on into the "data" section, and the data files get copied. In other words, you must prevent control from "falling through" a given section into the section governed by the next label.

Example 4: Use subroutines to clarify GOTO. The sort of batch file seen in Example 3 is commonly used for such tasks as installing new software. Like early BASIC programs, it can get pretty complicated when you have to trace the flow of control through a maze of GOTOs. One way to reduce the complexity is to use IF with a CALL statement to send control to a second batch file. (This statement is available starting with PC DOS 3.3.)

```
C:\>copy con: back.bat
@echo off
rem back up data or indexes
if %1==data goto :data
if %1==index goto :index

rem error
echo usage: back data or back index
goto :end
```

```
:data
call backdata
goto :end
:index
call backindx
:end
^Z
 1 file(s) copied
C:\>copy con: backdata.bat
echo insert data disk in A:
pause
copy *.dat a:
echo data files copied!
^Z
 1 file(s) copied
C:\>copy con: backindx.bat
echo insert index disk in A:
pause
copy *.inx a:
echo index files copied!
^Z
 1 file(s) copied
```

Here, the data and index file processing from the preceding example is "packaged" into two separate batch files. The IF statements go to labels followed by CALL statements that call the appropriate batch files.

On return, control goes to the GOTO :END statement, which sends control to the end of the batch file for exit. The advantage of this is marginal for a short batch file like this one, but if the processing for each choice is extensive, or if there are many choices, this approach makes for much cleaner and easier-to-maintain batch files. The slightly longer time it takes to call a separate batch file is usually not significant.

Note: You might be tempted to simplify further with statements such as `if %1==data call backdata`. The problem with this is that when control returns from the CALL, it eventually falls into the error processing section. If you then put a GOTO END in front of the error section, it is skipped all the time. The problem stems from the fact that you can't have multiple PC DOS commands on the same line.

Related Chapter Chapter 10–Batch Files

GRAFTABL

External Command

Compatibility	2.0	2.1	3.0	3.1	3.2	3.3	4.0	OS/2 (DOS mode)	OS/2 (prot.)
				▲	▲	▲	▲	▲	

Use the GRAFTABL command to enable the display of the extended ASCII character set in graphics mode.

Format `graftabl` *`option`*

Options ? displays the number of current code page and list of options.

/sta displays "status," the number of the code page currently being used. Can also be entered as /status.

page-number loads specified code page; see following.

Sample Use `graftabl 860`

Procedure If you don't remember the valid options, type `graftabl ?` to see the option list and the number of the current code page (if any) (Example 1). To find out which code page (if any) is being used, type `graftabl /sta`. To load the graphics information for the specified code page (and allow its display in graphics mode), type `graftabl` followed by one of the supported codes (you can find out which codes are supported by typing `graftabl ?` (see Example 1).

Related Commands CHCP switches between code pages in OS/2 or DOS mode.

CODEPAGE loads code pages in OS/2 or DOS mode.

COUNTRY specifies table for country-specific information.

DISPLAY.SYS enables code page switching with various graphics adapters.

DETAILED REFERENCE

Description Code pages are character sets that are loaded into memory; they reflect the use of different national languages. (For a complete discussion of code pages and their use, see Chapter 13 "International Language Support.") You initially set code pages with the codepage (or as part of using SELECT with PC DOS 4); and you select the current code page from the available ones with the CHCP command. These settings take care of the use of the code pages in text mode, but PC DOS requires extra support to display the complete (extended ASCII) character set in CGA-compatible graphics mode—that is, modes 4, 5, and 6 of the Color Graphics Adapter (CGA), Enhanced Graphics Adapter (EGA), or Video Graphics Array (VGA). This support is provided by issuing the GRAFTABL command with the appropriate code page number (437 for U.S.). The first time GRAFTABL is invoked, it becomes resident in memory; thus, it is only loaded once per session, although you can change the code page or query the status whenever you like.

Comments This command is only needed if you run applications that display text in graphics mode, and that use extended ASCII characters (those with codes 128 or higher). If you run such applications, it is easiest to put the appropriate GRAFTABL command in your AUTOEXEC.BAT file.

Examples Note: These examples use PC DOS 4. Earlier versions of PC DOS have similar displays with slightly less information. Support for the multilingual code page (850) was added with PC DOS 4.

Example 1: Get a list of options for GRAFTABL.

```
C:\>graftabl ?
Active Code Page: 437

DOS command line parameters supported:

    /STA - Request Status only
    ?    - Display this summary of parameters

    Code Pages available:
    437  - USA Graphic Character Set
    850  - Multi-lingual Graphic Character Set
    860  - Portuguese Graphic Character Set
    863  - Canadian French Graphic Character Set
    865  - Nordic Graphic Character Set
```

This lists the code pages supported by PC DOS 4; earlier versions have somewhat fewer.

Example 2: Load the multilingual code page graphic support.

```
C:\>graftabl 850
Previous Code Page: 437
Active Code Page: 850
```

This system has been configured to use the default code page, 437 (United States). The GRAFTABL command here switches to code page 850, the multilingual code page for international use. For this to work, both code pages must be loaded.

Example 3: Query the current status of GRAFTABL

```
C:\>graftabl /sta
Active Code Page: 850
```

This simply gives the number of the current code page.

Related Chapters Chapter 11–Customizing Your System
Chapter 13–International Language Support

GRAPHICS

External Command

Compatibility	2.0	2.1	3.0	3.1	3.2	3.3	**4.0**	OS/2 (DOS mode)	OS/2 (prot.)
	▲	▲	▲	▲	▲	▲	▲	▲	

Use the GRAPHICS command to give you the capability to print graphics screens by pressing the Print Screen (PrtSc) key.

Format `graphics printer-type profile-file options`

Options */r* prints white on black (as shown on the monitor). The default reverses black and white, which often saves ribbon and printing time when printing screens that contain a significant amount of empty space.

/b, with a color printer and the COLOR4 and COLOR8 printer types, prints the screen's background color. The default is to leave the background blank, which saves ribbon and printing time.

/lcd prints an exact copy of a liquid crystal (LCD) display, such as that on the IBM Convertible. Equivalent to *pb:lcd* (see following).

/pb:type and one of the "printbox" (size of printed image) types:

> *std* prints full sized image; specifies when you want a full size printed image from a computer with a small display, such as the PC Convertible laptop.
>
> *lcd* prints an image from an LCD display using its exact aspect ratio (vertical to horizontal pixel dimensions).

Sample Use `graphics graphicswide /r`

Procedure Type `graphics` followed by the printer type as given in Table R.9. (If the printer type is the default, graphics, and you will be using further options, you may use a comma rather than graphics.) Next, if you will be using a printer profile file other than the default GRAPHICS.PRO in the same directory as GRAPHICS.COM, give the name of your custom profile file, or the full path name if it is in a different directory. Finally, include any options you wish to use to control the manner of printing.

Note: if you usually use the same printer, it is convenient to put the GRAPHICS command in your AUTOEXEC.BAT file.

Table R.9 is for printers supported by PC DOS 4. Some of these printers are not officially supported by earlier PC DOS versions, but should work if downwardly compatible. For non-IBM printers, see whether your printer emulates one or more of the IBM printers listed.

Table R.9. *Graphics Printer Types*

Printer Profile File	Printers
GRAPHICS	For IBM 5152, 4201, 4202 (8.5-inch wide paper), 4207, 4208 (8.5-inch wide paper), 3812, and 5201 printers; the default printer type
GRAPHICSWIDE	For IBM 4202, 4208, and 5201 printers with 13.5-inch wide paper (PC DOS 4 only)

Table R.9. ***(cont.)***

Printer Profile File	Printers
COLOR1	For IBM 5182 with a monochrome screen or for printing monochrome from a color ribbon
COLOR4	For IBM 5182 with RGB (red, green, blue, black) ribbon
COLOR8	For IBM 5182 with YMC (yellow, magenta, cyan, black) ribbon
COMPACT	IBM Personal Computer Compact Printer (not supported by PC DOS 4)
THERMAL	For IBM 5140 (used with PC Convertible)

Related Commands

DEVICE installs device drivers.

MODE controls operation of printers, modems, and other devices.

PRINT sets up a print buffer and queue.

PRINTER.SYS supports code page switching.

SELECT installs a printer (PC DOS 4 only).

DETAILED REFERENCE

Explanation

In PC DOS systems, you can use the Print Screen key at any time to print the contents of a text screen. Additional support is needed for printing graphics screens. The GRAPHICS command installs a memory-resident program that allows you to use the Print Screen key to print a graphics screen that is currently being displayed.

Note: The varying relationship between the height and width of each pixel on the screen (the "aspect ratio") leads to printed images appearing to be "stretched" in height or width compared to their screen counterparts. The new VGA adapter, however, has a 1:1 aspect ratio, and printed VGA images have the same height/width relationship as the corresponding screen image.

Version 4

The GRAPHICS Command Supports EGA and VGA in Version 4

Prior to PC DOS 4, GRAPHICS supported the resolution of the CGA (Color/Graphics Adapter) only: 640 x 200 monochrome or 320 x 200 color. PC DOS 4 adds support for higher resolution images (EGA and VGA). The resolution and colors of the actual printed image are, of course, limited by the capabilities of your printer.

Comments

There is a tradeoff between exact representation of the screen image, printing time, and ribbon wear. For example, if you specify /r, all of the empty space on the screen is printed as black, and if you specify /b with a color printer, the empty space is printed in the background color. This prints an image that more closely matches what you see on the screen, but adds considerably to the time it takes to print the image and uses more ribbon.

Note: For a graphics screen showing black on white text, and for color charts, use the /r option. If you are printing an image containing a mouse pointer, do not move the mouse while printing is taking place, or a streak may be printed.

Constructing Printer Graphics Profiles: If you have a printer not listed in Table R.9 (or not compatible with one of those listed), you must create a file called GRAPHICS.PRO in the same directory as GRAPHICS.COM. (You can use a different file name; in this case, specify the file name in the GRAPHICS statement.) This process is rather technical, because it involves knowing the exact escape sequences used by your printer.

Examples Example 1: Set up for relatively "quick and dirty" graphics printing.

```
graphics
```

This gives you the default printer type GRAPHICS (used for most noncolor printers) and does not print black empty space on the screen. It assumes that you have the file GRAPHICS.PRO in the same directory as GRAPHICS.COM (probably C:\DOS).

Example 2: Set up for exact as possible color printing.

```
graphics color4 /r /b
```

Here, you specify the printer type (a color printer with a red, green, blue, black ribbon). You specify that black and white shown on the monitor will be printed exactly as shown, and that blank areas will be printed in the background color. The accuracy of the colors will depend somewhat on the printer.

Example 3: Use a custom printer setup.

```
graphics , c:\dos\myprint.pro /pb:lcd
```

Here, the default GRAPHICS printer type is indicated with a comma. A custom printer profile file C:\DOS\MYPRINT.PRO is then specified, followed by the printbox option for LCD displays.

Related Chapter Chapter 11–Customizing Your System

IF

Batch Command

Compatibility	2.0	2.1	3.0	3.1	3.2	3.3	4.0	OS/2 (DOS mode)	OS/2 (prot.)
	▲	▲	▲	▲	▲	▲	▲	▲	▲

Use the IF command in a PC DOS batch file to allow conditional execution of commands or other programs.

Format `if` *`condition command`*

Conditions *variable*==*string*; if the environmental variable or command-line parameter matches the string value, executes the specified command. (You could compare a literal string to a value, but that's not very useful.)

exist path name; if the file exists, executes the specified command. The current directory is searched for the command, unless you give a path name. The PATH and APPEND values are not used.

errorlevel number; if the error code returned by the previous command or program is greater than or equal to the specified number, executes the specified command. Normally error level 0 indicates successful execution of the preceding command or program; nonzero indicates some sort of error. Most PC DOS commands do not set errorlevel on error; however, see the appropriate reference entries for details.

not condition; if one of the above conditions is not true, executes the specified command.

Sample Use `if not exist data.bak copy data data.bak`

Procedure In a batch file command, type `if`, followed by a condition to be tested, in one of the formats given above. Next, give a command to be executed if the condition is true (or place `if not` before the condition if the condition is not true). This command can be anything that can be typed at the PC DOS prompt on one command line, including a PC DOS command or some other program to be run. You can also use a GOTO as the command to send control to a label based on the result of the IF test.

Related Commands GOTO transfers control to a labeled section of a batch file.

CALL executes another batch file from a batch file and returns.

DETAILED REFERENCE

Explanation The IF command is used for testing various conditions in a batch file. If the condition is true (or if the condition is false when not was used), the command following the condition is executed. The command can be anything you type on the command line or a GOTO command that transfers execution to a labeled portion of your batch file. (IF can also be used on the command line at the PC DOS prompt, so you can test conditions interactively.) The basic tests you can make are as follows.

Does a variable have a particular value? If, for example, you have an environmental variable called *sorted*, you can specify if %sorted%==yes. Notice that a variable must be surrounded by single percent signs; this notation obtains the value of the variable, which is then compared to the string specified after the double equal sign (yes, in this case). For more information on environmental variables, see Chapter 10, "Batch Files." This form of IF is illustrated in Example 1.

Does a command-line parameter have a particular value? You can also test the parameters that are entered on the command line when your batch file is run. %1 represents the first item on the command line following the batch file name, %2 the next item, and so on, up to %9. %0 represents the command or batch file name itself. (For more information on command-line parameters, see Chapter 10.) Thus, the test `if %1==print` in the command file LIST.BAT tests to see whether the user typed `list print`. See Example 2.

You can also test for a missing command-line parameter.

Either `if "%1"=="" echo not there` or `if (%1)==() echo not there` prints "not there" if nothing but the batch file name was typed on the command line.

Note: This is somewhat quirky and doesn't work with all earlier (pre-DOS 4) versions. If it doesn't work, you get a `@syntax error` message.

Does the specified file exist? The `if exist filename` tests to see whether the file named is in the current directory. If you give a path name, the specified directory is checked for the file. Note that the use of path names with this test is not supported in some earlier DOS versions. Also note that the current PATH, DPATH, and APPEND directories are not searched in this test. See Example 3.

Did the last program execute successfully? The `if errorlevel number` test tests whether certain PC DOS commands or other programs run successfully. The word *certain* is used because operation of this test depends on the preceding program setting the system's errorlevel to 1 or some other nonzero value if the program encountered an error in processing. Most PC DOS commands unfortunately do not set error codes; the FORMAT, REPLACE, BACKUP and RESTORE commands do, however (see Example 4), and more commands and other programs probably will have this capability in future versions of PC DOS. Remember that if `errorlevel number` tests for errorlevel being greater than or equal to number, multiple tests should be arranged so that they test for the highest value first, then the next highest, and so on.

Examples Example 1: Test an environmental variable. This might be used to control a C compiler by specifying the memory model to be used.

```
C:\BATCH>copy con: comp.bat
@echo off
if %model%==small scc
if %model%==medium mcc
if %model%==large lcc
echo %0: invalid model: must be small, medium, or large
^Z
 1 file(s) copied.
```

To test this batch file, create three small batch files called SCC.BAT, MCC.BAT, and LCC.BAT. You can put an ECHO statement in each for debugging purposes. Now, if you type `comp` followed by `small`, `medium`, or `large`, the appropriate batch file will be executed. If none of these options is typed on the command line, the last line (the error message) is executed. (The %0 in error messages is handy for debugging because it prints the name of the batch file itself.) Because executing a batch file from another batch file directly (not using the CALL command) terminates the current batch file, no GOTO is needed here to prevent execution "falling through" to the error message.

Example 2: Test a command-line parameter.

```
C:\BATCH>copy con: makedisk.bat
@echo off if %1==720 goto f720
if %1==144 goto f144
echo %0: must specify 720 (720K) or 144 (144MB)
goto end
:f720 format a: /n:9
goto end
:f144 format a:
:end
^Z
 1 file(s) copied.
```

It's not easy to remember the right set of options to use with certain commands—FORMAT is a good example (although DOS 4 provides an easier to remember set of options). The system user here has one floppy drive, A, so the "custom" format command assumes that this drive will be used. Now, if you type `makedisk 720`, you will make a 720K formatted disk (this assumes a PS/2 3.5-inch drive); if you type `makedisk 144`, you will make a 1.44MB disk. (See FORMAT entry for details on options.) If neither option is entered on the command line, the error message is given.

By the way, you can use a batch file like this to provide extra security against accidentally reformatting your hard disk. Rename the FORMAT command to something like XFORMAT, and change the references in the FORMAT.BAT file to XFORMAT. Now, you (and anyone who uses your system) who types FORMAT can only format disks in drive A!

Example 3: Test for the existence of several files.

```
C:\DBMS>copy con: checkdbs.bat
@echo off
for %%f in (bib.dat bib.inx bib.frm) do if not exist %%f call
missing.bat
^Z
 1 file(s) copied.
```

Here a FOR command and an IF command are combined to check the existence of a group of files. The FOR command executes the IF command three times, once for each file in the parentheses. Thus, the first time the IF command is executed, it tests for `if not exist bib.dat`. If the specified file does not exist in the current directory, its name is displayed by the ECHO statement. Here's what happens if you run this batch file and the files BIN.DAT and BIB.FRM are missing.

```
C:\DBMS>checkdbs
bib.dat missing
bib.frm missing
```

Example 4: Check whether a program ran successfully.

```
C:\DBMS> copy con: datadisk.bat
format a: /f:720
if errorlevel 1 echo %0: Format unsuccessful
^Z
 1 file(s) copied.
```

Here, the FORMAT command is executed, with the /f:720 parameter, available in DOS 4, specifying 720K formatted capacity. FORMAT is one of the PC DOS commands that can return an error code if it does not execute successfully. You can test this command file by leaving drive A empty. Here's what happens:

```
C:\DBMS>datadisk
Insert a new diskette in drive A:    ←Don't put in a disk
and press Enter when ready.
```

First, FORMAT reports a problem.

```
Not ready
Format terminated
Format another (Y/N)?   ←Type n here
```

Once FORMAT exits, the error code is returned to the batch file. Because it is 1, the batch file prints its own error message: `datadisk: format unsuccessful`.

Related Chapter Chapter 10–Batch Files

INSTALL

Setting

Compatibility	2.0	2.1	3.0	3.1	3.2	3.3	4.0	OS/2 (DOS mode)	OS/2 (prot.)
							▲		

In PC DOS 4, use the INSTALL setting in your CONFIG.SYS file rather than the AUTOEXEC.BAT file to load the memory-resident commands FASTOPEN, KEYB, NLSFUNC, or SHARE.

Format `install=`*`path:file.ext options`*

Options Use options as appropriate for the command you are loading. See the entry for specific commands for details.

Sample Use `install=c:\dos\fastopen.exe c:=(50,25)`

Procedure Begin a statement in your CONFIG.SYS file with `install=` followed by the complete path name, file name, and extension of the command or program you are loading. (You don't have to include the path if the file is in the startup directory, but you must always include the extension.) Follow this with any settings or options that you would normally use with the command or program.

To load multiple commands or programs, use a separate INSTALL statement for each.

If you have already placed a statement in your AUTOEXEC.BAT file that runs the program you are installing in CONFIG.SYS, remove the AUTOEXEC.BAT statement (or "comment it out" by placing REM in front of it).

Related Commands

FASTOPEN speeds access to disk file.

KEYB lets you select various keyboard configurations.

NLSFUNC sets up additional information needed for code page support.

SHARE includes PC DOS commands that can be loaded using INSTALL.

DETAILED REFERENCE

Explanation

Some PC DOS commands and other programs are designed to be loaded into memory to provide services that are available "in the background" while you are running your main application. An example is FASTOPEN, which provides buffers containing information about recently used files, speeding up repeated file access. Traditionally, such programs have been loaded by running them from the AUTOEXEC.BAT file. For example, the FASTOPEN example given above could also be accomplished using the following line in the AUTOEXEC.BAT file:

```
fastopen c:=(50,25)
```

With PC DOS 4, a "smarter," more efficient mechanism for loading memory-resident programs has been provided, using a strategy similar to that used for device drivers. By using an INSTALL statement instead of running the program from AUTOEXEC.BAT, you can take advantage of this improvement.

Note: The PC DOS 4 SELECT procedure automatically places the statement install=c:\dos\fastopen.exe c:=(50,25) in your CONFIG.SYS file if you accept the default settings. See the INSTALL entry for an explanation of this command, which improves file access speed.

Comments

INSTALL also appears to work with some other memory-resident programs, such as SideKick. It is unclear, however, what benefits may be gained.

Example

Example 1: Install network file sharing.

```
install=c:\dos\share.exe /f:4096 /l:40
```

This runs the SHARE command, providing 4096 bytes of space for network file control information and 40 file locks. See SHARE for details. Note that we had to include the .EXE extension.

Related Chapters

Chapter 11–Customizing Your System
Chapter 12–Installing a PC DOS System

JOIN

External Command

Compatibility	2.0	2.1	3.0	3.1	3.2	3.3	4.0	OS/2 (DOS mode)	OS/2 (prot.)
				▲	▲	▲	▲	▲	

Use the JOIN command to access files on one drive as though they were in a directory on another drive. This can simplify typing path names and allow easier access to virtual (RAM) disks.

Format

`join` ***`drive directory`*** joins a drive to a directory.

`join` displays the current join assignments.

`join` ***`drive`*** `/d` removes a join.

Option

/d removes a specified join.

Sample Use

```
join b: a:\driveb
```

Procedure

To join a drive to a directory, type `join` followed by the letter of the drive to be joined and a colon. Then, type the name of the directory on another drive to which the first drive is to be joined, using the drive specifier if it is not the current drive (Example 1).

The directory to which the drive is to be joined must be either nonexistent or empty. It must also be at the second level in the file system; that is, it must be an immediate subdirectory of the root directory. To find out which drives and directories are joined, type `join` (Example 3). To remove an existing JOIN, type `join` followed by the letter of the drive to be unjoined and a colon, followed by /d (Example 4).

Related Commands

ASSIGN assigns a different drive to a particular drive letter.

FDISK assigns logical drive letters to partitions.

SUBST uses a drive letter to stand for a directory.

TRUENAME reveals the path to the true location of a file.

DETAILED REFERENCE

Explanation

The JOIN command allows you to treat the files on a drive (such as floppy drive A) as though they belonged to a directory on another drive (such as drive C) This can be useful because it allows you to access files on the other drive with just the file name, with no need to use drive letters or to change the current directory. The usual case is to join the contents of the disk in a floppy drive to a directory on the hard drive.

Once a JOIN is made, the contents of the joined drive (including any directories and subdirectories on the drive) are treated as part of the specified directory. The file system of the joined drive is in effect "grafted onto" the directory (see Figure R.1). Any references to the drive letter of the joined drive are now treated as invalid.

Comments The directory to which you are joining the drive must either be nonexistent (in which case, it is created) or empty. If the directory is created, it is not removed when you terminate the JOIN. You cannot use a network drive for either the directory to be joined or the drive to which it is to be joined. JOIN can be used with a virtual (RAM) drive, however, (see Example 2).

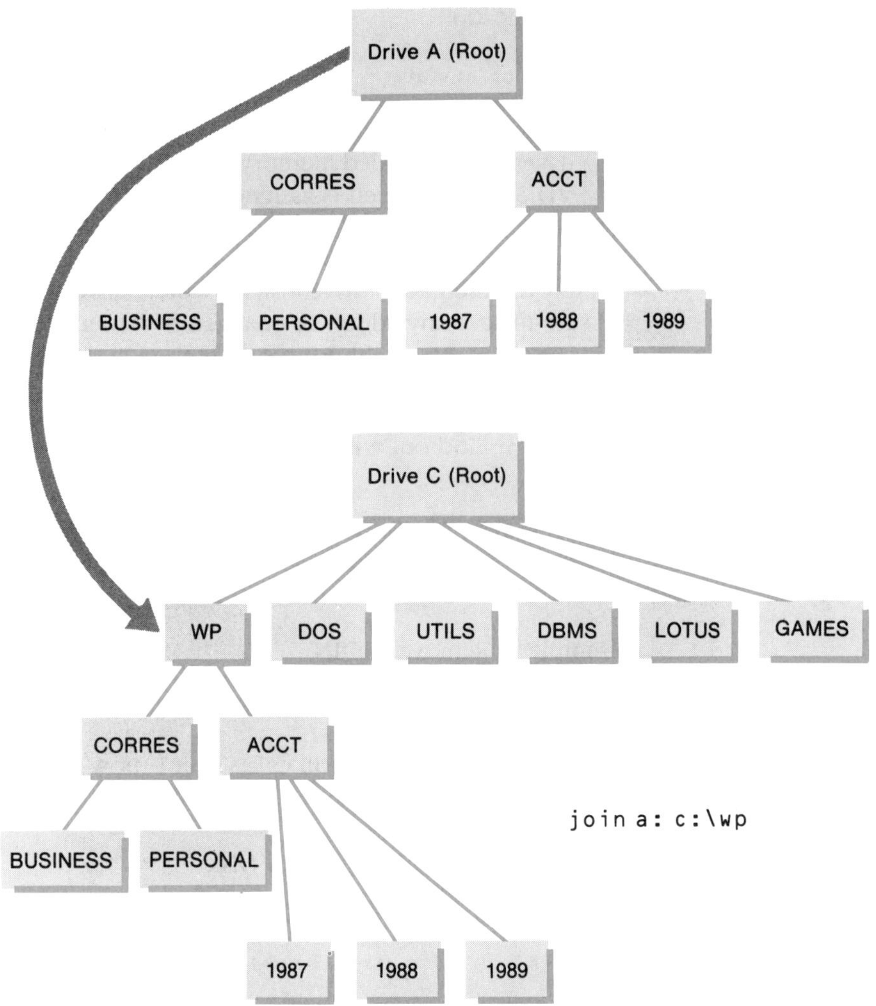

Figure R.1. ***Joining a directory.***

Some utility commands such as FORMAT, BACKUP, RESTORE, LABEL, and PRINT do not work properly with joined drives. This is noted in the Comments or Caution section of the reference entry for the affected commands. Note that JOIN will not work properly with substitute drive letters.

Examples Example 1: JOIN the contents of drive A to a directory on drive C.

```
C:\>join a: c:\ajoin
```

The directory AJOIN will be created if it does not exist. Note that it is a subdirectory of the root directory of drive C. The command DIR AJOIN will now show a directory listing of the contents of drive A. A command such as COPY LETTER A: will now fail (and give an error message) because the drive name A is not accessible while the JOIN is in effect.

Example 2: JOIN a virtual disk so that it can be used as a data directory with your application.

```
C:\>join c: a:\data
```

Here, you have a system with two floppy drives and no hard drive. Because you have some extended memory available, you create a virtual (RAM) drive (see VDISK.SYS), which is assigned the drive letter C. The JOIN command takes this whole disk and makes it equivalent to the DATA directory on drive A. If your program expects to use this directory for data files, it will now happily use the virtual drive instead. Note: As with all virtual disks, you must be sure to save any added or changed data to a "real" disk before you end your session. You could do this by removing the JOIN and then saving to a disk in drive A.

Example 3: Find out which JOINs are in effect.

```
C:\>join
A: => C:\ajoin
```

(If there are no JOINs in effect, nothing is displayed.)

Example 4: Remove a JOIN.

```
C:\>join a: /d
```

The directory C:\AJOIN still exists, but is now empty. The drive name A is again accessible.

Related Chapters Chapter 6–Managing Your Hard Disk
Chapter 7–All About Floppy Disks

KEYB

External Command

Compatibility	2.0	2.1	3.0	3.1	3.2	3.3	**4.0**	OS/2 (DOS mode)	OS/2 (prot.)
			▲	▲	▲	▲	▲	▲	▲

Use the KEYB command to select a keyboard layout other than the default standard U.S. keyboard, such as a French or German keyboard.

Format `keyb` *`layout,code-page,definition-file`* selects a layout by name.

`keyb` *`keyboard-id`* selects a layout by ID number.

`keyb` displays the keyboard status.

Option **Select from a Variety of Keyboard IDs in Version 4**
/id:keyboard-ID (PC DOS 4 only).

Sample Use

```
keyb sv,850
```

Procedure Note: You need to use KEYB only if you want to use a keyboard layout other than the default (U.S.) layout that comes with most PCs, or if you wish to use code page (character set) switching; thus most users will not need this command.

Before using KEYB, you should have installed the code pages you will be using; see Chapter 13, "International Language Support," for a discussion of code pages.

To use KEYB to specify a keyboard layout, follow `keyb` with the two-letter code for the keyboard layout you wish to use (see Table 13.1 in Chapter 13). If you wish to use a code page other than the default one for this keyboard, follow the keyboard ID with a comma and the correct code page number.

If a file other than the default KEYBOARD.SYS in your startup directory is to be used to provide keyboard configuration information, add a comma followed by the complete path name of the keyboard file (Example 1). If you are using PC DOS 4 and an enhanced keyboard that has more than one keyboard ID, and you wish to use the alternate ID, add `/id:` followed by the keyboard ID number (Example 2).

To specify a keyboard layout using the keyboard ID, follow `keyb` with the keyboard ID number (Example 3).

Version 4

For Most Efficient Operation in Version 4
PC DOS 4 users should load the KEYB command via the INSTALL setting in CONFIG.SYS, instead of running KEYB directly from AUTOEXEC.BAT. See Example 2 and the entry for INSTALL. Also, PC DOS 4 users should not use any keyboard definition files from earlier versions of PC DOS.

Note: The PC DOS 4 SELECT command prompts you for a keyboard layout and sets defaults according to your selections.

Related Commands COUNTRY sets date, time, currency, and sorting formats for a specified country.

ANSI provides extended keyboard and screen support.

DISPLAY.SYS provides screen support for code pages.

PRINTER.SYS provides printer support for code pages.

SELECT provides menu-driven selection of keyboard, country code, and so on (PC DOS 4).

DETAILED REFERENCE

Explanation PC DOS provides support for the keyboard layouts and code pages (character sets) needed for a variety of languages. For example, someone typing in

German needs the umlaut character (ü), which is not available on the standard U.S. keyboard. The KEYB command allows you to specify a keyboard layout, and, for some languages, one of two variant keyboard arrangements. The U.S. default keyboard is always available in ROM, and you can always switch back and forth between it and a keyboard you have installed.

Comments If you are using any program that redefines keys (such as ANSI.SYS commands or a memory-resident keyboard macro program), load or run the program after setting up the code pages and running KEYB.

Error Codes KEYB sets the error codes shown in Table R.10. (See chapter 10, "Batch Files," and the IF entry for an explanation of the use of these codes.)

Table R.10. ***KEYB Error Codes***

Value	Meaning
0	Successful execution and termination
1	Invalid language, code page, or syntax
2	Bad or missing keyboard definition file (possibly needs path name)
3	Could not create a keyboard table in resident memory
4	Error in communicating with CON: device
5	Code page requested, has not been prepared (also get an error message)
6	Translation table for selected code page not found in resident keyboard table
7	Incorrect PC DOS version (PC DOS 4 only)

Examples **Example 1**: Specify the German keyboard layout.

```
C:\>keyb gr,437,c:\dos\keyboard.sys
```

This KEYB statement, placed in the AUTOEXEC.BAT file, sets up the German keyboard layout, loads code page 437, and specifies that the keyboard information is to be loaded from the file C:\DOS\KEYBOARD.SYS. (If this file were in the startup directory, typically C:\, you would not have to specify the path and file name.)

Example 2: Specify keyboard layout and variant keyboard type. Use the INSTALL command for efficient loading of the keyboard information.

Version 4

Use INSTALL.COM in Your CONFIG.SYS File in Version 4

```
install=c:\dos\keyb.com fr,437,c:\dos\keyboard.sys/id:189
```

Here, an INSTALL statement is placed in the CONFIG.SYS file (PC DOS 4). Note that with INSTALL, the extension .COM must be included in the command name. When the CONFIG.SYS file is processed at startup, the French keyboard and code page 437 are loaded. The French keyboard has two variant keyboard IDs, 120 and 189. Since 120 is the default, /id:189 specifies the alternate keyboard.

Example 3: Select the primary British keyboard, using the keyboard ID.

```
C:\>keyb 168
```

This is an alternative way to select a keyboard. 168 is the primary keyboard ID for the United Kingdom. This is the equivalent of `keyb uk`.

Example 4: Display the current keyboard status.

```
C:\>keyb
Current keyboard code: US  code page: 437
Current CON: code page: 850
```

This indicates that the default U.S. keyboard is in use, but at some point the code page was switched to the multilingual code page 850.

Related Chapters Chapter 11–Customizing Your System
Chapter 13–International Language Support

External Command — LABEL

Compatibility	2.0	2.1	3.0	3.1	3.2	3.3	4.0	OS/2 (DOS mode)	OS/2 (prot.)
			▲	▲	▲	▲	▲	▲	▲

Use the LABEL command to attach a label to a disk's directory, or to change or delete an existing label. Such electronic disk labels allow you to quickly identify disks (via the DIR command) without removing them to read the physical label.

Format `label` ***`drive:label-text`*** assigns the specified label.

`label` ***`drive`*** shows the current label, if any, and prompts for a new label.

Sample Use `label c:startupdisk`

Procedure Type `label` followed by the drive letter (such as C) for the drive containing the disk to be labeled, if it is other than the current drive. Follow the drive letter immediately (no space) with the text of the label to be assigned to the disk. Labels can be up to 11 characters and can use any character acceptable for a file name. See Example 1.

If you omit the label text, you are shown the label (if any) for the specified disk and are prompted to type the label text. If you do not want to change the label, press Enter (Example 2).

Version 4

Each Disk Has a Volume Serial Number in Version 4
In PC DOS 4, you are also shown the volume serial number that was generated at the time the disk was formatted. You cannot change or delete this number; a new one is generated if you reformat the disk.

Related Commands

DIR shows the disk label with the directory.

CHKDSK shows the disk label with the disk and memory usage report.

FORMAT creates a label and volume number when a disk is formatted.

VOL displays the disk label and volume number (but does not allow you to change either).

DETAILED REFERENCE

Explanation

PC DOS allows you to attach a descriptive label to the directory for each floppy disk or hard disk. Labels are particularly useful for keeping track of which disk you currently have in which drive, and the label can be read by a program to ensure that the correct disk is in the drive.

A label can contain up to 11 characters. The characters that can appear in labels are the same as those that can appear in file names; a label must begin with an alphabetical character. (See Chapters 5,"PC DOS Files,"and 6,"Managing Your Hard Disk,"for file name rules.) Unlike a file name, a directory name has no period and three-letter extension. Do not confuse disk labels with the paper labels that are physically attached to disk jackets, or with the labels used in batch files with the GOTO command.

Comments

Do not use LABEL with disks for which ASSIGN, JOIN, or SUBST commands are in effect or which are in use on a network.

Examples

Example 1: Assign a disk label by specifying it in the command.

```
C:\>label a:startup
```

The label *startup* is assigned to the disk in drive A. This label will now appear when the directory for this disk is displayed.

Example 2: Use the LABEL command interactively.

```
C:\>label a:
Volume in drive A is STARTUP
Volume Serial Number is 3F6A-17CD
Volume label (11 characters, ENTER for none) pcdosboot    ←Type label and
                                                            press Enter
```

The label of the disk in drive C has been changed to *pcdosboot*.

Example 3: Delete a disk label.

```
C:\>label a:
Volume in drive A is PCDOSBOOT
Volume Serial Number is 3F6A-17CD
Volume label (11 characters, ENTER for none)?    ←Press Enter here
Delete current volume label (Y/N)?               ←Type y here
```

First, you press the Enter key when you are asked for a label. You are asked if you want to delete the current label. You do, so you type `y` and the label is deleted. (If you only want to know what the current label is, you type `n` at this point. If all you want is this information, however, it is easier to use the VOL command.)

Related Chapters Chapter 6–Managing Your Hard Disk
Chapter 7–All About Floppy Disks

Setting

LASTDRIVE

Compatibility	2.0	2.1	3.0	3.1	3.2	3.3	4.0	OS/2 (DOS mode)	OS/2 (prot.)
			▲	▲	▲	▲	▲		

Use the LASTDRIVE setting in your CONFIG.SYS file to specify the last drive letter you will be using and, thus, the total number of drives supported by the system. This command is normally needed only when you have a total of more than five physical and RAM drives.

Format `lastdrive=`*`drive-letter`*

Sample Use `lastdrive=g`

Procedure In your CONFIG.SYS file, begin a statement with `lastdrive=`. Follow this with the letter A–Z of the last drive that will be supported on your system. This letter must be at least far enough along in the alphabet to allow for all the physical drives currently installed. Thus, if you have two floppy drives and one hard drive, LASTDRIVE must be set to at least C. (Do not put a colon after the drive letter.) The default, if there is no LASTDRIVE statement, is lastdrive=e.

Related Commands ASSIGN assigns a drive letter to a different drive.

DRIVER.SYS assigns logical drive letters to additional physical drives.

SUBST uses a drive letter to stand for a path.

VDISK.SYS establishes a virtual (RAM) drive.

DETAILED REFERENCE

Explanation PC DOS automatically assigns drive letters to your built-in physical drives. For additional (virtual) or external (physical) drives, you may have to add a `device=driver.sys` statement to your CONFIG.SYS file. The default value lastdrive=e allows you to support five drive letters, which is usually enough for all of your physical drives. You normally need the LASTDRIVE statement only if you wish to use more than five drive letters. This can occur if you use one or more of the following to supplement your physical drive assignments:

virtual disks (RAM drives)

drive letters used with the SUBST command

network drives

Comments Any value you assign to LASTDRIVE must accommodate at least the number of physical drives in your system. If you use a "lower" drive letter than this, the statement will be ignored.

If you receive an `invalid drive specification` error message when attempting to access a drive, you may need to set LASTDRIVE.

Example Example 1: In addition to two floppy drives and two hard drives, allow drive letters for an add-on CD-ROM drive, a RAM drive, and four assignments to be used with the SUBST command.

```
lastdrive=j
```

You need a total of ten drives; there are ten letters available from a to j inclusive.

Related Chapter Chapter 11—Customizing Your System

MD (MKDIR)

Internal Command

Compatibility	2.0	2.1	3.0	3.1	3.2	3.3	4.0	OS/2 (DOS mode)	OS/2 (prot.)
	▲	▲	▲	▲	▲	▲	▲	▲	▲

Use the MD (or MKDIR) command to create a new directory on disk.

Format `md` *`path name`*

Sample Use `md c:\database`

Procedure Type `md` (or the synonym `mkdir`) followed by the path name for the directory you wish to create. The path name must include the drive letter unless the directory to be made is on the current drive. If the directory is to be a subdirectory of an existing directory, use a path name including the existing directory (Example 2). If no path name is specified, the new directory will be created as a subdirectory of the current directory on the current drive.

Related Commands APPEND specifies directories containing program data or overlay files.

CD changes the current directory.

DIR lists the contents of the specified directory.

PATH specifies directories containing executable programs.

RD removes a directory.

TREE displays the directory structure of a disk.

DETAILED REFERENCE

Explanation The MD command is used to create a new directory on disk. By setting up a logically organized group of directories and subdirectories, you can make it much easier to manage the hundreds of files usually found on a hard disk. Note that the root directory has a fixed maximum number of subdirectories (depending on disk format), but in good disk organization, only a few main directories are created from the root directory.

Comments MD will not erase and re-create an existing directory. To remove a directory, first use DEL to remove all of its files, and then use RD to remove the directory.

If the new directory will contain executable programs that you will want to run from anywhere in the file system, add the new directory to your PATH statement.

If the new directory contains data files that will be needed by programs, add it to your APPEND (DOS mode) statements.

Examples Example 1: Create a new subdirectory in the root directory on the hard disk.

```
C:\>md \utils
```

The directory UTILS is created as a subdirectory of the root directory (an initial backslash in a path name specifies the root directory). Note that if the prompt had read C:\>, you would have already been in the root directory, so you could have typed `md utils`.

Example 2: Create a new subdirectory several "branches" down the tree.

```
A:\>md c:\utils\disk\norton
```

Here the current drive is A, so you specify C in the path. A directory for Norton Utilities is created as a subdirectory of the DISK directory, which in turn, is a subdirectory of the UTILS directory, which in turn, is a subdirectory of the root directory of drive C

Related Chapter Chapter 6–Managing Your Hard Disk

MEM

External Command

Compatibility	2.0	2.1	3.0	3.1	3.2	3.3	4.0	OS/2 (DOS mode)	OS/2 (prot.)
							▲		

Version 4

Use the MEM command to obtain information about your current usage of regular PC DOS memory, extended memory, and expanded memory. Optionally, obtain debugging information showing the location of applications programs, device drivers, other memory-resident programs, and system data areas.

Format `mem option`

Options */program* obtains locations of programs as well as memory usage statistics.

/debug obtains the most complete listing of program and memory usage information.

MEM

Sample Use `mem /program`

Procedure To find out the total amount of regular, expanded, and extended memory in your system and the amount of each kind of memory currently available, type `mem`. To obtain this information plus a listing showing the locations of all programs in memory, type `mem /program`. To obtain a listing that includes all of the preceding information plus a listing of system device drivers and data areas, type `mem /debug`.

Related Commands CHKDSK obtains disk usage statistics, plus usage of regular memory.

XMAEM.SYS is a device driver to allow 386-based systems to use the XMA2EMS.SYS driver.

XMA2EMS.SYS is a device driver for IBM expanded memory boards.

DETAILED REFERENCE

Explanation This new command, introduced with PC DOS 4, responds to the need of modern PC users to keep track of not only the 640K of regular PC DOS memory, but of extended and expanded memory as well. Previously, only the CHKDSK command offered memory usage statistics, and these were limited to conventional PC DOS memory.

The MEM command, used without any options, gives a quick summary of how much of each kind of memory you have installed in your system and how much of each is still available. This can help you judge what combination of regular programs, memory-resident programs, and device drivers will fit in your available memory and still leave enough room for your main application program and its data.

The MEM /PROGRAM command, in addition to the memory usage statistics, gives a list of all the programs and device drivers in your system, including those PC DOS settings (such as FASTOPEN) and commands (such as PRINT and MODE) that load memory-resident code. (You may discover that you are routinely loading things from your CONFIG.SYS and AUTOEXEC.BAT files that you no longer need, and you can remove them and free some memory.)

The MEM /DEBUG command provides the most complete listing, including all the information provided by the /program option plus the locations of the built-in system devices and data areas. This is most useful for programmers developing memory-resident programs, because the information can help pinpoint memory allocation areas and conflicts between programs contending for the same area of memory.

Comments Extended memory is memory that is located above the 1MB address boundary. On IBM PS/2s that come with 1MB on the motherboard, 640K of the memory is regular PC DOS memory, and the other 360K, although physically contiguous, is addressed as though it started at 1MB. It is called "extended" because it addresses using an extension of the same segment/offset addressing used for regular memory. Expanded memory (EMS) is addressed by swapping portions ("pages") in and out of a "window" in conventional memory. Any expanded memory only shows up in the mem report if you have a properly installed expanded memory driver, such as the XMA2EMS.SYS driver included with PC DOS 4, or, for non-IBM expanded memory boards, a third-party driver that fully supports the LIM 4 specification.

Examples Example 1: Obtain a basic memory usage report.

```
C:\>mem
    655360 bytes total memory
    654336 bytes available
    446096 largest executable program size

   2097152 bytes total EMS memory
   2097152 bytes free EMS memory

    393216 bytes total extended memory
    262144 bytes available extended memory
```

This report is for an IBM PS/2 Model 50 with a total of 640K of onboard PC DOS memory, 360K of extended memory, and a 2MB expanded memory card. None of the expanded memory is currently in use; about 128K of the extended memory is being used by the disk cache.

Example 2: Obtain a memory usage summary and a list of programs currently in memory.

```
C:\>mem /program
  Address      Name         Size       Type
  -------      --------     ------     ------
  000000                    000400     Interrupt Vector
  000400                    000100     ROM Communication Area
  000500                    000200     DOS Communication Area
  000700       IBMBIO       002470     System Program
  002B70       IBMDOS       0088A0     System Program
  00B410       IBMBIO       00ADB0     System Data
                 EMM        0029C0      DEVICE=
                 DASDDRVR   0001E0      DEVICE=

                 IBMCACHE   003020      DEVICE=
                 MOUSE      002660      DEVICE=
                 ANSI       001190      DEVICE=
                            000380      FILES=
                            000100      FCBS=
                            000650      BUFFERS=
                            0001C0      LASTDRIVE=
                            000CD0      STACKS=
  0161D0       SKN          000090     Environment
  016270       IBMDOS       000020     -- Free --
  0162A0       FASTOPEN     002720     Program
  0189D0       COMMAND      001640     Program
  01A020       COMMAND      000100     Environment
  01A130       APPEND       001E20     Program
```

```
01BF60      MEM         000090     Environment
01C000      GRAPHICS    0014A0     Program
01D4B0      SKN         0141E0     Program
0316A0      PRINT       0016B0     Program
032D60      MEM         012F60     Program
045CD0      IBMDOS      059F20     -- Free --

  655360 bytes total memory
  654336 bytes available
  446096 largest executable program size
 2097152 bytes total EMS memory
 2097152 bytes free EMS memory
  393216 bytes total extended memory
  262144 bytes available extended memory
```

Here the report begins with a list of programs and their locations in memory (hexadecimal addresses). The first programs in low memory are the PC DOS "kernel" programs: IBMBIO and IBMDOS. IBMBIO's system data area includes a variety of device drivers (such as EMM, which happens to be the expanded memory driver for an Everex memory board), and data areas used for a number of CONFIG.SYS settings, including FILES, BUFFERS, and FCBS. Next, come a number of PC DOS commands that are residing in portions of memory: COMMAND (the command processor resident portion), APPEND, MEM (the currently running command), PRINT, and GRAPHICS. SKN is a version of the ubiquitous SideKick program. Notice that some commands (such as MEM) have separate areas for the program itself and for data used by the program.

The program listing is followed by the same memory usage summary given by the plain vanilla MEM command.

Example 3: Get a complete listing for debugging.

```
C:\>mem /debug
  Address      Name         Size       Type
  -------      --------     ------     ------

  000000                    000400     Interrupt Vector
  000400                    000100     ROM Communication Area
  000500                    000200     DOS Communication Area
  000700      IBMBIO        002470     System Program
                  CON                    System Device Driver
                  AUX                    System Device Driver
                  PRN                    System Device Driver
                  CLOCK$                 System Device Driver
                  A: - C:                System Device Driver
                  COM1                   System Device Driver
                  LPT1                   System Device Driver
                  LPT2                   System Device Driver
                  LPT3                   System Device Driver
                  COM2                   System Device Driver
                  COM3                   System Device Driver
```

```
                COM4                      System Device Driver
002B70      IBMDOS          0088A0      System Program
00B410      IBMBIO          00ADB0      System Data
                EMM         0029C0       DEVICE=
                DASDDRVR    0001E0       DEVICE=
                IBMCACHE    003020       DEVICE=
                MOUSE       002660       DEVICE=
                ANSI        001190       DEVICE=
                            000380       FILES=
                            000100       FCBS=
                            000650       BUFFERS=
                            0001C0       LASTDRIVE=
                            000CD0       STACKS=
0161D0      SKN             000090      Environment
016270      IBMDOS          000020      -- Free --
0162A0      FASTOPEN        002720      Program
0189D0      COMMAND         001640      Program
01A020      COMMAND         000100      Environment
01A130      APPEND          001E20      Program
01BF60      MEM             000090      Environment
01C000      GRAPHICS        0014A0      Program
01D4B0      SKN             0141E0      Program
0316A0      PRINT           0016B0      Program
032D60      MEM             012F60      Program
045CD0      IBMDOS          059F20      -- Free --

  655360 bytes total memory
  654336 bytes available
  446096 largest executable program size
Handle      EMS Name       Size
-------     --------      ------
    0                     000000
 2097152 bytes total EMS memory
 2097152 bytes free EMS memory
  393216 bytes total extended memory
  262144 bytes available extended memory
```

This listing is quite similar to that provided by mem /program; the main difference is that it includes the drivers for the built-in system devices (such as con: and prn:), and, as part of the memory usage summary at the end, provides a list of expanded memory handles currently in use (none in this case).

Related Chapter Chapter 11–Customizing Your System

MODE (Intro.)

External Command

Compatibility	2.0	2.1	3.0	3.1	3.2	3.3	4.0	OS/2 (DOS mode)	OS/2 (prot.)
	▲	▲	▲	▲	▲	▲	▲	▲	▲

Use the MODE command to specify the operation modes for devices, including parallel and serial ports, the video display, and the keyboard.

Note: Because of the extensive features provided by the MODE command, separate reference entries are provided for each of its major uses. Each entry contains its own sections for format, procedure, examples, related commands, and so on. The entries are

MODE (Introduction) is an overall discussion of MODE command (this entry).

MODE (Printer) discusses the use of MODE to specify parallel printer operation. This also includes redirecting parallel printer output to a serial printer.

MODE (Serial Communications) discusses the use of MODE to control the operation of the serial (asynchronous communication) ports.

MODE (Console) discusses the use of MODE for setting video display format and keyboard response rate.

MODE (Code Pages) discusses the use of MODE for preparing or changing code pages (PC DOS 3.3 and later).

Options The MODE command does not use option switches preceded by slashes (/), but rather device names and numbers separated by commas: for example, mode lpt1:132,8 means "set the printer to print 132 columns per line, 8 lines per inch."

Version 4

Syntax Allows More-Meaningful Statements in Version 4

PC DOS 4, in addition to adding a few new features to the MODE command, also provides an alternative syntax for specifying options. Prior to PC DOS 4, numeric options could only be entered as single numbers separated by commas, as shown in the Options section of this entry. Under PC DOS 4, you can use named specifications: for example, mode lpt1: cols=128 lines=8. Although this involves more typing, it is much clearer when you look back to see what you have done.

Note: This new syntax does not replace the previous one; rather it supplements it. This means that most of the old MODE commands in your AUTOEXEC.BAT file or elsewhere will continue to work, and you can continue to use the older syntax if you wish.

Sample Use A sample use for each major application of the MODE command is given in the appropriate MODE reference section.

Procedure To use the MODE command, read this entry for general information. Then, read the MODE reference entry for the kind of operation you need to control: parallel printer, serial port, display/keyboard, or code page switching.

If your MODE setting is to be used in every session, place the MODE command in your AUTOEXEC.BAT file so that it will be performed automatically at startup. You can also issue MODE commands at the command prompt as needed or place them in batch files for easier use.

Version 4

Use the MODE Command to Report Which Devices It Controls in Version 4
In PC DOS 4, you can obtain a listing of the status of all devices that `mode` supports by typing `mode`.

```
C:\>mode

Status for device LPT1:
-----------------------
LPT1: not rerouted
RETRY=NONE
Code page operation not supported on this device

Status for device LPT2:
-----------------------
LPT2: not rerouted

Status for device LPT3:
-----------------------
LPT3: not rerouted

Status for device CON:
----------------------
COLUMNS=80
LINES=25
Code page operation not supported on this device
```

You can also get the status of a particular port by typing `mode`, the port name, and optionally `/sta` or `/status`. (The status option, needed only with parallel ports, prevents MODE from removing any redirections affecting the specified port.) For example: mode lpt1: /sta displays the status of just the first parallel printer port, and, if its output is currently redirected to a serial port, does not remove this redirection.

Related Commands Because the majority of PC DOS commands are related in some way to one or more of the functions of the MODE command, the related commands for each major function of the MODE command are given in the appropriate MODE reference section.

DETAILED REFERENCE

Explanation The MODE command is a sort of "catchall" utility. As new devices became available (such as new video displays) or new capabilities were desired, additional features were added to the MODE command. Because the syntax and specification for each of the uses of MODE is different, it is useful to pretend that each of the major uses of MODE constitutes a separate command. That is why a separate reference entry is provided for each of the major uses of this command.

Examples A set of detailed examples for each major use of MODE is given in the appropriate MODE reference section.

Related Chapters Chapter 11–Customizing Your System
Chapter 13–International Language Support

MODE (Printer Control)

External Command

Compatibility	2.0	2.1	3.0	3.1	3.2	3.3	**4.0**	OS/2 (DOS mode)	OS/2 (prot.)
	▲	▲	▲	▲	▲	▲	▲	▲	▲

Use the printer control features of the MODE command to control the number of characters per line, the number of lines per inch, and the type of retry processing for a parallel printer. You can also redirect parallel printer output to a serial port.

Format

`mode` *`parallel port chars/line,lines/inch`*`,p` (pre-PC DOS 4)
`mode` *`parallel port=serial port`* redirects output from a parallel port to a specified serial port.

Version 4

Uses of the MODE Command Are Expanded in Version 4
`mode` *`parallel port`* displays status of parallel printer port (PC DOS 4 only).
`mode` *`parallel port`* `chars=`*`chars/line`* `lines=`*`lines/inch`* `retry=`*`retry-spec`* (PC DOS 4)
`mode` *`parallel port`* `/sta` (or `/status`) displays parallel port status without removing any redirection (PC DOS 4 only).

Sample Use

```
mode lpt2:132,8,p
```

Version 4

New Syntax Format for the MODE Command in Version 4
`mode lpt2: cols=132 lines=8 retry=r` (PC DOS 4)

Procedure Before you issue a MODE command involving a printer, make sure the printer is switched on and is "on line" rather than set to a local mode. With versions of PC DOS prior to 4, type `mode` followed by the name of the parallel port to be used; the colon following the port name is optional. Follow this with the number of characters per line (80 or 132) and number of lines per inch (6 or 8), separated by commas (Example 1). If you wish the printer to be retried when it is busy, add a comma followed by `p`. If you wish to omit any value and accept its default, put an extra comma in place of the value (Example 2).

Version 4

Syntax Changes in Version 4
You can use this same syntax in PC DOS 4. However, you can also type `mode` and the port name, followed by `cols=` and the number of columns per line; `lines=` and the number of lines per inch; and `retry=` followed by `e` (return error), `b` (return busy when port is

busy), or `r` (retry when busy). See Example 3 and later discussion. These specifications can be entered in any order; omitting a specification sets it at the default or the last setting it received in the current session.

To redirect output from a parallel port to a serial port, type `mode` followed by the name of the parallel port to be redirected, an equal sign, and then the name of the serial port to be used for output.

Note: Before doing this, you must have used a MODE command to initialize the serial port. See the MODE entry for serial devices/printers.

Three parallel ports are supported by the MODE command: lpt1:, lpt2:, and lpt3:. (prn: is a synonym for lpt1:). Four serial ports are supported for redirected output: com1:, com2:, com3:, and com4:, (aux: is a synonym for com1:).

To display the current status of a parallel or serial port, type `mode` followed by the port name (Example 5). You can also type just `mode` to get a report on the status of all supported devices.

Note: Typing `mode` followed by a port name also removes any redirection involving the specified port.

Version 4

Use the */sta* Option to Get a Report in Version 4

In PC DOS 4, you can type `mode` followed by a port name and `/sta` or `/status`. This reports the port status without removing any existing redirection.

Related Commands

AUTOEXEC.BAT is a file for MODE commands that are to be in effect for every session.

DEVICE installs drivers for printers and other devices.

GRAPHICS prints graphics screens.

NLSFUNC provides extended country information for code-page switching.

PRINT prints files in background.

PRINTER.SYS is a device driver to support code page switching on IBM printers.

DETAILED REFERENCE

Explanation

Most application programs, especially word processors and publishing programs, come with programs called printer drivers that control the printer from within the application. If you use only such applications, you will have no need to use MODE, except perhaps to redirect output from a parallel printer to a serial printer. (The documentation for your application should specify whether this is necessary; if you select a serial printer from your application and get no output, try redirection.)

The MODE command provides minimal printer control for print operations using PC DOS commands such as PRINT or through redirection of command output to the printer (such as type file1 > lpt1:).

Printer Retries: MODE also provides some control over how programs interact with the printer. Specifically, under versions of PC DOS prior to 4, you can use the p specification to try the printer again if it is busy and the printing operation has "timed out."

Specifying some form of retry makes a small part of the MODE command resident, using about 500 bytes of memory.

Version 4

Use the RETRY Specification in Version 4, If Your Application Program Has Trouble Printing

PC DOS 4 provides additional printer control specifications. The specification retry=b provides operation compatible with the p specification described previously, and replaces it. (Though the specification p is still accepted, you should use b for compatibility with future versions of PC DOS.) When this specification has been set, PC DOS returns a "busy" code when the printer is busy and provides retries.

The new specification retry=r tells the driver that the printer is ready and lets MODE handle the actual retries. With most applications, you should assume that the driver wants to handle the retries itself and add this specification only if your application's documentation mentions it or if you have problems, such as all of the data not being printed.

The specification retry=e returns an error code to the program when the printer is busy. This may be necessary if the printer's speed (and available printer buffer memory) is not enough to keep up with the rate at which characters are being sent to the printer; it is often needed in background processing or network situations.

Comments The chars (characters/line) setting does not "word wrap" (moving words that don't fit on a line to the next line). It merely chops the line off at that position and prints the rest on the next line. The use of MODE does not provide any of the print enhancements (such as boldface, underline, or fonts) provided by application printer drivers.

Examples Note: The actual messages shown here are from PC DOS 4. Messages from earlier versions of PC DOS are very similar.

Example 1: Set up parallel printer operation (pre-PC DOS 4).

```
C:\>mode lpt1: 132,8,p
LPT1: not rerouted


LPT1: set for 132


Printer lines per inch set


Infinite retry on parallel printer time-out
```

MODE says that output was not rerouted (such as to a serial port). It confirms that the number of columns and lines have been set. The "infinite retry" was specified with the p specification; it means that if the printer is busy, MODE retries it continuously.

Example 2: Set up parallel printer operation; use a default selection (pre-PC DOS 4).

```
C:\>mode lpt2: ,8,p
LPT2: not rerouted

Printer lines per inch set

Infinite retry on parallel printer time-out
```

Here, the second parallel port, lpt2:, is being set. The first comma stands for the missing columns/line specification. The lines/inch are set to 8, and the infinite retry is set. Columns/line retains its default value (80) unless some other value was set in a preceding MODE command.

Example 3: Set up parallel printer operation for a network (PC DOS 4).

Version 4

Using the RETRY Specification in Version 4

```
C:\>mode lpt1: cols=132 lines=8 retry=e

LPT1: not rerouted

LPT1: set for 132

Printer lines per inch set

Infinite retry on parallel printer time-out
```

←*See following*

Here, the new PC DOS 4 syntax is used. Due to an apparent bug, the `Infinite retry` message is printed regardless of the actual retry setting. However, if you use the command MODE LPT1: (see Example 5), the correct status, `No retry on parallel printer time-out`, is reported.

Example 4: Redirect printer output to a serial port.

```
C:\>mode lpt1:=com1:
LPT1: redirected to COM1:
```

(If you get a syntax error, try removing the colons; there may be a bug in early versions of PC DOS 4.) To remove this redirection, you can type `mode lpt1:`

Example 5: Display the status of the first parallel printer port.

```
C:\>mode lpt1:
LPT1: not rerouted

No retry on parallel printer time-out
```

Note that if you have a redirection in effect for lpt1: and wish to restore it, you have to reissue the redirection command now: for example, mode lpt1:=com1:

Related Chapter Chapter 11–Customizing Your System

MODE (Serial Communications/Printer)

External Command

Compatibility	2.0	2.1	3.0	3.1	3.2	3.3	**4.0**	OS/2 (DOS mode)	OS/2 (prot.)
	▲	▲	▲	▲	▲	▲	▲	▲	▲

Use the serial communications features of the MODE command to control the operation of modems, printers, or other devices connected to a serial (asynchronous communications) port.

Format `mode` *`serial port baud-rate, parity, databits, stopbits, pause, retry`* sets serial port operation (pre-PC DOS 4).

Version 4

The MODE Command Offers Expanded Control over Serial Ports in Version 4

`mode` *`serial port`* `baud=`*`baud-rate`* `data=`*`databits`* `stop=`*`stopbits`* `parity=`*`parity value`* `retry=`*`retry-type`*

`mode com` *`port-number:`* sets serial port operations (optional PC DOS 4 syntax).

`mode` *`serial port`* displays status of serial port (PC DOS 4 only).

Sample Use `mode com1:1200,e,8,1,p` (pre-PC DOS 4)

Version 4

Changes in Syntax Format in Version 4

`mode com1: baud=1200 data=8 stop=1 parity=e retry=r` (optional PC DOS 4 syntax)

Procedure To specify the operation of a serial port, type `mode` followed by the serial port name. Valid names are com1:, com2:, com3:, com4:, or aux: (the latter is a synonym for com1:). Colons following port names are optional.

Follow this with a series of numbers representing baud rate: 110, 150, 300, 600, 1200, 2400, 4800, 9600, or 19200. (19200 baud may not be supported on all machines.) When entering the baud rate, you may use only the first two digits if you wish. Follow the baud rate with the number of data bits (5, 6, 7, or 8); the number of stop bits (1, 1.5, or 2); the parity (n=none, o=odd, or e=even); and retry (p=retry indefinitely on busy). All items are separated by commas.

Note: The default number of databits is 7; the default parity is even; the default stopbits is 1 unless the baud rate is 110, in which case, the default stopbits is 2.

You must enter the baud rate. You can skip any other specification by using a comma to get the default (Example 2).

Version 4

Syntax Changes in Version 4

In PC DOS 4, you can use the preceding syntax. However, you can also spell out the specifications, using baud= followed by the baud rate, data= followed by the number of data bits, and stop= followed by the number of stop bits. You can use parity= followed by the parity (none, odd, even, mark, or space; the latter two parity values being additions to those supported by PC DOS 3.3). Note: Use the actual word *space*, not an actual space.

You can specify retry= followed by the retry value: e to return an error status when the port is busy, b to return the actual busy status, and r to return "ready" from a busy port to allow for repeated retries. See later discussion and Example 3.

The other values and defaults are as given for PC DOS 3.3 and earlier.

To display the current status of a serial port, type **mode** followed by the port name (Example 4).

Related Commands AUTOEXEC.BAT is a file for MODE commands that are to be in effect for every session.

DEVICE installs device drivers.

DETAILED REFERENCE

Explanation The serial ports are generally used for either a modem or a serial printer, although other devices, such as mice, can also be connected. Most applications software (such as communications programs or serial printer drivers) set up and manipulate the serial port directly. Therefore, you probably will not need to use the MODE command for this purpose unless your application's documentation specifies it or your programs do not access the port correctly.

Specifying *p* (pre-PC DOS 4) means that if the device reports that it is busy, it will be retried indefinitely until the access is successful. Specifying retry makes a small part of the MODE command resident, using about 500 bytes of memory.

Version 4

Using the RETRY Specification in Version 4

PC DOS 4 provides additional specifications for how retrying will be done with a serial printer or other serial device. The specification *retry=b* provides operation compatible with the p specification described earlier, and replaces it. (Though the specification p is still accepted, you should use *b* for compatibility with future versions of PC DOS.) It returns a "busy" code when the device is busy, and provides retries.

The new specification *retry=r* tells the driver that the device is ready and lets MODE handle the actual retries. It is generally used with the main (foreground) application. With most applications, you should assume that the driver wants to handle the retries itself and add this specification only if your application's documentation mentions it or if you have problems, such as not all of the data being printed.

The specification *retry=e* returns an error code to the program when the device is busy. This may be necessary, for example, if the printer's speed (and available printer buffer memory) is not enough to keep up with the rate at which characters are being sent to the printer; it is often needed in background processing or network situations.

Comments Before redirecting the output of a parallel port to a serial port (see the MODE (Printer Control) entry), you must initialize the serial port by using a MODE command as described here. See the documentation for your application for details; also make sure that any switches on the printer are set to the correct baud rate, data/stop bits, and parity.

If you use MODE for establishing direct communications with a remote device, make sure the settings for baud, data bits, stop bits, and parity match those for your software and those for the device (such as a bulletin board service) with which you are communicating.

Examples Example 1: Set the serial port.

```
C:\>mode com1:12,n,8,1,r

COM1: 1200,n,8,1,r
```

Notice that MODE echoes the new status that you just set; in this case, 1200 baud, no parity, 8 data bits, 1 stop bit, and continuous retry on busy.

Example 2: Use some default specifications.

```
C:\>mode com1:12,,8,1,

COM1: 1200,e,8,1,-
```

Here, commas are used in place of the parity and the retry status. As a result, the parity was set back to the default (even), and the retry was reset to -, meaning "none."

Example 3: Write a batch file that dials a number on a Hayes-compatible modem.

```
C:\>copy con: dial.bat
@echo off
mode com1:12,n,8,1 > nul
echo atdt%1% > com1:
^Z
 1 file(s) copied
C:\>dial 8489929     ←Dials the number
```

First, the serial port mode is set to a popular setting for bulletin boards (1200 baud, no parity, 8 data bits, 1 stop bit). The redirection to the null device gets rid of the message from MODE announcing the settings. The ECHO statement sends the characters atdt (the "attention, dial, tone" signal for Hayes-type modems) to the modem, followed by the phone number that was typed on the command line.

Example 4: Use the optional PC DOS 4 syntax.

Version 4

Syntax Format Changes in Version 4

```
C:\>mode com1: baud=24 data=8 stop=1 parity=odd retry=r

COM1: 2400,o,8,1,r
```

This specifies 24 (i.e., 2400) baud, 8 data bits, 1 stop bit, odd parity, and continuous retry if busy.

Example 5: Display the current status of the second serial port.

```
C:\>mode com1:

Status for device COM1:
-----------------------
RETRY=R
```

Unfortunately, this isn't very informative—only the retry status is given.

Related Chapter Chapter 11–Customizing Your System

External Command

MODE (Console-Display and Keyboard-Control)

Compatibility	2.0	2.1	3.0	3.1	3.2	3.3	**4.0**	**OS/2 (DOS mode)**	OS/2 (prot.)
	▲	▲	▲	▲	▲	▲	▲	▲	▲

Use the console control features of the MODE command to set the number of lines and columns for the video display, align or test the video display, and enable color or monochrome operation. You can also set the speed at which a key held down at the keyboard is repeated.

Format

`mode display-type,lines` specifies the mode for the video display and, optionally, the number of lines on the screen (must be 25, 43, or 50; 43 requires EGA or VGA, 50 requires VGA).

`mode display-typel,shift-direction,t` specifies the mode for the video display and, optionally, shifts and test aligns the screen interactively.

Version 4

New Features in Version 4

`mode con: cols=cols/line lines=lines on screen` specifies the number of columns per line and lines per screen (optional syntax for PC DOS 4 only).

`mode con: rate=keyboard repetition interval delay=repetition delay in quarters of a second` controls keyboard repetition (PC DOS 4 only).

`mode con:` displays status of console device (PC DOS 4 only).

Sample Use `mode co80,t` (pre-PC DOS 4 format)

Version 4

Examples of Using New Features in Version 4

`mode con: lines=50 cols=80` (Optional PC DOS 4 format)

`mode con: rate=16 delay=2` (Keyboard, PC DOS 4 only)

Procedure To specify the display mode, type `mode` followed by one of the following:

`40` = 40-character display
`80` = 80-character display
`bw40` = 40-character display, color graphics adapter with color disabled
`bw80` = 80-character display, color graphics adapter with color disabled
`co40` = 40-character display, color graphics adapter with color enabled
`co80` = 80-character display, color graphics adapter with color enabled
`mono` = monochrome display adapter (always has 80-character display)

Optionally, follow the display type with a comma and the number of lines per screen (25, 43, or 50; see Examples 1 and 2).

If your display is off center and cannot be adjusted at the monitor, you can add a comma followed by *r* to shift it right, or *l* to shift it left. It will be shifted two spaces if it is in an 80-column mode or one space in 40-column mode.

To adjust the screen interactively, you follow the shift specification with a comma followed by `t` (test). You will be asked if the screen is aligned properly. If you answer yes, the MODE command exits. If you say no, the screen shifts again in the same direction. This repeats until you answer yes (Example 3).

Note: PC DOS creates a buffer to hold the shifted screen contents, thus consuming some memory with each shift. Eventually, it will be unable to shift farther.

Version 4

Syntax Format Changes in Version 4

You can use the preceding syntax with PC DOS 4. However, you can also type `mode con:` followed by `lines=` followed by the number of lines per screen, and `cols=` followed by the number of columns (Example 4). The values for lines and columns are still limited to those given above. Use the pre-PC DOS 4 syntax if you wish to shift the screen or align it interactively. Do not attempt to mix the two kinds of syntax in the same command.

To specify how soon and how fast keys typed on the keyboard will repeat when held down, type `mode con:` followed by `rate=`, followed by a number between 1 and 32. See Table R.11 for the relationship between this value and the number of repetitions per second. To set the delay (the time the system will wait until it begins to repeat the key being pressed), add `delay=` followed by a number between 1 and 4, representing quarters of a second (Example 5).

To display the current status of the console display device, type `mode con:` (Example 6).

Related Commands ANSI.SYS is a driver for extended screen/keyboard control.

AUTOEXEC.BAT is a file for automatic execution of MODE commands at the start of every session.

BREAK specifies checking for Ctrl-Break keypress.

DEVICE installs device drivers.

DISPLAY.SYS is a driver to support code page switching on display.

GRAFTABL supports extended graphic characters on display.

GRAPHICS prints the contents of a graphic screen display.

KEYB loads alternative keyboard configurations.

SWITCH switches between extended and standard keyboard functions.

DETAILED REFERENCE

Explanation The various video display options of the MODE command are used mainly for switching between the standard text screen (25 lines by 80 columns) and the lower-resolution CGA text screen (25 lines by 40 columns) or the higher-resolution EGA (43 lines by 80 columns) or VGA (50 lines by 80 columns) displays. Of course, you must have the correct adapter and monitor installed for the format desired.

Note: The EGA includes the CGA formats; the VGA includes the CGA and EGA formats; all adapters include the MONO format.

Comments Some recent applications allow you to select the kind of screen format you want, and take care of setting the screen type for you. Conversely, MODE screen settings that you make at the PC DOS prompt usually have no effect inside an application, because the application usually resets the screen mode.

The keyboard options of the MODE command control two things: the number of times a key that is being held down repeats per second and how long the system waits after the initial keypress to begin repeating the key. The former is governed by the value of rate=, as shown in Table R.11.

As you can see, the number of repeats per second increases more rapidly as the value of the rate specification goes up.

The second specification, the delay, governs how long the system waits before it begins to repeat a key that has been held down. It is a number between 1 and 4, representing 1/4 second, 1/2 second, 3/4 second, or 1 second.

Note: If your program (such as a word processor) is slow about responding to keystrokes, changing this setting won't speed this response up, but it may improve your typing efficiency somewhat.

If you find that you are getting unwanted duplicate keypresses, try a value of

Table R.11. *Key Repetition Rates*

Value of Rate	Repeats/ Second	Value of Rate	Repeats/ Second
1	2.0	17	8.0
2	2.1	18	8.6
3	2.3	19	9.2
4	2.5	20	10.0
5	2.7	21	10.9
6	3.0	22	12.0
7	3.3	23	13.3
8	3.7	24	15.0
9	4.0	25	16.0
10	4.3	26	17.1
11	4.6	27	18.5
12	5.0	28	20.0
13	5.5	29	21.8
14	6.0	30	24.0
15	6.7	31	26.7
16	7.5	32	30.0

3 or 4 for the delay; this gives your finger more time to release the key. On the other hand, if keys that you want to repeat are not repeating quickly enough, experiment with a short delay (1 or 2) and possibly a higher repeat rate. By trial and error, you can arrive at the optimum keyboard response for your keyboard touch.

Examples Example 1: Set the video display to a 40-column color CGA text mode.

```
C:\>mode co40
```

(If you have a monochrome monitor, use bw40 instead.) This display may be useful if you have vision problems, because the characters are larger and thus easier to read.

Example 2: Set the display width to 80 columns.

```
C:\>mode 80
```

This sets the display to 80 columns with no effect on the current color status.

Example 3: Align and test the screen display.

```
C:\>mode 80,l,t
```

This shifts the display two character spaces to the left from its normal position. You are shown a row of numbers to help you see the screen alignment and then asked whether you see the rightmost numeral.

```
01234567890123456789012345678901234567890123456789012345678901234567890123
45678901234567890123456789
```

`Do you see the rightmost 9? (Y/N)` ← *Type y to continue shifting*

(If you were shifting to the right, you would be asked whether you see the leftmost 0 instead.) Type `y` if you see the numeral and the screen appears to be aligned correctly. Otherwisen type `n`; each time you do so, the screen is shifted another two spaces to the left.

Example 4: Write a batch file that displays a specified directory using 50 lines per screen.

Version 4

Varying the Lines per Screen in Version 4

```
C:\>copy con: vgdir.bat
@echo off
mode con: lines=50
dir %1 %2 %3 %4
pause
mode con: lines=25
^Z
 1 file(s) copied
```

This batch file uses the PC DOS 4 syntax to set the number of lines. The equivalents in PC DOS 3.3 are mode co80,50 and mode co80,25 respectively.

The MODE setting sets a 50-line color mode for the VGA (for EGA or to obtain slightly larger text, you could set a 43-line mode). The DIR command takes any path names and options from the batch file's command line. Its results are displayed in the 50 line mode, allowing for much larger listings to fit on one screen. The PAUSE command allows the user to view the listing and then press a key. Finally, another MODE setting restores the default mode.

Example 5: Set up the keyboard for a professional typist.

```
C:\>mode con: rate=32 delay=1
```

This sets the keyboard to wait for only 1/4 second before repeating a key, and once it starts repeating, to repeat it 30 times a second. This can make for fast cursor movement, but it requires a light, sure touch at the keyboard.

Example 6: Display the current status of the console device.

```
C:\>mode con:

Status for device CON:
----------------------
COLUMNS=80
LINES=25
Code page operation not supported on this device
```

Related Chapter Chapter 11–Customizing Your System

MODE (Code Page Management)

External Command

Compatibility	2.0	2.1	3.0	3.1	3.2	3.3	4.0	OS/2 (DOS mode)	OS/2 (prot.)
						▲	▲	▲	▲

Use the code page features of the MODE command in PC DOS 3.3 or 4 to prepare, select, activate, or refresh a code page or to display the code page status.

Note: Code pages are not needed by most users in the United States. They are used to provide national character sets for other countries and to provide access to an international multilingual character set. See Chapter 13, "International Language Support," for details.

Format

`mode` *`device`* `cp prep=((`*`code page(s)) code info. file`*`)` prepares one or more code pages.

`mode` *`device`* `cp sel=`*`code page`* selects an active code page (makes it the current code page).

`mode` *`device`* `cp ref` refreshes (reestablishes) a code page that has been lost.

`mode` *`device`* `cp /sta` displays the number of the active code page for the current device; it displays a list of available code pages if /sta is selected.

Note: Some of these specifications are abbreviations that can be typed in full if you wish: cp is the same as code page; prep is the same as prepare; sel is the same as select; ref is the same as refresh; and /sta is the same as /status.

Sample Use

`mode con: cp sel=850`

Note: Before preparing or using code pages with a particular device, make sure that you have installed the necessary device drivers for supporting code page switching on that device (see Chapter 13, "International Language Support," and the reference entries for the following related commands for details).

Procedure

To prepare one or more code pages for subsequent use, type `mode` followed by the device whose code page is to be prepared; valid devices are con:, prn:, lpt1:, lpt2:, or lpt3:. Follow this with `cp prep=`. Follow this with two opening parentheses and either a code page number or a list of code page numbers separated by commas.

Note: See Chapter 13 for a list of code pages by country.

Follow this with a single close parenthesis and a space. Next, type the name of the code page information file for the device being manipulated. PC DOS 3.3 and 4 provide the code page files listed in Table R.12

If the file is not in the current directory, give the complete path name. See Example 1.

To select a prepared code page (and make it the current or active one), type `mode` followed by the device name and `cp sel=` followed by the code page number.

To refresh (reload) an already prepared code page, type `mode` followed by the

Table R.12. *Standard PC DOS Code Page Files*

File	Device
4201.CPI	IBM ProPrinter
4208.CPI	IBM ProPrinter X24 and XL24 (PC DOS 4 only)
5202.CPI	IBM Quietwriter III Printer
EGA.CPI	EGA video display (also works with VGA)
LCD.CPI	LCD display for IBM Convertible

device name and `cp ref=`, followed by the number of the code page to be refreshed.

To display the code page status for a device, type `mode` followed by the device name. If you want a list of available code pages for this device to be displayed also, add /sta.

Related Commands CHCP specifies a new current code page for many devices at once.

COUNTRY specifies country information for code pages.

DEVICE installs devices needed for supporting code page switching.

DISPLAY.SYS is a device driver to support code pages on video displays.

GRAFTABL supports extended graphic characters on video displays.

NLSFUNC supports extended country information.

PRINTER.SYS supports code page switching on IBM printers.

DETAILED REFERENCE

Explanation Remember that the various drivers supporting code page use (such as DISPLAY.SYS and PRINTER.SYS) must be installed before you can use MODE to manipulate code pages. If you are using PC DOS 4, you will find that the SELECT installation program will query you about code page switching and set many defaults in your CONFIG.SYS and AUTOEXEC.BAT files accordingly.

Comments Code page switching is generally supported only for certain IBM printers, as shown in Table R.12. See your printer documentation for quirks involving particular printers.

If a printer or other device supports multiple code pages, and you want to skip a position in the code page list, put two commas in place of the missing number. For example, mode lpt1: cp prep=((850,,863) c:\dos\4210.cpi). If an incorrect or undefined code page is used in a code page list, the code page in that position becomes undefined. This can cause problems if you attempt to switch to that code page.

Examples Example 1: Prepare code pages for the video display.

```
C:\>mode con: cp prep=((437,850) c:\dos\ega.cpi)
MODE prepare code page function completed
```

MODE (Code Page Management)

This command copies the information for code pages 437 and 850 from the code page information file C:\DOS\EGA.CPI, preparing these code pages for use with the console device (the video display and screen).

Example 2: Select the multilingual code page for the printer.

```
C:\>mode lpt1: cp sel=850
MODE select code page function completed
```

This example assumes that you have already executed an appropriate code page prepare statement for the printer in port LPT1:.

Example 3: Refresh the preceding code page.

```
C:\>mode lpt1: cp ref
```

Because there can only be one active code page to refresh for a given device, no code page number is given.

Example 4: Display the code page status for the CON: device and a list of available code pages for that device.

```
C:\>mode con: /sta

Status for device CON:
----------------------
COLUMNS=80
LINES=25

Active code page for device CON: is 850
Hardware code pages:
  code page 437
Prepared code pages:
  code page 850

MODE status code page function completed
```

Related Chapters Chapter 11–Customizing Your System
Chapter 13–International Language Support

MORE

Internal Command

Compatibility	2.0	2.1	3.0	3.1	3.2	3.3	4.0	OS/2 (DOS mode)	OS/2 (prot.)
	▲	▲	▲	▲	▲	▲	▲	▲	▲

Use the MORE command to view text files screen by screen.

Format `more < `*`file name`*

Sample Use `more <letter.txt`

Procedure The easiest way to use MORE is with redirected input: follow MORE with the redirection operator (<) and the file name (or complete path name) of the file you wish to read. (See Chapter 8, "Advanced Use of the Command Line," for a discussion of redirection.) MORE can also be used with a pipe (see Example 2).

After each screen is displayed, press any key to view the next screen.

DOS Shell

The DOS Shell Lets You View Text Files and Control Scrolling
While using the DOS Shell, you can view the contents of a file by selecting File System from the Main Group on the Start Programs screen. Next, select the directory containing the file from the Directory Tree window and then select the file from the list in the right-hand window. Select View from the File menu. The file will be shown in a large window. Use the PageUp and PageDown keys to browse through the file. You can use the F9 key to toggle between regular ASCII and hexadecimal format.

Related Commands COMP compares contents of two files.

PRINT sends a file to the printer.

TYPE views contents of a file (continuous output).

DETAILED REFERENCE

Explanation The MORE command is a "filter" program: It normally receives its input from a specified file (by redirection) or from a program (via a pipe) and displays its output one screen at a time. Thus, it is useful for viewing files that are too long to fit on a single screen.

Comments UNIX users should note that the PC DOS MORE command has none of the browsing or searching features of the corresponding UNIX command. There are several excellent public domain or shareware file listing programs available, however, usually called LIST or MORE or some variant, that allow you to browse back and forth in files and even search for specified text. As noted earlier, DOSSHELL (available with PC DOS 4) also allows you to browse through files.

Note that many word processors include special formatting characters, and files created by such word processors are hard to read with MORE.

Examples Example 1: How not to use MORE.

```
C:\>more letter

Hmm. What's going on here?
Hmm. What's going on here?
I'm not seeing the letter!
I'm not seeing the letter!
^Z
```

You wanted to view the LETTER file but forgot to use the redirection operator (<) before the file name LETTER. The result is that MORE defaults to reading standard input—that is, whatever is typed at the keyboard. Each typed line is echoed. To get out of this, type a Ctrl-Z, which indicates end of file (in this case, end of standard input).

Example 2: Read the LETTER file one screen at a time

```
C:\>more <letter
```

Here, with redirection, MORE displays the contents of LETTER one screen at a time. At the end of each screenful of text, it prompts.

```
--More--
```

Press any key to see the next screen. Note that you can abort the operation of MORE and go back to the PC DOS prompt by typing Ctrl-C or Ctrl-Break.

Example 3: Use MORE in a pipeline

```
C:\>type letter | more
```

This performs the same function as Example 2, but uses a pipe. The TYPE command outputs the entire contents of LETTER at once. As the output is read by MORE from the pipe, it is broken into screens of text. This application of MORE might be useful if you have a no-frills program that generates lots of text and you want to view its output one screen at a time.

Related Chapters Chapter 5–PC DOS Files
Chapter 8–Advanced Use of the Command Line

NLSFUNC

External Command

Compatibility	2.0	2.1	3.0	3.1	3.2	3.3	4.0	OS/2 (DOS mode)	OS/2 (prot.)
						▲	▲		

Use the NLSFUNC command to provide display support for extended country information (used for setting date, time, and currency formats that vary with the country) and to enable use of the CHCP command for code page (character set) switching. See Chapter 13, "International Language Support," for a detailed discussion of code pages and their use.

Format `nlsfunc` *`country-information file`* (PC DOS 3.3)

Version 4

Use the NLSFUNC Command with the INSTALL Setting in Version 4

`install=nlsfunc.exe` *`country-information file`*
(in CONFIG.SYS; optional; PC DOS 4 only)

Sample Use `nlsfunc c:\dos\country.sys` (PC DOS 3.3 or 4)

Version 4

Use the NLSFUNC Command with the COUNTRY.SYS Driver and the INSTALL Setting in Version 4

`install=c:\dos\nlsfunc.exe c:\dos\country.sys` (PC DOS 4 only)

Procedure In PC DOS 3.3, type `nlsfunc` followed by the file name of the file containing country information. This is normally COUNTRY.SYS in your main PC DOS directory; if the file is not in the current directory, give the full path name. You will normally want to put the NLSFUNC statement in your AUTOEXEC.BAT file so that it will be executed at the start of each session.

Note: If you have a setting for COUNTRY in your CONFIG.SYS file, you need not specify the country information file with the NLSFUNC command.

Version 4

Using INSTALL = NLSFUNC.EXE in CONFIG.SYS Saves Memory in Version 4

In PC DOS 4, the recommended procedure is to begin a statement in your CONFIG.SYS with install=nlsfunc.exe. Remember to include the file extension .EXE. If NLSFUNC is not in the startup directory, give the complete path name. Follow this name with the name of the file containing country information, normally COUNTRY.SYS in the main PC DOS directory.

Note: PC DOS 4 users can run NLSFUNC from AUTOEXEC.BAT, using the procedure given previously for PC DOS 3.3 users. It is, however, more efficient to use the improved memory allocation provided by the INSTALL command and CONFIG.SYS as described here.

Related Commands CHCP changes among prepared code pages.

CONFIG.SYS is a file for installing NLSFUNC in PC DOS 4.

COUNTRY identifies the country for code page information.

DISPLAY.SYS is a driver for supporting code page switching on video display.

GRAFTABL provides support for extended graphics characters.

INSTALL loads NLSFUNC from CONFIG.SYS in PC DOS 4.

KEYB loads alternate keyboard configurations.

PRINTER.SYS is a driver to support code page switching on IBM printers.

SELECT helps set up code page switching while installing PC DOS 4.

SWITCHES disables extended keyboard functions.

DETAILED REFERENCE

Explanation The NLSFUNC command sets up additional information needed for code page support. It normally obtains this information from the file COUNTRY.SYS. Because NLSFUNC installs itself in memory, it need be run only once per session. PC DOS 3.3 users should run it from AUTOEXEC.BAT; PC DOS 4 users should run it via an INSTALL statement in their CONFIG.SYS file.

Comments NLSFUNC is part of a constellation of commands and settings used in code page switching. See Chapter 13, "International Language Support," for a complete discussion of the purpose of code pages, how to install code page switching, and how to use code pages during your work session.

Examples Example 1: Run NLSFUNC in PC DOS 3.3 via the AUTOEXEC.BAT file.

```
nlsfunc c:\dos\country.sys
```

This assumes that COUNTRY.SYS is in the C:\DOS directory. If you have the setting country=c:\dos\country.sys in your CONFIG.SYS file, you need not include the country file in your NLSFUNC command.

Example 2: Run NLSFUNC in PC DOS 4

Version 4

Installing NULSFUNC.EXE in the CONFIG.SYS File in Version 4

```
install=c:\dos\nlsfunc.exe c:\dos\country.sys
```

This statement goes in the CONFIG.SYS file. Remember that the file name extension (.EXE in this case) must be included with programs installed by the INSTALL command. Again, it is assumed that NLSFUNC is in the C:\DOS directory; if the country file is specified in a preceding COUNTRY setting in your CONFIG.SYS, it can be omitted here.

Related Chapter Chapter 13–International Language Support

PATH

Internal Command, Setting

Compatibility	2.0	2.1	3.0	3.1	3.2	3.3	4.0	OS/2 (DOS mode)	OS/2 (prot.)
	▲	▲	▲	▲	▲	▲	▲	▲	▲

Use the PATH command to specify the directories to be searched for executable files (programs). This allows you to run programs in other directories without having to specify their full path names.

Format `path` shows the current executable file search path.

`path` ***path name;...*** sets the executable file search path.

`path ;` removes the existing executable file search path.

Sample Use

```
path c:\;c:\dos;c:\dos\utils;c:\c5\bin;c:\wp;c:\database;
```

Procedure To display the current path, type `path` by itself (Example 1). To set a new path, type `path` followed by one or more path names, each followed by a semicolon, with no intervening spaces. Each path name should specify a drive and directory to be searched for program files. To remove the existing search path, you can type `path ;` (Example 3). Note that you don't have to remove the current path merely to change it; each new PATH command replaces the existing path.

Related Commands APPEND sets the search path for special data files.

AUTOEXEC.BAT is a file that sets automatically the path for your PC DOS session.

SET directly sets the path variable.

DETAILED REFERENCE

Explanation The PATH command allows you to specify the directories that will be searched for executable programs. (The APPEND command performs a similar function that allows your programs to search for needed overlay or data files.) Specifying a path for program files allows you to run a program from different parts of your file system rather than only from the directory containing the program. Thus, if your PATH contains the directory c:\wp, you can run WordPerfect from any directory containing correspondence or reports. (Chapter 6, "Managing Your Hard Disk," has more discussion and examples of the use of PATH in organizing your hard disk.)

Tip

Specify Your Most Frequently Used Directories First in Your PATH Statement
Because PC DOS will search the directories in the order specified, you gain a bit of extra speed by specifying directories containing the most frequently used programs first.

Although the PATH command can be used at the PC DOS prompt, it is normally put in the AUTOEXEC.BAT file, where it takes effect automatically at the start of each session.

DOS Shell

The DOS Shell Utility Provides Directory Access Similar to That of the PATH Command
If you are using PC DOS 4, you can eliminate much of the bother of keeping track of path names by using DOSSHELL to run programs and to find and manipulate files. DOSSHELL allows you to set up programs to be run from menus, without the user for whom you've set up the menus needing to know anything about paths. Through the shell's File System window, files can be found, selected, and manipulated without knowing their path names, although the path names are shown as you go along.

See Chapter 4, "Using DOSSHELL," for details. Even though DOSSHELL is convenient, especially for less experienced users, it is a good idea to learn about paths so that you can work effectively at the PC DOS prompt and can become comfortable with configuring your system via the CONFIG.SYS and AUTOEXEC.BAT files.

Comments Once set, the search path remains in effect until it is changed by executing a new PATH command (or the system is rebooted). Note that the value set by PATH is actually an environmental variable that can be displayed or changed by the SET command. (See Chapter 10, "Batch Files," for more discussion of environmental variables.) Thus, it can also be set in a batch file (or at the PC DOS prompt) with the SET command (see Example 4).

The path becomes part of the environment that is passed to every program when it is loaded. You can save some memory by loading memory-resident programs before defining a long path; this minimizes the duplication of path information.

When entering very long paths, you may get an `out of environment space` error. Because memory-resident programs are loaded just above the environment area, loading such a program limits your environment to 128 bytes or the current size, whichever is greater. You can increase the size of the environment by using the SHELL command to run COMMAND (see SHELL and COMMAND entries for details).

Examples **Example 1**: Show the program search path.

```
C:\>path
PATH=C:\DOS;C:\DOS\UTILS;C:\WP50
```

The value shown is simply the value of an environmental variable called PATH; thus you could also use the SET command to see the current path value as part of the list of environmental variables.

Example 2: Set a new search path.

```
C:\>path
c:\;c:\dos;c:\dos\utils;c:\c5\bin;c:\wp50;c:\db4
```

Notice that the path names are separated by semicolons. The specified path completely replaces the existing path; see Example 4 for a way to add to an existing path.

Example 3: Remove the current path.

```
C:\>path ;
```

Now, PC DOS will search only the current directory for programs and batch files. To run a program that is not in the current directory, you have to supply the complete path name.

Example 4: Write a batch file that adds a directory to the current search path. First, create this batch file.

```
C:\>copy con: addpath.bat
@echo off
path %path%%1;
^Z
 1 file(s) copied
```

The batch file runs the PATH command. The first value it gives it is %path%, which represents the current value of the PATH environmental variable; that is, the current search path. The %1; takes the value of the parameter typed on the command line when the batch file is run (which should be the directory to be added to the path) and adds it to the path with a semicolon (to separate it from any path names that are subsequently added). Here's an example of use, showing the current path before and after.

```
C:\>path
PATH=C:\;C:\DOS;C:\DOS\UTILS
addpath c:\wp
C:\>path
PATH=C:\;C:\DOS;C:\DOS\UTILS;C:\WP;
```

Related Chapters Chapter 5–PC DOS Files
Chapter 6–Managing Your Hard Disk
Chapter 7–All About Floppy Disks
Chapter 10–Batch Files

Batch Command

PAUSE

Compatibility	2.0	2.1	3.0	3.1	3.2	3.3	4.0	OS/2 (DOS mode)	OS/2 (prot.)
	▲	▲	▲	▲	▲	▲	▲	▲	▲

Use the PAUSE command in a batch file to halt processing temporarily so that the user can read a message or be prompted to perform an action.

Format `pause message`

Sample Use `pause Make sure the printer is turned on`

Procedure In a batch file, enter a statement beginning with the word PAUSE followed by an optional message to be displayed when processing is paused. When the user presses any key, batch processing resumes.

Related Commands ECHO displays a message without pausing.

REM places a nonexecutable remark in a batch file.

DETAILED REFERENCE

Explanation The PAUSE command is normally used in batch files for two purposes. First, you can use it to pause the display to allow the user to read some text before continuing. (You could also use it to display a message a screen at a time by putting a PAUSE command at the end of each screenful of text.) Second, you can use it to prompt the user to perform some action that must be done before processing can continue, such as inserting a disk in the drive, turning on the printer, and so on. Any message you place after the PAUSE command will be displayed at that point in the batch file's execution.

Comments If the user types Ctrl-C (or Break) in response to the pause, the batch file processing is halted. The user is asked if he or she wishes to continue batch processing: type `y` to continue, or `n` to abort processing of the batch file.

Although a message follows the word PAUSE, it is displayed only if ECHO is on. (It is the equivalent of using a REM statement before the PAUSE statement.) You can get more attractive results by having ECHO off and using an ECHO statement to display your message, followed by the PAUSE.

Example Example 1: In a batch file, use PAUSE to prompt for insertion of a disk.

```
C:\>copy con: datacopy.bat
@echo off
echo Copy Data Files to Backup Floppy
echo Insert data disk in drive A:
pause
copy *.dat a:
^Z
1 file(s) copied.
```

When the batch file is executed, the user sees

```
Copy Data Files to Backup Floppy

Insert data disk in drive A:
Press any key when ready    ←User inserts disk, presses a key
transac.dat
trail.dat
log.dat
 3 file(s) copied.
```

The `press any key . . .` prompt is "built in" to PAUSE and is issued automatically. Here an ECHO statement was used to precede the PAUSE prompt with the message `Insert data disk in drive A:`.

Related Chapter Chapter 10–Batch Files

PRINT

External Command

Compatibility	2.0	2.1	**3.0**	3.1	3.2	3.3	4.0	OS/2 (DOS mode)	OS/2 (prot.)
	▲	▲	▲	▲	▲	▲	▲	▲	▲

Use the PRINT command to print one or more files while you continue to do other work. PC DOS can print files created by applications without requiring that you remain within the application and wait for printing to finish.

Format `print` *`startup-options file name control-options`* installs the print facility and prints a file.

`print` *`control-options`* controls ongoing printing.

Options The following options can only be specified the first time PRINT is run in a given session:

/d:device specifies device to be used for printing.

/b size sets print buffer size in bytes: maximum, 16K; default, 512 bytes.

/u busyticks specifies number of clock ticks to wait for device; default is 1.

/m maxticks specifies number of clock ticks per turn at execution: 1-255, default is 2.

/s timeslice specifies number of clock ticks the main program can run before giving PRINT a chance to run: 1-255, default is 8

/q: quesize specifies number of files that can be waiting to be printed: 4-32, default is 10.

The following options can be issued at any time. They set "modes" that affect any files mentioned on the command line, and any other files mentioned in subsequent PRINT commands, until another mode is set.

/c sets a cancel mode, which cancels printing of all files mentioned on the command line and in subsequent PRINT commands until the /p option is used. It does not affect files already waiting to be printed.

/t sets the terminate mode. All files in the queue (waiting to be printed) are canceled. If a file is currently being printed, printing stops, the paper is advanced to the next page, and the printer alarm sounds. Any file whose name is mentioned on the command line after this option, however, is printed.

/p sets the print mode. All files mentioned on the command line and files mentioned in the subsequent PRINT command are added to the print queue for future printing, until the /c option is used.

Sample Use

```
print /p c:\dumpfile
```

Procedure

If you just want to start printing files with the default settings for buffer and processor usage, type `print` followed by name of the print device and the names of files you want to be printed. Global wildcards (* and ?) may be used to specify groups of similar files. (See Chapter 5, "PC DOS Files," for a discussion of wildcards.) If you do not specify a device, you will be prompted for it; press Return to accept the default of PRN: (which is the first parallel port, also called LPT1:) (Example 1).

If you want to specify operation of the printing facility in detail, you must do so before issuing any other PRINT commands. To do this, type `print`. To specify the size of the print buffer, add /b: followed by the buffer size in bytes. If you wish to control how much of the system's time is used for printing, add one or more of the /u:, /m:, and /s: options. See the Options section and the following discussion for details. To specify the maximum number of files that can be queued for printing, add the /q: option. Remember that the preceding four options can only be set once per session, and, if used, must be part of the first PRINT command issued (Example 2).

To set print mode, include the /p option in a PRINT command (Example 3). The preceding file (if any) given on the command line will be queued for printing. All files you mention in subsequent PRINT commands will also be queued, until you use the /c option.

To cancel the printing of the file currently being printed, include the /c option in a PRINT command (Example 4). The preceding file name (if any) mentioned in this command and all files mentioned in subsequent PRINT commands will be removed from the print queue, until the /p option is used.

To cancel the printing of all files waiting to be printed, use the /t option in a PRINT command (Example 5). If a file is currently being printed, it will also be stopped.

To show which files are waiting to be printed (in other words, the current contents of the print queue), type `print` (Example 6).

DOS Shell

How to Print a File Using the DOS Shell Utility

To print files from the DOS Shell, select File System from the Main Group on the Start Programs screen. Next, from the Directory Tree window, select the directory containing the file you want to print. Then, select the file(s) from the file list window. Finally, select Print from the File menu to send the file to the printer (or schedule it for printing if the printer is in use).

Related Commands

TYPE displays a file on the screen.

MORE displays a file one screen at a time.

DETAILED REFERENCE

Explanation

The PRINT command allows you to schedule files to be printed in the background while you do other work. While some applications (such as WordPerfect) allow you to edit one file while printing another, some other applications halt until printing is done. By using the application's print to disk command and then printing the formatted file from disk with the PRINT command, you can return to the application (or another one) and work on another file without waiting for the printer to finish.

When you first run PRINT, you can specify how much of the processor's time is used for printing and how much is available to your main or foreground application. You can also add more files to the print queue (the files waiting to be printed), remove files from the queue if you decide that you don't want to print them after all, and even cancel all pending print operations. If your printing needs are consistent from one session to the next, you will probably want to put the PRINT command in your AUTOEXEC.BAT files. If you need several different configurations, you can put them in separate batch files.

Before running PRINT, consider whether you need to specify buffer memory. If your printer has a large built-in buffer (such as many laser printers), you can skip the /b option (giving a default system buffer of 512 bytes) and let the printer handle the buffering.

On the other hand, if your printer has only a small buffer, such as many inexpensive dot-matrix printers, specify a large value for the /b option, perhaps the maximum of 16,384 bytes. Larger buffers allow more data to be moved to the printer, freeing the computer that much sooner.

If PRINT seems to be slowing down your main application, consider increasing the /s option. This option specifies a number between 1 and 255 that represents the "timeslice" or the number of clock ticks that the main program can run before PC DOS gives PRINT a turn at execution. The default is 2. You can try increasing it to higher values (such as 10 or 20) until you find a point where printing is continuous but your main application isn't noticeably slowed.

Another time not much data gets through to the printer is when the printer is unable to tell PRINT that it is ready quickly enough. In this case, consider increasing the /u option value and see whether there is improvement.

Increasing the /m option value somewhat can improve the efficiency of printing by allowing PRINT longer periods of execution.

Remember that increasing the values of the /u, /m, or /s takes processing time away from your main application, so use these options judiciously. If you are printing many files and find you cannot add more files to the queue, increase the /q option value.

Comments Before sending a file to be printed, make sure that the printer is turned on and is in the online mode. If a file you are printing is on a floppy disk, do not remove the disk until the file is actually printed. (Unlike some spooler programs that also do deferred printing, PRINT does not set up a temporary directory file containing files waiting to be printed. Rather, it reads the file from disk only when it is time to print it.)

Note that you cannot use PRINT to send a file in a word processor's "native" format directly to the printer. PRINT knows nothing about your word processor's special characters, fonts, formatting codes, etc. Most word processors, however, have an option to print a file to disk rather than to the printer. This puts a correctly formatted version of the file on disk, and you can use PRINT to print such formatted files.

Caution

Limitations Using the PRINT Command

PRINT cannot be used on a network server system. If your main application is timing-critical (such as a data acquisition system or some communications programs), you may not be able to use PRINT. As long as PRINT is printing or has data left to print, you cannot use the printer for other purposes (such as printing directly from a word processor or doing a screen dump).

PRINT constructs a full path name for every file to be printed. There is a maximum of 63 characters for the path name. This should not cause trouble unless you have deeply nested subdirectories.

Examples Example 1: Send all files beginning with the word REPORT (and followed by one character) to the print spooler for printing.

```
C:\>print report?
Name of list device ]PRN:[:    ←Type Enter to accept

  C:\TWG\PCDOSBIB\REPORT1 is currently being printed
  C:\TWG\PCDOSBIB\REPORT2 is in queue
  C:\TWG\PCDOSBIB\REPORT3 is in queue
```

Because the /d option was not used, you are asked which device to print to. Press Enter to accept the default (PRN:, which is the same as LPT1:). All files that match REPORT followed by a single letter or number will be printed. When multiple files are printed, a form feed is issued to start each file at the top of a new page.

As you can see, PRINT informs you about which file is being printed and which files are waiting to be printed.

Note: Remember that if you use PRINT in this way to print a file, without having previously set up the print facility as in Example 2, you will have to reboot if you wish to specify any of the setup options.

Example 2: Set up the PRINT facility.

```
C:\>print /d:lpt2: /b:4096 /u:10 /m:25 /s:50 /q:20
```

This command can be placed in the AUTOEXEC.BAT file instead of being executed at the PC DOS prompt. In order, the options specify that the second parallel port (LPT2:) will be used for background printing; a buffer of 4096 bytes (4K) will be allocated; PRINT will wait 10 clock ticks for the printer to be available; PRINT will use up to 25 ticks each time it executes; the main application can run for 50 ticks before turning over control to PRINT; and up to 20 files can be in the print queue at any one time.

Example 3: Add files to the print queue.

```
C:\>print /p report3 letter

  C:\TWG\PCDOSBIB\REPORT3 is currently being printed
  C:\TWG\PCDOSBIB\LETTER is in queue
```

The first file is printed; the second file, LETTER, goes into the queue. The print mode is now set: any files mentioned in subsequent PRINT commands will be printed (or sent to the queue), until the /c option is used.

Example 4: Cancel printing of a file (set cancel mode).

```
C:\>print letter /c
```

If the file LETTER is currently being printed, printing stops and a cancellation message is sent to the printer. If LETTER is still in the queue, it is removed from the queue. Any file names mentioned in subsequent PRINT commands will be taken as requests to cancel printing of these files, until a /p option is encountered. (Remember that when /p is used, the file named just prior to that option will be printed.)

Example 5: Empty the print queue.

```
C:\>print /t
```

All files in the print queue are canceled. If a file is currently being printed, printing stops and a message is sent to the printer. If a file is given on this command line (for example, print report4 /t), the file is sent to the printer.

Example 6: Show the current status of the print queue.

```
C:\>print
```

All files in the queue (waiting to be printed) are listed.

Related Chapter Chapter 11–Customizing Your System

Resource PRINTER.SYS

Compatibility	2.0	2.1	3.0	3.1	3.2	3.3	4.0	OS/2 (DOS mode)	OS/2 (prot.)
						▲	▲		

Use the PRINTER.SYS device driver to support code page switching (changing character sets) on various IBM printers. (This driver is not needed if you are not using code pages. For a general discussion of code pages and why you may want to use them, see Chapter 13, "International Language Support.")

Format

```
device=printer.sys device=(printer-type,hardware code page,
number of additional code pages)
```

Sample Use

```
device=printer.sys lpt1:=(4201,437,1)
```

Procedure In your CONFIG.SYS, begin a statement by typing `device=printer.sys`. (If the file PRINTER.SYS is not in the startup directory, give the full path name.) Follow this with the name of the port to be used: valid names are LPT1:, PRN: (same as LPT1:), LPT2:, and LPT3:. Without skipping a space, type an equal sign and an open parenthesis. Within the parenthesis, type the following three numbers, separated by commas: the printer type code (see Table R.13), the number of the hardware (built-in) code page, and the number of additional code pages. See the following explanation for valid values. Type a close parenthesis. See Example 1.

Note: you can specify up to three printers in the same DRIVER.SYS statement, by repeating the device, printer type, hardware code page, and additional code page specifications. See Example 2.

Once you have installed PRINTER.SYS, you can use appropriate MODE statements to prepare or change code pages.

Related Commands CHCP switches among prepared code pages.

COUNTRY specifies the country for code page information.

CONFIG.SYS is a file for installing device drivers.

DEVICE installs PRINTER.SYS.

DISPLAY.SYS supports code page switching on the video display.

MODE prepares and selects code pages.

PRINT prints files in the background.

PRINTER.SYS

DETAILED REFERENCE

Explanation PRINTER.SYS is a device driver that supports code page switching on the following IBM printers (see Table R.13). The printer type code is the first number used in the PRINTER.SYS statement.

Table R.13. ***Printers Supported by PRINTER.SYS***

Printer Type Code	Models	PC DOS Version
4201	Proprinter Family IBM 4201	3.3, 4
4201	Proprinter XL IBM 4202	4
4208	Proprinter X24 IBM 4207	4
4208	Proprinter XL24 IBM 4208	4
5202	Quietwriter III IBM 5202	3.3, 4

Hardware Code Pages: IBM printers typically have the code pages 437, 850, 860, 863, and 865 built in. These are character sets stored in read-only memory (ROM) chips in the printer. The two most commonly used are the U.S. standard code page (437) and the international multilingual code page (850). The hardware code page is the second number specified in the PRINTER.SYS statement. For printer types 4201 and 4208, only one hardware code page can be specified. For printer type 5202, you can specify either a single code page or a pair of code pages. In the latter case, the third number (additional code pages) must be 0.

Note: A MODE PREPARE statement is not needed for hardware code pages as it is for code pages loaded from disk.

The third number in the PRINTER.SYS statement specifies the number of additional code pages that will be prepared for the printer, up to a maximum of 12. These code pages will be loaded later from printer information files, through use of appropriate MODE commands. How this should be specified depends on the type of printer.

IBM Proprinters store certain code pages in read-only memory (ROM). When the printer is started, the hardware code page is copied into an area of random-access memory (RAM) in the printer. If you specify 0 for the last number, or do not specify it, PRINTER.SYS will copy one code page from the printer information file (such as 4201.CPI) to the printer's RAM to store it for ready use.

The IBM 5202 Quietwriter III allows you to use plug-in font cartridges, each of which provide several character styles for the same code page. You prepare a new code by physically changing the font cartridge. If you specify two hardware code pages, PC DOS assumes that these are the ones that are physically installed, and no code page preparation is needed for this device.

Comments In general, you must have genuine IBM printers to use these code pages, unless the documentation for your printer says that they are supported. Mere IBM mode or emulation is not sufficient.

Examples Example 1: Set up code pages for an IBM Proprinter XL.

```
device=c:\dos\printer.sys lpt1:=(4201,437,1)
```

Because the PRINTER.SYS file is not in the startup directory (C:\), the full path name is specified. The printer is connected to the first parallel port (LPT1:). The printer type is 4201 (even though the printer model is 4202; see Table R.13). The U.S. code page is specified as the hardware code page. Finally, room is provided for one more code page that can be prepared later with the MODE statement. (Typically, this will be code page 850.)

Example 2: Specify printers for two parallel ports.

```
device=c:\dos\printer.sys lpt1:=(4208,437,1)
lpt2:=(5202,437,850,0)
```

Notice that the second printer statement prepares two hardware code pages for the IBM 5202 printer: code pages 437 and 850. The additional code page's number must be 0 in this case.

Related Chapters Chapter 11–Customizing Your System
Chapter 13–International Language Support

Internal Command

PROMPT

Compatibility	2.0	2.1	3.0	3.1	3.2	3.3	4.0	OS/2 (DOS mode)	OS/2 (prot.)
	▲	▲	▲	▲	▲	▲	▲	▲	▲

Use the PROMPT command to change the appearance of and information contained in the PC DOS command-line prompt.

Format `prompt` *`characters`* changes the prompt.

`prompt` restores the default prompt.

Sample Use `prompt $n$g`

Procedure To define a new PC DOS prompt for the current session, type `prompt` followed by the text you want displayed as the prompt (Example 1). Note that certain characters must be entered using special character sequences; see Table R.14. To have a prompt automatically established at the start of each session, put a PROMPT command in your AUTOEXEC.BAT file. To restore the default prompt, type `prompt` without any other characters.

Related Commands ANSI.SYS performs special screen control functions as part of the prompt.

SET sets the prompt as an environmental variable.

AUTOEXEC.BAT is a file for setting the prompt for a DOS mode session.

VER displays the PC DOS version number.

DETAILED REFERENCE

Explanation The PROMPT command allows you to change the appearance of the command-line prompt. When specifying a new prompt, most characters can be entered just as they will appear, but some characters have to be entered using special sequences consisting of a dollar sign ($) followed by a particular character. These characters are listed in Table R.14.

Table R.14. ***Special Prompt Characters***

Enter	To Get
$$	$
$_	Return and Line Feed (skips a line)
$b	|
$d	Current date
$e	Escape character
$g	>
$h	Backspace (erases previous character)
$l	<
$n	Current drive
$p	Current drive and current directory
$q	=
$t	Current time
$v	PC DOS version number

Comments The prompt is actually part of the PC DOS environment; if you type `set`, the value of the variable PROMPT will be shown in the variable list. You can also change the prompt by assigning the prompt text to this variable. Because the prompt is in the environment, a prompt set while running a secondary processor has no effect on the prompt used by the primary processor. (See the COMMAND entry for a discussion of the PC DOS command processor.)

Using the PROMPT Command to Control the ANSI.SYS Driver
You can also include escape sequences recognized by ANSI.SYS in the prompt text, assuming you have installed this device driver (see the ANSI.SYS entry). In fact, this is the easiest way to put an ANSI command in a batch file. (See the ANSI.SYS entry for examples.)

Within a prompt, you could use this escape sequence facility to do things like clear the screen, display a help line at the top, and then display a prompt at the current cursor location.

The PC DOS 4 SELECT installation program places a PROMPT statement in your AUTOEXEC.BAT file that gives an informative prompt which shows the current drive and directory. Earlier versions do not do this; thus, you get the actual PC DOS default prompt that shows just the current drive. If you are using an earlier version of PC DOS, consider changing the prompt as shown in Example 1.

Examples Example 1: Create a prompt that shows the current drive and directory (not needed for PC DOS 4).

```
C:\>prompt $p$g
```

If you place this command in your AUTOEXEC.BAT file, you will always know the current drive and directory. The $p specifies the current drive and directory; the $g prints the > character. Thus, if the current directory is C:\DOS\UTILS, the PC DOS prompt is displayed as C:\DOS\UTILS>.

Example 2: Include a message in the prompt.

```
C:\>prompt TYPE EXIT TO RETURN TO WORD PROCESSOR
$_ $p$g
TYPE EXIT TO RETURN TO WORD PROCESSOR
C:\WP\DOCS>
```

Many application programs, such as WordPerfect, allow you to run a PC DOS command processor, issue file management commands at the PC DOS prompt, and then return to the application program where you left off. The prompt used by such programs often includes a message to remind you to type `exit` when you want to return to the application. This example simulates this technique. In this prompt, the message is displayed first. The special characters $_ issue a carriage return and a line feed to move the cursor to the beginning of the next line. The rest of the prompt is the same as in Example 1.

Example 3: Restore the default prompt.

```
C:\DOS\UTILS>prompt
C:\>
```

The default prompt shows just the current directory.

Related Chapters Chapter 10–Batch Files
Chapter 11–Customizing Your System

External Command — RECOVER

Compatibility	2.0	2.1	3.0	3.1	3.2	3.3	4.0	OS/2 (DOS mode)	OS/2 (prot.)
	▲	▲	▲	▲	▲	▲	▲	▲	▲

Use the RECOVER command to salvage readable data from a file with damaged disk sectors and to lock out bad disk sectors so they cannot be used to store data. Even if the directory is damaged, you can still recover most of the files by using this command.

Format `recover` *`file`* recovers a damaged file.

`recover` *`drive:`* recovers files on a disk with a damaged file allocation table.

Sample Use `recover a:\mail0721`

RECOVER

Procedure If you attempt to read (or load) a file and receive PC DOS error messages referring to bad data or an inability to read the file, type `recover` followed by the name of the affected file. (Use the path name if the file is not in the current directory.) PC DOS will copy the undamaged parts of the file to another part of the disk; the file name will not be changed. See Example 1.

If you attempt to read the directory of a disk (or otherwise access it) and receive PC DOS error messages indicating a general inability to read the disk (possibly because of a damaged directory), you can usually recover all of the undamaged files on the disk by typing `recover` followed by the drive name only. (If you don't specify the drive, the current drive will be used.) See the following discussion and Example 2.

Related Command CHKDSK examines the disk and attempts to repair the file allocation table.

DETAILED REFERENCE

Explanation The actual data in PC DOS files is stored on a series of disk sectors; the directory lists the names and certain characteristics of the files, and the file allocation table (FAT) records the actual locations of the sectors pertaining to each file. Problems such as physical wear or damage to a disk can make it impossible to read the data in the directory or on one or more of a file's sectors. When this happens, the PC DOS commands that deal with files (such as COPY or TYPE) report read errors. If the directory is damaged, files will not be accessible, even though their data may be undamaged. The RECOVER command allows you to copy the undamaged sectors of a file to a new, readable copy of the file. If the directory on the disk is damaged, you can use RECOVER to find the actual file data on the disk and make it accessible as a series of files, creating a new directory.

Comments Before running RECOVER, you might want to run CHKDSK; this will tell you whether the disk's FAT is intact. (If it isn't, error messages will refer to `FAT` or `File allocation table being bad`.) The CHKDSK command is much more informative than RECOVER in describing the problems found. If problems were found with the FAT, you can run `chkdsk /f` to fix them. Because RECOVER relies on the FAT, using CHKDSK here may allow better results. (In general, use CHKDSK to work with FAT problems such as lost sectors, and RECOVER to deal with actual physical damage to the directory or files.) If the FAT is intact, you can then run RECOVER to salvage as much of the file data as possible.

Note that because the recovery process skips over bad sectors, recovered files will be missing at least one sector of data. Therefore, it does little good to recover executable (program) files, which must be complete to function properly. On the other hand, recovering text files may save most of your work; with an editor, you may be able to restore missing parts from context, and remove any "garbage" that was recovered along with your text. (Recovered files include the remaining part of their last allocation unit of data, even if the actual file was shorter.) Note that if you use RECOVER with a wildcard, only the first file matching the wildcard will be recovered. When recovering an entire disk (due to an unreadable directory), if there are more files to be recovered than the maximum allowable in the root directory, you will have to copy the recovered files to another disk, then delete them from the original disk and run RECOVER again to continue recovery.

Examples Example 1: Recover a bad file on disk B.

```
C:\DOS>recover a:report1

Press any key to begin recovery of the
file(s) on drive A:

 51 of 51 bytes recovered
```

Although the message refers to "files," only the one file specified is recovered. Notice that you are told how many of the total bytes in the file were recovered. The recovered file will have the same name as the original, but it will reside on a (we hope) physically secure part of the disk. The bad sectors that were found will be marked as unavailable, so PC DOS will not use them in the future to store data. You can find out how many bytes have been locked out by running the CHKDSK command on the affected disk.

Example 2: Recover the files on a disk with a bad directory.

```
C:\DOS>recover a:

Press any key to begin recovery of the
file(s) on drive A:

3 file(s) recovered
```

Here, just the drive name is specified (perhaps after running chkdsk a: to check the status of the FAT). RECOVER in this case bypasses the directory and uses the sector list in the FAT to create a series of files. When you look at the directory of the disk, you see

```
 Volume in drive A has no label
 Directory of  A:\

FILE0001 REC      1024 10-23-90  10:15p
FILE0002 REC      1024 10-23-90  10:15p
FILE0003 REC      1024 10-23-90  10:15p
        3 File(s)     727040 bytes free
```

The files recovered are named FILE0001.REC through FILE003.REC. You can use the TYPE command (or an editor) to examine the contents of the files and then use RENAME to give them appropriate names. (It would also be a good idea to copy them to another disk, just in case . . .)

Related Chapters Chapter 5–PC DOS Files
Chapter 7–All About Floppy Disks

RD (RMDIR)

Internal Command

Compatibility	2.0	2.1	3.0	3.1	3.2	3.3	4.0	OS/2 (DOS mode)	OS/2 (prot.)
	▲	▲	▲	▲	▲	▲	▲	▲	▲

Use the RD (or RMDIR) command to remove a directory. The directory must be empty before you can remove it.

Format `rd` *`directory path name`* DOS mode.

Note: RMDIR is a synonym for RD.

Sample Use `rd c:\dos\temp`

Procedure Type `rd` followed by the path name of the directory to be removed. You cannot remove the current directory and, thus, you must use always at least the directory name (for a subdirectory of the current directory) or use a path name (for any other directories). If the directory is not empty, you will receive an error message and the directory will not be removed; use DEL to remove the files in the directory first (Example 1).

DOS Shell

How to Remove a Directory Using the DOS Shell Utility
While running the DOS Shell, you can remove a directory. First, select File System from the Main Group on the Start Programs screen. In the Directory Tree window, select the directory you wish to remove. Finally, select Delete from the File menu.

Related Commands DIR lists a directory.

DEL deletes files.

MD or MKDIR creates a directory.

DETAILED REFERENCE

Explanation The RD command is used to remove a directory. The directory must be empty before it can be removed; empty also means that the directory has no subdirectories. For example, if C:\PROGS\PHYSICS\STATS is a valid path, you can remove the STATS directory (if it is empty), but you cannot remove the PHYSICS directory until the STATS subdirectory (and any other subdirectories or files in the PHYSICS directory) has been removed.

Comments If you get a `directory not empty` message and the DIR command shows no files in the directory, you probably have hidden files in the directory. By issuing the CHKDSK /v command on the affected disk, the hidden files will be listed (along with the regular ones.)

DOS Shell

Common Problems in Removing a Subdirectory
The system files IBMDOS.COM and IBMBIO.COM are hidden. These files are in the root directory of the startup disk, and the

root directory cannot be removed anyway. Additionally, some applications create hidden files as part of a copy protection scheme.

In the case of the latter files, check your application's documentation under "uninstalling." If all else fails, there are various commercial, shareware, and public domain utilities that will remove hidden files. (They often have names like UNHIDE or CHMOD.)

The RD command cannot be used with directories that are being used in an active JOIN or SUBST command. Remove the JOIN or SUBST first. Be careful when removing a directory whose drive is affected by the ASSIGN command, because ASSIGN will direct your command to a different drive and may cause the wrong directory to be removed.

Examples Example 1: Remove a directory.

```
C:\>rd c:\dos\temp
Invalid path, not directory,
or directory not empty
```

Assuming you've given a valid path and directory name, this means that the directory is not empty (if the directory didn't exist, the message would refer to the system not being able to find the path specified). You must first delete the files. Then, you can remove the directory.

```
C:\>del c:\dos\temp\*.*
All files in directory will be deleted!
Are you sure (Y/N)?y     ←Type y to delete all files
```

Now, you can reissue the command RD C:\DOS\TEMP

Example 2: Write a batch file that removes a directory even if it is full.

```
C:\DOS\UTILS>copy con: wd.bat
@echo off
echo y | del %1\*.*
rd %1
```

The ECHO command sends a y along the pipe to the DEL command, answering its `are you sure` question. If you do want the command file to prompt you, remove the echo y | part. (If there are no files in the directory to be removed, a `file not found` error message will be shown—it can be ignored; the directory will still be removed.)

Related Chapter Chapter 6–Managing Your Hard Disk

REM

Batch Command

Compatibility	2.0	2.1	3.0	3.1	3.2	3.3	4.0	OS/2 (DOS mode)	OS/2 (prot.)
	▲	▲	▲	▲	▲	▲	▲	▲	▲

Use the REM statement in your AUTOEXEC.BAT file or other batch files to insert an explanatory comment or to make a command temporarily nonexecutable.

Format `rem comment` inserts an explanatory comment.

`rem existing statement` makes a statement nonexecutable.

Sample Use `rem load the custom device drivers`

Procedure To insert a comment in a batch file, type `rem` followed by the comment text (Example 1). Note that each new line of comment text must be preceded by REM. To make an existing statement nonexecutable, insert `rem` in front of the statement. This allows you to reactivate the statement at some later time without having to remember how to type it.

Version 4

Use the REM Command in Your CONFIG.SYS File in Version 4

In PC DOS 4, you can also use REM to comment out (make nonexecutable) statements in your CONFIG.SYS file. Actually, you can do so in earlier versions of PC DOS; you will get `unrecognized command in CONFIG.SYS` messages that you can ignore.

Related Command ECHO displays text in a batch file.

DETAILED REFERENCE

Explanation The REM statement allows you to insert a comment in a batch file, which can make the file easier to modify later. It is also sometimes useful to comment out an existing statement (such as one in AUTOEXEC.BAT) by inserting a REM in front of it. If you want the statement to become active again, simply remove the rem. A common use is to temporarily disable the loading of a memory-resident program for sessions in which you need the memory that it would ordinarily occupy (see Example 2).

Comments Note that the text of comments will be displayed when the batch file is run unless ECHO has been set to off.

Examples Example 1: Place comments in a batch file.

```
@echo off
rem find out if user wants to install on hard disk
if %1==h goto hard
rem not hard disk, so install on floppies
call flopinst.bat
goto end
```

```
:hard
call hardinst.cmd
:end
```

Here, the comments specify the purpose of testing the %1 command-line parameter and the two possibilities to be tested.

Example 2: Comment out a line in your AUTOEXEC.BAT file. Suppose that you are a regular SideKick user and have this line in your AUTOEXEC.BAT.

```
\desktop\sk
```

This means that SideKick will be run automatically at the start of each session. You know you are going to be running one of the monster-sized desktop publishing programs for a few days, and you can't spare the memory for SideKick. You can put `rem` in front of this line, reboot, and SideKick will no longer be loaded. When you don't need to do desktop publishing for awhile, remove the `rem`, and SideKick is loaded at the start of each session.

Related Chapters

Chapter 10–Batch Files
Chapter 11–Customizing Your System

Internal Command

REN (RENAME)

Compatibility	2.0	2.1	3.0	3.1	3.2	3.3	4.0	OS/2 (DOS mode)	OS/2 (prot.)
	▲	▲	▲	▲	▲	▲	▲	▲	▲

Use the REN (or RENAME) command to change the name of an existing file.

Format

`ren old-name new-name`

Note: RENAME is a synonym for REN.

Sample Use

`ren letter5 js0723`

Procedure

Type `ren` followed by the name of the file to be renamed, supplying the drive and directory name if the file is not in the current directory. Next, type the new name for the file (Example 1). To rename a group of files, use appropriate wildcard characters in the old name (Example 2).

DOS Shell

Renaming Files Using the DOS Shell Utility

With DOSSHELL, you can change the name of a file by first selecting File System from the Main Group on the Start Programs screen. Next, in the Directory Tree window on the left side of the screen, select the directory containing the file to be renamed. Finally, select Rename from the File menu.

Although PC DOS doesn't allow you to change the name of a directory from the command line, you can do so in DOSSHELL. Simply select the directory to be renamed, then select Rename from the File menu.

REN (RENAME)

Related Commands COPY copies a file.

DEL erases a file.

LABEL supplies or changes a disk volume label.

DETAILED REFERENCE

Explanation The REN command changes the name of a file (or a group of files) by revising the file's entry in the disk directory. It does not copy the file, nor can it move the file to another directory. (See Example 5, however, for a command that moves files.)

Comments Do not give a drive name or path name with the new name. If you give a path name, you will receive an error message, even if the path is the same as that of the original name.

Examples Example 1: Rename a file in the current directory.

```
C:\>ren test.bat printer.bat
```

Example 2: Rename a file in a different drive and directory.

```
C:\>ren a:\savegame\oldgame game1
```

Notice that you do not give a drive or path name with the new file name. The new file remains in the A:\SAVEGAME\OLDGAME directory.

Example 3: Rename a group of files using wildcards.

```
C:\>ren test? test?.bak
```

Here, all files with the name TEST followed by any one character are renamed to their original name plus the .BAK extension. For example, TEST5 would become TEST5.BAK.

Example 4: Use REN to change the file extension.

```
C:\>ren *.txt *.bak
```

In this case, any file with the .TXT extension will be renamed to the .BAK extension instead.

Example 5: Move a file to a different directory.

```
C:\UTILS>copy tempfile a:\accts\july90
C:\UTILS>del temptfile
```

You cannot move a file (rather than copy it) with a single PC DOS command. REN will not work, because it will not accept a new name for the file. However, you can copy a file to a destination directory, giving a new name, and then delete the original.

For convenience, you can write a batch file that can be used to move files to a different directory with the ease of a single command.

```
C:\BATCH>copy con: move.bat

@echo off
copy %1 %2
del %1
^Z
 1 file(s) copied.
```

This batch file moves a file (or a group of files specified with wildcards) by first copying the file to a file with the new path name and then deleting the original file. With this batch file, you can move a file like this: `move c:\stats\data a:\olddata`. You can add code to check for the presence of two parameters if you wish; however, using zero or one parameter will not harm anything, because the COPY and DEL commands in the batch file will issue error messages and abort.

Related Chapters Chapter 5–PC DOS Files
Chapter 6–Managing Your Hard Disk

External Command

REPLACE

Compatibility	2.0	2.1	3.0	3.1	3.2	3.3	4.0	OS/2 (DOS mode)	OS/2 (prot.)
					▲	▲	▲	▲	▲

Use the REPLACE command to replace specified files in one drive (or directory) with later versions from another drive or directory. You can also use REPLACE to selectively add files to a disk without erasing existing files.

Format `replace` *`file name destination options`*

Options

/s checks all subdirectories (and their subdirectories, etc.) on the source drive for files to replace.

/p prompts the user as each target file is found and asks whether it should be replaced.

/r replaces files on the destination even if they have the read-only attribute set.

/w prompts the user and waits for the user to press Enter (allows time to insert a floppy disk before beginning replacement process).

/a adds specified file(s) to the destination only if they do not already exist there. You cannot use this with the /s or /u options.

Version 4

The */u* Option Updates Files in Version 4

/u replaces files on the destination with source versions that have more recent dates and times (PC DOS 4 only).

REPLACE

Sample Use `replace a:\prog c:\utils`

Procedure Type `replace` followed by the name of the file you wish to use for the replacement. You can use wildcards to specify a group of replacement files. If the file is not in the current directory, give the appropriate path name. Next, type the name of the directory that you want to be searched for files to be replaced. (If you just specify the drive, the current directory for that drive will be used.) If you wish all files in all subdirectories on the destination drive to be searched, add the /s option. If you want to be prompted before each replacement is made, specify the /p option. If a file to be replaced has the read-only attribute set on the destination, you must specify the /r option. If you want to add files to the destination only if they are not already there (instead of replacing existing files), use the /a option. To replace files on the destination with more current source versions, specify the /u option.

Related Commands XCOPY selectively copies files (can also work with subdirectories).

RESTORE restores a file that has been stored on a disk by the BACKUP command.

DETAILED REFERENCE

Explanation The REPLACE command is most commonly used to find all the existing copies of a file (usually on a hard disk) and replace them with a revised version (perhaps on an update floppy provided by the manufacturer of an application program).

Comments Although REPLACE can be used to update many copies of a file on the hard disk, it is usually better to organize your hard disk so that there is only one copy of a given file—then you don't have to worry about updating several copies. If you use the PATH and APPEND commands, you can run a single copy of the application from anywhere in your file system. (See Chapter 6, "Managing Your Hard Disk," for details.)

Caution

Limitations of REPLACE
REPLACE does not check that the file being replaced is older than the replacement file unless you use the /u option in PC DOS 4. Also, because REPLACE can't change the name of the replacement copy, it cannot be used to install programs that use a new file name with each version.

REPLACE will not replace files with the hidden or system attribute set, such as the system files IBMBIO.COM and IBMDOS.COM.

Error Codes The REPLACE command, being one of the newer PC DOS utilities, sets the ERRORLEVEL value. You can thus test the command's success when it is used in a batch file by using the IF ERRORLEVEL statement. See the IF entry for details. The possible ERRORLEVEL values are shown in Table R.15.

Table R.15. ***REPLACE ERRORLEVEL Values***

Value	Meaning
2	None of the specified source files were found
3	Source or target path invalid or not found
5	At least one destination file was read-only, and the /r option was not specified
8	Insufficient memory for processing
11	Invalid parameters or invalid number of parameters used on the command line
15	An invalid drive was specified
22	Incorrect DOS version

Examples

For the first two examples, there are two directories, PROJ1 and PROJ2, with some letters in them.

```
C:\>dir proj1

 Volume label in drive C is DOSDISK.
 Directory of C:\PROJ1

.            <DIR>      7-24-90   5:10p
..           <DIR>      7-24-90   5:10p
LETTER2  TXT     1421   7-25-90   3:15p
LETTER1  TXT     1818   7-24-90   5:14p

C:\>dir proj2
 Volume label in drive C is DOS DISK.
 Directory of C:\PROJ2

.            <DIR>      7-24-90   5:10p
..           <DIR>      7-24-90   5:10p
LETTER2  TXT     1237   7-24-90   5:11p
LETTER3  TXT     1519   7-24-90   5:12p
     8 File(s)   5060608 bytes free
```

Example 1: Replace a file.

```
C:\>replace proj1\letter2 proj2 /u
Replacing C:\PROJ2\LETTER1.TXT
1 file(s) replaced
```

Notice that you don't specify a file name for the destination; it is the file specified in the source directory that will be searched for in the destination. Because LETTER2 is already in the destination directory PROJ2, it is replaced with the copy from PROJ1, which is a later version, because you gave the /u option. In versions of PC DOS prior to 4, where this option is not available, you must make sure that you are not replacing a newer file with an older one.

Example 2: Add the file LETTER1 to the PROJ2 directory. What happens if you try this?

```
C:\>replace proj1\letter1.txt proj2
No files were replaced
```

It doesn't work, because the default use of REPLACE can only replace a file that already exists at the destination. However, the following works:

```
C:\>replace proj1\letter1.txt proj2 /a
Adding C:\PROJ1\LETTER1.TXT

 1 file(s) added
```

The /a (add) option adds a file to the destination directory, but only if it's not there already. This can be more efficient than using COPY, because it doesn't copy over existing files.

Example 3: Replace every copy of a specified file on the hard disk.

```
C:\>replace a:arc.exe c:\ /s
Replacing file C:\ARC.EXE.
Replacing file C:\UTILS\ARC.EXE.
2 file(s) replaced
```

A common situation is to receive a new copy of a file or utility program on a floppy disk. You want to make sure that any and all copies of the file on your hard disk are replaced, but you're not sure where all the existing copies reside. Here, the /s (subdirectories) option is used, and the root directory of drive C is specified. This means that every file in every directory and subdirectory on disk drive C will be searched. In this example, two copies of ARC.EXE were found and replaced.

There is no PC DOS command that simply reports all the places on the disk where a particular file exists, although public domain versions of this utility are common in the PC DOS world (often called WHEREIS). However, if you know where one copy of the file in question is located, you can use a REPLACE command with the /p option to search a particular drive as though you were going to replace on that drive. REPLACE will report the location (path name) of each copy found, and you can just respond no to each prompt for replacement. (Another alternative is to run the TREE command, but the list it produces can be quite long.)

DOS Shell

Replacing Files Using the DOS Shell Utility

In PC DOS 4, DOSSHELL allows you to easily find and replace files manually. See Chapter 4, "Using DOSSHELL," for details.

Example 4: Write a batch file that automates replacement on a hard disk.

```
C:\UTILS>copy con: replall.bat
@echo off
echo Insert disk with replacement file in drive A:
replace a:%1 c:\ /s /u /w
```

```
^Z

 1 file(s) copied.
```

This batch file assumes you will use drive A as the source of your replacement file(s) and that C is your hard drive where updated copies will be placed. In the REPLACE command, the /s option ensures that every file on drive C will be checked; and the /u option ensures that only files older than replacement files will be replaced. The ECHO statement prompts the user to insert the disk in A, and the /w option causes the replacement to wait until the Enter key is pressed.

Related Chapter Chapter 6–Managing Your Hard Disk

External Command — RESTORE

Compatibility	2.0	2.1	3.0	3.1	3.2	3.3	4.0	OS/2 (DOS mode)	OS/2 (prot.)
	▲	▲	▲	▲	▲	▲	▲	▲	▲

Use the RESTORE command to restore files that have been backed up using the BACKUP command.

Format `restore backup-drive destination file name options`

Options */p* asks the user whether the old version of a file is to be restored, if a file on the destination disk has changed since the backup or is read-only.

/n restores files that do not exist on the destination disk (that is, were deleted since the last backup).

/m restores files whose copies on the destination disk have been modified since the last backup (replaces them with the older version).

/b:mm-dd-yy restores files on the destination disk that were last modified on or before the specified date.

/a:mm-dd-yy restores files on the destination disk that were last modified on or after the specified date.

/e:hh:mm:ss restores files on the destination disk that were last modified on or before the specified time.

/l:hh:mm:ss restores files on the destination disk that were last modified on or after the specified time.

/s, when restoring files, also restores any subdirectories involved that do not exist on the destination disk.

Sample Use `restore a: c:\*.* /s`

Procedure Type `restore` followed by, first, the letter of the drive containing the backup files, and, second, the name of the file, group of files, or directory that you wish to be restored. Follow this name with any options you wish to use; for example, if you only want to restore files that were last modified on or before, or on or after, a particular date or time, use the appropriate option as listed in the Options section. See the examples for how to handle common cases.

DOS Shell

Restoring Files Using the DOS Shell Utility
To restore files from a backup disk using DOSSHELL, select DOS Utilities from the Main Group on the Start Programs screen. Next, select Restore Fixed Disk. You will be prompted to enter path names and options.

Related Commands BACKUP backs up files that can be later restored.

RECOVER recovers partially damaged files or files from disks with damaged directories.

XCOPY copies files selectively according to the date or time of last modification.

DETAILED REFERENCE

Explanation You can use the RESTORE command only with files that have been backed up with the BACKUP command. You can use it to restore all of the files (including the complete structure of directories and subdirectories) from the backup disk, or you can restore files selectively according to their date and time of modification.

Error Codes RESTORE on exit returns error codes as shown in Table R.16. These codes can be tested in a batch file using the IF ERRORLEVEL statement (see the IF entry).

Table R.16 ***RESTORE ERRORLEVEL Codes***

Value	Meaning
0	Command executed successfully and normally
1	No files were found to restore
2	Some files not restored because of sharing conflicts (some other network user was using them)
3	User terminated command prematurely by pressing Ctrl-C
4	Command terminated due to unspecified error

Comments RESTORE will accept any format or size of disk, although the most common case is restoring to a hard disk from one or more floppies. If you are restoring files from a set of backup disks, you will be prompted when to insert the disks in the floppy drive.

RESTORE should never be used with drives that are referred to in an active JOIN, ASSIGN, SUBST, or APPEND command, because of bugs, confusion, and incompatibilities that may result. It is best not to use RESTORE on a network server, because one of the files eligible for replacement might be in use by a network user.

RESTORE will not restore the system files IBMBIO.COM, IBMDOS.COM, and COMMAND.COM. If you want to make the restored disk bootable, first use the SYS command to copy the first two of these system files to the hard disk and then use the COPY command to copy the COMMAND.COM file. Then, use RESTORE. As an alternative, you can use `format /s` (with any other options needed) to format a system disk and then do the RESTORE. This will destroy all existing data on the disk, however.

Examples Example 1: Restore a specific file from a backup disk. Suppose that you accidentally deleted or otherwise damaged a file on your hard disk. The easiest way to replace the file is to find a copy on some other disk and use the COPY command. If all you have are backup disks created by BACKUP, however, the files are not in a format suitable for COPY, so you must use RESTORE.

Tip

Restoring .LOG Files

If you use the /l option with the BACKUP command, a file called BACKUP.LOG will be created. This file contains a list of all the files backed up and the number of the backup disk containing each file. To restore a particular file, you can use the FIND command to find the file's entry in the log, insert the indicated disk in the floppy drive, and then run the RESTORE command. If the backup disk isn't disk 01, you will get a warning, but you can ignore this warning by pressing Enter, and the file will be restored. If there is no BACKUP.LOG, you will have to put successive disks in the drive until RESTORE finds the correct one.

```
C:\>restore a: c:\corres\letter5
Insert backup diskette 01 in drive A:
Strike any key when ready.    ←Press a key here

*** Files were backed up on 06-28-1990 ***
*** Restoring files from diskette 01 ***
\CONFIG.BAK                   ←File was found on the first disk
```

Example 2: Restore all files to the hard disk, including subdirectories.

```
C:\>restore a: c:\*.* /s
```

This specifies that files belonging to the root directory of drive C will be restored; the wildcards specify that all files will be restored; and the /s ensures that all directories of the root directory, their subdirectories, and any sub-subdirectories, and so on, will be restored.

Example 3: To be extra safe, have RESTORE prompt before replacing any files that have been modified or that are read-only.

```
C:\restore a: c:\sys /p
```

Here you want to restore files to the SYS directory on drive C (you are not restoring subdirectories). You specify the /p option to help you avoid losing more recent files accidentally. When RESTORE encounters a file that has been modified since the backup, it displays a message like this:

```
Warning!  File CONFIG.TMP was changed after the backup.
Replace the file (Y/N)?
```

Example 4: Restore only C program source files, regardless of their locations on the destination disk, that have been deleted since the last backup.

```
C:\>restore a: c:\*.c /s /n
```

The wildcard specifies that you want only files with the extension .c, traditional for C source files. The /n option is useful because it backs up the specified files only if they do not exist on the destination disk. This is a good way to restore accidentally deleted files (assuming, of course, that you've backed them up).

Example 5: Restore only files that have been modified since the last backup.

```
C:\>restore a: c:\data\*.* /m
```

This replaces with their earlier versions from the backup disk all files in the DATA directory that have been modified. This might be done if a program problem has corrupted your data and you need to go back to the last good copy of the database.

Example 6: Restore only files that were modified on or after June 1, 1990 at 5:00 PM.

```
C:\>restore a: c:\*.* /s /a:06-01-90 /l:17:00:00
```

Notice how the /a and /l are combined to specify the date and time.

Related Chapter Chapter 6–Managing Your Hard Disk

SELECT

External Command

Compatibility	2.0	2.1	3.0	3.1	3.2	**3.3**	**4.0**	OS/2 (DOS mode)	OS/2 (prot.)
			▲	▲	▲	▲	▲		

Use the SELECT command in PC DOS versions 3.0 through 3.3 to set up a bootable PC DOS disk that includes country-specific information, such as the formats for time, date, and currency.

Version 4

The SELECT Command Is Enhanced in Version 4
Use SELECT to configure a wide range of system options (including the COUNTRY information) through a series of menu screens.

Format

```
select country-code keyboard-code
select source drive destination country-code keyboard-code
```
(PC DOS 3.3)

Note: To use SELECT in PC DOS 4, you must boot a copy of the system distribution Install disk.

Sample Use

`select 049 gr` (PC DOS 3.0 through 3.2)

`select a: c:\dos` (PC DOS 3.3)

Boot System Install disk (PC DOS 4)

Procedure

To make a bootable configuration of PC DOS versions 3.0 through 3.2, type `select` followed by the country code and corresponding keyboard code. See Chapter 13, "International Language Support," for tables of country and keyboard codes. You must place a floppy disk containing the system files (such as a copy of your PC DOS distribution disk) in drive A and swap it with another floppy that will become a new copy of the system disk, configured with the selected country information. The drive must be drive A; other floppy or hard drives are not supported (but see the following discussion).

To make a bootable configuration of PC DOS version 3.3, type `select` followed by the source drive and then the destination drive (and optionally a directory path). If a source drive is not specified, drive A is assumed to be the source and drive B the destination. If the source drive is specified, a destination drive must be specified. Only drives A and B may be used (but see the following discussion). Follow the destination with the country code and corresponding keyboard code.

Version 4

Installing a Bootable Version 4 System Disk
To make a bootable configuration of PC DOS version 4, place a copy of your Install distribution disk in drive A and restart the system. The entire procedure from then on is menu-driven, complete with online help. For more information to help you make appropriate choices in installing PC DOS 4, see Chapter 12, "Installing a PC DOS System."

Related Commands

AUTOEXEC.BAT is a file where SELECT places commands to be run at startup.

CONFIG.SYS is a file where SELECT places the COUNTRY statement specifying which country is to be used for the format.

BACKUP and RESTORE save existing data on a hard disk before using SELECT to reformat it.

FDISK creates and manages hard disk partitions.

FORMAT prepares a disk for use; the /s option transfers system files (but does not select country information).

SYS transfers system files to an already-formatted disk (but does not select country information).

DETAILED REFERENCE

Explanation

The SELECT command in its various incarnations is intended to assist you in preparing a bootable configuration of PC DOS, complete with country-specific information. If you are using PC DOS 3.3 or earlier, are happy with the default U.S. format, and do not intend to use different character sets (code page switching), you need not use SELECT. In the case of a floppy disk, you can just format the disk with the /s option to transfer the three essential system files (IBMDOS.COM, IBMBIO.COM, and COMMAND.COM) to the new disk, copy whatever external PC DOS command files you will be needing, and optionally prepare CONFIG.SYS and AUTOEXEC.BAT files to configure the system. You could follow a similar procedure with a hard disk, although you should not format a hard disk without backing up any valuable data on it first for later restoration (see BACKUP and RESTORE). You may need to run FDISK first to create partitions. See FDISK and FORMAT entries for details.

If you wish to use a country format other than U.S., or want to do code page switching, you have two choices. Assuming you are making a bootable floppy disk, you can run SELECT, specifying the appropriate country and keyboard code, and the work of setting up the COUNTRY setting and KEYB command will be done for you. (You'll still have to install appropriate device drivers for the display and printer to enable them to support code pages, though.) Alternatively, you can perform all of the steps given in Chapter 13, "International Language Support," "by hand." (You must do the latter in any case if you are installing to a hard disk, because SELECT prior to PC DOS 4 does not support hard disks.)

Version 4

Use the SELECT Command to Install Version 4

If you are installing PC DOS 4, you must generally use the SELECT program by booting the Install system disk. You should do so regardless of whether you need country or code page information, because SELECT allows you to set a variety of other options as well, including priorities for memory versus disk use and the use of DOSSHELL.

In PC DOS 4, SELECT can install an updated version of PC DOS on your hard disk without having to reformat the hard disk. If your existing version is MS-DOS (rather than PC DOS), however, you will either have to reformat the disk or change the DOS signature in the system file by using DEBUG or a disk utility. As an alternative, you can install PC DOS 4 by hand. See Chapter 12, "Installing a PC DOS System," for details.

Comments The implementation of SELECT for PC DOS 3.0 through 3.2 uses the FORMAT command to prepare the new disk, the DISKCOPY command to copy the source disk to the destination (by swapping disks in drive A), and the DISKCOMP command to check the results of the copying. Because all the commands mentioned are external, they must be present on the source disk or somewhere in the current search path. The result of the operation of SELECT is a copy of the original system disk with the addition of a new AUTOEXEC.BAT file that loads the appropriate keyboard driver. (These versions of PC DOS use separate keyboard drivers for various country keyboards.)

The implementation of SELECT for PC DOS 3.3 uses FORMAT to prepare the new disk and then uses XCOPY to copy the three key system files; these external commands must be available somewhere in the search path. If you are using a high capacity (1.2MB or 1.44MB) drive, you must use a high capacity disk. Both AUTOEXEC.BAT and CONFIG.SYS files are created on the target disk; in this version of PC DOS, the KEYB command is installed to load the correct keyboard configuration instead of using separate keyboard drivers. The CONFIG.SYS file contains the COUNTRY setting. The codes used in these commands and settings correspond to the ones given on the command line when SELECT was run.

Version 4

SELECT Creates AUTOEXEC.BAT and CONFIG.SYS Commands and Settings in Version 4

Because PC DOS 4 requires the use of the system Install disk and prompts you to insert disks as needed, there should be no problem with files not being available. SELECT creates quite extensive AUTOEXEC.BAT and CONFIG.SYS files containing settings and commands for a variety of purposes.

Examples

Example 1: Create a bootable system disk with the French country information and keyboard code, under PC DOS 3.0, 3.1, or 3.2.

```
C:\>select 033 fr
```

033 is the country code for France; fr is the keyboard code. You will receive a message (the wording varies) warning you that SELECT erases everything; check that you have the correct disk in the drive, and type `y` to continue. You will be prompted for disk swaps as necessary. On the new disk, the AUTOEXEC.BAT file will contain

```
keybfr
```

to load the French keyboard. The CONFIG.SYS file will contain

```
country=033
```

Example 2: Create the same bootable disk under PC DOS 3.3.

```
C:\>select b: a: 033 fr
```

Here you can use two floppy disk drives, and put the source disk with the system files in drive B. (You can't use other drives such as C, however.) When SELECT is finished, the AUTOEXEC.BAT file on the new disk will look like this (the comments have been added):

```
path \;          ←Plus the rest of your current path
keyb fr,033      ←Installs French keyboard
echo off
date
time
ver
```

The CONFIG.SYS file will contain

```
country=033
```

Note: No example is given for PC DOS 4, because this version of SELECT provides extensive menu screens and online help. The AUTOEXEC.BAT and CONFIG.SYS files created by a "typical" installation of PC DOS 4 are shown and described in Chapter 12, "Installing a PC DOS System."

Related Chapters Chapter 11–Customizing Your System
Chapter 12–Installing a PC DOS System
Chapter 13–International Language Support

SET

Internal Command, Batch Command

Compatibility	2.0	2.1	3.0	3.1	3.2	3.3	4.0	OS/2 (DOS mode)	OS/2 (prot.)
	▲	▲	▲	▲	▲	▲	▲	▲	▲

Use the SET command to set the value of environmental variables to be used by PC DOS commands, batch files, and programs.

Format `set` displays the names and values of all environmental variables.

`set` *`variable-name=string`* creates a variable or gives a value to an existing variable.

`set` *`variable-name=`* removes a variable from the environment.

Sample Use `set comspec=c:\dos\command.com`

Procedure You can use SET either interactively or in a PC DOS batch file. To display a list of currently defined variables and their values, type `set` (Example 1). To create a variable, type `set` followed by the name of the variable and an equal sign. (Variable names follow the same rules as file names, except they can have no more than 8 characters.) Follow the equal sign with a string representing the variable's value (Example 2).

Note: Defining a variable replaces any existing variable that has the same name. To use the value of a defined variable in a batch file statement, precede and follow the variable name with percent signs (Example 3). To use a command-line parameter as a variable within a batch file, surround the parameter number with percent signs (Example 4). To remove a variable from the environment, type the variable name followed by an equal sign, without a following string (Example 5).

Related Commands APPEND sets the value of the APPEND variable.

AUTOEXEC.BAT is a file for setting variables automatically.

ECHO displays text, including the value of a variable.

IF tests the value of a variable.

FOR repeats the execution of a statement.

GOTO jumps to a label in a batch file.

PATH sets the value of the PATH variable.

DETAILED REFERENCE

Explanation The PC DOS environment maintains lists of variables that can be accessed by PC DOS commands, command or batch files, or other programs. For example, the list of directories that will be searched for executable programs is maintained as the value of a variable called PATH; executing the PATH command actually sets the value of this variable. The SET command allows you to list the currently defined variables, establish new variables, change or add to the value of a variable, or remove a variable from the environment.

Caution

Don't Use Spaces with the = Symbol

Be careful not to put a space before or after the equal sign when establishing or assigning to a variable. A statement such as `set path =c:\os2;c:\os2\progs` actually establishes a new variable whose name is the word *path* (including the space), instead of assigning to the actual PATH variable. A statement such as `alpha= on` actually gives alpha a value of *on* (including the preceding space).

PC DOS variables are not case sensitive, however. Path, path, and PATH refer to the same variable.

Comments If you use additional copies of the command processor (COMMAND.COM), each copy maintains its own separate environment (list of variables and their values). Changes made to the environment of an extra command processor do not affect the environment of the main processor from which it was run.

To set variables automatically at the start of each session, put the appropriate SET (or PATH or APPEND) statements in your AUTOEXEC.BAT file.

The default maximum size for the PC DOS environment is 127 bytes. If you use more than ten or so variables, or if your variables contain long strings such as path names, you may get the `out of environment space` error message. If so, you can increase the environment size (up to 32,768 bytes) by using the /e: option with the SHELL=COMMAND.COM statement in your CONFIG.SYS file.

Caution

Limitations of Environment Size

Once you load a memory-resident program (such as the PC DOS PRINT, MODE, or GRAPHICS commands, or programs like SideKick) and the environment already exceeds 127 bytes, it cannot be expanded further, and you will get an error message if you attempt to define variables whose values would require expansion of the environment.

In general, then, expand the amount of memory for variables by using the SHELL statement, if necessary, and then define the variables you will be needing in your AUTOEXEC.BAT file before loading memory-resident commands or programs. (If you think you will need to define more variables later, you can insert "dummy" variables in the AUTOEXEC.BAT file to reserve environment space for later use.)

Examples Example 1: Examine the contents of the environment.

```
C:\>set
COMSPEC=C:\COMMAND.COM
TEMP=c:\temp
PATH=C:\DOS;C:\DOS\UTILS;C:\WP50;C:\DOS\BATCH;C:\C51;C:\UTILS\;
APPEND=C:\DOS;C:\WP50;C:\C51;
INCLUDE=C:\C51\INCLUDE
PROMPT=$p$g
```

By typing `set` without a variable name, you obtain a list of the environment. Some key variables maintained by PC DOS commands include:

PATH: the search path for executable programs

APPEND: the search path for data files (DOS mode)

COMSPEC: the location of the command processor

PROMPT: the text to be displayed as a command prompt

Example 2: Assign values to some variables.

```
C:\>set home=c:\dos
C:\>set lib=c:\cpp\lib
C:\>set include=c:\cpp\include
```

Here, you create a new variable called *home* and give it a value, the directory name C:\DOS. You also redefine two existing variables, *lib* and *include*. (These variables are often used by compilers and other programming tools to point to the location of libraries and include files, but some applications use them, too. For example, the pop-up database Memory Mate allows you to use the variable MEMO_DIR to tell it where to find the current database.)

Example 3: Use the value of a variable in a statement.

```
C:\copy con: showincl.bat
@echo off
echo %include%
^Z
 1 file(s) copied
C:\>showincl
c:\cpp\include
```

In a batch file statement, placing percent signs around a variable name causes the name to be replaced by its value. For example, having defined the directory containing a database set dbms=c:\accts\yeardata, the batch file might later use cd %dbms% to change to that directory.

Example 4: Access a command-line parameter as a variable.

```
C:\>copy con: sdir.bat
set target=%1%
dir %target% | sort | more
^Z
 1 file(s) copied.
```

Any batch file can access whatever the user typed on the command line to run it. In batch file statements, the special parameter %1 is used to stand for the first item that was typed after the batch file name, %2 for the second item, and so on, up to %9 for the ninth item. The value of such a parameter (in other words, what was originally typed on the command line in that position) can be obtained in the same way as the values of other variables: by surrounding the parameter number with percent signs.

In this example, the value of the first parameter (the name of a directory typed by the user) is assigned to the variable *target*. The value of target is then used in the DIR statement, which generates the listing for the directory whose name was placed in target. The list is sent to SORT via a pipe and then to MORE to display the sorted directory a screen at a time.

In this example, of course, you could have simply used %1% rather than %target% in the DIR statement, but in a long, complicated batch file, it would be useful to assign command-line parameters to meaningful variable names for later use. See the chapters "Advanced Use of the Command Line" and "Batch Files" (Chapters 8 and 10) for more discussion and examples.

Example 5: Remove a variable from the environment.

```
C:\>set home=
```

Typing the variable name and an equal sign, but no value, removes the variable from the environment.

Related Chapters Chapter 8–Advanced Use of the Command Line
Chapter 10–Batch Files

External Command

SHARE

Compatibility	2.0	2.1	3.0	3.1	3.2	3.3	4.0	OS/2 (DOS mode)	OS/2 (prot.)
					▲	▲	▲		

Use the SHARE command to provide support for file sharing on a network. You can also use it to monitor the changing of floppy disks.

Format `share` *`options`* (PC DOS 3.2 and 3.3)

`install=share.exe` *`options`* (Recommended for PC DOS 4)

Options */f:file information space* specifies the number of bytes used to store file names plus file control information. Default is 2048 bytes.

/l:locks specifies the maximum number of file locks to be made available. Default is 20.

Sample Use `share /f:1024 /l:10` (PC DOS 3.2 or 3.3)

`install=c:\dos\share.exe /f:1024 /l:10` (PC DOS 4)

SHARE

Procedure For PC DOS 3.2 or 3.3, to install the SHARE facility, begin a statement with `share`. To specify the amount of space to be used for names and control of files in the network, specify `/f:` followed by the number of bytes to be allocated. To specify the maximum number of file locks to be used, type `/l:` followed by the number of locks. (File locks are special flags that prevent a file from being accessed when it is already in use by another user on the network.)

Version 4

Using INSTALL to Load SHARE in Version 4

For PC DOS 4, you can use the preceding procedure, but for efficient use of memory, use the INSTALL statement to load SHARE via the CONFIG.SYS file. Begin the statement with `install=share.exe`. (If the file SHARE.EXE is not in the startup directory, give the full path name.) You must include the extension .EXE in any case. To specify the amount of space to be used for names and control of files in the network, specify `/f:` followed by the number of bytes to be allocated. To specify the maximum number of file locks to be used, type `/l:` followed by the number of locks.

Related Commands AUTOEXEC.BAT is a file that runs SHARE automatically (PC DOS 3.2 or 3.3).

BUFFERS specifies the number of buffers to file information (for local use).

CONFIG.SYS is a file that loads SHARE automatically (PC DOS 4).

CTTY operates the computer from an external console.

FASTOPEN stores disk directory information in memory.

FCBS specifies the number of file control blocks and takes effect when file sharing is loaded.

FILES specifies the number of files that can be opened using file handles.

INSTALL loads SHARE via CONFIG.SYS (PC DOS 4).

VERIFY specifies verification of disk operations.

DETAILED REFERENCE

Explanation Any network needs a special facility to make sure that file access is carried on in an orderly way. If one user is using a file (for example, updating records in a database), and another user is given a copy of the same file to work with, what will the final file look like? Whose changes will be kept and whose discarded? Only one user can be allowed to work on a given piece of data at a given time. PC DOS networks use file-sharing rules and file locks to keep chaos at bay. From the programmer's point of view, file sharing works like this: When a program opens a file using system function 3DH, and SHARE has been loaded, a sharing code is used to determine what type of access other programs on the network may have to the file. A program that accesses a file can place a "lock" on it to make it temporarily unavailable to other programs. (More sophisticated applications lock individual data records, but allow the rest of the file to be shared.)

The /f option specifies the amount of space that will be set aside to hold the names and control information; for each file in use on the network, there must be room for the file name (including extension) plus 11 bytes. The default value, 2048, would thus hold about 100 files. No maximum value is specified in the IBM documentation.

The /l option specifies the maximum number of file locks that can be in use at a given time. The default provides for 20 files.

Note on share and the FCBS setting: If you have been using the default value of the FCBS setting (fcbs=4,0), SHARE adjusts the value to (16,8) for a larger number of files to be in use on the network. You can increase this setting if you receive a message referring to lack of file handles. See the FCBS entry. You can ignore these options unless you run into error messages that suggest that they need to be increased.

Version 4

Use SHARE with Hard Disk Partitions Greater Than 32MB in Version 4

If you are using a hard disk partition larger than 32MB, SHARE must be loaded into memory. A copy of SHARE.EXE must be in the root directory or the subdirectory specified in a SHELL statement in your CONFIG.SYS file.

Sensing Floppy Disk Changes: An additional capability of the SHARE command is to sense whether a disk drive door has been opened during a read or write operation. (This capability must be built into the drive hardware. Many AT-type and PS/2-type systems have this capability with their built-in drives; many earlier models and many external drives may not.) If SHARE is loaded and PC DOS detects that the drive door was opened during a read or write operation, it checks the disk volume label to see if it matches the information stored in memory. If it does not match, PC DOS issues a message requesting that the original disk volume be put in the drive. When the correct disk is inserted, the I/O operation is completed.

Examples

Example 1: Load network file sharing (pre-PC DOS 4).

```
share /f:1024 /l:10
```

This command would probably go in the AUTOEXEC.BAT file if the machine were dedicated as a network server. The values (1024 bytes for file information and 10 file locks) are half the default, suggesting a small network.

Example 2: Load network file sharing (PC DOS 4).

```
install=c:\dos\share.exe /f:4096 /l:40
```

This statement uses INSTALL to load SHARE via the CONFIG.SYS file. It provides for a larger network, with double the file information space and double the number of file locks allowed by the default settings.

Related Chapter

Chapter 11–Customizing Your System

SHELL

External Command

Compatibility	2.0	2.1	3.0	3.1	3.2	3.3	4.0	OS/2 (DOS mode)	OS/2 (prot.)
	▲	▲	▲	▲	▲	▲	▲	▲	

Use the SHELL statement in your CONFIG.SYS file to specify an alternative PC DOS command processor. You can also specify the amount of memory to be reserved for environmental variables by COMMAND.COM.

Format `shell=`*`processor options`*

Options The options available depend on the command processor loaded. When COMMAND.COM is specified, the following options can be used:

/p specifies that the command processor will remain permanently in memory. This option is always used when COMMAND.COM is loaded with the SHELL statement.

/e:bytes specifies size of environment for variables, from 160 to 32,768 bytes.

Version 4

Use the /MSG Option to Speed Error Reporting in Version 4
/MSG stores the text for all messages concerning command parsing or processing errors in memory. This speeds up operation when COMMAND.COM is run from a floppy disk.

Note: PC DOS 4 users should not confuse DOSSHELL with SHELL. DOSSHELL is a front-end program that runs from the actual shell, the command processor COMMAND.COM. It is run from the AUTOEXEC.BAT file or from the command line.

Sample Use `shell=command.com /p /e:512`

Procedure In your CONFIG.SYS file, begin a statement with `shell=` followed by the file name of the command processor to be used (usually COMMAND.COM). If the command processor is not in the startup directory, give the complete path name. Follow the file name with any options that you wish to specify for the command processor. To specify an environment size for COMMAND.COM, enter `shell=command.com /p /e:bytes` where *bytes* is a number between 160 and 32,768 (Example 1).

Related Commands COMMAND.COM is the default command processor for PC DOS.

COMSPEC specifies the location of DOS mode command processor.

DOSSHELL is the PC DOS 4 front-end program (not a shell installable by the SHELL statement).

DETAILED REFERENCE

Explanation The command processor is the program that interprets commands given by the user and runs application programs. The default command processor for PC DOS is COMMAND.COM. The SHELL statement allows you to specify a different command processor, such as a UNIX-style shell or a graphic, mouse-driven interface (Example 1). It also allows you to increase the size of the environment used to store variables, such as PATH (Example 2).

The default if no SHELL statement is given is shell=command.com /p.

Comments Programs that provide an alternative command processor should come with instructions specifying the correct SHELL statement. Note that if you are using a copy of COMMAND.COM that is not in the startup directory, you must also `set comspec=path name` where *path name* is the complete path to COMMAND.COM.

Examples **Example 1**: Increase the space for environmental variables for COMMAND.COM.

```
shell=command.com /p /e:1024
```

This is probably the most common use of the SHELL statement; the standard command processor COMMAND.COM is specified, with the /p option specifying that it resides permanently in memory. The /e option is used to specify that 1024 bytes (1K) be reserved for environmental variables. You can use a SHELL statement like this when you receive the error message `out of environment space`.

Example 2: Use an alternative command processor.

```
shell=csh.exe /i c:\unix\profile
```

Here it is specified that the command processor CSH.EXE (an emulation of the UNIX C shell) be loaded and run rather than COMMAND.COM. The /i option happens to be one recognized by this processor and specifies an initialization file.

Related Chapter Chapter 11–Customizing Your System

Batch Command

SHIFT

Compatibility	2.0	2.1	3.0	3.1	3.2	3.3	4.0	OS/2 (DOS mode)	OS/2 (prot.)
	▲	▲	▲	▲	▲	▲	▲	▲	▲

Use the SHIFT command in batch files to allow a batch file to access more than ten items of information from the command line.

Format `shift`

Sample Use `shift`

Procedure When you need to access more than 10 command-line parameters in a command or batch file, use the SHIFT statement. Each time you use the SHIFT statement, the command-line parameters are shifted one position to the left

(%9 becomes %8, %7 becomes %6 ... %1 becomes %0, and %0 is discarded). Example 1 shows how this works.

Related Command IF tests variables or command-line parameters.

DETAILED REFERENCE

Explanation When a command line is typed by the user, PC DOS keeps track of the items entered on the line and makes them available to batch files or programs. For example, if the user types the line

```
setup hard com1: vga
```

to run an installation program for a software package, the command file SETUP.BAT gains access to the following items:

Command-Line Parameter	Item
%0	setup
%1	hard
%2	com1:
%3	vga

The command file can test for these values and act accordingly. For example

```
rem determine kind of disk to be used
if %1%==hard goto hardinst
call flopinst
goto nextpart
:hardinst
call hardinst
:nextpart
...
```

A total of ten command-line parameters are thus accessible, numbered %0 through %9. If there may be more than ten items on the command line (including the name of the command file itself), you can use the SHIFT command to make the additional parameters accessible. See the examples for details.

Comments Note that each time you shift, the value of %0 is discarded and replaced by the value that was formerly in %1. You cannot recover discarded values. (If you need to discard a value that you may need later, you can first assign it to a "holder" variable via the SET command.)

Examples Example 1: Demonstrate the operation of the SHIFT statement.

```
C:\>copy con: shifter.bat
@echo off
echo %0 %1 %2 %3 %4 %5 %6 %7 %8 %9
shift
echo %0 %1 %2 %3 %4 %5 %6 %7 %8 %9
shift
echo %0 %1 %2 %3 %4 %5 %6 %7 %8 %9
^Z
 1 file(s) copied.
```

←Next, run the command line

```
C:\>shifter one two three four five six seven eight nine ten eleven
shifter one two three four five six seven eight nine   ←Results of echo
one two three four five six seven eight nine ten          statements
two three four five six seven eight nine ten eleven
```

The first ECHO statement lists ten command-line parameters, including the name of the command file itself, *shifter*, plus the words *one* through *nine*. When you SHIFT and look again, the parameter *shifter,* which had been in the first (actually zero) position has disappeared, and the parameters *one* through *ten* are shown. The next SHIFT accesses *two* through *eleven*.

Example 2: Write a batch file that processes a variable number of command-line parameters. Often you don't know how many items a command file will be called on to process. For example, suppose that you want to write a batch file that will give the TYPE command the capability to list an arbitrary number of files. (Normally, it can only display a single file.)

```
C:\DOS\BATCH> copy con: typer.bat
@echo off
rem type the next file
:typefile
if %1x==x goto end
type %1
rem check the next command-line parameter
shift
goto typefile
rem no more files
:end
^Z
 1 file(s) copied.
typer letter1 letter2 letter3 letter4   ←Contents of files will be displayed
                                          consecutively
```

The work is done in the section labeled *:typefile*. Command-line parameter %1 contains the first file name (remember that %0 is the name of the batch file itself). The test if %1x==x is a "trick" for testing for the absence of a command-line parameter; if %1 does not exist (and thus has a null value), the expression evaluates to if x==x, which is true. (You can't just specify if %1==, because this yields a syntax error.) If there is no file (%1 has a null value), the GOTO statement sends you to the end of the batch file. If the file is present, the following TYPE command lists its contents. Next, the SHIFT statement shifts all the parameters one position to the left, bringing the next file name (if any) into the %1 position. The GOTO statement repeats the test to see whether the parameter has a value, and so on, until every file specified on the command line is processed.

Related Chapter Chapter 10–Batch Files

SORT

External Command

Compatibility	2.0	2.1	3.0	3.1	3.2	3.3	4.0	OS/2 (DOS mode)	OS/2 (prot.)
	▲	▲	▲	▲	▲	▲	▲	▲	▲

Use the SORT command to put lines in a file into alphabetical order. You can also sort in reverse order or sort lines starting at a particular column position.

Format `sort` *`options`* is the basic format.

```
sort options < input-file>output-file (redirected input and output) command
| sort options > output-file (input from pipe and redirected output)
```

Options */r* reverses sort (z comes before a).

/+col sorts beginning at a specified column (column 1 is the default).

Sample Use `sort /+6 < data > sortdata`

Procedure To sort data from a disk file and save the results in another file, type `sort` followed by any options you want to use and then type < followed by the name of the file containing the data. Then type > followed by the name of the file that will contain the sorted data (Example 1).

To sort the data being output by a PC DOS command or other program, type the name of the command or program (and any appropriate options) followed by the pipe symbol | and then `sort` followed by any options. Redirect the output to a file by typing > followed by the name of the file in which the sorted data will be stored.

To sort data in reverse order (9 comes before 8, Z comes before A, and so on), use the /r option. To have SORT examine each line of data starting at a particular column, use the /+col option, where col is the number of the column where the text to be sorted begins.

Caution

Sorting Is Case-Sensitive in Versions 2.X
Versions of PC DOS prior to 3.0 sort in strict ASCII code order. In the ASCII code, all of the uppercase letters come before the lowercase ones. Thus Zelazny comes before astronaut. Starting with PC DOS 3.0, sorting is no longer case-sensitive, this means that letters are sorted in A–Z order regardless of case.

Related Command COUNTRY provides a country-specific sequence for sorting.

DETAILED REFERENCE

Explanation The SORT command sorts lines of data in ASCII order. Letters are sorted in alphabetical order, with no case distinction (that is, y comes before Z, even though in strict ASCII order all the uppercase letters come before the lowercase ones). Numerals come in the normal order (0 to 9). Other symbols (punctuation, etc.) follow the standard ASCII sequence, as modified by the "collation sequence" for the country specified in the country code and code page.

When SORT is used by itself, the standard input (typed at the keyboard) is read by SORT and then displayed on the screen in sorted order. The normal use of SORT, however, is to read in data from a disk file using input redirection (the < operator) and to place the sorted output in another file using output redirection (the > operator), as shown in Example 1. You can also use a pipe (|) to feed the output of a command or program to SORT and then display the sorted output on the screen or redirect it to a file (see Example 4). See Chapter 8, "Advanced Use of the Command Line," for more examples of redirection and the use of pipes.

The /r option causes the sort to be reversed (from highest to lowest ASCII values with upper- and lowercase treated as equivalent). Thus, zebra will come before antelope and 98 will come before 34.

The /+col allows you to treat the input data lines as records containing fields of data beginning at specified columns, as shown in Examples 2 and 3.

Version 4

SORTing Eccentricities

Because output redirection erases an existing file, you cannot use the same file for a SORT's input and output. When dealing with numbers, remember that they are treated as character strings by SORT; that is, 323 will come before 97. To sort numbers in numeric order, you must make sure they have the same number of digits (by adding leading zeroes where necessary, for example). Also, be careful about inserting leading spaces (blanks) when creating a data file for SORT. Because a blank is a character that comes before A in the ASCII alphabet,

```
 zebra
```

will come before

```
antelope
```

Examples The first three examples use the file ADDRESS.DAT.

```
C:\>copy con: address.txt
Watts, Leslie       1515 Bay St.        Lyme Center         NH   03769
Johnson, Jim        911 A St.           Prior Lake          MN   55372
Daniels, Richard    2451 19th St.       San Francisco       CA   94122
Roberts, Cathy      19 Orange St.       Tatamy              PA   18085
Able, Victoria      215 Shady Ave.      Stacy Fork          LA   41468
^Z
```

You can see that each line or record has been divided into five fields.

Field	Starts at Column
Name	1
Street address	20
City	40
State	60
ZIP code	65

Enough spaces have been typed following each field to reach the beginning of the next field. (Use spaces, not tabs. Spaces are needed because the /+col uses absolute column positions.)

Example 1: Sort the address list by last name.

```
C:\>sort < address.dat
Able, Victoria     215 Shady Ave.      Stacy Fork          LA   41468
Daniels, Richard   2451 19th St.       San Francisco       CA   94122
Johnson, Jim       911 A St.           Prior Lake          MN   55372
Roberts, Cathy     19 Orange St.       Tatamy              PA   18085
Watts, Leslie      1515 Bay St.        Lyme Center         NH   03769
```

Here, you get a default sort by the first column, in other words the last name. If you want to save the results of the sort in a file called NAME.DAT, you can type

```
C:\>sort < address.dat > name.dat
```

Example 2: Sort the address file by city.

```
C:\>sort /+40 < address.dat > city.dat
C:\>type city.dat
Watts, Leslie      1515 Bay St.        Lyme Center         NH   03769
Johnson, Jim       911 A St.           Prior Lake          MN   55372
Daniels, Richard   2451 19th St.       San Francisco       CA   94122
Able, Victoria     215 Shady Ave.      Stacy Fork          LA   41468
Roberts, Cathy     19 Orange St.       Tatamy              PA   18085
```

By specifying column 40, the start of the city field, you sort the records in order by city.

Example 3: Sort the address file by ZIP code in reverse order.

```
C:\>sort /+65 /r < address.dat > revzip.dat
C:\>type revzip.dat
Daniels, Richard   2451 19th St.       San Francisco       CA   94122
Johnson, Jim       911 A St.           Prior Lake          MN   55372
Able, Victoria     215 Shady Ave.      Stacy Fork          LA   41468
Roberts, Cathy     19 Orange St.       Tatamy              PA   18085
Watts, Leslie      1515 Bay St.        Lyme Center         NH   03769
```

The option */+65* specifies the ZIP code field. The */r* option specifies a reverse sort. Because all of the ZIP codes have five digits, they are sorted correctly.

Example 4: Sort the output of a PC DOS command.

```
C:\>copy con: sdir.bat
@echo off
dir %1 | sort
^Z
 1 file(s) copied.
C:\>sdir c:\pcdosbib\ref\sort.exa
     8 File(s)   5346432 bytes free
 Directory of C:\PCDOSBIB\REF\SORT.EXA
 The volume label in drive C is DOSDISK.
.            <DIR>      7-28-90   1:14p
..           <DIR>      7-28-90   1:14p
ADDRESS  DAT       356  7-28-90   1:16p
CITY     DAT       356  7-28-90   1:18p
REVZIP   DAT       356  7-28-90   1:18p
SDIR     CMD        22  7-28-90   1:23p
SDIR     TXT        50  7-28-90   1:24p
SORTED   DAT       356  7-28-90   1:16p
```

The batch file SDIR.BAT uses the DIR command to obtain the directory specified in the first command-line parameter (%1). This output is sent via a pipe (|) to the SORT command. It is serendipitous that the lines of the directory output referring to the directory path and volume label begin with a space; this puts them at the beginning of the listing instead of intermixing them with the directory entries. Because of the ASCII order, the special directory entries . and .. come before any regular file names. If you are going to be dealing with directories too long to fit on one screen, you might want to either save the output in a file (using redirection) or pipe the output to the MORE command so that it can be viewed one screen at a time.

Related Chapter Chapter 8–Advanced Use of the Command Line

Setting

STACKS

Compatibility	2.0	2.1	3.0	3.1	3.2	3.3	4.0	OS/2 (DOS mode)	OS/2 (prot.)
					▲	▲	▲		

Use the STACKS setting in your CONFIG.SYS file to change the number of stacks used for processing hardware interrupts. You do this only if you receive error messages referring to the stack or if the documentation for a device specifies it.

Format `stacks=(`*`frames,frame-size`*`)`

Sample Use `stacks=(12,64)`

Procedure In your CONFIG.SYS file, begin a statement with `stacks=(`. Specify the number of stack frames to be provided (from 8 to 64), a comma, and then the size of each stack frame in bytes (from 32 to 512), followed by a close parenthesis.

Related Commands BREAK controls processing of user interrupt (Break key).

CONFIG.SYS is a file for STACKS setting.

DETAILED REFERENCE

Explanation Hardware interrupts are signals sent by devices to PC DOS, informing it that some important action has taken place or that the device is ready for input or output. For example, pressing a key on the keyboard causes the keyboard to send a hardware interrupt.

When an interrupt is received, the current internal state of the processor (register contents, the location of the next instruction to be processed, and so on) is temporarily saved to an area of memory called a stack frame. Control then goes to a routine called an interrupt handler, which performs the operations necessary for dealing with the device. The information about the processor status is then retrieved from the stack frame, and the interrupted processing continues.

The STACKS setting allows you to increase the number of available stack frames, the size of the frames, or both. You need to use this setting only if the documentation for one of your applications requires it or if you receive an error message like `Internal stack overflow. System Halted.`

In this case, you will have to reboot. (If pressing Ctrl-Alt-Delete doesn't work, you will have to turn off the system's power, wait about ten seconds, and then turn it on again.)

At this point, check the documentation of whatever application you were running (or whatever special device you were using) when the system crashed. If you can't find any reference to the stack, try increasing the number of stack frames first. If that doesn't work, try increasing the size of the frames. Because the stack is a standard data structure, larger stack frames are seldom needed, except perhaps for interfacing with unusual devices.

Note: Increasing the number and/or size of stack frames reduces available memory for the application accordingly.

The default setting for IBM AT and PS/2 machines is 9 stack frames of 128 bytes each. For the PC, XT, and Portable PC, no hardware stacks are installed; if an application needs them, you must use the STACK setting.

Examples **Example 1**: Provide hardware stack support for an IBM XT.

```
stacks=(9,128)
```

This provides the same defaults as those automatically installed on the IBM AT or PS/2.

Example 2: Allow for 32 stack frames of 64 bytes each.

```
stacks=(32,64)
```

Related Chapter Chapter 11–Customizing Your System

External Command

SUBST

Compatibility	2.0	2.1	3.0	3.1	3.2	3.3	4.0	OS/2 (DOS mode)	OS/2 (prot.)
				▲	▲	▲	▲	▲	

Use the SUBST command to substitute a drive letter for a directory. You can use SUBST to create a shorthand for long path names or to "fool" an old application that does not recognize paths.

Format `subst` *`substitute-drive original drive or path`* substitutes a drive letter for a path.

`subst` displays current substitutions.

`subst` *`drive`* `/d` removes a substitution.

Option */d* deletes the substitution affecting the specified drive.

Sample Use `subst b: a:\`

Procedure To set up a drive substitution, type `subst` followed by the letter of the substitute drive, followed by the path for which it is to be substituted (Example 1). To display a list of substitutions currently in effect, type `subst` followed by the drive letter (Example 3). To remove a particular substitution, type `subst` followed by the letter of the affected drive, and the /d option (Example 4).

Note: Use SUBST when you want to substitute for part of a drive (in other words, a particular directory path). Use ASSIGN when you want to substitute a drive letter for an entire drive.

Related Commands ASSIGN assigns a drive letter to a different drive (doesn't work with path names).

AUTOEXEC.BAT is a file for setting up automatic substitutions.

DRIVER.SYS assigns logical drive letters to external drives.

FDISK assigns logical drive letters to hard disk partitions.

JOIN logically connects a drive to a directory.

LASTDRIVE sets the last available drive letter for substitutions.

TRUENAME reveals the path to the true location of a file.

DETAILED REFERENCE

Explanation The SUBST command allows you to create a shorthand in which you use a drive letter to stand for a path name. Occasionally, you may need to run older PC DOS applications that do not recognize path names, such as WordStar version 3.3. In this case, you can use the SUBST command to substitute a drive letter for the path name location of the data you will be working with. When you use the substitute drive letter, the PC DOS command processor automatically (and invisibly) substitutes the actual path name. More commonly, you can use SUBST to use drive letters for long path names. By referring to these drive letters, you can view directories, copy files, and so on, much more easily, because you no longer have to type (or remember) the long path names.

You can have multiple substitutions where several drive letters stand for the same path name; for example, after typing

```
C:\>subst p: c:\c51\bin
C:\>subst n: c:\c51\bin
C:\>subst r: c:\c51\bin
```

the commands DIR P:, DIR N:, and DIR R: will give exactly the same result.

Also, unlike the ASSIGN command, you can continue to use the original path whenever you wish. After executing subst s: c:\dos\progs, you can type either `dir s:` or `dir c:\dos\progs` to view this directory.

You can have substitutions take effect automatically at startup by putting the appropriate SUBST commands in AUTOEXEC.BAT.

Comments Drive letters used with the SUBST command must be within the range provided by the LASTDRIVE setting in your CONFIG.SYS. The default setting allows drive letters A through E. Therefore, if you want to use letters F, G, and H with SUBST, you would have to put the setting `lastdrive=h` in your CONFIG.SYS file. (You could, of course, have a higher setting.)

Caution

Some Commands Do Not Work with Substitute Drive Designations
Do not use the ASSIGN, BACKUP, DISKCOMP, DISKCOPY, FDISK, FORMAT, JOIN, LABEL, or RESTORE commands with substitute drive letters. Some of these commands, such as DISKCOPY and FORMAT, ignore substitutions and expect to work directly with "real" drives.

ASSIGN and JOIN also perform substitutions and will be misdirected if given names that are already substitutes.

Be careful in using CHDIR, MKDIR, PATH, or RMDIR with substitute names; make sure you understand which physical directory you are actually working with. You cannot use SUBST with network drives.

Examples Example 1: You have an old version of WordStar that does not recognize path names. You want to work on some letters in the directory B:\LETTERS while using WordStar in drive A.

```
A:\>subst d: b:\letters
```

Now, within WordStar, you can ask to retrieve D:LETTER6, and PC DOS will quietly substitute the actual path B:\LETTERS\LETTER6 without alarming WordStar.

Example 2: Create a shorthand form for long path names.

```
C:\>subst w: c:\wp\macros\techwrit
```

Now, if you wanted to copy the contents of this directory to drive A, you can type `copy w: a:`. (Note that LASTDRIVE must be set to w or "higher" for this to work.)

Example 3: Show the list of substitutions currently in effect.

```
C:\>subst
D: => B:\LETTERS
W: => C:\WP\MACROS\TECHWRIT
```

Example 4: Remove a substitution.

```
C:\>subst d: /d
```

Using the /d option removes the substitution of the drive letter D for the path B:\LETTERS. Notice that only the substitute drive letter is given, not the path for which it is a substitute.

Related Chapters

Chapter 6–Managing Your Hard Disk
Chapter 7–All About Floppy Disks
Chapter 11–Customizing Your System

Setting

SWITCHES

Compatibility	2.0	2.1	3.0	3.1	3.2	3.3	4.0	OS/2 (DOS mode)	OS/2 (prot.)
							▲		

Version 4

Use the SWITCHES setting in your CONFIG.SYS file in PC DOS 4 to specify the use of conventional keyboard functions on an extended keyboard. This is needed for applications that do not recognize the enhanced key functions of the new extended (101- or 102-key) keyboards.

Format

```
switches=/k
```

Options

/k prevents the use of extended keyboard functions and treats the extended keyboard as a conventional keyboard.

Sample Use

```
switches=/k
```

Procedure

To disable the extended keyboard functions, place the statement `switches=/k` in your CONFIG.SYS file. When the system is started, it will treat the extended keyboard as a conventional keyboard.

Related Commands

KEYB loads keyboard configurations.

MODE controls keyboard typing repetition.

SWITCHES

DETAILED REFERENCE

Explanation Newer IBM systems are provided with extended keyboards that recognize additional functions (for example, combinations involving the Alt and Ctrl keys with keypad and other special keys). Some older applications cannot deal with the extended keycodes properly. If you have such an application, you can use the SWITCHES setting in your CONFIG.SYS file to disable the extended keyboard functions, allowing your application to recognize the keyboard as a conventional one. You will, however, lose all extended keyboard functions until you remove this setting from CONFIG.SYS and reboot.

Comments When running applications that don't need this setting, you may wish to leave the SWITCHES setting in your CONFIG.SYS, but edit it by putting a REM in front of it to disable it. You can then remove the REM and reboot to go into conventional keyboard mode.

Example In the CONFIG.SYS file, disable the extended keyboard functions.

```
switches=/k
```

Related Chapter Chapter 11–Customizing Your System

SYS

External Command

Compatibility	2.0	2.1	3.0	3.1	3.2	3.3	**4.0**	OS/2 (DOS mode)	OS/2 (prot.)
	▲	▲	▲	▲	▲	▲	▲	▲	▲

Use the SYS command to copy the hidden operating system files IBMBIO.COM and IBMDOS.COM to a destination disk so that you can make it a bootable PC DOS disk. You can also use it to update the version of PC DOS on a disk.

Format `sys` *`drive:`* (PC DOS 3.3 and earlier)

`sys` *`source-drive: destination-drive:`* (PC DOS 4)

Sample Use `sys a:` (PC DOS 3.3 or earlier)

`sys c:\dos a:` (PC DOS 4)

To copy the hidden system files to another disk (for example, one in drive A), make the drive with the system files your current drive and then type `sys` followed by the drive letter for the drive containing the disk you are copying to (Example 1).

Version 4

Specify Both Source Drive and Destination Drive in Version 4

With PC DOS 4, you can specify a source drive other than the current drive (Example 2). Type `sys` followed by the source drive (the one containing the system files) and then the destination drive. If you omit the source drive, PC DOS assumes that the system files are on the current drive.

Related Commands

FDISK prepares partitions on a formatted hard disk.

FORMAT prepares a disk for use with OS/2 and can be used with the */s* option to copy system files

DETAILED REFERENCE

Explanation

The "core" files used by PC DOS (named IBMBIO.COM and IBMDOS.COM) are marked with the hidden attribute. This means that they cannot be copied with the regular COPY command. The SYS command copies these files from the root directory of the current drive (PC DOS 3.3 or earlier) or from a specified source drive (optional with PC DOS 4) to the specified destination drive. The two most common uses are to copy an updated version of the system files from a distribution floppy to the PC DOS startup drive, and to go in the opposite direction, copying the system files from the PC DOS startup drive to a floppy disk, as part of making the latter a bootable PC DOS disk.

Note: To make a bootable disk, you also need COMMAND.COM. SYS does not copy this file; use COPY to copy it after you've run SYS.

To format a new disk and make it bootable, it is easier to issue the command `format /s` with the specified drive. This has the advantage that, unlike SYS, it also copies COMMAND.COM to the new disk.

Comments

To copy the system files to a disk, the disk must either be newly formatted or already have the IBMBIO.COM and IBMDOS.COM files in place. In particular, IBMBIO.COM must reside at a particular fixed location on disk, from which it can be found at system startup. If a disk does not have the system files on it (in other words, is not a bootable disk), and does have other files, you cannot SYS to it without first removing the existing files. (This is not true with PC DOS 4; see following.) If a disk does have the system files from an earlier version of PC DOS on it (for example, a startup hard disk), you may be able to use SYS to update the system files from the distribution disk for a later version. This will work only if the old system files are not smaller than the new ones (but see following). If SYS reports that it was successful, you should also copy COMMAND.COM and all of the other PC DOS commands and utilities to the new disk, because commands for one version of PC DOS will not work with another version. If SYS reports that it was unable to copy the system files, you will have to back up all of the data on the disk (make two backups in case a disk happens to have bad sectors) and then run `format /s` to reformat the disk and copy the system files. You can then use the RESTORE command to place the original data on the disk. It is safest to follow the installation instructions that come with your version of PC DOS. (Also see Chapter 12, "Installing a PC DOS System.")

Version 4

Add the System to a Disk That Contains Files in Version 4

With PC DOS 4, you can use the SYS command with a disk containing existing files. If necessary, the SYS command will relocate existing files to allow it to place the system files correctly. There must be two unused directory entries available in the root directory, to accommodate the system files (not usually a problem), and of course, there must be room on the disk as a whole to store the system files. This means you can update a hard disk to PC DOS 4 without having to back it up, reformat it, and then restore the data.

Examples Example 1: Make a newly formatted disk bootable.

```
A:\
>c:
C:\>sys a:
copy \dos\command.com a:
```

First, you made drive C, which contains your system files, the current drive. COPY was then used to copy COMMAND.COM to the new disk. Alternatively, the steps could have been combined by typing `format a:/s`.

Example 2: In PC DOS 4, copy the system files from a disk in drive A to one in drive B.

Version 4

The Source Drive Need Not Be the Current Drive in Version 4

```
C:\>sys a: b:
```

The only difference is that PC DOS 4 allows you to specify a source drive that need not be the current drive.

Example 3: Update the PC DOS files on drive C.

```
A:\>sys c:
A:\>copy *.* c:\dos
```

First, you use SYS to copy the system files to drive C and then use COPY to copy all the other PC DOS files (including COMMAND.COM) to the C:\DOS directory on drive C. (You could have copied them to the root, but it's best to have as few files as possible in the root directory and neatly organize the other files in subdirectories.) You should then add `comspec=c:\dos\command.com` to your CONFIG.SYS file, put C:\DOS in your PATH setting, and give the full path name where necessary. As noted previously, SYS may not work, and you may have to back up drive C, reformat it, and then do the SYS. (It will definitely work with PC DOS 4, though PC DOS 4 comes with an installation program, SELECT, that is preferable to use because it allows you to set many options easily.)

Related Chapters Chapter 6–Managing Your Hard Disk
Chapter 7–All About Floppy Disks
Chapter 12–Installing a PC DOS System

Internal Command

TIME

Compatibility	2.0	2.1	3.0	3.1	3.2	3.3	**4.0**	OS/2 (DOS mode)	OS/2 (prot.)
	▲	▲	▲	▲	▲	▲	▲	▲	▲

Use the TIME command to set or display the system time.

Format `time` displays current time and prompts for new time.

`time hh:mm:ss.cc` sets the time (U.S. format).

`time hh:mm:ss.cc (a or p)` sets time with 12-hour clock (PC DOS 4).

Sample Use `time 12:30:15.00`

Procedure To display the current time, type `time`. If you do not wish to reset the time, press Enter in response to the prompt for the new time. To set a new time, respond to this prompt by entering the hours (0–24), minutes (0–59), seconds (0–59), and hundredths of a second (0–99). If you are using the U.S. format, separate the hours and minutes with a colon, the minutes and seconds with a colon, and the seconds and hundredths of a second with a period. (You can use periods in place of the colons if you wish.) An alternative way to set the time is to type `time` followed by the time in the format just discussed. This bypasses the prompt.

Note: The seconds and hundredths of a second values are optional, and default to 0 if not entered. In most cases, there is no need to enter them.

Version 4

Use 12-Hour Time with Version 4
In PC DOS 4, you can optionally specify the time using a conventional 12-hour (AM/PM) clock. To do so, follow the time immediately with *a* (AM) or *p* (PM). See Example 3.

Also, in DOSSHELL, the time is displayed in the upper right corner of the screen.

Related Commands COUNTRY is a CONFIG.SYS statement that sets time and date format (among other things).

DATE displays or sets the system date.

DIR displays times of file creation and modification.

PROMPT can incorporate the current time.

DETAILED REFERENCE

Explanation The TIME command displays the time as kept by the system clock. You can also use it to reset the time. Normally, you will not have to worry about maintaining the system time, except in case of failure of the clock battery, to set time for Daylight Savings or Standard Time, or when entering a new time zone. If you have no AUTOEXEC.BAT file, the TIME command will run automatically at startup, and you will be prompted for the time. This is a good reason to have at least a minimal AUTOEXEC.BAT file.

Comments There is little point in setting the hundredths of a second, because this precision is much greater than your physical ability to type the data.

Setting the Clock: On some systems, mainly those older PCs with clocks on expansion cards, you must also set the actual clock to the new time. On such systems, or on any system where the clock battery is replaced, you will have to run the appropriate utility for setting the clock. For add-on boards, the utility is supplied by the board manufacturer; on many AT-type systems, the utility is found on a Diagnostics or System Utility disk; and on PS/2s, it is found on the IBM PS/2 Reference Diskette.

Note: Due to a problem in the ROM BIOS, some IBM PS/2s can lose track of the time, even though the clock itself and the battery are fine. IBM dealers and some bulletin boards can supply a driver called DASDDRVR.SYS that fixes this problem.

Examples Example 1: Daylight Savings time begins today. Set the time one hour ahead.

```
C:\>time
Current time is: 18:31:35.50p
Enter new time: 19:32:00.00
```

←*Enter new time here*

The time was set one hour ahead and rounded up to the next minute to allow for the time it took to read the old time and type the new one. Note that the time was entered using the 24-hour clock: 19:32 is the same as 7:32 PM.

Example 2: An alternative way to set the same time:

```
C:\>time 19:32
```

Because the optional seconds and hundredths of a second were omitted, they will default to 0.

Example 3: In PC DOS 4, set the time using the AM/PM format.

Version 4

Setting 12-Hour Time in Version 4

```
C:\>time 9:45a
```

This sets the time to 9:45 in the morning.

Related Chapters Chapter 11–Customizing Your System
Chapter 13–International Language Support

TREE

External Command

Compatibility	2.0	2.1	3.0	3.1	3.2	3.3	4.0	OS/2 (DOS mode)	OS/2 (prot.)
	▲	▲	▲	▲	▲	▲	▲	▲	▲

Use the TREE command to display the contents of directories and subdirectories, showing how your disk is organized.

Format `tree drive: option` (PC DOS 3.3 and earlier)
`tree drive:path options` (PC DOS 4)

Options */f* lists files in each directory or subdirectory.

Version 4

An Alternate Graphic Character Set in Version 4
/a uses an alternate graphic character set. Works with all code pages and provides faster printing.

Sample Use `tree c:`

Procedure To obtain a list of all the directories and subdirectories on a disk, type `tree` followed by the letter of the drive and a colon.

Version 4

New Features for the TREE Command in Version 4
In PC DOS 4, you can specify the listing of a specific directory and its subdirectories; to do so, follow the drive letter with the path name for the directory. Note that to list an entire disk in PC DOS 4, you must include a backslash after the drive name, such as `c:\`. If you don't, only the current directory for that drive and its subdirectories will be listed.

You can also add the /a option to use alternate graphics characters and possibly faster printing.

For any version of PC DOS, use the /f option if you want the files in each directory or subdirectory to be listed. Because the list (particularly if it includes files) is likely to be long, you may wish to redirect it to a disk file (Example 2) or the printer (Example 3).

Related Commands DIR displays contents of a directory.

MKDIR creates a directory.

RMDIR removes a directory.

CD changes the current directory.

SUBST "fools" TREE into starting at a directory (needed only for PC DOS 3.3 or earlier).

DETAILED REFERENCE

Explanation Because hard disks can contain dozens of directories and subdirectories with hundreds of files, it is easy to lose track of the organization of your disk. Part of good organization is to create directories with meaningful names and to create subdirectories that reflect the logical division of the information involved. The TREE command can help you review your disk structure and possibly discover obsolete directories that could be eliminated or help you to devise a better organization.

TREE "walks" up and down the directory hierarchy. When it finds a directory, it lists the path to it and any subdirectories. It then does the same thing with each subdirectory, listing any of its subdirectories, and so on. If you specify /f, it also includes the names of all files found.

TREE

Comments In versions of PC DOS prior to 4, TREE works only with entire disks; do not specify a directory to start with, even the root directory. In other words, for drive C, use `tree c:`, not `tree c:\`. However, you can "trick" TREE into giving you a listing that starts at a particular directory (see Example 4).

Examples Example 1: List all the directories and subdirectories on drive C.

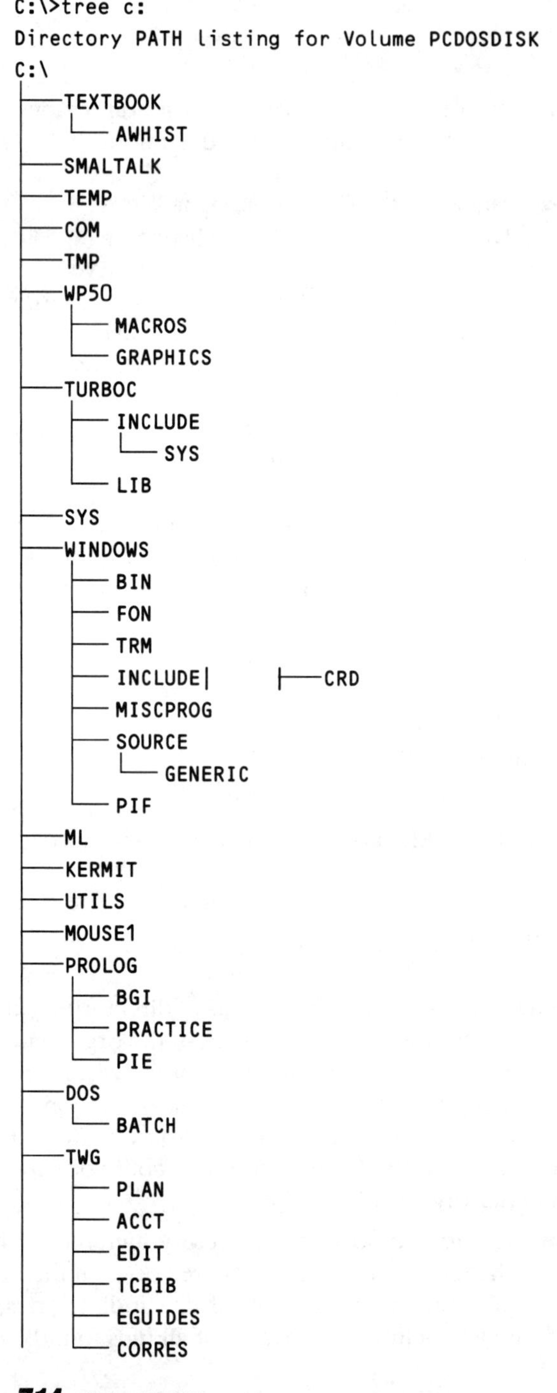

```
C:\>tree c:
Directory PATH listing for Volume PCDOSDISK
C:\
├───TEXTBOOK
│   └───AWHIST
├───SMALTALK
├───TEMP
├───COM
├───TMP
├───WP50
│   ├───MACROS
│   └───GRAPHICS
├───TURBOC
│   ├───INCLUDE
│   │   └───SYS
│   └───LIB
├───SYS
├───WINDOWS
│   ├───BIN
│   ├───FON
│   ├───TRM
│   ├───INCLUDE|          ├───CRD
│   ├───MISCPROG
│   ├───SOURCE
│   │   └───GENERIC
│   └───PIF
├───ML
├───KERMIT
├───UTILS
├───MOUSE1
├───PROLOG
│   ├───BGI
│   ├───PRACTICE
│   └───PIE
├───DOS
│   └───BATCH
├───TWG
│   ├───PLAN
│   ├───ACCT
│   ├───EDIT
│   ├───TCBIB
│   ├───EGUIDES
│   └───CORRES
│
```

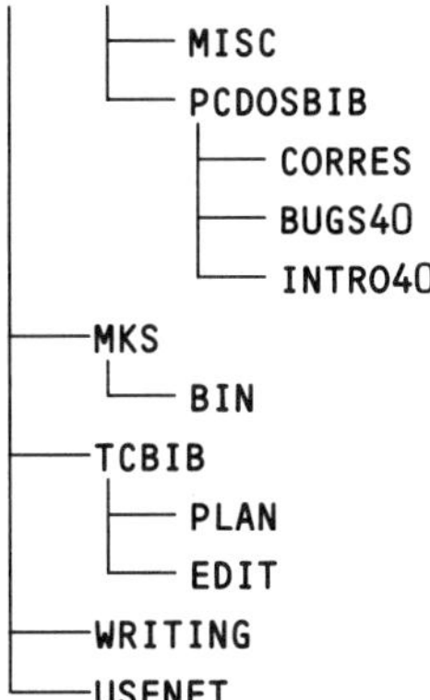

```
│    ├── MISC
│    └── PCDOSBIB
│         ├── CORRES
│         ├── BUGS40
│         └── INTRO40
├──MKS
│    └── BIN
├──TCBIB
│    ├── PLAN
│    └── EDIT
├──WRITING
└──USENET
```

Notice the outline-like format, with subdirectories indented under their parent directories. This example uses the default graphics character set for PC DOS 4; earlier versions use the regular character set.

Example 2: List the structure of a particular directory (PC DOS 4).

Version 4

Use TREE to Present the Structure of a Subdirectory in Version 4

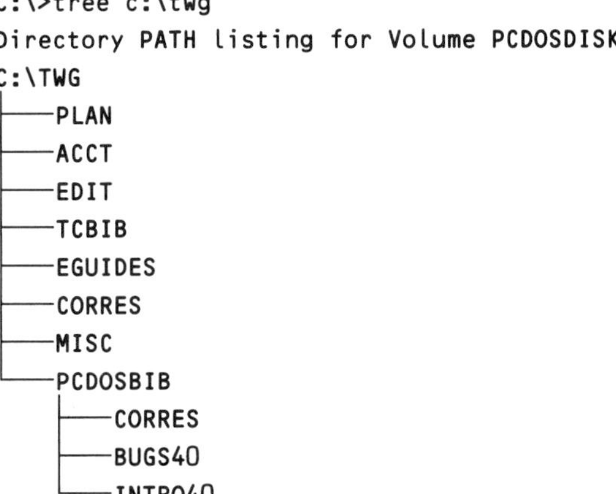

```
C:\>tree c:\twg
Directory PATH listing for Volume PCDOSDISK
C:\TWG
├───PLAN
├───ACCT
├───EDIT
├───TCBIB
├───EGUIDES
├───CORRES
├───MISC
└───PCDOSBIB
     ├───CORRES
     ├───BUGS40
     └───INTRO40
```

Example 3: List all the files in the C:\TWG directory and its subdirectories (PC DOS 4).

```
C:\>tree c:\twg /f /a
Directory PATH listing for Volume PCDOSDISK
C:\TWG\PCDOSBIB
|   REFLIST
|   DREFRS
|   DREFDF
|   DREFCD
|   DREFTX.BK!
|   GLOBAL
|   DREFAC
|   DREFTX
|   TECHQ
```

```
│
│  DOSTEMP
│  DREFGL
│  KBLAYOUT
│  ASKJIM
│  TYPER.BAT
│  DREFMR |    COMPAT
│  EX2
│  FILE1
│  EX3
│  FILE2
│  FILE3
│  OFF
├──CORRES
│      JS0908
│      JSP0907
│      REF
│      JSPC1013
├──BUGS40
│      SHELL1
└──INTRO40
       OUTLINE2
       OUTLINE
```

This is the same as the preceding example, except that all the files in each directory and subdirectory are listed. The /a specifies that regular rather than graphics characters be used; this speeds up the output.

Example 4: Send the TREE listing to a disk file, using redirection.

```
C:\>tree c: /f >treelist.dat
```

(Add a backslash after the c: if you're using PC DOS 4.) Here the listing includes files (/f option) and is redirected to the file TREELIST.DAT, where it could be printed or viewed using a word processor.

Example 5: Send the TREE listing directly to the printer.

```
C:\>tree c: > lpt1:
```

Example 6: Fool TREE into starting the listing at a particular directory; useful for versions of PC DOS prior to 4.

```
C:\>subst b: c:\twg
C:\>tree b: /f
```

This produces the same output as Example 2 but works with earlier versions of PC DOS. Here the SUBST command was first used to assign the drive letter B (a drive not in use on the system) to the path C:\TWG. Now, when you type `tree b: /f`, TREE sees just a drive letter and is happy, but the substitution causes the path C:\TWG to be actually sent to the directory listing routine.

Note: This may not work with all versions of PC DOS.

Related Chapters Chapter 6–Managing Your Hard Disk
Chapter 8–Advanced Use of the Command Line

Internal Command

TRUENAME

Compatibility	2.0	2.1	3.0	3.1	3.2	3.3	4.0	OS/2 (DOS mode)	OS/2 (prot.)
							▲		

Version 4

Use the TRUENAME command to reveal the true path location for files on drives affected by the ASSIGN, JOIN, or SUBST commands.

Format `truename` *`path`* finds the true path to a directory or file.

Sample Use `truename c:\letter5.doc`

Type TRUENAME followed by the path name for a directory or file that may have been affected by a drive assignment, join, or substitution. PC DOS will reply with a path containing the actual physical disk containing the file or directory.

Related Commands ASSIGN assigns requests involving a drive letter to another drive.

JOIN treats a drive as though it were part of a directory on another drive.

SUBST substitutes a drive letter for a long path name.

DETAILED REFERENCE

Explanation The ASSIGN, JOIN, and SUBST commands can be convenient in some circumstances: they can redirect disk accesses to a certain drive or allow you to specify future path names more easily. However, use of these commands creates a mildly schizophrenic situation where the names you are using to refer to directories and files no longer describe their real locations. PC DOS handles the translation between the name you use and the real path automatically, but sometimes you may want to know where a file really is. The TRUENAME command provides this information.

Comments The TRUENAME command does not appear in the PC DOS reference manuals and must therefore be considered to be undocumented. Because this command is merely informational, however, and affects no files, there is no harm in taking advantage of it.

Examples Example 1: Reveal the true location of a file.

```
join a: c:\work
C:\>dir \work\ref\temp

 Volume in drive C is PCDOSDISK
 Volume Serial Number is 1454-3E20
 Directory of  C:\WORK\REF

TEMP              9696 11-29-90  11:44a
        1 File(s)    5752512 bytes free

C:\>truename \work\ref\temp
A:\REF\TEMP
```

The JOIN command in effect grafts the entire file structure on drive A onto the directory WORK on drive C. Notice that the DIR command displays the file \WORK\REF as though it were stored on drive C, and gives the volume name, serial number, and free space for drive C. When the TRUENAME command is issued, however, the true location, A:\REF\TEMP is revealed.

Example 2: Find the location of a file referred to by a shorthand drive name.

```
C:\>subst w: \twg\upcdos\ref
C:\>truename w:header
C:\TWG\UPCDOS\REF\HEADER
```

The SUBST command is handy for assigning a shortcut for a long path name; here, the drive letter W is set to refer to the path \TWG\UPCDOS\REF on drive C. Suppose, however, that half an hour later, you don't remember where the file W:HEADER is really located? Again, the TRUENAME command comes to the rescue.

Related Chapter Chapter 6–Managing Your Hard Disk

TYPE

Internal Command

Compatibility	2.0	2.1	3.0	3.1	3.2	3.3	4.0	OS/2 (DOS mode)	**OS/2 (prot.)**
	▲	▲	▲	▲	▲	▲	▲	▲	▲

Use the TYPE command to list the contents of a text file on the screen.

Format `type` *`file name`*

Sample Use `type readme.doc`

Procedure To view the contents of a text file, type `type` followed by the name of the file. (Use the path name if the file isn't in the current directory.) You cannot specify multiple files or use wildcards; however, see Example 2 for a batch file that provides these capabilities.

Related Commands FOR allows TYPE to work with multiple files or wildcards.

MORE views files a screen at a time.

PRINT sends a file to the printer.

DETAILED REFERENCE

Explanation The TYPE command lists files on the screen. It should be used only with ASCII text files. Binary files will produce bizarre results, as various bytes will be interpreted as beeps, form feeds, graphics characters, etc.

Note: Many word processors, unless told to save files in plain ASCII format, produce files that contain special formatting codes and use ASCII values 128 and above, which display as various graphic symbols. Although you may be able to get the gist of the text by using the TYPE command, you will get better results by loading the file into the appropriate word processor and viewing it there.

Comments The data displayed by the TYPE command is not formatted in any way, other than the fact that any tab characters encountered skip the cursor to the next tab boundary (columns 8, 16, 24, and so on).

When viewing a file that is larger than one screen, you can use Ctrl-S to stop screen scrolling and Ctrl-Q to restart the display. A better alternative might be to use MORE < FILE rather than TYPE FILE to view a single file a screen at a time.

You can print the contents of a file that fits on one screen by pressing Shift-Print Screen. You can send a file of any length to the printer with TYPE FILE >PRN:, but it is better to use PRINT FILE because this gives you better control over the printing process.

Examples **Example 1**: Display the contents of a file.

```
C>type readme.doc
This file contains important information about E-Z-Word 4.0

To install this word processor, copy all of the
files from the distribution disk to your hard disk, by
using the command copy a:\*.* c:  You may wish to
create a subdirectory on your hard disk first, and
copy the files there instead.
```

Example 2: Create a batch file that allows you to use TYPE with multiple files and wildcards.

```
C:\>copy con: typeall.bat
@echo off
for %%f in (%1 %2 %3) do type %%f
^Z
 1 file(s) copied
```

This batch file uses a FOR statement to read up to three file names given on the command line. As a built-in feature, the FOR statement expands any file name with wildcards into a list of all matching file names. Now you can give the command

```
C:\>typeall note? letter
```

and you will execute the equivalent of

```
type note1
type note2
type note3
type letter
```

Related Chapter Chapter 5–PC DOS Files
Chapter 6–Managing Your Hard Disk

VDISK.SYS

Resource

Compatibility	2.0	2.1	3.0	3.1	3.2	3.3	**4.0**	OS/2 (DOS mode)	OS/2 (prot.)
	▲	▲	▲	▲	▲	▲	▲	▲	▲

Use the VDISK.SYS device driver to install a RAM (virtual) disk, allowing you to store programs and data files in memory for fast access.

Format `device=vdisk`*`capacity,sector-size,directory-entries options`*

Options

Version 4

Use VDISK with EMS Memory in Version 4
/e:maximum-sectors uses extended memory.
/x:maximum-sectors uses expanded memory.

Sample Use `device=vdisk.sys 360 256 32 /x:4`

Procedure To install a virtual disk, place a statement in your CONFIG.SYS file that begins with `device=vdisk.sys`. If the file VDISK.SYS is not in the root directory of your startup drive, specify the complete path name. Next, specify the capacity of the virtual disk in kilobytes (K), from 16 to 4096. (If you skip this value by putting a comma instead, you will receive the default of 64K. The maximum is the total amount of available memory in your system, unless you specify /e or /x, in which case, the absolute maximum is 16MB per virtual disk.) Next, give the sector size to be used, which must be 128, 256, or 512. (If you put just a comma, you receive the default of 128.)

Finally, specify the maximum number of directory entries to be allowed on the virtual disk. This number must be between 2 and 512; this is also limited by sector size as described later. The default value is 64.

Related Commands DISKCACHE is a alternative way to speed up access to programs and files with IBM PS/2.

CONFIG.SYS is a file containing VDISK.SYS statement.

DEVICE is a statement to install VDISK.SYS driver.

LASTDRIVE specifies range of drive letters that can be used.

DETAILED REFERENCE

Explanation The VDISK.SYS device driver allows you to create a virtual disk (sometimes called RAM disk). This allocates a block of memory that will be treated for most purposes like an additional disk drive.

Caution

Save to a Floppy or Hard Disk Before You Shut Off Power
A virtual disk is much faster than even a hard disk because all access is made directly to memory. On the other hand, the virtual disk (and any data on it) vanishes when the system is turned off. Thus, any data that is added or changed in the course of your work must be saved to a physical disk before you turn off the computer.

When a virtual disk is created, PC DOS assigns the next available drive letter to it; for example, if you already have floppy drives A and B and hard drive C, the virtual drive will be assigned the letter D. Multiple virtual drives can be installed by successive VDISK.SYS statements.

Note: If you already have five drives in use (letters A through E), you will need to include a LASTDRIVE statement in your CONFIG.SYS file allowing for additional letters; for example, lastdrive=g would allow you to use two more drives, including virtual drives.

Adjusting the Settings: Under certain conditions, VDISK.SYS will adjust the settings you specify. If you specify a size of less than 1K, the default value of 64K will be used. In any case, if less than 64K of memory is available, an error message will be issued, and no virtual disk will be installed. If the specified size for the virtual disk would leave less than 100K of memory available for other applications, the size will be adjusted downward until 100K is left.

The number of directory entries that you specify is adjusted upwards to the next sector size boundary. Thus, if you are using 128-byte sectors and specify ten entries, twelve entries will actually be used, because twelve 32-byte entries will fit in 384 bytes (3 x 128).

Tip

Determining Sector Size
In general, specify a large sector size, such as 512 bytes, if you will only be using a few files. This allows for more efficient movement of data to and from the virtual disk. On the other hand, if you will be using many small files, it is better to specify a smaller sector size, such as 128 bytes, because each file takes up at least one sector; smaller sectors minimize wasted space.

Version 4

Using the VDISK Driver with EMS Memory in Version 4
Many PC DOS users are familiar with the benefits of virtual disks and have often used them to put memory over 640K (otherwise useless to DOS) to good use for rapid access to programs and data.

(This extra memory can be addressed as either expanded or extended memory; see Chapter 11, "Customizing Your System," for an explanation of how these two methods differ.) Because many systems today have 1MB and more of memory, this is increasingly useful. PC DOS 4 now officially adds the ability to use expanded or extended memory to the VDISK driver. (If you are using an earlier version of PC DOS, there may be commercially available drivers that will still let you use expanded or extended memory; for example, Microsoft provides them for its MS Windows environment.)

Using VDISK with Expanded Memory: If you wish to use expanded memory for your virtual disk, specify the /x option. To use this option, the appropriate XMA2EMS.SYS statement must appear before the VDISK.SYS statement in your CONFIG.SYS file. Also, you must specify the /x option with your BUFFERS statement.

When Should You Use a Virtual Disk? Remember that an increasing number of applications such as WordPerfect or Microsoft Windows also have provisions for use of expanded (or sometimes extended) memory. Thus, it may be counterproductive to use a virtual disk (which requires that you copy programs and data between RAM and a physical disk) if your main application can be set to use the same RAM automatically. Another alternative for enhancing performance is to use a disk cache (IBM's DISKCACHE program, for example) to speed up access to your hard disk. Because you will probably want to use expanded or extended memory for the cache, you probably will not want to have both a virtual disk and a large disk cache. In general, it is recommended that you first allow any software that supports expanded or extended memory to use it; then experiment with the disk cache (possibly splitting memory between applications and the cache). If this is unsatisfactory, consider setting up a virtual disk for the application.

Also, in PC DOS 4, several commands (for example, BUFFERS and FASTOPEN) have been enhanced to allow use of expanded memory. When allocating a virtual disk, remember to allow for memory already used by such settings in your CONFIG.SYS file (in PC DOS 4, you can find out how much expanded or extended memory is available by using the MEM command after startup).

Note: VDISK always makes sure a minimum of 100K remains free, regardless of the size of virtual disk that you specify. Of course, 100K isn't enough to do much that is useful.

Problems with Extended Memory: When using extended (not expanded) memory, you may have problems using the virtual disk with applications that use very frequent interrupts (such as some communications or data acquisition programs). In this case, install the virtual disk in regular or expanded memory and see whether the problem goes away. If it does, try using extended memory instead, by setting the sector size to 128 and the number of sectors to transfer (in the /e option) to 1. Increase the latter value until problems occur and then subtract 1 for the final value.

Examples Example 1: You have a system with a hard disk and two floppy drives. In the CONFIG.SYS file, set up a 720K virtual disk.

```
device=c:\sys\vdisk.sys 720 256 64
```

Because you have put all device drivers in the SYS directory, you use the full path name to specify the driver. This virtual disk specifies a capacity of 720K of data, a sector size of 256 bytes, and a maximum number of 64 directory entries. (The last number could have been omitted, because 64 is the default, but it is often a good idea to specify default values—that way you will be reminded of them when you review the command.)

At startup, a brief message will notify you that the virtual disk has been installed and give the capacity, sector size, and maximum entries; the following is shown with PC DOS 4

```
VDISK version 3.40 virtual disk D:
   Buffer size: 720 KB
   Sector size: 256
   Directory entries: 64
```

Example 2: Set up a virtual disk with default sector size.

```
device=vdisk.sys 320 , 64
```

The comma represents the missing value for sector size; PC DOS will use the default of 128 bytes.

Related Chapter Chapter 11–Customizing Your System

Internal Command VER

Compatibility	2.0	2.1	3.0	3.1	3.2	3.3	4.0	OS/2 (DOS mode)	OS/2 (prot.)
	▲	▲	▲	▲	▲	▲	▲	▲	▲

Use the VER command to display a message announcing the version of PC DOS in use.

Format `ver`

Sample Use `ver`

Procedure Type `ver` to display a message indicating the version of PC DOS in use.

Related Commands COMMAND runs PC DOS command processor and displays version number.

PROMPT can be set to include the version number in prompt.

DETAILED REFERENCE

Explanation The VER command is most useful when you sit down in front of someone else's PC DOS system and want to determine quickly which version of PC DOS is running. The version number consists of two parts: the major version number, preceding the decimal point, and the minor version number, following it. Thus, a version number 3.2 would indicate an enhancement or revision of version 3.0, but not a fundamental reworking.

Note: Shortly after the release of PC DOS 4.0, IBM began distributing a version 4.01, containing fixes for a number of bugs. This version is identified only on the floppy disk label; the VER command still displays it as 4.0.

Comment You can include the PC DOS version number in the command prompt by including *$v* in a PROMPT command.

Example Show the version number.

```
C:\>ver
IBM DOS Version 4.00
```

VERIFY

Setting

Compatibility	2.0	2.1	3.0	3.1	3.2	3.3	4.0	OS/2 (DOS mode)	OS/2 (prot.)
	▲	▲	▲	▲	▲	▲	▲	▲	▲

Use the VERIFY command to have PC DOS check the accuracy of data that has been written to the disk.

Format `verify on` enables disk write verification.

`verify off` disables disk write verification.

`verify` displays current setting of VERIFY.

Sample Use `verify on`

Procedure To have all disk write operations automatically verified, type `verify on`. (You can also place this command in your AUTOEXEC.BAT file to have it executed automatically.) To turn off disk write verification, type `verify off`. To determine whether verification is on or off, type just `verify`.

Related Commands COPY, starting with PC DOS 3.3, does verification if /v option is specified.

XCOPY does verification if /v option specified.

DETAILED REFERENCE

Explanation By default, PC DOS does not verify that data has been written to disk correctly. Media defects can occasionally lead to data not being written correctly.

If you are concerned about this, you can set verification on, and PC DOS will verify that each disk write operation was performed correctly by attempting to reread the data. This added safety has the price of somewhat slower disk I/O performance; it is recommended that you experiment to see if this trade-off is acceptable for your application.

Comments If you want to verify a particular disk copy operation (regardless of the overall setting of VERIFY), you can use the /v option with the COPY (PC DOS 3.3 or higher) or XCOPY command.

Examples Example 1: Examine the current status of verification.

```
C:\>verify
VERIFY is off
```

Example 2: Turn verification on.

```
C:\>verify on
C:\>verify
VERIFY is on
```

Because VERIFY does not issue a confirming message, first `verify on` was typed and then just `verify` was typed to display the verification status.

Related Chapters Chapter 6–Managing Your Hard Disk
Chapter 7–All About Floppy Disks
Chapter 11–Customizing Your System

Internal Command

VOL

Compatibility	2.0	2.1	3.0	3.1	3.2	3.3	**4.0**	OS/2 (DOS mode)	OS/2 (prot.)
	▲	▲	▲	▲	▲	▲	▲	▲	▲

Use the VOL command to display the volume label of a specified disk. In PC DOS 4, the volume number is also displayed.

Format `vol drive:`

Sample Use `vol a:`

Procedure To display the volume label of a disk, type `vol` followed by the drive letter of the disk to be examined.

Related Commands FORMAT prompts for a disk label after formatting.

LABEL creates or changes a disk volume label.

DIR also displays the disk label.

DETAILED REFERENCE

Explanation The disk label is an optional identifying name of up to eleven characters that can be associated with a fixed or floppy disk. You can use the VOL command to display this label. If there is no label, you will be so informed.

Version 4

FORMAT Generates a Volume Serial Number in Version 4
In PC DOS 4, a volume serial number is also generated at the time a disk is formatted. This number is displayed along with the label by the VOL command.

Comments Disk labels are completely optional. You are prompted for a label at the time the disk is formatted. You can create or change a label on an already-formatted disk by using the LABEL command.

Example Examine the label on the disk in drive A.

```
C:\>vol a:
 Volume in drive A is WRITINGA
 Volume Serial Number is 1454-3E20
```

The volume serial number is used, starting with PC DOS 4.

Related Chapter Chapter 7–All About Floppy Disks

XCOPY

External Command

Compatibility	2.0	2.1	3.0	3.1	3.2	3.3	4.0	OS/2 (DOS mode)	OS/2 (prot.)
					▲	▲	▲	▲	▲

Use the XCOPY command to copy files or entire directories. You can copy all subdirectories of a specified directory. You can also select files to be copied by date or archive status.

Format `xcopy` *source drive, directory, or file destination drive or directory options*

Options */s* copies all subdirectories of specified directory, their subdirectories, and so on. Does not reproduce empty subdirectories.

/e is used with /s to copy subdirectories even if they are empty, reproducing the full tree structure at the destination.

/p prompts before copying each affected file.

/w prompts the user to insert a floppy disk on which to search for the source files.

/v verifies that the data was correctly written, for each copy.

/a copies archived files only (files that have been created or modified since the last time the BACKUP or XCOPY /M command was used). Does not change the archive setting of the copied files.

/m copies archived files only and clears the archive bit after the copy. This means that the file will not be copied again by this option unless it is subsequently modified (written to).

/d:mm-dd-yy copies only files that have been modified on or after the specified date. Use the date format appropriate for your country setting; the one shown is for the United States default.

Sample Use

```
xcopy c:\sys a: /s /e
```

Procedure

Type `xcopy` followed by a file name (wildcards may be used), a directory name, or a drive name (indicating the root directory of the specified drive). Follow this with the destination drive or directory, and any option(s) you wish to use (Example 1). When copying a directory, if you want all subdirectories containing files also to be copied, use the /s option (Example 2). If you want empty subdirectories to be included on the destination drive, use both the /s and /e options (Example 3). To have the user prompted before each file is copied, use the /p option (Example 4). To have the user prompted to insert the source disk from which files are to be copied, add the /w option. To have all copies verified (reread to check accuracy), use the /v option (Example 5). To have only files that have been modified since the last BACKUP command copied, use the /a option (Example 6). If you want such files to have their archive bits cleared after they are copied, use the /m options (Example 7) To have only files that have been modified on or after a specific date copied, use the /d option (Example 8).

Related Commands

COPY copies files or directories; cannot copy subdirectories.

DISKCOPY copies an entire disk sector by sector.

BACKUP is similar to XCOPY, but copies files in a special format that is not directly usable by other commands.

DETAILED REFERENCE

Explanation

The XCOPY command is a very versatile tool for copying files, directories, and whole branches of your file tree. Unlike COPY, XCOPY can copy subdirectories of the specified directory, including any subdirectories in the subdirectories, and so on. You can also copy only files that have been created or modified (written to) since the last time the BACKUP command was used, or files that have been modified on or since a specified date. These capabilities plus the ability to prompt for each copy enable you to write batch files that automate the copying of a directory (see Example 9).

Tip

Use the Right Copying Tool

It is important to familiarize yourself with the three commands that copy files: COPY, BACKUP, and XCOPY. Each has its uses. COPY is easiest to use for copying a whole directory (with no subdirectories) or a group of files selected by wildcard. It can also be used to concatenate (join together) files.

However, XCOPY can be better even for plain copying of a large number of files, because it reads as many source files as will fit into memory first, and then copies them as a group instead of reading and copying each file individually.

The BACKUP command is really designed to copy an entire disk (usually a hard disk) to a series of floppy disks. Files copied with the BACKUP command cannot be accessed directly; they must be copied back to the original disk using the RESTORE command. XCOPY operates best at a scope midway between that of COPY and BACKUP. Like BACKUP, it can copy subdirectories and copy selectively by modification status or date; like COPY, it copies in an immediately usable format. XCOPY is thus very useful for copying a branch of your file tree, such as a main word processing directory and the various subdirectories containing documents relating to various projects.

Note: The /m option is very useful, because it copies archived files only. These are files whose archive bit has been set; PC DOS turns this bit on when a file is created and whenever the file is modified (written to). The archive bit is turned off whenever a file is copied by the BACKUP command or by the XCOPY command with the /m option. This means that you can create a backup disk for a group of directories, run the XCOPY command periodically, and each time only the files that have been modified since the last backup will be copied.

Comment The /w option, which makes XCOPY wait until the user inserts a disk and presses a key, is really for use in batch files that you prepare for other users.

Tip

Copying the Contents of a Large Subdirectory to More Than One Disk

You can use XCOPY to copy more files than will fit on a single target disk. Specify the /s and /m options. When the current disk is filled, XCOPY displays a message to that effect and then exits. You can put another disk in and repeat the command. Because the archive bits of the files already copied are now off, they won't be copied again. Repeat this process until all the files in the source directory and any subdirectories have been copied. (Remember, however, that because of the /m option, all the files that were copied will now have their archive bits turned off.) This means that they will not be backed up if BACKUP is later used with the /m option.

Examples Some of the following examples use the set of directories shown in Figure R.2.

This set of directories represents a collection of bibliographical notes and other material related to books and films. Note that the directory BOOKS has the following subdirectories: COMPUTER, SCIFI, MYSTERY, and SPORTS. Some of these subdirectories have further subdirectories: SCIFI has the subdirectories MAGAZINE and FILM. Some directories (such as SPORTS) are empty. You will see how the various XCOPY options affect these directories.

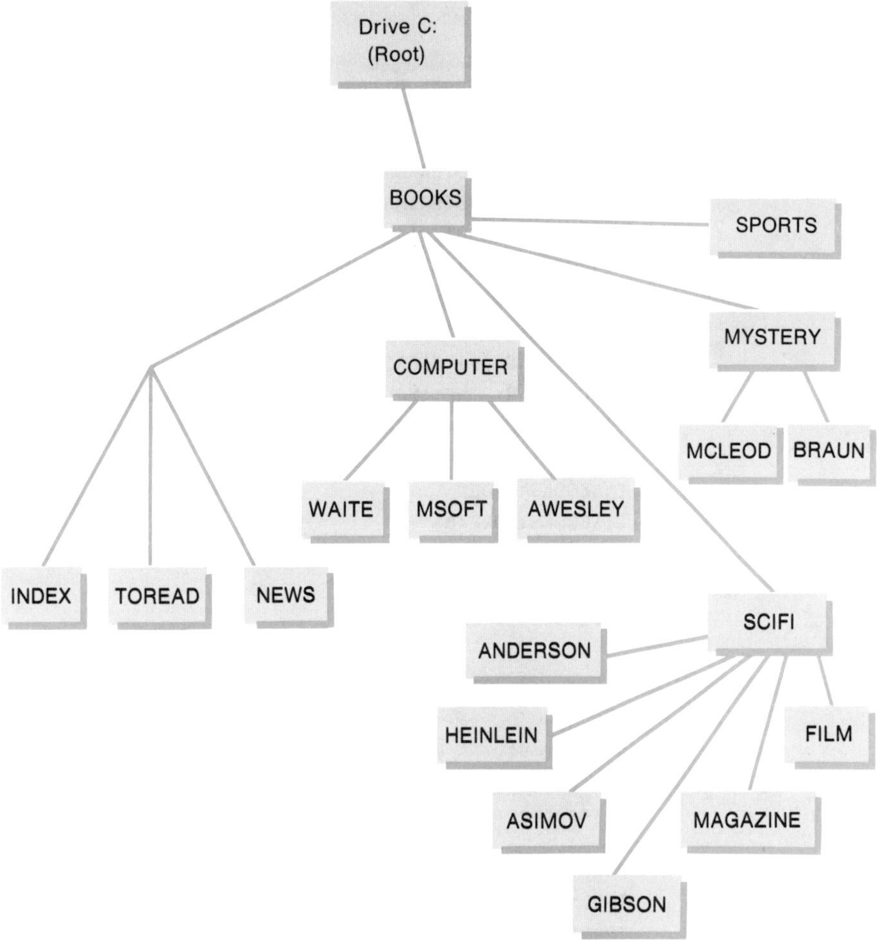

Figure R.2. ***A file tree to be copied.***

Example 1: Copy some files.

```
C:\>xcopy c:\books a:
Source files are being read...

:\BOOKS\INDEX
C:\BOOKS\TOREAD
C:\BOOKS\NEWS

 3 file(s) copied.
```

Here, XCOPY is being used as you might use COPY. Notice how the files are read as a group and then copied, speeding up the process. You can check the list of files copied to confirm your understanding of what is going on. Also notice that none of the subdirectories of BOOKS (such as SCIFI or MYSTERY) are copied.

Example 2: Copy all of the files in the BOOKS directory, including all the files in subdirectories.

```
C:\>copy c:\books a: /s
Reading source file(s)...

C:\BOOKS\COMPUTER\WAITE
C:\BOOKS\COMPUTER\MSOFT
C:\BOOKS\COMPUTER\AWESLEY
C:\BOOKS\SCIFI\ANDERSON
C:\BOOKS\SCIFI\HEINLEIN
C:\BOOKS\SCIFI\ASIMOV
C:\BOOKS\SCIFI\GIBSON
C:\BOOKS\MYSTERY\MCLEOD
C:\BOOKS\MYSTERY\BRAUN
C:\BOOKS\MYSTERY\SAYERS
C:\BOOKS\INDEX
C:\BOOKS\TOREAD
C:\BOOKS\NEWS

 13 file(s) copied.
```

When you examine the directory of drive A now, you see:

```
C:\>dir a:
 Volume in drive A is BOOKREVIEWS
 Directory of  A:\

NEWS              6144   8-03-90   7:36a
INDEX             9216   4-30-90   7:36a
TOREAD            6656   8-07-90   2:45p
        3 File(s)    707584 bytes free
```

As you can see, the empty subdirectory SPORTS was not copied.

Example 3: Copy all subdirectories, including empty ones.

```
C:\>xcopy c:\books a: /s /e
```

The same list of copied files will be displayed, but a directory of A will now also contain the empty subdirectories

```
C:\>dir c:\books

 The volume label in drive A is BOOKREVIEWS.
 Directory of A:\

NEWS              6144   8-03-90   7:36a
INDEX             9216   4-30-90   7:36a
TOREAD            6656   8-07-90   2:45p
COMPUTER     <DIR>       8-11-90   4:49p
```

```
SCIFI        <DIR>       8-11-90   4:49p
MYSTERY      <DIR>       8-11-90   4:49p
SPORTS       <DIR>       8-11-90   4:51p
     7 File(s)    585773 bytes free
```

Example 4: Prompt the user before each copy.

```
C:\>xcopy c:\books a: /p
```

Here, each file in BOOKS (but not its subdirectories) will be offered in turn for copying; for example,

```
C:\BOOKS\INDEX (Y/N)? y
C:\BOOKS\TOREAD (Y/N)? n
C:\BOOKS\NEWS (Y/N)? y

2 file(s) copied.
```

Example 5: Verify files after copying.

```
C:\>xcopy c:\books a: /s /v
```

Each file (including files in all subdirectories) is copied and then read back to verify that the copy is good. This is a good idea if you suspect that the disk is unreliable.

Example 6: Copy only files that have the archive bit set.

```
C:\>xcopy c:\books a: /s /a
```

Here, files that have been previously copied by the BACKUP command or by the command XCOPY /M will not be copied, unless they have been modified since the copy. This means that only changed files will be copied, saving considerable time. (This is called an incremental backup.) Note that because the archive bit isn't cleared by this option, the files will still be included in future copies made either by BACKUP or XCOPY /A.

Example 7: Copy only files that have the archive bit set, and clear the archive bit of such files.

```
C:\>xcopy c:\books a: /s /m
```

The only difference from the preceding example is that the archive bit of each such file will be cleared. This means that the files will not be copied by future BACKUP or XCOPY /M copies unless the files are subsequently modified. This option is handy for copying just the files you have worked with during the session. From the point of view of XCOPY, this option is more efficient than the preceding, but you will either have to make complete (nonincremental) backups to include the affected files on disks made by the BACKUP command or use the ATTRIB command later to selectively turn on the archive bits.

Example 8: Copy only files that have been modified on or after August 3, 1990.

```
C:\>xcopy c:\books a: /d:08-3-90

Reading source file(s)...

C:\BOOKS\NEWS
C:\BOOKS\TOREAD

 2 file(s) copied.
```

Note that the file \NEWS\INDEX, which has the date 04-30-90, was not copied.

Example 9: Write a batch file that keeps the backup disk for a project up to date.

```
C:\>copy con: update.bat
xcopy %1 a: /s /m /v
^Z
 1 file(s) copied.
```

To use this batch file, simply label a high-capacity floppy disk for use as the backup for your project. You can copy every file in your directory and its subdirectories the first time you make the backup, by typing a command such as

```
C:\>xcopy c:\writing a: /s
```

At the end of each subsequent session, invoke the batch file giving the main directory for the project: for example,

```
C:\>update c:\writing
```

Any files that have been modified since your last backup, whether they are in the \WRITING directory or one of its subdirectories, will be copied to the backup disk. Files that have not been modified will not be copied, thus saving much time.

Related Chapters

Chapter 6–Managing Your Hard Disk
Chapter 7–All About Floppy Disks

Resource

XMAEM.SYS

Compatibility	2.0	2.1	3.0	3.1	3.2	3.3	4.0	OS/2 (DOS mode)	OS/2 (prot.)
							▲	▲	

Use the XMAEM.SYS device driver to supported expanded memory with PC DOS 4 on 80386-based systems.

Format `device=xmaem.sys` *`expanded memory size`*

Sample Use `device=xmaem.sys` (statement in CONFIG.SYS)

Procedure To use expanded memory under PC DOS 4 on an 80386-based system, you must first place a statement in CONFIG.SYS installing the main expanded memory driver. The one provided with IBM PC DOS 4 is called XMA2EMS.SYS, and it has its own reference entry following this one. Following the DEVICE statement installing the main driver, begin a statement with `device=xmaem.sys`. (If the XMAEM.SYS driver is not in your startup directory, give the complete path name; for example, `c:\dos\sys\xmaem.sys`. If you wish all available memory on your expansion board(s) to be used as expanded (rather than extended) memory, you do not need to specify a memory size. If you wish only a portion of available memory to be used, reserving some for other purposes (perhaps a virtual disk), add the number of 16K "pages" to be used. In other words, divide the amount of memory in KB by 16 and give that number (see Example 2).

Related Commands MEM displays amount of expanded and extended memory available.

XMA2EMS.SYS is the main expanded memory driver, used alone on 80286-based systems.

DETAILED REFERENCE

Explanation Memory on 80386-based systems (such as the IBM PS/2 Model 80) is normally addressed as a continuous range of extended memory. Many applications and some PC DOS commands, however, cannot use extended memory but can use expanded memory, which is additional memory swapped into the main PC DOS memory through defined memory areas called pages. The XMAEM.SYS driver is designed to take the extended memory of an 80386 system and make it appear to the expanded memory driver as expanded memory. The expanded memory driver can then provide access to this memory for PC DOS and your applications.

Comments This driver emulates the IBM PS/2 80286 Expanded Memory Adapter/A. It may not work on non-IBM 80386 systems; if you have trouble, consult the manufacturer of the system or memory board.

Examples **Example 1**: Use all available extended memory as expanded memory.

```
device=c:\dos\sys\xmaem.sys
```

Example 2: Use 2MB of extended memory as expanded memory.

```
device=c:\dos\sys\xmaem.sys 128
```

In this case, the number of 16K pages was added. 2MB =2048K, and 2048/16 = 128.

Related Chapters Chapter 11–Customizing Your System
Chapter 12–Installing a PC DOS System

XMA2EMS.SYS

Resource

Compatibility	2.0	2.1	3.0	3.1	3.2	3.3	4.0	OS/2 (DOS mode)	OS/2 (prot.)
								▲	

Use the XMA2EMS.SYS device driver to use available expanded memory for some PC DOS commands and applications.

Note: If you have an 80386-based system, such as the IBM PS/2 Model 80, you must also install the XMAEM.SYS driver. See the preceding reference entry for details.

Format `device=xma2ems.sys` *`options`*

`device=xma2ems.sys` used without options, displays a list of available memory pages.

Options *frame=address* specifies the hexadecimal address (from A000 to E000) that will contain the EMS page frame. Specifying this designates the next four contiguous pages (usually P0, P1, P2, and P3).

Ppage-number[[[[[[[[[[[=address specifies the page number and address. Acceptable page numbers are P0, P1, P2, P3, P254, and P255. Addresses must be in an EMS page from A000 through E000 and begin a 16K contiguous memory area. If you specify P0, P1, P2, and P3, you cannot specify frame, because the first four pages represent the page frame.

/x:size specifies the total amount of expanded memory to be allocated, in 16K pages. The minimum is 4 pages (64K); the maximum (and default) is the total amount of memory available and must be an even multiple of 16K.

Sample Use `device=xma2ems.sys frame=d000`

Procedure Many of the options for this driver are quite technical, so start out simply. If you are going to use all of your expanded memory with applications and none for PC DOS commands, insert the statement given under the Sample Use section. This statement gives defaults that work with most EMS configurations. (If you are using an 80386-based system, make sure you have placed a `device=xmaems.sys` statement before the `device=xma2ems.sys` statement and that both statements refer to the same amount of memory if they use the /x option.)

Specify P254 if you want the VDISK.SYS and FASTOPEN features to use expanded memory. Specify P255 if you want the BUFFERS setting to use expanded memory (Example 1).

Specify pages P0, P1, P2, or P3 individually if there isn't a full 256K of contiguous memory following the frame address (Example 2). Remember that you do this instead of using the frame option.

After you have rebooted your system, use the MEM command to show that the expected amount of expanded memory is available (see Example 1). If you receive an error message while your CONFIG.SYS is processing this statement, if PC DOS or an application gives an error message indicating problems with expanded memory, or if the memory doesn't show up in the MEM statement, see the following discussion and Chapter 12, "Installing a PC DOS System."

Related Commands

CONFIG.SYS is a file for statements installing the expanded memory driver(s).

DEVICE installs device drivers.

MEM shows the amount of expanded and extended memory available.

XMAEM.SYS is a driver required to use expanded memory with an 80386-based system.

VDISK.SYS, FASTOPEN, BUFFERS can use expanded memory when the /x option is specified.

DETAILED REFERENCE

Explanation

Expanded memory is a way of making memory above the standard 640K available to your applications (and some PC DOS commands, such as FASTOPEN and BUFFERS). The XMA2EMS.SYS driver (working with the XMAEMS.SYS driver on 80386 systems) allows this memory to be used by applications that have the appropriate program code. Today, many major applications support expanded memory.

Comments

You may, from time to time, get error messages from PC DOS or applications indicating that expanded memory doesn't seem to be available or is not working properly. Chapter 11, "Customizing Your System," gives a series of steps that you can use to identify and possibly correct with expanded memory problems. It also provides further discussion of the use of addresses and other options given previously.

One major problem is that the XMA2EMS.SYS driver officially only supports the following:

- IBM 2MB Expanded Memory Adapter
- IBM PS/2 80286 Expanded Memory Adapter/A
- IBM PS/2 80286 Memory Expansion Option
- 80386-based systems on which the XMAEM.SYS works

At the time of writing, not all third-party memory boards emulate the IBM boards closely enough for the PC DOS expanded memory drivers to work. Note, however, that most board manufacturers provide their own expanded memory drivers. Try using the manufacturer's driver in place of the PC DOS one. If the driver specifies EMS 4 compatibility, it may work with your applications but not with certain PC DOS commands. This simply means that you won't be able to use expanded memory for such things as BUFFERS and FASTOPEN, which is only a minor nuisance. Check, however, to see whether your board manufacturer has written a driver that is fully compatible with PC DOS 4.

Examples **Example 1**: Use 1MB of your available expanded memory for PC DOS and applications. Specify a page frame at address D000 and specify the address for pages 254 and 255.

```
device=xma2ems.sys frame=D000 p254=C000 p255=C400 /x:64
```

The "frame" is the area into which expanded memory pages are "mapped." Here, it is specified as starting at the address D000. Because the locations of pages 254 and 255 are specified, the PC DOS commands that support expanded memory can use it. (If you receive error messages about memory conflicts, see Chapter 12, "Installing a PC DOS System.") The /x option specifies 64 16K pages; 64 * 16K = 1024K, or 1MB.

It is a good idea to verify that things are working properly by using the MEM command

```
C:\>mem

    655360 bytes total memory
    654336 bytes available
    110704 largest executable program size

   2097152 bytes total EMS memory
   2079152 bytes free EMS memory

    393216 bytes total extended memory
    262144 bytes available extended memory
```

This report shows that all EMS memory is available; check to see whether the total agrees with what you have specified in your XMA2EMS.SYS statement. If you are using some expanded memory for BUFFERS or other PC DOS commands, not all expanded memory will be shown as available.

Example 2: Specify individual pages rather than the frame address.

```
device=c:\dos\sys\xma2ems.sys p0=D000 p1=D400 p2=D800 p3=DC00
```

Here, the first four pages are specified instead of using the FRAME option. One reason for doing this is if there is a conflict between two memory boards such that the area after D000 is not contiguous, so you have to specify the address of four 64K pages separately (see Chapter 12, "Installing a PC DOS System"). Because pages 254 and 255 are not specified, this installation does not allow PC DOS itself to use expanded memory, although applications can.

Because no total amount of memory is specified, all available memory will be used.

Related Chapters Chapter 11–Customizing Your System
Chapter 12–Installing a PC DOS System

Appendix A
Error Messages

Like everything else you do, you learn to use PC DOS by trial and error. No matter how conscientious you are, you will make mistakes. Making mistakes and correcting them is an effective way to learn. That is why PC DOS contains error messages—to help you correct your mistakes.

The error messages that you will encounter most frequently are listed in this appendix. They are divided into two categories: those that refer to devices, such as your disk drive or keyboard, and those that refer to PC DOS commands or PC DOS itself.

Device Error Messages

Device error messages are displayed if PC DOS finds an error when it tries to use a device attached to your computer. These messages have a common format. It is easy to understand the message when you understand the format.

The format has two variations. The first is displayed when PC DOS has a problem reading (trying to get information from) a device:

```
type error reading device
Abort, Retry, Ignore?
```

The second variation appears when PC DOS has a problem writing (trying to send information to) a device:

```
type error writing device
Abort, Retry, Ignore?
```

Type defines the nature of the specific error and will vary with each instance.

Device refers to the piece of hardware involved in the error, such as a disk drive or a printer.

The second line of the message offers you three options to recover from the error; abort, retry, or ignore. PC DOS is waiting for you to enter one of these options from the keyboard.

Before you respond, check the obvious causes for the error. For instance, if the error concerns a disk drive, you may have left the drive door open or inserted the wrong disk.

When you have checked all the obvious causes, enter one of the three options:

`R` (Retry) PC DOS tries to perform the command again. This sometimes works even if you have not adjusted anything because the error might be minor and might not recur on the next try.

`A` (Abort) PC DOS stops the operation in progress. You should enter this response if `r` fails to correct the error.

`I` (Ignore) Causes PC DOS to retry the operation but ignore any messages it may encounter. It is not recommended that you use this response because it can result in losing the data that is being read or written.

The following messages are those that might appear in the *type* section of the error message.

`Bad call format` A driver is part of an operating system that controls a specific input/output device, such as a modem or printer. Each driver has specific codes in PC DOS. One such identifier is a length request header. This message means that an incorrect length request header was sent to the driver for the specified device. Consult your dealer.

`Bad command` The command issued to a device is invalid.

`Bad unit` An incorrect subunit number (driver code) was sent to the driver. Consult your dealer (see `Bad call format` also).

`Data` An error was detected while reading or writing data. Use the CHKDSK command to see whether your disk has a defective area.

`Disk` After three tries, a disk read or write error is still occurring. You may have inserted the wrong type of disk, or your disk may be inserted incorrectly. If neither is true, you may have a bad disk. If you receive this message, try the standard corrective procedures before removing the disk (CHKDSK /F, COPY *.*). You may be able to salvage data on the disk.

`File allocation table bad, drive d` This message always refers to a specific disk drive. It tells you that the file allocation table (FAT) on the disk in the indicated drive is faulty. If you receive this error, the disk is probably defective.

`No paper` There is no paper in your printer, or your printer is not turned on. Correct the problem and press R.

`Non-DOS disk` There is invalid data on the allocation table of the disk in the indicated device. The disk needs to be reformatted.

`Not ready` The device is not ready to read or write data. This may mean that the power is not turned on, the drive door is not closed, or there is no disk in the drive.

`Read fault` For some reason, the device cannot read or transmit data. The power may not be on, the drive may not contain a disk, or the device may not be configured properly for use with PC DOS.

`Sector not found` The sector holding the data you want cannot be located. The disk may be defective.

`Seek error` PC DOS cannot locate the proper track on the disk in the drive.

`Write fault` For some reason, the device cannot read or transmit data. The power may not be on, the drive may not contain a disk, or the device may not be configured properly for use with PC DOS.

`Write protect` You have instructed PC DOS to write to a disk that is write-protected (either temporarily by you or permanently by the manufacturer). Either insert a new disk or remove the write protection from the disk.

Additional Error Messages

The following is not a complete listing of error messages that may be received from PC DOS. Check your PC DOS manual if you cannot locate the message in the device error messages or in this section. Some error messages are associated with a specific command. When this is the case, the command name follows the error message.

`All specified file(s) are contiguous` CHKDSK. All the files are on the disk sequentially.

`Allocation error, size adjusted` CHKDSK. There was an invalid sector number in the file allocation table. The indicated file name was truncated at the end of the previous good sector.

`Attempted write-protection violation` FORMAT. You attempted to format a write-protected disk. Remove the disk and insert a new one.

`Bad command or filename`	You entered the command or file name incorrectly. Check the spelling and punctuation and make sure that the command or file you specified is on the disk in the indicated drive. You may be calling an external command from a disk that does not contain the command.
`Cannot edit .BAK filer--rename file`	To protect your data, you cannot access a file that has a .BAK extension. Rename the file using the REN command and give the copy a new name.
`Cannot load COMMAND, system halted`	While attempting to load the command processor, PC DOS found that the area where it keeps track of available memory is destroyed. Try booting PC DOS again.
`Contains XXX non-contiguous blocks`	CHKDSK. The indicated file has been written in sectors in different areas of the disk (rather than in sequential blocks). Because fragmented files take longer to read, it is probably best to copy the file so that it will be read sequentially.
`Disk boot failure`	While trying to load PC DOS, an error was encountered. If this message continues, use a backup PC DOS disk.
`Disk error writing FAT x`	CHKDSK. There was a disk error while CHKDSK was trying to update the FAT on the indicated drive. Depending on which of the file allocation tables could not be written, *x* will be a 1 or a 2. If both allocation tables are indicated, the disk is unusable.
`Duplicate filename or file not found`	The name you indicated in a RENAME command already exists in the current directory on the disk, or the file to be renamed is not on the disk in the specified drive.
`Entry error`	EDLIN. Your last command contains a syntax error.
`Error loading operating system`	An error was encountered when PC DOS tried to load from the hard disk. If the problem persists, load PC DOS from a floppy disk and use SYS to copy PC DOS to the hard disk.
`File cannot be copied onto itself`	You tried to give an already existing file name to a new file in the same directory.
`File not found`	The file named in a command parameter could not be found, or the command could not be found on the specified drive.

`Incorrect DOS version`	You tried to run a PC DOS command that requires a different version of PC DOS. This occurs only when you are using an earlier version of PC DOS and give a command found only in the later versions.
`Insufficient disk space`	There is not enough free space on the disk to hold the file you are writing. If you think there should be enough space, use CHKDSK to get a disk status report.
`Intermediate file error during pipe`	This message may mean that the intermediate files created during a piping procedure cannot be accommodated on the disk because the root directory of the default drive is full. Your disk may also be too full to hold the data being piped, or the piping files cannot be located on the disk.
`Invalid COMMAND.COM in drive d`	While trying to reload the command processor, PC DOS found that the copy of COMMAND.COM on the disk is a different version. Insert a disk containing the correct version of PC DOS.
`Invalid directory`	One of the directories in the specified path name does not exist.
`Invalid number of parameters`	The specified number of parameters does not agree with the number required by the command.
`Label not found` GOTO #	You have named a label in a GOTO command that does not exist in the batch file. Use EDLIN to review the GOTO command and make sure that all GOTO statements contain valid labels.
`No room for system on diskette` SYS	The specified disk does not contain the required reserved space for the system. (Is the system already on the disk?) You can solve this problem by using FORMAT/S to format a new disk and then copy your files to this disk.
`Syntax error`	The command was entered incorrectly. Check the format.
`Terminate batch job (Y/N)?`	You have pressed Ctrl-Break or Ctrl-C during the processing of a batch file. Press Y to end processing. Press N to stop the command that was executing when you pressed Ctrl-Break or Ctrl-C; processing will continue with the next command.

Appendix B
DOSSHELL Command Map

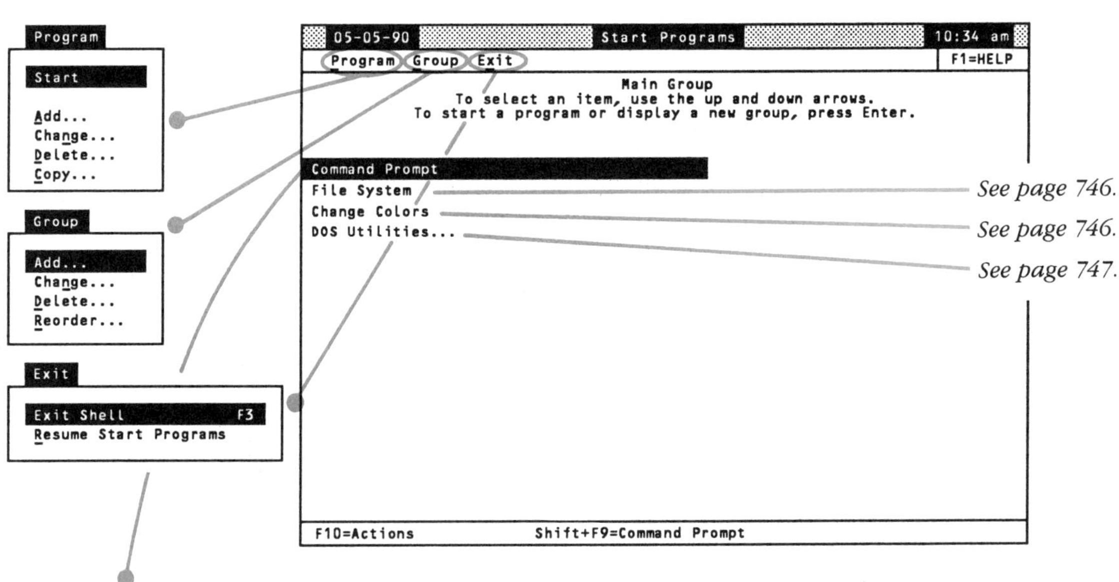

C:\DOS>

Type exit *to return to Shell.*

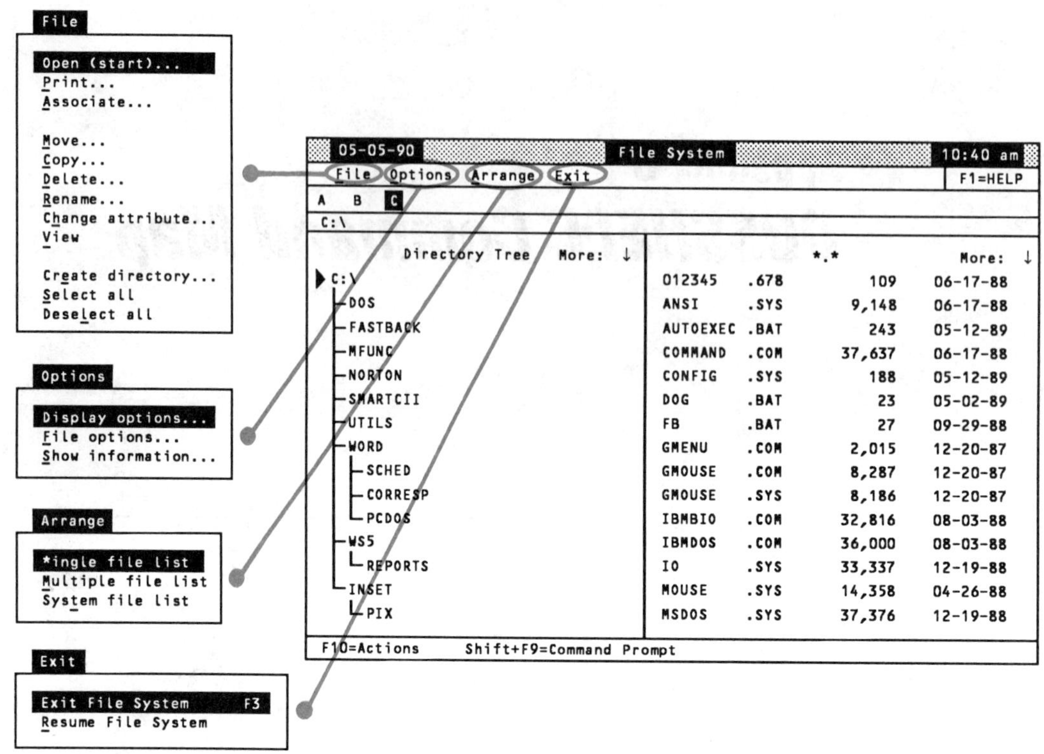
File
Open (start)...
Print...
Associate...
Move...
Copy...
Delete...
Rename...
Change attribute...
View
Create directory...
Select all
Deselect all
Options
Display options...
File options...
Show information...
Arrange
*ingle file list
Multiple file list
System file list
Exit
Exit File System F3
Resume File System
05-05-90 File System 10:40 am
File Options Arrange Exit F1=HELP
A B C
C:\
Directory Tree More: ↓
. More: ↓
C:\
DOS
FASTBACK
MFUNC
NORTON
SMARTCII
UTILS
WORD
SCHED
CORRESP
PCDOS
WS5
REPORTS
INSET
PIX
012345 .678 109 06-17-88
ANSI .SYS 9,148 06-17-88
AUTOEXEC .BAT 243 05-12-89
COMMAND .COM 37,637 06-17-88
CONFIG .SYS 188 05-12-89
DOG .BAT 23 05-02-89
FB .BAT 27 09-29-88
GMENU .COM 2,015 12-20-87
GMOUSE .COM 8,287 12-20-87
GMOUSE .SYS 8,186 12-20-87
IBMBIO .COM 32,816 08-03-88
IBMDOS .COM 36,000 08-03-88
IO .SYS 33,337 12-19-88
MOUSE .SYS 14,358 04-26-88
MSDOS .SYS 37,376 12-19-88
F10=Actions Shift+F9=Command Prompt

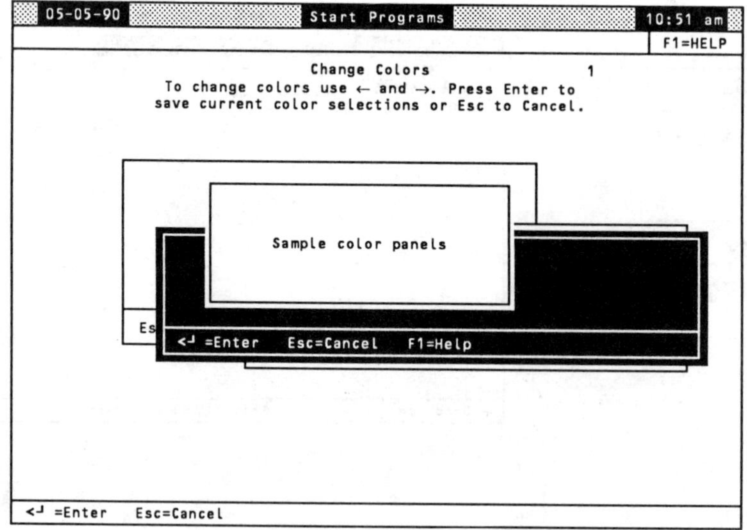
05-05-90 Start Programs 10:51 am
F1=HELP
Change Colors 1
To change colors use ← and →. Press Enter to
save current color selections or Esc to Cancel.
Sample color panels
Es
↵ =Enter Esc=Cancel F1=Help
↵ =Enter Esc=Cancel

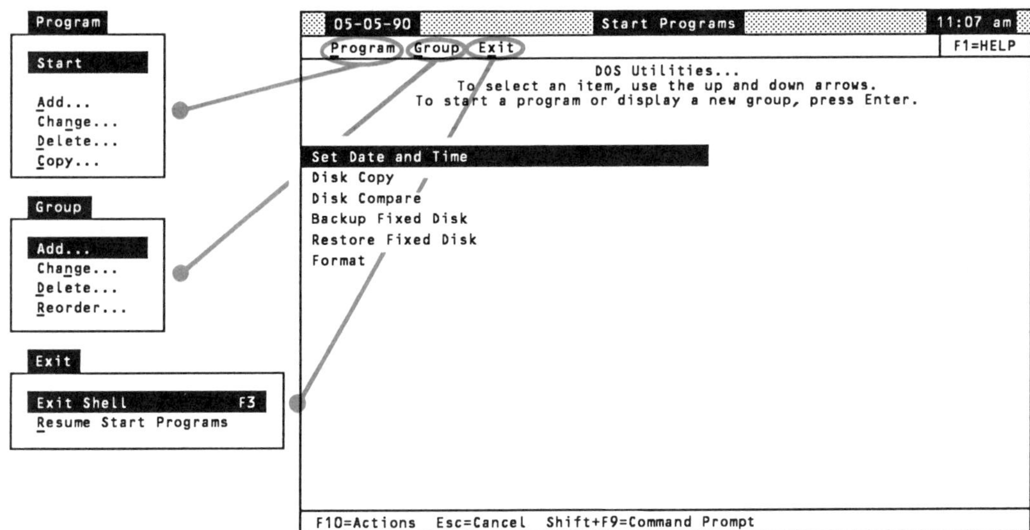
Program
Start
Add...
Change...
Delete...
Copy...
Group
Add...
Change...
Delete...
Reorder...
Exit
Exit Shell F3
Resume Start Programs
05-05-90 Start Programs 11:07 am
Program Group Exit F1=HELP
DOS Utilities...
To select an item, use the up and down arrows.
To start a program or display a new group, press Enter.
Set Date and Time
Disk Copy
Disk Compare
Backup Fixed Disk
Restore Fixed Disk
Format
F10=Actions Esc=Cancel Shift+F9=Command Prompt

Index

E

F

J

K

L

M

N

Q

R

T

The Waite Group's MS-DOS® Bible Third Edition

Steven Simrin

'his new edition of the classic *1S-DOS Bible* pays particular ttention to the Lotus/Intel Expand- d Memory Specification 4.0 and ncludes detailed explanations of all ew DOS 4.0 commands and func- ions. Completely updated to reflect he changes in DOS 4.0, the com- rehensive coverage includes the ew expanded batch language, disk ormats, device drivers, file struc- ures memory management, and erminate and stay resident pro- rams. The "Information Jump 'able" enhanced for easier and nore complete reference, and reviously undocumented features re highlighted.

'opics covered include:

- Starting MS-DOS
- Using DOSSHELL
- Directories, Paths, and Trees
- Installing a Fixed Disk
- MS-DOS Batch Files
- Redirection, Pipes, and Filters
- Configuring Your System
- Extended Keyboard and Display Control
- MS-DOS Connectivity
- EDLIN, the MS-DOS Text Editor
- Debug and Link
- Disk Structure and Management
- Memory Structure and Management
- Terminate and Stay Resident Programs
- MS-DOS Device Drivers
- Expanded Memory Specification

550 Pages, 7½ x 9¾, Softbound
ISBN: 0-672-22693-6
No. 22693, $24.95

The Waite Group's MS-DOS® Developer's Guide Second Edition

John Angermeyer and Kevin Jaeger

This new and expanded developer's guide covers the MS-DOS and PC-DOS™ operating systems up to Version 3.3, concentrating on techniques for developing application programs as well as memory resident programs and device drivers. The book is aimed at the serious programmer, developer, or "power user" with a significant understanding of MS-DOS.

Topics covered include:

- Structured Programming
- Program and Memory Management in the MS-DOS Environment
- TSRs
- EMS
- Real-Time Programming Under MS-DOS
- Installable Device Drivers
- Writing Programs for the Intel 8087/80287 Math Coprocessor
- LANs and MS-DOS
- Programming the Serial Port
- Programming the EGA and VGA
- Disk Layout and File Recovery Information
- Recovering Data Lost in Memory
- Differences Between MS-DOS Versions
- High-Level Languages
- Debugging

600 Pages, 7½ x 9¾, Softbound
ISBN: 0-672-22630-8
No. 22630, $24.95

Understanding MS-DOS®

Kate O'Day and John Angermeyer, The Waite Group

MS-DOS is a very powerful and intricate operating system, with millions of users. This operating system can be explored by beginning programmers to learn a hands-on approach at the keyboard.

Understanding MS-DOS introduces the use and operation of this popular operating system for those with little previous experience in computer hardware or software. The fundamentals of the operating system such as EDLIN, tree structured directories and pathnames, and such advanced features as redirection and filtering are presented in a way that is easy to understand and use.

Topics covered include:

- Organizing Data and Files
- Redirecting Input and Output
- Using the Text Editor EDLIN to Create and Edit Files
- Using Commands to Manage Files
- Special Function Keys and Key Combinations
- Creating Batch Files of Often Repeated Commands
- Create and Use Tree Structured Directories

240 Pages, 7 x 9, Softbound
ISBN: 0-672-27067-6
No. 27067, $17.95

The Waite Group's Tricks of the MS-DOS® Masters

John Angermeyer, Rich Fahringer, Kevin Jaeger, and Dan Shafer, The Waite Group

This title provides the personal user (not necessarily the programmer or software developer) with a wealth of advanced tips about the operating system and tricks for using it most successfully.

Also included are advanced tips on using popular software packages such as WordStar®.

Topics covered include:

- Secrets of the Batch File Command Language
- Secrets of Pipes, Filters, and Redirection
- Secrets of Tree-Structured Directories
- Discovering Secrets: A Debugger Tutorial
- Secrets of DOS Commands
- Secrets of Files
- Secrets of Free and Low-Cost Software
- Secrets of Add-on Software, Boards, and Mass Storage
- Secrets of System Configuration
- Secrets of Data Encryption

568 Pages, 7½ x 9¾, Softbound
ISBN: 0-672-22525-5
No. 22525, $24.95

Visit your local book retailer or call

800-428-SAMS.

The Waite Group's
Discovering MS-DOS®
Kate O'Day

This comprehensive study of MS-DOS commands such as DEBUG, LINK, and EDLIN begins with general information about operating systems. It then shows how to use MS-DOS to produce letters and documents; create, name, and manipulate files; use the keyboard and function keys to perform jobs faster; and direct, sort, and find data quickly.

It features a command summary card for quick reference.

Topics covered include:

- Introduction to MS-DOS
- What is a Computer System?
- What is an Operating System?
- Getting MS-DOS off the Ground
- System Insurance
- Editing
- Filing
- Batch Files
- Paths
- Input/Output
- Hard Disks
- Appendices: Error Messages, Reference Card

296 Pages, 7½ x 9¾, Softbound
ISBN: 0-672-22407-0
No. 22407, $19.95

The Waite Group's
MS-DOS® Papers
Edited by The Waite Group

MS-DOS Papers presents tutorials on fourteen of the most exciting topics in MS-DOS programming written by recognized experts and "gurus" in the computer industry. The book offers a close look at such important areas as the expanded memory specification (EMS), writing terminate and stay resident (TSR) programs, undocumented MS-DOS functions, how to program the Enhanced Graphics Adapter (EGA), and inner workings of MS-DOS systems.

Topics covered include:

- An Overview of MS-DOS
- A Fast File Search Utility
- PCnix: A UNIX-like Shell
- Adding Power to MS-DOS Programming
- Advanced MASM Techniques
- Undocumented MS-DOS Functions
- Terminate and Stay Resident Programming
- Data and File Security Techniques
- The Spy Utility: Investigating Windows
- MS-DOS Services for Device Drivers
- Sounder: A Musical Device Drive
- Programming the Enhanced Graphics Adapter
- Programming the Serial Port with C
- Enhanced Memory Specification (EMS)

608 Pages, 7½ x 9¾, Softbound
ISBN: 0-672-22594-8
No. 22594, $26.95

The Waite Group's
Desktop Publishing Bible
James Stockford, Editor

Publish high-quality documents right on your desktop with this "bible" that tells you what you need to know—everything from print production, typography, and high-end typesetters, to copyright information, equipment, and software.

In this collection of essays, experts from virtually every field of desktop publishing share their tips, tricks, and techniques while explaining both traditional publishing concepts and the new desktop publishing hardware and software.

Topics covered include:

- Publishing Basics: Traditional Print Production, Conventional Typography, Case Studies in Selecting a Publishing System, and a Comparison of Costs for Desktop and Conventional Systems
- Systems: The Macintosh, PC, MS-DOS, An Overview of Microsoft Windows, Graphics Cards and Standards, Monitors, Dot and Laser Printers, UNIX, and High-End Work Stations
- Software: Graphics Software, Page Layout Software, Type Encoding Programs, PostScript, and JustText
- Applications: Newsletters, Magazines, Forms, Comics and Cartooning, and Music

480 Pages, 7½ x 9¾, Softbound
ISBN: 0-672-22524-7
No. 22524, $24.95

The Waite Group's
Advanced C Primer++
Stephen Prata, The Waite Group

Programmers, students, managers, and hackers alike, will learn to master the C programming language. Anyone who knows the basics of C will learn practical C tips never before published. This in-depth coverage gives you rare and complete examination of video access ports, segmented memory, and registers.

Advanced C Primer++ takes the reader further than most C books on the market, showing how to manipulate the hardware of the IBM PC family of computers directly from C. Readers learn how to access routines in the Read Only Memory (ROM) of an IBM PC, how to use system calls in PC DOS from C and i/o ports, how to control the video screen, and to integrate assembly routines into C programs.

Topics covered include:

- Advanced C Programming
- Register and Bit Level System Control
- Hardware Operation for Beginners and Experienced Users
- Advanced Use of Pointers, Functions, Storage Classes, Arrays and Structures
- C Library Access
- Use of Assembly Language Modules
- Binary and Text File Input and Output

Includes chapter questions and answers.

512 Pages, 7½ x 9¾, Softbound
ISBN: 0-672-22486-0
No. 22486, $24.95

Visit your local book retailer or call
800-428-SAMS.

The Waite Group's
C Primer Plus, Revised Edition

Mitchell Waite, Stephen Prata, and Donald Martin

This revised and expanded edition of a best-seller presents everything you should know to begin programming in the exciting C language, now used by over 80 percent of the software community. The book is organized for quick learning and encourages problem solving through questions and exercises.

Topics covered include:

- Structure of a Simple C Program
- Variables, Constants, and Data Types
- Character Strings, *#define, printf( ), and scanf( )*
- Operators, Expressions, and Statements
- Input/Output Functions and Redirection
- Choosing Alternatives: *if, else,* Relational and Conditional Operators
- Loops and Other Control Aids
- How to "Function" Properly
- Storage Classes and Program Development
- The C Preprocessor
- Arrays and Pointers
- Character Strings and String Functions
- Structures and Other Data Delights
- The C Library and File I/O
- Bit Fiddling, Keywords, Binary Numbers, IBM® PC Music, and More

576 Pages, 7½ x 9¾, Softbound
ISBN: 0-672-22582-4
No. 22582, $24.95

The Waite Group's
Microsoft® C Bible

Nabajyoti Barkakati

Microsoft C Bible provides a thorough description of the 370 functions of the Microsoft C library, complete with practical, real-world MS-DOS-based examples for each function. Library routines are broken down into functional categories with an intermediate-level tutorial followed by the functions and examples.

Included are two "quick-start" tutorials, complete ANSI prototypes for each function, extensive program examples, and handy jump tables to help enhance learning.

Topics covered include:

- Overview of the C Language
- Microsoft C 5.0 Compiler Features and Options
- Process Control
- Variable Length Argument Lists
- Memory Allocation and Management
- Buffer Manipulation
- Data Conversion Routines
- Math Routines
- Character Classification and Conversion
- String Comparison and Manipulation
- Searching and Sorting
- Time Routines
- File and Directory Manipulation
- Input and Output Routines
- System Calls
- Graphics Modes, Coordinates, and Attributes
- Drawing and Animation
- Combining Graphics and Text

824 Pages, 7½ x 9¾, Softbound
ISBN: 0-672-22620-0
No. 22620, $24.95

The Waite Group's
Microsoft® C Programming for the PC, Revised Edition

Robert Lafore

This entry-level programming book assumes no previous knowledge of C as it moves quickly through the fundamentals of the language using step-by-step, hands-on tutorials. The author shows exactly what to do and how to do it, from simple topics to advanced features, moving the reader in an orderly fashion. The new edition is based on the 5.1 compiler and includes a chapter on the newest graphics features, the newest updates to Codeview, ANSI C prototyping, VGA graphics, MCGA control, and details on the QuickC optimizing compiler have been added.

Topics covered include:

- Getting Started
- C Building Blocks
- Loops, Decisions, Functions
- Arrays, Strings, and Pointers
- Keyboard and Cursor
- Structures, Unions, and ROM BIOS
- Memory and the Monochrome Display
- Library Graphics
- Direct CGA, EGA, and VGA Color Graphics
- New Microsoft Graphics Functions
- Files
- Larger Programs and Advanced Variables

750 Pages, 7½ x 9¾, Softbound
ISBN: 0-672-22661-8
No. 22661, $24.95

The Waite Group's
QuickC™ Bible

Naba Barkakati

This book, written for first-time programmers making the transition from Pascal or BASIC to C, is a complete, user-friendly reference to Microsoft's QuickC compiler.

The book shows how to accomplish such sophisticated procedures as using the environment and the PSP, provides complete details on video and graphics modes, and drawing and animation. It reveals little-known secrets of C programming, providing helpful, in-depth tips to make programming more organized and powerful. A pocket-size foldout reference card of all QuickC functions and commands is included, and unique compatibility boxes show portability with other compilers.

Topics covered include:

- Overview of the C Language
- Process Control
- Variable-Length Argument Lists
- Memory Allocation and Management
- Buffer Manipulation
- Data Conversion and Math Routines
- Character Classification and Conversion
- String Comparison and Manipulation
- Searching and Sorting
- Time Routines
- File and Directory Manipulation
- Input and Output Routines
- System Calls and Graphics Modes

900 Pages, 7½ x 9¾, Softbound
ISBN: 0-672-22632-4
No. 22632, $24.95

Visit your local book retailer or call 800-428-SAMS.

The Waite Group

100 Shoreline Highway, Suite 285 | Mill Valley, CA 94941 | (415) 331-0575
Compuserve: 74146,3515 | usernet: bplabs!well!mitch | AppleLink: D2097

Dear Reader:

Thank you for considering the purchase of our book. Readers have come to know products from **The Waite Group** for the care and quality we put into them. Let me tell you a little about our group and how we make our books.

It started in 1976 when I could not find a computer book that really taught me anything. The books that were available talked down to people, lacked illustrations and examples, were poorly laid out, and were written as if you already understood all the terminology. So I set out to write a good book about microcomputers. This was to be a special book—very graphic, with a friendly and casual style, and filled with examples. The result was an instant best-seller.

Over the years, I developed this approach into a "formula" (nothing really secret here, just a lot of hard work—I am a crazy man about technical accuracy and high-quality illustrations). I began to find writers who wanted to write books in this way. This led to coauthoring and then to multiple-author books and many more titles (over seventy titles currently on the market). As The Waite Group author base grew, I trained a group of editors to manage our products. We now have a team devoted to putting together the best possible book package and maintaining the high standard of our existing books.

We greatly appreciate and use any advice our readers send us (and you send us a lot). We have discovered that our readers are detail nuts: you want indexes that really work, tables of contents that dig deeply into the subject, illustrations, tons of examples, reference cards, and more.

The Waite Group's Using PC DOS is a good example of The Waite Group formula for a computer book. If you want to explore PC DOS from other angles, look for our other DOS books. *The Waite Group's Tricks of the MS-DOS Masters* is for power users and covers advanced MS-DOS topics and little-known tricks. *The Waite Group's MS-DOS Bible*, a sister book to this one, combines a command reference section with tutorial chapters.

If you'd like to extend your programming experience into the fast and powerful C language, study our book *Microsoft C Programming for the PC*. This book teaches you how to use the Microsoft C Compiler to write programs for PC DOS systems. To understand how the PC DOS operating system works, look for *The Waite Group's MS-DOS Developer's Guide*, which presents a thorough discussion of assembly language programming techniques, MS-DOS memory management, the LIM EMS 4.0 specification, writing programs for the EGA and VGA, and much more. You can find a list of all our titles in the back of this book, and if you let us know what you want, we'll try to write about it. Thanks again for considering the purchase of this title. If you care to tell me anything you like (or don't like) about the book, please write or send email to the addresses on this letterhead.

Sincerely,

Mitchell Waite
The Waite Group

The Waite Group Library

If you enjoyed this book, you may be interested in these additional subjects and titles from **The Waite Group** and Howard W. Sams & Company. Reader level is as follows: ★ = introductory, ★★ = intermediate, ★★★ = advanced. You can order these books by calling 800-428-SAMS.

Level	*Title*	*Catalog #*	*Price*	
	C and C++ Programming Language			
	Tutorial, UNIX & ANSI			
★	C Primer Plus, Revised Edition, Waite, Prata, & Martin	22582	$24.95	
★★	C++ Programming, Berry	22619	$24.95	
★★★	Advanced C Primer ++, Prata	22486	$24.95	
	Tutorial, Product Specific			
★	Microsoft C Programming for the PC, Revised Edition, Lafore	22661	$24.95	NEW
★	Turbo C Programming for the PC, Revised Edition, Lafore	22660	$22.95	
★★	Inside the Amiga with C, Second Edition, Berry	22625	$24.95	
	Reference, Product Specific			
★★	Microsoft C Bible, Barkakati	22620	$24.95	
★★	Quick C Bible, Barkakati	22632	$24.95	
★★	Turbo C. Bible, Barkakati	22631	$24.95	
★★	Essential Guide to ANSI C, Barkakati	22673	$7.95	
★★	Essential Guide to Turbo C, Barkakati	22675	$7.95	NEW
★★	Essential Guide to Microsoft C, Barkakati	22674	$7.95	NEW
	DOS and OS/2 Operating System			
	Tutorial, General Users			
★	Discovering MS-DOS, O'Day	22407	$19.95	
★	Understanding MS-DOS, O'Day & Angermeyer	27067	$17.95	
	Tutorial/Reference, General Users			
★★	MS-DOS Bible, Second Edition, Simrin	22617	$22.95	
	Tutorial/Reference, Power Users			
★★	Tricks of the MS-DOS Masters, Angermeyer & Jaeger	22525	$24.95	
	Tutorial, Programmers			
★★	MS-DOS Papers, Edited by The Waite Group	22594	$26.95	
★★	OS/2 Programmer's Reference, Dror	22645	$24.95	
★★★	MS-DOS Developer's Guide, Revised Edition, Angermeyer, Jaeger, et al.	22630	$24.95	
	UNIX Operating System			
	Tutorial, General Users			
★	UNIX Primer Plus, Waite, Prata, & Martin	22028	$22.95	
★	UNIX System V Primer, Revised Edition, Waite, Prata, & Martin	22570	$22.95	
★★	UNIX System V Bible, Prata and Martin	22562	$24.95	
★★	UNIX Communications, Henderson, Anderson, Costales	22511	$24.95	
★★	UNIX Papers, Edited by Mitchell Waite	22570	$26.95	
	Tutorial/Reference, Power Users and Programmers			
★★	Tricks of the UNIX Masters, Sage	22449	$24.95	
★★★	Advanced UNIX—A Programmer's Guide, Prata	22403	$24.95	
	Macintosh			
	Tutorial, General Users			
★	HyperTalk Bible, The Waite Group	48430	$24.95	NEW
	Tutorial/Reference, Power Users and Programmers			
★★	Tricks of the HyperTalk Masters, Edited by The Waite Group	48431	$24.95	NEW

Find it Fast

Note: Boldfaced page numbers refer to discussions in the Command Reference.

. . . continued from inside front cover.

The Waite Group's
Using PC-DOS

Waite Group Reader Feedback Card

Help Us Make A Better Book

To better serve our readers, we would like your opinion on the contents and quality of this book. Please fill out this card and return it to *The Waite Group*, 100 Shoreline Hwy., Suite A-285, Mill Valley, CA, 94941 (415) 331-0575.

Name ______________________

Company ______________________

Address ______________________

City ______________________

State _____ ZIP _________ Phone _________

1. How would you rate the content of this book?

- ☐ Excellent
- ☐ Very Good
- ☐ Good
- ☐ Fair
- ☐ Below Average
- ☐ Poor

2. What were the things you liked *most* about this book?

- ☐ Pace
- ☐ Content
- ☐ Writing Style
- ☐ Accuracy
- ☐ Examples
- ☐ Listings
- ☐ Reference
- ☐ Format
- ☐ Cover
- ☐ Index
- ☐ Jump Table
- ☐ 2nd Color
- ☐ Price
- ☐ Illustrations
- ☐ Construction

3. Please explain the one thing you liked *most* about this book. ______________________

4. What were the things you liked *least* about this book?

- ☐ Pace
- ☐ Content
- ☐ Writing Style
- ☐ Accuracy
- ☐ Examples
- ☐ Listings
- ☐ Reference
- ☐ Format
- ☐ Cover
- ☐ Index
- ☐ Jump Table
- ☐ 2nd Color
- ☐ Price
- ☐ Illustrations
- ☐ Construction

5. Please explain the one thing you liked *least* about this book. ______________________

6. How do you use this book? For work, recreation, look-up, self-training, classroom, etc?

7. Would you be interested in receiving a Pop-Up utility program containing the contents of this book? What would you pay for this?

8. Where did you purchase this particular book?

- ☐ Book Chain
- ☐ Small Book Store
- ☐ Computer Store
- ☐ Other: ______________________
- ☐ Direct Mail
- ☐ Book Club
- ☐ School Book Store

9. Can you name another similar book you like better than this one, or one that is as good, and tell us why?

10. How many Waite Group books do you own? _______

11. What are your favorite Waite Group books?

12. What topics or specific titles would you like to see The Waite Group develop?

13. What version of DOS are you using?

14. What computer are you using with DOS?

15. Any other comments you have about this book or other Waite Group titles?

Fold Here

From:

____

____

____

Place Stamp Here

The Waite Group, Inc.
100 Shoreline Highway, Suite A–285
Mill Valley, CA 94941

Staple or tape here

22679